TIMBER PRESS GUIDE TO
GARDENING IN THE PACIFIC NORTHWEST

TIMBER PRESS

Guide to
GARDENING
IN THE PACIFIC
NORTHWEST

Carol W. Hall & Norman E. Hall

TIMBER PRESS
Portland | London

All photographs not specifically credited were taken by the authors.

Photographs by Whitney Cranshaw, Frank Peairs, David Leatherman, and John Capinera courtesy the Gillette Entomology Club, Colorado State University.

Photographs by Ken Gray, Oregon State University, courtesy Annette Frahm, Local Hazardous Waste Management Program, King County, Washington.

Maps by Allan Cartography, Medford, Oregon.

Published in 2008 by

Timber Press, Inc.
The Haseltine Building
133 S.W. Second Avenue, Suite 450, Portland, Oregon 97204-3527
www.timberpress.com

2 The Quadrant, 135 Salusbury Road
London NW6 6RJ
www.timberpress.co.uk

ISBN-13: 978-0-88192-879-2
Printed in China

Library of Congress Cataloging-in-Publication Data
Hall, Carol W.
Timber Press guide to gardening in the Pacific Northwest / Carol W. Hall,
Norman E. Hall.
p. cm.
Includes bibliographical references and index.
ISBN-13: 978-0-88192-879-2
1. Gardening--Northwest, Pacific. 2. Plants, Ornamental--Northwest, Pacific. I.
Hall, Norman E. II. Title. III. Title: Guide to gardening in the Pacific Northwest.
SB453.2.N83H35 2008
635.909795--dc22   2008002926

A catalog record for this book is also available from the British Library.

CONTENTS

PREFACE

When Tom Fischer of Timber Press first approached us with the idea of writing a book on gardening in the Pacific Northwest, we were more than a little skeptical. (Are you quite sure you mean *us*?) We are not and have chosen not to be botanists, horticulturists, academics, nursery owners, lecturers, or collectors; we are simply longtime, dirt-under-the-fingernails gardeners who love plants and gardening.

We also love the Pacific Northwest. In fact, having lived in various parts of this incomparable region for a combined total of 116 years (and having gardened here nearly as long), we find it impossible to separate the two: to us, "gardening" *is* gardening in the Pacific Northwest. The longer we thought about it, the more it made sense to write this book—especially when we looked back at our own experiences with gardening guides.

As a very young and very green couple in Eugene, Oregon (where Norm was born and where we both grew up and were educated), we wanted to find out more about ornamental plants, for which we shared an enthusiastic but untutored passion, and especially about growing them without poisons. The only information we could find came from the eastern states. It advised us to mulch with ground corncobs or peanut shells (neither of which was even remotely available, although Douglas fir bark mulch was plentiful) and to acidify the soil for rhododendrons with pine needles (Pacific Northwest soils are naturally among the most acidic in the temperate world). It also told us how to prevent damage from insect pests that don't exist west of the Mississippi, but not how to deal with the common insect pests we did have. We muddled along happily enough on our own, learning from the best sources of all: the plants themselves.

By the time we moved to St. Helens, Oregon, we had discovered the *Sunset Western Garden Book* and other Sunset guides. While Sunset advice is excellent and thorough, we soon discovered almost all of it was geared toward conditions in California. We became adept at translating. "Regular garden watering" meant reasonably drought tolerant in Pacific Northwest summers; "fast growing" usually meant only slightly faster than slow growing in our cooler climate; "needs excellent drainage" meant likely to drown in our heavy soil over winter.

Our next move was to Courtenay on central Vancouver Island, British Columbia, where we began a new garden in semi-shaded woodland conditions. There we became interested in native plants, as well as intensely interested in non-native plants best suited to our climate. At the time, local nurseries carried few if any native plants; much of what they did carry were species highly recommended in eastern North America but inappropriate in the Pacific Northwest.

Information in national magazines, catalogs, and most books we could find was also largely inappropriate. Even lush, impressive estate gardens seemed to be trying to imitate East Coast or English estate gardens rather than featuring plants that excel in our own unique climate. Lacking regionally specific information, we made many mistakes; however, experience is an excellent teacher.

Creating our present full-sun garden on Denman Island, one of the Gulf Islands in the Strait of Georgia, presented many new challenges—not the least of which was a heightened appreciation of the importance of drought tolerance in the Pacific Northwest. (Summer droughts have been extreme in recent years; our only water source is a well.) Adding new and untried plants to our ever-expanding garden was exciting, but also frustrating. Although we were by then devouring gardening books, magazines, catalogs, and any other plant-specific information we could find, no single source of information was adequate, and none told us what we most wanted to know: why did some hardy plants that were theoretically well suited to Pacific Northwest conditions languish when actually planted in near-perfect manifestations of those conditions, while others thrived with little or no help?

Many sources described hundreds or even thousands of plants, but most gave physical descriptions only, implying all were as interchangeable as ties on a rack. Others included basic cultural requirements—sun or shade, moist or dry soil—but mentioned little or nothing about drought tolerance, tolerance of extreme winter wetness, disease resistance, tolerance of drizzly springs or heat-challenged summers, or even the type of soil preferred. None addressed what would happen 15 or 20 years down the road.

Translating, interpolating, and cross-referencing information from five or six not-quite-appropriate sources—British, Californian, continental North American—was a pain, but available books on gardening in the Pacific Northwest were of little help. Most made no differentiation between appropriate and inappropriate species as long as they combined well visually with other species. Others featured inspiring gardens and/or accomplished gardeners, but contained little useful information about actual gardening. Although plant selection in local nurseries was by now much more regionally appropriate, a plant's availability was (and still is) no guarantee of its success in real-life Pacific Northwest gardens. Ongoing economic realities mean most retail nurseries have little choice but to buy stock from mega-growers that ship continent-wide, and the minimal cultural information supplied with each plant assumes all climates equal.

Oddly enough, many of our gardening questions have been answered from non-gardening sources. For instance, we wondered for years why we never saw a full-sized *Ginkgo biloba* anywhere in the Pacific Northwest, even though the species is fully hardy here. (We thought at first it might be because of the taproot, but other taprooted plants such as hollies thrive here.) It was from reading a biography of Harry Truman that we finally found the answer. On his daily constitutional in retirement back in Missouri, Truman would stop to speak to a magnificent ginkgo. ("You're doing a good job," he would say.) Aha! If ginkgos thrive in Missouri's very hot, very muggy summers and sometimes brutally cold winters, it's no wonder they grow only so-so in the mild-summer, mild-winter Pacific Northwest. Other questions were answered from equally unlikely sources.

With some 11 million practicing or potential gardeners now living in the Pacific Northwest, we felt such roundabout methods of gathering information should not be required: a book addressing the concerns specific to this entire region's unique gardening conditions was certainly long overdue. We just never imagined we would be the ones to write it.

Knowing that plants have been around for millions of years longer than humans and that each has its own profound reasons for doing whatever it does, we approached the subject with humility. We finished with even deeper humility. As much as we thought we had found out about certain plants, and as much as we thought we knew about the Pacific Northwest, where we have both spent a lifetime, we learned a great deal more about both and will never stop learning. Writing this book sharpened our own understanding of gardening in the Pacific Northwest considerably. We sincerely hope the information contained in it will be helpful to fellow gardeners.

ACKNOWLEDGMENTS

Many people lent kind assistance to the completion of this book. We would especially like to acknowledge the contributions of the following people: Ingrid Hoff, horticultural manager of the University of British Columbia Botanical Garden and Centre for Plant Research, for reading Part 4 and offering helpful comments; Judy Newton, retired education coordinator for the University of British Columbia Botanical Garden, for reading and critiquing Chapter 4 and also for the generous loan of several slides; Heide Hermary of Gaia College near Duncan, B.C., for the equally generous loan of her slides; Mary Rabourne of the King County (Washington) Department of Natural Resources and Parks, for facilitating the use of insect images from the booklet *Good Bugs Guide—Stop Before You Spray*, written by Annette Frahm, Brendan Jordan, and Andrea Imler.

We would also like to thank Linda Gilkeson, a renowned expert on Integrated Pest Management in British Columbia and beyond, for the use of several slides and for her assistance in locating other sources of insect images. We are especially grateful to Whitney Cranshaw, Professor/Extension Specialist and Advisor of the Gillette Entomology Club at Colorado State University, for making special arrangements for the use of photographs from the Gillette Entomology Club Image Collection as well as the generous use of his own insect images.

Special thanks go to Franni Bertolino Farrell, our editor and new friend at Timber Press, for her quick, efficient, and always good-humored skill in streamlining the organization and format of this book, smoothing out the bumps, and catching the numerous typos that escaped our own proofreading. Her many sensitive and sensible small changes added up to one big improvement overall.

Most of all we would like to thank Tom Fischer, Editor-in-Chief at Timber Press, for suggesting this book in the first place and for many other things: steering us through a maze of unfamiliar processes, answering our many questions, loaning one of his own photos, making helpful suggestions along the way, having our crude hand-sketched maps beautifully transformed by a cartographer, and patiently allowing us—several times—to extend our deadline. Without his help, we never would have started this book, let alone completed it.

In writing this book, we have referred to many major and minor sources, including numerous peripheral sources not listed in our selected bibliography. However, any errors contained in the book are exclusively our own.

PART ONE

THE REGION

Where exactly is the Pacific Northwest? Everyone knows and uses the term, but what geographical area it applies to varies wildly.

To some, the Pacific Northwest is a coastal strip of western North America between San Francisco in the south and the Aleutian Islands in the north. Others tinker with this definition, placing the southern limit at about Eugene, Oregon, and/ or the northern limit somewhere near Seward, Alaska. A common broad definition includes all of Oregon, Washington, and Idaho, plus northern California, southern British Columbia, and sometimes western Montana. A common narrow definition (its popularity rising in direct proportion to the distance of the speaker from the Pacific Northwest) is the dripping-wet rainforest portion of Washington's Olympic Peninsula, where Seattle is presumed to be located.

Political boundaries confuse the issue even more. To many Americans, the Pacific Northwest is the states of Oregon, Washington, and Idaho; to others it is confined to those parts of Washington and Oregon west of the Cascades. To many Canadians, it means Vancouver Island and the Lower Mainland of British Columbia, perhaps with the area around Bellingham, Washington, or even Seattle thrown in for good measure.

In gardening terms, however, the Pacific Northwest is much easier to locate. This region of unique garden opportunities and challenges is defined by a unique set of givens: a shared climate not quite like any other in the world, intertwined geographic features that influence the climate, and a common natural distribution of native vegetation. The several different political jurisdictions of the region even have a commonly shared cultural history that influences gardening practices.

The obvious western boundary of this region, the Pacific Ocean, is all-important; the influence of this enormous body of water is the single most important factor defining the Pacific Northwest climate. The eastern boundary, the Cascade Range (which becomes the Coast Mountains north of the Fraser River just on the Canadian side of the international border) is equally indisputable, since this continuous north-south chain of lofty mountains brings the influence of the Pacific Ocean to an abrupt halt. West of the mountains, the climate is very mild and very moist, especially in winter; east of the mountains it's much

Douglas fir, coastal form (*Pseudotsuga menziesii* var. *menziesii*)

colder in winter, much hotter in summer, and much, much drier, creating completely different gardening conditions.

Northern and southern boundaries of the Pacific Northwest are not as sharply defined geographically, but in gardening terms they might as well be flagged with flashing red lights. Once you go much further north than Campbell River on Vancouver Island, the ever-increasing influence of the cold Pacific Ocean begins to shift the climate into one that is perpetually moist, cloudy, and uniformly cool year-round.

Gardening conditions on the northern tip of Vancouver Island are still similar to those on the west coast of the island, which is unmistakably a part of the Pacific Northwest, but north of here (about 51° North latitude on the sparsely populated mainland coast of B.C.), differences between high and low temperatures become smaller and light intensity starts to diminish even on clear days. Although summer days are increasingly longer, the angle of the sun is increasingly lower, and gardening conditions beyond this point are not those of the Pacific Northwest, but those of coastal Alaska.

The southern boundary of the Pacific Northwest is equally distinct. Although often drawn at the Oregon–California border at 42° North latitude, political boundaries have nothing to do with gardening. On the coast, Crescent City, California, enjoys gardening conditions virtually identical to those of Brookings and Gold Beach in Oregon; the characteristics of coastal California's northern redwood-forest climate (very damp, but with half our rainfall and warmer nights) are not fully apparent until just north of Eureka.

The same relationship exists inland. There is no discernible difference between gardening conditions on the north (Oregon) slopes of the heavily forested Siskiyou Mountains and those on their south (California) slopes—at least until the point where Mount Shasta in the Cascade Range looms up on the east. It's only after negotiating the steep descent from here to the valley floor and seeing the palm trees lining the streets of Redding, California, that you know you've suddenly entered a whole new gardening world.

Within these boundaries of the Pacific Ocean, the Cascade Range, and about 51° North latitude and 41° North latitude, normal climate and vegetation patterns are remarkably consistent. Winters are almost identically mild, with only short periods (and sometimes none) of moderate frost, but are invariably wet to very wet. Steady rain is the usual winter precipitation; snow is infrequent and rarely stays long on the ground, although deeper snowfalls are an unpredictable hazard almost everywhere. Spring is long, cool, and moist, with rainfall very gradually tapering off to mere showers.

Summer temperatures vary considerably more, ranging from cool to moderately warm to hot, but summer nights are cool even in the hottest subregions. Everywhere, though, summers are dry: over 80 percent of annual precipitation falls between October and April, and very little if any rain falls between July and mid-September. Although it appears to be a moist-temperate climate similar to that of the British Isles or New Zealand, the Pacific Northwest climate is actually a modified Mediterranean climate, defined as one with wet winters and very dry summers.

Fall (more accurately called Indian summer, since it usually means September and early October) is pleasantly warm and comfortably dry, with a few welcome showers easing the drought. However, summer's long dry spell is truly broken only by heavy rains that begin in earnest in late October, following the Mediterranean pattern, and reach their heaviest monthly totals in November. Actual amounts then decrease slightly but remain very high until February, when they begin their slow tapering off.

The actual amount of annual precipitation varies considerably due to the rain-enhancing or rain-shadow effects of our many mountains, but exactly the same pattern exists everywhere. When graphed by month from January to December, the resulting line resembles a skipping rope held high at both ends but nearly touching the ground in the middle. This is the mirror image of average monthly temperatures, which when graphed from January to December make a hill-shaped curve.

Given the consistency of climate throughout the region, it's not surprising that the natural vegetation throughout the Pacific Northwest is also remarkably similar. Species found abundantly everywhere include bigleaf maple (*Acer macrophyllum*), red alder (*Alnus rubra*), western red cedar (*Thuja plicata*), western hemlock (*Tsuga heterophylla*), Pacific dogwood (*Cornus nuttallii*), tall Oregon grape (*Mahonia aquifolium*), low Oregon grape (*M. nervosa*), salal (*Gaultheria shallon*), snowberry (*Symphoricarpos albus* var. *laevigatus*), salmonberry (*Rubus spectabilis*), thimbleberry (*R. parviflorus*), the ubiquitous sword fern (*Polystichum munitum*), and a host of other trees, shrubs, perennials, and bulbs. Wetter, cooler areas include Sitka spruce (*Picea sitchensis*) and shore pine (*Pinus contorta* var. *contorta*); warmer, drier areas include Garry oak (*Quercus garryana*) and Pacific madrone (*Arbutus menziesii*).

However, the most abundant and unmistakable Pacific Northwest plant of all is Douglas fir (*Pseudotsuga menziesii*), the conifer that practically defines the Pacific Northwest. (The variety that grows on the eastern side of the Cascades and into the Rocky Mountains and the Sierra Nevada, *P. m.* var. *glauca*, is a much shorter tree with bluer foliage; the ubiquitous coastal form of Douglas fir is *P. m.* var. *menziesii*.)

The presence of this so-familiar conifer is overwhelming. Although it merges in the north with Sitka spruce, in the south with various pines, and along the Pacific with shore pine and hemlock, its presence is a defining characteristic of the landscape, history, economy, and ecology of the entire Pacific Northwest. This is the dominant tree of forests once so vast that all our mountain slopes and even our lowlands were completely covered with timber.

For well over a century, Douglas fir was a mainstay of the logging economies of western Oregon, western Washington, and southwestern B.C. Although forestry has taken a beating in all three jurisdictions in recent years, it is still an enormously important part of all three now-diversified economies. Douglas fir is the main species used for reforestation, both for timber and recreational use. Its wood frames our houses. Its protected giants shade and perfume our parks and hiking trails. Its saplings, grown and groomed on plantations, are our Christmas trees.

Being so perfectly adapted to the Pacific Northwest climate and conditions, Douglas fir sprouts and grows with abandon in any clearing, soon making mini-forests in disturbed open ground even in highly urbanized settings. So pervasive is the presence of this tree that it would be very hard for anyone in the Pacific Northwest to go through a single day without laying eyes on this species, either at close range or in the distance.

In the end, this ready-made test may be as good a definition of the Pacific Northwest as any. If you see *Pseudotsuga menziesii* var. *menziesii* as a matter of course in your normal daily life, you're in the Pacific Northwest. If you don't, you're not.

CHAPTER 1

Climate, Soil, and Weather Patterns

First-time visitors to the Pacific Northwest are always bowled over by the sheer abundance of its lush greenery and the seeming benignity of a climate that keeps winters comfortably mild and summers comfortably cool. When they realize a good percentage of this greenery retains its emerald hue year-round, they're convinced this place is a perfect Eden for plants.

They're half right. It takes only a quick glance around to see that the Pacific Northwest truly is an Eden for plants—but it's an Eden far, far from perfect. It usually takes rueful personal experience before gardeners new to the region discover just how plant-unfriendly this place can be. The same discovery is made with distressing frequency by longtime residents of the Pacific Northwest who have just taken up gardening, and even by seasoned gardeners who move from one part of the region to another.

In spite of the seeming ease with which plants grow here, gardening success is dependent on a thorough understanding of the peculiarities (some would call them perversities) of the unique climate of this corner of the world, and of the interrelated geographic features governing that climate. More importantly, it requires that gardeners adapt their plant selection, gardening techniques, and gardening schedules to fit these immutable givens.

BASICS OF THE PACIFIC NORTHWEST CLIMATE

Location

Part of the reason for our temperate climate is obvious: the Pacific Northwest lies almost exactly halfway between the equator and the North Pole. (Salem, Oregon, straddles the 45th parallel.) However, this alone does not fully account for its mild winters. Portland is at the same latitude as Montreal, Quebec; Seattle at that of Duluth, Minnesota; Campbell River, British Columbia, at that of Kyiv, Ukraine. However, normal winter temperatures throughout the Pacific Northwest seldom drop below 10°F (-12°C).

Summer temperatures are likewise unexplained by location alone. Salem, Oregon, is slightly further south than Milan, Italy, but Pacific Northwest summers are considerably cooler than those of northern Italy, especially at night. Although high temperatures can briefly top 100°F (38°C) in the Rogue, Willamette, and eastern Fraser Valleys, typical highs are 75–85°F (24–30°C)

inland and considerably cooler on the coast. Summer nights are even chillier, seldom exceeding 55–60°F (13–16°C) in mid-summer even in our warmest subregions (see the next chapter for descriptions of the various subregions and the differences between them). The factor responsible for both phenomena is the Pacific Ocean.

The Pacific Ocean

Because large bodies of water heat up and cool down much more slowly than land masses, the Pacific Ocean—the largest body of water on the planet—is warmer in winter and cooler in summer than the land adjoining it. In winter, the warm, slow-moving North Pacific Current is aimed directly at the Pacific Northwest—between about 40° and 50° North latitude. Air masses in the northern hemisphere move from west to east, so by the time they arrive onshore in winter, they have traversed huge expanses of relatively warm ocean and are approximately the same temperature as the water: about 45°F (7°C). This is exactly the average midwinter high temperature throughout the Pacific Northwest. Frost is very rare right on the coast, but since the winter-warming effect of the ocean diminishes with distance from it, subfreezing (but still mild) temperatures can and do occur inland.

In summer, the situation is reversed, and air is cooled by the time it reaches land. In fact, it's considerably cooler than could be expected, because it passes over the cold California Current that flows southward from southern British Columbia to Baja California. This major ocean current, being at its largest and strongest in summer, keeps northeastern Pacific waters from warming to much more than the upper 50s F (13–15°C) in summer even in the most protected coves. Such temperatures make swimming a decidedly short-lived pleasure (longtime residents take fiendish delight in enticing innocent visitors to jump right in), and the air masses arriving onshore are not much warmer than the water. Sweaters, fleeces, and/or windbreakers are an essential part of summer wardrobes on the coast, especially at night and in early morning.

The Pacific Ocean is also the cause of the high humidity that characterizes the entire Pacific Northwest in winter and most parts of it year-round. Fog, low cloud, and gray overcast skies

The Pacific Northwest

are the norm from October to February whenever it is not actually raining; from February to April, conditions are cool, very damp, and only marginally less gray. Even in what appear to be dry (non-rainy) conditions, humidity is clearly visible at night in the beam of a flashlight or vehicle headlights.

Semi-permanent pressure areas

The very mildness of the climate year-round tends to sabotage its reputation as an Eden for plants. Mild winters mean insects overwinter far more easily than they do in colder climates. High humidity from the strong marine influence means fungal diseases are rampant in spring (see Chapter 15). Cool summer days and even cooler nights limit the success of late bloomers and late-ripening fruit. The growth of trees and shrubs native to continental climates is compromised, since sustained heat is needed to ripen their new wood before winter. On the coast, even getting tomatoes to ripen can be a challenge.

These drawbacks may seem fairly minor, and they are. But that's before factoring in the seasons. In the Pacific Northwest, there are not four, but two: wet and dry.

All winter, a massive low-pressure trough in the Gulf of Alaska dominates our weather. Since air circulates counterclockwise around low-pressure systems, the air arriving onshore in winter comes from the southwest—directly from Hawaii, which is why it's often called the Pineapple Express—and is very, very mild. Since warm air holds more moisture than cold air, it's also very, very moist.

When these warm, moist air masses hit our coastal mountains, which they usually do with considerable force, they rise and cool. As they cool, they release their moisture as rain, giving the Pacific Northwest coast the highest average annual precipitation in North America. Most of it falls when the effect of the low-pressure area is strongest, between October and February.

In late spring, this massive low-pressure area weakens and moves north of the Aleutian Islands, and an equally massive high-pressure ridge begins to build off the Oregon–California coast. By July, this ridge is so strong that virtually all moisture-bearing Pacific weather systems are deflected by it and cannot reach land, although a few weakened systems do sneak around its northern edge.

The ridge holds until late September, when it weakens and starts moving south, making way for the strengthening semi-permanent low-pressure area to move in once again. But while the high-pressure ridge holds sway between July and September, very little rain falls anywhere in the Pacific Northwest. In spite of our high annual rainfall, drought tolerance is an increasingly important factor in choosing garden plants.

Since air circulates clockwise around high-pressure areas, summer air masses arriving onshore come from the northwest—directly from the Arctic—and are of course very cold. Since cold air cannot pick up or hold much moisture even though it travels over water, summer winds are not only very cool, but very dry. These winds, which are most brisk on the coast, exacerbate the dryness of already dry summer gardens. As air masses move south and east over the land, they lose velocity and become warmer, but remain dry since there is no moisture to pick up.

Dry soil in August

The northwestern portion of the Pacific Northwest is coolest, dampest, and windiest in summer; the southeastern portion is warmest, driest, and least windy.

Mountains, rain, and rain shadows

So far, plants in the Pacific Northwest have to deal with mild but very wet winters and cool but very dry summers. This is of course the opposite of Eden-like conditions; plants need ample moisture while they're growing and blooming in summer (when ours get little or no rain) and only minimal amounts when they're dormant in winter (when ours get an overabundance). And even this too-simple scenario leaves out the complicating influences of our many mountains on rain—or lack of it.

Newcomers to the Pacific Northwest are sometimes let in on some local folk wisdom. "If you can see Mount Rainier (or Mount Hood, or Mount Baker, or the Three Sisters, or the North Shore Mountains, or simply "the mountains"), it means it's going to rain." As the newcomer mentally stores this useful bit of information for future reference, the story continues. "And if you can't see Mount Rainier (or whatever mountain), it means it *is* raining."

It's only a slight exaggeration, at least between October and April, when we get over 80 percent of our annual precipitation. Warm, moist air masses coming in off the Pacific release their moisture when they rise over mountains, and the Pacific Northwest has no shortage of mountains. Not just isolated snow-capped peaks, but whole major mountain ranges: the Coast Mountains and Vancouver Island Ranges (note the plural) in British Columbia; the Olympic Mountains, northern Cascade Range, and the mountain-sized Willapa Hills in Washington; the Coast Range, Cascade Range, and Siskiyou Mountains in Oregon; the Klamath Mountains and the southernmost peaks of the Cascade Range in southern Oregon and northern California.

The higher the mountains and/or the closer to the Pacific, the more intense and more frequent the rain. The relatively low Coast Range, being the first obstacle in the path of the Pineapple Express, gives gardens on its western slopes an average annual precipitation of at least 75 in. (1905 mm). On the southwestern slopes of the much higher Olympic Mountains, average annual precipitation is 150 in. (3810 mm), making this area the only temperate rain forest in North America. At the peak of Mount Olympus, precipitation is closer to 200 in. (5080 mm).

At the uninhabited weather station of Henderson Lake, just east of Barkley Sound on Vancouver Island, the Pineapple Express routinely collides head-on with high, steep mountains to give average annual precipitation of 262 in. (6655 mm)—a North American record—and record annual precipitation of 373 in. (9474 mm). This is obviously a fluke of circumstance, but the common designation of the whole region as the Wet Coast is undeniably accurate—at least in winter.

Rainfall in the inland areas between major mountain ranges is not nearly as high, of course, but only in the Pacific Northwest would annual precipitation averaging between 36 and 60 in. (914 and 1524 mm) be considered low to moderate. Again, the higher amounts occur on the western slopes of the Cascade Range as clouds rise up their very high slopes, cool, and release their moisture.

But the equation is not quite as simple as mountains = rain. It all depends on which side of the mountains you're on. Clouds that drop their moisture on western or southwestern slopes are that much drier once they clear the mountains; the higher the mountains they have to climb, the less moisture is left in them. Almost nothing is left by the time clouds clear the Cascades (Coast Mountains in British Columbia); precipitation east of these major ranges drops suddenly to near-desert or even true desert levels.

Similarly, the overlapping mountain ranges in southern Oregon and northern California are very wet on their southwestern slopes, but create a rain shadow on their northeastern slopes. Rainfall in the Rogue Valley around Medford is barely one-third what it is right on the coast. Significant rain shadows also exist on the eastern coast of Vancouver Island and the mainland coast (aptly known as the Sunshine Coast) of B.C.

The most extensive rain shadow within the Pacific Northwest is cast by the Olympic Mountains that are so super-wet on their southwestern slopes. In their lee, the northern coastal strip of the Olympic Peninsula gets a scant 15–27 in. (381–686 mm) of precipitation annually. Nearby areas—the southern tip of Vancouver Island, the San Juan Islands, and even the northern part of Washington around Bellingham—are similarly affected, having much lower rainfall than could be expected.

It's a whole new story in summer, of course, since weather systems come from the northwest instead of the southwest and are channeled in completely different directions, but again the mountains have profound effect. Depending on their orientation, they can funnel or deflect cooling and/or drying winds, greatly influencing local garden conditions.

FALLOUT FROM THE BASIC CLIMATE

By now it's obvious that plants in Pacific Northwest gardens have to be thoroughly drought-tolerant in order to survive the warmest two months of the year with little or no rain, yet be able to survive regular and prolonged deluges of cold rain in winter. They should also be highly resistant to fungal diseases and not be dependent on prolonged summer heat, and of course be attuned to the peculiarities of local garden conditions—excess rain, very little rain, and/or cooling and drying summer winds. But they also have to put up with some even more plant-unfriendly consequences of our supposedly perfect climate.

Time warps

To begin with, the regular changing of the guard of our low-pressure and high-pressure areas sometimes gets out of synch with the seasons. If the low-pressure area lingers, winter can continue well into June, with cooler-than-normal temperatures and non-stop rain creating havoc with spring planting schedules and greatly increasing the incidence of fungal diseases. At the other end of the season, our long, warm, fairly dry, very pleasant Indian summers of four to six weeks tend to be longest and strongest after an abnormally early killing frost in September.

Summer sometimes continues right into November—not necessarily with warm temperatures, but certainly with dry conditions. Conversely, winter can arrive in fall, as it did in November 1985 when subfreezing temperatures damaged many plants before they were fully dormant. (Many still had their leaves.) Spring often puts in a brief early appearance in midwinter, prompting plants to break dormancy; their tender growth buds are then killed by frost.

Less often, the high-pressure ridge arrives early, bringing summer in April. This may seem a pleasant development, but for plants, it's devastating: summer means drought, and without rain, plants cannot leaf out, flower, or grow as they're programmed to do in spring. (Gardeners grit their teeth in dry springs when people say "Isn't this great weather we're having?") Although gardens can be watered, irrigation does not replace all the benefits of natural rainfall, even in gardens; outside our gardens, native plants suffer greatly when this happens.

Sometimes the time warps continue through the year, as they did in 2004. June came in April, bringing drought, and August came in June, bringing high heat to gardens already parched. Fortunately, October then came in August, bringing continuous rain, but it was already too late for many plants. No colorful fall foliage was seen that October; leaves were simply too dry and exhausted.

Frost and snow have a regular habit of arriving at inconvenient times. Late frosts are a fact of life here, since the continuous rains that keep our winters so mild protect us from low temperatures only while they remain continuous. When the rains start to diminish, so does the protection. Except in our coldest-winter subregions, most gardens in the Pacific Northwest have experienced at least one frost-free winter—only to get severe frost in late March or April, just after most new buds have broken dormancy.

Snow also has its own schedule. White Christmases are extremely rare (we have personally experienced two in 60-plus years), but white Valentine's Days are not. Snow is likely in late November, although it invariably melts before Christmas; it can even come in early November before all the leaves are off the trees, greatly increasing the risk of damage. Snow is even more likely in late February or early March, when it's very wet and heavy and likewise increases the risk of damage.

Hardy in Siberia, tender in the Pacific Northwest

Conventional wisdom holds that gardeners can safely grow any plant in their own hardiness zone or lower. Not in the Pacific Northwest. Sometimes we can't even grow plants that perfectly match our hardiness zones, Zones 7 to 9.

Although low temperatures may be identical, Zone 7 in the Pacific Northwest is simply not the same as Zone 7 in Virginia, Tennessee, or Arkansas. Our Zone 8 is a far cry from the Zone 8 of Georgia, Alabama, or Mississippi, and our narrow southern coastal strip of Zone 9 bears no relationship at all to the Zone 9 of northern Florida, southern Louisiana, or coastal Texas. (We once tried growing okra; it was a colossal flop.) It bears repeating that hardiness zones are a very crude indicator of plant suitability, indicating nothing at all about high temperatures, humidity (or lack of it), the relative length of summer or winter, or a plant's inherent robustness or weakness. Gardener beware.

Plants in the medium range of cold hardiness, Zones 4 to 6, tend to be those native to continental climates with long hot summers and long cold winters. Here again our mild climate proves a drawback; it's often too mild in summer to sufficiently ripen the new growth of woody species. The result is winter dieback, even though the species is much hardier than it need be for our winter temperatures.

Woody species hardy to Zones 1 to 3 tend to perform even more poorly in our mild winters. For instance, although Siberian larch (*Larix sibirica*) is as solidly cold-hardy as a plant can get, it rarely survives very many of our winters. Programmed to remain deeply dormant through a very long, very cold winter, it interprets our mild spells in January or February as the signal to break dormancy at long last. The tender new buds are then nipped by a mild frost of only a few degrees, and that's that. No new ones will regrow. Russian olive (*Elaeagnus angustifolia*), a shrub considered impossible to kill in cold-winter zones, is another non-starter in the Pacific Northwest.

There are exceptions, of course, but in general, woody plants that do well in continental climates are not well suited for the Pacific Northwest—and vice versa. Very often, species or cultivars described as "difficult" in general North American gardening guides are the very ones that do best in the Pacific Northwest, while those considered "easy" do poorly. Flowering crabapple cultivars, roses, shade trees, rhododendron cultivars, and fruit varieties are prime examples. Plants that sound exceptional in nationwide plant catalogs can thus turn out to be major disappointments, especially if they're described as "easy to grow." Our mild climate is perfect for growing difficult plants; it's only the easy ones that give us problems.

Acidic soil

Soils in high-rainfall areas are almost always strongly acidic, and ours are no exception. Liming our gardens is a necessity, and for lawns, fruit trees, and vegetable gardens, a perpetual necessity. Acidic soils also tend to be infertile, and, despite the misleading visual cues of towering conifers and the dense undergrowth of Pacific Northwest forests, often are.

Our most highly acidic soils are those on the rainy coast; on the almost-as-rainy windward slopes of our many mountains, they're almost as acidic. Coastal soils are also the most infertile, with mountain soils a close second; both need regular fertilizing if they're to grow a wide range of garden plants. The alluvial soils of our major river valleys are rich, but are still strongly acidic. Since most garden plants prefer a fertile soil that's only slightly acidic, there are soil adjustments to be made no matter which part of the Pacific Northwest we garden in.

Water tables

As well as being acidic, the soils in our most heavily populated river valleys are very heavy—the result of fine particles being washed down from the mountains by numerous rivers over many millennia. When our high winter rainfall combines with runoff from our many mountains, it cannot drain away fast enough, and water tables rise right to the surface of the soil. This of course does roots no good, since they must have air as well as water to survive. Plants may be in little danger of freezing in mild Pacific Northwest winters, but they're often in grave danger of drowning.

Another consequence of super-mild spells in winter is that if heavy rains combine with unseasonable snowmelt in the mountains, rivers can and do flood their banks. Widespread rowboats-in-the-street flooding is now largely controlled by dams, but is not eliminated; major flooding occurred in Washington in November 1990 (the Interstate 90 Lake Washington Floating Bridge sank) and throughout western Oregon and Washington in February 1996 and December 2007. Local flooding remains an expected hazard, especially close to any mountains.

Most likely flooding times are late December/early January, when the mild Pineapple Express is heavily laden with rain, and in May, when snowpacks normally begin melting. The latter seldom causes serious problems for gardeners, but can wreak havoc with farm planting since heavy tractors cannot be driven over mushy fields.

High winter water tables limit the number of deep-rooted trees we can grow, which partially accounts for the noticeable lack of large deciduous shade trees in our landscapes. It also contributes directly to the number of tall conifers that blow down in winter storms. All our very tall native conifers have unbelievably shallow root systems, and when the soil is saturated, they literally have nothing to cling to.

Local flooding in late December

Since our strongest winds coincide with our heaviest rains, these trees have no way to brace themselves against the wind, and down they come. In heavily treed areas, good garden sites—not to mention house sites—are those that either take prevailing winter wind direction into account or are enhanced by selective logging. The few tall, scraggly conifers left standing in newly cleared subdivisions are especially vulnerable to blowdown because they have suddenly lost the sheltering protection of surrounding trees.

In summer, of course, the high water tables that cause these problems sink out of sight, and sometimes out of reach of plant roots. In rural areas, shallow wells often run dry just at the point where water is most desperately needed by garden plants. The importance of choosing species that are reliably drought tolerant becomes painfully obvious here—but of course all these plants must also be able to survive saturated and occasionally flooded soil in winter.

Snow
It snows in the Pacific Northwest. Maybe not every year in every place, but snow occasionally falls even in coastal southern Oregon and northern California. Most of it melts quickly, if not immediately, and accumulations of more than about 6 in. (15 cm) are unusual except on the Cascade slopes and other high elevations.

The reaction of Pacific Northwesterners to predictable and expectable snow, especially in our larger cities, causes people from cold-winter climates to shake their heads in disbelief. Snow alerts warn of possible accumulations of 0.5–1 in. (1.2–2.5 cm), schools close for ankle-deep drifts, and half the population stays home from work at the sign of the first snowflake. The other half jumps into their cars to stock up on groceries and other necessities for the duration.

Such reactions seem laughable, but with most municipalities owning no genuine, single-purpose snowplows and having limited supplies of sand and salt on hand (after all, snowfalls are usually fleeting), snow is a very real hazard to transportation—especially since the slush tends to refreeze and most people don't bother to equip their vehicles with snow tires. It really is safer to stay home, at least until the streets are cleared. While there, we can do what's necessary in our gardens whenever it snows.

Given our usually light (and sometimes absent) snowfalls, wrapping upright conifers and other vulnerable plants with snow netting may seem an undue precaution. However, the supposed advantages of our mild winters again come back to haunt us. Since it usually snows here when temperatures are barely below freezing, our snows are very wet, and consequently very heavy. Even a very moderate snowfall of 4–5 in. (10–13 cm) is capable of causing widespread limb breakage. Pacific Northwest gardeners who routinely brush even light layers of fresh snow off their hedges and vulnerable trees and shrubs aren't being paranoid, but prudent. Even very light layers of snow tend to partially melt, then freeze to limbs and evergreen leaves, adding considerable weight.

Blowdown of native conifer

Snow on contorted filbert (*Corylus avellana* 'Contorta')

The situation is even worse when temperatures fluctuate from subfreezing to just above freezing, bringing alternating snow and rain. Rain soaks into snow that has already accumulated on branches, filling all the tiny air spaces. When the temperature drops, this becomes ice, which is even heavier than wet snow. Additional layers of snow that fill with rain and then freeze add up to weight that can literally be unbearable even for strong-limbed trees such as oaks. The scenario of alternating snow and rain usually occurs during the night, making it almost impossible to deal with (although dedicated gardeners have been known to set their alarm clocks for midnight snow-brushing detail). Some snow damage is almost inevitable, though, and all that can be done is to remove broken limbs as soon as possible.

Outflow winds and ice storms

The continuous north-south mountain chain of the Cascades and Coast Mountains is broken only by two major west-flowing rivers, the Columbia and the Fraser, and the valleys they have created. (The almost canyon-like valley of the Columbia is very narrow, which is why it's called the Columbia River Gorge.) In normal conditions, these corridors allow Pacific air masses moving from west to east to bring mild, moist conditions far inland. However, the corridors also work in reverse. Air always flows from high-pressure areas toward low-pressure areas, so when barometric pressure is high east of the mountains and low west of them, air flows from east to west.

Although this can happen in summer, bringing hot, dry interior air into the Pacific Northwest, it happens most often in winter, when our low-pressure area is strongest and the dry air east of the mountains is coldest. The result is a blast of very cold continental air blowing from the east, chilling everything in its path. The effects of outflow winds from the Columbia River Gorge routinely extend to the east sides of Portland and Vancouver (Washington); very strong outflows can cause sharp temperature drops deep into the Willamette Valley and northward well into Washington. Although most likely to occur in late December and again in early March, outflow conditions are a possibility any time in winter.

Winter outflow winds from the eastern Fraser Valley chill communities all along the Fraser River, including Vancouver

(B.C.) at its mouth, and often spill right over the Strait of Georgia to cause sudden severe drops in temperature in the San Juan Islands, the southern tip of Vancouver Island, and on the northern and eastern coasts of the Olympic Peninsula. Because this cold air is blocked by mountains just north of Vancouver, it also spills south to chill the area around Bellingham, Washington. Outflow conditions also occur through all the major mountain passes (and in B.C., major inlets), but their effects are more localized and usually not as severe.

Sudden freezing is of course not good for plants, especially not-so-hardy species, and they also don't appreciate the extra doses of sleet or wet snow they get while surrounding areas are getting normal rain. But these are the least of the problem. If cold outflow winds chill an area to below freezing just before the situation reverts to normal and it rains again, raindrops turn to ice the instant they contact a frozen surface.

Tree limbs and shrubs (not to mention roads and utility wires) then quickly become coated with beautiful but very heavy ice, causing extensive damage. Often but misleadingly called silver thaws, these ice storms are usually short-lived but can wreak havoc on gardens in a matter of hours. There is nothing gardeners can do in this situation except wait it out and avoid touching any plant; even super-flexible grasses and perennial stems become brittle as glass when encased in ice.

Big Freezes and Big Snows

Once every 15 to 20 years or so, strong winter outflow conditions coincide with super-cold Arctic air that has been drawn deep into the continent. Frigid air then spills through every major and minor river valley, mountain pass, and inlet, and the entire Pacific Northwest experiences a Big Freeze.

In these infrequent but regularly occurring conditions, average low temperatures can suddenly drop by two hardiness zones. Temperatures hover at or below 0°F (-18°C) for two weeks or more, causing wholesale losses of Zone 8 plants, defoliating broadleaved Zone 7 plants such as English holly, and even killing native plants. These Big Freezes extend as far as southern California, bringing ice and snow and causing extensive damage to citrus crops.

There is little or nothing gardeners can do about Big Freezes except clean up, cut back, and start over—and perhaps hedge

Aftermath of high wind

our bets by not filling our gardens too exclusively with border-line-hardy plants. However, some established Zone 8 species have proven root-hardy enough to survive Big Freezes, although at considerable setback to their top growth.

In the last century or so, Big Freezes have occurred in 1924, 1935, 1949–50, 1968–69, 1972 (many records still stand), and 1989. Only slightly less noteworthy are what could be called mini–Big Freezes, in which temperatures do not drop quite so low (only to about 10°F, -12°C), but remain low for longer periods and/or are accompanied by deep snow. Recent mini–Big Freezes occurred in 1979, 1983–84, 1990–91, and 2006–07.

Big Snows, the result of cold outflow winds colliding with the Pineapple Express, are usually much more localized, although deep snow covered the entire Pacific Northwest in January 1950. These deep snows, being lighter and more powdery than our usual wet snows, actually do relatively little harm to plants. Plastic greenhouses often collapse, and the ground can get super-saturated when massive amounts of snow are suddenly washed away by subsequent rain, but the worst danger of Big Snows is probably to smaller plants being inadvertently stepped on by gardeners trying to brush snow off larger plants.

However, Big Snows can cause considerable havoc in gardens where snow is usually light or absent. In snow-challenged Eugene, Oregon (where the standard response to "It's starting to snow" is "Is it sticking?"), a total of 47 in. (119 cm) of snow fell in January 1969, including 34 in. (86 cm) in one day. The same weather system dumped 6–12 in. (15–30 cm) of snow on the even more snow-challenged Oregon coast.

In super-mild Seattle, over 21 in. (53 cm) of snow fell in one day in January 1950; more recently, a total of 18–24 in. (45–60 cm) fell in Puget Sound in four days in late December 1996. In the same storm, still remembered in British Columbia as "The Blizzard of '96," a total of over 48 in. (120 cm) of snow fell in Mediterranean-like Victoria, with a record 25 in. (64 cm) in one day; in Vancouver, the four-day total was almost 60 in. (150 cm).

Ill winds

Wind is not usually a problem in the Pacific Northwest; even on the coast, where strong winds are normal, gardens and gardeners soon learn to adapt. However, when we do get regionwide high winds, we get them in spades. The danger to gardens is usually not so much from direct damage, such as trees being uprooted, but from being smashed by very large trees, usually native conifers, falling on them. Broken tree limbs also become deadly missiles in high winds and can wreak havoc on smaller plants.

Our most recent regionwide high winds, in December 2006, hit at near-hurricane force at Seattle-Tacoma International Airport and at 50 mph (80 kmh) in downtown Seattle. A series of intense windstorms that month caused widespread damage throughout the Pacific Northwest but especially in northern Washington and southwestern B.C.; in Vancouver's heavily forested Stanley Park, 10,000 trees were blown down. In January 1993, a severe windstorm with gusts well over hurricane force (the Inaugural Day Storm) also caused extensive damage throughout Puget Sound. But the all-time record for widespread wind damage belongs to the storm of 12 October 1962.

Known in northern California, Oregon, and Washington as the Columbus Day Storm and in B.C. (where it hit in late afternoon and evening) as Typhoon Freda, this massive windstorm that blew out of a clear blue sky carried sustained winds of 55 mph (89 kmh), with gusts of 116 mph (187 kmh) in downtown Portland and gusts of 150 mph (241 kmh) at Naselle on the southern coast of Washington.

Hopefully, this typhoon (the Pacific equivalent of a hurricane) will remain a record; its damage was incalculable. In addition to the loss of 48 lives and costs in the hundreds of millions of (1962) dollars, many fruit and nut orchards were totally destroyed and 15 billion board feet of timber were blown down. Damage to individual gardens can only be imagined; in some areas, two out of every three houses were damaged.

The scars of the Columbus Day Storm/Typhoon Freda can still be seen today on now-mature timber trees with double or triple trunks; these grew to replace normal leaders that were snapped off when they were saplings.

AN EDEN AFTER ALL

By now it may seem the Pacific Northwest is a perfect hell for plants, but a little reflection puts all these imperfections into proper perspective. Once we acknowledge the quirks and peculiarities and drawbacks of our climate as basic gardening guidelines, instead of ignoring them (or worse, trying to combat them), this place really is an Eden.

We may not be able to do anything about Big Freezes or Big Snows or infrequent devastating high winds, but we can choose from among hundreds of garden-worthy species from all over the world that will hold up beautifully to these known hazards. We can't make our heavy wet snows any lighter, but we can wrap our upright conifers (even if winter turns out to be snowless) and gently brush or shake fresh snow off our vulnerable plants while it's still loose.

We can't turn our seasons upside down to get more of our abundant annual rainfall in summer and less of it in winter, but our heavy winter rains really are what keep our Eden green year-round. Besides creating ideal conditions for broadleaved evergreens and conifers, they fully recharge our depleted water tables, wells, and reservoirs to supply us with sufficient water for irrigating next summer.

Very often no summer irrigation is needed after all, at least for established plants. The heavy soils of our densely populated river valleys hold moisture far into the dry season and release it slowly. In these conditions, a great many beautiful plants from around the world are highly drought tolerant—and more amazingly, highly tolerant of wet winters at the same time (see Chapter 4).

Even with our winter monsoons, soil drainage is less of a problem than it first appears. Coastal soils, being sandy-silty in texture, are naturally well drained and easily accommodate the drenching rains that fall on them all winter. Any site on a slope, whether a minor rise in a particular garden or an entire garden on a slope of a hill or mountain, is also well drained.

As for the heavy soils in our river valleys, even these are basically well drained. It's true these soils are very heavy—that is, a

Himalayan blue poppy (*Meconopsis betonicifolia*)

shovelful seems to weigh a ton—but instead of being pure sticky, gooey clay, they're actually clay-based loams, with plenty of silt and sand and even modest amount of organic matter mixed in. These are precisely the elusive and seemingly contradictory "moisture-retentive but well-drained" soils so often called for. If their drainage does need improving, it's easy to do so by working in large amounts of bulk organic materials.

We can't do anything about our long, cool, very moist springs, but these very conditions are what prolong the colorful blooms of some of the most beautiful flowering shrubs, trees, bulbs, and perennials known to man. So what if our cool, damp springs make it almost impossible to grow hollyhocks or flowering almonds? They make it ridiculously easy to grow rhododendrons, flowering dogwoods, erythroniums, and Himalayan blue poppies.

We can't do anything about our heat-challenged summers, but so what if we can't ripen Granny Smith apples or get crape myrtles (*Lagerstroemia indica*) to flower in most areas? We can easily grow bumper crops of raspberries, strawberries, and blueberries, and our sunny but cool summers are perfect for roses, clematis, lilies, and lavender.

We can't stop winter rains from leaching calcium from our soils and making them acidic, but would we really want

Acid-loving plants thrive beautifully in our imperfect Eden.

them to? These acidic soils are perfect for growing rhododendrons and azaleas, heaths and heathers, vacciniums, camellias, flowering dogwoods, magnolias, maples, a wide assortment of broadleaved evergreens such as pieris, and a huge assortment of conifers and ferns.

With the addition of lime, we can also grow a much wider range of plants—even lime-lovers such as lilacs and mock oranges, if we so choose. It's much easier to raise the pH of acidic soils to accommodate lime-lovers than it is to lower the pH of alkaline soils to accommodate acid-lovers. It's also easier to water plants in dry summers than it is to keep water-shy species such as ceanothus dry in wet-summer areas. And it's far easier to provide heat-lovers with a warm microclimate, such as the south side of a wall, than it is to try to keep plants cool in hot-summer areas.

As a matter of fact, we seem to come out on the right side of the equation every time. Our Eden is definitely imperfect, but its imperfections are possible to work with. In many instances, they even work to our advantage—as long as we acknowledge the absolute reality of their existence. In a nutshell, this is the key to successful gardening in the Pacific Northwest.

CHAPTER 2

Subregions of the Pacific Northwest

Winter is what gives the Pacific Northwest its reputation in the rest of the world for being very mild, very wet, and very much the same all over. And it is—in winter. Between November and February, a forecast of rain, highs of 45°F (7°C) and lows of 34°F (1°C) could apply anywhere from northern Vancouver Island to just across the Oregon–California border, and from the breakers of the Pacific to the slopes of the Cascades. Indeed, nearly identical winter conditions, varying only by a degree or two and the intensity of the rain, sometimes persist over the entire region for two or three weeks at a time.

But for gardeners, weather conditions that count the most are those that occur spring through fall—and in the various parts of the Pacific Northwest, these can be as different from each other as night and day. The seven subregions we have identified are based on major differences in annual rainfall, high and low temperatures in both summer and winter, length of growing season, topography, soils, and natural vegetation. The dividing lines between adjacent subregions are of course not sharp; climates blend and blur into each other so that the climate of a community near the edge of one subregion is strongly influenced by that of its neighboring region(s).

This is especially true of the area around Roseburg, which we have included in the Willamette subregion even though it shares almost as many characteristics with the Rogue subregion. Arguably, the Umpqua Valley deserves a subregion of its own, but this would open the door to similar arguments for parts of other subregions and create a balkanization that would render all the maps meaningless. We have opted for clarity, even at the expense of oversimplification.

We have shown the mountainous areas separately for three reasons. First, we wanted to give a graphic depiction of how they cause the different rainfall patterns, rain shadows, prevailing winds, sun exposure, and other climatic factors that so strongly influence local gardening conditions. We have differentiated between mountains higher and lower than 5000 ft. (1524 m) to give some idea of the relative importance of these factors as well as the steepness of the surrounding terrain.

Secondly, we believe that leaving mountains off climatic maps—especially maps of the Pacific Northwest—is highly misleading. For instance, the central section of the Pacific Coast subregion does not blend and blur into the Willamette subregion; the two distinct climates are separated by mountains that belong in neither subregion but greatly influence the climate of both.

One of our pet peeves is that most climatic maps either ignore the Pacific Northwest mountains completely, declaring the entire region Zone 8, or give them the barest nod by designating most mountains Zone 7 and the high peaks of the Cascades Zone 6. This is accurate enough in that winter temperatures probably do not go much lower than the Zone 7 (0°F, -18°C) at the tops of the Vancouver Island Ranges, the Olympic Mountains, or the Siskiyou Mountains, or much lower than the Zone 6 (-10°F, -23°C) in the high Cascades.

But what such numbers fail to mention is that these winter-low temperatures may remain in effect for nine, ten, or even 12 months of the year. From our own garden in the Gulf Islands, we see Vancouver Island mountaintops that are completely covered with snow from October until at least April, with isolated patches of snow never quite disappearing from northeast-facing depressions even in August. Nearby is an enormous, permanent, age-old glacier—in Zone 7. Designating the high Cascades Zone 6—a very accommodating gardening climate as the term is commonly understood—is even more ludicrous, given their perpetually snow-clad peaks and their elevations far above timberline.

Our third reason for excluding the mountainous areas is that they are very sparsely populated. Surprisingly large portions of them are virtually uninhabited except for seasonal cabins and facilities related to logging or to recreational pursuits such as skiing and camping. The Olympic Mountains, for instance, are almost entirely included in the Olympic National Park, and the park is surrounded by the Olympic National Forest. North of Powell River on the mainland coast of British Columbia, human habitation does not (at least at this time) extend more than a mile or so inland from the edge of salt water. In Oregon, with the exception of small communities along the major mountain passes, the middle and upper slopes of the Cascades south of Mount Hood are truly the Wilderness Areas they are designated.

People living in small communities along the many smaller rivers that drain both slopes of the Coast Range may take

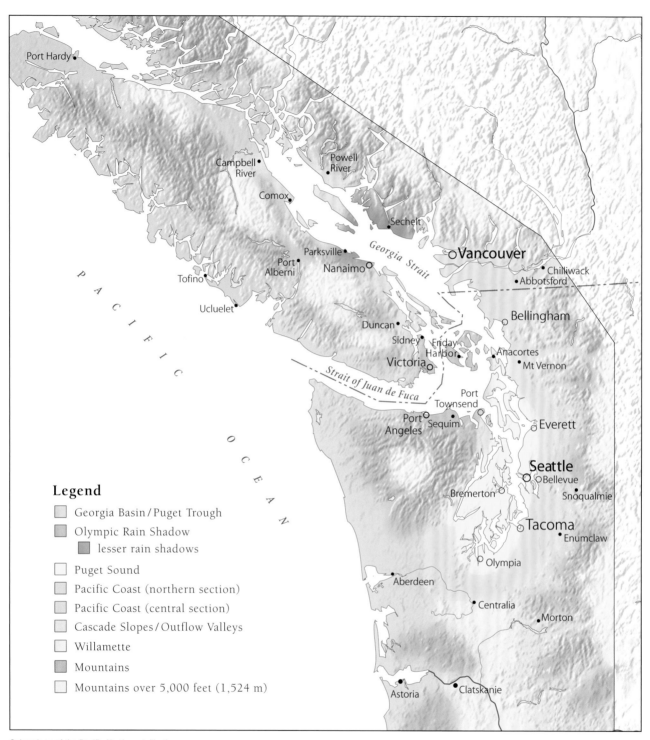

Legend

- Georgia Basin / Puget Trough
- Olympic Rain Shadow
  - lesser rain shadows
- Puget Sound
- Pacific Coast (northern section)
- Pacific Coast (central section)
- Cascade Slopes / Outflow Valleys
- Willamette
- Mountains
- Mountains over 5,000 feet (1,524 m)

Subregions of the Pacific Northwest, North

exception to being considered marginal or even nonexistent, and they would be perfectly justified. Again, however, showing all these smaller river valleys would have made our already complicated maps almost incomprehensible. To any of you who feel slighted, and to any homesteaders living on any "uninhabited" mountain slopes anywhere in the Pacific Northwest, we apologize: we do know you exist.

However, it is precisely because the mountainous areas of the Pacific Northwest are so sparsely inhabited that few of the 11 million of us who live in this unique region are fully aware of the profound influence of these mountains on our climate, our weather, and our gardening conditions. Devising these maps certainly opened our own eyes to some new understandings; we hope they will do the same for others.

PACIFIC COAST

Elevation: Sea level to 200 ft. (60 m)

Soil: Highly acidic, light-textured, marginally fertile; heavier and moderately fertile in coastal valleys of Oregon

Annual precipitation: 75 in. (1905 mm) or more

Average temperature, August:

Northern section: High 65°F (18°C), low 50°F (10°C)

Central and southern sections: High 68°F (20°C), low 52°F (11°C)

Average temperature, January:

Northern section: High 45°F (7°C), low 34°F (1°C)

Central section: High 50°F (10°C), low 38°F (3°C)

Southern section: High 55°F (13°C), low 42°F (5°C)

Average last frost: 1–15 March

Average first frost: 15–30 November

Growing season: 240–270 days; very low heat units

Humidity: High year-round; frequent morning fog

Winds:

Northern section: Brisk in summer, west to northwest; strong in winter, southwest to southeast. Frequent winter storms often reach hurricane strength of 64 knots (73 mph, 117 kmh)

Central section: Brisk in summer, northwest to north; strong in winter, south to southwest. Frequent winter storms, with two or three reaching hurricane strength each winter. Winds along mouth of Columbia River moderate in summer, west; moderate to strong in winter, east

Southern section: Moderate to brisk in summer, north to northwest; light to moderate in winter, usually south. Occasional winter storms reaching gale force of 34 knots (39 mph, 63 kmh) or stronger

Because of its length, this subregion is divided into northern, central, and southern sections. The northern section is north of Ucluelet, B.C.; the central section is between Ucluelet and Cape Blanco, Oregon; the southern section is south of Cape Blanco. The southern section and most of the central section are shown on the map on page 31.

Seldom exceeding 12 miles (19 km) in width, this very long, narrow subregion lies between the ocean's edge and the coastal mountains, which in places jut out almost to the ocean's edge. It also includes the lowlands at the northern tip of Vancouver Island, along with its northeastern coast and the adjacent mainland, and extends surprisingly far inland along numerous inlets and rivers.

Communities along the lower Chehalis, Umpqua, and Rogue Rivers definitely experience coastal-type climates; along the much broader expanse of the lower Columbia, a coastal flavor penetrates as far as Clatskanie, Oregon, almost 40 miles (64 km) inland. Port Alberni, situated at the head of the Alberni Inlet that almost bisects Vancouver Island, is also strongly affected by the Pacific Ocean—it was hit by a tsunami in 1964—even though it's much closer to the east coast of the island than to the west coast.

Western red cedar, hemlock, salal, sword fern, Pacific rhododendron, and other moisture-loving native species provide the background and context for coastal gardens, as do the wind-swept silhouettes of shore pines. In the northern section, Sitka spruce begins to predominate, as it does all the way to Alaska; in the southern section, redwoods and Oregon myrtle/California bay laurel (*Umbellularia californica*) give notice of overlap with the climate of coastal California.

Throughout this subregion, the influence of the Pacific Ocean is overwhelming. Winters are very mild (hard frost is rare, although we have personally seen ice right on the beach near Florence, Oregon) and summers are very cool, even when the sun does shine. Other coastal constants include frequent fog, frequent wind, and above all, high rainfall. The average annual precipitation that totals more than 6 ft. (1.8 m) here is actually just a minimum: Aberdeen, Washington, gets 83 in. (2108 mm); Tillamook, Oregon, 90 in. (2286 mm); Tofino, British Columbia, 130 in. (3302 mm); the western slopes of the Olympics 150 in. (3810 mm). Most of this falls in winter—sometimes as sleet or wet snow in the northern section—but amazingly, drainage is seldom a problem in this subregion's sandy-silty soils.

Rain diminishes to a mere trickle by late summer and early fall. Since this is also when cooling winds finally diminish, the warmest temperatures of the year come in August rather than July. Summer highs can easily reach 78°F (25°C); anything warmer is a heat wave.

The fine weather between August and early October brings hordes of tourists, many of whom believe the coastal climate is always this benign. Inland locals flock to the coast then too, but also like to visit in January or February. It's just as wet as everywhere else then, if not wetter, but temperatures can be warmer by a good five degrees Fahrenheit (three degrees Celsius), and salt air is a great winter tonic.

Rhododendrons and azaleas grow to perfection throughout this subregion, as do other ericaceous plants such as pieris, pernettya, heaths and heathers, enkianthus, leucothoe, huckleberries, bearberry (kinnikinnick), and ornamental vacciniums. So do hydrangeas, camellias, escallonias, hebes, hardy fuchsias, primulas, mahonias, maples, hollies, astilbes, hostas, ferns, and most conifers, including the highly wind-tolerant monkey puzzle. Cool-season ornamental grasses grow as easily as the abundant hay crops that feed the cows that give the milk for Tillamook's famous cheese. Blueberries and cranberries grow to perfection in the moist, acidic soils; both are grown commercially here.

Moisture-loving Japanese species grow to perfection in this subregion, and most plants from China and northeastern Asia also thrive here. The cool, moist, nearly frost-free climate is also ideal for many semi-tender species from the Himalaya, especially if they're protected from strong winds; those from New Zealand and southern Chile thrive even in windy conditions. All Zone 8 plants can be safely grown here; Zone 9 plants can be grown in the open in the southern section and with protection elsewhere.

But Zone 8 or 9 plants needing a long hot summer for flowering, fruiting, or ripening of wood are ruled out: the necessary heat units just don't exist. Plants originating in hot-summer, cold-winter continental climates are very unhappy here, as are heat-loving Mediterranean plants such as grapes and figs. However, lavender and rosemary grow beautifully as long as winter drainage is good. Cool-weather vegetables such as peas, lettuce, potatoes, cabbages, kale, and Chinese vegetables thrive on the coast; heat-loving tomatoes, corn, peppers, eggplant, and melons do not. A small greenhouse—or a large one—is a good investment for coastal vegetable growers.

Any plant subject to fungal disease is subject in spades on the coast, and roses and fruit trees must be chosen with disease resistance as top priority. (Rugosa roses are great, apples are iffy; don't even think about peaches.) Early-season clematis and perennials are generally more successful than late bloomers, which are prone to mildew. Fleshy-rooted perennials such as baby's breath and hardy gloxinias tend to rot over winter, and a high water table in the northern section limits deep-rooted plants there year-round.

Shelter from wind is extremely important, but cooling summer winds cause more garden headaches than the much stronger winter winds. Even non-dormant plants can handle winter's strong, mild, wet winds unless they have very large evergreen leaves (not a good idea here), but brisk northern winds in summer can cool gardens even more than the lack of sun—which is another problem. "Plant in shade" is a garden directive that should be banished on the coast. Virtually all so-called shade-lovers are perfectly happy in full sun, or what would be full sun if it appeared through the fog and clouds more often.

On the plus side, gardeners in this subregion never have to worry about ice storms, heavy snow, or late killing frosts, and seldom need to irrigate. Bragging rights include being easily able to grow such "finicky" plants as artichokes and Himalayan blue poppy (*Meconopsis betonicifolia*). Above all, coastal gardeners can grow the widest possible range of temperate-climate rhododendrons, including the more tender species and cultivars.

Ucluelet, B.C., and Florence, Oregon, each hold a well-attended annual Rhododendron Festival; Brookings, Oregon, holds a yearly Azalea Festival. Tofino, B.C., is home to Painted Mountain, a spectacular hilltop rhododendron garden, and also hosts the fairly new Tofino Botanical Gardens. At the other end of the subregion, near Coos Bay, Oregon, is Shore Acres State Park Botanical Garden.

CASCADE SLOPES/OUTFLOW VALLEYS

Elevation: Cascade slopes 400–1200 ft. (122–366 m); outflow valleys 60–400 ft. (18–122 m)

Soil: Thin, acidic, and moderately fertile on Cascade slopes; deep, heavy, and fertile in outflow valleys

Annual precipitation: 50–70 in. (1270–1778 mm)

Average temperature, July: High 75–82°F (24–28°C), low 52°F (11°C)

Average temperature, January: High 43°F (6°C), low 32°F (0°C)

Average last frost: 15–30 April

Average first frost: 15–31 October

Growing season: 160–180 days; moderately high heat units

Humidity: High in winter, moderate in summer

Winds: Light to moderate in summer, west to northwest; moderate in winter, southwest to west except for occasional strong easterly winds in outflow valleys and mountain passes

This subregion (the southern portion of which is shown on the map on page 31) includes the lower western slopes of the Cascades along their entire length, from where they merge with the Coast Mountains of British Columbia in the north to where they disappear in the maze of Klamath and Siskiyou Mountains in the south. It also includes the Columbia Gorge, the eastern Fraser Valley, higher elevations in the smaller river valleys, and all mountain passes on the west side of the Cascades. Terrains differ widely here, but weather patterns are the same, with drier, slightly warmer summers and wetter, slightly colder winters than in the flatter lands just to their west.

The Cascade slopes face almost due west, giving them long exposure to hot, baking afternoon sun in summer so that peak temperatures often reach 95°F (35°C) or more. But in winter, the same orientation limits the hours of exposure to much weaker sun—when it does shine—keeping this subregion on the chilly side.

The mild, wet, vigorous weather systems that roar in off the Pacific in winter still have plenty of moisture to spare after passing over the relatively low coastal mountains. They release some of it over the low-lying regions between mountain ranges, but being slightly warmed there, they're able to retain a considerable amount. As saturated clouds rise up the much higher Cascade slopes, they cool, releasing torrents of precipitation—not quite as much as on the coast (only 5 ft., 1.5 m annually on average, often as snow)—but considerably more than on the flatter lands between the mountain ranges. As always, there are exceptions; Hood River (an honorary member of this subregion, although technically just outside it) is in the rain shadow of Mount Hood and so gets only half this amount.

The outflow valleys share similar conditions because of their proximity to the mountains, but add a unique factor of their own. Under certain conditions, they funnel air from east to west, the reverse of the natural air flow. The most pronounced effect occurs along the Fraser and Columbia Rivers, where relatively low-level passages through the mountains provide the most direct links between the mild, moist climate of the Pacific Northwest and the harsher, drier climate east of the Cascades.

In summer, these occasional east winds bring even hotter, drier conditions to this subregion. In winter—most predictably in late December and early March—they bring very cold interior air that causes sudden drops in temperature, freezing rain, sleet, snow, and/or ice buildup. Depending on severity, these effects can extend all the way to I-5 (the north-south interstate highway) and even cross the Strait of Georgia to chill the Olympic Peninsula. (For more on this phenomenon, see "Outflow Winds and Ice Storms" in Chapter 1.)

Because of its west-facing orientation, this subregion is slow to warm up in spring. April may see a light snow at higher elevations, frost is not unusual in early May, and even early June temperatures can come perilously close to frost at night. However, it's also slow to cool down in fall, and hard frost comes surprisingly late in most years.

In short, gardeners in this subregion face long, hot, dry summers; relatively cold winters punctuated by truly cold spells; dirty weather in early and late winter with a strong possibility of snow or ice damage; and sudden unpredictable changes in temperature year-round.

What thrives in these conditions? An amazing variety of hardy plants: deciduous and coniferous trees, fruit trees, small fruits, grapes, roses, a great many shrubs (rhododendrons flourish on the heavily timbered mountain slopes), woodland plants, virtually all perennials, vines, groundcovers, ornamental grasses, and bulbs. Tremendous crops of vegetables and berries grow in the rich soils of the eastern Fraser Valley. (Abbotsford is the second largest producer of raspberries in North America, just behind California.) With the exception of more tender species such as Asian pears, fruit trees of all kinds thrive here, especially in the partial rain shadow around Hood River.

Many tough, adaptable plants from Asia Minor and the Caucasus, northeastern Asia, China, and the Balkans thrive here. All Zone 6 plants are fully hardy; Zone 7 plants are also hardy but may need protection from sudden freezes and late frosts. Although temperatures seldom actually go much below 10°F (-12°C), sudden weather changes mean Zone 8 plants are unlikely to succeed here except in protected microclimates.

This is not the place for plants of weak constitution, or for very early bloomers. (Fortunately, late springs keep premature budding to a minimum.) Trees and shrubs need to be chosen with resistance to snow or ice damage in mind—no weak-branched or brittle-limbed plants need apply. Own-root roses are a much safer bet than grafted varieties, since they will regrow if the canes are winter-killed. The range of broadleaved evergreens is slightly more limited here than in most other subregions, but those hardy to Zone 7 should do just fine, especially in the shelter of conifers.

Climatic benefits in this subregion include lower insect populations (colder winters kill them off) and fewer problems with fungal diseases. Since both wetness and warmth are necessary for the spread of airborne fungi, colder springs are an advantage: by the time temperatures finally warm up, the rain has all but stopped. As a result, plants that are tricky to grow elsewhere actually like it here. The Hood River area (including the Washington shore) grows over 14,000 acres (5666 ha) of apples, cherries, peaches, and pears, leading the world in production of Anjou pears; wine grapes are also grown commercially.

The exact western boundary of this subregion is hazy, but an incredible concentration of nursery stock is grown in the 20-mile (32-km) stretch between low-elevation Portland, which is definitely not included here, and Sandy (elevation 967 ft., 295 m), which definitely is. Here, major wholesale nurseries such as tree growers J. Frank Schmidt & Son supply varied markets all across the United States and Canada.

The situation is similar in the eastern Fraser Valley. The Heather Farm and Classic Miniature Roses in Sardis (near Chilliwack) is a major Canadian mail-order supplier, and Valleybrook Gardens in Abbotsford is one of the largest wholesale producers of herbaceous perennials (trademarked Heritage Perennials) in North America. Many other general and specialty nurseries, orchards, vineyards, and farms are also located in this unique subregion. Minter Gardens, a popular privately owned display garden, is located in Chilliwack, B.C.

GEORGIA BASIN/PUGET TROUGH

Elevation: Sea level to 400 ft. (122 m)

Soil: Moderately fertile but often shallow; glacial till common. Rich alluvial soil in lower Fraser Valley, Skagit Valley, and smaller river valleys

Annual precipitation: 45–55 in. (1143–1397 mm); in lesser rain shadow areas, 35–40 in. (889–1016 mm)

Average temperature, July: High 72°F (22°C), low 55°F (13°C)

Average temperature, January: High 45°F (7°C), low 34°F (1°C)

Average last frost: 1–15 April

Average first frost: 15–31 October

Growing season: 180–220 days; moderate heat units

Humidity: High in winter, moderate in summer

Winds: Light to moderate in summer, northwest to west; strong in winter, southeast to south, often reaching storm force of 48 knots (55 mph, 89 kmh). Occasional cold easterly outflow winds in lower Fraser Valley (spilling as far south as Bellingham), especially in late December and early March

The best way to visualize this subregion is to imagine the rim of an oblong bowl filled with water. Although not steeply sloped itself, this narrow rim is surrounded by steep mountains on all but its southernmost end. From all directions, it slopes downward from this outer rim to sea level or close to it at its inner circumference. (Due to its unique characteristics, Puget Sound itself is a separate subregion.)

In its center—floating in the bowl of the Strait of Georgia, so to speak—are the Gulf Islands, so named when the strait was presumed to be a gulf, closed off at its northern end. The rim of the bowl is breached by the Strait of Juan de Fuca and by the Olympic Rain Shadow subregion, which differs from this one mainly in its lower rainfall.

With both mountain and marine influences, the motto of this subregion could well be "moderation in all things." Summers are not overly warm, but winters are not overly cold. It's seldom terribly wet, and seldom terribly dry. Skies are not always filled with endless sun, but neither are they predominantly cloudy or foggy. Soils are not highly fertile—except in the lower Fraser Valley and other river valleys—but they're far from infertile.

Typical high temperatures in summer are seldom more than 86°F (30°C); in winter, they're seldom lower than 20°F (-7°C). Heavy winter rains are punctuated by brief appearances of the sun, and summer's normal drought is usually punctuated by a few brief showers. Spring is cool and damp; fall is warm and dry. Several snowfalls of minor consequence occur most winters, but a deep snowfall of 30 in. (75 cm) or more can be expected about once a decade somewhere in the subregion.

Some parts of this subregion get a little more rain than the average, while other parts (identified as lesser rain shadows on the map on page 24) lie in partial rain shadows and get considerably less. In Washington, Bellingham and Mount Vernon are just grazed by the Olympic rain shadow; in British Columbia, Parksville, Sechelt, and virtually all the Gulf Islands lie in modest to moderate rain shadows. In keeping with the character of this subregion, both moisture-loving native species and those that indicate drier conditions are found throughout its extent. In fact, western red cedar, Sitka spruce, and hemlock can often be found almost side by side with Garry oak, Pacific madrone, and native pines.

A very wide range of plants can be grown in this accommodating climate—everything from roses to rhododendrons, alpines to conifers, fruit trees to bulbs. Although the entire subregion is theoretically in Zone 8, in reality only the inner, waterside rim of this sloping subregion is truly Zone 8; gardens at higher elevations are more often Zone 7b or even 7a. However, all plants in Zone 7 are perfectly hardy here (although those needing long, hot summers may not flourish), and in favorable microclimates or with special protection, most Zone 8 plants can be grown successfully. Plants most likely to flourish are those from Japan, China, and northeastern Asia, hardier species from New Zealand and southern Chile, hardier Mediterranean natives, and plants from northern Europe and the Balkans.

Plants that don't appreciate this subregion's climate are those that prefer drier, more continental climates with shorter, more sharply defined springs. Peach leaf curl is endemic here unless peaches and their relatives are grown under cover. Lilacs often suffer from bacterial blight unless protected with copper sprays, and apricots (both fruiting and flowering) are a lost cause. Fungal diseases of all sorts can wreak havoc on a wide variety of plants if June is warm and wet—even fences get covered with fungus then—but gardeners here soon learn which species are worth coddling and which it's best to give up on, based on prevailing local conditions.

Most vegetables do well here, but tomato varieties must be chosen carefully to get ripe fruit before September. Peppers and eggplants are best grown in a greenhouse; ripe melons and figs are usually a see-if-you-can-do-it proposition. Excellent crops of potatoes can be grown here; fruit trees (other than peaches and apricots) give satisfactory performance, neither outstanding nor disappointing. Grapes can be grown successfully—some crops are grown commercially—but varieties must be well suited to local conditions.

The long, cool springs that characterize this subregion are perfect for berry crops, and thousands of commercial acres produce outstanding crops of strawberries, raspberries, blueberries (20 million lbs., 9 million kg per year), cranberries (37 million lbs., 17 million kg per year), and other specialty berries, especially on the fertile alluvial soils of the lower Fraser Valley.

A very wide range of perennials, bulbs, and general nursery stock is also grown here.

This abundance is echoed on a smaller scale in the Comox Valley and the Cowichan Valley (surrounding Duncan) on Vancouver Island, and especially in the Skagit Valley surrounding Mount Vernon, Washington. Among other agricultural honors, this fertile valley holds the distinction of being the best location in the entire Pacific Northwest in which to grow tulips. The Washington Bulb Company there grows more than 12,000 acres (4856 ha) of tulips and other bulbs, and the month-long Skagit Valley Tulip Festival draws thousands of visitors every April.

Other horticultural establishments of note include Christianson's Nursery in Mount Vernon (trees, shrubs, perennials, and over 800 varieties of roses) and Clearview Horticultural Products in Aldergrove, B.C. (growers and continent-wide suppliers of clematis and other vines).

Many public and private display gardens are also found in this plant-friendly subregion. Milner Gardens and Woodland is located at Qualicum Beach (near Parksville) on Vancouver Island, and Bellingham, Washington, boasts at least three rose gardens. Major public gardens in Vancouver include the University of British Columbia Botanical Garden, the Van Dusen Botanical Garden, the Bloedel Conservatory at Queen Elizabeth Park, and the Dr. Sun Yat-Sen Classical Chinese Garden.

OLYMPIC RAIN SHADOW

Elevation: Sea level to 200 ft. (60 m)

Soil: Moderately fertile but thin, with outcrops of bedrock; glacial till common. Fertile and moderately deep in parts of Saanich Peninsula and northeastern shore of Olympic Peninsula

Annual precipitation: 15–27 in. (381–686 mm)

Average temperature, July: High 70°F (21°C), low 54°F (12°C)

Average temperature, January: High 45°F (7°C), low 38°F (3°C)

Average last frost: 15–31 March

Average first frost: 15–30 November

Growing season: 230–250 days; moderately low heat units

Humidity: High in winter, moderately low in summer

Winds: Brisk in summer, west to southwest; strong in winter, southwest to southeast, including some reaching storm force of 48 knots (55 mph, 89 kmh). Winter winds light on northeastern shore of Olympic Peninsula

In the rain-drenched Pacific Northwest, this subregion stands out for having annual precipitation on a par with southern California. In winter, moisture-laden southwest weather systems rolling in off the Pacific dump virtually all their load on the Olympic Mountains, leaving very little moisture for the areas in their lee. Included in this major rain shadow are the northeastern shore of the Olympic Peninsula, Victoria and most of the Saanich Peninsula at the southern tip of Vancouver Island, the San Juan Islands, and the northern half of long, narrow Whidbey Island and nearby Anacortes in Washington. In summer, when lesser weather systems come from the northwest, the same area is sheltered in the lee of the Vancouver Island Ranges.

Being smack in the center of both rain shadows, the small Washington town of Sequim (pronounced "skwim") gets only about 15 in. (381 mm) of rain per year—the same amount as Los Angeles—and nearby Port Townsend gets only very slightly more. Areas further from the center of the Olympic rain shadow, including Port Angeles, Victoria, Friday Harbor, and Anacortes, get considerably more precipitation (25–27 in., 635–686 mm), but this is still barely half the amount that falls on neighboring subregions. The influence of this major rain shadow extends as far as Sidney on the Saanich Peninsula and Bellingham in northern Washington.

The geology of the subregion is also unique. During the ice ages, glaciers moving down from the north repeatedly bulldozed the area; in many cases their tremendous weight scraped soil right down to bedrock. As they melted, the whole area was submerged under water. When the land rebounded, the shelf-like edge of the Olympic Peninsula and most of the Saanich Peninsula held a layer of fertile marine silt—but elsewhere, good soil is to be found only in pockets mixed unpredictably with areas of rocky soil, swamp, or bare rock.

Because of its mild winters, low rainfall, and heat-retaining rocky outcroppings, this subregion warms up early and quickly in spring. Summers are dry and sunny, but a strong marine influence usually holds peak summer temperatures to below 80°F (27°C). Fall is pleasantly cool and dry. Even though cold rain and high humidity makes winters feel chilly, actual temperatures seldom dip below 28°F (-2°C).

Snow is scarce in most years, although a heavy snowfall can occur every ten or 15 years. Even in normal years, though, winter comes with a caveat: easterly outflow winds from the Fraser Valley can chill the entire area, dropping 20 degrees Fahrenheit (11 degrees Celsius) in a matter of hours. Conflicting weather systems can buffet the Victoria area in winter with high winds from any of several directions.

This dry, seaside subregion has a true Mediterranean climate, albeit on the cool side of that range. Naturally, many Mediterranean plants flourish here—not just those from Greece or Italy, but those originating in California or Mexico, southern Africa, and southern South America. Bulbs also do very well, especially those originating in the Mediterranean or parts of Asia Minor where winters are wet and mild and summers are very dry. All Zone 8 plants are hardy here (although some heat-lovers may need a south-facing wall); New Zealand and southeastern Australian natives flourish with attention to their water needs. Many Zone 9 plants can be grown with protection.

Where soil exists, it is of good quality, and virtually all fruits and vegetables that don't require extra-warm conditions can be grown successfully. So can cold-tender crops such as kiwis and Asian pears. Strawberries can usually count on ideal ripening weather in June, and good crops of figs can be ripened if grown against a warm wall. (Although its name may give pause, Desert King is the variety best suited for Pacific Northwest conditions.)

Summer drought, not surprisingly, is the biggest concern here. Plants needing constant summer moisture are not necessarily ruled out, but gardeners soon learn to group water-lovers together or to limit their extent. Some gardeners—especially those relying on scarce well water—choose to garden with drought-tolerant plants only. Fortunately, a great many species, including many Pacific Northwest natives, are drought tolerant in the relatively cool summers of this subregion.

Other gardening challenges include salt spray and cooling summer winds, which can be quite brisk. Thin soils and solid bedrock also limit the success of deep-rooted species. However, some plants perform better here than anywhere else in the Pacific Northwest.

Mild winters with less rainfall mean winter-blooming species such as sasanqua camellias and *Viburnum ×bodnantense* 'Dawn' can be admired more often, and early bloomers such as star magnolias can flower unmolested by harsh weather. Bulbs also get the ideal dry conditions they need after flowering; lilies are grown commercially in Port Townsend, and narcissus and other bulbs on the Saanich Peninsula. Until recently, Vantreight and Sons cultivated some 750 acres (304 ha) of bulbs there, making the company the largest producer of daffodils in Canada and the second largest in North America.

This is also a world-class climate for lavender, second only to that of Provence, France. Some 50 varieties are grown commercially in several locations, but most notably in Sequim, which hosts the popular three-day Sequim Lavender Festival every summer.

Many excellent public, private, and display gardens grace this subregion. The world-famous Butchart Gardens (100 years old in 2004) are located on the Saanich Peninsula, and the Horticulture Centre of the Pacific is located near Victoria. The latter is particularly noted for its Doris Page Winter Garden, which features some 500 varieties of plants of winter interest in the climate of the Pacific Northwest.

PUGET SOUND

Elevation: Sea level to 500 ft. (152 m)

Soil: Moderately infertile to moderately fertile; varying deposits of silt, sand, gravel, clay, and muck, often mixed

Annual precipitation: 36–50 in. (914–1270 mm)

Average temperature, July: High 76°F (24°C), low 55°F (13°C)

Average temperature, January: High 46°F (8°C), low 34°F (1°C)

Average last frost: 15–28 February

Average first frost: 1–15 November

Growing season: 240–260 days (less in Olympia); moderate to moderately high heat units

Humidity: High year-round; slightly lower on summer afternoons

Winds: Mild to moderate year-round; mainly northwest in summer, south or southwest in winter

Consisting of all the lands within Puget Sound and a narrow rim of land surrounding it, this profoundly marine-influenced subregion is second smallest in physical size, but by far the largest in terms of population. Approximately three and one-half million people, most of whom have at least a passing interest in gardening, make their home here.

The international reputation of this area for "raining all the time" is greatly exaggerated; annual precipitation here is actually less than in most places in the Pacific Northwest. In the Tacoma–Everett corridor, which includes Seattle and the bulk of the subregion's population, precipitation is only 36–39 in. (914–991 mm) annually. Olympia and Bremerton, being more exposed to southwest weather systems in winter, do get slightly more, but their totals are still only two-thirds that of the Pacific Coast subregion.

The catch is that although most rain falls between October and February—it's not unusual to have 30 straight days of measurable precipitation in winter—the rest is spread out over the remaining months as interminable drizzle. Light showers occur even in summer. The average number of days per year with at least some cloud cover is 226; morning fog is frequent even on cloudless days.

With so much moderating moisture all around, winters here are very mild, with few hard frosts. However, short-lived snowfalls can be expected in most years. Seattle, situated in the path of cold winter air flowing down from Snoqualmie Pass, gets twice as much snow—12 in. (30 cm) annually—as Everett just to the north or Tacoma just to the south. Unlike the super-cold outflow blasts from the Fraser Valley and the Columbia Gorge, this cold air is not enough to ice things up, but just cold enough to nudge cold rain into snow.

Summers can be surprisingly warm here, especially if offshore (east) winds blow away morning fog quickly. Temperatures can easily reach 85–90°F (29–32°C) or even higher, making it possible to grow a very wide range of plants. A steady breeze blows year-round, but strong winds seldom develop.

Puget Sound soil is a mixture that almost defies description. The glaciers that scraped most of the clay soil from the San Juan Islands and southern Vancouver Island spread it over Puget Sound, mixing it with finer, more alkaline sea-bottom silt as they advanced. When they melted, they left behind the tons of sand, gravel, rocks, and boulders accumulated in their movements, and all this is now mixed with the clay and the silt in unpredictable layers and heaps throughout the area.

The weight of the glaciers also created a very compacted layer of hardpan that rose close to the surface as the land rebounded. Today, soils in the area are a hodge-podge mix of sand and silt, clay and gravel, overlaid in some cases with a thin, much more recent layer of peat or muck. One garden here can have soil of completely different texture, composition, drainage, fertility, and pH than that of a garden just down the street.

A further legacy of the glaciers is a surprisingly hilly terrain and numerous shallow depressions, both small and large (up to 40 ft., 12 m across). Both these feature can play havoc with cold air flow in winter, either helping or hurting individual gardens.

Due to its climate and soils, Puget Sound is not really the perfect place for vegetable gardens; Washington's main agricultural and fruit-growing area is east of the Cascades. However, adequate late-summer heat means corn, tomatoes, and even melons ripen well. Most small fruits, including kiwis, thrive here, but grape varieties must be very carefully chosen to avoid mildew. With enough determination, tree fruits can also be grown, although many show their resentment of high year-round humidity by developing fungal problems.

However, for nursery stock and ornamentals, the Puget Sound climate is close to ideal. Rhododendrons absolutely love the mild, year-round moist atmosphere (our native Pacific rhododendron is the state flower of Washington), and so do virtually all other broadleaved evergreens. The special affinity of moisture-loving Japanese species for this place is reflected in the many Japanese gardens—public and private, formal and informal—found here; even bamboos thrive in this climate.

Not surprisingly, the more tender moisture-loving species from the Himalaya, China, New Zealand, and southern Chile thrive here—but so do semi-hardy plants from the Mediterranean and southern Africa. Conifers of every description grow with abandon. Sun-shy hydrangeas, camellias, pieris, and hostas excel, as could be expected, but so do roses, dahlias (the official flower of Seattle), peonies, ornamental grasses, and other sun-loving species. Keeping those problematic frost pockets in mind, all Zone 8 plants can be grown here; Zone 9 plants can be grown near the water and/or with protection.

Drawbacks of this mild, moist climate include the usual suspects: fungal diseases, mildew, and lack of sunlight. The good air circulation provided by constant breezes helps alleviate some fungal problems, but growing roses without black spot or apples without scab is a challenge. When soil dryness, increased fog, and the mildest breezes of the year coincide in late summer, mildew is rampant; mildew-prone perennials such as monarda, garden phlox, and lungwort are not the best choices here.

Balancing these drawbacks is a greatly reduced need for summer irrigation. (Three weeks with only a few light showers is a drought.) With no worries about late killing frosts or high winds, this is the best subregion in the Pacific Northwest for growing large-leaved, somewhat tender species such as *Cardiocrinum giganteum*, gunnera, timber bamboo, and very large-leaved rhododendrons.

The urban sophistication of this subregion is reflected in the many specialty nurseries in the area as well as the number of general nurseries catering to collectors and connoisseurs. The growing popularity of native plant gardening and nature preserves also reflects the fierce determination of most Puget Sound residents to live and garden as naturally as possible in a highly urbanized setting. Organic, environmentally friendly gardening methods are almost a religion here, and stewardship programs available through Seattle's Center for Urban Horticulture are very popular.

Many major botanical and display gardens are featured in this populous subregion. Among the most prominent are Bellevue Botanical Garden, Lakewold Gardens Estate in Lakewood (near Everett), Meerkerk Rhododendron Gardens on Whidbey

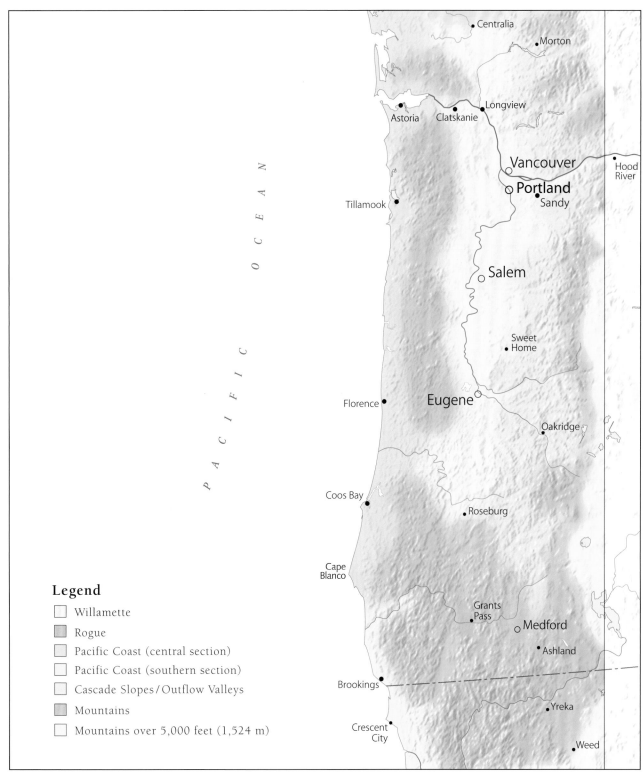

Legend

- ☐ Willamette
- ▨ Rogue
- ☐ Pacific Coast (central section)
- ☐ Pacific Coast (southern section)
- ☐ Cascade Slopes / Outflow Valleys
- ▨ Mountains
- ☐ Mountains over 5,000 feet (1,524 m)

Subregions of the Pacific Northwest, South

Island, Kruckeberg Botanic Garden in Richmond Beach (north of Seattle), Elisabeth Carey Miller Botanical Garden in Seattle, Washington Park Arboretum at the University of Washington in Seattle, Bloedel Reserve on Bainbridge Island (west of Seattle), the Rhododendron Species Foundation and Botanical Garden in Federal Way (between Seattle and Tacoma), Point Defiance Park in Tacoma, and Elandan Gardens in Bremerton. As well, the very popular Northwest Flower and Garden Show, the third largest in North America, is held in Seattle every year in early February.

WILLAMETTE

Elevation: 40–640 ft. (12–195 m)

Soil: Deep, rich, heavy

Annual precipitation: 40–48 in. (1016–1219 mm); less in Roseburg

Average temperature, July: High 82°F (28°C), warmer in Roseburg; low 55°F (13°C)

Average temperature, January: High 46°F (8°C), low 34°F (1°C)

Average last frost: 1–15 April; earlier in Portland

Average first frost: 1–15 November

Growing season: 200–260 days; moderately high to high heat units

Humidity: High in winter, low in summer

Winds: Light in summer, north to northwest; light to moderate in winter, south to southwest. Some gale force winds of 34 knots (39 mph, 63 kmh) in late fall; cold easterly outflow winds east of Portland, especially in late December and early March

Dominated by the famed, fertile Willamette Valley—the broad, nearly flat intermountain expanse between Eugene and Portland—this subregion also includes similar areas just to the north and south of the valley itself.

In the north, fertile soils and virtually the same climate are found along both banks of the Columbia River between Portland and Longview, Washington. In the more inland area around aptly named Centralia (it experiences coastal, mountain, Puget Trough, and valley floor influences in roughly equal measures), temperatures are slightly milder both summer and winter, and soils are slightly shallower and less fertile.

In the south, fertility is high in the Umpqua Valley surrounding Roseburg, but the influence of the Rogue subregion is apparent in its hillier terrain, shallower soils, hotter summers, and lower rainfall. Roseburg itself, in the rain shadow of some of the higher mountains of the Coast Range, gets only 28 in. (711 mm) of precipitation annually.

The entire subregion is often described, quite accurately, as having coastal winters and continental summers. Winter rain is moderate by Pacific Northwest standards, since southwest storm systems lose much of their moisture and most of their wallop in crossing the Coast Range. But it falls almost daily between mid-October and April, so that mild, wet winters and long, cool, drizzly springs are sometimes hard to tell apart. Frequent temperature inversions between fall and spring, in which cooler air is trapped beneath warmer air, create high-level fog or low-level cloud, keeping skies gray even when it's not raining. The return of real sunshine here in April cannot be overappreciated.

Because of the near-constant regime of moist, mild air in winter, frost is seldom deep or prolonged (Big Freezes excepted), and snow is usually wet and short-lived. However, strong easterly outflow conditions every few years can suck cold air down the mountain passes of the Cascades, and if this collides with rain-laden clouds, the result is a foot and a half or so (45 cm) of snow. If the cold air remains right around the freezing point, rain falling through it turns to ice as soon as it touches any chilled surface, including plants. Fortunately, these "silver thaws," although fairly frequent, seldom cause serious damage.

Summers here are moderately hot and definitely dry. Rain usually stops abruptly in mid-June and does not return, except for a couple of light showers, until mid-September. Typical temperatures in late July and August are usually well into the 90s F (32–35°C), and at least a few days over 100°F (38°C) can be expected throughout the subregion every summer.

Fall is long, warm, and very usable. Fog is frequent, due to low winds and temperature inversions, but it's still warm enough to ripen grapes; the wine industry here is thriving. Portland, with its semi-sheltered location and the moderating influence of the Columbia River, enjoys a growing season of 279 days and slightly milder temperatures both summer and winter—except, of course, for those nasty outflow winds roaring down the Gorge.

In the entire Pacific Northwest, this is the only subregion with large areas of level or even near-level land. (Residents here take their terrain for granted and are truly astonished the first time they see the rest of the Pacific Northwest from the air.) It's also the most rock-free, since the glaciers did not come this far south. With a solid Zone 8 climate that even accommodates heat-lovers, just about anything short of citrus fruit and tropical plants can be grown here, including Zone 9 plants in protected microclimates.

These near-ideal growing conditions are what prompted thousands of pioneer settlers—most of whom didn't know beans about farming when they started out—to pull up stakes in Illinois or Kentucky or Missouri in the 1840s and hit the Oregon Trail. They were not misguided. The Willamette subregion is still a prime producer of filberts or hazelnuts (more than 25,000 tons annually, accounting for virtually all North American production), walnuts, cherries, raspberries and other cane berries, strawberries, blueberries, vegetables of every description, grass seed, mint, roses, rhododendrons, ornamental trees and shrubs, perennials, and general and specialty nursery stock.

The only drawback here is water: there's either not enough or too much of it. Summer irrigation is a necessity for all but well-established, deep-rooted, or naturally drought-tolerant species. In winter, soil may become waterlogged or even flooded as numerous rain-swollen rivers and streams flow into bottomlands faster than they can be drained away. Of the two, summer irrigation is the greater problem; wells and even reservoirs outside the Willamette Valley proper can run dry. Within the valley, a huge aquifer only 20 ft. (6 m) or so beneath the soil surface makes irrigation look easy, but there is growing concern about pollution and overuse from ever-increasing urbanization.

Other minor and not-so-minor problems include fungal diseases in spring and late frosts, which in these mild winters means any hard frost past February. In early summer, entire crops of nearly ripe sweet cherries can be ruined in an hour by rain, which causes the fruits to swell and split their skins. Plants with thin, delicate leaves and those needing cool, constantly moist conditions can also suffer in summer unless very well sited and pampered.

But drawbacks pale beside the advantages of gardening in this fertile and benign subregion. Specialty growers and general nurseries are too numerous to name, but rhododendrons, magnolias, Japanese maples, lilies, roses, perennials, and more are all grown commercially for national, continental, and even worldwide markets. Many fine rhododendron, rose, and estate gardens are also located here.

Major botanical and display gardens in the Portland area include the Berry Botanic Garden, the Portland Classical Chinese Garden, the Portland Japanese Garden, and the Hoyt Arboretum. Portland also hosts the annual Portland Rose Festival—100 years old in 2007—and its famed Grand Floral Parade, better known locally as the Rose Parade. A fairly new (2001) botanical garden, The Oregon Garden, is located in Silverton, Oregon (near Salem).

Given that there are more colleges and universities in this one subregion than in many entire states or provinces, it's not surprising that gardening here has a strong educational flavor. Classes in gardening and conservation offered by various institutions of higher learning are always well attended, and lectures on specific garden subjects are popular. However, since a keen interest in nature, wilderness, and native plants is equally strong, garden clubs are just as likely to organize a hike as a lecture. Mount Pisgah Arboretum near Eugene is among the largest of the unique hybrid parks—part tree reserve, part living museum, part nature education laboratory—that are becoming popular here and throughout the Pacific Northwest.

ROGUE

Elevation: 640–3466 ft. (195–1056 m)

Soil: Moderately fertile to moderately infertile; high mineral content; may be deficient in one or more essential elements

Annual precipitation: 19–28 in. (483–711 mm)

Average temperature, July: High 90°F (32°C), cooler in Weed; low 52°F (11°C)

Average temperature, January: High 45°F (7°C), low 30°F (-1°C)

Average last frost: 1–15 May

Average first frost: 15–30 September

Growing season: 140–180 days; high heat units

Humidity: High in winter and early spring, with frequent fog; very low in summer

Winds: Light year-round, north to northwest. Some high winds during summer thunderstorms (direction variable); a few southwest winds reaching storm force of 48 knots (55 mph, 89 kmh) in winter

Situated where the Cascade, Siskiyou, and Klamath Mountains meet and overlap, this subregion is a collection of well-defined microclimates tied together by their overwhelming mountain influence. Differences in elevation, exposure, slope, and air flow affect temperature, rainfall, and length of growing season, but differences are minor compared to the similarities that make the entire subregion unique.

The typical pattern of mild, wet winters and dry summers still holds sway here, but with more mountain influence and less marine influence, days are hotter, nights are colder, and seasons more pronounced than anywhere else in the Pacific Northwest. Precipitation is also much lower due to southwesterly winter storms being blocked by the Klamath and Siskiyou Mountains.

The resulting rain shadow limits the area between Medford, Oregon, and Yreka, California, to just 19 in. (483 mm) of precipitation annually. Even Grants Pass, Oregon, although more exposed to Pacific storms, is in enough of a rain shadow to hold precipitation there to 28 in. (711 mm) annually. Tiny Weed, California, nestled in the very lap of Mount Shasta at an elevation of 3466 ft. (1056 m), is fully exposed to winter rains, but since it verges on the dry Californian climate, its precipitation is still far less than average for the Pacific Northwest. Very little rain falls anywhere in the subregion between late June and early October except for scattered thundershowers.

This is where native vegetation begins its shift from the cool-moist species of the Pacific Northwest to the hot-dry species of California. Fewer water-lovers (bigleaf maple, black cottonwood, salal) and more dry-feet species (Garry oak, madrone, manzanita) are seen here, and California species such as tanoak (*Lithocarpus densiflorus*), knobcone pine (*Pinus attenuata*), and black oak (*Quercus kelloggii*) start becoming common. Choice broadleaved evergreen trees such as canyon live oak (*Q. chrysolepis*) and golden chinquapin (*Chrysolepis chrysophylla*) are also much more common here than in the rest of the Pacific Northwest.

Summers here are definitely hot as well as very dry, with daytime highs frequently reaching 100°F (38°C) in late July and early August. However, nights are definitely cool, often in the high 50s F (13–15°C) even in midsummer. On clear days in winter, temperatures also rise considerably above the Pacific Northwest norm, but then fall slightly below average at night.

Winters are surprisingly mild, given such high elevations—Medford is at 1382 ft. (421 m); Ashland at 1951 ft. (595 m); Yreka at 2625 ft. (800 m). Zone 7 plants are generally hardy here, but may need protection in sudden sharp cold spells, especially if there is no snow cover. (Snowfall is heavy on the mountain peaks, but usually light and transient in the populated valleys.) Due to low winds and frequent temperature inversions, fog is frequent and may last for days.

Spring and fall both come abruptly here. In April, daytime highs take a sudden upward leap of ten degrees Fahrenheit (five degrees Celsius) or more, quickly building to comfortable shirt-sleeve weather, but nighttime frost lingers well into May and even early June. Frost can be expected again in September, even though daytime temperatures remain warm to hot. Precipitous cooling in October quickly brings both high and low temperatures down to early winter levels.

Lower rainfall and suddenly warm, dry springs mean fungal diseases are much less of a problem than anywhere else in the Pacific Northwest. Lilacs, peaches, apricots, flowering almonds, peonies, roses, apples, hollyhocks, and other plants so prone to various blights, fungi, scab, dieback, rust, or leaf spots in other subregions grow beautifully unblemished here. Since warm, dry springs are also perfect for bees and other pollinating insects, fruit trees also bear abundant crops. Early frosts rule out varieties needing an unusually long growing season, but high heat units all summer means tree fruits and vegetables ripen satisfactorily before frost.

Grapes, which can be challenging in the wetter springs and cooler summers of other subregions, find a near-perfect home here. The many types of wine produced in the various microclimates—some of which rival France's Bordeaux region—are fast gaining an international reputation. Roses also grow disease-free in the area's sunny days and cool nights; although most Jackson & Perkins roses are grown in California, the company's test and display gardens are located in Medford.

Most perfectly suited of all, especially to the soils and climate of the Rogue Valley surrounding Medford, are pears. This and southern France are the two best places in the world for growing these luscious fruits, and some of the oldest pear orchards in the United States are located here. The 10,000 acres (4047 ha) of present-day orchards produce many thousands of tons of pears annually—mainly Bartlett, Anjou, Bosc, and Comice—for domestic and international markets.

Not surprisingly, a Pear Blossom Festival is held in Medford every April. (It's indicative of the outdoorsy, recreation-oriented lifestyle prevalent here that this is linked with an 8-mile, 13-km, Pear Blossom Run.) The well-known Medford firm Harry and David, which got its start many decades ago selling gift packages of perfect pears, is now the world's largest shipper of fancy fruits and gift foods.

Cold-hardy, drought-tolerant plants from China, Asia Minor and the Caucasus, and the Balkans all grow beautifully here; so do hardier Mediterranean species and drought-tolerant European species. The only plants not likely to thrive in this subregion (besides those hardy only to Zone 8) are those needing cool, moist conditions all summer, such as tiarellas or candelabra primroses. Very early bloomers are also not a good bet except in very sheltered locations. For many ornamental plants, open shade (such as on the eastern or northern side of a building or fence) is often preferable to a site in full sun.

A few broadleaved evergreens (camellias, ceanothus) may not be fully hardy in all locations; others, such as pieris, rhododendrons, and Japanese azaleas, definitely need summer watering as well as the cool relief of an eastern or northern exposure. However, hardy, drought-tolerant broadleaved species such as mahonia, manzanita, and Japanese holly (*Ilex crenata*) can easily be grown in sun or shade in any location.

Drought is the main concern, especially if sources of irrigation are limited, but a surprising variety of plants are drought tolerant here. Alpine plants, for instance, are naturally at home in this mountain-influenced climate, thriving in the warm, sunny days and cool nights with their roots tucked behind sheltering rocks. The long-established Siskiyou Rare Plant Nursery in Medford specializes in alpines and other plants from around the world that thrive in this climate. One of its introductions, the highly drought-tolerant *Gaura lindheimeri* 'Siskiyou Pink', is a popular perennial across the continent.

CHAPTER 3

What's Different about Gardening Here

It's not just our climate that's unique; everything about the Pacific Northwest is just a little bit different from everywhere else. Even its physical existence. Our corner of the world began as odd bits and slices of unattached land called terranes somewhere out in the Pacific. Over many eons, these slowly drifted eastward and plastered themselves onto the North American continent, creating our major mountain chains as they collided. The seam of the Cascades is still unresolved, as evidenced by the number of peaks that are dormant—not extinct—volcanoes.

In spite of the incredibly mountainous terrain created by these geologically ancient collisions, virtually all Pacific Northwesterners live in the relatively scarce lowlands between mountains. And in spite of our region having a profound marine influence, it's quite unlike other major maritime regions, including the east coast of North America and the coast of southern California. Our major settlements, including our major ports, are all located 50–60 miles (80–95 km) from the open ocean. (There's good reason for this: the misnamed Pacific Ocean is anything but peaceful except in summer.) The coast itself is very sparsely populated, and the vast majority of our population is squeezed into a narrow corridor extending from Oregon's Willamette Valley through the eastern shore of Washington's Puget Sound to the southwestern tip of mainland British Columbia and the southern half of the east coast of Vancouver Island.

This brings up another peculiarity of the Pacific Northwest. Unlike other well-defined physical/climatic/ecological entities with a shared history, such as Switzerland or Florida or the United Kingdom, the Pacific Northwest is artificially divided into two nations, three states, and one province—but with only a portion of each of those states and province included. However, our patchwork political allegiances do not appreciably affect our day-to-day reality; Pacific Northwesterners north and south have more affinity with each other than with their respective counterparts "back East" or even on the other side of the Cascades. Especially when it comes to gardening. Throughout the Pacific Northwest, we all garden a little bit differently in much the same way.

TIMING IS EVERYTHING

To begin with, our seasons do not coincide with the standard calendar. Summer is July and August, when it's dry and warm ("hot" by our standards) and the sun shines all day. Fall is September and October, when days are pleasantly warm, nights are nippy, and it's still dry and sunny most days. Winter is November and December, when continuous pelting rain and uniformly dark skies mean having to have the lights on all day when indoors and having to don a waterproof parka or carry an umbrella when outdoors. (Unless you're between the ages of 13 and 18, in which case you'd rather look and feel like a drowned rat than be caught dead with either non-cool item.)

The rest of the year, January to June, is more or less spring: cool, wet, and drizzly. It's true that winter can put on a repeat performance, especially in March, or even put on a surprisingly good imitation of real winter by getting suddenly cold in January. It's also true that beautifully mild, sunny, early-summer days can occur in April, or even February. But however uneven it is, the reality of this very long transition from winter to summer, with rains gradually diminishing and temperatures gradually rising, greatly influences our gardening schedules not just in spring, but throughout the year. Our warm, dry falls—being the exact reverse of our cool, moist springs—further solidify the nonstandard timing of our gardening tasks.

In most of the rest of North America, spring comes much later than it does in the Pacific Northwest, but it also comes suddenly and very briefly. ("Spring came on a Tuesday last year.") Where this is the case, it's prudent to plant everything as early as possible before the heat of summer arrives. But in our case, even though spring begins as early as January, patience is the watchword.

Heavy soils are very slow to warm even when the sun does shine, and our cool, moist spring weather keeps them cold and sluggish far into April and even May. It's fine to plant hardy nursery stock as soon as the ground can be worked—bare-root trees, roses, and small fruits can and should be planted in early March. But we soon learn (sometimes the hard way) to hold off on more tender woody plants, annual and vegetable transplants, and seeds.

Pot marigolds (*Calendula officinalis*)

Although daytime temperatures can be quite balmy in April, our cool spring nights keep our soils colder than it seems they should be, and nothing is gained by early planting. Even if seeds or roots don't rot and tender top growth is not killed by late frosts, plants will not actually start growing until the soil begins to warm up. There's no rush anyway; in our climate, hot weather won't arrive until at least July.

At the other end of the season, fall is an ideal time for planting, especially conifers, vines, specimen trees, hardy broad-leaved evergreens, and lawns. In September and early October, the warm ground is perfect for root growth and the soon-to-come rains will keep them well watered; our mild winters pose little or no threat of harm to new plantings. Fall plantings are thus well on their way to becoming established by spring and generally outperform spring plantings, which need plenty of water just as soil moisture is diminishing. However, border-line-hardy species, smaller deciduous plants, and warm-season grasses (including bamboos) are best planted in spring.

Since winter-kill due to cold is not a problem in our climate, fall is also an excellent time for pruning hedges, lifting and dividing perennials, cutting back spent top growth, and general tidying up in the garden. Doing these things in fall instead of in spring doesn't make that much difference to plants, but it does to gardeners. Such chores are pleasant in warm, dry fall; in cold, wet spring, even when the weather permits, they're disagreeable enough that many of them are let go until it's too late in the season to do them at all.

ANNUALS, BIENNIALS, AND SHORT-LIVED PERENNIALS

It seems logical that summer annuals grow the same way everywhere, but here again things are just a little bit different in the Pacific Northwest. For instance, snapdragons, sweet alyssum, nasturtiums, and even trailing petunias (all of which are actually very tender perennials) sometimes survive our mild winters and begin regrowing. Some true annuals such as cornflower (*Centaurea cyanus*), California poppy (*Eschscholzia californica*), and poached egg flower (*Limnanthes douglasii*) self-seed so faithfully that many gardeners are surprised to learn they're not perennial. Pot marigold (*Calendula officinalis*) not only self-seeds but is so well adapted to our long stretches of cool, moist weather that it can be seen in sporadic bloom year-round, even in midwinter.

Naturally, annuals that like cool weather are very happy in our climate. Sweet peas grow spectacularly well; the only challenge is to get them planted early enough without having the seeds rot in our cold, wet spring soils. (Presprouting works for some.) At the other end of the season, fall-planted flowering cabbage and kale remain in great shape until at least December and sometimes even overwinter, making spectacular cone-shaped towers as they go to seed.

Other annuals that excel in our climate include cosmos, which can bloom into November; lobelia, which blooms happily all summer if cut back and fertilized in July; and nemesia, which likes our cool summer nights. Garden heliotrope (*Heliotropium arborescens*) also likes our cool but sunny summers; this old-fashioned tender perennial with deep purple flowers and a delicious cherry-pie fragrance is usually grown as an annual but can be overwintered in very mild gardens.

All the other standbys and newer introductions also bloom beautifully all summer, but "shade" annuals such as fuchsias, impatiens, fibrous begonias, tuberous begonias, and coleus need special treatment. Being native to subtropical regions, these plants like warm shade and are not happy in our very cool, sometimes dank coniferous shade; in all but our hottest river valleys, they do best with at least four hours of morning sun. New Guinea impatiens, being a tropical plant, absolutely needs a warm site and is often happiest in full sun (with adequate watering) as long as it is not too intense.

In all cases, shade annuals should not be planted out until the soil warms—the blooming of lilacs is usually a good indicator. Once they're comfortably settled in conditions to their liking, though, these annuals, tender bulbs, and tender perennials thrive all summer and into September. Fuchsia baskets can even be overwintered by cutting them back and keeping them on the dry side (but not completely parched) in a cool bedroom until next April, when they can gradually be given more water, warmth, and light.

The lingering coolness of our May nights also affects the planting time of tropical and subtropical shade annuals—and of sun-loving tender bulbs and perennials such as canna

lilies, osteospermum, or gerbera daisies, for that matter. They simply will not grow while soil temperatures remain cool. Better late than early is the key to success; mid- to late May (lilac time again) is usually best. For recommended planting times, see the lists of "Annuals to Plant" under March, April, and May in Part 2, the gardening calendar.

Our slow-to-warm soils also affect the planting of heat-lovers such as zinnias, verbena, strawflowers, annual statice, and basil. Mildew can be a problem while holding transplants until the soil warms, but this is preferable to seeing them keel over in cold, wet soil. These annuals do very well once the weather does warm up, but annuals that require sustained high heat, such as Madagascar periwinkle (*Catharanthus roseus*, syn. *Vinca rosea*), are usually a major disappointment.

With the exception of hollyhocks, which are hopelessly prone to rust in all but our driest subregions, biennials excel in our climate and soils. Sweet William (*Dianthus barbatus*), Canterbury bells (*Campanula medium*), and English daisies (*Bellis perennis*) grow like weeds, and common foxglove (*Digitalis purpurea*) grows so well that it has officially become a weed. It's now considered invasive, since its tall, stately spires can be found on any hike through the edges of second-growth forest. (Cultivars and other species of *Digitalis* are still considered acceptable.)

Tender canna lily and sun-loving annuals

Bowles' Mauve wallflower (*Erysimum* 'Bowles' Mauve')

Winter pansies in early February

Forget-me-nots (*Myosotis*) and wallflowers (*Erysimum cheiri*, syn. *Cheiranthus cheiri*) are commonly set out as small transplants in fall to provide welcome color in early spring. However, the very popular Bowles' Mauve wallflower (*Erysimum* 'Bowles' Mauve') is not a biennial and is best planted in spring. Although this sun-loving evergreen perennial is hardy only to Zone 8 and dislikes wet winters, it's a must-have for its shrub-sized mounds of gray-green foliage and its non-stop purple flowers. Sometimes starting into bloom as early as late February, it keeps on pushing out flowers at the end of long stalks right through October and up to hard frost.

Naturally, such effort often exhausts the plant, but in very well-drained, well-limed soil that's not too rich, it may survive for three to five years. In colder or less well-drained gardens it's well worth growing as an annual; cuttings taken in late June root easily and are good insurance.

In terms of sheer numbers, our most popular annuals (actually short-lived perennials) by far are pansies (*Viola* ×*wittrockiana*), which are planted by the zillions in both spring and fall. They love our long spells of cool, moist weather; although they dislike both summer heat and winter cold, these delicate-looking little flowers are surprisingly tough and can take just about any non-extreme setting that's not too dry. In our coolest subregions, they can take full sun; in our hottest river valleys, a cool semi-shady site is best. Given the differences between our subregions, these cheerful and well-loved flowers are in bloom somewhere in the Pacific Northwest in every month of the year.

Although sold as spring pansies and winter pansies, blooming time in reality largely depends on when the seeds were started. However, the choice of color, size, form (plain-edged, ruffled, or semi-double), and markings (with or without faces or lines) is far greater in spring. Spring pansies bloom from early spring until the heat of midsummer, then again in cooler fall weather until temperatures drop. Regular deadheading prolongs bloom; in our cooler-summer subregions, spring pansies bloom continuously all summer and into September.

Many winter pansies are in fact slightly hardier to cold, especially those displaying an appropriately cool shade of blue or purple that reflects the strong strain of *Viola cornuta* in their genetic makeup. Winter pansies bloom through fall, during mild spells in winter and again in early spring; in our mildest-winter subregions they may bloom continuously through winter. However, complex hybridization sometimes results in unexpected surprises. We once planted a winter pansy that refused to bloom all fall or winter, starting into bloom only in March; it then bloomed non-stop through August.

Pansies make colorful hanging baskets in earliest spring, brighten borders and planters all summer, combine beautifully with flowering kale and cabbage in fall, and cheer our winters in mild spells. They do not normally self-seed, but are so indispensable and inexpensive that they're well worth replacing both spring and fall. Watch for slugs, which love them almost as much as gardeners do.

LAWNS

Pacific Northwest lawns grow, need mowing, and get overrun with dandelions just as they do everywhere else, and the basics of seeding (or laying sod), mowing, watering, fertilizing, dethatching, aerating, and managing weeds are the same. Still, growing and maintaining a lawn in this mild, moist corner of the world is again just a little bit different than it is anywhere else.

Seeding a new lawn

Although achieving a putting-green type lawn is more a matter of preparation, maintenance, and proper mowing than of seed pedigree, seed mixture does have a direct bearing on lawn performance. Kentucky bluegrass is a poor choice for the Pacific Northwest, since it needs lots of lime and has shallow roots that dry out quickly in our summer drought; deeper-rooted fescues and fine-leaved perennial ryegrasses are much better suited. Fescues have the added advantage of being somewhat shade tolerant and also hold up well to kids, dogs, and frequent foot traffic.

Although the habit of planting lawns in spring dies hard, September is a much better time for starting a new lawn in our climate. In spring, the soil is cold and seeds take a long time to germinate (meanwhile, hungry birds eat their fill); the new lawn must then be watered regularly just as natural rainfall is diminishing. In September, the opposite is true: seeds sprout quickly in the warm soil, and while they must be kept moist until the rains begin, nature very shortly takes over, bringing regular and generous warm rain. Our mild winters do new lawns absolutely no harm, but seeding should begin at least six weeks before the first expected frost to allow for adequate root growth.

Mowing

Only in the Pacific Northwest is it common to see people in winter jackets and knit caps out mowing their lawns in February, but this is yet another consequence of our mild winters. At the other end of the season, our warm fall rains also stimulate lawns into lush new growth, so mowing is often necessary well into November, when declining temperatures finally check its growth.

In between, it grows so fast in April that it needs mowing every four or five days, but frequent showers make it hard to co-ordinate need with sufficiently dry opportunity to mow. We start getting a reprieve in June as rain tapers off to almost nothing, but even if we choose not to irrigate lawns in summer, it's still a good idea to mow every ten days or so just to keep perennial weeds from getting the upper hand.

Is blond beautiful?

Given our normal summer drought and the increasing concerns over water supply and overuse, many Pacific Northwesterners are choosing to let their lawns go dormant in summer. The sight of straw-colored ("blond") grass takes some getting used to, but this is just cultural conditioning. How many of us think dormant deciduous trees "just don't look right" in winter when they're leafless?

The choice to water a lawn in summer is a personal one (although people on limited-supply private wells, ourselves included, have little or no choice), and no one should be intimidated into not watering through political correctness. However, there are good reasons for letting lawns go blond in summer.

All lawn grasses are cool-season grasses, growing rapidly in spring, going dormant in the heat and drought of summer, reviving quickly with fall rains, and remaining green but not growing in winter. Their natural dormant season (summer) gives the roots a chance to rest and recuperate; keeping them growing against their natural inclination tends to weaken them and make them even more dependent on artificial irrigation. And the amount of water needed to keep a lawn green in our dry summers is sobering.

It takes 1 in. (2.5 cm) of water per week to keep a lawn growing steadily, so a modest-sized lawn of 40 ft. × 65 ft. (12 m × 20 m) needs approximately 1600 gallons (6057 liters) of water per week. Assuming a normal dry season of ten to 12 weeks, this adds up to 16,000–19,200 gallons (60,557–72,680 liters) per summer—just when water reserves are lowest and many garden plants are beginning to show signs of water stress.

Dormant lawns green up again with breathtaking speed in the first fall rains, growing so rapidly they even need mowing again. However, going blond is not the only option for reducing lawn-related water use; reducing the size of the lawn by replacing parts of it with drought-tolerant, low-maintenance ground-covers is another popular option.

Lime

Our high fall-through-spring rainfall leaches calcium from the soil, lowering the pH and leaving it acidic. Since lawn grasses prefer a pH closer to neutral, lime must be applied regularly to counteract the acidity and raise the pH to a more grass-friendly level.

The higher the annual rainfall, the more acidic the soil. In the low-rainfall Rogue and Olympic Rain Shadow subregions, it's advisable to test the soil with an inexpensive pH kit before liming, but on the high-rainfall coast, most lawns need liming yearly. (If there are many clam or oyster shells nearby, the soil may be alkaline; if in doubt, test before liming.) In inland gardens where rains are not quite as heavy, liming every other year may be sufficient.

A healthy soil high in organic matter tends to leach calcium more slowly, so once the target pH of 6.0–6.5 is reached, annual testing is recommended before automatically liming. Do not lime if the pH is 6.0 or above.

The best time to spread dolomite lime is in fall, so that soon-to-come heavy rains can wash it down to the root zone by spring. However, March is also good. Dolomite lime (calcium

Fairy ring mushrooms in lawn

magnesium carbonate) is most beneficial in the long run but is very slow-acting, especially on heavy soils; plain ground limestone (calcium carbonate) gives quicker but less long-lasting results.

By far the best way to apply lime is with a wheeled spreader, of which there are two types. Broadcast spreaders that fling the lime out give more even coverage, but care must be taken that lime is not flung into nearby beds of acid-loving plants. Drop spreaders place the lime more precisely, but these must be guided carefully to avoid both overlaps and missed edges on adjacent passes. In either case, the lime should be in granular form or prilled (temporarily glued into tiny balls), not powdered; powdered lime clogs both types of spreaders and creates unbelievable clouds of dust.

Mushrooms, moss, and rust

Mushrooms spring up like, well, mushrooms when soil is damp on the surface but drier underneath. Since this combination is normal in early fall, it's not surprising to find a great many mushrooms popping up in lawns in October. They're also common in late spring when the soil starts drying out but showers are still frequent.

Most mushrooms are quite harmless if not eaten (never take the risk—some species can be deadly), but they should be knocked over before the caps open to keep them from proliferating. The back of a garden rake works well for larger amounts; for just a few mushrooms, a well-aimed foot does the trick.

Fairy rings, though, are a more serious matter. The first sign of a fairy ring is a circle or partial circle of very dark green grass. Mushrooms then appear all along its circumference, looking like seats for ethereal sprites. The grass then starts dying—and unlike bare spots due to various other causes, these bare places remain bare. Grass refuses to grow even when reseeded, so the exposed soil is soon colonized by weeds.

Eliminating the possibility of some types of fairy rings is a horrendously complicated and expensive procedure, so the best way to deal with them is to pick and destroy any mushrooms as soon as they appear. Some of these can be very small, so it's worth combing through the grass in the dark rings to find them all. As long as the mushrooms are prevented from maturing, the grass will not die, and the ring will most likely disappear within a year or so.

Lawn moss

Most people associate moss with excessively damp, shady conditions, but the main cause of lawn moss is an overly acidic soil. Poor drainage, low fertility, and shade also encourage moss, but as long as the soil is strongly acidic, even lawns on well-drained fertile soil in full sun will soon host robust patches of moss. The moss problem can get so acute that some people give up and accept more moss than lawn in small areas, especially if acid-loving plants surround it. However, lawn moss can be effectively controlled with regular liming, which raises the pH of the soil and makes growing conditions unsuitable for moss.

Lime will not kill existing moss, though; if the amounts are beyond what can be raked out, it must first be killed with a proprietary product containing ferrous (iron) sulfate. Water it in well, wait until the moss blackens, then rake it out and plant grass seed in the bare spots. Ferrous sulfate, a naturally occurring substance, is ecologically safe, but be careful not to spill any on concrete walks or driveways; the iron can leave indelible rust-colored stains.

Lawn rust can appear in late summer or early fall on grass stressed by drought, especially if soil fertility is low. Kentucky bluegrass is especially prone to rust, which appears as yellowish or reddish brown powdery spots on the blades. Rust can also appear on lawns that are sprinkled daily instead of being watered deeply once a week. Although its appearance can be rather alarming, rust is rarely a problem; fall rains will soon bring water to thirsty roots, and the rust will not overwinter.

Leatherjackets

Most people new to the Pacific Northwest have never heard of leatherjackets, which are the larvae of the European crane fly. These skinny grayish brown larvae, which are about 2 in. (5 cm) long when fully grown, live under the sod and are seldom seen even though they're a fact of life here: they find our mild, moist winters and springs very much to their liking. However, although leatherjackets do eat grass roots, the harm they cause has been greatly exaggerated.

In the past, many homeowners terrorized by the prospect of large unsightly patches of dead grass routinely applied chemical insecticides to their lawns every year in early spring. In the past, perhaps not coincidentally, such practice was big business: according to a Washington State University Extension survey done by master gardeners in Whatcom County, homeowners in

Birds will soon provide natural control of the minor leatherjacket damage on this lawn.

the Puget Sound area alone spent about $13 million in 1999 for insecticides—usually diazinon—to control leatherjackets.

However, with increased interest in non-toxic pest control and the recent de-listing of diazinon for homeowner use (it has been found in drinking water sources and salmon-bearing streams, and is toxic to birds), leatherjacket populations have actually decreased. Between 2001 and 2006, no lawns tested by the master gardeners had leatherjacket populations serious enough to treat, and most lawns had none at all.

The most likely explanation for this is that the natural predators of leatherjackets—birds, bats, frogs, yellowjackets, and beneficial insects such as ground beetles—are no longer being killed off. It may also be that with more gardeners letting their lawns go dormant in summer, fewer of the eggs laid by adult crane flies in early fall are surviving due to the dryness of the soil.

The life cycle of leatherjackets begins in September with the mating of adult crane flies—very large, alarming-looking but completely harmless flying insects that resemble daddy long-legs—and the laying of eggs in the soil. No chemicals control the adults; if they're of concern, they can be swatted. If you see many crane flies in September and are still watering your lawn, stop: the eggs need moisture to survive. There's no trade-off here; with fall rains arriving in a matter of weeks, the grass won't even have time to go seriously blond.

The larvae that soon hatch underground feed on grass roots, doing most of their damage in winter and early spring, but dead patches (assuming there are enough leatherjackets to cause them) may not show up until the weather warms in May or June. Leatherjackets will always be present in the Pacific Northwest, but the good news is that even large populations are easily tolerated by healthy lawns, making any kind of treatment unnecessary.

To check for leatherjackets in early spring, cut a 12 in. × 12 in. (30 cm × 30 cm) square in the lawn, pry up the sod temporarily, and count any larvae in the square. Up to 25 is no cause for concern at all; up to 50 can still be well tolerated. Even 80 leatherjackets per square foot do not cause serious damage.

Even if high numbers are found, the best recourse is to leave them for the birds. Starlings love them and are very efficient at finding them, so never shoo them off your lawn in April when they congregate there. Robins and beneficial insects also help out considerably. Leatherjackets can also be flooded out: soak any high-population areas with a hose, forcing the leatherjackets to the surface, then pick them up (wear disposable gloves if you're squeamish) and drop them into a bucket of soapy water.

Weeds

Dandelions abound in Pacific Northwest lawns, just as they do everywhere else. However, they can appear here as early as January and persist until late May, when plantain takes over. As hot dry weather arrives, plantain gives way to hawkweeds, which resemble dandelions on a smaller scale. Hawkweeds, which have an amazing ability to grow, flower, and go to seed on even the driest summer-dormant lawns, persist until fall.

The solution to all three, as well as to other broadleaved perennial lawn weeds such as dock, is to remove them by the root. The most effective and easiest-to-use tool is the kind with two pincer-like prongs used from a standing position. Center the prongs over the weed, step on the foot support to force the prongs into the soil, then push the handle to the side using the foot support as a fulcrum. This causes the weed, trapped between the two prongs, to be pulled out by the roots. The procedure is so curiously relaxing and satisfying that many gardeners are secretly sorry to run out of weeds.

A squirt of plain white vinegar from a squeeze bottle discourages regrowth from any roots left behind. If the divots left by the dandelion puller are objectionably large, they can be filled in with soil or a mixture of sand and peat moss; they'll soon be covered as the surrounding grass creeps in.

The best defense against aggressive annual weeds such as chickweed or veronica is a healthy, vigorously growing lawn. Besides maintaining a pH of 6.0–6.5, clippings should always be left on the lawn, since these are the best natural fertilizer of all. (Natural grasslands, among the world's most fertile soils, are fed only by their decayed top growth.) A mulching mower is a lawn's best friend, chopping the clippings into fine bits that decay quickly. Contrary to popular belief, clippings do not cause thatch, which is the accumulation of old but not decomposed grass stems and roots.

By mowing high (at least 2 in., 5 cm) and mowing often (never removing more than one-third the length of the blades at one time), most weeds are soon crowded or shaded out, and the

Even imperfect lawns are an integral part of ornamental gardens.

few that remain pose no problem except to gardeners intent on a perfect lawn. This is where our expectations need some adjustment. Clover, for instance, is very beneficial to lawn grasses since it supplies nitrogen; it's also an excellent nurse crop for new lawns. As the grass grows thicker and more vigorously, even clover is largely shaded out.

The lawn as an ornamental element

Lawns are often taken for granted, but they're an integral part of any ornamental garden. The popular notion that their only function is to provide "negative space" to set off the more showy elements of the garden is simply wrong. Gardens are not static, two-dimensional paintings to be looked at, but living, three-dimensional (four, if you count time) space to be experienced. Lawns actually add a very positive space, one that enables us to walk right up to our beds and borders, or, when used as broad paths, even through them.

Regarding their size and shape, lawns have a welcome plasticity about them: they can be made smaller or larger, their contours can easily be modified, and they don't object at all to having large holes cut into them to accommodate yet another ornamental plant—for which they will again provide a perfect backdrop of textureless green carpet that goes with everything. Their living presence (which includes their delicious fresh-mowed scent) just cannot be replaced by gravel, mulch, or concrete pavers; lawnless gardens always look as if they're lacking a vital element. Because they are.

When considered as a groundcover, which they are, lawns are even more remarkable. No other plant could put up with so much abuse—being walked on, run on, played on; total summer drought; neglect—and still grow as effortlessly and uncomplainingly as lawn grasses grow in the Pacific Northwest. Even the amount of maintenance time required for mowing, weeding, and liming (and watering if desired) is small compared to the time required to maintain any other ornamental planting of comparable size.

Lawns are rarely perfect, whether in the Pacific Northwest or anywhere else. They're currently in disfavor precisely because of the huge amounts of water, pesticides, and chemical fertilizers expended on them in the past in trying to make them perfect. But since healthy, naturally grown lawns actually need none of these things, don't be tempted (or pressured) into getting rid of all lawn grass. Even with a few bumps here, a few weeds there, a few thin spots, a few mushrooms, and a little moss, lawns play a vital and irreplaceable role in ornamental gardening. Who cares if they're not perfect? Nothing else in the Pacific Northwest is- and yet somehow, all of it works together beautifully.

VEGETABLE GARDENS

In August, Pacific Northwest vegetable gardens are pretty much the same as vegetable gardens everywhere else, with all crops (especially zucchini) producing like mad. But throughout the rest of the year, they're more than a little different. Where else but in the Pacific Northwest can vegetables be harvested all fall and winter and even in very early spring as well as in summer?

Spring planting

In the first place, as with annuals, there's no reason to rush spring planting. It's true that broad beans and peas should be in as early as possible, but with our soils often cold, wet, and uncooperative in very early March, such plantings are likely to rot even if gardeners are brave enough to attempt them. If they don't rot, any growth will be imperceptible. (We once got so organized that we actually got our potatoes planted before St. Patrick's Day, 17 March; not a shoot appeared until our more usual potato-planting date of late April.)

If conditions are favorable in early March, by all means go ahead and plant, but if they're not, there's nothing lost by waiting two or three weeks, or even more. Since our springs last until June, there's no deadline of coming hot weather to beat. If anything, "early" crops planted slightly later, when the soil starts warming, tend to outperform very early plantings because they have not had their growth checked. This is somewhat true even for warm-weather crops: many gardeners have ruefully watched volunteer tomato seedlings pop up in June and proceed to outgrow their carefully nurtured and coddled tomato transplants set out in May.

Except in the warmer Rogue and Willamette subregions, our cool summers are not particularly friendly to vegetable gardens. Beefsteak tomatoes can be disappointing, since they need long, hot summers, but nearly every gardener has a favorite early-ma-

Scarlet runner beans

turing tomato variety that succeeds in local conditions. Oregon Spring is an old reliable standby, shrugging off our cool spring weather; there are many other excellent newer varieties. Scarlet runner beans are also popular in many gardens for their ability to grow and produce in less-than-perfect bean-growing temperatures. As well as being highly ornamental with their red flowers that attract hummingbirds, they produce abundant crops that are delicious and tender if picked young.

Raised beds, which help warm the soil earlier, have received a lot of press in recent years and are favored by some gardeners. However, raised beds also dry out much faster in summer and need frequent watering. Finding non-toxic, rot-resistant, affordable construction materials that will not attract too many sowbugs can also be a challenge. There's no denying that raised vegetable beds are attractive, but whether or not they're worth it in our climate is another matter.

Clubroot

Most vegetables prefer a soil just on the acidic side of neutral, about pH 6.0–6.5. However, wholesale liming of the vegetable garden is not always a good move; potatoes, for instance, prefer a more acidic soil and get scabby if exposed to fresh lime.

On the other hand, brassicas or members of the cabbage family (including broccoli, Brussels sprouts, Chinese cabbage, cauliflower, collards, kale, and kohlrabi) need a pH near neutral (6.8–7.0). In acidic soil they suffer from clubroot, a fungal disease that causes knobby, misshapen roots and stunts growth to the point of woody, shriveled inedibility. The fungus overwinters in the soil, so in addition to liming the soil where brassicas are to be grown, these crops should be rotated so that none of them are grown in the same soil for at least three consecutive years.

In new gardens, the fungus may be well established thanks to brassica-family weeds such as mustard; control may take several years. Repeated cultivation of garden soil and building up its fertility seem to help in keeping clubroot at bay, but yearly liming is still a necessity, especially in high-rainfall areas. Lime should be applied in fall so it can be washed down to the root zone by spring planting time. It takes little time, effort, or expense to do this every year; in return, members of the cabbage family grow beautifully large and succulent in our cool, moist climate. Summer watering is of course necessary and should never be skimped; a mulch of straw or hay around the roots helps immeasurably.

Winter gardening

Perhaps the most important and unique characteristic of Pacific Northwest vegetable gardens is that they do not need to be "put to bed" in fall. Frost-tender crops come out, of course, and are replaced by a cover crop of fall rye, but a good half of the garden can remain for fresh eating all fall, through winter, and up until planting time next spring.

Root crops—potatoes, carrots, parsnips, winter beets, winter radishes, and rutabagas or Swede turnips—can be left right in the ground, where they will be kept in ideal storage conditions of high humidity and low but not freezing temperatures. A thick mulch of straw or hay is of course necessary insurance against sudden cold snaps and excess rain, but root crops keep so well in these refrigerator-like conditions that they're still in prime condition next March or even April. There is always a small chance of losing crops to a Big Freeze or local flooding, but the large potential benefit of leaving them in the ground is well worth the very small potential risk of losing them.

Other crops can be mulched at their bases and left standing all winter. Kale, collards, leeks, and late cabbage remain in prime condition all winter; Swiss chard is knocked back by subfreezing temperatures but always roars back again and puts on phenomenal fresh growth in late winter. Broccoli, Brussels sprouts, Chinese cabbage, celery, and parsley remain in good condition through December in most winters; in very mild winters, broccoli will even produce small but tasty new buds in March.

"Winter gardening" is a somewhat misleading term; it really should be "winter-eating gardening." It's important to remember that although these crops are harvested in fall and winter, they must be planted by July at the latest in order to have time to grow to maturity. However, broad beans can be planted in September for very early (and more reliable) spring harvest; garlic planted in September will mature by July. Transplants of

MORE VEGETABLE GARDENING

For more on vegetable garden preparation, recommended planting times, and harvesting, see the monthly to-do lists in Part 2. For more details on winter vegetable gardening, a good reference is *Winter Gardening in the Maritime Northwest: Cool Season Crops for the Year-Round Gardener* by Binda Colebrook (Seattle, Washington: Sasquatch Books, 1998).

sprouting broccoli and winter cabbage can also be set out in late summer; these will overwinter and start producing much earlier than will spring transplants.

Four-year vegetable crop rotation

Balancing early and late plantings, summer and winter crops, pH preferences, stored/standing crops and cover crops, fertilizer needs (some vegetables are heavy feeders, others prefer leaner soil), and rotation needs to avoid disease can become a logistical nightmare. The following yearly rotation, with plot B following plot A, plot C following plot B and so on, is our own invention; it has worked well for us. Except for brassicas, which are non-negotiable, the placement of specific crops can be tinkered with to suit personal personal preference and needs; a few workable alternatives are given.

Plot A: Brassicas (cabbage family)

Crops: Broccoli, Brussels sprouts, cabbage, Chinese cabbage, cauliflower, collards, kale, kohlrabi. Because they are winter crops and have similar needs, leeks and Swiss chard are also best in this bed; celery may also go here.

Needs: Deep, fertile, nearly neutral soil (pH around 6.8–7.0).

Preparation: After harvesting in early fall, last year's plot D (this year's plot A) will have had a generous layer of manure or compost dug in, been planted with fall rye, and generously limed. Turn under the rye as early as the ground can be worked in spring.

Planting and harvest: Transplant early crops about three weeks after turning the fall rye under; plant midseason and late crops (seeds or transplants) from April to June. Harvest when mature; late crops can be mulched for fall-winter harvest.

Plot B: Root crops

Crops: Carrots, parsnips, potatoes*, rutabagas (Swede turnips), winter beets, winter radishes.

Needs: Fertile soil, not too alkaline (pH around 6.5); high in phosphorus and potassium but not in nitrogen. No fresh manure (causes hairy roots) or lime (causes potato scab).

Preparation: Soil is left reasonably fertile but somewhat less alkaline by plot A. Extra phosphorus (bone meal or rock phosphate) and potassium (greensand or kelp meal) can be added at planting time.

Planting and harvest: All crops can be planted early, midseason, and/or late. Harvest when mature; late crops can be covered with mulch and stored in the ground all winter.

Plot C: Legumes, cool-weather crops, and salad crops

Crops: Broad beans, green beans, lima beans, peas; celery, green onions, lettuce/salad greens, spinach, summer beets, summer (bunching) radishes, summer turnips, storage onions, garlic. Cucumbers, summer squash, and/or zucchini may also go in this bed.

Needs: Legumes (peas and beans) adapt to any soil type and need little or no extra fertilizer as long as soil is high in organic matter. Except for lettuce, all other crops need or tolerate slightly acidic soil (pH 6.0–6.5). Most need only moderately fertile soil; onions and leafy crops need extra nitrogen.

Preparation: Soil is left moderately acidic and moderately fertile by plot B. Turning under the straw or hay used for its winter mulch adds organic matter. Extra nitrogen for onions and leafy crops can be added at planting time, as can extra lime (if necessary) for lettuce.

Planting and harvest: All crops except green beans and lima beans (both warm-weather crops) can be planted as soon as the ground can be worked; salad crops can be sown in succession. Most crops are repeat-harvesters. At summer's end, dig plot over, plant fall rye, and lime lightly.

Plot D: Warm-weather crops

Crops: Corn, cucumbers, eggplant*, melons, peppers*, pumpkin, summer squash, tomatoes*, winter squash, zucchini. Green beans and annual herbs may also go in this bed.

Needs: Fertile soil; adequate lime (pH around 6.5).

Preparation: Soil fertility is replenished by legumes from plot C and the turned-under rye. Lime applied last fall ensures a pH level acceptable to all crops, although lime-tolerant peppers may appreciate more. Compost or aged manure can be dug in at planting time or applied as top dressing.

Planting and harvest: Plant only after danger of frost is past and soil is warm. Melons, peppers, and eggplants may not be suitable crops in cool-summer subregions; even in warmer areas, delay their planting until temperatures are above 50°F (10°C) at night. Crops are harvested as they mature, but all are finished by early fall at the latest. This leaves plenty of time to dig in compost or manure, plant fall rye, and lime heavily in preparation for the brassica crops that will once again occupy the soil as plot A in spring.

---

*   To avoid late blight and other soilborne diseases, no members of the nightshade family—potatoes, tomatoes, eggplants, or peppers—should occupy the same soil for at least three years. A foolproof way to keep them separated, even though they belong to different plots, is to always plant potatoes on the same end of their plot (north, east, closest to the house, or whatever) and tomatoes, eggplants, and peppers always on the opposite end of theirs (south, west, farthest from the house).

CHAPTER 4

Where Our Plants Come From

Although the gardening climate of the Pacific Northwest is far from perfect, its very imperfections allow us to grow a great many different plants from very different parts of the world. The cosmopolitan nature of our gardens is taken for granted here, but some of the juxtapositions commonly seen are really quite astonishing.

Our own garden serves as a typical example. In one small partially shaded bed next to our driveway, a maple native to Japan is underplanted with a bulb native to the southern tip of Chile. Beside the maple are spireas native to Japan and a yew native to the Mediterranean and Europe; behind it, a daylily native to China is underplanted with *Primula* 'Wanda', a hybrid of several species native to the Caucasus. This is backed by bergenias native to eastern Siberia, sword ferns native to the Pacific Northwest, and a hybrid mahonia, a cross of one species from the Himalaya and another from eastern Asia.

Across from the mahonia are several hellebores native to the Balkans and Asia Minor, some hardy geraniums native to Europe, a boxwood and some ivy-leaved cyclamen native to the Mediterranean, and a cedar native to eastern North America. In back is a hedge of western red cedar native to the Pacific Northwest.

On the sunny side of the driveway, in a bed not watered regularly in summer, a weeping yellow cedar native to the Pacific Northwest is underplanted with the groundcover *Rubus rolfei*, native to Taiwan. Bordering the bed are crocosmias native to southern Africa and hoop petticoat daffodils native to the Mediterranean; in between are hebes native to New Zealand, box honeysuckles (*Lonicera nitida*) native to China, a Russian sage (*Perovskia atriplicifolia*) native to the Caucasus, and a tiger lily (*Lilium lancifolium*) native to China.

The origins of these plants, all of which are commonplace in Pacific Northwest gardens, were not even considered when choosing them. The essential criterion was the suitability of the site for each plant's needs; beyond that, we simply liked their looks together.

But that plants from such utterly disparate origins can grow in the same site at all, let alone not look out of place with each other, is a phenomenon not widely appreciated—especially since the exchange usually does not work in reverse. We can easily grow plants from the Mediterranean, but most of our own native plants cannot be easily grown in the warmer, much drier Mediterranean. We can grow plants from Siberia, Asia Minor, and New Zealand in the same bed, but most plants native to any one of these places cannot be grown successfully in either of the other two.

Incredibly, it is the drawbacks of the Pacific Northwest climate, not its merits, that make such wholesale accommodation possible. It is our summer drought that enables us to grow plants from the bone-dry Mediterranean and the western side of southern Africa. It is our heat-challenged but sunny summers that enable us to grow choice alpines and rock plants from the Pyrenees, the Alps, the Caucasus, the Himalayas, the Andes, the Sierra Nevada, and other mountain ranges, including our own. It is our very mild, unvaryingly moist (dare we say monotonous?) winters that make broadleaved evergreens from New Zealand and southern Chile such a good fit here, especially on the problematically windy Pacific Coast.

Without the incessant drizzle that keeps our winter temperatures much milder than they would be without it, we could not overwinter plants from southeastern Australia or the eastern side of southern Africa outdoors. Without the heat that builds up in August due to our long summer drought, we could not ripen the berries, fruits, or even the wood of many plants from central Europe, eastern North America, or parts of China. Without our high annual rainfall and high humidity, we could not grow plants from Japan or the Himalaya with nearly as much ease.

Yes, we have challenges in accommodating plants that need winter dryness, such as those from the Caucasus; or plants that need regular summer water, such as those from eastern North America. However, it's fairly easy to meet such challenges. More importantly, even these apparent drawbacks work in our favor. It is precisely because plants from other parts of the world tend to fit into Pacific Northwest conditions slightly imperfectly that the danger of them becoming invasive is minimized.

The ornamental plants mentioned in this chapter are just a few of the better-known and most widely available. We have not included plants with very widespread native distribution, but in many cases a plant listed as native in one region is also native in at least one other neighboring region. This is especially

NATIVES, EXOTICS, AND INVASIVE ALIENS

The introduction of non-native plants (also called exotic or alien species) always carries an inherent risk of invasiveness. It's not that invasiveness is exclusively the domain of exotic plants; aggressively spreading Pacific Northwest natives such as false lily-of-the-valley (*Maianthemum bifolium* subsp. *kamtschaticum*, syn. *M. dilatatum*), northern reed grass (*Calamagrostis canadensis*), or salal (*Gaultheria shallon*) can quickly take over large areas, especially in damp soil. Even some of our most annoying invasive weeds, such as horsetails and the ankle-grabbing trailing blackberry (*Rubus ursinus*), are native plants.

However, the greatest risk of invasiveness comes from alien ornamental plants that are perfectly adapted to their new settings. Ironically, these are the wonder plants of gardens: those that adapt easily to a wide range of soils and conditions, are perfectly comfortable with our rainfall patterns and seasonal temperatures, and need no watering, fertilizing, lifting, dividing, staking, pruning, or coddling. They also tend to be impervious to insects and diseases, and are often so happy in their adopted homes that they self-seed or spread quickly by rhizomes or stolons.

The lines between well-adapted plants, aggressive spreaders, easily naturalized species, and invasive alien species are by no means cut and dried. Much depends on locale, and simplistic solutions such as banning all plants that appear on any list of alien invasive species are not very helpful. For instance, baby's breath (*Gypsophila paniculata*) is a noxious weed east of the Cascades because it proliferates like crazy in dry, light-textured soil, but on this side of the mountains, most gardeners have trouble keeping it alive over winter. It has naturalized locally in the low-rainfall Olympic Rain Shadow subregion but is not considered invasive there; in areas of heavy, winter-wet soils, it poses no threat at all.

A lot also depends on perspective. Some of us see invasive aliens under every tree (or sometimes, as in the case of Norway maple, as the tree itself), while others deny any problem exists, pointing out that the natural world is always in flux. However, the examples of deliberately introduced Scotch broom (*Cytisus scoparius*), purple loosestrife (*Lythrum salicaria*), and English ivy (*Hedera helix*) loom large. Any very adaptable plant that reproduces itself rapidly, outcompetes surrounding plants, is hard to eradicate, and is not checked by natural predators (insects or grazing animals) is potentially invasive.

There are no easy answers, including gardening with native plants only. Man's fascination with pretty plants from strange places is at least as old as civilization itself, and is probably an inborn aspect of being human. Responsible ornamental gardening does not mean eschewing exotic plants, but it does require following common-sense guidelines:

➤ Be extremely leery of any plant that self-seeds prolifically, spreads rapidly, or overwhelms other garden plants. This goes for old favorites such as some cottage-garden perennials as well as newer introductions. If at all possible, phase these thugs out of your garden.

➤ Keep all spreading and/or self-seeding plants well away from property lines, especially near natural wooded areas. Confine spreading bamboos and aggressively spreading groundcovers in escape-proof containers or between impenetrable barriers such as buildings and paved areas.

➤ Be especially vigilant about keeping aggressive spreaders or self-seeders away from streams, rivers, lakes, beaches, and wetlands, since these areas are most vulnerable to invasion.

➤ Deadhead perennials after bloom to prevent seed set. Double-flowered forms are also a good choice; the extra petals are modified stamens, so the plants are sterile or very nearly so.

➤ Avoid self-seeding species with very deep, extensive root systems.

➤ Keep an open mind about new threats from widely planted species such as butterfly bush (*Buddleja davidii*). Sometimes it is simply a critical mass of seed availability that pushes a species into the invasive category (e.g., *B. davidii* itself, but not its cultivars, is now noxious in Oregon.)

➤ Respect plant quarantine regulations, especially when ordering plants or seeds from another country. Red tape can be a pain, but in this case it exists for several good reasons (e.g., ramorum blight and tip dieback).

➤ Enjoy the many well-adapted and beautiful plants, both exotic and native, that have proven themselves well behaved in the Pacific Northwest.

---

true where civilizations are oldest: it's no coincidence that the native/naturalized range of many "Eurasian" plants closely follows the various Silk Roads and other ancient trade routes.

JAPAN

Japan, our closest neighbor to the west, is arguably our closest horticultural connection as well. Many of our most popular and indispensable plants have Japanese origins—Japanese anemones (*Anemone* ×*hybrida*), Japanese angelica tree (*Aralia elata*), Japanese (evergreen) azaleas, Japanese flowering crabapple (*Malus floribunda*), Japanese flowering cherries, Japanese holly (*Ilex crenata*), Japanese iris (*Iris ensata*), Japanese larch (*Larix kaempferi*), Japanese maples, Japanese painted fern, various Japanese pines (black, red, and white), Japanese silver grass (*Miscanthus sinensis*), Japanese spurge (*Pachysandra terminalis*), Japanese stewartia (*Stewartia pseudocamellia*), and Japanese wisteria (*Wisteria floribunda*)—and that's just for starters.

Japanese maple foliage in fall

Pieris japonica 'Mountain Fire'

Magnolia stellata 'Royal Star'

With the common names of more than 150 other plants also beginning with "Japanese," it's no wonder so many of us refer to our gardening styles, only half-jokingly, as "Japamerican" or "Japanadian." In truth, we simply can't imagine gardening in the Pacific Northwest without at least some of these plants, or without some of numerous excellent plants bearing the species epithet *japonica*.

Although many people (and even some dictionaries) still use japonica as a common name for flowering quince (*Chaenomeles* species, of which *C. japonica* is one), the term simply means "of Japan." So do the epithets *japonicum* and *japonicus*; scores of genera from *Acer* to *Zoysia* contain a species "of Japan." Among the most essential to Pacific Northwest gardens are *Aucuba japonica*, *Camellia japonica*, *Cercidiphyllum japonicum*, *Cryptomeria japonica*, *Euonymus japonicus*, *Fatsia japonica* (Japanese aralia), *Kerria japonica*, *Mahonia japonica*, *Pieris japonica*, *Primula japonica*, *Skimmia japonica*, *Spiraea japonica*, and *Styrax japonicus* (Japanese snowbell).

Then there are the other garden essentials whose names give no hint of their Japanese origins—*Enkianthus campanulatus*, virtually all *Hosta* species, *Hydrangea macrophylla* and *H. paniculata*, many important lilies (*Lilium auratum*, *L. longiflorum*, *L. speciosum*), *Magnolia kobus*, *M. sieboldii*, star magnolia (*M. stellata*), *Weigela florida*, and the winter hazels *Corylopsis pauciflora* and *C. spicata*. *Rosa rugosa* is also native to Japan, as is *R. multiflora*, an ancestor of many ramblers, climbers, and all the modern roses we know as floribundas. So is *Rhododendron degronianum* subsp. *yakushimanum* and several other outstanding *Rhododendron* species.

Of course, many plants native to Japan are also native to neighboring eastern Siberia, Korea, and especially to China. To be scrupulously accurate, no plants are native to Japan's geologically young volcanic islands; all were introduced somewhere back in the mists of time. But the Japanese have always honored their own native plants to such an extent that many species—particularly chrysanthemums, flowering cherries, and maples—have uniquely Japanese associations.

Interest in other regional species such as bamboos, camellias, flowering quince, peonies, and pines has historically been shared with China; for instance, *Sophora japonica* is known both as Japanese pagoda tree and Chinese scholar tree.

There have to be good reasons for so many Pacific Northwest horticultural staples coming from the same relatively small corner of the world, and there are. Both regions are full of mountains of volcanic origin; both have moderately to strongly acidic soils; both have mild climates due to strong marine influence; both are known for their high rainfall. In fact, Japan's annual precipitation of about 80 in. (2000 mm) closely matches the heavy rainfalls of our Pacific Coast subregion. Both regions also enjoy warm, dry falls; both have wet but mild winters with no severe or long-lasting freezes; both have cool, drizzly springs with even cooler spring nights.

Summer, though, is a different story. Unlike our own, Japanese summers are both hot and humid: June is the rainiest month of the year, and the southernmost Japanese islands lie at the same latitude as northern Mexico. However, in northern Japan and at higher elevations even in the extreme south (where the tiny, mountainous, horticulturally rich island of Yakushima or Yaku Jima is located), temperatures are similar to ours.

Not surprisingly, many Japanese species need regular summer watering in our climate, although most shrubs and trees are at least moderately drought tolerant when established. A few (aucuba, kerria, spirea) are admirably drought tolerant in normal summers, but no Japanese species should be assumed to be tolerant of extensive summer drought until proven otherwise.

On the plus side is just about everything else about Japanese plants, including the ability to shrug off our winter monsoons (with good drainage, of course) and wet, drippy springs. Even our reduced light levels contribute to their comfort. Although many Japanese plants are considered woodland or shade-loving species, most can be grown here with only light shade or even in the open as long as they're watered in summer and protected from intense sun and drying winds.

Japanese plants have long drawn interest across the Western world, as evidenced by the species epithets *kaempferi, mariesii, maximowicziana, sargentii, sieboldii, thunbergii,* and *veitchii.* These respectively commemorate the plant explorers and/or expedition backers Englebert Kaempfer (German), Charles Maries (British), Carl Maximowicz (Russian), Charles Sprague Sargent (American), Philipp Franz von Siebold (German-born Dutch), Carl Peter Thunberg (Swedish), and John Gould Veitch or his son James Henry Veitch (British).

In recent times, gardens around the world (and especially in the Pacific Northwest) have benefited from ongoing Japanese hybridization of camellias, clematis, flowering dogwoods, flowering cherries, flowering kale and cabbage, hostas, hydrangeas, Japanese maples, and rhododendrons.

NORTHEASTERN ASIA

The contrast between mild, maritime-influenced Japan and cold, continental-influenced northeastern Asia could not be more pronounced, even though they are close geographic neighbors. At first glance, the Pacific Northwest also seems to have nothing in common with eastern Siberia, Sakhalin Island, northern Korea, and northeastern China (Manchuria), where temperatures in winter (the dry season) can reach -40°F (-40°C). Yet even as our gardens benefit so greatly from so many Japanese plants, they also accommodate certain plants from northeastern Asia beautifully.

Other than its dry, very cold winters, northeastern Asia actually shares many similarities with the Pacific Northwest, especially along the Amur River, which forms the border between northern China and southeastern Siberia. This cool-temperate region of coniferous forests has annual rainfall on a par with

Cornus alba 'Elegantissima'

that of Seattle, along with similar summer temperatures. Even winter is not necessarily bitterly cold here, since the surrounding mountains help deflect prevailing frigid continental winds from the river valley itself.

Naturally, plants such as Korean fir (*Abies koreana*) that grow near the tops of the mountains are adapted to extreme cold and are not good fits for mild-winter gardens at low elevations. Very cold-hardy deciduous trees from this region such as Dahurian larch (*Larix gmelini*) are even more unsuitable; our mild spring-like Februarys prompt them into growth too early, leaving them mortally vulnerable to even the mildest frost in March.

Other eastern Siberian deciduous trees such as Amur cork tree (*Phellodendron amurense*) and Siberian peashrub (*Caragana arborescens*) grow here, although not very happily; with so many other better-suited choices available, there is little reason to choose either of these. (We must admit that 'Pendula', the weeping form of Siberian peashrub, is quite pretty.)

Much better adapted to our gardens are Amur maple (*Acer tataricum* subsp. *ginnala*, formerly *A. ginnala*), which makes a well-behaved small tree or multi-trunked shrub that can be relied on for fiery red fall color, and Amur maackia (*Maackia amurensis*), a small, pretty tree with bluish white summer flowers and a dislike of hot summers. Even better adapted is the Siberian crab (*Malus baccata*), whose cultivar 'Jackii' and the *M. ×robusta* hybrids derived from it are among the best-suited flowering crabapples of all for Pacific Northwest gardens. Also very well adapted are *Clematis macropetala, C. tangutica,* and the decorative pink-variegated *Actinidia kolomikta,* a relative of kiwi vine. Japanese yew (*Taxus cuspidata*), widespread in northeastern Asia, is an excellent choice in very cold, windy, or high-elevation gardens where other yews might suffer winter damage.

One of the best-suited of all plants from this region is *Cornus alba,* a shrub dogwood much valued for its red winter stems that are brightest in cold weather. Although several species are similar, including our native *C. sericea* (formerly *C. stolonifera*), *C. alba* will take either moist or dry soil and is reasonably drought tolerant in our summers, especially in partial shade. *Cornus alba* 'Sibirica', a more refined selection of the species, is popular for its particularly brilliant winter stems. The yellow-variegated 'Gouchaultii' and especially the white-variegated

'Elegantissima' make this species a popular choice year-round, since the light foliage brightens up shady corners so beautifully. The hard-to-find 'Kesselringii' (green leaves and purple-black winter stems) makes a great combination with either.

One of our most beautiful deciduous rhododendrons is also native to northeastern Asia. *Rhododendron schlippenbachii* (royal azalea) should be sited where it will not be exposed either to winter warming or to late spring frosts; although very cold-hardy, its exquisite pale pink flowers and reddish new foliage can be damaged if they break dormancy too early. However, the early-blooming evergreen *R. dauricum* needs no special protection.

Perennials native to northeastern Asia include *Paeonia lactiflora*, which grows reasonably well here and is very popular in spite of being prone to botrytis blight in our damp springs, and the winter-flowering *Bergenia crassifolia*, which is very well suited to our climate but not nearly as popular as it should be. Its flowers and leaves can be blackened by late hard frost, so it needs a sheltered site in spite of being hardy to Zone 3. (If late frost does hit, plants will quickly recover and even rebloom.) *Delphinium grandiflorum* is also native to northeastern Asia.

Perennials native to both northeastern Asia and northern Japan include balloon flower (*Platycodon grandiflorus*), the lovely, scented, early-blooming *Hemerocallis lilioasphodelus* (formerly *H. flava*), Japanese iris (*Iris ensata*), the fall-blooming *Sedum spectabile*, soft, feathery silver mound (*Artemisia schmidtiana*), and the groundcover *Waldsteinia ternata*. The popular shrub *Euonymus alatus* (burning bush), prized throughout the Pacific Northwest for its outstanding fall foliage, is also native to both areas.

As might be expected, some plants originating in this less-than-ideal climate are so tough and well adapted that they become invasive in milder climates. The common or tawny daylily, *Hemerocallis fulva*, is blacklisted in Oregon, Washington, and most other states as an invasive garden escapee; although nearly sterile, it spreads quickly via underground stolons and will regrow from very small remnants left in the ground.

Much more of a problem is giant knotweed, *Polygonum sachalinense*. This huge (up to 10 ft., 3 m), handsome herbaceous perennial with heart-shaped leaves and somewhat bamboo-like stems is very well adapted to our climate, spreads very aggressively by deep underground stolons, and is very difficult to eradicate, making it undesirable in British Columbia and noxious in Washington and Oregon.

Two very similar species that are only slightly less gigantic are Japanese knotweed (*Polygonum cuspidatum*, now *Fallopia japonica*), and Himalayan knotweed (*P. polystachyum*, now *Persicaria wallichii*). Both were introduced via England as ornamental plants; both are equally aggressive and equally noxious. All three species are common in roadside ditches and disturbed sites but are unlikely to invade gardens unless deliberately introduced. (If it does happen, cut them to the ground and cover them closely for a full growing season, cutting off any new growth as soon as it appears.) Never be tempted to dig up a root of any of these deceptively attractive Asian natives; you'll live to regret it.

Wisteria sinensis 'Alba'

CHINA

The debt owed to China by the entire gardening world cannot be overestimated. This is especially true in the Pacific Northwest, where rhododendrons from the Himalayan border of western China find such an excellent home, but other plants from other parts of China are equally important to our gardens. For example, without the hybridization of *Rosa chinensis* with non-Chinese species, we would have no repeat-blooming roses, nor any true red ones; without the Chinese native *Clematis lanuginosa*, we would have no large-flowered, long-blooming clematis.

This vast country contains every climate imaginable, from steppe, prairie, desert, and rocky plateau to coastal plain, temperate forest, subtropical broadleaved forest, tropical rain forest, and subalpine and alpine conditions. Moreover, its ancient civilization, which dates back at least 4000 years, has always revered plants for their beauty as well as their utility. Many plants now grown as favorites around the world—chrysanthemums, magnolias, herbaceous and tree peonies, weeping willow, wisteria—are Chinese natives that have been carefully cultivated since ancient times.

China gave the world apricots, peaches, some plums, and the flowering varieties of these, including *Prunus mume*. Also native to China are the sweet orange (*Citrus sinensis*), the sour orange, the Mandarin orange, and many other types of citrus fruits. Every genus of bamboo is represented somewhere in China; so is every genus of conifer except *Araucaria*. (Even here, the Chinese fir, or *Cunninghamia lanceolata*, somewhat resembles the monkey puzzle and is sometimes substituted for it.) China is the home of the dawn redwood (*Metasequoia glyptostroboides*) and the maidenhair tree (*Ginkgo biloba*)—both "living fossil" deciduous conifers thought to be long extinct—as well as a third rare deciduous conifer, the golden larch (*Pseudolarix amabilis*).

Then there are the rhododendrons. China's western provinces of Sichuan and Yunnan are home to approximately three-quarters of the world's 800-plus *Rhododendron* species (including some deciduous and evergreen azaleas) prized both for their own merits and for their essential contributions to our finest hybrids. To this day, the remote rugged mountains of western China continue to be a source of new horticultural

Three-quarters of the world's 800-plus species of *Rhododendron* are native to western China. This one is *R. oreotrephes.*

Chinese witch hazel (*Hamamelis mollis*)

introductions well suited to Pacific Northwest gardens, such as the trillium-like *Paris polyphylla.*

But China's greatest gift to gardens, including our own, comes from a unique and intertwined combination of geography, climate, and culture. On the whole, China's climate is the exact opposite of ours: wet in summer and dry in winter. Heavy monsoons soak the southeast from May to October, which is our dry season, and cold but dry air from Siberia and Mongolia spills southward from northern China in winter.

There are of course wide variations, but the overwhelming feature of China's rainfall pattern is its unpredictability. The monsoons often fail, bringing devastating drought and—at least in the past—subsequent famine. Conversely, they can be unusually intense, bringing widespread flooding and subsequent famine. Both conditions have occurred regularly but unpredictably since time immemorial, causing untold human misery.

If an upside to such widespread suffering is possible, it is this: because Chinese plants have had to survive both unexpected drought and unexpected flood for eons, most Chinese plants—at least the ones suitable for temperate climates—are reliably drought tolerant without being overly sensitive to wetness, as are plants from regions that are always dry.

This characteristic has been the savior of many a Pacific Northwest garden in recent years. In our own garden, all the Chinese natives have come through the repeated, abnormally extended droughts of the past few years with flying colors. Since more abnormal drought (perhaps mixed with a few super-wet winters) has been all but promised us in the foreseeable future, plants native to China will undoubtedly become even more indispensable in years to come.

Adding even more to the adaptability of these plants is the historical Chinese veneration of the traditional and the time-proven, the symbolic and the auspicious. For ages, the same plants cultivated in the warm, wet south were cultivated in the cold, dry north, and vice versa. From the plants' viewpoints, it was either adapt or perish—and over a few thousand years, they adapted. Chinese plants tend to tolerate both heat and cold remarkably well, regardless of their original ecological niches,

and are tolerant of a wide range of soil types. (This does not apply to rhododendrons native to China, since this genus was largely ignored in ancient Chinese culture.)

With such awe-inspiring adaptability, it's not surprising that many plants considered native to the places they were first seen in antiquity by Europeans are actually native to China. Plants whose species epithets should rightfully be *chinensis* or *sinensis* (both mean "from China") include the apricot, *Prunus armeniaca* (from Armenia); the peach, *Prunus persica* (from Persia or modern-day Iran); the weeping willow, *Salix babylonica* (from Babylon or modern-day Iraq); the crape myrtle, *Lagerstroemia indica* (from India); and the hardy hibiscus, *Hibiscus syriacus* (from Syria). This also applies to many if not most of the dozens of plants with the species epithet *japonica* ("from Japan").

Unfortunately, a few of the plants most highly regarded in Chinese culture are not quite adaptable enough to make the switch from China's mainly dry winters and early springs to the super-saturated winters and early springs of the Pacific Northwest. Peaches, nectarines, apricots, and all their flowering kin are very prone to peach leaf curl, fungal twig blights, and/or bacterial twig blights here, making them not-so-good choices in all but our driest subregions.

Herbaceous peonies, being native to the cold, dry north of China and neighboring Siberia, are also highly subject to botrytis blight in our climate—although that doesn't stop us from growing these beautiful flowers by the thousands. (Tree peonies, native to the wetter, milder regions of western China, are less bothered by fungal diseases in our climate.)

Fortunately, this leaves a huge number of very adaptable, very beautiful ornamental plants well suited to Pacific Northwest growing conditions. We are especially indebted to the Chinese love of winter-blooming flowers, which has given us Chinese witch hazel (*Hamamelis mollis*), several winter hazels (*Corylopsis*), winter jasmine (*Jasminum nudiflorum*), wintersweet (*Chimonanthus praecox*), *Skimmia japonica* var. *reevesiana*, and flowering quince (*Chaenomeles speciosa*). Close on their heels come more early-blooming favorites such as our deliciously fragrant winter daphne (*Daphne odora*), several *Camellia* species, and nearly all *Forsythia* species, whose Chinese name means "welcome to spring."

As well, the species epithets of some of our most popular garden plants commemorate famous Westerners from the golden age of plant exploration (19th and early 20th centuries) in China. Most notable are *davidii* (Père Jean Pierre Armand David), *delavayi* (Abbé Jean Marie Delavay), *farreri* (Reginald Farrer), *forrestii* (George Forrest), *fortunei* (Robert Fortune), *henryi* or *henryana* (Augustine Henry), and *wilsonii* (Ernest "Chinese" Wilson).

MORE PLANTS FROM CHINA

Deciduous trees
Cornus kousa var. *chinensis*, dove tree (*Davidia involucrata*), many flowering crabapples, empress tree (*Paulownia tomentosa*), golden rain tree (*Koelreuteria paniculata*), paperbark maple (*Acer griseum*), tree of heaven (*Ailanthus altissima*)

Conifers
Juniperus chinensis, *J. squamata*, Oriental cedar or biota (*Platycladus orientalis*)

Shrubs
Several barberries, beautyberry (*Callicarpa bodinieri*), beauty bush (*Kolkwitzia amabilis*), box honeysuckle (*Lonicera nitida*), *Buddleja davidii*, Chinese holly (*Ilex cornuta*), many cotoneasters, many deutzias, heavenly bamboo (*Nandina domestica*), *Mahonia japonica* Bealei Group, most photinias, several pieris, several spireas, several lilacs (including the dwarf species), many viburnums, windmill palm (*Trachycarpus fortunei*)

Perennials
Anemone hupehensis, several astilbes, bleeding heart (*Dicentra spectabilis*), most daylilies, hardy gloxinia, most ligularias, many primulas, *Rodgersia*, white mugwort (*Artemisia lactiflora*—the popular dark-leaved *A. l.* Guizhou Group is named for a Chinese province)

Annuals
China aster (*Callistephus chinensis*), balsam (*Impatiens balsamina*)

Bulbs
Many lilies, including tiger lily (*Lilium lancifolium*), *L. henryi*, and white trumpet lily (*L. regale*)

Vines
Boston ivy (*Parthenocissus tricuspidata*), evergreen clematis (*Clematis armandii*), several actinidias (including the edible fuzzy kiwi, *Actinidia deliciosa*, and the hardy kiwi, *A. arguta*), Chinese trumpet vine (*Campsis grandiflora*), many honeysuckles, *Schizophragma integrifolium*, star jasmine (*Trachelospermum jasminoides*), many other borderline-hardy jasmines

THE HIMALAYA

Often called the roof of the world, this high-altitude region of often-disputed political boundaries includes the Kashmir region, Nepal, Bhutan, Tibet, northern Myanmar (formerly Burma), and the northern Indian states of Assam, Sikkim, and Manipur. For horticultural purposes, it also includes part of the southwestern Chinese province of Yunnan. Although famed for its frigid, snow-covered peaks (*Himalaya* means "abode of snow"), this region is located in subtropical latitudes, giving it a very complicated climate. Sudden and steep differences in elevation mean climatic zones are separated vertically, not horizontally; several utterly different zones can occur within the same few miles on a map.

Of greatest importance to Pacific Northwest gardens is the temperate rainforest zone, which lies between the subtropical foothills and the subalpine zone (also a valuable source of plants) just below the tree line. Here, conditions resemble our own to a remarkable extent, being cool and moist for most of the year, with mild winters seldom dipping below freezing for very long and summers that are never truly hot. Soils are moderately to strongly acidic, and the year is divided into wet and dry seasons—but in mirror image to ours, with Himalayan monsoons arriving in summer, not winter.

However, the Himalayan dry season (winter) is never truly dry; although little rain falls, humidity remains very high due to frequent fog and mists. Numerous high-elevation valleys that act as "walled gardens" protect plants within them from fierce mountain winds; to some extent these also moderate summer weather, creating partial rain shadows from the warm, very wet monsoons.

Putting all these conditions together, many plants from the Himalaya are considered very tricky to grow, needing cool but never truly cold conditions, acidic soil that remains moist but not wet, protection from severe frost and high winds, and a good light level—neither too shady nor too bright—that somehow mimics the cloud-covered skies of a subtropical summer.

If such conditions are hard to imagine, think of cool, misty Scotland, which is home to some of the largest and most comprehensive collections of Himalayan plants outside their native habitat. Much closer to home, think of the cool, moist climates of the Pacific Coast and Puget Sound subregions: given a lightly sheltered site with adequate wind protection, conditions in these two subregions are close to perfect for these plants. The Georgia Basin/Puget Trough subregion is also a very good home for Himalayan plants, although light woodland shade and/or the protection afforded by conifer "walls" is advisable.

Choice, much-coveted Himalayan plants that grow easily in these moister, cooler subregions include blue-flowered *Corydalis cashmeriana* and *C. flexuosa*, the towering, fragrant trumpets of giant lily (*Cardiocrinum giganteum*), and the sky-blue flowers of Himalayan blue poppy (*Meconopsis betonicifolia*). Other choice floral beauties include *Lilium mackliniae*, *L. nepalense*, and several nomocharis; several rock jasmines (*Androsace*), and many species of *Primula*, including *P. beesiana*, *P. capitata*, *P. denticulata* (drumstick primrose), *P. florindae* (giant cowslip), *P. sikkimensis*, and *P. vialii* (pagoda primrose).

Pink-flowered Himalayan clematis (*Clematis montana* var. *rubens* 'Pink Perfection')

Himalayan birch (*Betula utilis* var. *jacquemontii*)

Choice but semi-tender (Zone 8b) Himalayan species easily grown in our mildest subregions include the pink-flowered *Magnolia campbellii*, *Mahonia lomariifolia* (parent of the magnificent winter-flowering *M.* ×*media* hybrids), and Paul's Himalayan Musk, a rampant, very fragrant hybrid rambler involving the Himalayan species *Rosa brunonii*.

Elsewhere in the Pacific Northwest, growing these and many other Himalayan species can be a challenge due to winter cold, summer heat, low rainfall, and/or low humidity. However, our universally cool nights (a requisite of most Himalayan species) are an ace in the hole, so the challenge is worth meeting. Best results come with a cool, sheltered eastern or northern exposure that is not too dark; protection from sudden, severe, or late frosts and strong winds; and regular summer watering with frequent misting.

But not all Himalayan plants need coddling. This region has also given us a few plants we'd rather not have, including Himalayan blackberry and Himalayan jewelweed or policeman's helmet (*Impatiens glandulifera*). A goodly number of perennials with invasive tendencies, such as chameleon plant (*Houttuynia cordata*) and most fleeceflowers (*Fallopia*, *Persicaria*, *Polygonum*) are also native to the Himalaya.

Fortunately, other Himalayan natives that also thrive with no special care in Pacific Northwest gardens (other than summer watering as needed) are highly valued. Leading the list is the beautiful *Clematis montana*; not far behind are birchbark cherry (*Prunus serrula*), *Cedrus deodara*, *Euphorbia griffithii*, *Geranium clarkei*, *G. himalayense*, Himalayan honeysuckle (*Leycesteria formosa*), several species of *Pyracantha*, and several choice mountain ashes, including *Sorbus cashmiriana* with its marble-sized white fruits and *S. hupehensis* var. *obtusa* with its pink fruits.

Deserving special mention is *Betula utilis* var. *jacquemontii* (Himalayan birch), which is by far the best choice for Pacific Northwest gardeners who simply must have a white-barked birch. Although this species is subject to all the many ills that plague birches in our climate (aphids/honeydew, borers, leaf miners, woodpeckers and sapsuckers, canker, and dieback), it is considerably less susceptible. It's also by far the most beautiful of white birches; its dazzling, pure white bark remains smooth and attractive from sapling stage through maturity. It also handles normal summer drought with fewer complaints than other birches, and is hardier (Zone 5) and more adaptable than many Himalayan species.

Of particular value to Pacific Northwest gardens, both in their own right and for their role in hybridizing, are the countless *Rhododendron* species (some of them somewhat tender) native to the Himalaya. Although far too numerous to list, these include *R. arboreum*, *R. barbatum*, *R. campanulatum*, *R. campylogynum*, *R. cinnabarinum*, *R. calostrotum* subsp. *keleticum*, and *R. thomsonii*.

Plants bearing the species epithets *farreri*, *griffithii*, *hookeri*, *thomsonii*, or *wardii* are almost certain to be native to the Himalaya; these respectively honor early Western plant explorers Reginald Farrer, William Griffith, Joseph Dalton Hooker, John Thomson, and Frank Kingdon Ward, most of whom also collected in China. Naturally, such epithets as *cashmiriana*, *himalayense*, *nepalense*, *sikkimense*, *tibetica*, and *yunnanense* (and their variants, *cashmeriana*, *himalayensis*, *yunnanensis*) also indicate Himalayan natives. The list of Himalayan plants suitable for Pacific Northwest gardens continues to grow as new plants from the region are introduced by Dan Hinkley, founder of the highly regarded Heronswood Nursery and now with Monrovia, and other modern plant explorers.

ASIA MINOR/CAUCASUS

Exactly what to call this part of the world, where eastern Europe meets and overlaps with western Asia, is a bit of a dilemma. In the past, parts of it have been known as Turkestan, Anatolia, Thrace, the Caucasus, Persia, the Byzantine Empire, and the Ottoman Empire; in the present, parts are known as the Near East, the Middle East, the eastern Mediterranean, and southwestern Asia. For plant-suitability purposes, this area includes all of Turkey; northern Syria, northern Iraq, and northern Iran; and the area between the Black Sea and the Caspian Sea, which includes Armenia, Azerbaijan, Georgia, and southwestern Russia.

Like the volatile mix of peoples, civilizations, religions, histories, and cultures that co-exist in this ancient and often blood-soaked region, its geographies, climates, and plants defy a common categorization. The Mediterranean coasts of Turkey, Syria, and Lebanon have—not surprisingly—Mediterranean climates, with very mild, wet winters (although not nearly as wet as ours) and very dry summers. The Black Sea coast of northern Turkey has a temperate climate very much like that of the Willamette subregion, with mild but damp winters, moderate but dry summers, and very little wind. Mountainous interior Turkey, Iran, and the Caucasus all have longer and colder winters, ranging from moderately wet to very dry.

Parts of southwestern Russia and northern Iran have benign climates with temperatures closely approximating ours, but as this area merges into the Central Asian countries of Turkmenistan and Afghanistan, the climate becomes colder in winter, much hotter in summer, and much, much drier (precipitation of less than 10 in., 250 mm annually). Plants from this section are thus not well suited to most parts of the Pacific Northwest, except perhaps for the Rogue subregion. Examples include foxtail lily (*Eremurus*), Russian olive (*Elaeagnus angustifolia*), and Lombardy and Theve's poplars (*Populus nigra* 'Italica' and *P. n.* 'Afghanica'), which grow but are highly subject to insects and disease in wetter climates.

Most parts of the Asia Minor/Caucasus region have much drier winters than ours; yearly precipitation even in wet-winter areas never exceeds about 20 in. (508 mm). (Whatever their precise origins, good winter drainage for these plants is imperative, especially in heavier soils.) But what all parts of this region have in common with the Pacific Northwest, and what makes their plants so useful and valuable here, is mild, rainy springs followed by dry summers. Even the extremely dry mountains of northern Iran are a tremendously rich source of hardy spring bulbs, all of which have the good sense to emerge and set seed during this brief opportunity, then go dormant for the long, dry summer and long, dry winter.

The range of plants native to the various parts of this region is truly astounding. Wine grapes originated here, as did fruiting cherries, pears, fruiting quince (*Cydonia oblonga*), and, most likely, apples and crabapples. So did filberts or hazelnuts (75 percent of the world's supply is grown in northern Turkey), "English" walnuts (once called Persian walnuts), and sweet chestnuts. Ornamental trees include Oriental spruce (*Picea*

Star of Persia (*Allium cristophii*)

orientalis), *Parrotia persica*, and most likely the flowering plum, *Prunus cerasifera*.

If the species epithets of some of these plants sound familiar, they should. Many of our most popular and familiar plants commemorate this area of the world with the epithets *orientalis*, meaning "eastern" (in the sense of being east of Europe, as in Oriental carpets or the Orient Express); *persica*, meaning "from Persia" (Iran); *sibirica* or *siberica*, meaning "from Siberia" (usually western Siberia); *tatarica*, referring to the Tatar peoples of Central Asia; *byzantina* or *byzantinus*, referring to the Byzantine Empire, and *caucasica*, a reference to the Caucasus Mountains. Not a few common names also begin with the adjectives Persian, Russian, Siberian, or Turkish.

A few examples of well-known shrubs and vines from this area include *Daphne mezereum* (February daphne) and several other *Daphne* species, *Clematis orientalis* (orange peel clematis), Persian ivy (*Hedera colchica*), *Fallopia baldschuanica* (Russian vine, silver lace vine), smoke tree (*Cotinus coggygria*), Tatarian honeysuckle (*Lonicera tatarica*), *Pyracantha coccinea*, and willow-leaved pear (*Pyrus salicifolia*). The ancestors of damask roses and the Persian yellow rose (*Rosa foetida* 'Persiana') are also native to this region.

Of special note are the *Rhododendron* species native to the Caucasus, all of which are cold-hardy, very adaptable, and have been used extensively in hybridizing. *Rhododendron ponticum*, which has naturalized in Europe and the British Isles, is the parent of many older hybrids; the dwarf species *R. ungernii* and *R. smirnowii* have more recently added their cold hardiness and excellent foliage to newer hybrids. The deciduous species *R. luteum* (formerly *Azalea pontica*), prized for its powerfully but sweetly scented yellow flowers, is still popular even on its own.

Perennials and groundcovers from this region are, like its peoples, incredibly tough, resilient, and adaptable survivors, enduring all kinds of less-than-perfect growing conditions except poor drainage, which may be fatal in winter. A little lime is beneficial in strongly acidic soils, but not absolutely imperative. All are very drought tolerant, making them invaluable in the dry Rogue and Olympic Rain Shadow subregions; since most are also tolerant of cold and extremes of temperature, they're also excellent choices in the Cascade Slopes/Outflow Valleys subregion. All are very easy to grow in all subregions. In fact, with their constitutions attuned to adverse growing conditions, some may spread more than is wanted in more congenial circumstances. A few—such as comfrey (*Symphytum*), which regrows from the smallest piece of root—are notorious for this habit.

Some of the most familiar perennials from this region include *Astrantia maxima*, baby's breath (*Gypsophila paniculata*), *Brunnera macrophylla*, several catmints (*Nepeta*), *Crambe cordifolia*, dame's rocket (*Hesperis matronalis*), fernleaf yarrow (*Achillea filipendulina*), German or Tatarian statice (*Goniolimon tataricum*), many hardy geraniums, *Helleborus orientalis* (parent of *H.* ×*hybridus*), *Iris sibirica*, lamb's ears (*Stachys byzantina*), lady's mantle, lemon balm (*Melissa officinalis*), several leopard's banes (*Doronicum*), Maltese cross (*Lychnis chalcedonica*), milky bellflower (*Campanula lactiflora*), Miss Willmott's ghost (*Eryngium giganteum*, named for her habit of surreptitiously spreading its seed in other people's gardens), and the vigorous spreader known as Mrs. Robb's bonnet (*Euphorbia amygdaloides* var. *robbiae*), so named because the first specimen sent back to Europe was packed in a hatbox belonging to a Mrs. Robb.

Still others include Oriental poppy (*Papaver orientale*), painted daisy (*Tanacetum coccineum*), Persian cornflower (*Centaurea dealbata*), several species of *Primula* (including the ancestors of *P.* 'Wanda'), rose campion (*Lychnis coronaria*), Russian sage (*Perovskia atriplicifolia*), many salvias, *Scabiosa caucasica*, Siberian iris, and many veronicas, including the superb *Veronica umbrosa* 'Georgia Blue'. A great many alpines and rock garden plants are native to the Caucasus. Particularly valuable are aubrieta, alpine wall cress (*Arabis alpina* subsp. *caucasica*), *Anchusa azurea*, *Gentiana septemfida*, several dwarf fleabanes (*Erigeron*), and several navelworts (*Omphalodes*).

These plants alone make a major contribution to Pacific Northwest gardens, but the greatest gift of this region to all temperate gardens is its incredible variety of hardy spring bulbs. Except for daffodils, most of which are native to the Mediterranean region to its west, and taller tulips, which are native to the Central Asia region to its east, virtually all of our familiar spring bulbs come from this region.

All hyacinths, most grape hyacinths (*Muscari*), most squills (including the favorite bright blue *Scilla siberica* 'Spring Beauty'), and a huge number of fritillaries come from here. So do many *Crocus* species, including most fall-blooming crocus and colchicums. Nearly all the very early-blooming bulbs—*Iris danfordiae*, *I. reticulata*, *Cyclamen coum*, *Eranthis* Cilicica Group, glory-of-the-snow (*Chionodoxa*), *Puschkinia scilloides*—and many snowdrops (*Galanthus*) are also native here.

Later bloomers include many early-blooming, low-growing species tulips such as *Tulipa greigii* and *T. kaufmanniana*, several *Corydalis* species, several *Ranunculus* species, a great many *Allium* species (especially the taller ones with globe-shaped flowers), and the Madonna lily (*Lilium candidum*).

THE MEDITERRANEAN

The images usually conjured up by the word "Mediterranean"—figs, grapes, and olive trees basking in warm, perpetual-summer conditions under skies that are always bright and sunny—make this area of the world seem to have almost nothing in common with the cool, moist Pacific Northwest, especially during our seven-month rainy season. However, our wet-winter, dry-summer climate is actually a closer match to the Mediterranean pattern than to any other climate in the world.

Mediterranean plants, which include many species not usually thought of as native to that part of the world, are invaluable here for their high natural drought tolerance coupled with a similar tolerance of torrential rain in winter (as long as drainage is good). Since our unnaturally extended summer droughts of recent years are likely to continue, Mediterranean natives seem destined to become even more valuable in local gardens.

In many ways, the Pacific Northwest has bona fide Mediterranean credentials itself. All Mediterranean-type climates occur in relatively narrow coastal strips on the western or southern edge of continents; all have oceans or large seas on their windward sides; all have mountain ranges for interior boundaries. This combination of factors always creates wet winters and dry summers, both of which are much milder than those on the other side of the mountains.

Of the lands actually bordering the Mediterranean Sea, only some—southern Spain, southern France, most of Italy, the Adriatic coast, all of Greece, southwestern Turkey, western Syria, Lebanon, and the Atlas Mountains region of northern Algeria and Morocco—actually have Mediterranean climates; Libya, Egypt, and Israel, lacking the necessary causal factors, do not. Portugal has a true Mediterranean climate, even though it does not border that particular body of water; so do the southwestern tip of South Africa, coastal southwestern Australia, central Chile, and coastal southern California.

One major difference between a true Mediterranean climate and our modified version of one is winter and summer temperatures. Lands with true Mediterranean climates lie between latitudes 30° and 45° (North or South) and have very mild, nearly frost-free winters; consequently, many Mediterranean natives are not terribly cold-hardy and need winter protection in most parts of the Pacific Northwest. Others, however, are hardy to Zone 5; a great many more are hardy to Zone 7.

Summer temperatures are also somewhat warmer than ours (especially at night) but are never scorching hot; normal summer highs are in the high 80s F (low 30s C). Lack of adequate warmth for Mediterranean natives such as figs or bay trees can be a bit of a problem in the Pacific Coast and Puget Sound subregions, but a southern exposure and/or warm wall can help a lot.

This disparity is more than offset by the number of Mediterranean plants ideally suited to coastal conditions of wind, salt spray, and porous, not-too-fertile soil, such as lavender, lavatera, *Arbutus unedo*, and *Viburnum tinus*. In the cool-summer Olympic Rain Shadow subregion, which has the most Mediterranean-like climate in all the Pacific Northwest, conditions for such plants are near perfect.

Lavatera ×*clementii* 'Rosea'

As could be expected of dry-climate plants, most Mediterranean natives are lime-tolerant, but this does not necessarily mean they must have neutral or alkaline soil. Only the most strongly acidic soils need amendment to please these quite adaptable plants. Full sun is almost a given (in the Pacific Northwest, most Mediterranean plants need all the sun they can get, but a few are also remarkably shade tolerant).

Since Mediterranean plants can expect warm-season drought for seven or eight months of every year, their drought tolerance in Pacific Northwest summers is guaranteed, even in full sun. Our higher rainfalls and cooler summers do not displease them; in fact, since "tolerate" and "like" are two different things, most probably prefer a bit more water than they would get at home, especially in spring and early summer.

However, there is one extremely important caveat: since their roots search wide and deep for summer water in soil that is usually light and porous, all Mediterranean plants need excellent winter drainage, especially in heavier soils. Although Mediterranean winter rains (which begin suddenly in October, just as they do here) can be heavy, they are of considerably shorter duration, diminishing by January to what we would call showers and rarely causing the water table to rise. With very few exceptions, saturated soil is not well tolerated by Mediterranean plants; standing water can be fatal.

Mediterranean plants ideally suited to Pacific Northwest conditions are those whose natural range extends to the British Isles and Mediterranean introductions that have thrived there for centuries. English holly and English yew are examples of the former; "English" boxwood and "English" lavender, of the latter.

Many dwarf evergreen shrubs and subshrubs commonly used as perennials or groundcover in the Pacific Northwest also have Mediterranean origins. Besides many species of lavender and heath (*Erica*), these include several artemisias, candytuft (*Iberis sempervirens*), St. John's wort (*Hypericum calycinum*), dusty miller (*Senecio cineraria*), *Euphorbia characias*, germander (*Teucrium*), Jerusalem sage (*Phlomis fruticosa*), lavender cotton (*Santolina chamaecyparissus*), lithodora, rosemary, rue (*Ruta graveolens*), most thymes, and *Vinca major*.

A few herbaceous perennials native to the Mediterranean include bear's breeches (*Acanthus mollis*), Cupid's dart (*Catananche caerulea*), gold dust plant (*Alyssum saxatile*), king's spear (*Asphodeline lutea*), many mulleins (*Verbascum*), red valerian

(*Centranthus ruber*), and most wallflowers (*Erysimum*, including all plants formerly classed as *Cheiranthus*). Snapdragons, which thrive in Pacific Northwest gardens and sometimes overwinter here, are semi-tender Mediterranean perennials.

Hardy spring-blooming bulbs are very well represented, with virtually all *Narcissus* species being native to the western end of this region. Other Mediterranean bulbs include several species each of crocus, grape hyacinth, ornithogalum, snowdrops, and squill (*Scilla*). *Anemone blanda* (Grecian windflower), *A. coronaria*, many low-growing alliums, hardy fall cyclamen (*Cyclamen hederifolium*), Spanish bluebells, the fall-blooming *Sternbergia lutea*, and winter aconite (*Eranthis hyemalis*) are also native here.

Being fully hardy in our climate and perfectly suited to a dry-summer dormant season, Mediterranean bulbs should not be lifted in summer, as is sometimes recommended in general gardening books; they need year-round residence in the soil to multiply and look their best. Avoid regular summer watering of areas containing Mediterranean bulbs, since they expect and need dry summers.

Mediterranean trees, shrubs, and vines that excel in our climate include Algerian ivy (*Hedera canariensis*), Atlas cedar (*Cedrus atlantica*), *Clematis cirrhosa*, *C. viticella* (parent of many important hybrids), *Juniperus sabina* (parent of many hybrids), pineapple broom (*Cytisus battandieri*), Portugal laurel (*Prunus lusitanica*, which looks better and is far better suited to our climate than English laurel), rock roses (*Cistus*), strawberry tree (*Arbutus unedo*), and laurustinus (*Viburnum tinus*). Several species of hardy pines and evergreen oaks are also native to the Mediterranean; in Zones 8 and 9, many more species such as bay tree (*Laurus nobilis*) and Italian cypress (*Cupressus sempervirens*) can also be grown.

Some Mediterranean natives have adapted so well to our climate that they're almost too much at home here. Creeping St. John's wort, vinca, and mulleins are well known for their aggressive spreading; English holly and Portugal laurel have naturalized and are listed as invasive in parts of the Pacific Northwest.

On an even more ominous note, all brooms—*Genista* species, Spanish broom (*Spartium junceum*), and *Cytisus* species, including the notorious Scotch broom, *C. scoparius*—are originally native to the Mediterranean. So is salt cedar (*Tamarix ramosissima*), an invasive species now considered noxious in most areas. Unwelcome guests, yes—but a telling example of just how great a natural affinity exists between Mediterranean plants and the Pacific Northwest.

EUROPE

The greatest similarity in cultural conditions between the Pacific Northwest and Europe is human culture. Whether or not we're of European descent personally, most of us have been conditioned to identify emotionally with European history, literature, and art, all of which refer quite often to native plants. As a result, we somehow automatically think European natives belong in our own gardens, whether or not they're actually well suited to the peculiar Pacific Northwest climate, soils, and (plant) cultural conditions.

Fortunately, important similarities in climate mean many European plants do in fact make themselves right at home here. The two regions share similar latitudes, with temperatures in the same ballpark spring through fall. (Winters in Central and Eastern Europe can be considerably colder than ours.) Excepting the Pacific Coast subregion with its very heavy rainfalls, the two regions have a similar range of annual precipitation; both also have fertile, heavy soil in their densely populated river valleys and sandier, siltier soils on their coasts.

However, precipitation is more or less evenly spread through the year in Europe; if anything, spring or summer months (depending on location) bring slightly more rain than average, and winters are not nearly as wet as ours. Most European soils also tend to be close to neutral or even slightly alkaline, although soils in northern Europe are more acidic.

With these differences in mind, most European natives thrive in the Pacific Northwest as long as they're watered as necessary in summer, provided with good winter drainage, and limed appropriately. A few examples so familiar we take them for granted include *Aquilegia vulgaris*, chamomile, *Clematis alpina*, common snowdrop (*Galanthus nivalis*), Dutch (large-flowered) crocus, English daisies (*Bellis perennis*), English bluebells (*Hyacinthoides non-scripta*), French pussy willow (*Salix caprea*), *Daphne cneorum*, all hardy heaths and

Philadelphus coronarius 'Aureus'

heathers, common hop (*Humulus lupulus*), common lilac (*Syringa vulgaris*), lily-of-the-valley, *Lonicera periclymenum*, Norway spruce (*Picea abies*), ornamental elderberries (*Sambucus nigra*, *S. racemosa*), ornamental hazel (*Corylus avellana*), sweet mock orange (*Philadelphus coronarius*), tall bearded iris, *Viburnum opulus*, and *Vinca minor*.

Such familiar plants as raspberries, currants (red, black, and white), and gooseberries are also European natives; so are several important rose species, including *Rosa gallica*, *R. glauca*, and *R. spinosissima*. The sweet briar rose (*R. rubiginosa*, syn. *R. eglanteria*) likes Pacific Northwest conditions so much that it has naturalized in many areas.

Many European natives have in fact made themselves a little too much at home here, and not a few are now considered potentially (if not actually) invasive. Common foxglove, common hawthorn (*Crataegus monogyna*), English ivy, European white birch (*Betula pendula*), European mountain ash (*Sorbus aucuparia*), golden chain tree (*Laburnum anagyroides*), Norway maple, spurge laurel (*Daphne laureola*), and Scots pine (*Pinus sylvestris*) are all blacklisted as undesirable species somewhere in the Pacific Northwest, although their cultivars—at least for now—are considered to have acceptable manners. However, all forms of purple loosestrife (*Lythrum salicaria*) and traveler's joy (*Clematis vitalba*) are listed as noxious weeds in most parts of the Pacific Northwest.

Other European natives never seem quite at ease here. The performance of European ash (*Fraxinus excelsior*), common or European beech (*Fagus sylvatica*), English hawthorn (*Crataegus laevigata*, especially double-flowered hybrids), common or European hornbeam (*Carpinus betulus*), European linden (*Tilia ×europaea*), and English oak (*Quercus robur*) is satisfactory but rarely spectacular in the Pacific Northwest; somehow, even given ideal conditions, these species always seem like very polite but slightly homesick visitors.

On the other hand, European perennials take to our gardens as a duck takes to water, especially when they're appropriately limed. Examples not already mentioned include many artemisias, carpet bugle (*Ajuga reptans*), virtually all dianthus, gas plant (*Dictamnus albus*), many hardy geraniums, *Primula veris*, *P. vulgaris*, *Pulsatilla vulgaris*, snow-in-summer (*Cerastium tomentosum*), sun rose (*Helianthemum*), and many species of thalictrum, thrift (*Armeria*), veronica, and yarrow (*Achillea*).

Almost every perennial or herb with the species epithet *vulgaris* ("common") is also likely to be a European native; so are the majority of plants with "wort" (an old Anglo-Saxon word for herbaceous plant) in their common names, such as lungwort, masterwort, sandwort, and soapwort. In addition, many of our most familiar alpines such as *Primula auricula*, many gentians, and most saxifrages come from the European Alps, the Pyrenees, or the Carpathian Mountains.

From a Pacific Northwest perspective, one of the most important regions of Europe is northern Germany and the Netherlands, where recent plant-breeding programs seem tailor-made for our gardens. It's no accident that many newer top-rated astilbes, heaths and heathers, ornamental grasses, roses, and witch hazels have German or Dutch names. Happily, all these

Rosa glauca

species and more from ongoing European breeding programs grow to perfection in our gardens.

The other region of Europe with conditions closely akin to those of the Pacific Northwest (but quite unlike those of northern Europe) is the Balkan region. With a modified Mediterranean climate and strong maritime influence, this region has wet winters and dry summers that closely resemble our own. A mountainous terrain and heavy soils make the two regions even more similar. The only major difference is that Balkan soils are more alkaline than ours, so most Balkan natives benefit from regular liming here.

There are far too many Balkan natives to list them all, but notable species include many campanulas, hardy geraniums, and hellebores, common horse chestnut (*Aesculus hippocastanum*), *Lilium martagon*, *Rhododendron myrtifolium*, Serbian spruce (*Picea omorika*), and many beautiful forms of hardy spring bulbs.

THE BRITISH ISLES

Oddly enough, for a region renowned worldwide for its gardens and gardeners, the British Isles are notably lacking in native plants exclusively their own. "English" boxwood and "English" lavender are native to the Mediterranean region; "English" laurel, "English" oak, and "English" walnut to Eastern Europe and/or Asia Minor. It's true that English holly and English yew are

native to the British Isles, but they're also native to the Mediterranean; the native ranges of English daisies, English hawthorn, and English ivy include most of Europe. So do the native ranges of all the hardy heaths and heathers so indelibly associated with England and Scotland.

British authorities themselves can't agree on which plants are indigenous and therefore deserving of protected-species status. With a history of trade with the European continent that stretches back more than 2000 years (not to mention a land bridge in prehistoric times), this is entirely understandable. However, this region's greatest gift to gardeners, and especially those in the Pacific Northwest, is not British plants; it is the long and widespread interest of its peoples in gardening, hybridizing, and seeking out ornamental plants from all parts of the globe.

Blessed with a climate capable of accommodating the widest possible range of plants—not to mention the willingness of its gardeners (especially well-heeled ones) to build greenhouses, conservatories, protective covers, alpine troughs, ferneries, and more for species not so easily accommodated—the British Isles are a plant-lover's paradise. Over 70,000 named plants from every corner of the earth are available commercially. Thorough knowledge of each and every plant can be found somewhere in the region; the Royal Horticultural Society is one of the world's leading authorities on horticultural taxonomy (naming and classifying plants correctly).

Summer-blooming heaths and heathers

British gardening expertise is especially important to Pacific Northwest gardeners, since our climates are very similar. Most North American gardening advice is geared to a continental climate, and even West Coast advice tends to be strongly skewed toward the climate of California, making most of it inappropriate for us. But Britons garden in a climate noted for its mild but gray winters, relatively cool summers, frequent rain and/or cloud cover, and high humidity for most of the year.

If a British gardening book says a certain plant is best in full sun, we can take their word for it; if it says a certain plant needs shade, it does, even in our most sun-challenged subregions. We also share the British risks of late frosts in spring, wet snow in winter (when we do get any), and delayed summers, with cool temperatures lingering into June and high temperatures peaking in late July or August.

However, the Pacific Northwest is not England. Our summers are considerably warmer and much drier ("drought" in England is officially defined as two weeks without rain), our winters are slightly colder (many parts of the British Isles are Zone 9), and our rains are much heavier, especially in fall and winter. Annual precipitation in fog-famed London is only 20 in. (508 mm); by comparison, annual precipitation in Seattle is 36 in. (914 mm); in Portland 40 in. (1016 mm); in Vancouver, British Columbia, 47 in. (1200 mm). (We won't even get into annual precipitation on the west coast of Vancouver Island.) Our soils also differ considerably; most British gardens overlie limestone or "chalk" and

are slightly alkaline. However, soils in Scotland and Ireland can be quite acidic.

Because of these differences, some translations are necessary when applying British advice to Pacific Northwest gardens. To start with, our warmer summers and higher rainfalls mean most plants grow faster here than they do in the British Isles. A good rule of thumb is to increase estimated plant sizes at a given age by at least half. British plant-spacing recommendations, especially for hedging, are also crowded by our standards; most can be safely doubled.

"Hardy only in the southwest and Ireland" indicates a plant needing nearly frost-free conditions, but "needs a warm wall" doesn't mean much of anything to us, since our summers are warm enough to ripen most ornamental fruits without such measures. "Difficult" plants are often those needing deep acidic soil, such as golden larch (*Pseudolarix amabilis*); such plants we can grow with ease. But alpines needing to be "grown under glass" or "protected from winter wet" are definitely non-starters in our climate; these would drown in our first October storm.

British advice to "grow in lime-free soil" or in soil with "not a trace of lime" has caused many a Pacific Northwest gardener to become paranoid about lime, even to the point of omitting bone meal because bones contain calcium. Relax. Such advice is natural where deep roots cannot avoid reaching a limestone base, but in our naturally acidic soils, bone meal is a small drop in a very large bucket. Since there is a ten-fold difference between whole-number pH readings, an initial sprinkling of dolomite lime on previously uncultivated soil (to boost earthworm activity and encourage beneficial microorganisms) is extremely unlikely to cause problems for even the most sensitive acid-loving plants.

With or without translation, though, British advice on fruits and vegetables is simply not applicable here. Because of the differences in our summer climates and soils, named varieties of fruit are rarely the same (although a few English apples such as Bramley's Seedling, Cox's Orange Pippin, and Tydeman's Red have made the transition); vegetables are even more mutually exclusive. British tomatoes are almost exclusively grown in greenhouses, winter squash is considered exotic, and sweet corn ("maize") is more likely to be grown for ornamental value than for eating.

Other cultural differences point out the simple but inescapable fact that we Pacific Northwesterners are not British. Some of us enjoy practicing elaborate pruning and training techniques, or maintaining huge perennial borders or rose gardens, or spending many hours a week clipping, pruning, lifting, deadheading, tying up, spraying, and nipping and tucking, but most of us prefer low-maintenance gardens with a more natural look. We're also much more inclined to use organic fertilizers and non-toxic methods of pest control. Even favorite choices in roses and rhododendrons, for which we share a passion, are remarkably different.

However, British horticultural knowledge remains unsurpassed in both depth and breadth (often making very enjoyable reading), and the pleasure of looking at photographs of famous British estate gardens never pales. Keeping in mind the translations and caveats necessary for our own conditions, British advice is an invaluable aid to Pacific Northwest gardeners.

NEW ZEALAND

An unusual degree of affinity exists between the Pacific Northwest and New Zealand, our closest neighbor to the west in the southern hemisphere. New Zealand's South Island in particular, which occupies latitudes corresponding to those of Oregon and southern Washington, seems strangely familiar with its mild, maritime climate and its emerald-hued landscape backed by snowcapped mountains. It's perhaps not surprising that most North American visitors to New Zealand are from the West Coast.

Strangely enough, this affinity may go back millions of years. According to one geologic theory, a major slice of the Pacific Northwest began its volcanic existence somewhere near New Zealand before drifting northeastward over the equator (at approximately the speed toenails grow) and crashing into the northwestern coast of North America about 100 million years ago.

Be that as it may, horticultural affinity between the two regions is particularly strong. With its mild winters, moderate summers, and high humidity, New Zealand is an ideal climate for growing camellias and magnolias. Although neither is native there, both genera owe some of their most outstanding hybrids to New Zealanders; the names Les Jury (camellias)

Hebe ochracea

and Felix Jury (magnolias) are known worldwide. Other hybrid ornamental plants extensively grown and developed in New Zealand (although not native there) include Japanese maples, pieris, flowering dogwoods, witch hazels, rhododendrons, and lilies, all of which also grow to perfection in our own climate.

As for New Zealand native plants, the three best known and most widely appreciated in the Pacific Northwest are carexes, hebes, and the wonderfully spiky, slightly tender New Zealand flax, *Phormium tenax*. (Kiwi fruits, although popularly associated with New Zealand and grown commercially there, are native to China.)

Two evergreen silver-foliaged New Zealand shrubs gaining in popularity, especially in mild seaside gardens, are the daisy bushes (*Olearia*) with their tiny white aster-like flowers, and *Brachyglottis* 'Sunshine' (syn. *Senecio* 'Sunshine') with its cheerful yellow daisies. *Podocarpus nivalis* (alpine totara), a dwarf conifer resembling a small, refined spreading yew, is also gaining in popularity. But, for a couple of reasons, we are just beginning to get better acquainted with the rest of this country's many beautiful and unique species.

In the first place, New Zealanders themselves, like most Westerners, have only recently started appreciating the garden value of their own native plants. However, they are rapidly making up for lost time, and Pacific Northwest gardens—especially those in coastal areas—are among the beneficiaries. New Zealand natives make superb seaside plants, being extremely tolerant of wind, salt spray, mist, and fog. They also take exposure to full sun (light shade in hot-summer valleys), heavy rain, and air pollution; most tolerate infertile soil. Amazingly, many are also fully drought tolerant in our normal summers. Although New Zealand has no dry season per se, its mountains create many rain shadows, and it is not unusual to have local summer droughts lasting four to six weeks.

Unfortunately, with the exception of most carexes and some hebes, many New Zealand species are only borderline hardy—Zone 8 at best—and even then, their winter survival is chancy. It's not that our winters are that much colder, but our combination of winter cold and wetness is definitely not to their liking. Although they are not picky about soil type or texture, all New Zealand plants (except for carexes) are renowned for needing excellent drainage, especially in winter. They also do not appreciate our late frosts or long periods of very cold rain.

Because of their need for protection from excess winter wetness as well as winter cold, many New Zealand plants are best grown in containers and tubs, spending their summers outdoors and their winters in protected quarters—indoors, under a sheltered patio roof, or in a conservatory or unheated greenhouse.

Luckily, the role of indoor/outdoor patio plant is one for which New Zealand plants—evergreen shrubs and small trees in particular—seem custom-designed. With their exotic, almost tropical good looks, low maintenance, pest and disease resistance, and ease of overwintering, these plants are prized as patio specimens even where they're fully hardy.

A few of these are already well known, such as *Cordyline australis* (cabbage palm) with its multi-branched upright trunk and long, bold, sword-like evergreen leaves that resemble dracaenas but are held in palm-like heads. Related to agaves, it can grow to tree-like proportions in very mild gardens. The highly variable but always attractive lancewoods (*Pseudopanax*) are also increasingly used as indoor/outdoor plants.

Where hardy, the small shrub *Corokia cotoneaster* is gaining popularity as an outdoor plant, but its wiry contorted branches, tiny leaves, and small bright orange fruits make it an excellent tub plant anywhere. The same goes for the New Zealand tea tree or manuka (*Leptospermum scoparium*), a small, tiny-leaved evergreen shrub completely covered with very small flowers in May and June. The species itself has single white flowers, but the most popular cultivars have double flowers of pink or red.

New Zealand broadleaf (*Griselinia littoralis*), a large shrub perfect for patio tubs as well as for windy coastal gardens, has dense, leathery evergreen foliage the color of Granny Smith apples. Karos (*Pittosporum* species, most of which are native to New Zealand) are also excellent garden plants wherever they're hardy, and excellent container plants wherever they're not.

Less familiar, semi-tender (Zone 9) evergreen shrubs and small trees native to New Zealand include *Clianthus puniceus* (kaka beak); several low-growing, wiry-branched *Coprosma* species; white-flowered, malva-like ribbonwoods (*Hoheria*); and shade-tolerant *Lophomyrtus* ×*ralphii* hybrids with their puckered bronze or copper leaves. All make splendid tub plants and will undoubtedly become much more popular as they become more available.

Another New Zealand plant creating a lot of interest recently is *Clematis paniculata* (syn. *C. indivisa*), a semi-tender species that has generated several beautiful hybrids. Male forms have delicate, almost plumeria-like white flowers with yellow stamens and pink anthers; some are fragrant. All are short climbers ideally suited to container culture and will remain evergreen if wintered indoors or in a very sheltered site.

Of particular interest to lovers of New Zealand are kowhai (*Sophora* species, especially *S. tetraptera*), which is New Zealand's national flower, and pohutukawa or New Zealand Christmas tree (*Metrosideros excelsa*). The former somewhat resembles a laburnum, but with even more beautiful clusters of tubular yellow flowers followed by decorative seed pods resembling strands of beads. The latter has small, glossy, dark green leaves covered with bright red bottlebrush flowers in summer (which of course arrives in the southern hemisphere in December) and

is impervious to wind and salt spray. Both are evergreen and, although tender in our climate, are well worth growing in large containers such as half-barrels.

AUSTRALIA

Australia may seem a very unlikely source for plants suitable for Pacific Northwest gardens—and for cold-hardy plants, it is. But a surprising number of borderline hardy Australian plants are popular here, and like New Zealand plants, make excellent container plants that lend a slightly exotic air to decks and patios in summer. In Zones 8 and 9, they can even be grown outdoors, although at the risk of loss in cold or excessively wet winters.

Although the popular image of Australia is hot and dry, southeastern Australia and especially the large southern island of Tasmania have climates closer to that of New Zealand, and in fact share several important genera including *Leptospermum*, *Pittosporum*, and *Podocarpus*. Contrary to expectations, plants from these regions dislike heat as much as they do cold, and prefer moderately moist, cool, acidic soil that's very well drained, especially in winter. However, although some tolerate shade in their native habitats, most need as much sun as they can get in our climate.

Best known of all Australian plants are the eucalyptuses, of which the cider gum (*Eucalyptus gunnii*) is especially prized for its rounded, slivery-blue juvenile foliage. One of the hardiest species, it will survive temperatures of 0°F (-18°C) or even lower when established, although it does look a bit out of place in a rainforest setting. Moderately hardy (Zone 8) are the low-growing evergreen shrub called Australian fuchsia (*Correa*), valued for its fuchsia-shaped winter flowers, and several shrubby evergreen eucryphias, valued for their large, exquisite white flowers with golden stamens. The pretty little round-leaved mint bush, *Prostanthera rotundifolia*, is also moderately hardy, although protection from cold or dry winds is advisable.

Less hardy (Zone 9) but popular as flowering evergreen patio plants are Australian honeysuckle (*Banksia*), the related *Grevillea* (especially the silk oak, *G. robusta*), the various brightly colored bottlebrushes (*Callistemon*), and the somewhat similar-looking *Melaleuca*.

Grevillea 'Canberra Gem'. Photo by Judy Newton

Perhaps most coveted of all Australian plants in the Pacific Northwest is the Tasmanian tree fern, *Dicksonia antarctica* (Zone 9), whose huge, exotic, ferny fronds are almost irresistible. Although finding space to overwinter it can be a problem (it almost requires dedicated conservatory space), it is in fact much easier to grow than the truly tropical Hawaiian tree fern (*Cibotium chamissoi*). Given rich soil, regular watering, occasional misting, and protection from hot sun, Tasmanian tree ferns are actually quite at home in Pacific Northwest summers.

Other Australian plants are very familiar to our gardens as annuals. Swan River daisy (*Brachyscome iberidifolia*) and Tasmanian fan flower (*Scaevola cuneiformis*) are both long-blooming, must-have blue flowers for our hanging baskets and planters. Australian natives indispensable for dried flower arrangements are the multi-hued annual strawflower (*Xerochrysum bracteatum*, formerly *Helichrysum bracteatum*) and the somewhat similar pink-flowered *Rhodanthe chlorocephala* subsp. *rosea* (formerly *Helipterum roseum*). All need sun and good drainage.

SOUTHERN AFRICA

Due to a cold ocean current from Antarctica, the southern tip of Africa has a much more temperate climate than could be expected from its position just outside the tropical zone of the southern hemisphere. Moreover, within its overall warm-temperate climate are several unique subclimates, ranging from desert to Mediterranean to moist temperate to sultry subtropical. Not surprisingly, a wide range of plant types are represented; ten percent of all known plant species are found in this small corner of the world. Most are found in the Mediterranean-type climate of the southwest Cape, where the treeless scrubland of the Fynbos ("fine bush") is located.

Named for its amazing collection of mainly shrubby, drought-tolerant evergreen plants with needle-like leaves, this small region hosts some 9000 separate plant species, most of which do not exist anywhere else in the world. All are extremely well adapted to infertile, very well-drained acidic soil and to long, dry, but not terribly hot summers with cool nights. So far not a bad fit for the Pacific Northwest, but southern African winters, although wet in this region, are not nearly as wet as ours, nor are they quite as cold.

Although most of the plants found here are not fully hardy in our climate, all make excellent container subjects and thrive beautifully in our summer gardens. Best known are the indispensable bedding plants popularly known as geraniums (*Pelargonium* hybrids). Proteas, restios (beautiful reed-like plants related to grasses and rushes), and some 600 tender and semi-hardy *Erica* species are also widespread in the Fynbos.

So are many members of the daisy family very familiar to summer gardeners, including *Euryops* (daisy tree), *Felicia amelloides* (blue marguerite), *Gazania*, *Gerbera* (Transvaal daisy), and three genera all confusingly called "African daisy"—the borderline-hardy perennials *Arctotis* and *Osteospermum* and the annual *Dimorphotheca*. Many succulents are also found here, including jade plant (*Crassula ovata*), most species of *Aloe*, and several genera known as ice plant—hardy *Delosperma*, tender *Lampranthus*,

SOUTHERN AFRICAN BULBS

These are just a few of the most popular and most readily available bulbs from southern Africa; many others are available from specialty sources. Bulbs listed as borderline hardy can be grown outdoors in subregions with long, warm, dry summers, although at the risk of loss in a winter cold snap. A site near a warm wall is good, especially if its eaves give some protection from excess winter wetness. In all cases, good to perfect winter drainage is required. Again, all make excellent container subjects and are easily overwintered indoors or in a cool greenhouse. Tender corms (family Iridaceae) can be lifted in fall and the new corms stored dry after discarding the old, exhausted corms.

Family Alliaceae
Borderline hardy: *Agapanthus africanus* (lily of the Nile)
Tender: *Tulbaghia violacea* (society garlic)

Family Amaryllidaceae
Borderline hardy: *Amaryllis belladonna* (belladonna lily), *Nerine bowdenii*
Tender: *Clivia miniata* (Natal lily), *Crinum × powellii*, *Haemanthus coccineus* (blood lily)

Family Araceae
Hardy: *Zantedeschia* (calla lily)

Family Hyacinthaceae
Borderline hardy: *Eucomis* (pineapple lily)
Tender: *Galtonia candicans* (summer hyacinth), *Ornithogalum thyrsoides* (chincherinchee)

Family Iridaceae
Hardy: *Crocosmia*
Borderline hardy: *Babiana* (baboon flower), *Dierama* (angel's fishing rod, fairy wand), *Ixia* (African corn lily), *Schizostylis coccinea* (crimson flag lily), *Watsonia* (bugle lily)
Tender: *Freesia*, *Gladiolus*, *Sparaxis* (harlequin flower), *Tritonia*

Crocosmia × crocosmiiflora

and the annuals *Dorotheanthus bellidiformis* (Livingstone daisy) and *Mesembryanthemum crystallinum*.

Except for annual species, all the plants just named make fine indoor/outdoor plants everywhere in the Pacific Northwest, and some can even survive outdoors in our mildest subregions. However, since all have a definite aversion to our unrelenting winter rains and our cold, wet winter soil—especially heavy soil—container culture is almost always preferable even in Zone 9.

From the eastern side of southern Africa, where rainfall is more plentiful but winter is the dry season, come the shrub-sized evergreen perennials known as Cape fuchsias (*Phygelius capensis*) and the familiar, brightly colored red hot pokers (*Kniphofia* hybrids), both of which are fully hardy and very popular in the Pacific Northwest. Red hot pokers (available in a range of sizes and colors that do not always include red) are hardy to Zone 5 and drought tolerant in our normal summers, but do not appreciate cold, heavy rains filling their hollow crowns in winter. In our higher-rainfall subregions, a thatch-like winter covering of straw is advisable.

Borderline-hardy perennials from southern Africa include the shrubby, blue-foliaged *Melianthus major* and the floriferous bubblegum-pink forms of *Diascia*, popularly used as long-blooming annuals in hanging baskets. Bird of paradise (*Strelitzia reginae*) and Cape primrose (*Streptocarpus*), both tender conservatory plants, are also native to this region.

Perhaps most unique of all southern African plants are the many bulbs found here, especially those of the family Iridaceae, of which gladioli are the best known. Most come from the cooler, more mountainous eastern regions that experience summer rain and dry winters; crocosmias and calla lilies (*Zantedeschia*) in particular need ample moisture in summer. Callas can even take boggy soil in summer, but since they need fairly dry soil during their winter resting period, they're best lifted for winter in high rainfall subregions. The short, beautiful *Rhodohypoxis baurii* and its many hybrids are theoretically cold-hardy here, but since these bulbs absolutely need very dry winters, container culture is highly advisable in our climate.

TEMPERATE SOUTH AMERICA

Although relatively few in number, the plants native to temperate South America are of special importance to Pacific Northwest gardeners, especially those in coastal areas. The region known as Patagonia—the southern tip of South America between about 40° South latitude and the Strait of Magellan at about 53° South latitude—is almost a mirror image of the Pacific Northwest location in the northern hemisphere.

Southern Chile in particular has a mild, maritime-influenced climate very similar to our own, being neither very cold in winter nor very warm in summer. Both regions experience high rainfall due to weather systems from the Pacific dumping their moisture on the western slopes of north-south mountain ranges; an arid rain shadow exists east of the mountains in both areas. Both have moderately to strongly acidic soil.

The match between southern Chile and the Pacific Coast subregion is near perfect, since both have no real dry season

Leaves of monkey puzzle or Chilean pine (*Araucaria araucana*)

and are subject to strong winds (often salt-laden) nearly year-round. Chilean plants are also very well suited to inland gardens, although they need summer watering there; in Zone 7 and below, some may need winter protection. Most are best in partial shade inland but can take full sun in coastal areas.

Chilean natives include such favorites as escallonias (all species), the beloved monkey puzzle (or Chilean pine), and *Gaultheria mucronata* (syn. *Pernettya mucronata*). Other important Chilean plants include many of our most beautiful barberries such as *Berberis buxifolia*, *B. darwinii*, and *B. ×stenophylla*, a hybrid of two Chilean species. All are hardy but should be protected from cold, drying winds in winter and intense sun in summer. Slightly more tender but worth trying in a sheltered site is the white-flowered *Eucryphia glutinosa*, which is one of the hardiest and most beautiful eucryphias and the only deciduous one.

Also native to Patagonia are several southern beeches, including the best known, *Nothofagus antarctica*. (Several other species of *Nothofagus*, some of them evergreen, are native to New Zealand and/or Australia, indicating a geologic connection between these areas at one time; other shared genera include *Eucryphia* and *Podocarpus*.) Our popular, drought-tolerant pampas grass hails from the warmer, drier Argentine half of Patagonia; the orange-flowered *Buddleja globosa* grows in the Andes.

Many flowering plants native to temperate South America have bright tubular flowers, often red, to attract hummingbirds for pollination. Best known is the hardy fuchsia, *Fuchsia magellanica*, which is indispensable in Pacific Northwest gardens for summer-long color as well as for attracting hummingbirds like a magnet. Root-hardy in all subregions, it makes excellent evergreen hedges on the coast but behaves more like a woody perennial in colder areas, dying to the ground in winter.

Two other shrubs very attractive to hummingbirds are the beautiful but borderline hardy Chilean firebush (*Embothrium coccineum*) and Chilean glory flower (*Eccremocarpus scaber*), both of which bear fiery red flowers. Since hummingbirds abound throughout South America, Central America, and Mexico, many more red-flowered shrubs and perennials, most of them somewhat tender, are native to these regions.

The Chilean Andes have not yet been as thoroughly explored for plants as some of the other mountain ranges of the world, and will undoubtedly yield many more plants well suited to

Pacific Northwest gardens. Among the Andean perennials and bulbs already well known are Peruvian lilies (*Alstroemeria*), several species of *Calceolaria*, the popular garden geums (*Geum chiloense*), garden heliotrope (*Heliotropium arborescens*), several well-behaved *Oxalis* species, and many verbenas, both hardy and tender. All thrive in our climate.

Colorful summer annuals native to the southern Chilean Andes include butterfly flower or poor man's orchid (*Schizanthus*) and painted tongue (*Salpiglossis*). Our ubiquitous, self-seeding garden nasturtiums (*Tropaeolum majus*) are native to the northern Chilean Andes, as are several borderline-hardy *Tropaeolum* vines such as the yellow-flowered canary creeper and the orange-red flame creeper.

TROPICAL AND SUBTROPICAL SOUTH AMERICA AND CENTRAL AMERICA

Few climates could be as different as those of the New World tropics and the Pacific Northwest, but even here there are a few surprises. Although the popular image of the tropics is one continuous hot, steamy jungle, variables such as elevation, air flow, and shade create several different subclimates that support an amazing diversity of plant habitats.

Not surprisingly, most tropical and subtropical species are too tender to grow outdoors here, and even as summer plants some of these need warmer, much more humid summers than we can give them. However, we can easily supply the cooler temperatures, acidic soil, and moderate but reliable humidity needed by plants of the mountains or of the cool forest understory. Some of these are even sufficiently hardy to survive our winters.

One of the hardiest (Zone 7) and most exotic-looking is giant gunnera (*Gunnera manicata*), native to southern Brazil. Truly a giant among herbaceous perennials, this foliage plant sports heavily textured, slightly prickly rhubarb-like leaves that can exceed 8 ft. (2.4 m) in diameter. Even its brownish, cone-like summer flowers are awesome—they can be hip-high.

This is not a plant for small gardens—or dry ones—but the temptation to try one is great, especially since few other climates in North America combine the reasonably cool summers, mild winters, and reliable humidity it needs. Give it very rich soil that remains constantly moist (not boggy) in summer but is well drained in winter, along with protection from strong wind and hot sun. As a precaution against cold spells and excessive rain in winter, protect the crown by folding a few spent leaves over it in late fall.

Even more exotic-looking are the Brazilian natives known as passion flowers (*Passiflora*), of which the blue-flowered *P. caerulea* is one of the hardiest (Zone 7b) and most popular. The flowers of these vines, so bizarre and yet so perfectly formed that they're often mistaken for artificial decorations, are guaranteed to draw attention from midsummer to fall.

A few other tropical natives are also suitable for outdoor growing in our region in the right conditions. Once established, the coral tree (*Erythrina crista-galli*) is hardy to Zone 8 and can grow into a substantial-sized shrub. The pineapple guava (*Acca*

Gunnera manicata

sellowiana, syn. *Feijoa sellowiana*) is best classed as semi-hardy, although it is grown outdoors in some very mild Pacific Northwest gardens. Both also make fine specimens for conservatories or indoor/outdoor patio containers.

Favorite tender bulbs from the American tropics include tuberous begonias, caladiums, and bold-leaved, sun-loving canna lilies, all of which grace our summer gardens, and the amaryllis (*Hippeastrum*) and tuberous-rooted gloxinias (*Sinningia*) we're so fond of growing indoors. Popular patio or conservatory plants include bougainvillea, shade-tolerant orchid cactus (*Epiphyllum*), *Mandevilla* (especially *M.* ×*amabilis* 'Alice du Pont'), and the stunning princess flower (*Tibouchina urvilleana*) with its velvety leaves and large flowers of deep royal purple. Christmas cactus (*Schlumbergera*) and flowering maple (*Abutilon*) are time-honored, even old-fashioned houseplants that enjoy summers outdoors; well-known annuals include semi-succulent moss rose (*Portulaca*) and bright red *Salvia splendens*.

Our vegetable gardens owe a substantial debt to subtropical South America, Central America, and southern Mexico. Corn, green beans, and winter squash are all native to this part of the world; all are grown commercially in the Pacific Northwest, especially in our warmer, most fertile river valleys. Green beans in particular are very well suited to our climate and at one time were a major crop in the Willamette Valley. In the not-so-distant past, thousands of young teenagers (including both of us) bought their school clothes and earned spending money for the year by picking pole beans all summer at the princely rate of two and one-half cents a pound.

An incredible number of important plants belonging to the nightshade family (Solanaceae) are native to subtropical South America and Central America. Best known is the potato, native to the Andes of Peru and Bolivia, which does especially well in the cool, acidic soils of our cooler subregions. Other edible plants that thrive best in our warmer subregions include the tomato, bell peppers, and an assortment of chili peppers such as cayenne and jalapeño. On a more dubious note, tobacco, another member of the nightshade family, also originated in the subtropics of Central and South America.

Popular ornamental members of the family Solanaceae native to this region include angel's trumpets—both the shrubby, downfacing *Brugmansia* species and the annual, upfacing *Datura* species—and the fragrant, semi-hardy potato vine, *Solanum jasminoides*. Even more familiar are the subtropical New World members of this family grown as annuals in our summer gardens: browallia, flowering tobacco (*Nicotiana*), and petunia. *Salpiglossis* (painted tongue) and *Schizanthus* (butterfly flower), both native to Chile, are also members of the nightshade family.

MEXICO AND CALIFORNIA

Although Mexico's overall climate is much hotter and drier than ours, we share one very important characteristic with its high-altitude mountainous interior: cool summer nights, along with sunny but not terribly hot summer days. This explains our phenomenal success in growing such Mexican natives as dahlias, Mexican feather grass (*Stipa tenuissima*), and cosmos, which bloom here from early summer to hard frost. The fragrant-flowered evergreen shrub *Choisya ternata* (Mexican orange) also thrives in our climate, although a winter-sheltered site is advisable in all but the mildest gardens.

Both the short, small-flowered "French" marigolds (*Tagetes patula*) and the tall, large-flowered "African" marigolds (*T. erecta*) are actually Mexican natives; so are zinnias. Although the latter are prone to mildew in our cooler subregions, at least until the weather warms up, they thrive beautifully in our hotter river valleys. The white-edged foliage annual called snow-on-the-mountain (*Euphorbia marginata*), which just happens to combine perfectly with our more brightly colored summer favorites such as dahlias, zinnias, and marigolds, is also native to Mexico.

Although only semi-hardy in our climate, woolly-leaved pineapple sage (*Salvia elegans*) and equally woolly Mexican oregano (*Lippia graveolens*) are both popular as potted herbs, and the endless fascinating textures of the many succulent, drought-tolerant *Echeveria* species make them must-haves for urban and balcony gardens. Of course, the most popular Mexican plant of all time is the tender poinsettia, *Euphorbia pulcherrima*.

Good drainage and full sun (or at least bright light) are the two most important requirements for growing Mexican plants; summer watering is of course necessary for annuals, summer bulbs, and containerized plants.

Plants native to both Mexico and California tend to be very drought tolerant when established—even water-hating—since they come from a true Mediterranean-type climate with very low rainfall. While some evergreen oaks and manzanitas (*Arctostaphylos*) are not fully hardy everywhere in the Pacific Northwest, others are at least borderline hardy. More importantly, they're well adapted to wet winters (although not quite as wet as ours) and dry summers. In our climate, all need as much sun as they can get, along with excellent winter drainage.

Most successful in the Pacific Northwest are the hardier California lilacs (*Ceanothus*), of which the hardiest, best-suited,

Hybrid dahlias in midsummer

and most popular of all is *C. impressus* 'Victoria' (often sold as *C. thyrsiflorus* 'Victoria'). This potentially huge cultivar can grow to 8 ft. (2.4 m) tall and even wider, but like all ceanothus, it accepts pruning very well and is easily kept smaller with regular trimming right after flowering. *Ceanothus thyrsiflorus*, another of the hardiest species, is best represented by the naturally low-growing, wide-spreading *C. t.* var. *repens*, often used as a ground-cover in commercial plantings.

Ceanothus gloriosus 'Point Reyes' is another popular wide-spreading groundcover type; *C.* 'Puget Blue' (sometimes considered a selection of *C. impressus*) is upright and bushy. All ceanothus are subject to root rot in warm, wet soil, and although they're less prone to this problem in our cooler climate than they are in California, summer irrigation of established plants should be avoided.

California tree poppy (*Romneya coulteri*) also grows well here as long as winter drainage is near perfect; so do most shrubby and herbaceous penstemons. Scarlet larkspur (*Delphinium cardinale*) grows well here but dislikes our wet winters; it's best treated as an annual. Light-textured soil is advisable for all.

Needing some winter protection in addition to full sun and excellent drainage is the yellow-flowered, vine-like flannel bush (*Fremontodendron*), of which the long-blooming *F.* 'California Glory' (a cross between Mexican and Californian species) is most popular. The beautiful white-flowered tree anemone (*Carpenteria californica*) grows well in a warm site in sun or light shade, but winter protection may be needed in Zone 7. Neither should be watered in summer once established.

Two beautiful California natives even trickier to grow in our rainier subregions are mariposa lily (*Calochortus*) and *Lewisia cotyledon*, both of which are native as far north as the Siskiyous. Both need extremely well-drained soil—lewisias are sometimes deliberately planted sideways in rock walls—and are very sensitive to summer watering. However, their beauty is such that many of us keep trying despite the odds.

There's no such problem with California poppy (*Eschscholzia californica*), which is also native to coastal Oregon and is widely naturalized throughout the Pacific Northwest. Although the state flower of California, it seems to like our cooler summers and wetter winters just as well as those of its warmer, drier homeland, and the affection is returned by Pacific Northwest gardeners. This long-blooming summer annual self-seeds freely but never aggressively, and its cheerful orange flowers are welcome in both our cultivated and wildflower gardens.

EASTERN NORTH AMERICA

Although the Pacific Northwest is an integral part of North America geographically, politically, and culturally, a strong horticultural divide exists between east and west. Eastern summers are hotter, rainier, and much more humid than ours, with warm, muggy nights; in the northern half, winters are much colder.

Creeping California lilac (*Ceanothus thyrsiflorus* var. *repens*)

Annual precipitation is roughly the same as ours, but is spread fairly evenly throughout the year, with no dry season. But most striking of all is the difference in our natural vegetation: forest trees in eastern North American are deciduous hardwoods; ours are coniferous softwoods.

Our lack of eastern hardwood trees sometimes leaves us with a sense of cultural disconnect. We have no red or scarlet oaks (*Quercus rubra* and *Q. coccinea*) to set our hills ablaze in fall, and no sugar maples (*Acer saccharum*) to tap for syrup in late winter. We have no spreading chestnuts (*Castanea dentata*) for village smithies to stand under, and no white ash (*Fraxinus americana*) or hickories (*Carya*) for garden tool handles or to threaten recalcitrant young scholars with. None of our residential streets are shaded by tall, leafy, native North American elms (*Ulmus americana*), sycamores (*Platanus occidentalis*), basswoods (*Tilia americana*), or beeches (*Fagus grandifolia*).

Even more disconcertingly, none of these fare well in our climate even when introduced. Although they live, they're clearly not happy and don't come close to reaching the sizes they do in their native habitats. Even our maple-friendly climate does not suit most eastern maples well. Some selections and hybrids of red or Canadian maple (*Acer rubrum*) do well in our climate, but the species itself is underwhelming, seldom if ever reaching its majestic potential. Sugar maple (*A. saccharum*) is almost universally disappointing, and silver maple (*A. saccharinum*) should be avoided at all costs, since its heavy, brittle limbs are prone to breakage in our wet snows and wilder fall windstorms.

However, there are some definite bright lights from back East. Sweetgum (*Liquidambar styraciflua*) and tulip tree (*Liriodendron tulipifera*) both grow very well in the Pacific Northwest, although again neither reaches its full size. The fact that sweetgum is a member of the witch hazel family (Hamamelidaceae) and tulip tree a member of the magnolia family (Magnoliaceae) undoubtedly has something to do with this, since all hardy members of both families thrive beautifully in our climate.

One eastern native hardwood that does reach impressive size on deep, moist, fertile soils (such as near a river) is black walnut (*Juglans nigra*). Where well suited, it makes a truly magnificent specimen, but don't plan on growing much underneath it—including a lawn—since its roots inhibit the growth of other plants. Don't plan on feasting on black walnuts, either: single trees produce very few nuts, and these are encased in husks so hard they can be driven over without cracking.

Pin oak (*Quercus palustris*) also thrives in our climate, being far less sensitive to our soggy winters (*palustris* means "of swamps or marshes") than most oaks, including our own natives. However, it also tolerates our normal summer drought. Its distinctive pyramidal shape and reliable fall color make it a good shade tree, but leave plenty of room for its wide-spreading lower branches. On young trees, deciduous leaves that hang on all winter before dropping give a rare bonus of privacy in winter as well as in summer.

Perennials native to eastern North America can leave Pacific Northwest gardeners feeling perplexed. Although we constantly read about the low maintenance, drought tolerance, and ease of growth of North American native wildflowers, something very

Fall foliage of *Quercus palustris*

important—water—is missing from the equation in our corner of the world. Sun-loving eastern natives such as coreopsis, gaillardia, *Liatris spicata*, obedient plant (*Physostegia*), purple coneflower (*Echinacea purpurea*), rudbeckia, and spiderwort (*Tradescantia*) may be drought tolerant where summer rain is a given, but they definitely need at least a few good soakings in our dry summers, even when established.

In a notable exception, one of the Pacific Northwest's favorite drought-tolerant perennials comes from the southeastern United States. The exotic-looking *Yucca filamentosa*, which reminds us of the hot, arid southwest, is much better suited to our cooler, moister climate than are any of the true desert species. It's also reliably cold-hardy and takes our wet winters in stride, provided it has good drainage.

However, other sun-loving eastern perennials such as Joe Pye weed (*Eupatorium purpureum*), cardinal flower (*Lobelia cardinalis*), giant blue lobelia (*L. siphilitica*), turtlehead (*Chelone*), and the astilbe-like queen of the prairie (*Filipendula rubra*) need very moist, even boggy soil in summer. It's no accident that many of the perennials most prone to mildew in our climate—especially *Aster novi-belgii* hybrids, bee balm (*Monarda didyma*), and garden phlox (*Phlox paniculata*)—are native to eastern North America. However, as long as plentiful moisture can be supplied, all these perennials grow well here. The same goes for moisture-loving eastern trees and shrubs such as Carolina silverbell (*Halesia carolina*), tupelo (*Nyssa sylvatica*), and summersweet (*Clethra alnifolia*).

Eastern shade-lovers are another story, especially if woodland conditions are recommended. Eastern woodland soil is deep, rich, moist, and humusy; our woodland soil is thin, infertile, highly acidic, and dry all summer. By adding compost, copious leaf litter, summer water, and a touch of lime to our shady areas, we can succeed tolerably well with eastern plants such as foamflower (*Tiarella cordifolia*), which needs considerably more water than West Coast native *Tiarella* species, and black cohosh (*Actaea racemosa*, syn. *Cimicifuga racemosa*). However, eastern true woodlanders such as Jack-in-the-pulpit (*Arisaema triphyllum*) and Virginia bluebells (*Mertensia virginica*) are usually a lost cause. (Incidentally, *virginica*, *virginicus*, or *virginiana* can indicate origin anywhere on the East Coast; to the 17th-century

Fothergilla gardenii in October

Englishmen who bestowed these names, the entire region was "Virginia.")

Yet another disconnect between east and west is the theoretical similarity between the Pacific Northwest and the southeastern United States. Both have similar precipitation and high humidity, both have acidic soil, and winter low temperatures are virtually identical. However, our summers are drier, shorter, and much, much cooler. Although southeastern natives such as pecans, pawpaws, and persimmons are all cold-hardy here, we lack the summer heat and high humidity to ripen them successfully. The same goes for *Franklinia alatamaha*, a small flowering tree that needs a long, hot, very humid summer to produce its late-blooming flowers and to ripen its wood.

However, the Appalachian region of the southeastern states is a real treasure trove for Pacific Northwest gardens. Here, cooler summers and thinner, slightly less fertile acidic soils more closely approximate our own conditions. The few eastern hardwood trees that do succeed in the Pacific Northwest—sweetgum, tulip tree, black walnut, pin oak—all grow in the Appalachians, although not necessarily exclusively; mountain silverbell (*Halesia monticola*) is even better suited to our climate than is Carolina silverbell.

Other Appalachian natives that do well in the Pacific Northwest include Carolina allspice (*Calycanthus floridus*), sorrel tree or sourwood (*Oxydendrum arboreum*, a member of the family Ericaceae), and the green-leaved American smoke tree, *Cotinus obovatus*, which is better suited to our conditions than the more popular purple-leaved *C. coggygria*. Flowering dogwood (*Cornus florida*) is also very well suited to our climate but has unfortunately become very prone to dogwood anthracnose, even in its native habitat. Mountain laurel (*Kalmia latifolia*) theoretically does well in our gardens, but difficulties in traditional methods of propagation make it scarce, and tissue-culture propagation makes it prone to sudden collapse.

Best suited of all to our gardens are the many Appalachian members of the genera *Hamamelis* (witch hazel), *Hydrangea, Magnolia,* and *Rhododendron. Fothergilla gardenii*, a small shrub related to the witch hazels, is especially at home in the Pacific Northwest; although preferring moist soils, it accepts our summer drought with little or no ill effects. (Our specimen, planted on a lightly shaded slope, has shrugged off several extended droughts.) Showy white bottlebrush flowers in spring, handsome witch hazel–like rounded leaves, brilliant red fall color, and a graceful winter silhouette make it an ideal all-season shrub here.

A fascinating fact concerning the four genera so well represented in the Appalachians is that the same genera are also well represented in China—and in few if any other places in the world. Several theories exist to explain this. One is that all these genera were once common worldwide but were wiped out elsewhere by glaciers or increasing aridity. Another is that the two land masses were joined before the Atlantic Ocean formed between northeastern North America and Europe. A more bizarre theory is that Appalachia was once an island near China; a more prosaic one, simply that similar habitats led to similar evolution and adaptation.

Whatever the explanation, a tantalizing connection between the plants of Appalachia and China is undeniable. In addition to witch hazels, hydrangeas, magnolias, and rhododendrons, several more genera are represented by very similar species in both places. The trumpet vine *Campsis radicans* is native to Appalachia; *C. grandiflora* to China. Boston ivy (*Parthenocissus tricuspidata*) is native to China—it arrived in Boston in the era of clipper ships—and Virginia creeper (*P. quinquefolia*) to Appalachia. Several species of *Stewartia* grow in each region; Appalachian natives *Halesia, Juglans, Liquidambar, Liriodendron,* and *Nyssa* all have Chinese counterparts. The only two hardy fringe trees are *Chionanthus retusus*, native to China, and *C. virginicus*, native to Appalachia. Several more genera, including *Panax* (ginseng), show the same coincidence of distribution.

Plants native to the cooler, cloudier, less fertile northern section of eastern North America include highbush blueberries (*Vaccinium corymbosum*) and cranberries (*V. oxycoccos*), both of which thrive in our cool, acidic soil and are important economic crops in our wetter subregions. The ornamental, diminutive *V. vitis-idaea* subsp. *minus* is also native to northeastern North America.

Most important to Pacific Northwest gardens is *Thuja occidentalis*, parent of so many of our favorite dwarf conifers and hedging plants. (The epithet *occidentalis*, meaning "western," is somewhat confusing since its native habitat is on the eastern side of the continent, but it was named for a habitat that was—and still is—west of Europe.) All cultivars of this important conifer thrive in our gardens, but many need regular summer water to look their best, and none tolerate extended summer drought.

THE PACIFIC NORTHWEST

Having surveyed an assortment of beautiful garden plants from all over the world, we return to the Pacific Northwest to find a wealth of garden-worthy native plants right in our own backyards. Ironically, following the law of human nature that always makes the plants on the other side of the fence look greener (or redder, or bluer), many of our own natives have been prized in other countries far longer than they have been here.

Ocean spray (*Holodiscus discolor*), Lewis's mock orange (*Philadelphus lewisii*), great camas (*Camassia leichtlinii*), and several

RECOMMENDED PACIFIC NORTHWEST NATIVE PLANTS

Acer circinatum (vine maple)

Adiantum aleuticum (western maidenhair fern)

Allium cernuum (nodding onion)

Blechnum spicant (deer fern)

Camassia (camas)

Chamaecyparis nootkatensis (yellow cedar)

Cornus nuttallii (Pacific dogwood)

Cystopteris fragilis (fragile fern)

Erythronium (avalanche lily, fawn lily, glacier lily, trout lily)

Mahonia aquifolium (Oregon grape)

Mahonia nervosa (Cascade Oregon grape)

Polystichum braunii (Braun's holly fern)

Polystichum munitum (western sword fern)

Rhododendron macrophyllum (Pacific rhododendron)

Rhododendron occidentale (western azalea)

Ribes sanguineum (flowering currant)

Spiraea douglasii (hardhack)

Thuja plicata (western red cedar)

Tsuga heterophylla (western hemlock)

Tsuga mertensiana (mountain hemlock)

Sedum spathulifolium 'Cape Blanco'

of our erythroniums have been popular in Europe for decades; flowering currant (*Ribes sanguineum*), Oregon grape (*Mahonia aquifolium*), and snowberry (*Symphoricarpos albus* var. *laevigatus*) have been cultivated by the British for nearly 200 years. (To be fair to ourselves, we had other priorities back then, such as staying alive.)

Today, however, with native plants enjoying unprecedented attention all over the world, we are embracing our own natives with unbridled enthusiasm, both in the sense of conservation and as cultivated (not wild-collected) ornamentals that are splendidly adapted to our unique climate. Some of these are profiled in detail as recommended plants in Part 3 (see sidebar); a few other must-haves are described here.

One of the most popular Pacific Northwest natives already in cultivation is *Arctostaphylos uva-ursi* (bearberry), widely known as kinnikinnick. The species is common throughout the northern hemisphere, but the pink-flowered 'Vancouver Jade', introduced in the 1980s by the Plant Introduction Scheme of the Botanical Garden of the University of British Columbia (PISBG), is extremely popular in commercial plantings as a dense, low-maintenance, evergreen groundcover in sun or light shade. Very drought tolerant and a good soil stabilizer, it's especially valuable on large banks.

Also in wide cultivation is our low-growing, sun-loving, drought-tolerant *Sedum spathulifolium*, popular for its tightly congested succulent leaves of bluish gray that turn reddish purple in very cold weather. Its best-known cultivar, 'Cape Blanco', named

for the westernmost point of the contiguous United States on the Oregon coast, has intensely glaucous new foliage and is suitable for rock gardens, small-scale groundcover, and even between paving stones. Starry yellow flowers in spring are a bonus; some gardeners remove them to better enjoy the foliage.

Our native Pacific bleeding heart (*Dicentra formosa*) is a herbaceous perennial with beautiful ferny foliage that makes an excellent small- to medium-scale groundcover in partial shade to cool sun. Its delicate pink flowers bloom continuously from May to October in moist conditions, and nearly as long in quite dry shade. Its popular hybrid *D.* 'Luxuriant', a cross with *D. eximia* from eastern North America, resembles it closely but is more compact and has deeper pink flowers.

Deserving of far greater popularity is Lewis's mock orange (*Philadelphus lewisii*), named for Captain Meriwether Lewis of the Lewis and Clark Expedition. The species, which is the state flower of Idaho, is mainly found in drier regions east of the Cascades and is naturally drought-tolerant; *P. l.* 'Galahad', a selected form, is beginning to become popular here. *Philadelphus lewisii* var. *gordonianus*, the natural form found on our side of the mountains, sails through our normal summer droughts but also performs beautifully in our wet winters, provided it has good drainage. Tall and upright in form, it blooms prolifically in late May and June with single, sweetly scented white flowers that have a natural grace unmatched by double-flowered cultivars.

Commemorating Captain William Clark of the Lewis and Clark expedition is the beautiful *Clarkia amoena* (godetia), a taprooted annual that also goes by the wistful name farewell-to-spring. Its large, abundant azalea-like flowers in shades of pink bloom in late May and June. Since it does not like to be transplanted, it should be direct-seeded in a sunny place in early April.

Some Pacific Northwest natives have gone mainstream in a big way through hybridization with other species. Our western form of snowberry, *Symphoricarpos albus* var. *laevigatus*, was crossed with other North American species to produce the pink-fruited *S.* ×*doorenbosii* 'Magic Berry' and other hybrids less prone to suckering. (On a large scale, snowberry itself makes a wonderful, indestructible, drought-tolerant thicket in sun or shade, but it does need room to spread.) Our native lupine *Lupinus polyphyllus*, so often used as a bank stabilizer along

Pacific bleeding heart (*Dicentra formosa*)

Philadelphus lewisii var. *gordonianus*

highways, was the main species used in the development of the colorful Russell hybrids.

Fortunately, more and more Pacific Northwest natives are becoming available even in non-specialty nurseries. Evergreen huckleberry (*Vaccinium ovatum*) is an outstanding medium-sized evergreen foliage shrub capable of thriving in dry shade, although it is also happy in full sun. The selected form 'Thundercloud' is particularly outstanding, with small pinkish heather-like flowers in spring, large blue-black berries in fall, and coppery new foliage. This plant is best grown from seed, or better yet, purchased from a reputable native plant nursery; cuttings root easily but very few of them strike (start growing new shoots).

Also increasingly available are several species of our native perennial shooting stars (*Dodecatheon*). Members of the primrose family with similar cultural needs, these small but showy plants have unique pink or reddish cyclamen-like flowers with very strongly reflexed petals. Western rattlesnake plantain (*Goodyera oblongifolia*), a shade-loving evergreen ground orchid found in our forests, has leaves beautifully marked like snakeskin—a feature early settlers took as signifying a natural remedy for snakebite. Even salal (*Gaultheria shallon*) is becoming more available through nurseries, as it should be. European gardeners have long appreciated its beautiful, leathery, evergreen foliage, which is most compact in cool sun.

But however much we admire them in the wild, other native plants are still sadly underrepresented in our own gardens. June-blooming ocean spray (*Holodiscus discolor*), long popular in Europe, does have a slightly rangy growth habit, but its gorgeous lacy sprays of creamy white flowers that slowly fade to ivory, then buff, then tan make it an ideal back-of-the-border shrub in sun or partial shade.

Western trumpet honeysuckle (*Lonicera ciliosa*) is a beautiful nonrampant climber with interesting round twinned leaves that clasp the stem between them. Its bright red-orange clusters of tubular flowers that attract hummingbirds are not scented, but are a knockout visually. Pacific ninebark (*Physocarpus capitatus*) makes a large, handsome background shrub with its small, densely packed maple-shaped leaves that are almost completely covered in May by rounded clusters of slightly scented white flowers.

CAN'T FIND A NATIVE PLANT NURSERY?

For a list of retail and wholesale nurseries in Oregon, Washington, or British Columbia that carry at least some native plants, go to the Web site PNW Native Plant Sources at http://www.tardigrade.org/natives/nurseries.html. The site also has links to native plant organizations and other useful information.

Baldhip rose (*Rosa gymnocarpa*), a very appealing, nearly thornless rose with a very dainty appearance, also deserves far greater recognition, especially since it grows so well in shade. Although its tiny single pink flowers, small rounded leaves, and persistent bright red huckleberry-like hips are all on a miniature scale, the shrub itself can grow as tall as a person.

Other beautiful natives that should be used more frequently in garden sites that mimic their natural habitats include red huckleberry (*Vaccinium parvifolium*), which grows best on rotting logs in cool sun or light shade, and vanilla leaf (*Achlys triphylla*), which loves humus-rich sites in deep shade. Many people are surprised to find that the popular houseplant known as piggyback plant or mother-of-thousands (*Tolmiea menziesii*) is a hardy Pacific Northwest native; all it needs is a moist, shady site and perhaps a bit of winter protection in our coldest subregions.

However, some Pacific Northwest natives, especially trees, do not adapt well to cultivated garden conditions. If you have a mature Garry oak (*Quercus garryana*), Pacific dogwood (*Cornus nuttallii*), or Pacific madrone (*Arbutus menziesii*) on your property, cherish it—and care for it by leaving it alone. Do not fertilize it, do not water it in summer, and do not cultivate the soil underneath it. Keep the area around it free of weeds, lawn grass, and exotic plants, but do try to introduce appropriate native groundcover plants, preferably by seed. Drought-tolerant *Mahonia nervosa* is often found naturally under these species; another good bet is trailing snowberry (*Symphoricarpos mollis*),

Ocean spray (*Holodiscus discolor*)

a low-growing relative of the taller, more common *S. albus* var. *laevigatus*. Two very useful native groundcovers that are moderately drought tolerant in shade are fringecup (*Tellima grandiflora*) and inside-out flower (*Vancouveria hexandra*).

All these and many, many more well-adapted and beautiful plants are available through native plant nurseries that have perfected propagating techniques using mother stock grown from seeds or cuttings. All reputable native plant nurseries display a prominent notice that none of their products have been collected in the wild. If no such notice is given, do not patronize that nursery.

DO NOT DIG

Never dig up native plants in the wild, no matter how abundant they look, unless the site is slated for imminent destruction. Many native species are locally endangered, and increasing numbers of others are protected by law. More importantly, the survival of fully grown native transplants, especially when in flower, is so appallingly low that a native plant dug is essentially a native plant destroyed.

Most native plants sprout readily from seed, and as long as production is locally abundant and the species is not endangered (check locally), small amounts of seed may be gathered when ripe. A few cuttings may also be taken in July or August provided no harm is done to the parent plant. Common courtesy—and increasingly, the law—requires the collector to ask permission of the landowner, whether private or public, before collecting. An excellent source of information on propagating native plants is *Gardening with Native Plants of the Pacific Northwest* by Arthur R. Kruckeberg (Seattle: University of Washington Press, 1996).

PART TWO

A TWELVE-MONTH GARDENING CALENDAR

In the Pacific Northwest there is no definite dividing line between one gardening year and the next. Like the Arctic sun that dips close to the horizon in summer but never quite sets, our gardening activities slow in winter but never come to a complete stop. We simply turn around one day, in the midst of what we thought were late-winter tasks, and realize it's actually early spring.

Dividing blooming times into months is always somewhat arbitrary, since some plants come into bloom during the first few days of any given month and others not until the last few days of the same month. However, using more vague terms such as early spring, mid-spring, and late spring does not help much. Throughout the entire region, early spring is March; mid-spring is April; late spring is May. If the main daffodil season is March in the Willamette Valley and April on Vancouver Island, it's because daffodils are considered to bloom naturally in early spring or mid-spring, depending on the location of the gardener.

From May through mid-February, blooming times are remarkably consistent throughout the Pacific Northwest, but late winter/early spring blossoming can vary considerably even within the same garden. For instance, our own flowering plum trees have bloomed as early as 1 March and as late as 1 April. A great many factors influence just when the first camellia buds will open or exactly when the first Japanese flowering cherries will bloom.

Naturally, temperatures rise and sunlight intensifies earlier in the year in the southern parts of our region than in the northern ones. Lighter soils warm up faster than heavier soils, lower elevations warm up faster than higher elevations, and southern exposures warm up faster than northern exposures. Proximity to salt water, amount of cloud cover, and local terrain also add their influences. Rather than try to deal with all the possible variations in all subregions, we have placed spring blooming times in the month they normally or usually occur in our own garden and local area, which is in the late-middle part of the range. We trust this will help gauge expected blooming times for specific gardens in other areas.

Weather patterns described for each month are those that can normally be expected in most years—but what is normal any more? Weather in this part of the world has been particularly atypical in recent years, and it seems that in almost every month some record is set somewhere in the Pacific Northwest for unseasonably warm, cold, wet, dry, windy, sunny, or overcast weather. Weather conditions described here are those that can be expected, but not necessarily those that will occur.

The plants listed in the calendar are those most likely to be readily available. Most are well suited for all subregions, but of course all have their own preferences for moisture, sunlight, temperature, soil type, and winter conditions. The lists are not meant to be exhaustive; we have not included annuals, tender perennials, herbs, or water plants, and the native plants listed are only a few of the most noteworthy. We have included some semi-hardy perennials and bulbs since these can be grown in our milder subregions, but have limited truly tender bulbs to those most widely grown. We have deliberately and to the best of our knowledge excluded species with weedy tendencies and especially those considered invasive anywhere in the Pacific Northwest.

Many more garden-worthy plants well suited to local conditions and microclimates are available from specialty sources. For more choices or more specific cultural information, consult a local garden center or horticultural society.

The flowering period of many plants covers two, three, or even more months, but we have listed each plant only in the month in which it normally begins flowering. (Some are listed again for fall or winter interest.) Plants that bloom for at least two months are marked with an asterisk (*), so when choosing plants for simultaneous bloom in any given month, be sure to refer back to the long bloomers of the two or three preceding months as well.

Hamamelis mollis in full flower

The photographs illustrating each month were all taken in the authors' garden.

JANUARY

Here in the Pacific Northwest, the New Year almost always begins with wild and woolly weather of some sort, usually high winds (hurricane force is not uncommon on the coast, especially in the northern section) and/or torrential rains (we once got 7 in., 175 mm, by 7 January). Less frequently, there may be a subfreezing cold snap or a heavy snowfall of 12 in. (30 cm) or more.

None of this fazes Pacific Northwest gardeners. Come 1 January, we start looking for—and finding—signs of spring. Regardless of the fact that winter is less than two weeks old, afternoons are lengthening perceptibly, skies are a lighter shade of gray, and conversations are peppered with enthusiastic reports of daffodils coming up, snowdrops and primroses in full bloom, and fat buds of *Helleborus foetidus* almost ready to burst open. But whether or not such optimism is warranted depends on which of our three versions of the remainder of January—cold, wet, or super-mild—will ensue.

Naturally, the coldest temperatures of the year are most likely in January, and a normal cold spell of just a few degrees below freezing is not such a bad thing now. It does no harm to still-dormant deciduous plants, or even to most broadleaved evergreens, and helps kill off overwintering insect pests. Cold spells also bring out the brightest winter foliage colors of conifers, Scottish heathers, and heavenly bamboos, and the brightest bark on coral bark maples, shrub dogwoods, willows, and other winter-interest plants.

If we're going to get one of our infamous Big Freezes, it will almost surely come in January, and these deep freezes are another story. But as long as they're preceded by a few inches of insulating snow, as they usually are, and are not accompanied by high winds, relatively little harm to gardens is likely other than the unavoidable loss of borderline-hardy plants.

A wet January may see downpours of 2–3 in. (50–75 mm) of rain in 24 hours, which in itself is no big deal. As we're fond of saying, at least we don't have to shovel it. But if heavy rain collides with the tail end of a cold snap, it can—and often does—fall in the form of snow, which translates to 20–30 in. (50–75 cm) of white stuff that definitely does need shoveling.

Barring outright flooding, plants absolutely love wet Januarys, especially on the seemingly unending days of heavy mist/constant drizzle/light rain/frequent fog for which our winters are renowned. As for people, well, it takes time to learn to love Pacific Northwest winters. But somehow, when the air is still, and skies are that almost glowing pearl-gray, and that ever-present drizzle/fog/mist mutes all colors into subtle heather tones and makes even rocks appear soft-edged, we know we could never forsake this cool, moist corner of the world for winters in, say, Arizona.

The third type of January is everybody's favorite: gentle rains, frequent sunny periods, and mild, frost-free temperatures that feel more like late March than January. This is when more and more bulbs, perennials, and deciduous groundcovers pop out of the ground with every passing day, and flower buds swell noticeably on trees and shrubs. But welcome as this early growth is, it's also cause for concern that it might succumb to hard frost in February or March. Then again, we may not get another frost at all, but just glide effortlessly into real spring. If we're really lucky, we may even hear choruses of frogs on mild evenings in late January.

Cold, wet, or super-mild, January brings the ever-faithful blooms of witch hazels and the tiny, powerfully fragrant flowers of sarcococcas. Snowdrops, winter aconites, spring snowflakes, and primroses can also be counted on in January, and winter-blooming heaths become more colorful every day. By month's end, snow crocuses and *Cyclamen coum* are beginning to flower, tulips are pushing up leaves, and hellebore buds are fat and swollen, with a few actually in bloom. Garlic shoots are up, chives are almost big enough to harvest, and even that most unmistakable harbinger of spring, the dandelion, may make an appearance.

This is when it's a real joy to get out and poke around in the garden, getting reacquainted with old favorites and delighting in seeing new acquisitions starting into growth. Ready-made winter chores such as pruning fruit trees are no chore at all, and we gardeners can even be found inventing outdoor tasks just for an excuse to get our hands back into the dirt. But we don't tax ourselves. After all, by the calendar, we have only just arrived at deepest midwinter.

OF FRESH SEASONAL INTEREST IN JANUARY
* interest continues until March or later

Ornamental and shade trees
Acer griseum and cultivars* (paperbark maple)—bark

Acer palmatum 'Sango-kaku'* (coral bark maple)—bark

Betula utilis var. *jacquemontii* and cultivars* (Himalayan birch)—bark

Corylus maxima (edible filbert)—catkins

Conifers
Cryptomeria japonica and cultivars* (Japanese cedar)—foliage

Larix species and cultivars* (larch)—cones on bare branches

Shrubs
Calluna vulgaris and cultivars* (Scottish heather)—winter foliage

Cornus alba, C. sanguinea, C. sericea and cultivars* (shrub dogwoods)—stems

Erica ×*darleyensis*, early cultivars* (winter-blooming heath)—flowers

Hamamelis ×*intermedia*, early cultivars (witch hazel)—flowers

Hamamelis mollis and cultivars (Chinese witch hazel)—flowers

*Hibiscus syriacus** (hardy hibiscus)—stems

Kerria japonica and cultivars*—stems

Sarcococca species and cultivars* (sweet box)—scented flowers

Perennials
Helleborus foetidus and cultivars (stinking hellebore)—flowers

Primula vulgaris and cultivars* (English primrose)—flowers

Bulbs and bulb-like plants
Cyclamen coum and cultivars (winter cyclamen)—flowers

Eranthis species and cultivars (winter aconite)—flowers

Galanthus species and cultivars* (snowdrop)—flowers

Leucojum vernum and cultivars (spring snowflake)—flowers

TO DO IN JANUARY

➤ Cut limbs from discarded Christmas tree and use for extra cold protection around borderline-hardy plants or new plantings.

➤ Prune grapes. (If pruned later, grapes will bleed sap profusely.)

➤ Prune larches as needed.

➤ Begin pruning fruit trees as weather permits.

➤ Spray fruit trees and susceptible ornamentals with lime sulfur and/or dormant oil as needed. Read labels thoroughly for correct timing and to ensure compatibility; spray only if weather forecasts do not include either rain or freezing temperatures for the next 24 hours.

➤ Harvest winter vegetables as needed.

➤ Check stored flower bulbs for rot or shriveling. Discard rotten bulbs; if shriveled, sprinkle with water and recheck in a few days.

➤ Indulge in a few brightly colored potted primroses or forced miniature daffodils to enjoy indoors in a cool, bright spot until late February, when they can be planted outdoors.

➤ Cut branches of flowering quince for indoor forcing.

➤ Start making a wish list for spring planting of nursery stock. Firm up orders for vegetable and annual seeds from catalogs.

FEBRUARY

February is the wild card of the year. February 1989 (which continued a Big Freeze that started in late January) felt like Siberia, with one snowfall after another and temperatures hitting 0°F (-18°C) or below. February 2005 was dry, perpetually sunny, and warm enough to pass for April. Anything in between can also happen, including local flooding as snow melts in the mountains in warm spells. February 1996 saw record flooding in Oregon and Washington when a brief subfreezing snap was followed by four days of heavy rain.

Still, some things about February are as regular as clockwork. Leaf buds start swelling on currants, gooseberries, shrubby potentillas, and *Spiraea* 'Arguta'. Native red alders actually turn red as their catkins grow. Filbert catkins are in their full glory,

Catkins of *Corylus avellana* 'Contorta' with *Helleborus* × *hybridus*

and pussy willows appear on both native and cultivated species. (*Salix caprea* 'Kilmarnock', a small weeping form, is especially beautiful.) Almost all witch hazel cultivars are in bloom now no matter what the weather.

Bees start coming out to look for pollen on sunny days (willows, winter-blooming heaths, and snow crocus can be lifesavers now) and birds start pairing off, sitting together quietly on bare tree branches. A tree frog or two may be heard, though seldom seen. And on any clear day, people may be seen outdoors without jackets—sometimes in shorts—finding any excuse to stand, sit, or even lie in the weak but now palpably warm sunlight and soak it up.

In February, it's disturbingly easy to forget for a few moments not just what month it is, but what season. A warm breeze embedded in a cold air mass—is this October or March? Drizzle so fine that the only way to "see" if it's raining is to step outside and check—is this January or April? It's definitely not spring yet, but it's not winter, either. This in-between time (not-spring? prelude to spring?), one of the most distinguishing characteristics of the Pacific Northwest, is one we take for granted and even grouse about, but it's so much a part of our existence we'd surely feel quite lost without it.

February's in-bloom list is not long but is very welcome as proof that a whole new season is actually underway (even if we do often get a short-lived snowfall around the middle of the month). February's flowers are not super-late-bloomers, but super-early. As in spring. In fact, if February is mild, the end of the month is high gloating season as we casually mention to friends and relatives in colder climes that our daffodils, early rhododendrons, forsythias, or even—in favored sites—star magnolias and early-blooming cherries are in full flower. Victoria even holds an annual tongue-in-cheek flower count (that's individual blossoms, not plants) mainly for gloating purposes.

We're considerably more subdued if a cold snap follows a mild January. (February is often the reverse of January, being dry if January was wet, mild if it was cold, cold if it was mild.) This is when emerging leaf buds can easily get nipped by temperatures only a few degrees below freezing, especially if they're exposed to early morning sun. Pacific Northwest gardeners quickly learn from experience how important it is to site early-budding species where the sun won't hit them until late morning, after frost is gone.

February's lengthening days and increasing warmth make it tempting to rush out and start planting, but caution is the watchword. Assuming the ground is not frozen or covered with snow (you never know with February), it's safe to plant bare-root fruit trees and roses by month's end, along with conifers and still-dormant deciduous trees and shrubs. But it's best to hold off on broadleaved evergreens, smaller plants, anything remotely tender, and especially any plant just about to bloom. Winter may be on its last legs, but it ain't over until early March has its predictable say.

IN FRESH BLOOM IN FEBRUARY

* blooms until April or later

Ornamental and shade trees
Cornus mas and cultivars (Cornelian cherry)

Prunus mume (Japanese apricot)

Prunus ×*subhirtella*, very early cultivars (spring cherry)

Salix species and cultivars (willow)

Shrubs
Chaenomeles species and cultivars* (flowering quince)

Chimonanthus praecox and cultivars (wintersweet)

Corylus avellana 'Aurea' (golden filbert)

Corylus avellana 'Contorta' (contorted filbert)

Corylus maxima 'Purpurea' (giant purple filbert)

Daphne mezereum and cultivars (February daphne)

Daphne odora 'Aureomarginata' (variegated winter daphne)

Hamamelis ×*intermedia*, midseason cultivars (witch hazel)

Rhododendron hybrids: 'Bric-à-brac', 'Conemaugh', 'Gable's Pioneer', 'Olive', 'Praecox', and others (cold weather delays bloom)

Rhododendron species: *R. barbatum*, *R. dauricum*, *R. mucronulatum*, *R. pemakoense*, and others (cold weather delays bloom)

Perennials

Arabis procurrens 'Variegata'* (variegated alpine wall cress)

Bergenia crassifolia and cultivars* (winter-blooming bergenia)

*Helleborus ×hybridus** (Lenten rose)

Helleborus niger and cultivars (Christmas rose)

Primula polyantha hybrids* (polyanthus primrose)

Primula ×pruhonicensis and cultivars*

Viola odorata and cultivars (sweet violet)

Viola ×wittrockiana and cultivars* (winter pansy)

Bulbs and bulb-like plants

Anemone blanda and cultivars* (windflower)

Crocus ancyrensis, C. chrysanthus, C. tommasinianus and cultivars (snow crocus)

Galanthus elwesii and cultivars (giant snowdrop)

Iris danfordiae and cultivars

Iris reticulata and cultivars

Narcissus 'February Gold'

Vines

Clematis cirrhosa and cultivars

TO DO IN FEBRUARY

➤ Finish dormant spraying of fruit trees and susceptible ornamentals.

➤ Finish dormant pruning of trees and shrubs before buds swell. Do not prune maples, birches, or walnuts now: they will bleed sap. Instead, prune these in early summer.

➤ Prune Group C clematis down to two healthy buds on each stem. Tie up and tidy Group A and Group B clematis.

➤ Check conifers for spruce aphids, balsam woolly adelgid, and hemlock woolly adelgid; spray as necessary with insecticidal soap.

➤ Cut back all deciduous ornamental grasses and prune or comb out evergreen grasses as needed.

➤ If at all possible, attend the Northwest Flower and Garden Show in Seattle.

➤ Sow seeds of early vegetables and annuals indoors.

➤ Shop early for best selection of tuberous begonias to start indoors.

➤ Start cleaning up garden by removing debris, cutting back old perennial stems, pruning out obviously dead branches, and so on.

➤ Mow lawn if weather permits, setting blade higher than normal to reduce shock to grass and leave ample protection from possible cold spells to come.

➤ Dig all remaining root vegetables by month's end.

➤ Add a fragrant, blooming *Jasminum polyanthum* to your conservatory or houseplant collection.

Prunus cerasifera 'Pissardii' with shrubs and blue windflowers (*Anemone blanda*)

MARCH

The trade-off for getting glimpses of spring in January is that we get winter in March. This month almost invariably comes in like a lion, bringing cold wind, sleety rain or hail, sudden temperature drops—and, in inland areas, a better-than-even chance of wet snow.

We gardeners soon learn to expect this annual practical joke of Mother Nature, which usually melts within the day. But we can't always just laugh it off—and we can't let February's deceptively mild spells seduce us into removing snow protection too early. The worst case of wet snow we have ever personally experienced came in early March: it was the consistency of sticky concrete. We could hear branches breaking all around us for hours, including in well-established stands of native trees.

Winter's last kick at the can may come as late as mid-month (it often coincides with spring break for school kids), especially along the Columbia Gorge, on the east sides of Portland and Vancouver, Washington, and in the eastern Fraser Valley. Another of Mother Nature's little jokes is to celebrate the first day of spring by giving us eight or ten straight hours of miserably cold rain, making us wonder if she hasn't somehow made the seasons go in reverse.

However, once she's gotten these things out of her system, she relents and lets us enjoy early spring, Pacific Northwest style. Native Indian plum (*Oemleria cerasiformis*) and snowberry are always the first to leaf out, followed closely by native salmonberry and Japanese flowering crabapple (*Malus floribunda*). Forsythia, whose Chinese name means "welcome-to-spring," lights up our gardens, and native skunk cabbage (*Lysichiton americanus*, euphemistically renamed swamp lantern) lights up our waterways. Flowering plums, early-blooming flowering cherries, and Japanese fruiting plums burst into full bloom; pieris, mahonia, and early-blooming rhododendrons and camellias add their welcome color, and the delicious scents of early-blooming viburnums fill the air.

Winter-blooming heaths are now at their peak, and *Anemone blanda* makes broad carpets of mauve-blue. Dutch crocus, early to midseason daffodils, and early tulips display their Easter-themed hues, punctuated by the impossibly bright blue of Siberian squill. Early-blooming primrose species, bergenia, and lungwort also add to the "spring is here" picture.

With so much in bloom already, it can be bewildering and slightly frustrating to see that many trees and shrubs are not yet in full leaf even by month's end. But they have good reason. The combination of wetness, cloud cover, and wind chill that makes gloves and warm jackets so mandatory for March gardening keeps our heavy soils as efficiently chilled as any refrigerator or cold-storage facility.

Daytime highs are just now reaching the growth-inducing threshold of 60°F (15°C), and it will be several more weeks until they're sustained. Meanwhile, nighttime lows are still in the low 40s F (4–7°C) at best, and frost is still normal in all noncoastal areas. With days now longer than nights, the sun does its best to warm things up, but it's a long, slow, incremental process frequently interrupted by rain or clouds. (Although rain no longer comes down in buckets as it does in late fall and winter, the finer-textured showers of March do come often.)

But skies are considerably brighter now, even when they're overcast—they're almost luminescent then—and the sun often shines right after showers. Or even during them. There are lots of rainbows in late March. A signal, perhaps, that in spite of all the false starts, setbacks, teasers, and double whammies of the past few weeks, genuine, unmistakable, nonreversible spring is here at last.

IN FRESH BLOOM IN MARCH

* blooms until May or later
(R) suitable for rock gardens

Ornamental and shade trees

Magnolia kobus and cultivars

Magnolia ×*loebneri* and cultivars

Magnolia stellata and cultivars (star magnolia)

Prunus ×*blireana*, *P. cerasifera* and cultivars (flowering plum)

Prunus pendula, *P. sargentii*, *P.* ×*subhirtella*, *P.* ×*yedoensis* and early cultivars (Japanese flowering cherry)

Shrubs

Abeliophyllum distichum and cultivars (white forsythia)

Berberis thunbergii and cultivars (Japanese barberry)

Camellia, early species and cultivars*

Chaenomeles species and cultivars* (flowering quince)

Corylopsis species and cultivars (winter hazel)

Forsythia species and cultivars

Mahonia aquifolium and cultivars (Oregon grape; Pacific Northwest native)

Mahonia japonica and cultivars

Pieris species and cultivars*

Prunus ×*cistena* and cultivars (dwarf purple-leaved plum)

Rhododendron hybrids: 'Bo-peep', 'Christmas Cheer', 'Cilipinense', 'Etta Burroughs', 'Ginny Gee', PJM Group, 'Rosamundi', 'Shamrock', 'Snow Lady', and others

Rhododendron species: *R. macabeanum*, *R. moupinense*, *R. schlippenbachii*, and others

Ribes sanguineum and cultivars (flowering currant; Pacific Northwest native)

Rubus spectabilis and cultivars (salmonberry; Pacific Northwest native)

Spiraea prunifolia 'Plena' (bridal wreath spirea, shoe-button spirea)

Viburnum ×*burkwoodii* and cultivars

Perennials

Arabis species and cultivars (R)* (wall cress)

Aubrieta species and cultivars (R)* (rock cress)

Bergenia cordifolia and cultivars* (heartleaf bergenia)

Draba aizoides (R)*

Erysimum 'Bowles' Mauve'* (Bowles' Mauve wallflower)

Euphorbia characias subsp. *wulfenii* and cultivars*

Gentiana verna and cultivars (R)* (spring gentian)

Helleborus argutifolius and cultivars (Corsican hellebore)

Lysichiton americanus (skunk cabbage, swamp lantern; Pacific Northwest native)

Petasites frigidus var. *palmatus* (coltsfoot; Pacific Northwest native)

Primula auricula and cultivars (R)*

Primula denticulata and cultivars (R)* (drumstick primrose)

Pulmonaria species and cultivars* (lungwort)

Bulbs and bulb-like plants

Chionodoxa species and cultivars (glory-of-the-snow)

Crocus vernus and cultivars (Dutch crocus)

Narcissus, early and midseason species and cultivars (daffodil)

Puschkinia species and cultivars

Scilla siberica and cultivars (Siberian squill)

Tulipa fosteriana, T. greigii, T. kaufmanniana and cultivars; several other species tulips

Vines
Akebia quinata and cultivars (chocolate vine, sausage vine)

Clematis armandii and cultivars (evergreen clematis)

Groundcovers
Mahonia repens and cultivars (creeping mahonia; Pacific Northwest native)

Veronica umbrosa 'Georgia Blue'*

TO DO IN MARCH

➤ Prune roses.

➤ Prune conifer hedges as needed.

➤ Prune established butterfly bushes (*Buddleja davidii* cultivars) to 24 in. (60 cm) or less as soon as new growth starts to expand.

➤ Prune out and dead, damaged, or diseased wood on trees, shrubs, and small fruits such as gooseberries. If disease is suspected, disinfect pruning tools after each cut.

➤ Prune vigorous summer-blooming shrubs such as snowberries, ninebarks, and *Hypericum* 'Hidcote' by one-third to keep them compact and bushy. Prune other summer-flowering shrubs as needed.

➤ Shear daboecias (St. Dabeoc's heath) as low as possible without cutting into bare wood.

➤ Clean up herbaceous perennials, removing any old growth still remaining.

➤ Divide and transplant midseason and late-blooming perennials as needed.

➤ Clean up vegetable garden, removing all plants except Swiss chard, kale, leeks, sprouting broccoli, and any others still producing. Remove straw or mulch hay to allow soil to warm up.

➤ Plant bare-root or potted trees, shrubs, roses, vines, small fruits, rhubarb, asparagus, groundcovers, and perennials.

➤ Transplant any midseason or late-blooming shrubs needing relocation.

➤ Spray blight-susceptible species with fixed copper before average daytime temperatures rise above 60°F (15°C).

➤ Sow seeds of tender annuals and warm-weather vegetables indoors.

➤ Mow lawn at normal height as needed. If weather permits, apply environmentally safe moss killer. Rake out and dispose of dead moss, then spread dolomite lime to discourage regrowth.

ANNUALS TO PLANT IN MARCH

Vegetables
Seed potatoes (early varieties), onion sets, garlic (if not planted in fall); seeds of broad beans, leaf lettuce, mustard greens, parsley, peas, spring radishes, spinach

Flowers
Sweet peas

➤ Sprinkle dolomite lime around lilacs, mock oranges, deutzias, and other lime-lovers.

➤ Bring overwintered tender shrubs and patio plants into brighter light. Water sparingly until growth resumes.

➤ Take cuttings of overwintered geraniums (pelargoniums) and fuchsias. Pot up when well rooted.

➤ Stock up on packaged summer-blooming bulbs and bare-root perennials (bleeding heart, lily-of-the-valley, phlox, peonies, daylilies, hostas, and others) while selection and prices are good.

➤ Plant perennials, true lilies, and crocosmias as soon as possible, but hold back on dahlias, gladioli, and other tender bulbs until danger of local hard frost is past and soil warms enough that you can stand to keep your hands in it.

➤ Remove snow netting by end of month except in Cascade Slopes/Outflow Valleys subregion and at higher elevations, where it's best to play it safe until mid-April.

APRIL

No matter how much time has been spent in the garden during March, April always comes as a shock. Now that we're past the equinox, daylight extends well into evening (thanks in part to Daylight Savings Time), and we all suddenly feel like Rip Van Winkle, wondering how we went from being slightly ahead in our garden tasks to being two weeks behind.

Part of it has to do with the sheer volume of growth that seems to have appeared overnight. In other parts of the continent, June may be the month of most phenomenal growth, but in the Pacific Northwest, it's April that busts out all over. Lawns, for instance, grow so fast it's almost scary. New leaves clothe virtually all trees and shrubs (excepting a few recalcitrants such as beautyberry, hardy hibiscus, walnuts, and oaks), and an amazing number of species come into flower.

Magnolias, midseason flowering cherries, early to early midseason rhododendrons, several *Clematis* species, and many fruit trees—cherries, pears, early apples, European plums, and (where adapted) peaches—are in full, glorious bloom. Midsea-

Top to bottom: *Prunus* 'Kanzan', *Spiraea* 'Arguta' (white), late-blooming winter heaths, *Spiraea japonica* 'Goldflame' (foreground)

son tulips overlap with late daffodils, hyacinths, and other earlier bulbs. Many groundcovers begin flowering now, and early rock garden perennials create their own carpets of bright color. Hummingbirds return in full force and are seldom far from any native flowering currant.

In the vegetable garden, the last of overwintered kale, collards, and Swiss chard push out super-tender, super-sweet new leaves before going to seed. Rhubarb clumps grow bigger by the day, purple sprouting broccoli is almost ready to harvest, and chives, Welsh (perennial) onion, sorrel, and lovage are already harvestable.

Nature outdoes herself in April, clothing huge, mature weeping willows and bigleaf maples in an unimaginably fresh shade of light golden green and setting them against clear blue skies. The first truly warm days of the year stir gentle breezes that caress our skin, release the delicious honey scent from the leaves of native black cottonwoods (*Populus trichocarpa*), and prompt robins and red-winged blackbirds into exuberant song. In April, all our senses are overwhelmed with a sweetness that would be cloying if it weren't so utterly pure, natural, and unaffected.

But eventually we have to tear ourselves away from these entrancing pleasures and focus on April's essential gardening tasks. Some of the less welcome things that bust out all over in April include horsetails, dandelions, cool-weather annual weeds, fast growing grassy weeds, and new generations of leatherjackets and slugs. Nature helps out considerably on the latter two—just-hatched starlings forage diligently on lawns for leatherjackets, and garter snakes emerging from hibernation relish young, tender slugs—but keeping up with weeds is up to us gardeners.

A two-week stretch of clear weather can be expected sometime during the month, bringing unusually high daytime temperatures combined with mild but definite frost at night. With daytime temperatures reaching as high as the mid 70s F (low 20s C) in noncoastal gardens, it's tempting to rush the season, but it's still definitely chilly in the shade, and official last-hard-frost dates do not come with guarantees. Still, this dry spell is an excellent time to prepare vegetable gardens and flower beds and start planting cold-hardy annuals.

It's also a warning sign to keep a watchful eye on soil moisture. April showers are usually adequate, but if this month's mini-drought is abnormally prolonged, as it was in 2004 (our own garden did not get one drop all month), even native plants can suffer. Roots need ample moisture to sustain all those brand-new leaves, flower buds, and growth buds, so it's actually more important to water now (if necessary) than in summer, when new growth has already filled out. But for now, all the promised flowers, top growth, and root growth scheduled for May and June is just that—a promise, with fulfillment dependent on April moisture.

IN FRESH BLOOM IN APRIL

* blooms until June or later
(R) suitable for rock gardens

Ornamental and shade trees

Acer species and cultivars (maple)

Amelanchier species and cultivars (serviceberry)

Arbutus menziesii and cultivars (Pacific madrone; Pacific Northwest native)

Cercis canadensis and cultivars (redbud)

Halesia species and cultivars (silver bell, snowdrop tree)

Magnolia, most deciduous species and cultivars

Malus, early and midseason species and cultivars (flowering crabapple)

Prunus serrulata, midseason and late cultivars (Japanese flowering cherry)

Pyrus species and cultivars (flowering pear)

Shrubs

Andromeda polifolia and cultivars* (bog rosemary)

Aronia species and cultivars (chokeberry)

Aucuba japonica and cultivars

Berberis, most species and cultivars (barberry)

Camellia, midseason and late species and cultivars*

Fothergilla species and cultivars

Kerria japonica and cultivars

Leucothoe fontanesiana and cultivars

Osmanthus delavayi and cultivars

Potentilla fruticosa and cultivars* (shrubby cinquefoil)

Prunus laurocerasus and cultivars (cherry laurel)

Rhododendron, early and early midseason species and hybrids

Sambucus racemosa var. *pubens* (red-berried elder; Pacific Northwest native)

Skimmia japonica and cultivars

Spiraea 'Arguta' (bridal wreath spirea)

Spiraea thunbergii and cultivars (garland spirea)

Viburnum carlesii and cultivars (Korean spice viburnum)

Viburnum davidii

Viburnum tinus and cultivars (laurustinus)

Perennials

Ajuga pyramidalis 'Metallica Crispa' (R)

Aurinia saxatilis and cultivars (R)* (cloth of gold)

Bellis perennis and cultivars (R)* (English daisy)

Brunnera macrophylla and cultivars* (Siberian bugloss)

Caltha palustris and cultivars (marsh marigold)

Convallaria majalis and cultivars (lily-of-the-valley)

Corydalis cashmeriana and cultivars (R)*

Darmera peltata and cultivars (umbrella plant; Pacific Northwest native)

Dicentra formosa and cultivars* (Pacific bleeding heart; Pacific Northwest native)

Dicentra spectabilis and cultivars (old-fashioned bleeding heart)

Doronicum species and cultivars* (leopard's bane)

Epimedium species and cultivars (barrenwort)

Erigeron compositus and cultivars (R)* (alpine fleabane)

Erysimum linifolium 'Variegatum'*

Euphorbia, most species and cultivars (spurge)

Gentiana acaulis and cultivars (R)* (mountain gentian)

*Hemerocallis lilioasphodelus** (lemon daylily)

Iberis sempervirens and cultivars (R)* (candytuft)

Lithodora diffusa and cultivars (R)*

Omphalodes species and cultivars (navelwort)

Phlox divaricata and cultivars (R)* (woodland phlox)

Phlox douglasii, P. stolonifera and cultivars (R) (creeping phlox)

Phlox subulata and cultivars (R) (moss phlox)

Potentilla cinerea (R)*

Potentilla neumanniana 'Nana' (R)* (alpine cinquefoil)

Primula sieboldii and cultivars (R) (Japanese star primrose)

Primula vulgaris, double-flowered cultivars (R) (double English primrose)

Pulsatilla vulgaris and cultivars (R) (Pasque flower)

Saxifraga ×*arendsii* and cultivars (R)* (mossy saxifrage)

Tiarella species and cultivars* (foamflower)

Viola ×*wittrockiana,* spring-blooming cultivars* (pansy)

Biennials

Erysimum cheiri and cultivars* (wallflower)

Myosotis sylvatica and cultivars (forget-me-not)

Bulbs and bulb-like plants

Anemone nemorosa and cultivars

Camassia quamash (camas, quamash; Pacific Northwest native)

Erythronium species and cultivars (fawn lily, trout lily, avalanche lily, dog's-tooth violet; many native to Pacific Northwest)

Fritillaria species and cultivars (fritillary, several native to Pacific Northwest)

Hyacinthoides non-scripta (English bluebell, wood hyacinth)

Hyacinthus orientalis and cultivars (hyacinth)

Iris ×*hollandica* (Dutch iris)

Iris ×*pumila* (dwarf bearded iris)

Muscari species and cultivars (grape hyacinth)

Naiocrene parvifolia (spring beauty; Pacific Northwest native)

Narcissus, midseason and late species and cultivars (daffodil)

Ranunculus asiaticus and cultivars (Persian buttercup)

Trillium species and cultivars (several native to Pacific Northwest)

Tulipa, midseason species and cultivars (tulip)

Vines

Clematis alpina and cultivars

Clematis macropetala and cultivars (downy clematis)

Groundcovers

*Ajuga reptans** (carpet bugle)

Arctostaphylos uva-ursi and cultivars* (bearberry, kinnikinnick)

Galium odoratum (sweet woodruff)

Luzula species and cultivars* (wood rush)

Maianthemum bifolium subsp. *kamtschaticum* (false lily-of-the-valley; Pacific Northwest native)

Pachysandra terminalis and cultivars (Japanese spurge)

Sedum acre 'Aureum' (golden stonecrop)

Vinca species and cultivars* (periwinkle)

Waldsteinia ternata (barren strawberry)

ANNUALS TO PLANT IN APRIL

Vegetables

Seed potatoes (midseason and late varieties); seeds of beets, carrots, Chinese vegetables, mustard greens, parsnips, rutabagas, Swiss chard, turnips; transplants of broccoli, Brussels sprouts, cabbage, cauliflower, celery, collards, kale, lettuce, leeks, green onions, parsley, and most other herbs except basil and pineapple sage. Harden off transplants before planting out.

Flowers

Seeds of godetia (sow in place), nasturtium; transplants of ageratum, annual candytuft, annual dianthus, bacopa, brachycome, calendula, cornflower, dusty miller, lobelia, marguerite, marigold, nicotiana, pansy, petunia, snapdragon, sweet alyssum. Harden off before planting and be prepared to cover at night if frost threatens.

TO DO IN APRIL

➤ Till or dig in fall rye before it reaches 10 in. (25 cm) in height. Let rot for two weeks, till or dig again, then plant cold-hardy vegetables (see sidebar).

➤ Finish planting trees, shrubs, roses, vines, and woody perennials, including borderline-hardy species.

➤ Plant or transplant ornamental grasses and bamboos.

➤ Watch for fertile (spore-bearing) horsetails. Pick off heads before they open, seal in zippered plastic bags, and dispose of in garbage.

➤ Dig out dandelions in lawn before they go to seed.

➤ Aerate, dethatch, and fertilize lawn as needed. Seed bare or thin patches with overseeder mix or fine-textured perennial rye.

➤ Mow lawn every five to seven days, ideally when not wet. Even in showery weather, do not let it go for more than a week. Knock over any mushrooms before they open to prevent spores from dispersing.

➤ Water containers and new plantings during dry spells.

➤ Make sure all hoses, sprinklers, and built-in irrigation systems are in good working order in case they're needed.

➤ Weed as much as possible to stay ahead of thistles and other deep-rooted perennial weeds and cool-season annuals such as chickweed.

➤ If in doubt whether a woody plant is dead or simply still dormant, scratch the bark of a small branch gently with your thumbnail to expose the cambium layer. If the color is green, it's alive; if yellowish, it's dying back; if brown or white, it's dead. Use hand pruners to snip off small sections of branch, proceeding if necessary to larger branches, until a ring of green cambium indicates live wood. If none is found, cut whole plant close to ground; it may resprout from roots. Give it until June before giving up on it.

➤ Shear Scottish heathers and summer-blooming heaths, cutting just below last year's flowers but not into bare stems.

➤ Prune boxwoods, lavender, and subshrubs such as artemisias, caryopteris, and ceratostigma as needed.

➤ Place peony rings or supports around peonies before they bloom.

➤ Bring overwintered tender geraniums (pelargoniums) and tender perennials to brighter light; gradually increase watering as growth resumes.

➤ If red-headed ants (fire ants) are a local problem, band trunks of blooming fruit trees with sticky paste to prevent ants from climbing trunks and eating sugar-rich blossoms.

➤ If weather is mild and rainy, keep an eye out for fungal diseases and treat accordingly.

➤ If possible, attend a Cherry Blossom Festival. Seattle and Vancouver, B.C., both host one, as do several smaller cities.

➤ Plant cold-hardy annuals (see sidebar) as soon as local danger of hard frost appears to be over.

MAY

On the subject of weather, May blows both hot and cold. The first part of the month can be surprisingly cool, with daytime highs only into the mid-50s F (12–14°C) and nights that come uncomfortably close to frost. It's even possible to get an unseasonable late-late frost in exposed inland gardens or at higher elevations. However, these are relatively rare, and May's initial coolness merely serves to prolong the flowers of all the midseason rhododendrons, deciduous azaleas, and evergreen azaleas that bloom in such profusion this month.

Close on the heels of this cool spell, May usually produces a sudden hot spell, with temperatures soaring into the mid-80s F (29–30°C). This happens so often that it's a personal standing joke between us, using Canada's Celsius measurements, that May goes from zero (freezing) to 30 (86°F) in six days.

High humidity lingering from spring showers makes it seem even hotter than it is, and, since none of us are acclimatized yet, heat exhaustion is actually a very real risk following heavy physical exertion. With the summer solstice only a few weeks away, sunburn is another very common consequence of doing too much at one stretch in the garden.

But who can blame us for wanting to spend all our time outdoors in May? It's not just that so many different kinds of plants come into bloom now, but that so many of them bloom in such extravagant style. It's as if the whole world is putting on a sumptuous garden party, and the urge to participate in it—especially after May's brief hot spell subsides—is irresistible.

Malus 'Prairie Fire', top left; *Rhododendron* 'Gold Dust', center right. In foreground, *Erica* ×*darleyensis* cultivars 'Silberschmelze' and 'Ghost Hills' are in their seventh month of bloom.

Rhododendrons, including the spectacular large-flowered hybrids, are at their peak now, with bright deciduous azaleas and evergreen azaleas filling in any possible color gaps. Late-flowering magnolias and Japanese flowering cherries are joined by flowering dogwoods, flowering crabapples, laburnums, hawthorns, and the flamboyant, almost subtropical blooms of majestic horse chestnuts.

Vines are not to be outdone, with massive displays of wisteria, *Clematis montana* cultivars, Group B hybrid clematis, and early honeysuckles. Nor are groundcovers, most of which seem to be in bloom this month. Nor are perennials, which pop into bloom in almost daily succession. Nor are bulbs (alliums, camas lilies, bearded iris, late tulips), nor cool-season ornamental grasses. Even conifers put on their freshest, spiffiest new growth for the festive occasion. Apple and quince blossoms add a touch of simple grace, and our native Pacific dogwoods, western trumpet honeysuckles, and the broad, almost rose-like white flowers of thimbleberries add their quiet elegance to the scene.

The only uninvited guest is Scotch broom, whose yellow flowers are a reminder that this is the time to cut large plants and pull small ones to prevent their spread by seed. There are also plenty of weeds to deal with, a fair amount of deadheading

to do, and—since the soil is slowly but surely beginning to dry out—watering to keep up with. New plantings naturally take top priority on the watering schedule, but close attention to soil moisture of all plants—especially those in full bloom, about to bloom, or just finishing bloom—will pay off handsomely in plant health and vigor that cannot be duplicated by any amount of catch-up watering in summer.

May's most pressing task, though, is getting all flower beds, containers, and hanging baskets planted up and getting the vegetable garden in before the end of the month. May's up-and-down temperatures sometimes leave a very small window of opportunity for doing all this, what with protecting tender transplants from frost one day and from sunburn the next, but the May long weekend (Memorial Day in the U.S., Victoria Day in Canada) is perfectly timed for last-minute planting.

If nighttime temperatures are still below 55°F (13°C), as they are in most subregions, it's best to hold off planting heat-lovers such as basil, peppers, eggplant, zinnias, and portulaca until early June. But as long as summer's main performers are in by month's end, all is well. This done, we gardeners can even take a well-deserved break, stopping to smell the roses that are already beginning to bloom.

IN FRESH BLOOM IN MAY

* blooms until July or later
(R) suitable for rock gardens

Ornamental and shade trees

Aesculus species and cultivars (horse chestnut)

Caragana arborescens 'Pendula' (weeping Siberian peashrub)

Cornus, most species and cultivars (flowering dogwood)

Crataegus species and cultivars (hawthorn)

Davidia involucrata (dove tree, pocket handkerchief tree)

Laburnum species and cultivars (golden chain tree)

Magnolia acuminata and cultivars (cucumber tree)

Magnolia liliiflora 'Nigra'*

Magnolia sieboldii*

Malus, midseason and late species and cultivars (flowering crabapple)

Sorbus species and cultivars (mountain ash)

Shrubs

Berberis julianae and cultivars

Ceanothus species and cultivars* (California lilac)

Choisya ternata and cultivars* (Mexican orange)

Cornus alba, *C. sanguinea*, *C. sericea* (shrub dogwoods)

Daboecia cantabrica subsp. *scotica* and cultivars*

Daphne ×*burkwoodii* and cultivars

Daphne cneorum and cultivars (garland daphne)

Deutzia species and cultivars

Enkianthus campanulatus and cultivars (redvein enkianthus)

Erica ×*stuartii* 'Irish Lemon'*

Exochorda ×*macrantha* 'The Bride' (pearlbush)

Gaultheria mucronata and cultivars

Genista lydia (Lydia broom)—not invasive

Hebe, early species and cultivars

Ilex species and cultivars (holly)

Kalmia angustifolia and cultivars (sheep laurel)

Kalmia latifolia and cultivars (mountain laurel)

Kolkwitzia amabilis and cultivars (beauty bush)

Lavandula dentata and cultivars* (French lavender)

Lavandula stoechas and cultivars* (Spanish lavender)

Ledum groenlandicum (Labrador tea; Pacific Northwest native)

Photinia species and cultivars

Pyracantha, most species and cultivars (firethorn)

Rhododendron, midseason species and hybrids, including most deciduous and evergreen azaleas

Rosmarinus officinalis and cultivars (rosemary)

Rubus parviflorus (thimbleberry; Pacific Northwest native)

Spiraea nipponica 'Snowmound'

Spiraea ×*vanhouttei* (bridal wreath spirea)

Syringa pubescens subsp. *patula* 'Miss Kim' (Miss Kim lilac)

Syringa vulgaris (common lilac)

Viburnum, most species and cultivars

Weigela species and cultivars

Roses

Rosa foetida 'Bicolor' (Austrian copper rose)

Rosa rugosa and cultivars

Rosa xanthina 'Canary Bird'

Perennials

Achillea tomentosa and cultivars (R)* (woolly yarrow)

Acinos alpinus (R) (alpine calamint)

Alchemilla alpina (R)* (alpine lady's mantle)

*Amsonia tabernaemontana**

Anacyclus pyrethrum var. *depressus* (R)* (Atlas daisy)

*Anchusa azurea**

Androsace species and cultivars (R) (rock jasmine)

*Anemone sylvestris** (snowdrop anemone)

Antennaria dioica and cultivars (R) (pussytoes)

Aquilegia species and cultivars (columbine)

Arenaria species and cultivars (R) (sandwort)

Armeria species and cultivars (R)* (thrift)

Aster alpinus and cultivars (R) (alpine aster)

Centaurea montana and cultivars (perennial cornflower)

Cerastium alpinum var. *lanatum* (R) (alpine cerastium)

Cerastium tomentosum (R) (snow-in-summer)

Chrysogonum virginianum (R)* (golden star)

Corydalis, most species and cultivars (R)*

Dianthus, most species and cultivars (R)* (pink)

Dicentra eximia and cultivars* (fringed bleeding heart)

Dictamnus albus and cultivars (gas plant)

Dodecatheon meadia and cultivars (R) (shooting star)

Dryas octopetala and cultivars (R) (mountain avens)

Erinus alpinus and cultivars (R)* (fairy foxglove)

Erodium species and cultivars (R)* (storksbill)

Euphorbia griffithii and cultivars*

Filipendula vulgaris and cultivars* (dropwort)

Geranium, early species and cultivars* (cranesbill, hardy geranium)

Geum species and cultivars* (avens)

Gypsophila repens and cultivars (R)* (creeping baby's breath)

Helianthemum species and cultivars (R)* (sun rose)

Heuchera sanguinea and cultivars* (coral bells)

×*Heucherella* cultivars*

Incarvillea delavayi and cultivars* (hardy gloxinia)

Iris sibirica and cultivars (Siberian iris)

Lavatera species and cultivars* (tree mallow)

Leontopodium alpinum (R) (Edelweiss)

Lewisia cotyledon and cultivars (R)*

Linum perenne and cultivars* (blue flax)

Lychnis alpina and cultivars (R) (alpine campion)

Meconopsis betonicifolia and cultivars* (Himalayan blue poppy)

Meconopsis cambrica and cultivars* (Welsh poppy)

Paeonia species and cultivars (peony)

Papaver species and cultivars* (poppy)

Penstemon fruticosus and cultivars (shrubby penstemon; Pacific Northwest native)

Persicaria affinis and cultivars* (dwarf fleeceflower)

Phlox maculata and cultivars (meadow phlox)

Polemonium caeruleum and cultivars* (Jacob's ladder)

Polygonatum species and cultivars (Solomon's seal)

Primula ×*bulleesiana* and cultivars (candelabra primrose)

Primula japonica and cultivars* (Japanese primrose)

Primula vialii (R)* (pagoda primrose)

Saxifraga paniculata and cultivars (R) (encrusted saxifrage)

Saxifraga ×*urbium* and cultivars (London pride)

Sedum, most dwarf species and cultivars (R)* (stonecrop)

Silene acaulis and cultivars (R)* (moss campion)

Sisyrinchium species and cultivars (R) (blue-eyed grass)

Thalictrum aquilegiifolium (columbine meadow rue)

Thermopsis species (false lupine)

Thymus, most species and cultivars (thyme)

Trollius species and cultivars (globe flower)

Bulbs and bulb-like plants

Allium, early and midseason species and cultivars (flowering onion)

*Anemone coronaria** (poppy-flowered anemone)

Asphodeline lutea and cultivars (king's spear)

Calochortus species and cultivars (Mariposa lily; native to West Coast mountains)

Camassia, most species and cultivars (camas, quamash; Pacific Northwest native)

Dierama species and cultivars (angel's fishing rod, fairy wand)

Eremurus species and cultivars (foxtail lily)

Iris germanica, early and midseason cultivars (bearded iris)

Iris setosa (Arctic iris)

Leucojum aestivum (summer snowflake)

Ornithogalum species and cultivars (star of Bethlehem)

Oxalis adenophylla and cultivars (Chilean wood sorrel)

Tulipa, midseason and late cultivars (tulip)

Vines

Clematis Group B hybrids

Clematis montana and cultivars (Himalayan clematis)

Decumaria barbara

Lonicera ciliosa (western trumpet honeysuckle; Pacific Northwest native)

Lonicera periclymenum 'Belgica' (Early Dutch honeysuckle)

Schisandra species and cultivars

Wisteria species and cultivars

Groundcovers

Ceanothus gloriosus 'Point Reyes'

Cornus canadensis (bunchberry; Pacific Northwest native)

Cotoneaster dammeri and cultivars

Genista pilosa 'Vancouver Gold'*—not invasive

Geranium macrorrhizum and cultivars (bigroot geranium)

Isotoma axillaris 'Blue Star'* (blue star creeper)

Lamium galeobdolon 'Hermann's Pride' (yellow archangel)—not invasive

Lamium maculatum and cultivars* (spotted deadnettle)

Lysimachia nummularia and cultivars (creeping Jenny)

Ornamental grasses

Deschampsia cespitosa and cultivars* (tufted hair grass)

Festuca species and cultivars* (fescue)

Helictotrichon sempervirens and cultivars* (blue oat grass)

ANNUALS TO PLANT IN MAY

Vegetables and herbs

Transplants of tomatoes; seeds of beans and corn; seeds or transplants of cucumbers, pumpkins, summer squash, winter squash, zucchini; in appropriate subregions, if soil is warm, transplants of basil*, cantaloupes and other melons*, peppers*, pineapple sage*, watermelon*

Tender bulbs

Freesia, dahlia, gladiolus (plant every two weeks for continuous bloom), sparaxis, tigridia

Flowers

Set out bedding geraniums (pelargoniums), ivy geraniums, Martha Washington geraniums, fuchsias, tuberous begonias; transplants of bidens, browallia, celosia, coleus*, diascia, fibrous begonia, gazania, helichrysum (strawflower), impatiens, larkspur, lisianthus, nemesia, New Guinea impatiens*, portulaca*, rudbeckia, salpiglossis (painted tongue), scarlet sage, scaevola, schizanthus, stocks, verbena*, zinnia*; seeds or transplants of cosmos and sunflower

* Delay planting until early June if nighttime temperatures remain lower than about 55°F (13°C)

TO DO IN MAY

➤ Finish planting and transplanting perennials.

➤ Water newly planted nursery stock regularly.

➤ Plant up annual containers and hanging baskets early in the month; set out at mid-month but be prepared to protect or take down in adverse weather.

➤ Water rhododendrons, azaleas, and other established plants in full bloom during dry spells. Fertilize with light dressing of compost after bloom.

➤ Deadhead early rhododendrons as they finish blooming.

➤ Check rhododendrons, yews, and other susceptible plants for signs of root weevils, which are now at peak populations.

➤ Harvest rhubarb by pulling stalks with a slight twisting motion (do not cut); harvest asparagus by cutting stalks with a sharp knife held at a 45° angle to prevent damage to emerging stalks (do not pull). Stop harvesting both after six to eight weeks or when new stalks become thinner and weaker, whichever comes first.

➤ Snap off faded flowers of tulips and other spring bulbs as they finish blooming (unless seeds are wanted for naturalizing), but leave foliage to feed bulbs until it withers naturally.

➤ Deadhead perennials as they finish blooming.

➤ Stake tall perennials such as delphiniums before they reach full height.

➤ Shear winter-blooming heaths lightly as needed.

➤ Cut unwanted Scotch broom (pull small plants) before flowers have a chance to set seed.

➤ Watch for larvae of currant sawfly on currants and gooseberries—plants can be defoliated in a matter of days. If many small dark green "caterpillars" are seen, spray with pyrethrin-based insecticidal soap, not *Bacillus thuringiensis* var. *kurstaki*. Larvae are not true caterpillars, so BTK is ineffective on them.

➤ Keep up with weeds, especially noxious plants such as bindweed.

➤ Plant annual flower beds, being sure to harden off small transplants before setting out.

➤ Plant vegetable garden (harden off transplants first); keep soil moist until all seeds have sprouted.

JUNE

June is no longer spring-like, but neither is it true summer. At its very beginning, sure signs that spring's over include snow-like drifts of native black cottonwood "cotton" that pile up everywhere, the roadside blooming of California poppies, cornflowers, and oxeye daisies, and the imposition of sprinkling restrictions, which in many jurisdictions begin 1 June no matter what the weather. Yet with summer's heat, drought, and sometimes glaring brightness still on the distant horizon, June is a brief, almost charmed interlude allowing both garden and gardener to take a much-needed breather.

After spring's endless kaleidoscope of color, the gentle and pervasive blues of June—ceanothus, campanulas, hardy geraniums, delphiniums, lavender, and even the ubiquitous swaths of Crystal Palace lobelia—are welcome balm to almost-fatigued eyes. The unbelievably lush green jungles of fresh growth surrounding us both inside and outside our gardens (the payoff for all those months of interminable rain) are also at their height of soothing, cool freshness.

Except for the Pacific Coast subregion, where cool rains and even cooler winds usually make June one of the more disagreeable months of the year, even the weather is soothingly mild in June—neither too wet nor too dry; too hot nor too cold. As usual, though, there are exceptions. Rain can continue right through the solstice, giving the question "What is so rare as a day in June?" an ironic twist. At the opposite extreme there may be an unseasonably early heat wave, such as the one that broke records throughout the Pacific Northwest in 2006. But in our memories and expectations, June will always be mild and benign—except, of course, on the coast.

Despite relatively calm floral displays, June never lacks color or variety. Roses, especially the larger climbers and ramblers, are now at their peak of perfection. Korean dogwoods are in full pink or white bloom, and mock oranges (including our floriferous

Clockwise from top right: *Spiraea nipponica* 'Snowmound', *S. japonica* 'Lisp' (Golden Princess), *Carex comans*, *Alchemilla mollis*, *Geranium* 'Johnson's Blue'

native, *Philadelphus lewisii* var. *gordonianus*) add sweet fragrance as well as simple, timeless beauty. The huge mounds of beauty bush and variegated weigela that began blooming late in May continue their majestic presence, and Asiatic lilies add their cheerful accents of bright or pastel color. Herbaceous perennials now bloom in full force, with taller border types taking center stage as the shorter rock garden types begin to wrap up their blooming seasons. Outside our gardens, the bright red fruits of red-berried elder and the exquisite lace-curtain flowers of ocean spray (*Holodiscus discolor*) grace our borrowed scenery.

Whether or not to let the lawn go summer-dormant is a matter of personal choice, but June is when lawn grasses begin their natural (and intelligent) resting season. As well as being good for the grass itself, this is also an excellent way to gauge the amount of moisture left in the soil, now that we're at the tail end of our seasonal rains and fast approaching our normal summer drought. June's usually mild weather can be deceptive, but lawns never lie: the first sign of browning is a signal to make sure all plants that need water now—those newly planted, those in flower or just about to flower, and of course the vegetable garden—get their fair share.

There are plenty of other garden tasks to do in June, but none of them are overly demanding, strenuous, or disagreeable. With spring's hectic pruning, digging, planting, transplanting, and fertilizing tasks behind us, and summer's busy harvesting season not yet here, there is ample opportunity to establish a pleasant daily rhythm of regular maintenance. But even with daily watering, weeding, and deadheading, we still have plenty of time left to experience the simple joy of being alive and soaking up the sights, scents, textures, and tastes of our gardens in June's long, long hours of daylight.

IN FRESH BLOOM IN JUNE

* blooms until August or later
(R) suitable for rock gardens

Ornamental and shade trees
Chionanthus species and cultivars (fringe tree)
Cornus kousa and cultivars (Korean dogwood)
Gleditsia triacanthos and cultivars (honey locust)
Styrax japonicus and cultivars (Japanese snowbell)
Styrax obassia (fragrant snowbell)
Tilia cordata and cultivars (littleleaf linden)

Shrubs
Abelia ×*grandiflora* and cultivars* (glossy abelia)
Buddleja globosa and cultivars*
Callicarpa bodinieri var. *giraldii* 'Profusion' (Profusion beautyberry)
Cistus species and cultivars* (rock rose)
Cotoneaster, most species and cultivars
Daboecia cantabrica and cultivars* (St. Dabeoc's heath, Irish bell heather)
Erica ciliaris, early cultivars* (Dorset heath)
Erica cinerea and cultivars* (bell heather)
Erica ×*stuartii*, most cultivars*
Erica tetralix and cultivars* (cross-leaved heath)
Erica ×*watsonii* and cultivars*
Erica ×*williamsii* and cultivars*
Escallonia species and cultivars*
Fremontodendron californicum and cultivars* (flannel bush)
Fuchsia magellanica and cultivars* (hardy fuchsia)
Gaultheria shallon (salal; Pacific Northwest native)
Hebe, many species and cultivars
Holodiscus discolor* (ocean spray; Pacific Northwest native)
Hydrangea quercifolia and cultivars* (oak-leaved hydrangea)
Hypericum species and cultivars* (St. John's wort)
Lavandula angustifolia, most cultivars* (English lavender)
Paeonia suffruticosa and cultivars (tree peony)
Philadelphus species and cultivars (mock orange)
Physocarpus species and cultivars (ninebark)
Rhododendron, late species and hybrids
Sambucus, most species and cultivars (elderberry)

Spiraea douglasii (hardhack; native to the Pacific Northwest)
Spiraea japonica, most cultivars* (Japanese spirea)
Stephanandra species and cultivars
Syringa pubescens subsp. *microphylla* 'Superba'* (dwarf lilac)
Viburnum opulus 'Roseum' (snowball bush)

Roses
Nearly all species and hybrids

Perennials
Achillea species and cultivars* (yarrow)
Aconitum species and cultivars* (monkshood)
Alchemilla mollis and cultivars* (lady's mantle)
Aruncus species and cultivars (goat's beard)
Astilbe, most species and cultivars*
Astrantia species and cultivars* (masterwort)
Campanula species and cultivars* (bellflower)
Catananche caerulea* (Cupid's dart)
Centaurea dealbata (Persian cornflower)
Clematis ×*durandii** and cultivars
Clematis integrifolia and cultivars*
Coreopsis species and cultivars* (tickseed)
Crambe cordifolia (sea kale)
Delphinium species and cultivars*
Dicentra 'Luxuriant'*
Digitalis grandiflora and cultivars* (yellow foxglove)
Digitalis ×*mertonensis** (strawberry foxglove)
Digitalis purpurea* (common foxglove)
Echinops species and cultivars* (globe thistle)
Erigeron species and cultivars* (bugbane, fleabane)
Eryngium giganteum* (Miss Willmott's ghost)
Filipendula species and cultivars (meadowsweet)
Gaillardia species and cultivars* (blanket flower)
Gaura lindheimeri and cultivars* (butterfly gaura)
Geranium, most species and cultivars* (cranesbill, hardy geranium)
Gunnera manicata (giant gunnera)
Gypsophila paniculata and cultivars* (baby's breath)
Heliopsis helianthoides var. *scabra* and cultivars* (false sunflower)
Hemerocallis, early and midseason hybrids* (daylily)
Heuchera species and cultivars
Hypericum olympicum and cultivars (R)*
Iris ensata and cultivars (Japanese iris)
Jasione species and cultivars* (sheep's bit)
Kniphofia species and cultivars* (red hot poker)
Leucanthemum ×*superbum* and cultivars* (Shasta daisy)
Limonium platyphyllum* (sea lavender)

Linum flavum and cultivars* (golden flax)

Lupinus species and cultivars (lupine)

Lychnis chalcedonica and cultivars* (Maltese cross)

Lychnis coronaria and cultivars* (rose campion)

Lysimachia punctata and cultivars* (yellow loosestrife)—
not invasive

Malva moschata and cultivars* (musk mallow)

Monarda didyma and cultivars* (bee balm, bergamot)

Nepeta species and cultivars* (catmint)

Oenothera species and cultivars* (evening primrose)

Platycodon grandiflorus and cultivars* (balloon flower)

Primula florindae and cultivars* (giant cowslip)

Rodgersia species and cultivars

Romneya coulteri and cultivars* (Matilija poppy, California tree
poppy)

Roscoea species and cultivars

Sagina subulata and cultivars (R) (Irish moss, Scots moss)

Salvia, most species and cultivars* (garden sage)

Santolina chamaecyparissus and cultivars (R) (lavender cotton)

Saponaria ×lempergii 'Max Frei' (R)* (Max Frei soapwort)—
not invasive

Scabiosa species and cultivars* (pincushion flower)

Sempervivum species and cultivars* (hen and chicks, houseleek)

Sidalcea species and cultivars* (prairie mallow)

Stachys byzantina and cultivars (lamb's ear)

Tanacetum coccineum and cultivars* (painted daisy)

Tanacetum parthenium and cultivars* (feverfew)

Teucrium species and cultivars (germander)

Thymus pseudolanuginosus (R) (woolly thyme)

Thymus serpyllum and cultivars (R) (creeping thyme,
mother-of-thyme)

Tradescantia Andersoniana Group cultivars* (spiderwort)

Veronica, most species and cultivars* (speedwell)

Bulbs and bulb-like plants

Agapanthus species and cultivars* (lily of the Nile)

Allium, midseason and late species and cultivars (flowering
onion)

Alstroemeria species and cultivars* (Peruvian lily)

Babiana species and cultivars* (baboon flower)

*Cardiocrinum giganteum** (giant lily)

Iris germanica, midseason and late cultivars (bearded iris)

Ixia hybrids (African corn lily)

Lilium, Asiatic hybrids

Watsonia species and hybrids

Zantedeschia species and cultivars* (calla lily)

Vines

Actinidia kolomikta and cultivars

Aristolochia species and cultivars (Dutchman's pipe)

Clematis, most Group C hybrids*

Clematis tangutica and cultivars* (golden clematis)

Clematis viticella and cultivars*

Dicentra scandens and cultivars* (climbing bleeding heart)

Lonicera ×brownii 'Dropmore Scarlet'* (Dropmore Scarlet
honeysuckle)

Lonicera ×heckrottii 'Gold Flame' (Gold Flame honeysuckle)

Lonicera japonica and cultivars* (Japanese honeysuckle)

Lonicera periclymenum 'Serotina'* (Late Dutch honeysuckle)

Passiflora, most species and cultivars* (passion vine)

Groundcovers

Gaultheria procumbens and cultivars (wintergreen)

*Hypericum calycinum** (St. John's wort, rose of Sharon)

Rubus rolfei and cultivars (Taiwan creeper)

Tanacetum haradjanii

Ornamental grasses

Arrhenatherum elatius var. *bulbosum* 'Variegatum' (variegated
bulbous oat grass)

Calamagrostis ×acutiflora and cultivars* (feather reed grass)

*Stipa tenuissima** (Mexican feather grass)

TO DO IN JUNE

➤ Water new plantings, containers, and the vegetable garden
regularly; make sure plants just coming into bloom have
ample water.

➤ Watch for insect damage, especially from aphids, tent
caterpillars, root weevils, leaf-chewing beetles, and
slugs and snails. Although insect activity is at a peak in
June, strange-looking or unidentified insects should not
automatically be destroyed; most are harmless or even
beneficial (see Chapter 16). Learn to identify ladybug larvae
(which are very prevalent now), lacewings, rove beetles, and
other beneficial insects commonly seen in June.

➤ With the sun's rays now at their most intense, be prepared
to protect new plantings with shade cloth in prolonged
sunny weather. Rig up a frame of some sort to keep cloth
from actually touching plants.

➤ Mow lawn every seven to ten days, even if growth is slow, to
prevent faster-growing weeds from flowering and setting seed.

➤ Deadhead rhododendrons. Wear disposable gloves to
keep hands from being coated with sticky substance that is
almost impossible to wash off.

➤ Watch the Portland Rose Festival's Grand Floral Parade ("the
rose parade")—in person, if possible; on television if not.

POT-AND-BAG PROPAGATION

1. Fill 6 in. (15 cm) diameter pots with coarse builder's sand (never beach sand) or coarse potting mix. Water well.

2. Select healthy, vigorous shoots, preferably non-flowering, that grew this year. Test for ripeness by bending a sample shoot back on itself: it should snap cleanly. If it bends without breaking, it's immature; if it tears raggedly, it's over-ripe.

3. Take cuttings 6–8 in. long (15–20 cm), making sharp cuts just below a leaf node. Keep cuttings in a zippered plastic bag, kept out of direct sun, if the next steps will be delayed (for example, when taking cuttings in a friend's garden).

4. Remove growing tips, including any flowers, and strip leaves off lower halves. If remaining leaves are large, cut them in half to reduce transpiration.

5. Insert lower end of each cutting into potting medium up to lowest leaf, spacing so leaves do not touch those of other cuttings. Rooting hormone is not necessary.

6. Water well.

7. Insert blunt twigs, popsicle sticks, or bent wire around edges of pot to hold surface of bag off cuttings.

8. Place whole pot inside white (not clear) kitchen garbage bag. Tie top, leaving plenty of air inside bag.

9. Place bagged pot in cool, shady area—under a deciduous tree is perfect. Check periodically for moisture. If too dry, add water; if slimy wet, leave bag open for a few hours.

10. After six to eight weeks, check for rooting, indicated by new growth in leaf axils. If growth is not satisfactory, wait a couple more weeks.

11. If growth looks good, gently tip pot on side and tease out fragile new rooted cuttings. Pot up individually (do not fertilize except for a bit of bone meal); water well.

12. Grow on in semi-shaded area until fall. Robust growers, especially evergreens, can be planted out in fall, but most deciduous subjects are best held over winter in a protected spot and planted out in spring.

➤ Deadhead roses and perennials as needed.

➤ Tie up canes of climbing roses as needed.

➤ Thin plantings in vegetable garden as needed.

➤ Pick (and eat) strawberries regularly.

➤ Weed, weed, weed.

➤ Prune rhododendrons and deciduous azaleas if necessary; shear evergreen azaleas lightly after blooming.

➤ Clip back "candles" (new growth) of pines as needed.

➤ Cut back fall-blooming asters and chrysanthemums by half to force multiple branching for more blooms on more compact plants in fall.

➤ Cut back tall or vigorous artemisias by half to prevent unwanted flowers and encourage denser foliage.

➤ Pick sweet peas and edible peas regularly (even if not used) to prevent seed set and keep up production.

➤ Pull (do not cut) root suckers on trees and roses. Cutting will only result in more suckers, and this is the time of year they are easiest to dislodge by pulling. Most should snap out of their sockets cleanly by applying backward pressure at the point of attachment, leaving a smooth, bowl-shaped depression. Use vise grips to get a better grip on slippery-barked or tenacious suckers.

➤ Take semi-hardwood cuttings of flowering shrubs and vines (see sidebar). Good shrub candidates for pot-and-bag propagation include buddleja, ceanothus, escallonia, forsythia, hebe, hydrangea, kerria, laurels (*Prunus*), lavatera, lavender, mock orange, photinia, pieris, potentilla, rhododendrons and azaleas, rosemary, spireas, most viburnums, and weigela. Vines to try include deciduous clematis, honeysuckle, passion vine, Virginia creeper, and wisteria.

JULY

With the exception of the central and northern sections of the Pacific Coast subregion, where cool temperatures and some summer rain can be expected, normal July weather throughout the Pacific Northwest can be summed up in three words: sunny, hot (to us, at least), dry. Occasionally there is one last blast of March-like weather—it's not terribly unusual for Fourth of July fireworks to be rained out, or for Canada Day celebrations (1 July) to be miserably cold, windy, and wet—but early July is when a massive high pressure ridge should be getting firmly established off the Oregon–California coast.

Once this happens, corresponding conditions of drought can arrive with alarming speed. There's still ample moisture in the air—dew falls in the night, and distant hills are blue with haze—but lawns now start to turn blond, moisture-loving plants show signs of stress, and deep cracks begin to appear in unamended clay soil. Some thunderstorms can be expected near any of our mountains, but except in the Rogue subregion these are not an inevitable feature of summer. For all practical purposes, natural rainfall is now firmly turned to OFF, and any plant needing extra moisture must find it at the end of a hose.

Fortunately, a great many perennials are drought-tolerant when established, so July gardens can overflow with color as those that begin flowering in midsummer overlap with those that started in June. Since heavier soils are the rule here rather than

Hebe cupressoides (center) with summer-blooming shrubs and lilies

the exception, one or two deep soakings should see all of them through the summer, even if no rain falls until September.

Assuming adequate irrigation, early July is when the vegetable garden kicks into high gear, with warm-season crops such as tomatoes, peppers, squash, zucchini, basil, cucumbers, melons, and beans all putting on phenomenal growth. (We once actually watched a bean vine in action as it groped its blind way around a pole.) Heat-loving annuals such as zinnias, verbenas, and lavateras also relish the arrival of real heat.

Small fruits now ripen in quick succession. Late strawberries are joined by raspberries, currants (red, black, and white), and gooseberries early in the month, and only slightly later by blueberries. Sweet cherries are also ready for picking any time after 1 July, and the earliest Japanese plums soon follow.

The last two weeks of July are often the warmest of the year, with temperatures in the major river valleys routinely into the 90s F (30s C). This is when the Rogue and Willamette subregions can get stinking hot, reaching as high as 104°F (40°C) for several days. Even now, though, nights are mercifully much cooler, dipping into the mid- to high 60s F (high teens C). This is when we Pacific Northwesterners, gardeners and non-gardeners alike, spend more time in our shady, wonderfully comfortable backyards than in our houses, sometimes sleeping as well as eating outdoors.

Long day length means long, relatively cool evenings. (In our area, the July sun doesn't set until well after 9:00 p.m., and twilight lingers long afterward.) This is the perfect time for those

gardening tasks that would seem too much like work in the heat of the day—or for just sitting back and enjoying the peaceful, time-suspended equilibrium of a typical Pacific Northwest evening in high summer.

IN FRESH BLOOM IN JULY

* blooms until September or later
(F) followed by attractive fruits or berries in fall

Ornamental and shade trees

Catalpa bignonioides and cultivars (Indian bean tree)

Koelreuteria paniculata and cultivars (golden rain tree)

Liriodendron tulipifera and cultivars (tulip tree)

Magnolia grandiflora and cultivars* (southern magnolia)

Stewartia pseudocamellia and cultivars (Japanese stewartia)

Shrubs

Brachyglottis 'Sunshine'

Buddleja davidii* (butterfly bush)—cultivars only; species is considered invasive

Carpenteria californica (bush anemone)

Cotinus coggygria and cultivars (smoke tree, purple-leaved smoke tree)

Cytisus battandieri (pineapple broom)

Erica ciliaris, most cultivars* (Dorset heath)

Erica vagans cultivars* (Cornish heath)

Hebe, many species and cultivars

Hydrangea, most species and cultivars*

Indigofera species and cultivars (indigo)

Lavandula angustifolia 'Twickel Purple'*

Lavandula ×intermedia and cultivars* (lavandin)

Nandina domestica and cultivars (F) (heavenly bamboo)

Olearia ×haastii and cultivars (daisy tree)

Spiraea japonica var. *albiflora**

Symphoricarpos species and cultivars (F) (snowberry)

Yucca filamentosa and cultivars (Adam's needle)

Roses
Rosa 'The Fairy'*

Perennials
Acanthus mollis and cultivars* (bear's breeches)

Agastache foeniculum and cultivars* (anise-hyssop)

Aster ×frikartii 'Mönch'*

Clematis heracleifolia and cultivars*

Echinacea purpurea and cultivars* (purple coneflower)

Eryngium, most species and cultivars (sea holly)

*Gentiana septemfida** (everyman's gentian)

*Goniolimon tataricum** (German statice, Tatarian statice)

Hemerocallis, midseason and late cultivars* (daylily)

Hosta species and cultivars (plantain lily)

Liatris spicata and cultivars* (blazing star)

Ligularia species and cultivars

Lobelia species and cultivars* (cardinal flower, giant blue lobelia)

*Lysimachia clethroides** (gooseneck loosestrife)

Macleaya cordata (plume poppy)

Origanum species and cultivars* (oregano)

Penstemon barbatus and cultivars (beard-tongue)

Penstemon digitalis 'Husker Red'*

Perovskia atriplicifolia and cultivars* (Russian sage)

Phlox paniculata and cultivars* (garden phlox)

Phygelius species and cultivars* (cape fuchsia)

Physostegia virginiana and cultivars* (obedient plant)

Rudbeckia species and cultivars* (black-eyed Susan, coneflower)

Salvia verticillata 'Purple Rain'*

*×Solidaster luteus** (solidaster)

Stokesia laevis and cultivars* (Stokes' aster)

Tanacetum vulgare var. *crispum** (fernleaf tansy)

Teucrium species and cultivars (germander)

Bulbs and bulb-like plants
Canna hybrids* (canna lily)

Crocosmia, early and midseason hybrids*

Dahlia hybrids*

Eucomis species and cultivars (pineapple lily)

Gladiolus hybrids*

Lilium henryi

Lilium hybrids: trumpet lilies, early Oriental lilies, early Orienpets

Vines
Clematis, late-blooming Group C hybrids*

Clematis orientalis and hybrids* (orange peel clematis)

*Clematis texensis**

Fallopia baldschuanica (F) (Russian vine, silver lace vine)

Humulus lupulus and cultivars (hop)

Hydrangea anomala subsp. *petiolaris* (climbing hydrangea)

Schizophragma hydrangeoides and cultivars (Japanese climbing hydrangea)

*Schizophragma integrifolium**

Trachelospermum jasminoides and cultivars (star jasmine)

Ornamental grasses
Acorus species and cultivars (sweet flag)

Briza media and cultivars* (quaking grass)

Chasmanthium latifolium (northern sea oats)

Panicum virgatum and cultivars* (switch grass)

TO DO IN JULY

➤ Water vegetable garden, containers, and new plantings regularly, preferably in early morning.

➤ Mulch moisture-lovers; water as needed.

➤ Mulch established beds after deep watering to conserve moisture.

➤ Water compost pile to keep moist; turn as needed.

➤ Keep up with weeding.

➤ Deadhead annuals, perennials, and roses as needed.

➤ Continue taking semi-hardwood cuttings of shrubs (especially broadleaved evergreens) as wood ripens.

➤ Cut back early-blooming annuals and perennials for second flush of growth.

➤ Shear lavenders when blooms fade.

➤ Prune spring-flowering shrubs as needed.

➤ Prune maples, birches, walnuts, and other trees that can't be pruned in spring because of profuse bleeding of sap then.

➤ Hose down spruces every two weeks to discourage spider mites.

➤ Start ornamental cabbage and kale from seed.

➤ Plant seeds of sprouting broccoli (purple is best) and kale to overwinter for early spring crops.

➤ Stop watering garlic when tops turn yellow and droop. To harvest, pull bulbs and shake off excess dirt but do not wash; do not cut stems. Dry in warm, airy place for seven to ten days until skins are white, papery, and slightly shiny. (If drying in open air, bring in at night.) Trim roots; braid stems and store by hanging in a cool, dark, airy place.

AUGUST

If the hottest temperatures of the year don't come in late July, they're bound to come in early August. Once this peak heat wave has passed, high temperatures slowly start to level off (except in the Rogue subregion, where they remain high all month), but even with this slight decline, it's still warm to hot everywhere, even on the coast.

Drought is now inescapable. Non-irrigated clay soils ring hollow underfoot, normally hard-packed gravel paths are as loose as dune sand, and sandy soils are like deserts. Forests are tinder-dry, and smoke from major forest fires often gives the August sky a distinctive color and smell. (We both admit to an odd nostalgia for smoky skies, stemming from our respective childhoods in the Willamette Valley. Back then, before stringent air pollution controls, widespread field burning of grass seed crops took place every year in late August, darkening the sky for miles around for at least a week.)

With sprinkling restrictions in force in urban areas and wells running low to dry in rural areas, water for irrigation is now at a premium. August is when the worth of drought-tolerant plants and the value of mulch simply cannot be exaggerated.

As surprising as it may seem, a good number of shrubs, perennials, bulbs, and other plants just now coming into bloom are very well suited to our summers (once they're well established, of course), and many of these will continue to bloom until hard frost. Our native Pacific dogwood, *Cornus nuttallii*, even puts on a repeat performance by reblooming in August, sometimes almost as profusely as in May.

Paradoxically, it's the heat and drought of August that enable many plants to flourish in our otherwise cool and moist climate. Warm-season grasses (most of them native to continental climates) require August's heat to flower well, and many ornamental trees and shrubs also need this extended heat to ripen their new woody growth before winter. To stay reliably perennial, dormant spring bulbs such as daffodils, tulips, and hyacinths need this dry summer baking period every bit as much as they need a moist winter chilling period. The dry heat of August also ripens the early tree fruits—Japanese plums, Bartlett pears, Yellow Transparent and other summer apples, and (in appropriate subregions) peaches, nectarines, and apricots.

Miscanthus sinensis 'Silberfeder' (left), *Rosa glauca* with ripening hips (right), *Crocosmia* ×*crocosmiiflora* (foreground)

Dry heat also ripens the Himalayan blackberries that grow everywhere, making August and early September the only time of year this invasive plant is not roundly cursed. In fact, crop failure in cool, wet summers brings laments for the pies, jams, syrups, and wines that won't materialize. (Near forested areas, failed blackberry crops may also bring black bears into backyard apple trees.)

In the vegetable garden, August brings an embarrassment of riches, with the abundance and variety of ripe vegetables necessitating frequent freezing, canning, or giving away of produce. Filberts (hazelnuts) may start adding to the harvest at month's end, but be sure to crack open a goodly sample before gathering for drying; the "blanks" or empty shells always fall first. Nuts are not ripe enough for drying until they fall free of their husks.

Crickets start their chirping about mid-month, signaling the bittersweet beginning of the end of summer. Suddenly, evenings are noticeably shorter, but glorious clear-sky sunsets (red sky at night, sailors' delight) are fair compensation.

In late August, a light rain shower or even thundershower can be expected, bringing welcome (if insufficient) moisture and respite from heat. It may be that these showers wash summer's accumulated dust from the air, because when skies clear again, there's a subtle but unmistakable difference in the quality of the sunlight. Summer is now on the wane. Fall is coming.

IN FRESH BLOOM IN AUGUST

* blooms until hard frost
(F) followed by attractive fruits or berries

Ornamental and shade trees

Cornus nuttallii (Pacific dogwood; Pacific Northwest native)—rebloom

Oxydendrum arboreum (sorrel tree)

Shrubs

Aralia elata and cultivars (Japanese angelica tree)

Calluna vulgaris and cultivars* (Scottish heather)

Caryopteris ×*clandonensis* and cultivars* (bluebeard)

Ceratostigma willmottianum and cultivars (hardy plumbago)

Clerodendrum species and cultivars (glory bower)

Clethra alnifolia (sweet pepper bush)

Cotinus obovatus (American smoke tree)

Hebe, late species and cultivars

Heptacodium miconioides* (seven son flower of Zhejiang)

Hibiscus syriacus and cultivars* (hardy hibiscus)

Hydrangea aspera Villosa Group

Hydrangea paniculata 'Tardiva'*

Itea ilicifolia (hollyleaf sweetspire)

Leycesteria formosa (Himalayan honeysuckle)

Sorbaria sorbifolia (false spirea)

Perennials

Actaea simplex and cultivars* (bugbane, snakeroot)

Anemone ×*hybrida* 'Robustissima'*

Artemisia lactiflora and cultivars* (white mugwort)

Astilbe chinensis var. *taquetii* and cultivars (fall astilbe)

Boltonia asteroides (Bolton's aster)

Calamintha nepeta and cultivars (calamint)

Ceratostigma plumbaginoides* (blue leadwort)

Chelone obliqua and cultivars* (turtlehead)

Eupatorium species and cultivars* (Joe Pye weed, boneset)

Kirengeshoma palmata and cultivars* (yellow waxbells)

Rudbeckia laciniata 'Herbstsonne'*

Veronicastrum virginicum* (culver's root)

Bulbs and bulb-like plants

Crocosmia, midseason and late hybrids*

Cyclamen hederifolium* (ivy-leaved cyclamen)

Gladiolus murielae (Abyssinian sword lily)

Lilium hybrids: late Oriental lilies, late Orienpets

Lilium lancifolium and cultivars (tiger lily)

Lilium speciosum and cultivars (Japanese showy lily)

Vines

Campsis species and cultivars (trumpet vine)

Clematis terniflora* (sweet autumn clematis)

Ornamental grasses

Miscanthus sinensis, most cultivars* (Japanese silver grass)

Pennisetum species and cultivars* (fountain grass)

Schizachyrium scoparium (little bluestem)

TO DO IN AUGUST

➤ Keep watering vegetable gardens, new plantings, containers, and moisture-lovers as needed.

➤ Cut out canes of raspberries that bore fruit; thin and tie in new canes.

➤ Move containerized plants into partially shaded area to prevent heat stress.

➤ Finish major pruning of all woody plants by mid-month to allow resulting new growth time to harden off before winter.

➤ Keep up with deadheading of roses and perennials.

➤ Pick beans, zucchini, summer squash, cucumbers, and tomatoes regularly to prevent seed set and curtailed growth.

➤ Stop watering onions when stem tips turn yellow, then push all stems over to ground to start ripening process. Pull bulbs with stems intact (do not wash) and dry in a warm, dry, airy place for seven to ten days or until stems are shriveled and skins are papery-dry and slightly shiny. (If drying in open air, bring in at night.) Cut stems to about 1 in. (2.5 cm) from bulb tops; store in dry, cool, dark place.

SEPTEMBER

In most years, September brings what many of us consider the most pleasant weather of the year, especially in the Pacific Coast subregion. It's no longer summer—although afternoon temperatures can still feel like it—but fall has not quite arrived. A few golden or ruddy tints do make early appearances in some foliage, but for the most part, leaves remain stubbornly green.

Although a few showers can be expected, most days are comfortably warm, with just a hint of invigorating cool breeze, and skies are blue or sprinkled with fleecy white clouds. (As always, there are exceptions—we can remember a few full-fledged November-type storms in September, including one on Labor Day.) Daytime temperatures begin to fall slowly, but nighttime lows now fall rapidly, and mornings are decidedly chilly, with heavy dew. Morning fog—a given in the Puget Sound and Pacific Coast subregions—may appear anywhere now. Soils remain warm and dry, but with cooler temperatures and some light showers, they at least won't get any drier now.

The combination of warm soil and cooler temperatures, along with the prospect of prolonged wet, mild weather to come,

Spiderweb and yews

makes September a perfect time for planting trees, shrubs, vines, roses, perennials, and lawns. Roots establish quickly in the still-warm soil, and plants can be assured they will not dry out or be subjected to sudden heat spells, as can happen with spring planting.

Unfortunately, September's combination of dry soil, warm days, cool nights, and moisture on foliage creates perfect conditions for powdery mildew. Everything from deciduous azaleas to roses to native bigleaf maples to zucchini leaves can be affected, but this is rarely cause for alarm; silver-white foliage is just another sign of September in the Pacific Northwest.

More than any other month, September looks both forward and backward as well as at the present. It's a very colorful month, with many plants that began blooming in August (Scottish heathers, hardy hibiscus, ornamental grasses, hardy cyclamen) just hitting their stride. Some shrubs and perennials that began blooming in July, June, or even May (for example, shrubby potentilla) are still going strong, and many roses put out enthusiastic new flushes in response to cooler temperatures. All these are joined by such September favorites as pampas grass, miscanthus, fall asters, chrysanthemums, and the leafless blooms of autumn crocus.

Group B clematis—the ones that bloomed in May and June—put on a good second show in September. Some rhododendrons, notably dwarf reds and dwarf blues, also rebloom modestly, as do a few shrubs such as spireas. The first of the

season's colorful fall and winter berries also become prominent now: take your pick (depending on genus, species, and cultivar) of yellow, orange, red, pink, white, blue, purple, or black.

When nighttime temperatures consistently fall below about 50°F (10°C), plant growth starts slowing to a halt. Annuals, including vegetables, complete their life cycle by going to seed; deciduous plants begin the process of going dormant; broadleaved evergreens and conifers slow to a near standstill. Regardless of official first-frost dates, a light frost can be expected anytime after mid-month in any exposed, noncoastal area, especially if skies clear at night after a showery day. Ironically, this first mild frost—expected or unexpected—is usually followed by three to six weeks of beautifully mild Indian summer. Keeping a sharp weather-eye out and having a good supply of floating row cover on hand can make the difference between a short season and a long one.

It's a good thing September weather is so pleasant, because gardening tasks are tripled in addressing past, present, and future. There's right-now harvesting (midseason apples and pears, European plums, filberts, walnuts, corn, tomatoes, and other vegetables); spent perennials to be cut back and divided (a much more pleasant task in warm, dry September than in cold, wet March); and bulbs and other plants to get into the ground for next year's bloom. September's to-do list is one of the longest and most varied of the year. (Gardeners in the Puget Sound, Pacific Coast, and Olympic Rain Shadow subregions can put off some of these chores—but not all of them—until October.)

Daylight now decreases by only a few minutes per day, but with so much to do, precious minutes add up, and many a Pacific Northwest gardener finishes September chores by flashlight. But the following morning, the garden looks as if no one has set foot in it for a hundred years: mist-covered spiderwebs cover everything, even blocking paths and imprisoning garden tools. A sunlight-diffused light fog only adds to the illusion that time has stopped. But gardeners can't pause to enjoy this fantasy world for long; this is September, and there's not a moment to be wasted.

OF FRESH SEASONAL INTEREST IN SEPTEMBER
interest continues until November or later

Ornamental and shade trees
Arbutus menziesii (Pacific madrone; Pacific Northwest native)—fruits

Cornus florida 'Welchii' (tricolor dogwood)—foliage

Cornus mas (Cornelian cherry)—fruits

Malus species and cultivars* (flowering crabapple)—fruits

Sorbus species and cultivars (mountain ash)—fruits

Shrubs
Aralia elata and cultivars (Japanese angelica tree)—foliage

Aronia melanocarpa 'Autumn Magic'—fruits, foliage

Aucuba japonica and cultivars*—fruits

Berberis species and cultivars* (barberry)—fruits

Ceratostigma griffithii (hardy plumbago)—flowers

Cornus sanguinea 'Midwinter Fire'—foliage

Cotoneaster species and cultivars—fruits

Forsythia species and cultivars—foliage

Gaultheria procumbens* (wintergreen)—fruits, foliage

Osmanthus heterophyllus and cultivars—flowers

Sambucus nigra subsp. *caerulea* (blue elder; Pacific Northwest native)—fruits

Skimmia species and cultivars*—fruits

Viburnum davidii—fruits

Viburnum opulus and cultivars*—fruits, foliage

Roses

Rosa 'Fru Dagmar Hastrup'—fruits, flowers, foliage

Rosa glauca—fruits

Rosa rubiginosa* (sweet briar rose)—fruits

Rosa rugosa and hybrids—fruits, flowers

Perennials

Anemone ×hybrida and cultivars (Japanese anemone)—flowers

Aster species and cultivars—flowers

Chrysanthemum, early hybrids—flowers

Euphorbia, many species and cultivars (spurge)—foliage

Primula polyantha (polyanthus primrose)—flowers (rebloom)

Sedum spectabile 'Brilliant'—flowers

Sedum 'Vera Jameson'—flowers, foliage

Tricyrtis species and cultivars (toad lily)—flowers

Viola ×wittrockiana and cultivars (winter pansy)—flowers

Bulbs and bulb-like plants

Amaryllis belladonna and cultivars (belladonna lily)—flowers

Colchicum autumnale and cultivars (autumn crocus, meadow saffron)—flowers

Crocus kotschyanus, C. speciosus and cultivars (fall-blooming crocus)—flowers

Crocus sativus and cultivars (saffron crocus)—flowers

Nerine bowdenii and cultivars—flowers

Sternbergia lutea—flowers

Vines

Ampelopsis brevipedunculata and cultivars (porcelain vine)—fruits, foliage

Clematis Group B hybrids—flowers (rebloom)

Clematis tangutica and cultivars* (golden clematis)—seedheads

Vitis species and cultivars (ornamental grape)—foliage

Ornamental grasses

Arrhenatherum elatius var. *bulbosum* 'Variegatum' (variegated bulbous oat grass)—foliage (regrowth)

Cortaderia selloana and cultivars* (pampas grass)—flower plumes

Miscanthus sinensis, late cultivars*—flower plumes

TO DO IN SEPTEMBER

➤ Stop irrigating when nighttime temperatures consistently fall below 50°F (10°C).

➤ Bring in any houseplants that have summered outdoors. (Wash foliage with insecticidal soap and inspect soil for insects first.)

➤ Pick midseason apples and European plums as they ripen. If wasps are a problem, pick in evening.

➤ Pick midseason pears. As with all pears, these must be picked while still slightly green, as they ripen from the inside out.

➤ Gather filberts and walnuts daily to prevent mice, squirrels, and birds from getting more than their fair share. Wear gloves when handling walnuts—indelible deep brown stain disappears only as new skin grows.

➤ Dry filberts for storage when harvest is complete.

➤ To protect lower trunks of young fruit and nut trees from winter cracking, sunscald, and insects, paint with white interior latex paint (no fungicides, no oil paints) mixed half and half with water.

➤ Take rose cuttings.

➤ If frost threatens, pick all frost-tender vegetables, including winter squash. (Halloween pumpkins can be left on the vine, but frost affects keeping qualities of edible squash.) Pick squash with stems attached; wash skins with weak bleach solution to remove dirt and bacteria that may cause rotting. Let cure in warm, dry, airy place for four or five days or until thumbnail will not dent skin. Store, not touching, in cool, dry place. Green tomatoes will ripen slowly over four to six weeks if placed in layers in a clean cardboard box, separated by layers of newsprint. Store box in a cool, dark place; check frequently for ripe tomatoes.

➤ Pull and compost residues of vegetable crops as they ripen; plant fall rye in their places.

➤ Plant garlic.

➤ Stop watering late-season potatoes when tops die down. For immediate use, dig, wash, and store in dark, very cool but frost-free place; for winter storage crops (assuming good drainage), cover with 6 in. (15 cm) of clean straw or mulch hay.

➤ Mulch winter-storage vegetables crops with clean straw or mulch hay.

➤ Lift and divide early and midseason perennials as needed. September is the only time recommended for dividing peonies.

➤ Cut back stems of spent perennials; add new mulch as needed. Do not cut back ornamental grasses yet, since they add valuable fall and winter interest. Stems of true lilies (*Lilium*) should not be pulled or cut until they have completely withered and separate easily from bulbs.

➤ Lift and store pelargoniums (tender geraniums).

➤ Plant new lawns, allowing at least six weeks before hard frost; keep seeds moist until rains begin.

➤ Plant conifers, especially hedges. Water well until rains start in earnest.

➤ Plant roses, vines, fruit trees, ornamental trees, hardy broadleaved evergreen shrubs, hardy early-blooming deciduous shrubs, and early and midseason perennials. (Borderline-tender plants, late bloomers, and most ornamental grasses are best planted in spring.) Water well.

➤ Plant non-dormant bulbs—autumn crocus, fall-blooming crocus, hardy cyclamen, true lilies, and bearded iris—as soon as purchased. Plant daffodils and snowdrops while soil is still warm to ensure good root growth.

➤ Plant starts of wallflowers and forget-me-nots for spring bloom.

OCTOBER

An expression commonly heard in early October is "when the weather breaks" or "before the weather breaks." This is no figure of speech. Sometime in October, usually around mid-month, Indian summer comes to an abrupt end: dark clouds roll in, the heavens split open, and water pours out. Unlike September's showers, this is real rain—1–2 in. (25–50 mm) at a time—and from now on, dawn is likely to see beautiful but ominous pink-tinged clouds heralding the arrival of yet another Pacific weather system within 24 hours. In some years, sunny shirt-sleeve weather does continue until late in the month, but the feeling of "we'll pay for this later" is usually validated by a sudden sharp frost or even sleety snow right around Halloween.

October rain is welcomed by Pacific Northwest gardeners, not just because it's perfect for all those plants tucked into the ground in September, but because it's so mild. After flirting with frost in late September or early October, temperatures actually go up when the rains begin. Daytime highs reach into the mid-60s F (high teens C) or higher, and nighttime lows are seasonally balmy, in the mid-40s to low 50s F (6–12°C).

October gardening tasks follow the weather. If it's not raining, jobs that require not getting wet take priority. If it is raining, well, just pull on a raincoat—no insulating sweater or fleece required—and continue planting bulbs, vines, perennials, shrubs, and trees. In our own garden, we have kept planting in these drenching mild rains as late as the first week of November, as happy (and as wet) as clams.

As in other temperate climates, October is the month of colorful foliage. Pacific Northwest fall colors are naturally subtle—with the exception of our native vine maple, our borrowed

Mixed fall foliage with last blooms of summer-flowering *Erica vagans* 'Saint Keverne' (left foreground) and *E. v.* 'Mrs. D. F. Maxwell' (right foreground)

scenery lacks the brilliant scarlets and blazing oranges of the eastern part of the continent—but are every bit as treasured. When bigleaf maples and black cottonwoods once again turn clear yellow; and are combined with the deep reds and maroons of Pacific and red-twig dogwoods (the latter bearing startlingly white berries), the yellow-oranges of serviceberries, the tawny golden browns of native willows, and the bright highlights of red huckleberries—all set against a backdrop of somber dark green Douglas firs—we wouldn't trade our Pacific Northwest fall colors for all the maples and oaks in New England.

That's not to say brighter colors are lacking in our fall gardens. Many well-adapted introduced trees (Japanese maple, sweetgum, Persian parrotia) and shrubs (witch hazel, burning bush, fothergilla) are worth growing for their fall foliage alone. These are joined by a carnival of colors displayed by many plants usually overlooked for their fall contributions, such as spireas, euphorbias, and hardy geraniums.

If these fall leaves of red, orange, yellow, or purple seem to glow even on dull days, it's because they do. The phosphorus contained in them actually gives off light, as can be seen by holding a piece of white paper close to them. A whole tree or large shrub can even cast its colored light onto white interior walls well inside a house.

Adding to October's foliage colors are the blooms of chrysanthemums, asters, fall sedums, winter pansies, and the flower-like foliage of ornamental cabbages and kales. Deciduous grasses add their fall tints, and even the fading foliage of daylilies and hostas are beautiful as they change from yellow to buff to pale straw. A hint of summer is still visible in such stalwart annuals as cosmos, fibrous begonias, pot marigolds, and ageratum. Fall berries and fruits, many of them now at their peak, complete the picture with their promise of persisting through winter.

November may arrive, weather-wise, in the last week of October, bringing all-day heavy rains and a drop in temperatures. Halloween is either drenched with rain, visited with high winds, or spookily calm, clear, and cold, with wisps of fog. But whichever way it goes, it's obvious by 31 October that a threshold has been crossed. Winter, Pacific Northwest style, has arrived.

OF FRESH SEASONAL INTEREST IN OCTOBER
* interest continues until December or later

Ornamental and shade trees
Acer species and cultivars (maple)—foliage

Amelanchier species and cultivars (serviceberry)—foliage

Betula species and cultivars (birch)—foliage

Cercidiphyllum japonicum and cultivars (katsura)—foliage

Cornus species and cultivars (flowering dogwood)—foliage

Crataegus species and cultivars (hawthorn)—fruits

Liriodendron tulipifera and cultivars (tulip tree)—foliage

Magnolia ×*loebneri* 'Ballerina'—fruits

Magnolia sieboldii and cultivars—fruits

Malus species and cultivars (flowering crabapple)—fruits, foliage

Parrotia persica and cultivars (Persian parrotia)—foliage

Quercus, most species and cultivars (oak)—foliage

Stewartia species and cultivars—foliage

Conifers
Ginkgo biloba and cultivars (maidenhair tree)—foliage

Pseudolarix amabilis (golden larch)—foliage

Taxus species and cultivars—fruits

Shrubs
Arbutus unedo and cultivars* (strawberry tree)—fruits, flowers

Aronia melanocarpa 'Autumn Magic'*—fruits

Berberis species and cultivars (barberry)—foliage

Callicarpa bodinieri var. *giraldii* 'Profusion'* (Profusion beautyberry)—fruits

Cornus sericea and cultivars (red-twig dogwood; Pacific Northwest native)—foliage, fruits

Cotinus obovatus and cultivars (American smoke tree)—foliage

Enkianthus campanulatus and cultivars—foliage

Euonymus alatus and cultivars—foliage

Fothergilla species and cultivars—foliage

Hamamelis species and cultivars (witch hazel)—foliage

Hydrangea macrophylla and cultivars (mophead hydrangea, lacecap hydrangea)—faded flowerheads

Hydrangea paniculata and cultivars (tree hydrangea)—faded flowerheads

Hydrangea quercifolia and cultivars (oakleaf hydrangea)—foliage

Kolkwitzia amabilis and cultivars (beauty bush)—fruits

Nandina domestica and cultivars* (heavenly bamboo)—fruits

Rhododendron species and cultivars (deciduous azalea types)—foliage

Spiraea japonica and cultivars (dwarf spirea)—foliage

Vaccinium species and cultivars—foliage

Viburnum opulus and cultivars—foliage

Viburnum plicatum and cultivars (doublefile viburnum)—foliage

Perennials
Aster novi-belgii, late cultivars (New York aster)—flowers

Aster pilosus var. *pringlei* 'Monte Cassino'*—flowers

Chrysanthemum and *Dendranthema* cultivars—flowers

Euphorbia polychroma and cultivars (cushion spurge)—stems

Sedum 'Herbstfreude'* (Autumn Joy sedum)—flowers

Annuals and biennials
Flowering kale and cabbage

Lunaria annua and cultivars (money plant, honesty)—seed pods

Ornamental corn

Ornamental gourds

Physalis alkekengi (Chinese lantern)—seed pods

Bulbs and bulb-like plants
Schizostylis coccinea and cultivars (crimson flag lily)—flowers

Vines
Parthenocissus quinquefolia and cultivars (Virginia creeper)—foliage

Parthenocissus tricuspidata and cultivars (Boston ivy)—foliage

Groundcovers
Cornus canadensis (bunchberry; Pacific Northwest native)—fruits, foliage

Euonymus fortunei 'Coloratus'* (purple wintercreeper)—foliage

Ornamental grasses
Hakonechloa macra and cultivars (Hakone grass)—foliage

Miscanthus purpurascens (flame grass)—foliage

Miscanthus sinensis, variegated cultivars*—flower plumes, foliage

Miscanthus sinensis 'Gracillimus'* (maiden grass)—flower plumes, foliage

Molinia species and cultivars (moor grass)—foliage

TO DO IN OCTOBER

➤ Pick late apples, late pears, and fruiting quince.

➤ Finish gathering walnuts. Dry in very warm, airy place until shells are completely dry before storing in a cool, dry place.

➤ Plant tulips, crocus, hyacinths, alliums, and all other hardy spring-blooming bulbs. Plant daffodils and garlic if you didn't get around to it in September.

➤ Store Halloween pumpkins in a cool, dry place (not in contact with bare soil) until it's time to carve them.

➤ Continue planting shrubs and trees, especially conifers. Make sure new plants are well staked against wind.

➤ Lift dahlias, gladioli, begonias, and other tender bulbs for winter storage when hard frost blackens leaves.

➤ If necessary, dig and transplant any shrubs established for no more than three years.

➤ Prune cedar hedges and yews as needed. Smaller prunings can be placed around tender plants, new plantings, or containerized plants for added protection against frost.

➤ Bring hardy containerized plants to shelter under an overhang so they won't drown over winter.

➤ Cut back late-blooming perennials as they finish blooming, but leave foliage on borderline-hardy or new plants as winter protection.

➤ Cut back overly tall non-shrub roses, especially if recently planted, by about half to protect against wind-rock.

➤ Cut back Group C clematis (unless trained into a tree) by half or more to minimize wind damage, but leave final pruning until late winter.

➤ If any potted plants need to be held over for spring planting, group them together, pot-tight, in a sheltered spot but not in a rain shadow. Place mulch or conifer boughs around the perimeter to protect pots from severe freezing and/or overheating in winter sun.

➤ Spread dolomite lime on lawns and gardens as needed.

➤ Spread 1–2 in. (2.5–5 cm) of compost or well-rotted manure over flower beds and around the drip line of shrubs and trees.

➤ Wrap columnar-shaped plants, especially conifers, with netting to keep them from splaying out in snow or heavy rain. Black plastic bird netting is almost invisible but not terribly strong; black mesh deer fencing is more expensive but will last for years.

➤ Do one last weeding of deep-rooted perennial weeds such as dandelions and thistles to deprive their roots of stored energy over winter.

➤ Protect maples, oaks, and flowering cherries from larvae of the winter moth by banding tree trunks with sticky paste such as Tanglefoot.

➤ Look around all sides of the house and roof for branches that could contact them under the weight of snow or heavy rain. Prune accordingly.

➤ Make a fall planter using seasonally appropriate flowers and foliage.

➤ Near the end of the month, pot up amaryllis and prepared (pre-chilled) hyacinths for bloom in time for Christmas. (Nice gift idea, too.)

NOVEMBER

November is, in a word, wet. November rain is in a class by itself, not just for its high frequency and intensity, but because of often being accompanied by high winds that drive it nearly horizontal. You haven't been wet until you've been out in a Pacific Northwest November rainstorm for more than 30 seconds without a waterproof parka. (Forget water-resistant.)

There are lulls between storms, of course, but everything outside will now remain wet for the duration, even on rare sunny days. There may be a week or so of high pressure—"fair weather," according to the barometer—but this too brings wetness; warmer upper air overlying cooler air at ground level creates a liquid-atmosphere fog that goes right through you.

With all this moisture around, there is usually little frost, although an unseasonable cold snap such as the record-breaking one in November 1985 is always a possibility. Usually, though, temperatures are relatively mild and almost identical throughout the entire region, with highs in the low 50s F (10–12°C) and lows in the high 30s F (3–5°C). But, being so wet, November always feels a lot colder than it really is. Former neighbors of ours from Calgary, Alberta, where it gets to 40 below, were quite justified in their annual complaints about the coldness of Pacific Northwest Novembers at 40 above.

After being housebound by hard rains for 24 hours or more, the urge to get outside and do some active physical work can be overwhelming. This is when serious gardeners are commonly seen in full-cover rain gear even when it's not raining. Such protection (the yellow ones are known as banana suits) is an excellent way to keep bodies warm and clothes mud-free, thus making rough work such as clearing brush actually enjoyable.

In November's wet soil, even the roots of Scotch broom, wild roses, and Himalayan blackberry can be dislodged with soul-satisfying finality. Leather gloves are a must in November, and not just for dealing with the prickles and thorns of blackberries and roses; real leather is the only material that keeps hands tolerably warm even when soaking wet.

In spite of its wetness, the November garden has a seasonal grandeur all its own. The leaves of flowering cherries, among the last to turn color, blanket the ground with orange, pink, and gold, and the starry leaves of sweetgum trees (*Liquidambar styraciflua*) turn red, orange, purple, green, and yellow all at the same time. Larches put on an incomparable show as their needles turn blazing orange-gold, and the fruits of flowering crabapples and beautyberries (*Callicarpa*) are stunning on bare branches.

Hints of a whole new season now start to appear as winter-flowering shrubs and trees such as *Prunus* ×*subhirtella* 'Autumnalis', *Viburnum* ×*bodnantense* 'Dawn', and *V. tinus* 'Spring Bouquet' push out a few tentative flowers. Some early winter-blooming heaths and sasanqua camellias are approaching full bloom, and the prominent winter buds of pieris, skimmias, and even dwarf conifers such as *Picea abies* 'Clanbrassiliana' are living proof that a whole new year's worth of gardening awaits in the not-so-distant future.

In the last week or so of November, snow is a very real possibility in all inland areas. This first snowfall of the season, even though it never amounts to much and won't stick around long, is invariably wet and heavy and has considerable potential for causing plant damage.

With any luck, all deciduous leaves will have already fallen, preventing major snow buildup and subsequent breakage of branches. However, wet snow like this should always be gently brushed or shaken off vulnerable plants and hedges, because it's likely to melt and then refreeze into heavy blocks of ice that are impossible to remove without causing even more damage. From now on, it's a good idea to keep a snow-dislodging tool such as an old corn broom at the ready. Just in case.

Fallen leaves of *Prunus cerasifera* 'Pissardii' with *Viburnum rhytidophyllum* (right) and fall foliage of *Kerria japonica* 'Pleniflora' (background)

OF FRESH SEASONAL INTEREST IN NOVEMBER
* interest continues until January or later

Ornamental and shade trees
Liquidambar styraciflua and cultivars (sweetgum)—foliage

Prunus hybrids (Japanese flowering cherry)—foliage

Prunus ×*subhirtella* 'Autumnalis' (autumn-flowering cherry)—flowers

Conifers
Larix species and cultivars (larch)—foliage

Metasequoia glyptostroboides (dawn redwood)—foliage

Picea abies 'Clanbrassiliana'—growth buds

Shrubs
Camellia sasanqua and cultivars*—flowers

Cotoneaster franchetii*—fruits

Erica carnea 'King George'*—flowers

Erica ×*darleyensis* 'Silberschmelze'*—flowers

Ilex species and cultivars* (holly)—fruits

Kerria japonica 'Pleniflora'—foliage

Mahonia japonica 'Hivernant'*—foliage

Pieris species and cultivars*—flower buds

Skimmia japonica 'Rubella'*—flower buds

Symphoricarpos albus var. *laevigatus** (snowberry; Pacific Northwest native)—fruits

Viburnum ×*bodnantense* 'Dawn'—flowers

Viburnum tinus 'Spring Bouquet'—flowers

Perennials
Sedum, late species and cultivars—seedheads, stems

Groundcovers
Arctostaphylos uva-ursi and cultivars* (bearberry, kinnikinnick)—fruits

TO DO IN NOVEMBER

➤ Finish planting tulips and other hardy spring bulbs.

➤ Drain, clean, and store garden hoses.

➤ Turn off water supply to outside taps to prevent pipes from freezing—you never know when the next Big Freeze will come.

➤ Empty any containers still holding summer annuals; wash, dry, and store.

➤ Spread dolomite lime around root zone of lilacs, mock oranges, and deutzias.

➤ Rake up and burn any leaves suspected of harboring disease (for example, black spot).

➤ Brush large fallen leaves off conifers and broadleaved evergreens to keep them from smothering foliage.

➤ Use all healthy deciduous leaves for mulch or winter protection. Leaves on lawns can be shredded in place using a mulching mower; they add valuable nutrients to the grass. Larger leaves from elsewhere can also be spread on the lawn, raked into windrows, then run over with a lawn mower before being used as mulch wherever some is needed.

➤ Dig, repair, and clean drainage ditches as necessary.

➤ Clear overgrown brush by cutting back tops and digging out roots.

DECEMBER

In the Pacific Northwest, it's a good thing December ushers in the holiday season. If we didn't already have Christmas (or New Year's Eve, or Hanukkah, or the winter solstice, or Kwanzaa, or whatever you choose to celebrate), we'd have to invent a joyful shared holiday just to take our minds off our unrelentingly dismal weather.

This is of course the darkest month of the year in all northern temperate regions, but it's hard to explain to outsiders just how dark and gloomy our Decembers can be. In our own area, just south of the 50th parallel, the sun starts fading behind the mountains shortly after 3:30 p.m. and doesn't reappear—if you can call the slightly lighter tinge to the sky reappearing—until well after 8:00 the next morning. On rainy days, which are plentiful, it never really does get what could normally be considered light. By this time of year, in fact, we hardly remember what light is—gray skies have been the norm for so long that rare patches of blue look disturbingly artificial, like old-fashioned hand-tinted photographs.

Except in the mildest southern and central sections of the Pacific Coast subregion, December usually brings low temperatures hovering right around the freezing mark. This is when winter mulch proves its worth—not by keeping roots warm, but by preventing them from being heaved out of soil that's constantly freezing, thawing, and refreezing. Hoarfrost, which is what we get when dew precipitates as ice crystals instead of water, can easily heave fist-sized rocks above the soil line.

These off-again, on-again freezing temperatures may bring rain, sleet, wet snow, genuine snow (but almost never at Christmas), alternating rain and snow, cold fog (including ice fog in northern coastal sections), or, most unwelcome of all, freezing rain. These "silver thaws" create ethereal but potentially lethal garden effects as delicate, ice-encased stems become brittle as glass; even larger branches can snap under the weight of ice. The only recourse, unfortunately, is to keep well away from iced-up plants to avoid accidentally breaking them.

Given December's weather options, it's no wonder we Pacific Northwesterners take advantage of every half-reasonable opportunity that presents itself to get outside. Although there is little actual gardening to do, there is much to appreciate. Deciduous trees and shrubs, for instance. Their freshly revealed, sometimes astonishingly beautiful architecture reminds us that both evergreen and deciduous plants are essential in any year-round garden.

Colorful berries, showy cones and seed pods, and prominent winter buds abound now, and are joined by the fresh blooms of winter-flowering shrubs such as Jelena witch hazel, several mahonia cultivars, winter jasmine, and early-blooming winter heaths. This is also when ornamental grasses become a daily fascination as they sway with the wind, spread fountain-like in wet weather, and stand up straight—in many cases, with leaf tips tightly curled—when it's colder and drier.

Mid-month finds many of us busily scouting for seasonal plant material for wreaths and centerpieces, not to mention eagerly looking forward to bringing a real conifer tree (fresh-cut, cultured, or potted) indoors. Everybody has a favorite species for this important role, but for most of us, indoor holiday decorating is practically defined by the scent of freshly cut Douglas fir in one guise or another. Outdoors, myriad colorful lights in both private and public gardens brighten the darkness and lift our spirits.

Late December often brings a surge of very mild, very wet weather, possibly causing local flooding as snowpacks melt in local mountains and heavy rains fall on ground already saturated. High winds are also common now, especially along the Strait of Juan de Fuca and all along the Pacific Coast.

High winds plus saturated soil equals widespread tree blow-down, but not in our own gardens, we hope; deodar cedar (*Cedrus deodara*), Nootka cypress (*Chamaecyparis nootkatensis*), and hemlocks (*Tsuga*) are all notorious for blowing over and should be avoided in areas known to be windy. But in saturated soil, even Douglas firs blow down frequently and in fact account for most of our winter power outages.

But who cares? With the solstice past, days are officially getting longer, and the way we count seasons here, that means winter is all but over. So have another eggnog, browse through a good plant book or seed catalog, and sit back and enjoy this brief time-out from gardening, because there's very little such free time remaining. Amid all the hubbub of the holidays, the tips of snowdrops, early daffodils, and even daylilies are already pushing quietly through the soil.

OF FRESH SEASONAL INTEREST IN DECEMBER
interest continues until February or later

Ornamental and shade trees

Catalpa bignonioides and cultivars* (Indian bean tree)—seed pods

Liquidambar styraciflua and cultivars* (sweetgum)—fruits, twigs

*Quercus garryana** (Garry oak; Pacific Northwest native)—branching pattern

Winter foliage of *Mahonia japonica* 'Hivernant'

Quercus palustris and cultivars* (pin oak)—persistent leaves

Tilia species and cultivars* (linden)—seed pods

Shrubs

Corylus avellana 'Contorta'* (contorted filbert)—bare branches

Erica carnea, early cultivars* (winter-blooming heath)—flowers

Euonymus alatus and cultivars* (burning bush)—twigs

Garrya elliptica (coast silk tassel; native to West Coast)—catkins

Hamamelis ×intermedia 'Jelena'—flowers

Hamamelis ×intermedia 'Pallida'—flowers

*Jasminum nudiflorum** (winter jasmine)—flowers

Lonicera fragrantissima, L. ×purpusii (winter honeysuckle)—flowers (tiny but fragrant)

Mahonia ×media and cultivars—flowers

Nandina domestica and cultivars* (heavenly bamboo)—foliage, fruits

Perennials

*Iris unguicularis** (winter iris)—flowers

Groundcovers

Luzula sylvatica and cultivars* (greater wood rush)—foliage

Ornamental grasses

Calamagrostis ×acutiflora 'Karl Foerster'*—flower stems

Carex species and cultivars* (sedge)—foliage

Miscanthus sinensis and cultivars (Japanese silver grass)—foliage, dried flower plumes

TO DO IN DECEMBER

➤ Pot up paperwhite bulbs early in month for holiday bloom.

➤ Make mental notes of possible garden improvements, additions, or deletions. Check these out over time as you walk around the garden; if they still seem right, mark appropriate times to do them on the new year's calendar.

➤ Cut early-blooming miscanthus close to the ground (or not, if flower plumes are still decorative) once foliage starts to break up.

➤ After wet snow or high wind, check for any broken or split branches and cut them off to prevent further tearing of bark. It's enough for now just to get the weight off; final pruning can wait until March.

➤ As weather permits, work on crazy-paving paths, stone walls, or placement of large rocks. All-leather gloves not only protect fingers from painful pinches, but keep hands comfortably warm even when soaking wet.

➤ Refurbish garden tools by sharpening blades and cleaning metal surfaces (baking soda works best for removing ground-in green gunk). If long-handled tools feel rough, sand them and apply boiled linseed oil (not raw) or good-quality paste wax. Dispose of used rags in water-filled sealed container to prevent spontaneous combustion.

➤ If possible, drain any garden puddles that stand more than a few hours. Do not walk on garden soil when soggy, and avoid walking on water-saturated lawns.

➤ Check mulch frequently for disturbance by birds, especially around crowns. Repair as needed.

➤ Dig root vegetables (potatoes, carrots, parsnips, rutabagas or Swede turnips, winter beets) and harvest winter greens (kale, collards, Swiss chard, Brussels sprouts, leeks) as needed.

➤ Gather fresh plant material for holiday decoration. Conifer branches, with the exception of hemlock (needles fall off immediately), are a great place to start, but holly, other berries, bare twigs, faded flowerheads, seed pods, and even fern fronds all add special touches. Local stands of native Garry oak may even sport clumps of mistletoe. Place all such plant materials in cool settings well away from sources of heat or open flames, including candles.

➤ Make sure seed in bird feeders is always fresh and dry. Wet seed can mold and make birds sick, so keep feeders under shelter and dispose of all wet seed in the garbage.

➤ Keep cut Christmas trees well watered.

PART THREE

RECOMMENDED PLANTS

When someone asked Duke Ellington what kind of music was best—jazz, classical, pop, blues, country/western, gospel, other—his response was that there are only two kinds of music: good and bad. We feel the same way about plants. Whether native or non-native, ornamental or utilitarian, commonplace or obscure, species or hybrid, longtime classic or new introduction, there are only two kinds of plants: those that are well adapted to Pacific Northwest conditions and those that are not.

This section is not meant to be encyclopedic, even within any one genus; it is in fact blatantly biased toward our personal favorites. But since our favorites are invariably those most perfectly adapted to Pacific Northwest conditions—climate, soil, and the sometimes-perverse vagaries of our growing season—we can guarantee their appropriateness. We're not above fudging a bit for some favorites by adding a bit of lime, improving winter drainage, or even doing some regular pruning, but low maintenance and self-sufficiency are priorities with us, as they are for most busy gardeners.

The selected plants profiled here are also naturally healthy, vigorous, and hardy everywhere in the Pacific Northwest. Although some are best suited to our cooler, damper subregions and others to our warmer, drier areas, all are adaptable enough to be grown anywhere with just a bit of extra care. Few if any are hard to find or difficult to establish; the whole point of this book is to encourage the planting of species and cultivars most likely to succeed with the least amount of special pains necessary.

All selections are well mannered, with no bad habits such as rampant suckering or self-seeding; we have excluded any with invasive or weedy tendencies. Almost all are at least reasonably drought tolerant when established, and most have multi-season interest. Last but by no means least, all are as beautiful to look at as they are beautifully adapted.

The sizes, growth rates, and water needs given for each selection are within the context of Pacific Northwest conditions only and cannot be applied elsewhere. This is especially true of the inclusion of Zone 9, by which we mean only the very mild-winter southern section of the Pacific Coast subregion. Summers in this area are much, much cooler than in any other Zone 9 area in North America, such as northern Florida; the closest comparison would be the Zone 9 climate of southwestern England and Ireland.

Since all plant sizes are approximate, the metric equivalents of U.S./imperial measurements are also approximate. For instance, 36 in. is given as 90 cm, not 91.4 cm. Hardiness zones are based on the USDA (United States Department of Agriculture) model, which is fast becoming the world standard (see "Plant Hardiness Zones," in the back matter of this book, where both Fahrenheit and Celsius temperatures are given for each hardiness zone). Again, equivalent Celsius temperatures have been rounded to the nearest degree, as they are in standard Canadian hardiness zone charts; for example, 0°F is -18°C, not -17.8°C, and 10°F is -12°C, not -12.2°C. Canadian gardeners can rest assured that Zone 7 (or 8, or 9, or 6) is Zone 7 (or 8, or 9, or 6) north of the 49th parallel as well as south of it.

We would love to have included many more plants that thrive everywhere in the Pacific Northwest, as well as some genera such as *Primula* that grow to perfection in some subregions but not in others. We had to draw the line somewhere; however, at least from our highly prejudiced viewpoint, none of those we have included could have been left out.

For information on any "possible problem" listed but not described in the text, please refer to the index.

CHAPTER 5

Ornamental and Shade Trees

Ornamental trees in May, authors' garden. Left to right: *Prunus* 'Kanzan', *P.* 'Shirofugen' (light pink, background), *Malus* 'Prairie Fire', *Acer shirasawanum* 'Aureum'.

Trees are not just the crowning glory of any garden, but its structural underpinning. Only the height and mass of trees make a garden truly three-dimensional, and the choice of species and cultivars is crucial in determining basic garden design. Everything else depends on these largest, slowest growing, and most permanent of garden plants—character and seasonal focus of the whole garden; the size, placement, and compatibility of nearby plants; the amount and degree of shade created 15 years down the road.

No other plant type needs more careful attention to site suitability, mature size, and personal satisfaction—especially since any one choice necessarily excludes others. (Few of us have estate-sized gardens.) So it's just as well that our choices among ornamental and shade trees are not unlimited.

Although it seems as if the mild climate and benign conditions of the Pacific Northwest would make it easy to grow any and all ornamental and shade trees, quite the opposite is true. Our relatively thin, acidic soils severely limit the success of large eastern North American species such as hickories, elms, oaks, ashes, and chestnuts; our dry summers make water-loving species such as birches, poplars, and weeping willows very poor choices except where soil is constantly moist in summer.

PLANTING A B&B SPECIMEN

To gardeners, B&B does not mean "bed and breakfast," but "balled and burlapped"—the form in which larger and/or more sensitive specimen trees and shrubs are sold. Instead of being grown in containers, these valuable plants are field-grown in heavy clay-based soil that keeps their roots compact; when they're ready for sale in early spring, they're dug up with their roots encased in a ball of this heavy soil. The ball is immediately wrapped in burlap held tightly in place with twine.

Never pick up a B&B specimen by the trunk: you may pull the roots out of the soil and/or break them. Instead, lift it by grasping the twine on both sides of the trunk (two people are a definite help here), or better yet, save your back by using a dolly, cart, or wheelbarrow. Do not disturb the root ball in any way, including removing any roots growing through the burlap; both burlap and twine should stay in place until the specimen is in place in the planting hole. In sunny or dry weather, keep the root ball moist by covering it with mulch (even damp newspapers will do) until it can be planted.

Dig the hole three times wider than the root ball but no deeper; the top of the ball should be no deeper than the surface of the surrounding soil. The soil in the hole should not be enriched except for a couple of handfuls of bone meal at the bottom, since enrichment creates an artificial "pot" roots are reluctant to grow out of. If at all possible, though, choose a site on well-drained, medium to heavy loam to make their transition out of the clay ball easier. If fertility is low, a thin layer of compost can be spread on top of the soil (not touching the trunk) after planting.

Lower the specimen into the hole holding it by the twine, not the trunk; when it's positioned well, cut the twine in several places and pull out as much as you can without disturbing the root ball. Then untie the burlap where it's wrapped around the trunk and cut off the loose ends. Don't try to pull the burlap out from under the root ball; this can make it fall apart and break the roots growing through it. Both burlap and twine are made of natural materials and will soon rot; meanwhile, roots will easily grow right through them. Backfill the hole and water in well; when all the soil is settled, spread a layer of mulch over the area but keep it from touching the trunk.

It will take some time for roots to grow out from the clay ball, so for the first few months, direct the water where the roots are—right under the trunk—soaking them deeply once a week rather than with a few dribbles every day. Newly planted trees need regular deep watering every two to three weeks through the first summer and usually the second; by the third summer, watering can usually be reduced to once a month unless it's unusually dry or the plant shows signs of stress. Beyond three years, the specimen should be well established, with whatever drought tolerance is expected of its species.

Although all three are widely planted, water stress makes them vulnerable to disease, insect damage, and attack by sapsuckers and woodpeckers; their aggressive water-seeking roots can crack foundations and ruin septic fields.

Some trees such as the highly drought-tolerant acacias don't like our wet winters (especially combined with cold); others such as mimosa or silk tree (*Albizia julibrissin*) don't like our cool summers. Still others such as London plane (*Platanus ×hispanica*), eastern redbud (*Cercis canadensis*), and many hawthorns (*Crataegus*) don't like our damp, drizzly springs, which make them prone to fungal diseases. And a few otherwise well-suited and attractive ornamental trees simply have bad habits—staghorn sumac (*Rhus typhina*), for instance, has invasive suckering roots.

Fortunately, trees that do grow well in the Pacific Northwest include some of the most beautiful and highly desirable species in the world. Larger well-adapted species not profiled in this chapter include sweetgum (*Liquidambar styraciflua*), tulip tree (*Liriodendron tulipifera*), linden (*Tilia*), hornbeam (*Carpinus*), and horse chestnut (*Aesculus*), of which the compact red-flowered *A. ×carnea* 'Briotii' is especially striking. In our hot-summer valleys, larger heat-loving species such catalpa, ginkgo, dove tree (*Davidia involucrata*), and Japanese pagoda tree (*Sophora japonica*) also grow well.

Smaller flowering trees that grow well everywhere in our region include serviceberry (*Amelanchier*) and golden chain tree (*Laburnum*); small trees best suited to cool, acidic soil with regular summer watering include silverbell (*Halesia*), stewartia, and styrax (especially *Styrax japonicus*), all of which bear beautiful white flowers. Sourwood (*Oxydendrum arboreum*) also grows well in cool, acidic conditions if given constant moisture; in our climate, it remains a small tree. Persian parrotia (*Parrotia persica*) has beautiful fall foliage and is well suited to our climate and soils, but its limbs are brittle and easily broken in wet snow or high wind.

Many other small ornamental trees are suitable for appropriate microclimates, but beware the all-too-common desire to plant a rare tree, or at least one that no one else has. If an ornamental tree is not widely available, there's probably a good reason it's not. If an outstanding and highly suitable new species is found, or a fantastic new hybrid developed, growers will be way ahead of gardeners in trying to get their hands on it.

The following trees are deciduous except for *Magnolia grandiflora*, which is reliably evergreen. Sizes given are what can be expected at the threshold of maturity (about 20 years) in average Pacific Northwest conditions. However, all will grow larger in time—some considerably larger—so plan for the future: measure twice, plant once.

ACER (MAPLE)

Origin: Temperate regions of northern hemisphere

Hardiness zones: Varies

Size: Varies

Season of interest: Spring through fall; excellent fall foliage color

Exposure: Cool sun to light shade, protected from intense sun and drying winds

Soil preference: Rich, moisture-retentive but well drained; slightly to moderately acidic

Water needs: Drought tolerant when established

Maintenance needs: Low

Subregions best suited: All

Possible problems: Verticillium wilt, leaf scorch, powdery mildew

Maples are so well suited to the Pacific Northwest that it would be hard to imagine a landscape without either native or introduced species—or both. Most unmistakable of all is our magnificent native bigleaf maple, *Acer macrophyllum*, which can reach truly impressive size (over 100 ft., 30 m) on moist, deep soil. Its massive presence is a defining feature of our forests and roadsides, especially when its huge leaves turn bright yellow in fall. Larger than those of any other maple in the world, these leaves regularly reach 12 in. (30 cm) across; we have measured some with a length of more than 15 in. (38 cm) not counting the stem.

Its numerous two-winged seedpods that float down like miniature helicopters (much to the delight of children) cause such abundant self-seeding that it's considered a pest by some, yet bigleaf maple is losing ground to urbanization so rapidly that some jurisdictions have given it protected-species status. If you have a mature bigleaf maple on your property, cherish it; although far too large for general use as a garden tree, we can't afford to lose this majestic native tree through complacency.

Our much smaller native vine maple is well suited to garden use; so is Douglas maple (*Acer glabrum* var. *douglasii*), an underused native species particularly suited to drier areas. Among introduced species, Japanese maples (*A. palmatum*) are extremely well suited and by far the most popular. Other well-suited species include paperbark maple (*A. griseum*), whose exfoliating reddish brown bark rivals that of Pacific madrone; Amur maple (*A. tataricum* subsp. *ginnala*), a small, tough tree with fiery red fall color; and several species with green-and-white striped bark, all known as snakebark maple: *A. capillipes*, *A. davidii*, and *A. pensylvanicum*. Of the three, *A. davidii*, a Chinese species, is best adapted to most areas of our region.

A few maples should be avoided. Sugar maple (*Acer saccharum*) and silver maple (*A. saccharinum*) do not perform well and are disease-prone in our climate; *A. negundo* (box elder, Manitoba maple) is weedy and invasive, although its variegated cultivars such as the popular 'Flamingo' are beautiful and well behaved.

All maples appreciate our abundant rainfall, moisture-retentive acidic soils, and relatively cool summers; all dislike intense sun, high heat, alkaline soil, and dry conditions. Like fair-skinned people who are prone to sunburn, maples have thin

Acer circinatum foliage in early October

leaves that are prone to leaf scorch under any of these adverse conditions. (By the end of a dry summer, even our native bigleaf maples show severe leaf scorch.) Regular summer watering is important for young trees and will prevent leaf scorch even in older specimens, but is not absolutely necessary for mature trees; in our climate, all maple species are reliably drought tolerant when established and will leaf out next spring as if nothing had ever happened.

However, always suspect verticillium wilt if leaf scorch appears on only one branch. All maples, and Japanese maples in particular, are susceptible to this soilborne disease, which can become rampant in wet, warm springs. Healthy stock (always buy from a reputable nursery), good sanitation, recognition of early symptoms, and prompt intervention are the best defenses.

Pruning should be avoided. Maples have the unique ability to shed nonessential branches as they grow, and all—particularly Japanese maples—look best when allowed to develop their own naturally graceful forms. If necessary to raise the canopy, control size, or remove diseased limbs, prune in dry conditions in early summer only; maples will bleed sap profusely if pruned in late winter or early spring. Fall/early winter pruning is also acceptable in theory but is rarely practicable, since this is our monsoon season.

An ancient Oriental gardening rule says that maples should always be planted to the west of a dwelling. Superstition? Maybe so, but for viewing gloriously colored maple leaves in fall with late afternoon sunlight streaming through them, there is no better placement.

Green-leaved seedling of *Acer palmatum* in summer

Acer circinatum (vine maple). Native to the Pacific Northwest. Well-loved forest dweller with a very lax, almost vine-like habit in shade; habit in sun is a shrubby small tree, often with multiple trunks. Widely adaptable, it grows well in full sun to full shade, moist to dry soil. In shade or on rich, moist soil, its rounded leaves with seven or nine lobes turn yellow in fall; in full sun or on leaner, drier soil, they turn blazing red and orange. Fall colors come early, especially in sun, but remain for a long time, making vine maple a number one choice for fall foliage. Bright red seedpods held almost horizontally are another attractive feature.

Even though it's not native anywhere in eastern Asia, vine maple is very closely related to Japanese maple (*Acer palmatum*); grafts are compatible, and several hybrids exist. More intriguingly, vine maple is not native to Vancouver Island, although it grows abundantly on the mainland to the south, east, and north. This curious fact supports the theory of the island's late geologic arrival in the Pacific Northwest.

Vine maple is especially effective in groups, with its multiple trunks giving the effect of a small grove. Ideal in native/natural gardens, its fall foliage is shown to perfection against dark green native conifers. The species is highly drought tolerant when established and of very low maintenance; like all native plants, it should be fed sparingly. However, its few cultivars are considerably less adaptable, needing some coddling along with careful siting. Height in sun 15–20 ft. (4.5–6 m); Zones 5 to 9.

'Monroe'. First and best-known cultivar; discovered in 1960 in the Cascades of southern Oregon by Warner Monroe of Port-land. Almost eerily like a laceleaf Japanese maple; green leaves are very deeply divided and habit is a shrubby mushroom-shaped mound growing very slowly to about 10 ft. (3 m). However, branches are not at all weeping, but held stiffly upright. Needs reasonably rich soil in partial shade; fall color is yellow. Often grafted on *Acer palmatum* rootstock, negating vine maple's higher drought tolerance and greater cold hardiness.

'Pacific Fire'. Yellow-green leaves (tinged pink in spring) turn clear yellow in late summer and drop early, revealing a coral-red trunk almost as bright as that of *Acer palmatum* 'Sango-kaku'. (Some consider it brighter.) Best in good, moist soil in light shade; less vigorous than species. Upright, almost columnar growth to 15 ft. (4.5 m).

Acer palmatum (Japanese maple). Native to Japan. Ideally suited to Pacific Northwest conditions and by far the most popular ornamental tree in our area. With their incredible range of size, habit, leaf type, and foliage color—not to mention the relatively small size of even the largest cultivars—it's no wonder many gardens host several. These always-graceful trees may be anything from specimens to weeping shrub-like accents to miniature trees in containers.

We gardeners are the beneficiaries of the mind-boggling genetic variability inherent in this single species. As with Japanese flowering cherries, Japan's mountainous terrain provides a range of habitats differing widely in elevation, exposure, and soil type; with their strong natural variability from seed and a

Acer palmatum 'Butterfly' in late spring

Acer palmatum 'Osakazuki' in spring

Acer palmatum 'Osakazuki' in fall

Acer palmatum 'Shindeshōjō' in spring

tendency toward sports (natural genetic mutations), Japanese maples soon filled every niche.

Human intervention over the last few hundred years—collecting, planting in different areas, hybridizing, cloning—further increased both the variability and adaptability of Japanese maples. Although thousands of names are known and over 500 cultivars are available commercially, almost all Japanese maples will grow in any well-drained site that's not too hot and dry in summer or too cold and dry in winter.

However, since ideal conditions include plenty of moisture, relatively cool growing conditions, summer sun that's not too hot or intense, and moisture-retentive, slightly acidic loam, it's no wonder they thrive particularly well in our climate, especially in cool sun. Although all cultivars grow well in partial shade, only variegated or golden-leaved forms require it; red-leaved forms—even the delicate-looking laceleaf types—will turn bronze or greenish in shade. Established trees tolerate our normal summer droughts very well; however, all look better with a couple of deep soakings in summer, especially if the weather is hotter or drier than normal.

In our hot-summer river valleys, an eastern or northern exposure open to the sky is advisable, since intense sun causes leaf scorch. Drying winds and terribly dry soil also cause leaf scorch, so windy sites should be avoided and light soils improved with copious amounts of bulk organic soil amendments. Expect some leaf scorch on newly planted specimens for the first summer or two. This does not indicate a dislike for sun, but merely reflects the temporary inability of the new root system to keep up with the leaves' demand for water. Always watch closely for signs of verticillium wilt, to which Japanese maples are unfortunately very susceptible; the initial signs are often mistaken for leaf scorch or water stress.

Like rhododendrons, Japanese maples should never be planted deeply; their extensive but not very deep fibrous roots need access to air. Plant them with the upper surface of the root ball even with the level of the surrounding soil, then cover the root zone with a moderate layer of coarse Douglas fir bark mulch to help keep roots cool and conserve moisture.

Although grafted named cultivars are most popular, Japanese maple seedlings should definitely not be ignored. These variable small-leaved green trees are very healthy and very robust, growing to about 25 ft. × 30 ft. (7.5 m × 9 m); they make wonderful specimen or shade trees, especially if their canopy is raised as they grow. New growth is tinged pink; fall color is an attractive blend of soft yellow, orange, pink, and peach.

The overwhelming number of cultivars available—far too many, considering their similarities—can be bewildering. A more unfortunate complication is that many of the more obscure cultivars have weak constitutions and/or look almost grotesquely deformed. Although they may appeal to collectors, such cultivars need special care and do not make good garden plants.

The following selections of *Acer palmatum* are all strong and reliable, even though some grow very slowly. All are hardy in Zones 6 to 9 and are proven performers in Pacific Northwest gardens. Despite their hundreds of variations, the upright, tree-like Japanese maples are always recognizable by their distinctive, very graceful leaves divided into five or seven (occasionally nine) lobes radiating outward like fingers from the palm of a hand—hence *palmatum*. Tree size as well as leaf size varies considerably; smaller cultivars are very popular for training as bonsai.

Many have bright new growth in spring, with somewhat more subdued hues in summer; almost all have outstanding fall foliage color. (The popular red-leaved cultivars, with blazing red fall foliage, are described separately.) All—even true dwarfs—have a definite tree-like form, often with multiple trunks. Growth is upright at first, spreading wider with age.

'Beni-komachi'. Small, twiggy, semi-dwarf; deeply divided leaves are crimson-red in spring, greenish red with red edges in summer, bright red in fall. (*Beni* means "red"; *komachi* means "dwarf" or "beautiful little girl.") Very slow growth to 6 ft. (1.8 m); good in containers.

'Butterfly'. Small, quite deeply divided leaves of gray-green edged creamy white are tinged pink in spring; fall color is magenta and red. Any branches that revert to plain green should be removed in summer. Best in light shade; slow upright growth to 12 ft. (3.6 m).

'Katsura'. Small leaves on densely branched tree are orange-yellow with deeper orange margins in spring, becoming yellow-green in summer. Fall color is bright yellow-orange, bringing to mind the foliage of *Cercidiphyllum japonicum* (katsura). Upright at first, becoming rounded; moderate growth to 20 ft. (6 m).

'Osakazuki'. Large leaves emerge reddish in spring, soon turning bronze-green, then deep green for summer. In fall, they suddenly and surprisingly turn fire-engine red, the brightest of any Japanese maple. Excellent in full sun; leaves do not burn. Very healthy and robust; a reliable classic. Moderate growth to 20 ft. (6 m).

'Sango-kaku' (coral bark maple). Widely planted for its winter bark of brilliant coral-red. Small leaves are light green edged red in spring, turning plain green in summer; fall color is bright orange/yellow/peach. Best in cool sun; not as vigorous as some cultivars but worth pampering. Narrow upright growth (name means "coral tower") to 15 ft. (4.5 m).

'Shigitatsu-sawa'. Relatively large leaves of light green with dark green veining have attractive netted look. New growth is tinted pink; fall color is reddish green. In the form 'Aka-shigitatsu-sawa', leaves are overlaid with red all season, becoming bright red in fall. Both need good light but protection from hot sun to bring out the best leaf pattern. Both grow slowly to 15 ft. (4.5 m).

'Shindeshōjō'. Very small leaves are brilliant pinkish red in spring; color lasts into early summer. Summer color is reddish green with a few white flecks; fall color, reddish orange. Slow growth to 10 ft. (3 m); good in containers.

'Shishigashira' (lion's head maple). Unmistakable form with very densely packed small leaves that are fantastically crinkled and twisted. New growth is bright green, darkening in summer; fall color is bright yellow-orange. Best viewed at close range; popular in containers. Despite distorted, congested leaves, growth is healthy and quite vigorous; can reach 20 ft. (6 m) but is usually smaller.

Acer palmatum 'Shishigashira' in summer

Acer palmatum var. *dissectum* 'Crimson Queen'

'Ukigumo' (floating clouds maple). Small tree with small, slightly twisted leaves of light green speckled white and pink; a few leaves are entirely white or pink. White spotting becomes more pronounced in maturity, appearing very pastel greenish white at a distance. Needs bright light for best color but can burn in hot sun; best in open shade. Slow growth to 12 ft. (3.6 m).

Red-leaved Japanese maples
Graceful yet substantial-looking small, upright trees, often multi-trunked; average mature size of 15 ft. × 20 ft. (4.5 m × 6 m) makes them excellent specimens. Leaves are largest and most robust of Japanese maples, often with a lustrous sheen. Best in full sun; red-purple foliage turns bronze-green in shade. Color is deepest and brightest in spring and early summer, becoming slightly bronzed by late summer before turning brilliant red in fall.

'Bloodgood'. Still the standard for the type. Wide leaves with satiny surfaces hold their deep red color until late summer. Very strong grower; largest of the red-leaved cultivars.

'Burgundy Lace'. Very graceful leaves, almost as deeply divided as a laceleaf. New growth is burgundy-red, becoming bronze-green by late summer. Best in cool-summer subregions; leaf tips can burn in hot sun but lose their red color in shade.

'Moonfire'. Compact tree with very large leaves of almost black-red; does not bronze out.

'O-kagami'. Purple-red new leaves mature almost black-red with very shiny surfaces; name means "great mirror." Tree matures slightly smaller than most red-leaved cultivars.

'Trompenburg'. Unusual shiny leaves of deep purple-red are deeply divided with each lobe rolled downward over its midrib, giving a strong, bold look. Turns reddish green to bronze by late summer. Vigorous.

Acer palmatum var. *dissectum* (laceleaf Japanese maple). Also called weeping Japanese maples, the delicate-looking cultivars of this variety are more shrub-like in habit, making dense mushroom-shaped mounds. Leaves are very deeply divided and habit is weeping, giving a look that is very different from the tree-like forms. Both combine beautifully, with the range of sizes, textures, and foliage colors offering unlimited possibilities.

Although very slow growing, most laceleaf cultivars can easily reach 8 ft. (2.4 m) in height and more in width (many are even larger with age); a common mistake is not leaving them enough room. Size can be controlled by light trimming in June, but a mature full-sized laceleaf Japanese maple is a truly magnificent sight. Trunks need to be staked upright for several years to allow branches to cascade downward.

Despite their fragile appearance, red-leaved forms are best in cool sun; open shade is preferable if sun is very intense. Leaf tips may burn for the first couple of summers, but will soon adapt.

'Crimson Queen'. Foliage is nearly black-red in summer, bronzing slightly by late summer before turning bright red.

Acer palmatum var. *dissectum* Dissectum Viride Group

Acer palmatum var. *dissectum* 'Inaba-shidare' in late summer

Habit is low, dense, and strongly weeping. Takes heat and full sun without burning as long as soil moisture is adequate.

Dissectum Atropurpureum Group. Often sold as *Acer palmatum* 'Dissectum Atropurpurea'; commonly called red laceleaf Japanese maple. Variable in color, form, and performance; can be very satisfactory but will not have exact characteristics of named (cloned) cultivars.

Dissectum Viride Group. Often sold as *Acer palmatum* 'Dissectum Viridis'; commonly called green laceleaf Japanese maple. Dense cascading foliage is brightest green in light shade, becoming deep yellow and gold in fall. Not as popular as red-foliaged forms, but should be much more widely planted for their excellent performance and refreshingly cool summer color. 'Green Lace' and 'Waterfall' are good varieties that thrive in sun or shade; both have excellent clear yellow fall foliage.

'Inaba-shidare'. Purple-red foliage does not bronze; turns brilliant red in fall. Habit is more upright and vigorous than most. (Inaba is a red-leaved rice plant; *shidare* means "cascading" or "weeping.")

'Orangeola'. Spring leaves of bright orange-red mature reddish green, with new summer growth retaining orange-red color. Foliage turns dark red in late summer before becoming bright orange-red for fall. Vigorous upright habit, but matures smaller than most laceleafs.

'Red Dragon'. Deep purple-red foliage holds its color longer in summer than any other strongly weeping red-leaved cultivar; fall color is bright scarlet.

'Seiryû' (Blue-green Dragon). Unusual among laceleaf forms in being upright and tree-like in form, eventually to 15 ft. (4.5 m). Bright bluish green leaves are tipped red in spring, turning to yellow and gold with red highlights in fall. Best in light shade; very graceful.

'Tamukeyama'. Deep burgundy-red foliage does not bronze and is very scorch-resistant, even in full sun; turns scarlet in fall. Known in Japan since 1710 (named for Mount Tamuke) and still considered the best red laceleaf form by many. Open, semi-weeping habit; if grafted high, can become tree-like in maturity.

Related taxa

Commonly listed with and displayed as Japanese maples, the following maples enjoy the same cultural conditions as *Acer palmatum* and have similar looks and growth rates.

Acer buergerianum (trident maple). Native to China; naturalized in Japan. Small ivy-shaped leaves with three lobes are very shiny; new growth is red. Good long-lasting fall color of red, orange, and purple. Species is slow growing upright tree to 20 ft. (6 m), but is best known for its shrub-like dwarf cultivars (many containing the word *yatsubusa*, Japanese for "dwarf") that are popular in containers and for training as bonsai.

Acer japonicum 'Aconitifolium' (fernleaf maple). Large, deeply divided leaves with each wide lobe further divided, giving a feathery or fern-like texture. Foliage is reddish in spring, bright green in summer; long-lasting fall foliage is fiery red, orange, and gold. Likes well-drained heavy soil; tolerates our

Acer palmatum var. *dissectum* 'Orangeola' in fall

Acer shirasawanum 'Aureum' in late spring

Acer palmatum var. *dissectum* 'Seiryû' in summer

normal summer drought in cool sun or light shade. Slow upright growth to 15 ft. (4.5 m).

Acer shirasawanum 'Aureum' (syn. *A. japonicum* 'Aureum'; golden full moon maple). Nearly round, 11-lobed leaves closely resembling those of vine maple are a beautiful clear yellow in spring, darkening slightly to greenish yellow in summer. Pink flowers and red seedpods make an attractive contrast. In fall, leaves turn red and orange starting at tips, briefly leaving circular golden "full moons" in centers. Needs good light for best color but burns badly in intense sun; best site is one in open shade or shaded between 11:00 a.m. and 4:00 p.m. Likes well-drained heavy soil and is drought tolerant in light shade. Outstanding in cool-summer subregions. Slow rounded growth to 10–15 ft. (3–4.5 m).

Acer platanoides (Norway maple). Native to Europe but widely naturalized in temperate regions; considered invasive in northeastern North America, where it outcompetes native maples in hardwood forests. Also considered invasive on moist river banks in the Pacific Northwest, but with the nearest maple forests half a continent away, the threat of invasion is much less significant.

The self-seeding species itself should nonetheless be avoided, but cultivars are much less aggressive and pose no problems in residential gardens. Fast growth rate, pleasing form, beautiful foliage, and good resistance to pests and diseases make them good choices for large shade and specimen trees; strong limbs

Acer platanoides 'Crimson Sentry' in summer

hold up well to wet snow. Deep fibrous roots make them thoroughly drought tolerant and scorch-resistant but not always easy to garden under; vigorous groundcovers are often the best solution. Watch for root girdling. Zones 4 to 9.

'Crimson King'. Well-known, well-behaved shade tree; black-red leaves turn bright deep red in fall. Yellow spring flowers are showy among new leaves, which emerge glowing red. Upright rounded growth to 40 ft. × 30 ft. (12 m × 9 m).

Acer platanoides 'Drummondii'

Acer rubrum 'Franksred' (Red Sunset) in fall

Acer 'Warrenred' (Pacific Sunset) in fall

'Crimson Sentry'. Sport of 'Crimson King' with densely foliaged columnar habit; good in confined spaces or for accent. 25 ft. × 15 ft. (7.5 m × 4.5 m).

'Deborah'. Massive but not overwhelming. New leaves emerge red-maroon, turning dark bronze-green in summer; fall color is deep gold. 45 ft. × 40 ft. (13.5 m × 12 m).

'Drummondii'. Large leaves of light green strongly variegated creamy white. Needs rich, moist soil and protection from hot or intense sun to look its best, but makes a striking feature when well grown. Any branches that revert to plain green should be removed promptly. Slow growth to 25 ft. × 20 ft. (7.5 m × 6 m).

'Globosum'. Small tree with dense globular crown makes perfect lollipop shape; good in small spaces and under utility wires. 15 ft. (4.5 m) high and wide.

Acer rubrum (red maple). Native to eastern North America. The only eastern maple that performs consistently in the Pacific Northwest; although it seldom reaches full potential in size, fall color is reliable even in our mildest subregions. Trees are drought tolerant and healthy, with no serious problems. Zones 4 to 9.

'Franksred' (Red Sunset). Smallish green leaves on upright, vigorous tree turn deep orange and red in early fall; much used as a street tree. To 40 ft. × 30 ft. (12 m × 9 m).

'October Glory'. Dense, almost perfectly globular crown of glossy green leaves turns deep clear red in late fall; colors best in hot-summer valleys. To 30 ft. (9 m) high and wide.

Acer 'Warrenred' (Pacific Sunset). Hybrid of *A. platanoides* and *A. truncatum*, native to China; resembles a smaller Norway maple. Very glossy leaves emerge purple-red, maturing dark green; fall color is bright yellow-orange with orange-red highlights. Very healthy and vigorous. Upright growth to 30 ft. (9 m).

Cercidiphyllum japonicum in fall

CERCIDIPHYLLUM JAPONICUM (KATSURA)

Origin: Japan and China

Hardiness zones: 4 to 8

Size: 20–30 ft. × 15–20 ft. (6–9 m × 4.5–6 m); eventually larger

Season of interest: Fall (foliage color); spring (new leaves)

Exposure: Cool sun to partial shade

Soil preference: Deep, rich, moisture-retentive but well drained; acidic

Water needs: Moderate

Maintenance needs: Low

Subregions best suited: Puget Sound, Georgia Basin/Puget Trough, Pacific Coast

Subregions not suited: None

Possible problems: Leaves burn in hot sun or dry soil

Refined, well-behaved specimen tree; beautiful in all seasons. Multi-trunked habit and arching branching pattern give it a very appealing winter silhouette. In early spring, new heart-shaped leaves on nodding stalks are deep burgundy, resembling those of redbud (*Cercis*), which gives its generic name (meaning "leaves like *Cercis*"). Leaves gradually turn bluish green, retaining their burgundy veining until early summer. Best show of all comes in fall, when leaves turn beautiful shades of yellow/ peach/orange and release a light but noticeable fragrance of burnt sugar as they fall.

Although it can eventually reach 40 ft. (12 m) or more, katsura (its Japanese name) always appears graceful; its small, neatly arranged leaves gives the tree an airy, elegant look, something like a birch—but without any of birch's problems: katsura is one of the most pest- and disease-free of all ornamental trees. Its non-aggressive root system is also very congenial, allowing the planting of woodland or shade-loving plants beneath it.

Adequate soil moisture is very important, especially for young trees. Although drought tolerance increases with maturity, katsura's thin leaves will always tend to scorch in dry soil, dry winds, or hot sun. Regular deep watering in summer is necessary in warmer and/or drier subregions; mulch and/or the placement of leafy shrubs on its south side help considerably by keeping the roots cool.

One of very few ornamental trees that grows well in moderate shade, katsura is an ideal choice for gardens hemmed in by tall conifers or tall buildings. In our hotter river valleys, afternoon shade is almost mandatory; in coastal areas full sun is fine and brings out the best fall color. Leave it plenty of space; the arching branches spread almost horizontal in maturity.

'Morioka Weeping'. Similar to *Cercidiphyllum japonicum* f. *pendulum* in size and habit, but branches arch up and outward before becoming strongly weeping. Effect is somewhat like weeping birch, especially in maturity. Vigorous.

f. *pendulum* (syn. *Cercidiphyllum magnificum* f. *pendulum*; weeping katsura). An even more graceful tree; main trunk grows upright, with weeping branches that are rather stiff when young. Weeping habit and gracefulness increase with maturity. Excellent choice on north or east side of tall, dark green conifers. 15–20 ft. × 10–15 ft. (4.5–6 m × 3–4.5 m); eventually taller.

CORNUS (FLOWERING DOGWOOD)

Origin: China, Korea, Japan, North America

Hardiness zones: Varies

Size: Varies

Season of interest: May to July (showy bracts); fall (foliage and fruits)

Exposure: Light shade to cool sun, protected from hot or intense sun

Soil preference: Cool, high humus content, moisture-retentive but well drained; acidic

Water needs: Moderately to fully drought tolerant when established

Maintenance needs: Low

Subregions best suited: All

Possible problems: Dogwood anthracnose (see sidebar), powdery mildew

The term "flowering dogwood" can be a bit confusing, since all member of the genus *Cornus* bear flowers. Shrub dogwoods (*C. alba*, *C. sanguinea*, and our native *C. sericea*) all bear clusters of small white flowers; Cornelian cherry (*C. mas*), a shrub-like European tree, bears small yellow flowers on bare branches in late winter. Even bunchberry (*C. canadensis*), a North American native groundcover, bears tiny true flowers and showy white petal-like bracts that are actually modified leaves. In addition, flowering dogwood is the widely used common name of *C. florida*, a species native to eastern North America.

However, most Pacific Northwesterners use the term "flowering dogwood" to mean any of the tree forms that bear long-lasting flower-like bracts of white or pink in late spring and early summer. (The small true flowers in the center of these bracts produce showy red fall fruits that attract birds.)

Few flowering trees are more gracefully beautiful or natural-looking than these trees that love the conditions of woodland edges—and few flowering trees are more sensitive to growing conditions that differ from these conditions. Fortunately, the Pacific Northwest can provide exactly what they need: plenty of moisture in winter and spring, slightly to moderately acidic soil, and summers on the cool side, with sunlight that's not too hot or intense (especially important for pink cultivars). Flowering dogwoods have no objection to our heavy soils as long as they're well drained; most species (including our native *Cornus nuttallii*) prefer heavy soil, which allows them to handle our normal summer drought with ease.

Of course these conditions do not occur everywhere, even within the same garden, so it's up to us gardeners to find or create sites that provide them. Siting flowering dogwoods well is nine-tenths of their success; once happily established in a congenial spot, they're very undemanding and in fact are best left undisturbed.

The bark of all flowering dogwoods is very thin and tender, making the trunks vulnerable to sunburn in summer and bark splitting in winter. In addition, any wounds in the sensitive bark (including the most careful pruning cuts) are slow to heal, making them potential entry points for fungal diseases.

In nature, flowering dogwoods are smart enough to grow on the north or east side of tall conifers or other forest trees so that afternoon shade protects their tender bark. Mature trees also grow their own shade, either in the form of low-growing branches or multiple trunks well clothed with leaves. There are three excellent reasons for never removing these lower branches or any of the multiple trunks: it leaves the bark of the lower trunk unprotected, invites diseases to enter the pruning cuts, and spoils the graceful natural form of the tree.

As important as shade is for the bark, especially on the trunk, flowering dogwoods are not true shade-lovers; they need at least four to six hours of direct but cool sun (morning and/or late afternoon) to bloom well. On the cool, sun-challenged coast, they can take full sun. Little fertilizer is needed, but a reasonably fertile soil high in organic matter is a requirement. Mulch helps take the place of the leafy forest litter these trees depend on in their natural habitats to keep their roots cool and see them through droughts.

The worst site for a flowering dogwood, both culturally and visually, is in the middle of a lawn with grass up to its trunk. Not only will it look forlorn there, but it won't get the cool, partially shaded conditions it needs. It may also be exposed to high-nitrogen fertilizer and regular summer watering, both of which can cause problems, and to the potentially lethal hazard of string trimmers.

In nature, flowering dogwoods are never found standing alone like this, but always in close association with other trees, including other dogwoods. Not surprisingly, these forest-edge trees fare best (and definitely look best) in the company of other trees. A perfect site visually as well as culturally is in the lee of large, dark-foliaged conifers. Their liking for company is also an excuse to plant several dogwoods in close proximity, which is another visually and culturally perfect siting.

Ideal sites are large beds or borders backed by taller trees that provide afternoon shade. These beds can be beautifully completed by the addition of low-growing, acid-loving shrubs, ferns, and groundcovers; spring-blooming bulbs are also natural companions. New specimens need careful planting and summer watering for their first two or three years, but once established, will provide decades of incomparable low-maintenance beauty.

Cornus controversa (giant dogwood). Native to Japan and China. Very wide-spreading horizontal branches give a tiered or layered look. Similar in effect to *C. alternifolia* (pagoda dogwood), a native of eastern North America (another of those China/

DOGWOOD ANTHRACNOSE

This fungal disease specific to flowering dogwoods was introduced simultaneously on both the east and west coasts of North America in the mid-1970s. Appropriately called *Discula destructiva*, the fungus proceeded to devastate natural stands of both *Cornus florida*, native to eastern North America, and *C. nuttallii*, our native Pacific dogwood.

The disease begins as leaf spots or blotches, then proceeds to kill entire leaves (dead leaves tend to remain on branches). If not checked, it invades small branches, then larger branches, especially the lowest ones. Dogwood anthracnose is not necessarily fatal; some established native plants have lived with the disease for many years, and a few have more or less recovered. It is, however, very serious and potentially lethal, especially to very young, very old, or very stressed trees.

No cure has yet been found, and fungicides of any kind are only partially effective, so the best solution is to choose disease-resistant species and cultivars. For vulnerable existing specimens, the disease is best managed or prevented by reducing environmental stresses. Infection is least likely in healthy, well-sited trees; stressed or injured plants are most vulnerable, especially during mild, moist weather in late spring and early summer. (About the only blessing of our recent droughts has been the retreat of dogwood anthracnose.)

Never prune a flowering dogwood if it can possibly be avoided, since any opening in the bark creates an entry for the fungus. (Needless to say, don't go anywhere near a flowering dogwood with a string trimmer.) However, since the fungus overwinters in dead tissue, any dead twigs should be cut off as soon as practicable. Do this during prolonged dry weather only, disinfecting pruning tools after each cut; the same applies to any larger branches that must be removed.

Avoid high-nitrogen fertilizer, since succulent new growth is also vulnerable to infection. Do not water established specimens, especially of *Cornus nuttallii*, unless severely stressed by drought. If necessary, water deeply at ground level to avoid wetting the foliage. Mulch the root zone to conserve moisture in summer, but keep mulch from actually touching the trunk.

Dogwood anthracnose (*Discula destructiva*). Photo by Heide Hermary

Make sure the site is shady enough to protect the tender bark, but not so shady that foliage cannot dry quickly after rain. Air circulation should also be good; nearby vegetation may need some thinning. Gather and dispose of all leaves that fall any time between spring and fall; also pull off and destroy any dead, shriveled leaves remaining on the tree.

eastern North America coincidences), but even better suited to our climate; appears to be immune to dogwood anthracnose. Does not have the typical showy bracts of other flowering dogwoods; small white flowers are like those of shrub dogwoods, in rounded clusters. Small blue-black fruits attract birds; fall colors are mainly reds and purples. Pruning the horizontal branches would be a crime, so leave it lots of room. To 30 ft. × 40 ft. (9 m × 12 m); Zones 5 to 9.

'June Snow'. Fast growing and wide-spreading; large rounded flowerheads of creamy white can reach 6 in. (15 cm) in diameter. Fall foliage is orange, yellow, red, and purple.

'Variegata'. White-variegated leaves are striking, especially in light shade where it's best sited. Small but profuse creamy white flowers in May add to breathtaking effect. Smaller than species but still wide-spreading; much larger than similar *Cornus alternifolia* 'Argentea'. 15 ft. × 20 ft. (4.5 m × 6 m).

Cornus 'Eddie's White Wonder'. Hybrid of *C. florida* and our native *C. nuttallii* made in the 1940s by nurseryman Henry M. Eddie of Vancouver, British Columbia; patented in 1964. Vigorous, floriferous tree closely resembles *C. nuttallii* but is far easier to transplant and much more adaptable to garden conditions. Excellent choice for native/natural gardens or simply for incomparable look of *C. nuttallii* without its problems. Despite high susceptibility of both parents to dogwood anthracnose, hybrid vigor gives it moderate to good disease resistance. Drought tolerant; performs beautifully in Pacific Northwest conditions when well sited. To 30 ft. × 20 ft. (9 m × 6 m); Zones 6 to 9.

Cornus 'Eddie's White Wonder'

Cornus florida 'Welchii' in summer

Cornus florida (flowering dogwood). Native to eastern North America. Species and its scores of beautiful cultivars are no longer recommended due to high susceptibility to dogwood anthracnose; whole native stands have been decimated since the 1970s. One bright note is that a few healthy specimens found in otherwise devastated stands appear to have natural immunity; several, such as 'Appalachian Spring', have already been cloned. Keep in mind that all cultivars of *C. florida* are best suited to the warmer, more humid summer conditions of eastern North America.

One cultivar that continues to do well in the Pacific Northwest and appears to have good disease resistance is 'Welchii' (syn. 'Tricolor'), a shrub-like form with leaves beautifully variegated cream, yellow, and pink. Fall color is deep pink and maroon. Best in light shade with regular summer watering. Slow growth to 12–15 ft. × 10–12 ft. (3.6–4.5 m × 3–3.6 m); Zones 6 to 9.

Cornus 'KN30-8' (Venus). Newer hybrid made by Elwin Orton of Rutgers University in New Jersey; parentage is three-quarters *C. kousa* and one-quarter *C. nuttallii*. Compact, wide-spreading tree is covered with very large (to 6 in., 15 cm) four- to six-petalled bracts of pure white. Very promising; appears to be vigorous, drought tolerant, and highly disease-resistant. To 20 ft. × 25 ft. (6 m × 7.5 m); Zones 6 to 9.

Cornus kousa (Korean dogwood). Native to Korea and Japan. Best-adapted introduced species for the Pacific Northwest and by far the most resistant to dogwood anthracnose. Large shrub or small tree with spreading habit; blooms heavily in June and July with narrow, slightly pointed four-petalled bracts of creamy white. Conspicuous orange-red fruits, fall foliage color of bronze and red, and pleasing winter silhouette make it a four-season plant. Needs acidic soil; drought tolerant in light shade to cool sun. 20 ft. × 15 ft. (6 m × 4.5 m); Zones 4 to 9.

var. *chinensis* (Chinese dogwood). Taller, more tree-like variety native to China. Larger leaves and larger bracts than species; fall foliage is deep burgundy and red. Very drought tolerant and cold-hardy, but some authorities consider it slightly less disease-resistant than species. However, the selected form 'Milky Way' is considered highly disease-resistant; it has prolific, long-lasting bracts of pure white.

'Samzan' (Samaratin). Sport of 'Milky Way' with attractively wavy, gray-green leaves with wide margin of creamy white. Best in light shade.

'Satomi'. Wide overlapping bracts of deep pink; good show of bright red fruits. Fall foliage is deep burgundy and red. Best in cool conditions; highly resistant to dogwood anthracnose.

Cornus kousa var. *chinensis*

Cornus kousa 'Satomi'

Cornus nuttallii

Cornus 'Rutgan' (Stellar Pink)

Cornus nuttallii (Pacific dogwood). Native to the Pacific Northwest; provincial flower of British Columbia. Much loved for its large, long-lasting white bracts of four to six petals in May and June; often reblooms in August. Strawberry-like fruits attract birds; fall foliage is subtle but colorful blend of deep gold, rose, and maroon. Tragically, it is also susceptible to dogwood anthracnose. The worst of the devastation that began in the 1970s appears to be over, however, and native plants still stand-

ing may have natural resistance (see previous sidebar for tips on how best to prevent infection).

Difficult to transplant and not well adapted to garden conditions (the look-alike hybrid 'Eddie's White Wonder' makes an excellent substitute). Existing native trees are best honored by not pruning, not feeding, and not watering in summer: they're perfectly adapted to our wet-winter, dry-summer climate, especially on heavier soils. To 50 ft. × 40 ft. (15 m × 12 m); Zones 6 to 9.

Cornus Stellar Series. Series of newer hybrids of *C. florida* and *C. kousa* bred for high disease resistance by Elwin Orton at Rutgers University. Vigorous, wide-spreading plants are compact and very floriferous as well as disease-resistant; resemble *C. kousa* in flower form, habit, and blooming time (June and July). Showy fall fruits and fall foliage of deep reds and burgundies.

'Rutban' (Aurora). Creamy white bracts with almost round petals bloom heavily; fall foliage is brilliant red.

'Rutdan' (Celestial; originally sold as Galaxy). Round-petalled bracts open greenish white but mature bright white; highly resistant to powdery mildew.

'Rutgan' (Stellar Pink). Large bracts with wide overlapping petals are soft pink at tips, shading to white at centers. Very graceful appearance.

Magnolia 'Susan'

The other two hybrids, crosses of the same species but using different cultivars, are the most different of the group.

'Jane'. Late-blooming, very fragrant flowers are pinkish purple on outside, white on inside. Vigorous.

'Pinkie'. Latest to bloom (May). Large cup-shaped flowers are pale purplish pink on outside, white inside. Compact grower.

Magnolia 'Elizabeth'. Hybrid of *M. denudata* and *M. acuminata*. First and most famous of yellow-flowered magnolias, selected in 1978. Large, well-formed flowers that bloom just as leaves appear are cream-colored in cool weather, primrose-yellow in warmer weather, especially when they first open. Vigorous multi-trunked tree to 25 ft. (7.5 m) high and wide; midseason. Zones 4 to 9.

Magnolia 'Galaxy'. Hybrid of *M. liliiflora* 'Nigra' and the exotic, semi-tender *M. sprengeri* var. *diva*, native to the Himalaya. Large, prolific reddish purple buds open to waterlily-shaped flowers of rich, deep purplish pink, lighter on insides. Very long blooming season. Sister seedling 'Spectrum' has fewer but larger, more intensely colored flowers. Both can reach 30 ft. (9 m) in height; 'Galaxy' has a strongly pyramidal form. Both early; Zones 5 to 9.

Magnolia grandiflora (southern magnolia). Evergreen. Native to southeastern United States, evoking "Gone with the Wind" genteel elegance. Can reach 90 ft. (27 m) in its native habitat, but rarely gets over 40 ft. (12 m) in the Pacific Northwest, even in the Willamette subregion, where it is best suited and commonly planted as a street tree. Widely tolerant of growing conditions, but at its magnificent best where summers are hot, soils are deep and moisture-retentive (preferably light-textured), and winds are light; large, leathery, glossy green leaves that can reach 10 in. (25 cm) can be torn to shreds in strong winter winds.

Perfectly formed, lemon-scented, pure white flowers may be over 12 in. (30 cm) in diameter. Although individual flowers last only two to four days, they're produced from July to October and are followed by decorative orange-red seedpods.

'Edith Bogue'. Full and bushy in form, with narrow leaves that hold up well to wet snow. Most cold-hardy cultivar. Zones 5 to 9.

Magnolia grandiflora. Photo by Tom Fischer

'Russet'. Compact and fast growing, with narrowly pyramidal habit; excellent for smaller gardens. Narrow leaves with orange-brown tomentum (dense, felt-like short hairs) on undersides. Large, fragrant flowers bloom at a young age. Zones 6 to 9.

'Samuel Sommer'. Large oval leaves with rusty brown tomentum; flowers are 10–14 in. (25–35 cm) in diameter. Dense, compact growth on fast growing rounded tree; considered the finest cultivar by many. Zones 7 to 9.

'Victoria'. Particularly hardy plant found in Victoria, British Columbia; popular in cooler-summer parts of the Pacific Northwest. Broad, handsome leaves have reddish tomentum; flowers are medium-large and profuse. Zones 6 to 9.

Magnolia 'Iolanthe'. Hybrid with same parentage as 'Atlas'. Profuse, bowl-shaped, outfacing flowers of soft lilac-pink, lighter on inside, are 10 in. (25 cm) in diameter; bloom over a long season. Huge fuzzy buds are attractive in late winter. 20 ft. (6 m) high and wide; early. Zones 6 to 9.

Magnolia liliiflora (Mulan, lily magnolia). Native to China; long cultivated throughout eastern Asia. Lily-shaped upright flowers vary from dark pink to purple; flower over a long season. Species itself is seldom grown, but it and its cultivar 'Nigra' are

Magnolia ×loebneri 'Leonard Messel'

Magnolia ×loebneri 'Merrill'

Magnolia ×soulangeana 'Alba'

Magnolia sieboldii

extremely important in magnolia breeding. 15 ft. (4.5 m) high and wide; midseason. Zones 4 to 9.

'Nigra'. Vigorous form with deep purple flowers, lighter inside; exceptionally long blooming season.

Magnolia ×loebneri. Hybrid of *M. kobus*, a Japanese species with star-like white flowers, and *M. stellata*. Masses of fragrant, star-like flowers with many strap-shaped tepals bloom at a much earlier age than *M. kobus*; slightly later blooming time than *M. stellata* means flowers are less likely to be damaged by frost. Hybrid vigor, wide adaptability, compact size, and resistance to wind make these outstanding cultivars. To 15 ft. (4.5 m) high and wide; midseason. Zones 4 to 9.

'Ballerina'. Fragrant white flowers with up to 30 tepals are tinged pink at base; decorative red seedpods follow in fall. Can become small tree. Midseason.

'Leonard Messel'. Chance seedling; rapidly becoming a favorite worldwide. Large, frost-resistant flowers with 12 tepals are pale pink in cooler weather; rich lilac-pink in warmer weather. Midseason.

'Merrill'. Vigorous plant with large, dazzling white flowers with up to 12 tepals. Can reach 30 ft. (9 m) in height and width in time. Midseason.

Magnolia ×soulangeana 'Picture'

Magnolia ×soulangeana 'Rustica Rubra'

Magnolia sieboldii. Native to Japan, Korea, and China. Usually small and shrubby, but can reach 15 ft. (4.5 m) in height and width. Small, nodding, very sweetly scented flowers of pure white with prominent red stamens open a few at a time between late May and July. Decorative seedpods of bright pink follow. Needs site protected from late frosts, which will not harm plant but can kill flower buds. Excellent in smaller gardens and in containers. Zones 7 to 9.

Magnolia ×soulangeana (saucer magnolia). Named for Etienne Soulange-Bodin, a French cavalry officer in the Napoleonic wars who famously remarked, following those debacles, that it would have been better if both sides had stayed home and planted their cabbages. Further observing that gardening is "one of the most agreeable guarantees" of a peace-loving world, he founded France's Royal Institute of Horticulture; his crossing of *M. denudata* and *M. liliiflora* resulted in the spectacular and widely variable tree named after him.

Numerous clones exist, with flowers varying from tulip-shaped to cup-and-saucer-shaped to goblet-shaped; colors are various combinations of white and pinkish purple. All eventually become wide-spreading, multi-trunked trees to 25 ft. (7.5 m) high and wide, or larger. Lightly fragrant flowers start

opening in midseason, escaping most frosts; established plants may bloom for six to eight weeks. Zones 7 to 9.

'Alba' (syn. 'Alba Superba'). Pure white tulip-shaped flowers with hint of pinkish purple at bases. Early to midseason.

'Lennei'. Enormous goblet-shaped flowers, reddish purple on outside and creamy white on inside. Upright, vigorous small tree. Midseason.

'Lennei Alba'. Profuse flowers of ivory-white resemble those of *Magnolia denudata*. Early to midseason.

'Picture'. Large, upright, cup-and-saucer white flowers are streaked rosy purple from bases to mid-tips of tepals; vigorous plant. Midseason.

'Rustica Rubra'. Similar to 'Lennei' except that goblet-shaped flowers are rosy purple on outside, white on inside. Midseason.

'San Jose'. Fragrant goblet-shaped flowers, deep pink on outside and white on inside; color is most intense in warm weather. Midseason.

Magnolia stellata (star magnolia). Native to Japan. Slow growing, densely branched shrub eventually wider than tall. White flowers with strap-shaped tepals, sometimes tinged pink. Very early (late January in protected sites in the Willamette subregion); flowers are breathtakingly beautiful on bare branches, but often spoiled by frost. Leaves are smaller than those of most magnolias, giving a more delicate look even when not in flower. Usually to 10 ft. × 12 ft. (3 m × 3.6 m), but can become small tree. Zones 4 to 9.

'Jane Platt'. Very floriferous, each flower having up to 30 tepals of deep, rich pink. Named for Jane Kerr Platt of Portland, Oregon, who grew it as *Magnolia stellata* 'Rosea', a much lighter pink clone.

'Royal Star'. Pale pink buds open to many-tepalled flowers of icy white. Blooms two to three weeks later than species, escaping worst frosts, but still needs sheltered site.

'Waterlily'. Beautifully formed flowers are larger than species and have more tepals than 'Royal Star', but are not as dazzling white.

Malus floribunda

MALUS (FLOWERING CRABAPPLE)

Origin: Northern temperate regions worldwide, especially northeastern Asia

Hardiness zones: 4 to 9

Size: Varies

Blooming season: April and May

Exposure: Full sun, good air circulation

Soil preference: Heavy, moderately fertile; slightly acidic

Water needs: Drought tolerant when established

Maintenance needs: Low to moderate

Subregions best suited: All

Possible problems: Cedar-apple rust, fireblight, powdery mildew, scab

The Pacific Northwest may not be the most ideal place for flowering crabapples—many would be happier in more continental climates with less constant humidity—but their merits are such that most of us can't imagine gardening without them.

Unlike many flowering trees, crabapples remain small even in maturity, making them suitable for smaller gardens. They also take well to pruning, with no concerns over inviting disease or spoiling their shape. Along with roses and other members of the family Rosaceae, they love the heavy soils of our river valleys, sending their roots deep and wide to make them thoroughly drought tolerant.

They're also perfectly content in moist soil and don't object even if drainage is a bit slow, as long as water never stands on their roots. They take heat, cold, and the vagaries of our spring weather with aplomb. They don't even mind rocky soil, which is a major bonus in the glacial till so widespread north of Olympia.

Their beautiful flowers, small and single but very profuse, bloom for only a short time in spring, but this is balanced by their long second season of interest in fall and winter, when their small but highly decorative "crabs" provide welcome seasonal color. Some of these persist all winter; others are relished by birds, who ignore them when they first ripen but devour

them as soon as they begin to ferment. Plant crabapples where you can observe the highly entertaining antics of slightly tipsy birds in late fall, but be sure to shoo them away before they get too inebriated and become easy prey for cats.

Because larger-fruited varieties are often called "edible crabapples," many people assume the much smaller fruits of flowering crabapples are at least somewhat toxic. They definitely are not. Although too small to be worth picking or preserving, all are unquestionably edible (as long as they have not been sprayed), making them good choices where small children are around.

One downside to flowering crabapples is that their prodigious blooming temporarily exhausts the trees, giving them a forlorn morning-after-the-night-before look for a week or two. Root suckering is another minor annoyance, even on own-root trees; these are easily dealt with by pulling (not cutting) suckers in early June, when they detach most readily.

A far more serious problem is susceptibility to disease—especially, in our climate, scab. Cedar-apple rust, which requires the presence of junipers as an alternate host, is uncommon in our area, as is fireblight; mildew is always a possibility in late summer but is far less a concern than scab, which is endemic in our mild, wet springs.

Unfortunately, cultivars with poor scab resistance—and their numbers are legion—have given all flowering crabapples an undeserved bad name. Purple-foliage cultivars in particular seem to be scab-susceptible; names to avoid include 'Liset' (also prone to mildew), 'Pink Spires', 'Profusion', 'Radiant', 'Red Barron', 'Royalty' (also prone to fireblight), and 'Thunderchild'. The older purple-brown 'Hopa' (whose name in the Pacific Northwest should be 'Hopeless') should be avoided like the plague, as it is very susceptible to disease in our climate.

Weeping crabapples, including the popular 'Red Jade' and 'Weepcanzam' (Weeping Candied Apple) also seem more prone to disease here, although some newer weeping forms look promising. Miscellaneous crabapples to avoid in our climate include 'Echtermeyer', 'Makamik', 'Spring Snow', 'Van Eseltine', and *Malus ioensis* 'Plena' (syn. 'Bechtel').

It should be noted that the cultivars just mentioned may perform perfectly well in climates differing from ours (even 'Hopa' excels in southern California). Unfortunately, because they are often highly rated in general reference books and nationwide magazines, many of these are still offered for sale locally. This just goes to show the importance of choosing cultivars well suited to particular climates, especially a climate as unique as ours. The good news is that many newer flowering crabapples are highly resistant to scab and other diseases and perform beautifully in moist, cool Pacific Northwest springs.

"Large" crabs are those 0.5 in. (12 mm) or larger; "small" crabs are those ⅜ in. (10 mm) or less. "Persistent" refers to fruit that remains on the tree well into winter. Scab will always be the main concern in our climate, but rest assured that none of the scab-resistant cultivars included here are highly susceptible to any other disease.

Malus baccata 'Jackii'. Sometimes listed as *M. b.* var. *jackii*; species is native to Korea, northern China, Manchuria, and Siberia.

Large, profuse, early-blooming flowers of pure white are set off by deep green healthy foliage; crabs are purplish red. Large, vigorous tree to 25 ft. × 20 ft. (7.5 m × 6 m) has long been popular in the Pacific Northwest. Highly resistant to scab and mildew; very slightly susceptible to fireblight.

Malus 'Cardinal'. Bright magenta-pink flowers and large red crabs; purple-red glossy foliage holds its color all summer. Large spreading tree to 15 ft. × 25 ft. (4.5 m × 7.5 m) has excellent scab resistance but is very slightly susceptible to fireblight. One of the most disease-resistant purple-foliaged crabapples to date.

Malus 'Evereste'. Bright red oval crabs reaching 2 in. (5 cm) are highly decorative as well as edible; if not picked, they persist well into winter. Although tree is large and rounded in form, weight of fruits can bend branches into permanently weeping shape. Fragrant white flowers in spring are showy. Disease-resistant tree appears to be immune to scab. To 20 ft. (6 m) high and wide.

Malus floribunda (Japanese flowering crabapple). Native to Japan. Bright red buds open to unbelievably profuse flowers that are white on insides and pink on outsides, giving three-toned effect. Small yellow crabs, sometimes flushed red. Light green foliage appears very early on semi-weeping, wide-spreading tree to 15 ft. × 25 ft. (4.5 m × 7.5 m). Somewhat susceptible to fireblight and not always that great for scab resistance, but graceful, irregular form and unsurpassed floral display keep it popular.

Malus 'Jewelberry'. Pink buds open to white flowers with pink margins fairly late in season; large, bright red crabs are persistent. Healthy green foliage on dwarf spreading tree to 8 ft. × 12 ft. (2.4 m × 3.6 m). Very slight susceptibility to fireblight; excellent resistance to scab.

Malus 'Louisa'. Strongly weeping form with blush-pink flowers and dark green glossy foliage; small yellow crabs. Graceful small tree to 15 ft. (4.5 m) high and wide; needs staking to establish upright trunk. Good resistance to most diseases, including excellent resistance to scab; one of the most promising disease-resistant weeping forms.

Malus 'Prairie Fire'. Sometimes listed as 'Prairifire'. Late-blooming deep red buds open to large flowers of bright raspberry-red; color changes daily, becoming rose-red infused with a smoky blue that somehow never approaches purple. Fades to an indescribable color; "pinkish gray" doesn't do it justice. New leaves emerge dark red, becoming red-tinted green by summer; bright bronze-orange in fall. Abundant small crabs start out purple, turn bright red. Vigorous semi-weeping tree to 20 ft. (6 m) in height and width. Very slightly susceptible to fireblight, but impervious to scab and other diseases.

Malus 'Purple Prince'. Dark rose-red flowers and maroon crabs; foliage emerges purple, turning bronze-green in summer. Vigorous upright tree with spreading branches, to 20 ft. (6 m) high

Malus 'Prairie Fire'

and wide. Slightly susceptible to mildew, but much less so than similarly colored 'Liset'. Excellent resistance to scab makes it a good replacement for maroon-red flowers and crabs of once-popular 'Royalty'.

Malus ×*robusta* 'Red Sentinel'. Showy red buds open to white flowers blushed pink; foliage is bright green and glossy. Large, bright red crabs persist all winter and even into spring. Vigorous, vase-shaped upright tree to 20 ft. × 12 ft. (6 m × 4.2 m). Highly resistant to scab and other diseases.

Malus 'Strawberry Parfait'. Large light pink flowers have deeper pink margins, giving two-toned effect; small dark red crabs are persistent. Leaves emerge reddish purple, turning deep green by summer. Large, irregular-shaped tree to 18 ft. × 25 ft. (5.5 m × 7.5 m) has unique character. Very slight susceptibility to fireblight, but excellent resistance to scab and other diseases.

Malus transitoria 'Schmidtcutleaf' (Golden Raindrops). Species, native to northwestern China and Tibet, is known as cutleaf crabapple for its narrow, deeply lobed leaves, which give the tree a delicate appearance and provide good fall color. Red buds open to small white flowers; tiny but abundant crabs are bright golden yellow. Excellent resistance to scab and most other dis-

Malus ×zumi 'Professor Sprenger'

eases, but slightly susceptible to fireblight. Upright, vase-shaped tree to 20 ft. × 15 ft. (6 m × 4.5 m).

Malus ×zumi var. *calocarpa* (redbud crabapple). Native to Japan. Dark red buds open to profuse white flowers; abundant small red crabs are persistent and very decorative. Large, vigorous, rounded tree to 20 ft. × 25 ft. (6 m × 7.5 m). Very slight susceptibility to mildew, but excellent resistance to scab and other diseases.

Malus ×zumi 'Professor Sprenger'. Red buds open to fragrant flowers of white blushed pink; large, abundant crabs of an unusual bright orange persist all winter, providing welcome seasonal interest. Vigorous tree to 20 ft. (6 m) high and wide. Somewhat susceptible to fireblight but highly resistant to scab and other diseases.

PRUNUS (JAPANESE FLOWERING CHERRIES)

Origin: Japan

Hardiness zones: 5 to 9

Size: Varies

Blooming season: February to May

Exposure: Full sun

Soil preference: Fertile, slightly acidic; moisture-retentive but well drained

Water needs: Moderately drought tolerant when established

Maintenance needs: Low

Subregions best suited: All

Possible problems: Bacterial blight, blossom brown rot, gummosis, cherry bark tortrix, pear slug, tent caterpillar, winter moth

The true harbinger of spring in the Pacific Northwest is not the first crocus or the first daffodil, but the cry "The cherries are blooming in [whatever city or town is nearest]!" Exactly which cultivars these are doesn't much matter to most people, but everyone knows the blooms heralded so ecstatically are those of Japanese flowering cherries, as opposed to those of Euro-

WHAT WAS THAT NAME?

Keeping the proper names of Japanese flowering cherry cultivars straight is a daunting task. There is the usual shuffling and reshuffling into different species, with the added complication that many familiar trees once classed as selections of *Prunus serrulata* are now considered hybrids. There is also a trend to revert to their original Japanese names, which is only fitting and should have been done long ago. However, only some Japanese names (such as 'Amanogawa') are actual names; many are merely descriptive and keep reappearing in different configurations that are bewildering to English speakers. A short crash course in Japanese proves helpful.

beni. Red

higan. Very early flowering (literally "spring equinox")

kiku. Extremely double-flowered (literally "chrysanthemum")

sakura. Flowering cherry (this becomes *-zakura* in the middle of a word)

sato-zakura. Cultivated (as opposed to wild) flowering cherry

shidare. Cascading or weeping

shiro. White

yae. Double-flowered

In the descriptions offered here, we have tried to strike a balance between taxonomic correctness, most widespread usage, and just plain intelligibility. Fortunately, name changes sift through the nursery industry very slowly, so any of the synonyms given should identify the same tree.

pean, North American, or Asian species. For various biological, geographical, cultural, and historical reasons, these trees are uniquely Japanese—and nowhere outside Japan are they more popular, or better adapted, than in the Pacific Northwest.

The ancestors of Japanese flowering cherries were found in China and Korea as well, but these trees grew especially well on the rich, well-drained, slightly acidic, well-watered volcanic slopes of Japan's mountains. Being naturally variable and capable of interbreeding freely, there were soon many distinct natural hybrids flourishing in the innumerable microclimates afforded by different elevations, exposures, and local conditions. Beginning over 1000 years ago, Japanese peasants would transplant especially appealing saplings to their villages, where they self-propagated and interbred further with local species and natural hybrids.

Specific trees having special significance were deliberately propagated and given names. Some of these have been grown for centuries, changing only slightly over the years through natural mutation and local adaptation, and sometimes even coming true (or nearly true) from seed. Two of the oldest and most

Fallen cherry blossom petals

widely grown "species," *Prunus* ×*subhirtella* and *P.* ×*yedoensis*, are acknowledged hybrids and are unknown in the wild.

Gardeners all over the world have benefited from this long hybridization process, since only the healthiest, most vigorous, and most widely adaptable trees (as well as the most beautiful) were selected and reselected. However, we in the Pacific Northwest are especially fortunate in having growing conditions very similar to those of their native habitat. Our abundant annual rainfall is roughly equal; our winters are almost identical, with lots of rain and some frost, but no severe cold. (These trees cannot abide winters that are cold, dry, and sunny.) Our springs are also similar, with mild, damp days and chilly nights that prolong bloom; our warm, dry Indian summers echo Japan's warm, dry Octobers that are necessary for setting next year's flower buds.

The main difference is that rain falls throughout the year in Japan; in southern Japan rain is actually heaviest in June, just when we are drying out. Nonetheless, established trees easily handle our normal summer droughts, provided there has been adequate rainfall in April and May. Ample water is needed before, during, and immediately following bloom and must be supplied if rains do not appear.

Full sun and good air circulation are needed to avoid fungal diseases. Very early and early-blooming cultivars (especially those with double flowers) should be chosen carefully in the Puget Sound and Pacific Coast subregions, where blossom brown rot—a disfiguring but non-lethal fungal disease—can be a problem. Good drainage is also crucial: Japanese flowering cherries planted in poorly drained sites will first start oozing sap (a condition known as gummosis), more than likely leading to full-blown bacterial blight and canker. Canker can be treated, but unless drainage is improved the tree will probably decline and die. Gummosis can also be a symptom of any undue growing stress, including severe drought, so the cause must always be identified and corrected.

In the 1970s, an incurable virus was a serious problem in the Pacific Northwest (and even more serious in Japan), but the disease seems to have finally run its course and is no longer a threat. All Japanese flowering cherries sold in the West are now grown from certified virus-free stock.

Caterpillars are the number one nuisance pest, with tent caterpillars and winter moth larvae being the worst culprits. The cherry bark tortrix is more potentially serious, since damage is done by very small larvae hidden beneath the bark. Tiny holes with accumulations of very fine sawdust indicate their presence; the tunnels they make into the tree invite disease. Young trees, very old trees, and those under stress are most vulnerable. The best (and only) defense is to keep trees healthy by providing good air circulation and sunlight, feeding adequately, and watering during dry spells. Pruning should be avoided; cuts provide openings in the bark where the adult tortrix can lay eggs.

Pruning in general should be avoided, since it serves no purpose and spoils the shape of these trees. Mature tree size and especially width should be carefully considered when choosing a specimen: nothing looks more maimed than a flowering

FLOWERING CHERRY BLOOMING TIMES

Blooming time can vary with the weather, especially with early bloomers, but the blooming sequence is always the same. In most years, this is what can be expected:

Very early: Mid-March or earlier

Early: Mid-March to early April

Early midseason: Early to mid-April

Midseason: Mid- to late April

Late: Late April to early May

Prunus 'Amanogawa'

cherry with its limbs hacked off to fit a space too small for it. If possible, find out what rootstock has been used. All cherry roots sucker to some extent, but some rootstocks (such as our native bitter cherry, *Prunus emarginata*) are unacceptably profuse with suckers.

Although Japanese flowering cherries were rare anywhere in the West until the 20th century, the Pacific Northwest has rapidly made up for lost time. Victoria, Seattle, and Vancouver, B.C, are especially noted for their numerous street trees. Victoria has about 3000 trees of 23 different varieties; in Seattle, over 40 percent of the many thousands of street trees are Japanese flowering cherries. (Seattle also hosts a Cherry Blossom and Japanese Cultural Festival every April.) Vancouver, with over 36,000 trees in bloom at its annual Cherry Blossom Festival, is well on its way to achieving its ambition of becoming "the cherry tree capital of the West Coast."

Prunus 'Accolade'. Hybrid of *P. sargentii* and a selected form of *P. ×subhirtella*. Profuse semi-double flowers of deep rich pink held in drooping clusters; early bloom. Small but vigorous tree with good fall color. To 20 ft. (6 m) high and wide.

Prunus 'Amanogawa' (Heaven's River). Translated name is the Japanese term for what Westerners call the Milky Way. Unmistakable for fastigiate shape, like small Lombardy poplar. Large, lightly fragrant, light pink semi-double flowers fade to very pale pink. Early midseason bloom. Strong upright form when young, to 20 ft. × 6 ft. (6 m × 1.8 m), but branches do arch outward in maturity to 10 ft. (3 m) or more.

Prunus 'Berry' (Cascade Snow). Broadly columnar tree with dark green leaves; nice fall colors of yellow/orange/bronze. Large, single, snow-white flowers bloom early midseason; tree is exceptionally healthy and seems impervious to disease in our climate. This is a Japanese cultivar of uncertain origin, but the parent plant was found at the Berry Botanic Garden in Portland. Often sold as 'Cascade Snow'. To 25 ft. × 20 ft. (7.5 m × 6 m).

Prunus 'Kanzan' (syns. 'Kwanzan', a now-obsolete rendering of the name in the Roman alphabet, and 'Sekiyama'; both mean "bordering mountain," a term with poetic significance). A sato-zakura (cultivar) grown in Japan since the 17th century; most popular flowering cherry and quite possibly the most popular flowering tree in the Western world. Extremely adaptable, vigorous, healthy, and reliable, with exuberant midseason display of large, fully double flowers of dark pink set off by copper-colored new foliage that makes them appear even brighter. This exuberance and brightness is dismissed by some as gaudy, but so what? Spring itself is exuberant and gaudy.

Tree is distinctively vase-shaped when young, with stiffly angled branches, but becomes more fountain-shaped in maturity, especially when loaded with flowers. To 30 ft. × 25 ft. (9 m × 7.5 m) or more.

Prunus 'Kiku-shidare-zakura' (chrysanthemum weeping cherry, double weeping cherry). "Chrysanthemum" aptly describes the almost globular pompoms of clear pink flowers that bloom in early midseason. Branches extend sideways before weeping at tips, becoming thick and inflexible as they mature. The sport 'Cheal's Weeping', which is now considered by most authorities to be the same clone, is reputed to have thinner, more pliable branches but does not flower as profusely.

Prunus 'Kanzan'

Prunus 'Shirofugen'

Prunus 'Shirotae'

Usually grafted onto an upright stem, making a permanently dwarfed, mushroom-shaped mound to 6 ft. × 10 ft. (1.8 m × 3 m) or wider. Best in formal or Japanese-themed settings. New non-weeping branchlets on main framework will not revert to upright growth but will eventually arch, then weep; cutting them off gives a rigid, even grotesque look.

Prunus pendula (syn. *P. ×subhirtella* 'Pendula'; single weeping cherry, weeping spring cherry). Slender, gracefully drooping branches like those of weeping birch, often weeping to ground. Tiny single flowers of pale pink bloom early, before leaves emerge, giving delicate, see-through effect. Often grafted onto an upright trunk, making a mushroom-shaped small tree that will never grow higher than the graft. Can become quite large, to 25 ft. × 20 ft. (7.5 m × 6 m), if the natural leader is trained upright.

'Pendula Rosea'. Dark pink buds open to clear pink flowers.

'Pendula Rubra' (syn. 'Beni-shidare'). Buds deep reddish pink; dark pink flowers fade to clear pink.

Prunus 'Pink Perfection'. Somewhat similar to 'Kanzan', which is probably one of its parents; large, double flowers that bloom midseason are clear pink with no hint of purple. Tree is similarly vase-shaped when young but outer branches are more drooping at tips. Not as vigorous as 'Kanzan'; often grafted onto the trunk

of a more vigorous species or onto birchbark cherry (*P. serrula*) for the beauty of its mahogany-colored bark.

Prunus sargentii (Sargent cherry). Native to high mountains in northern Japan; one of the hardiest species. Single flowers of bright, deep pink bloom early; sour purple-black fruits follow in summer. Young foliage is bronze-red, turning beautiful orange-red early in fall. Bark is dark reddish brown. Species is large, rounded tree to 40 ft. × 30 ft. (12 m × 9 m); several narrowly upright forms such as 'Rancho' are available.

Prunus 'Shirofugen'. White-flowered form of 'Fugenzo', the Japanese classic cultivated since the 1500s. (Name literally means "white-Fugen," Fugen being the name of an important Buddhist saint.) Latest to bloom, often not until May. Large, slightly flattened double flowers open from pink buds; become white when fully open, then fade to purplish pink, resembling those of 'Kanzan'. Young foliage is coppery red. Vigorous, wide-spreading tree to 20 ft. × 30 ft. (6 m × 9 m) or wider.

Prunus 'Shirotae' (syn. 'Mount Fuji'). Short, extremely wide-spreading tree with very large semi-double flowers of pure white. Early bloom; thin-petalled flowers can be damaged by frost in colder subregions but are resistant to blossom brown rot. Broad

Prunus ×*subhirtella* 'Autumnalis Rosea' in early March

Prunus ×*yedoensis* 'Akebono'

form needs lots of room; mature trees are rarely over 15 ft. (4.5 m) in height but can be 40 ft. (12 m) in width, with branch tips drooping almost to ground. Branches may need support in old age. Unsuitable for small spaces, but superb in a large garden setting against a backdrop of dark conifers.

Prunus ×*subhirtella* (spring cherry, higan cherry). Best known by its cultivars, all of which have slender, graceful branches and small, somewhat bell-shaped single flowers.

'Autumnalis' (syn. 'Jugatsu-zakura', literally "tenth-month" or "October cherry"; autumn-flowering cherry). A few very small, very pale pink flowers open in October or November and continue to open in warm spells throughout fall and winter. However, main blooming begins in late February or early March, with slightly larger flowers. Small tree to 15 ft. (4.5 m) high and wide. Needs well-drained fertile site in sun. Because it blooms while rains are still heavy, needs very good air circulation to avoid blossom brown rot. Plant where slightly fragrant winter flowers can be enjoyed up close; even main flowering is not showy from a distance.

'Autumnalis Rosea'. Flowers are a more definite shade of pink, fading lighter.

'Pendula Plena Rosea' (syn. 'Yae-beni-shidare'; double pink weeping cherry). Semi-double flowers of deep pink; early midseason bloom.

'Rosea' (rosebud cherry). Some question exists as to ancestry; may be a deeper pink-flowered form of upright, long-lived (several hundred years) *Prunus pendula* var. *ascendens*. Large spreading tree to 25 ft. (7.5 m) in height and width.

'Whitcomb' (Whitcomb cherry). A Pacific Northwest exclusive. In the 1920s, Washington grower David Whitcomb supplied Seattle-area nurseries with propagating stock of this tree, which may or may not be a dark-flowered selection of 'Rosea'. Small, single, dark pink flowers bloom very early (mid-February in Seattle), fading to white. Tree is large, vigorous, and healthy, although reportedly more prone to disease in recent years. Very popular in the Puget Sound subregion; succeeds elsewhere in the Pacific Northwest where microclimates provide very mild winters and protection from late frosts. Sometimes sold as 'Whitcombii'. To 25 ft. × 35 ft. (7.5 m × 9 m).

Prunus 'Taihaku' (great white cherry). Very large, pure white single flowers, 2.5 in. (6 cm) in diameter, bloom early midseason amid copper-colored leaves. Foliage turns orange in fall. Vigorous rounded tree to 25 ft. × 30 ft. (7.5 m × 9 m) or more. This ancient cultivar was almost lost to cultivation. For unknown reasons, all specimens in Japan were extinct by the 1920s; happily, in 1923, a single specimen was found in an English garden, where it was being choked out by other vegetation. This was propagated and reintroduced to Japan.

Prunus 'Ukon'. Large semi-double flowers of unusual but attractive greenish yellow bloom in midseason, contrasting beautifully with bronze-green new leaves. Foliage turns purple-red in fall. Tree is vigorous and healthy, vase-shaped when young but wide-spreading in maturity. To 25 ft. × 40 ft. (7.5 m × 12 m).

Prunus ×*yedoensis* (Yoshino cherry). Very graceful tree blooms early, with medium-sized, lightly fragrant flowers of pale pink appearing before leaves. Very free-flowering. Slender, arching branches make umbrella-shaped tree to 35 ft. × 25 ft. (10 m × 7.5 m).

'Akebono' (Daybreak). Semi-double flowers of soft pink on small, graceful tree to 20 ft. (6 m) high and wide. This American introduction ('Amerika' in Japan) has met with increasing popularity since its 1920 debut; early flowers hold up well to rain and late frosts and are highly resistant to blossom brown rot. Excellent cultivar, especially for smaller gardens.

PRUNUS (FLOWERING PLUMS)

Origin: Balkans, Asia Minor, Central Asia, eastern Asia

Hardiness zones: 4–5 to 9

Size: Varies

Blooming season: Late February to April

Exposure: Full sun

Soil preference: Rich; moisture-retentive but well drained

Water needs: Moderately drought tolerant when established

Maintenance needs: Low

Subregions best suited: All

Possible problems: Tent caterpillars, fall webworm, shot-hole fungus

Like Japanese flowering cherries, with which they are sometimes confused, these adaptable trees have a very long history of cultivation and are best known by their hybrids. All bloom mainly in March, just before leafing out, and differ from flowering cherries in their smaller, subtly fragrant, usually single flowers; their more compact, densely branched growth habit; and most obviously by their purple or reddish summer foliage.

One of the most welcome signs of the approach of spring, flowering plums are long-lived and cling tenaciously to life even under the most adverse conditions—a fact that seems to invite scorn. (It has become fashionable to dismiss them as plebian, or worse, tacky.) However, when their few but essential needs are met, specimens are a joy to behold in any season.

Chief among these needs is full sun. Although they will grow in considerable shade, this encourages fungal diseases that can cause twig blight and eventually kill whole branches. They also appreciate summer heat—as much as they can get in our relatively cool climate. They do not like wet or poorly drained soil; although they easily survive our normal summer drought, they suffer badly in prolonged drought, especially if spring has been dry. Young specimens need regular summer water for their first few years, and adequate water in April and May is essential at any age.

Pruning should be restricted to initial training or repair (branches are fairly brittle and easily broken by snow). Over-pruning results in numerous long, upright, unbranched shoots, or water sprouts, which should be removed. Caterpillars can be a nuisance but are rarely serious. Damage from shot-hole fungus (one of several diseases causing tiny leaf spots that eventually fall out, leaving tiny holes in new leaves) is widespread but cosmetic only; holes are virtually invisible amid summer's dense foliage.

The small red plums of *Prunus cerasifera*, which attract birds, are sweet and quite tasty for fresh eating, but do not keep well and are not suitable for preserving. Cultivars vary widely in their setting of crops, so the desirability or undesirability of fruit is an important factor in choosing among them.

Prunus ×blireana

Prunus ×blireana. Hybrid of *P. cerasifera* 'Pissardii' and a selected form of *P. mume* (Japanese apricot), a very early-blooming species native to China but long cultivated in Japan. Small, graceful tree blooms about two weeks earlier than other flowering plums. Fragrant, bright pink flowers are fully double and—for a plum—very large at 1 to 1.5 in. (2.5 to 4 cm) in diameter. Size and color of flowers, which bloom for several weeks, draw attention from several blocks away, especially since few other plants of any size are in bloom so early. Foliage emerges reddish, becoming mixed with bronze-green by summer; fall foliage is reddish bronze. Sets little or no fruit. To 20 ft. × 15 ft. (6 m × 4.5 m), with dense but slender branches and a gnarly trunk. Needs a sunny, airy site in fertile well-drained soil; preferably sheltered from strong winds and excessive rain while in bloom.

'Moseri'. Tree is slightly larger and less dense; double flowers are pale pink. Sometimes sold as 'Light Pink Blireana'.

Prunus cerasifera (cherry plum). Native to somewhere between the Middle East and China; cultivated since the 1500s but now unknown in the wild. Species itself is seldom grown but is used for rootstock on several kinds of stone fruits and on purple-leaved flowering cultivars. On the latter, suckers arising from rootstock are clearly identifiable by green leaves and pure white flowers; these should be removed as soon as noticed.

'Frankthrees' (Mount St. Helens). Light pink flowers; purple foliage emerges early and holds deep color all summer. Fall foliage is purplish red; sets little or no fruit. Tolerance of extremes of temperature make it a good choice for Cascade Slopes/Outflow Valleys subregion. Fast growing rounded tree to 20 ft. (6 m) in both dimensions.

'Pissardii' (purple-leaved plum). Very popular cultivar; found circa 1880 as a natural sport in the garden of the Shah of Persia (Iran) by the head gardener, one Monsieur Pissard. Very heat-tolerant—temperatures can reach 122°F (50°C) in Iran—but widely adaptable. Profuse, lightly fragrant flowers open white from pink buds, contrasting beautifully with dark trunk; fade to light pink. Foliage emerges coppery red, passing through brown and reddish green stages before settling on deep burgundy-purple for summer. Good dark red fall color. In normally rainy springs, sets moderate crops of fruit, but if weather is warm and sunny while in bloom (allowing bees to forage) can set bumper crops. Can be used as a pollinator for Japanese-type fruiting plums, which bloom at same time. Fast growing rounded tree to 25 ft. × 20 ft. (7.5 m × 6 m); more with age.

'Thundercloud'. Light pink flowers fade to rose-pink; foliage emerges coppery red, then turns deep purple for summer. Fall color reddish. Usually sets little fruit but can set heavy crops if March is warm and dry. To 20 ft. (6 m) in height and width; widely planted.

'Vesuvius'. Light pink flowers and purple-black foliage on small, upright tree to 18 ft. × 12 ft. (5.5 m × 3.6 m). Fall foliage purplish red; sets little or no fruit. Needs warm site; tolerance of heat and drought make it good choice for Rogue subregion and hot-summer valleys.

Prunus ×cistena (dwarf purple-leaved plum; dwarf purple-leaved sand cherry). Hybrid of *P. cerasifera* 'Pissardii' and North American native sand cherry, *P. pumila* var. *besseyi*; very cold-hardy. Multi-stemmed shrub, only 6–8 ft. (1.8–2.4 m) tall, looks like a dwarf 'Pissardii'. Fragrant flowers are pale pink, fading darker. Good in containers; can be trained to a single trunk as miniature tree. Sets light crops of small, dark purple fruits.

'Big Cis'. Very similar but twice the size, reaching 15 ft. × 12 ft. (4.5 m × 3.6 m). Can be used as large multi-stemmed shrub or trained as small tree.

Prunus cerasifera 'Pissardii'

Prunus cerasifera 'Thundercloud'

PYRUS SALICIFOLIA 'PENDULA' (WEEPING WILLOW-LEAVED PEAR, WEEPING SILVER PEAR)

Origin: Species native to the Caucasus

Hardiness zones: 4 to 9

Size: 12–15 ft. × 10–12 ft. (3.6–4.5 m × 3–3.6 m)

Blooming season: March and April

Exposure: Full sun

Soil preference: Deep, heavy, moisture-retentive but well drained

Water needs: Very drought tolerant when established

Maintenance needs: Moderate

Subregions best suited: All except Cascade Slopes/Outflow Valleys

Possible problems: Brittle limbs may break in wet snow or ice storms

Pyrus salicifolia 'Pendula'

Clusters of creamy white flowers with dark stamens that adorn bare weeping branches in earliest spring are very pretty, but main attraction is its foliage. The slender, graceful willow-shaped leaves open silvery green but soon turn truly silver with a faint green cast, keeping their garden-brightening color right up until October, when they briefly turn yellowish brown before dropping. Small, knobby, inedible brown fruits may remain on the branches until late November, neither adding to nor detracting from the tree's looks.

Where adapted, weeping silver pear is an invaluable addition to Pacific Northwest gardens, adding the well-known and incomparable effects of silver foliage in satisfying quantity while remaining small enough to fit into the smallest gardens. Better yet, its silver suits our climate. Most silver-foliaged plants are native to arid regions and look lovely in dry, bright sunny weather, but are reduced by rain, fog, or even heavy dew to a bedraggled mess no self-respecting cat would drag in. Not so with weeping silver pear, which looks great rain or shine, in cool weather or hot, under overcast skies or in bright sun.

Even more unusual for a silver-foliaged plant, most of which need light soil with excellent drainage (and can drown in our wet winters), silver weeping pear thrives year-round in our heavy soils. Usually grafted onto quince or hawthorn rootstock, its roots go straight down into the subsoil, making it thoroughly drought tolerant in our longest, driest summers. Yet these deep roots also tolerate rain-soaked soil all winter, even tolerating short periods of saturated soil. Because the tree is so well anchored, there is no danger of blowdown even in super-wet windstorms.

Besides being remarkably free of diseases and insects, silver weeping pear grows so quickly and vigorously that no extra fertilizer is ever needed. (Nitrogen in particular should be avoided; it could theoretically encourage fireblight, although actual infections are rare west of the Cascades.) Still, it is not without drawbacks.

Pruning, for instance, is a bewildering prospect, since the stiff, overlapping, mainly weeping branches grow in any direction they feel like, including straight up. The best compromise is to prune any weeping branches that contact the ground; any that cross over the center of the tree; and any that threaten to make its overall form too lopsided. The rough aim should be to maintain a broadly conical "haystack" outline, but the tree may have other ideas.

Crawling underneath the spine-equipped weeping branches to pick up bucket loads of fallen fruit in late November can also be counted as a negative, but the most serious drawback is the tree's high susceptibility to snow damage. Like all ornamental pears, its limbs are brittle, and its dense overlapping branches tend to hold even more snow than other trees. Breakage is almost inevitable in wet snow.

However, because of its rapid and eccentric growth pattern, even the loss of a major limb is soon disguised. Our own tree has been clobbered many times over, but has always come back strong—although in slightly altered outline every time.

ROBINIA PSEUDOACACIA 'FRISIA'
(FRISIA BLACK LOCUST)

Origin: Species native to the Appalachian region of North America

Hardiness zones: 4 to 9

Size: 20–40 ft. × 15–20 ft. (6–12 m × 4.5–6 m); can be larger

Season of interest: Spring to fall

Exposure: Cool sun to light shade

Soil preference: Heavy but well drained; average fertility

Water needs: Drought tolerant when established

Maintenance needs: Low

Subregions best suited: All

Possible problems: May sucker if grafted onto species rootstock

Robinia pseudoacacia 'Frisia'

If sited carefully, this tree has the potential of lighting up the whole garden from spring through fall with breathtaking and reliable beauty. A sport of *Robinia pseudoacacia* found in a Dutch nursery in the 1930s, 'Frisia' has inherited all the good features of its parent, including wide adaptability and disease resistance. Its beautiful and airy compound leaves cast pleasant, filtered shade that is never heavy or dank, and its drought tolerance is legendary, even in our extended summer droughts. (Like its parent, it actually likes our heavy soils.) It has also inherited the pendent clusters of white flowers in late spring that are very fragrant and attract bees.

Its outstanding feature, though, is its foliage. Yellow-gold in spring, it remains bright chartreuse-yellow all summer long, never burning or fading, and displays its best color in cool-summer climates such as ours. Fall color is not long-lived, but the leaves do briefly turn pure yellow before falling in early October.

Amazingly, this tree has inherited none of the considerable faults of its parent, which include vicious thorns ('Frisia' bears small thorns on new shoots only), self-seeding to the point of invasiveness ('Frisia' sets very little seed), and rampant root suckering that produces thorny new shoots as far as 20 ft. (6 m) from the trunk ('Frisia' does not sucker). Brittle limbs are another species problem that seems muted or nonexistent in 'Frisia'; local specimens, at least, seem unaffected by wet snow and came through the tree-decimating windstorms of December 2006 unscathed.

The considerable merits of 'Frisia' led to a meteoric rise in its popularity in the 1980s, which led to the propagation of this naturally small, non-suckering tree onto rootstock of the species for faster growth and quick sales. Unfortunately, this created a much larger tree than most people could reasonably have anticipated; grafted trees can eventually reach 60 ft. (18 m). Worse, it created a root-suckering problem where none existed. If planted in a lawn, these roots are subject to nicking by lawnmowers or string trimmers and will start sending up stout, thorny, green-leaved suckers.

Finding a specimen of 'Frisia' on its own roots may be difficult, but even grafted specimens can still be enjoyed by giving them enough space and keeping them out of lawns. Plant 'Frisia' in a permanent garden bed where no digging will take place, or surround the tree with low-maintenance permanent groundcover. In either case, the leafy but open canopy will allow plenty of light and natural rainfall to reach the ground, even in maturity; the small individual leaf segments disintegrate quickly and will never smother plants underneath them.

One more planting caveat: although 'Frisia' will survive without complaint—or water—in even the hottest sun without burning, its color will be less than spectacular there. Unlike most golden-foliaged plants that fry to a crisp in intense sun, 'Frisia' protects itself by turning a rather unbecoming (some would say sickly) shade of yellowish green. Full sun is perfect for this tree in our cooler subregions, but in hot-summer valleys its full potential is best realized by planting it on the east or north side of tall, dark conifers—a setting as perfect esthetically as it is culturally.

CHAPTER 6

Conifers

Dwarf conifers in June, authors' garden. Clockwise from top right: *Thuja occidentalis* 'Woodwardii', *Cryptomeria japonica* 'Vilmoriniana', *T. o.* 'Boisbriand', *Picea mariana* 'Nana', *T. o.* 'Rheingold' (yellow). At top left is *Taxus baccata* 'Fastigiata'; below white lilies is *Abies balsamea* 'Nana'.

Since the natural habitat of most conifers is on the upper, middle, or lower slope of some mountain, it's no wonder the Pacific Northwest abounds in native conifers. Our many mountain ranges are host to red cedar, yellow cedar, spruce, hemlock, yew, various pines, several true firs, a couple of false cypresses, and even a smattering of juniper and redwood in addition to our ubiquitous Douglas fir. Indeed, we're so overwhelmed by conifers that some people might wonder why we deliberately plant introduced species in our gardens.

The answer is simple: our moist winters, moderate summers, and acidic soils make near-perfect garden conditions for conifers of many types. Our native species supply our magnificent "borrowed scenery," our tallest and stateliest shelter trees, and in many cases our hedges (not to mention the wood for our houses and garden structures). However, the more compact and dwarf cultivars better suited to today's smaller gardens tend to come from species native to other parts of the world. Interestingly, most of the dwarf forms are nature's own handiwork.

Many conifer species are subject to natural mutations that cause growth on a single branch to become very tightly congested. If cuttings are taken of these growths (called witches' brooms), they will form roots, giving rise to a new, permanently miniaturized plant that grows very slowly. *Chamaecyparis* (false cypress), *Cryptomeria* (Japanese cedar), *Picea* (spruce), and *Tsuga* (hemlock) are particularly prone to forming witches' brooms, making them a treasure trove of garden-worthy (and garden-sized) conifers.

Far from being static green foils for brighter flowering plants, garden conifers may have foliage of blue, silver, gold, white-variegated, yellow-variegated, blue-green, or gray-green, with additional winter hues of orange, bronze, dark red, or reddish purple. They also offer a wide range of sizes, textures, and habits: narrowly upright, prostrate, perfectly rounded, weeping, widely or narrowly pyramidal, mounding, or picturesquely irregular.

Indispensable in the winter garden, garden conifers are ideal year-round companions for heaths and heathers, providing ever-changing but never-clashing color combinations. The addition of ornamental grasses, a few acid-loving shrubs such as deciduous rhododendrons (the kind we used to call deciduous azaleas), some spring-flowering bulbs, and perhaps a hebe or two makes an outstanding low-maintenance combination that's horticulturally rare. (Not to get too smug about it, but ours is one of very few climates in the world conducive to growing all these plant groups simultaneously.)

As ideal as our climate is for conifers, growing them is not entirely problem-free. Their native mountain habitats provide good to excellent drainage, but most gardens in the Pacific Northwest are located where the "good" soil is—in river valleys and bottomlands, where drainage is often less than adequate in winter. A site with good winter drainage is of prime importance, since even moisture-loving conifers such as redwoods like their soil spongy, not waterlogged.

Size is another quandary. Dwarf conifers in particular grow very slowly at first, but eventually get much larger than most gardeners anticipated. This not only makes long-range landscaping plans a bit of a challenge, but means pruning will probably be necessary at some point. However, this point may not be reached for ten, 15, or even 20 years.

Feeding conifers is seldom a problem—mountain slopes are rarely covered with deep, fertile soil—but clean air is vital. Needle-type conifers rely on small pores located on the undersides of their needles to "breathe" (in botanical terms, exchange gasses), making them very sensitive to air pollution, dust, and even chimney smoke.

This gas-exchanging function may also have something to do with the great size conifers attain on thin mountain soils of low fertility. Where do they get the nitrogen necessary for such growth? It's perhaps no coincidence the earth's atmosphere is made up of nearly 80 percent nitrogen, with less than 20 percent oxygen and about one percent other gasses. At any rate, no conifer will thrive in polluted air.

Most of the conifer genera and species not listed here can be grown well somewhere in the Pacific Northwest, but not every-

where. For instance, our well-adapted native true firs (*Abies*) are too large for most gardens, but most non-native *Abies* species prefer climates colder than ours, with some summer rain and better winter drainage. (Given summer watering and good drainage, *A. balsamea* 'Nana' is a popular dwarf.) *Podocarpus* species, native to the southern hemisphere, prefer slightly warmer winters and can do without our summer droughts. *Sequoia sempervirens* (coast redwood), although native to the southern Oregon coast, also needs too much summer water to be ideally adapted to most parts of the Pacific Northwest.

Cedrus species (true cedars) include such knockouts as *C. atlantica* (Atlas cedar) and *C. deodara* (Himalayan cedar), but most forms eventually grow too large for the average garden. Being shallow-rooted, *C. deodara* also has the disconcerting habit of blowing down in moderately strong winds once it reaches a certain size.

Junipers are so widely grown and so adaptable they needn't be covered here at all, except to mention they need excellent drainage, a bit of dolomite lime in the soil (they tend to suffer from magnesium deficiency here), and no more than light shade. They also prefer lower rainfall and lower humidity than most of our subregions offer.

The deciduous conifers are novel and beautiful, but *Larix* species (larch) prefer wetter summers and colder, longer winters than ours. (Here, larches tend to break dormancy too early in our mild winters and get caught by late frosts.) Both *Metasequoia glyptostroboides* (dawn redwood) and the broadleaved, deciduous *Ginkgo biloba* are widely admired as living fossils, but dawn redwoods need lots of summer water and humidity, and ginkgos would much prefer much hotter, more humid summers. However, all these and more can be grown in suitable microclimates, sometimes with spectacular success.

There is only one conifer to avoid, and that, ironically, is a Pacific Northwest native. *Chamaecyparis lawsoniana* (Port Orford cedar, Lawson cypress), a timber tree native to southwestern Oregon and northern California, is the parent of dozens of horticulturally valuable cultivars, many with beautifully colored foliage. Unfortunately, this species is highly prone to a *Phytophthora* fungus that causes a fatal root rot. The fungus also infects needles, branches, and trunks; whole stands of native trees have been decimated. Our heavy soils and moist atmosphere are conducive to the proliferation of this fungus, especially in warm, wet weather. Good drainage helps, but since there is no fully reliable prevention and no cure once contracted, some nurseries refuse to carry Lawson cypresses. Although root rot is by no means inevitable (many fine old specimens of these trees can be seen throughout the Pacific Northwest), it is a very real risk that should be seriously considered.

Note: Almost all conifers are cool-climate plants, and Zones 8 and 9 are included here only in the context of Pacific Northwest summers. Other regions that share our minimum winter temperatures, such as Texas (Zone 8) or northern Florida (Zone 9), have much hotter summers than ours and are not suitable climates for most of the conifers described here.

Sizes given are approximate but are what can be expected in the Pacific Northwest after 25 to 30 years.

ARAUCARIA ARAUCANA (MONKEY PUZZLE, CHILEAN PINE)

Origin: Chile

Hardiness zones: 7 to 9

Size: To 30 ft. (9 m); eventually taller

Exposure: Full sun

Soil preference: Moderately fertile; moisture-retentive but well drained

Water needs: Moderate in youth; drought tolerant in maturity

Maintenance needs: Low

Subregions best suited: All

Possible problems: None serious

A distinctive profile of sparse branches spaced around its trunk with geometrically precise symmetry make this conifer unmistakable: its rigid, persistent spine-like leaves look like something off the back of a dinosaur. One flush of growth per year makes it possible to determine a tree's age by counting the layers of branches.

Trees are either male or female, but gender cannot be determined until maturity at about 15 years. Male catkins are held in clusters the size and shape of bananas, while female cones are the size and shape of muskmelons. Cones take three years to ripen and may weigh 10–15 lbs. (4.5–7 kg) apiece; most shatter when ripe but occasionally fall intact.

Monkey puzzle is very slow growing and in need of some coddling (consistent watering, excellent drainage, protection from cold winds) for the first ten years; it then grows rapidly for the next 20 to 30 years, eventually slowing and developing a dense, broadly rounded crown. The tree is remarkably free of pests and diseases and is exceptionally windfirm. Longevity (century-old specimens are not uncommon) and distinctive character make it a good legacy or memorial tree, but leave it plenty of room to grow: a pruned monkey puzzle is a travesty.

CHAMAECYPARIS (FALSE CYPRESS)

Origin: Japan, Taiwan, North America

Hardiness zones: 5 to 9

Size: Varies

Exposure: Full sun to light shade

Soil preference: Moderately fertile; moisture-retentive but well drained; acidic

Water needs: Varies

Maintenance needs: Low

Subregions best suited: All

Possible problems: None serious

Araucaria araucana

Chamaecyparis nootkatensis 'Pendula'

Chamaecyparis obtusa 'Fernspray Gold'

Chamaecyparis obtusa 'Nana Gracilis', approximately 15 years old

Scale-like leaves on flattened branches and small decorative cones on some species give this genus a superficial resemblance to true cypresses (*Cupressus*). Most species are widely adaptable and usually drought tolerant in our climate, but they do appreciate ample moisture in both the soil and the atmosphere. They dislike cold, drying winds and prolonged exposure to hot sun or very strong winds; most are best in sheltered but not heavily shaded sites.

Chamaecyparis nootkatensis (Nootka cypress, yellow cedar). Native to the Pacific Northwest. Species itself is rarely grown in gardens, but does make a beautiful hedge if kept clipped. Foliage and close-grained wood both have a distinctive pungent odor. Shallow roots make tall specimens prone to blowdown; even hedges are not advisable in areas exposed to high winds. Prefers cool weather and high humidity, but is quite adaptable. Drought tolerant when established.

'Compacta'. Semi-dwarf form with dense, yellow-green foliage; good in large tubs if sheltered from wind. To 8 ft. × 4 ft. (2.4 m × 1.2 m).

'Green Arrow'. Essentially a narrower form of 'Pendula', with short horizontal or weeping branches clothed in long weeping branchlets. To 30 ft. × 8–10 ft. (9 m × 2.4–3 m).

'Pendula' (weeping Nootka cypress). A tree of genuine character, with very long weeping branches, some of which turn sharply upward again. Long branchlets hang straight down from them like dense curtains. Branches that weep to ground before turning upward act as "elbows" to lean against, making the tree windfirm once it's large enough. Leader must be trained upright for several years. To 30 ft. × 15–20 ft. (9 m × 4.5–6 m).

Chamaecyparis obtusa (Hinoki cypress). Native to Japan. Dwarf forms with richly textured foliage are indispensable in Japanese-themed gardens. Very slow growing for many years, they later grow much faster; overgrown dwarfs can have their character changed to that of small trees by removing lower limbs. Reliably drought tolerant when established, Hinoki cypresses tolerate heat but dislike drying winds or very dry atmosphere.

'Fernspray Gold'. Small to medium-sized shrub with long, narrow sprays of foliage resembling fern fronds; color is deep gold highlighted with bright yellow in spring. Needs protection from wind and hot sun. Best with regular light pruning to maintain density. To 5 ft. × 4 ft. (1.5 m × 1.2 m).

'Gracilis'. Tall upright form with very dark green foliage held in cup-like sprays; practically begs for placement near a Japanese stone lantern or interesting large rock. Narrow width makes it unlikely to outgrow its allotted space. To 20 ft. × 5 ft. (6 m × 1.5 m).

'Kosteri'. Versatile small to medium-sized shrub with dense, flattened branchlets; pleasingly irregular in shape, often flat-topped. Foliage is bright green in summer, olive-green to bronze

Chamaecyparis pisifera 'Boulevard'

Mature *Chamaecyparis pisifera* 'Filifera Aurea' pruned to small tree form

in winter. Takes more exposure than most forms, but looks best with some shelter. To 5 ft. (1.5 m) high and wide.

'Nana Gracilis'. Popular form with dense, very dark green foliage held in small shell-like sprays. Extremely slow growing (a fraction of an inch per year) for ten to 15 years, then grows moderately fast, eventually becoming small tree. To 36 in. × 24 in. (90 cm × 60 cm) in 15 years; eventually to 12 ft. × 6 ft. (3.6 m × 1.8 m) or more. Very easy to confuse when young with 'Nana', a much harder-to-find true miniature reaching less than 2 ft. (60 cm) high and wide even after several decades. Plants sold as 'Nana' often turn out to be 'Nana Gracilis'.

Chamaecyparis pisifera (Sawara cypress). Native to Japan. Source of many dwarf and semi-dwarf forms with unusual foliage color and/or texture. Prefers moist, fertile, acidic soil with shelter from hottest sun and strong winds. Brightest color and finest foliage texture are best maintained with regular but conservative trimming; any large atypical branches should be removed promptly.

'Boulevard' (syn. 'Cyanoviridis'). Dense, soft, all-juvenile foliage is silvery greenish blue in summer, purplish blue-gray in winter. Best kept lightly pruned; does not resprout from old wood. Eventually a small, somewhat open tree. Needs excellent drainage but dislikes dry soil. To 10 ft. × 8 ft. (3 m × 2.4 m).

'Filifera' (threadleaf cypress). Large shrub with distinctive dark green, drooping, cord-like foliage; good background plant or large filler. Widely adaptable and problem-free, but best pruned occasionally to prevent legginess. Drought tolerant when established. To 8 ft. × 6 ft. (2.4 m × 1.8 m).

'Filifera Aurea' (golden threadleaf cypress). Similar to 'Filifera' but smaller, to 6 ft. × 4 ft. (1.8 m × 1.2 m); golden foliage darkens slightly in winter.

'Filifera Nana' (dwarf threadleaf cypress). Dense, spreading dwarf form. To 4 ft. × 6 ft. (1.2 m × 1.8 m).

'Golden Mop'. Similar to 'Filifera Nana' but smaller, with bright yellow foliage. To 3 ft. × 5 ft. (0.9 m × 1.5 m). Several similar forms are available.

Related species

×*Cupressocyparis leylandii* (Leyland cypress), an intergeneric cross of *Chamaecyparis nootkatensis* and Monterey cypress (*Cupressus macrocarpa*), is very fast growing and tempting for privacy hedging, but results are often disappointing. Plants are very sparsely branched for the first few years, making privacy negligible; older, bushier specimens are slow to establish and prone to blowdown. Continued rapid growth in later years requires frequent pruning to keep to a manageable height, and tall hedges are not windfirm. But it does have a beautiful texture and looks great when kept trimmed. The selection 'Castlewellan Gold' is slightly smaller, denser, and slower growing, with attractive gold-tinged new growth that is brightest in full sun. It too makes a nice hedge if trimmed regularly.

Cryptomeria japonica Elegans Group in November

Cryptomeria japonica 'Sekkan' in early summer

Cryptomeria japonica 'Spiralis'

CRYPTOMERIA JAPONICA (JAPANESE CEDAR, SUGI)

Origin: Japan

Hardiness zones: Varies

Size: Varies

Exposure: Sheltered site in cool sun to light shade

Soil preference: Moderately fertile; moisture-retentive but well drained; acidic

Water needs: Low when established

Maintenance needs: Low

Subregions best suited: Puget Sound, Pacific Coast, Georgia Basin/Puget Trough

Subregions not suited: Cascade Slopes/Outflow Valleys

Possible problems: Prone to damage from snow or ice

Species itself is a very important timber tree in Japan, where it is known as *sugi* and honored as the National Tree. Parent of many unusual dwarf forms and collectors' plants, all remarkably free of pests and diseases but tricky to site. Foliage shows its best color in sun, but can burn in hot sun or in winter sun when covered with frost. Plants love high rainfall and humidity, but wet snow can break limbs, especially on *Cryptomeria japonica* Elegans Group. Cold winds, late frosts, and very dry conditions are also not to their liking.

Cryptomeria japonica 'Vilmoriniana' in February

Picea abies 'Inversa'

'Elegans Compacta'. Compact, shrub-sized form of Elegans Group with very dense, soft foliage. To 6 ft. × 2 ft. (1.8 m × 0.6 m).

Elegans Group. Rounded columnar form with fluffy, finely textured, soft-to-touch foliage, sea-green in summer, deep reddish purple in winter. Needs shelter from cold winds and wet snow. Slow growing to 15 ft. × 6 ft. (4.5 m × 1.8 m). Zones 7 to 9.

'Sekkan' (syn. 'Sekkan-sugi'). Outstanding foliage color of bright creamy yellow, darkening only slightly in winter. Needs bright light but protection from hot sun, especially when young. Fairly fast growing to 10 ft. × 6 ft. (3 m × 1.8 m). Zones 7 to 9.

'Spiralis'. Unusual drooping foliage with needles twisted spirally around branchlets like so many ringlets. Remains bright green year-round. Very slow growing, especially in youth; habit is dense and spreading, but may develop upright shoots as it ages. To 3 ft. × 5 ft. (0.9 m × 1.5 m). Zones 6 to 9.

'Vilmoriniana'. Very slow growing dwarf form, popular for over 100 years. Very fine, tightly congested, slightly prickly foliage grows in rigid, irregular mound; deep sea-green in summer, reddish purple in winter. Protect from late frosts and from early morning sun in winter. To 30 in. × 36 in. (75 cm × 90 cm). Zones 6 to 9.

PICEA (SPRUCE)

Origin: Temperate regions in northern hemisphere

Hardiness zones: Varies

Size: Varies

Exposure: Full sun

Soil preference: Average to rich loam; well drained

Water needs: Drought tolerant when established

Maintenance needs: Low

Subregions best suited: Depends on species

Possible problems: Spider mites, spruce aphids, Cooley spruce gall aphids

Although renowned for cold hardiness, spruces fit the mild-winter climate of the Pacific Northwest like a glove. Our moderate summers approximate those of high mountain habitats; our overcast winter skies mimic the light levels of the far north. Our

Picea abies 'Nidiformis'

high fall-to-spring rainfall pleases them, yet their extensive root systems allow them to thrive in our summer droughts. These roots are incredibly long and pliable (native peoples used them as rope) and need plenty of room. Never confine a spruce, even a miniature, in a permanent container; it will eventually suffer.

Caution is advisable whenever planting any irresistibly small spruce, since "slow growing" does not always mean "perpetually tiny." A few forms do remain small forever, but most eventually require considerably more space than can be imagined at planting time, and a few become impressively large within 20 years or so. Give all dwarfs plenty of growing room, especially near immovable objects such as houses. While waiting, perennials or short-lived shrubs can fill in the slack. Any branches that revert to normal size should be cut out as soon as noticed, or the whole plant will eventually end up timber-tree-sized.

Beginning in late winter, *Picea* species may start losing inner needles to spruce aphids, a pest unique to mild-winter areas. If not checked, plants can become nearly defoliated, with only tufts of newest growth remaining at branch tips. Blue spruces, especially if grown in shade or other less-than-ideal conditions, are particularly prone to attack. Trees can readily recover from one year's damage, but repeated infestations—the result of not checking for spruce aphids early enough in the year—may prove fatal.

The presence of this pest is easily checked, starting in February, by vigorously shaking or tapping a branch over a piece of

Picea glauca var. *albertiana* 'Conica'

Picea mariana 'Nana'. This specimen is over 20 years old.

stiff white paper. If small, dull green aphids fall onto the paper, spray with insecticidal soap every two weeks until mid-June or until aphids no longer appear on the test paper. If inner needles fall off in summer, especially on Alberta spruce, the problem is more likely to be spider mites.

Damage from Cooley spruce gall aphids, most likely to be found on native Sitka spruce and Colorado blue spruce, is easy to recognize. Greenish purple galls, 1–2 in. (2.5–5 cm) in length, form at tips of branches and soon turn hard and brown, resembling miniature pineapples. Aphids living inside the galls cause defoliation, leaving bare, gall-infested branch tips. Damage is best controlled by cutting off and burning galls as soon as noticed. For further protection, spray trees with insecticidal soap just as new growth buds burst open in May.

Cooley spruce gall aphids are also found on Douglas fir, where they appear as tiny white flecks on needles but do not form galls. Control on Douglas fir is rarely necessary, but the appearance of aphids on them is a warning to check spruces nearby.

Picea abies (Norway spruce). Native to northern and central Europe. Parent of innumerable witches' brooms, all maintenance-free and highly resistant to insects and disease. Drought tolerant when established; fine in light shade. Afternoon shade is advisable in hot-summer valleys. Zones 3 to 9.

'Acrocona'. Dark green, semi-pendulous branches bear bright red male flowers and large, attractive cones even at a young age. To 7 ft. (2.1 m) in both dimensions.

'Clanbrassiliana'. Neat, compact habit and prominent brown winter buds; popular for nearly 200 years. To 2 ft. × 3 ft. (60 cm × 90 cm), larger in great age.

'Inversa' (syn. 'Pendula'; weeping spruce). Prostrate form to 10 ft. (3 m) or more, usually trained to a short upright trunk and allowed to cascade downward.

'Little Gem'. Witches' broom of 'Nidiformis'; very appealing miniature version, but, unlike bird's nest spruce, prone to spider mites.

'Nidiformis' (bird's nest spruce). Flat-topped form with indented center resembling nest; popular and reliable. Impervious to pests and diseases. New growth is bright green, soft, slightly pendulous. To 2 ft. × 6 ft. (0.6 m × 1.8 m).

Picea glauca (white spruce). Native to Canada and northeastern United States. Likes cool conditions; eastern or northern exposure recommended in hot-summer valleys. Watch for spider mites. Zones 2 to 9.

var. *albertiana* 'Conica' (dwarf Alberta spruce). Very popular, densely foliaged form much abused for its perfectly conical Christmas-tree shape. Soft, light green new growth in May. Prone to spider mites; appreciates some watering as well as occasional misting in dry summers. Accepts light shade but keeps best form in full sun. Slow growing, but can easily reach 7 ft. (2.1 m) high and wide in 20 years.

var. *albertiana* 'Laurin'. Witches' broom of dwarf Alberta spruce. Perfect miniature replica barely 18 in. × 8 in. (45 cm × 20 cm) in ten years; good in rock gardens. Eventually to 4 ft. × 3 ft. (1.2 m × 0.9 m) or more.

'Densata' (Black Hills spruce). Very slow growing, densely branched form with beautiful dark, almost black-green foliage. Eventually becomes a large pyramidal shrub or small tree, 10 ft. × 8 ft. (3 m × 2.4 m) or more.

Picea mariana (black spruce). Native to Canada and northeastern United States; Zones 3 to 9.

'Nana' (dwarf black spruce). Extremely slow growing dwarf with tiny, tightly congested blue-green needles. Often confused

Picea omorika 'Pendula'

Picea pungens 'Hoopsii'

with *Picea glauca* 'Echiniformis' and sold as such. Highly resistant to insects and disease. Excellent in rock gardens; needs northern or eastern exposure in hot-summer valleys. To 12 in. × 24 in. (30 cm × 60 cm) in 25 years.

Picea omorika (Serbian spruce). Native to the former Yugoslavia. Narrow, steeple-shaped tree with short, dark green pendulous branches that turn up at tips to reveal silvery undersides. Good in heavy soils, acidic or alkaline; takes full sun to medium shade. Thoroughly drought tolerant when established and highly resistant to insects and disease. To 30 ft. × 6 ft. (9 m × 1.8 m); eventually taller. Zones 5 to 9.

'Nana'. Dwarf form with very dense foliage; silvery undersides of needles show to advantage. To 4 ft. (1.2 m) high and wide.

'Pendula'. Pencil-slim form with short, weeping branches that hug trunk, turning up at very tips. To 20 ft. × 3 ft. (6 m × 0.9 m).

Picea pungens (Colorado spruce). Stiff blue-green needles on rigid branches give a formal look; *P. pungens* Glauca Group (Colorado blue spruce) has even bluer needles. Cultivars (almost always grafted) have silvery blue foliage and are very popular as specimens. All need full sun. Blue spruces take heat and drought well, but performance is iffy in foggy, cool-summer gardens

unless perfectly sited. Good drainage is essential, especially in winter. Grafted cultivars need training in early years to develop strong leader and upright form. Prone to spider mites, spruce aphids, and Cooley spruce gall aphids, but regular checking prevents serious damage. Very slow growing; eventually to 20 ft. × 8 ft. (6 m × 2.4 m) or more. Zones 2 to 9.

'Endtz'. Extremely slow growing, gray in winter, silver-blue in summer.

'Hoopsii'. Considered one of the bluest of blue spruces. Gangly at first; needs training for several years.

'Koster'. Older compact cultivar still valued for regular shape and good year-round blue color.

'Moerheimii'. Small, densely branched form with intensely blue-silver needles.

Several good nonstandard forms are also available. 'Globosa' is dense and rounded (eventually a short, broad pyramid) with bright blue new growth; 'Fat Albert' and 'Iseli Fastigiate', both introductions from Iseli Nursery in Boring, Oregon, are respectively widely pyramidal and narrowly upright in form. All have dense foliage and excellent blue color.

There are also several prostrate forms of blue spruce, but all tend to throw up leading shoots that must be removed to maintain a low-growing habit.

PINUS (PINE)

Origin: Temperate regions, mainly in northern hemisphere

Hardiness zones: Varies

Size: Varies

Exposure: Full sun

Soil preference: Very well drained; low to average fertility

Water needs: Drought tolerant when established

Maintenance needs: Low to moderate

Subregions best suited: Depends on species

Possible problems: European pine shoot moth, white pine blister rust

The genus *Pinus* has something of a split personality. Many species are extremely drought tolerant, thriving in poor soil and high heat, while others prefer cool conditions, a moist atmosphere, and moist but well-drained soil. Many are superb windbreaks; others suffer in either hot or cold winds.

Amazingly, some (by no means all) "hot-dry" pines are adaptable to coastal conditions; some "cool-moist" pines can also thrive in dry soil and high temperatures. Our native shore pine/lodgepole pine illustrates this dichotomy nicely. Shore pine (*Pinus contorta* var. *contorta*), so common in our moist coastal areas, is a small, irregular tree with a usually twisted trunk. But on the much drier, hotter eastern slopes of the Cascades this same species grows tall, sturdy, and so perfectly straight that native peoples used it for supporting their dwellings. Hence its other name, lodgepole pine (*P. contorta* var. *latifolia*).

Whatever their differences, pines share two absolute needs: full sun and excellent drainage. Large specimens can get into trouble on thin but heavy soil as roots go deep seeking moisture in summer drought; they can then drown in winter when water tables rise. Yellowing needles usually indicates poor drainage, not lack of fertilizer (pines prefer not-too-rich soil); unless drainage is improved, yellowing specimens may decline and die. Dwarf forms are more adaptable, but large pine specimens are best planted on a slope unless soil is deep sand or glacial till.

Dwarf and semi-dwarf pines look best and are most easily kept to reasonable size with regular pruning. Unlike most other conifers, there is only one flush of growth per year; the long, thin, upright new shoots in early summer are called candles for obvious reasons. Cutting candles by one-third, one-half, or even more after they have reached full length (but before needles fill out) keeps plants compact and bushy. Pruning at this time allows for the formation of next year's growth buds on uncut portion; pruning at any other time does not. Pines do not resprout from old wood, so if repair pruning is necessary, cut back to a large branch or even the main trunk; do not leave a stub.

Larvae of the European pine shoot moth—tiny, brown, black-headed caterpillars about 0.25 in. (6 mm) long—may bore into growth buds of pines in midsummer; infested buds become sticky with pitch. New growth the following spring, if it develops at all, is distorted. Any pine may be affected, but damage is more likely on pine species with needles in bundles of two.

To control, cut off and burn damaged shoots as soon as noticed. If badly infested, spray with insecticidal soap mixture containing pyrethrum, or with *Bacillus thuringiensis* var. *kurstaki* (BTK) in late June. Spray again in ten days.

Pine species with needles in bundles of five may be affected by white pine blister rust if currants or gooseberries are grown in the same area. Blister-like swellings appear on branches in late fall or winter and rupture in spring, releasing orange spores that spread in wind. Cankers may form, causing profuse flow of pitch; branches may die beyond cankers. Spores blown onto currant or gooseberry plants in spring can remain alive there over summer, then be blown back to pines in fall to start a new infection.

If blisters or cankers are found, prune at least 4 in. (10 cm) below the infected area and burn all diseased wood. Reinfection

Pinus aristata

will occur as long as currants or gooseberries remain in same garden, so either they or the pine will have to go.

The mountain pine beetle is a very serious pest of native forest pines on the eastern side of the mountains, especially on lodgepole pine (*Pinus contorta* var. *latifolia*) and ponderosa pine (*P. ponderosa*). Stands of western white pine (*P. monticola*) are also vulnerable; the beetle may also attack naturalized stands of Scots pine (*P. sylvestris*). Individual trees, especially of non-native species, are unlikely to be attacked; so far, the problem seems confined to large stands of pine forests, which are not common on the west side of the mountains.

However, since beetle populations expand in mild winters, their spread may be inevitable, and anyone with a stand of native pines on their property should be aware of the potential risk. Information concerning management of the mountain pine beetle is available in Washington and Oregon from local State Forestry offices or County Extensions; in B.C., contact the local office of the Ministry of Forests and Range.

Pinus aristata (Rocky Mountain bristlecone pine). Needles in fives. Native to the southwestern Rocky Mountains. Some specimens are known to be over 2400 years old; some specimens of its close relative *P. longaeva* (Great Basin bristlecone pine), the oldest living thing on earth, are over 4000 years old. Dense, dark green needles and cones are flecked all over with aromatic white

Pinus parviflora

Pinus thunbergii in candle, late May

Pinus thunbergii 'Sayonara'

is often double. Needs acidic soil and prefers moist, cool atmosphere; best in coastal areas. Protect from hot and cold drying winds. Moderately fast growth to 25 ft. × 15 ft. (7.5 m × 4.5 m). Zones 3 to 9.

'Umbraculifera' (Tanyosho pine, tabletop pine). Semi-dwarf form with multiple trunks and broad, spreading, flat-topped crown; numerous small cones are decorative. Removing lower limbs from older specimens gives Japanese-garden effect; shows off beautiful bark. Very slow growing; eventually to 12 ft. × 15 ft. (3.6 m × 4.5 m).

Pinus mugo Pumilio Group (dwarf mugo pine). Needles in twos. Native to central Europe. Overused in commercial plantings, but invaluable for cast-iron constitution in difficult sites. Thrives in heat, cold, intense sun, drought, wind, poor soil; adaptable to all situations except deep shade and poor drainage. Best with candles trimmed closely every year to maintain size and bushiness. Seedling forms are variable; finest choices are named varieties such as 'Gnom', 'Humpy', or 'Mops'. Can be kept at 2 ft. × 4 ft. (0.6 m × 1.2 m). Zones 2 to 9.

Pinus nigra subsp. *nigra* (Austrian pine). Needles in twos. Native to Europe. Strong, robust grower with large limbs and rounded crown. Dense, dark green needles to 6 in. (15 cm) long. Very hardy and durable; good in hot, dry areas but also in coastal areas. Excellent windbreak. To 30 ft. × 20 ft. (9 m × 6 m). Zones 3 to 9.

resin. Prefers dryish soil and atmosphere, but accepts coastal conditions well. Moderate growth in early years, then slowing. To 10 ft. × 5 ft. (3 m × 1.5 m) in 30 years; eventually larger. Good in containers. Zones 4 to 9.

Pinus densiflora (Japanese red pine). Needles in twos. Native to Japan, Korea, northern China. Hardy and adaptable; resembles Scots pine except needles are bright green, not blue-green. Attractive reddish bark; trunk tends to lean picturesquely and

Pinus parviflora (Japanese white pine). Needles in fives. Native to Japan and Taiwan. Small to medium tree, broad and flat-topped in maturity. Short, slightly twisted blue-green needles show silvery undersides. Best in well-drained soil in coastal conditions, but adaptable to drier areas. Takes shaping well; can be used for bonsai. Clustered egg-shaped cones are bluish when young. To 20 ft. (6 m) in height and width. Zones 5 to 9.

Glauca Group. Slower growing than species, with bluer foliage. Broadly pyramidal; eventually wider than tall.

'Templehof'. Vigorous form with short, thick, glaucous-blue foliage; faster growing than species.

Pinus thunbergii (Japanese black pine). Needles in twos. Native to Japan and Korea. Species is timber tree in its native maritime habitat; grows to perfection in coastal areas, where it tolerates salt spray. Also tolerates heat, drought, poor soil; excellent windbreak. Very amenable to pruning; popular for bonsai and bonsai-inspired shaping of garden specimens. Needles grayish green to bright green; dark trunks with textured bark often lean at angle. Prominent white winter buds with silky white hairs are very attractive. To 15 ft. × 8 ft. (4.8 m × 2.4 m). Zones 5 to 9.

'Sayonara'. Widely sold as 'Yatsubusa' (Japanese for "dwarf"). Low-growing, spreading form with long green needles and white winter buds. To 4 ft. × 6 ft. (1.2 m × 1.8 m); eventually wider.

'Thunderhead'. Compact form with dense, dark green foliage; bright white of winter buds and new candles contrasts beautifully. Slow growing to 8 ft. × 6 ft. (2.4 m × 1.8 m); can easily be kept smaller.

Pseudolarix amabilis in October

PSEUDOLARIX AMABILIS (GOLDEN LARCH)

Origin: Southwestern China

Hardiness zones: 5 to 9

Size: To 30 ft. (9 m) high and wide; eventually more

Exposure: Full sun

Soil preference: Fertile; moisture-retentive but well drained; acidic

Water needs: Moderate when young, moderately drought tolerant when mature

Maintenance needs: Low

Subregions best suited: All

Possible problems: None serious

This beautiful deciduous conifer is reputed to be hard to grow—and it probably is, outside the Pacific Northwest or similar area providing the moist, lime-free soil it requires. Related to and resembling larch (*Larix*), with slender, graceful branches, it bears tufts of long, light green needles that turn clear golden yellow in fall. Small rounded cones on bare branches add winter interest; good choice for a large year-round specimen.

Very slow growing at first, then somewhat faster, eventually making a broad-based cone. Reaches its largest size in moist soils where summers are hot; cooler, drier summers keep it considerably smaller. Can be maintained at the size of a large shrub by pruning in midwinter.

Needs ample water when young, but is much less water-dependent than true larches; tolerates our normal summer drought when established. Breaks dormancy later than larches, so late frosts are not a problem, but young specimens may suffer dieback at tips from cold winter winds. Established specimens are perfectly hardy and free of pests, diseases, and problems.

SEQUOIADENDRON GIGANTEUM (GIANT SEQUOIA)

Origin: Western slopes of Sierra Nevada, California

Hardiness zones: 6 to 9

Size: To 30 ft. × 12 ft. (9 m × 4.2 m); eventually more

Exposure: Full sun

Soil preference: Moderately fertile; moisture-retentive but well drained

Water needs: Drought tolerant when established

Maintenance needs: Low

Subregions best suited: All

Possible problems: None serious

Sequoiadendron giganteum 'Pendulum'

Sequoiadendron giganteum

Eternally fascinating, this conifer is the largest living thing on earth as well as the second oldest (right after bristlecone pines). Better suited to Pacific Northwest conditions than its taller but less massive cousin, coast redwood (*Sequoia sempervirens*); giant sequoia is hardier to cold, less reliant on constant high humidity, and is fully drought tolerant once established.

Long, lush, cord-like leaves and reddish brown bark are both beautifully textured; very attractive background specimen on larger properties. Slow growing when young, it speeds up with maturity, but in our climate is unlikely to get anywhere near

record size. Insects and diseases are rare; a well-planted specimen should last quite a few lifetimes.

'Glaucum'. Bluish green foliage; even slower growing than species. To 20 ft. × 8 ft. (6 m × 2.4 m); eventually more.

'Pendulum' (weeping giant sequoia). More odd than beautiful, but much loved (especially by children) for seemingly impossible height-to-width ratio and unpredictable, spiraling leanings that make it resemble some fantastic prehistoric monster. Leader needs training upright for several years; young specimens may need protection from wet, heavy snow that could push them over. Slow growth to 30 ft. × 2 ft. (9 m × 0.6 m).

TAXUS (YEW)

Origin: Temperate regions, mainly in northern hemisphere

Hardiness zones: Varies

Size: Varies

Exposure: Full sun to full shade

Soil preference: Well drained; average to moderate fertility

Water needs: Very drought tolerant when established

Maintenance needs: Low to moderate

Subregions best suited: All

Possible problems: Root weevils, root rot

Amazingly adaptable, yews are prized for their ability to thrive in full shade (a feat unmatched by any other conifer) but are equally happy in full, hot sun. They take moderately acidic to moderately alkaline soil, light to heavy soil texture, high to fairly low fertility. Once established, specimens are diehard drought tolerant, even in full sun, but also accept our heavy rains and long wet season as long as drainage is good to excellent. Yews are so sensitive to waterlogged soil that water standing over their roots for 24 hours can kill them, especially if the weather is warm.

Beautifully textured foliage ranges from darkest black-green to bright creamy yellow. Form may be upright, spreading, rounded, or spikily irregular and can be pruned into any shape imaginable, including hedges. Plants are either male or female; female forms bear attractive, bright red, cup-like fruits in early fall. Seeds contained in these fruits (but not the fruits themselves) are highly toxic to people and animals if eaten, as are needles and branches. Non-seed-bearing male forms can be identified by numerous clusters of light tan, peppercorn-sized pollen sacs that release huge clouds of dust-like pollen when brushed against in early spring.

Yews are extremely healthy and are bothered by only one pest, the larvae of root weevils. Unfortunately, since yews are one of their favorite foods, larvae can kill young specimens by completely girdling the bark at or just below soil level. Young specimens also need protection from cold winter winds and intense hot sun, but established specimens are impervious to weather.

All yews sprout freely from old, bare wood, even when cut almost to the ground after many years of neglect, so specimens

Taxus baccata 'Fastigiata'

Taxus baccata 'Fastigiata Aureomarginata'

Taxus baccata 'Repens Aurea'

Taxus cuspidata var. *cuspidata*

need never outgrow their spaces. Even neglected hedges can easily be rejuvenated. Although slow growing in their first few years, established yews put on 6–12 in. (15–30 cm) of growth per year.

Taxus baccata (English yew). Species itself is seldom grown; not nearly as attractive or horticulturally valuable as its numerous cultivars. Widely adaptable and can be pruned, but regular pruning should start early to avoid thick, stiff branch stubs. Zones 6 to 9.

'Fastigiata' (Irish yew). Female. Strong-growing columnar form, becoming elliptical with age. Its shape and very dark green foliage make a strong, steadfast, personage-like presence. Needs tying or wrapping with netting in winter to keep branches from splaying in snow. May need pruning after many years to maintain form and manageable size. To 15 ft. × 4 ft. (4.5 m × 1.2 m).

'Fastigiata Aureomarginata' (golden Irish yew). Usually male. Similar to 'Fastigiata' but with needles edged yellow; brightest

Hedge of *Taxus* ×*media* 'Hicksii'

in spring, gradually fading to old gold. Needs sun to maintain color. To 12 ft. × 3 ft. (3.6 m × 0.9 m).

'Repandens' (spreading yew). Low-growing, slowly spreading form with deep green foliage. Branches may grow at upward angle; can be pruned to maintain low habit. Very slow growth to 2 ft. × 6 ft. (0.6 m × 1.8 m); eventually wider.

'Repens Aurea' (golden spreading yew). Male or female. Similar to 'Repandens' but more vigorous, with golden-edged foliage. New growth bright orange-yellow. Needs sun to maintain color; may need pruning to maintain size. To 3 ft. × 8 ft. (0.9 m × 2.4 m); eventually wider.

'Semperaurea'. Male. Slow growing dwarf form with rounded habit and long, bright yellow needles; new growth orange-gold. Needs sun to maintain color. To 5 ft. (1.5 m) high and wide.

Taxus cuspidata (Japanese yew). Hardier and shrubbier than English yew; leaves are deep green, yellowish on undersides, sometimes slightly twisted. Best with regular pruning. Sun or shade; very adaptable. Zones 5 to 9.

var. *cuspidata*. Male or female. Dense, mid-green foliage on broadly conical shrub. Vigorous grower to 12 ft. × 8 ft. (3.6 m × 2.4 m); easily kept smaller with regular pruning. Sometimes sold as 'Capitata'.

var. *nana*. Male. Dense, dark green foliage on dwarf, spreading shrub. Best with occasional pruning to maintain bushiness. Slow growth to 2 ft. × 5 ft. (0.6 m × 1.5 m). Usually sold as 'Nana'.

Taxus ×*media*. Hybrid of *T. baccata* and *T. cuspidata*. Best known for vigorous but compact upright forms that make excellent hedging. Zones 5 to 9.

'Brownii'. Male. Dense, dark green foliage. Habit upright at first, then spreading. Growth 6 in. (15 cm) per year; unpruned, to 12 ft. × 15 ft. (3.6 m × 4.5 m).

'Hicksii'. Female. Most popular hedging form. Very dark green foliage, upright habit. Growth 12 in. (30 cm) per year; unpruned, to 20 ft. × 8 ft. (6 m × 2.4 m).

Thuja occidentalis 'Golden Globe', left; *T. o.* 'Woodwardii', right

THUJA (CEDAR)

Origin: Temperate regions in northern hemisphere

Hardiness zones: Varies

Size: Varies

Exposure: Full sun to light shade

Soil preference: Average to moderate fertility; moisture-retentive but well drained

Water needs: Varies

Maintenance needs: Low to moderate

Subregions best suited: All

Possible problems: None serious

The common generic name for *Thuja* is supposedly arborvitae, but in the Pacific Northwest these widely planted conifers are universally called cedars. We also call *Chamaecyparis nootkatensis* yellow cedar and *Calocedrus decurrens* incense cedar, although neither is any more a true cedar (*Cedrus*) than is any thuja. What, then, do we call *Cedrus* species? True cedars, of course. Or, to be perfectly clear, *Cedrus*.

Most valuable as hedging, cedars (*Thuja*) also make good specimens, accents, foundation plantings, and general landscaping companions. All prefer soil on the moist side and can be stressed by summer drought (some types more than others), but soon revive in fall and winter rains. Cedars are opportunistic,

growing whenever conditions are favorable (fall, winter, spring, or summer), so unless summer drought is exceptional, their annual growth is not compromised.

Wet springs followed by dry summers can cause cedar flagging; most green-leaved forms are also subject to winter browning, a physiological response to very cold weather. Young specimens and newest foliage are most affected, turning bronze, brown, or purplish; normal green color returns with milder weather. Golden-foliaged forms turn deep gold to coppery orange in winter. (Same response, more esthetically pleasing.)

When used as hedging, pruning should begin the season after planting, just nipping tops. Yearly conservative pruning results in much denser, more finely textured hedge than if pruning is delayed until the desired height is reached. Hedge sides should be canted inward at the top to allow sunlight and rain to reach lower branches and to prevent tops from splaying in snow.

Thuja occidentalis (eastern white cedar). Native to northeastern North America. Very hardy; lightly aromatic foliage is relished by deer. Does not sprout from bare wood, so pruning should never extend past foliage. Globular forms should be shaped to broad mounds (not globes); lower branches will atrophy if sun and rain cannot reach foliage. Most are best with at least some summer water. Zones 3 to 9.

'Golden Globe'. Dwarf form with naturally rounded habit. Foliage is greenish yellow in summer, old gold in winter;

Thuja occidentalis 'Rheingold' in June

Thuja plicata 'Zebrina'

Thuja occidentalis 'Smaragd'

Thujopsis dolabrata

CEDAR HEDGE SPACING

Thuja occidentalis 'Pyramidalis'	24–30 in. (60–75 cm)
Thuja occidentalis 'Smaragd'	24 in. (60 cm)
Thuja plicata	36 in. (90 cm)

To find the number of plants needed for a hedge, divide the length of the property by the appropriate spacing and add one. Never be tempted to plant a cedar hedge on a berm to gain instant privacy. The raised area will dry out quickly in summer; even with normal watering, plants will be severely stressed and may die.

best color in sun. Several other similar forms are available. Slow growth to 5 ft. (1.5 m) in height and width; can be kept smaller.

'Pyramidalis' (pyramidal cedar). Columnar form with rounded top and dense foliage held in shell-like sprays. Mid-green in summer, olive to pea-green in winter. Best with regular summer water; suffers in drought. Moderate growth to 10 ft. × 2.5 ft. (3 m × 0.75 m); eventually taller but easily maintained at hedge height.

'Rheingold'. Unusual dwarf form with bright butter-yellow new foliage turning coppery orange in winter; best color in sun. Young plants are mounding in form, with all-juvenile foliage resembling heath. Older plants become broadly pyramidal with mostly cord-like adult foliage, but effect is still dainty. Dependent on summer water. To 5 ft. × 4 ft. (1.5 m × 1.4 m).

'Smaragd' (Emerald). Danish columnar form with sharply pointed tip and dark green foliage held in vertical sprays. Retains color all winter. Very popular for hedging but can grow unevenly if plants receive differing amounts of sunlight or water. Best in sun; needs good soil and good drainage. Moderately drought tolerant when established. Agonizingly slow growth, especially for privacy hedge, but eventually to 12 ft. × 3 ft. (3.6 m × 0.9 m). Good vertical accent.

'Woodwardii'. Medium-sized globular, spreading form with mid-green foliage, bronzing lightly in cold winters. Very reliable and durable in all weather; moderately drought tolerant. Slow to moderate growth to 4 ft. × 6 ft. (1.2 m × 1.8 m). Eventually considerably wider if not pruned, but regular light pruning will maintain a reasonable girth.

Thuja plicata (western red cedar). Native to the Pacific Northwest. Familiar timber tree with massive straight trunk; furrowed, peeling reddish brown bark; wonderfully aromatic foliage. Too large (200 ft., 60 m) for garden use except as hedging, but present in most gardens in form of wood: straight-grained, lightweight, aromatic, rot-resistant, and perfect for decks, gazebos, sheds, fences, and trellises.

As a hedge, prefers moist soil and atmosphere, but tolerates normal summer drought. Moderate to fast growth; can be kept at 4 ft. (1.2 m) to 10 ft. (3 m) indefinitely, but needs vigorous annual trimming on sides as well as top. More deer-resistant than *Thuja occidentalis*, although young plants are vulnerable. Best in sun; hedges in shade are subject to non-lethal but unsightly keithia blight that causes small holes and dead leaf tissue at branch tips. To control, spray with fixed copper in March and early October. Zones 5 to 9.

'Excelsa'. Vigorous selected form with larger, fleshier foliage and faster growth rate; more resistant to keithia blight.

'Zebrina'. Variegated form splashed and streaked yellow; brightest in sun. Good for smaller, shorter hedges but a bit eye-wearying for boundary hedges. Makes a good large specimen to 30 ft. × 12 ft. (9 m × 4.2 m) or more.

THUJOPSIS DOLABRATA (ELKHORN CEDAR, HIBA CEDAR)

Origin: Japan

Hardiness zones: 5 to 9

Size: To 20 ft. × 10 ft. (6 m × 3 m); eventually more

Exposure: Cool sun to partial shade

Soil preference: Moderately fertile; moisture-retentive but well drained

Water needs: Drought tolerant when established

Maintenance needs: Low

Subregions best suited: Puget Sound, Pacific Coast, Georgia Basin/Puget Trough

Subregions not suited: None

Possible problems: None serious

Hard-to-find relative of *Thuja*; most closely resembles *T. plicata* but on exaggerated scale, with large, fleshier, scalier foliage that somehow looks reptilian. Undersides of shiny mid-green leaves are bright silver, making beautiful pattern.

Extremely slow growing (almost petrified) for first few years, then speeds up, eventually making broadly conical tree. Can be kept shrub-sized by pruning in early spring. Prefers moist soil and atmosphere, but adaptable to all reasonable soils and conditions. Tolerates considerable shade without contracting fungal blights. Needs protection from heavy, wet snow.

Foliage often shows isolated white variegation; the cultivar 'Variegata' is unstable.

Tsuga canadensis 'New Gold'

Tsuga canadensis 'Pendula'

Hemlock woolly adelgid and balsam woolly adelgid (both white, cottony-looking aphids) may suck juices from needles; repeated infestations can cause defoliation and even death. Inspect undersides of foliage regularly, starting in February; if aphids are found, spray with insecticidal soap and repeat in one week if necessary. Inspect again in July and September; spray as necessary.

Tsuga canadensis (eastern hemlock). Native to northern parts of eastern and central North America.

'Gentsch White'. White-variegated dwarf with rounded form, becoming conical; foliage is brightest in midsummer, appearing white from distance. Foliage can burn in hot sun but loses brightness in shade; an eastern or northern exposure is best. Regular light pruning ensures brightest new growth. To 5 ft. × 3 ft. (1.5 m × 0.9 m).

'Jeddeloh'. Low, spreading form with gracefully drooping branches and distinctive shallow "bird's nest" in center. Foliage light gray-green; very finely textured. Best in light shade. To 2 ft. × 4 ft. (0.6 m × 1.2 m).

'New Gold'. Semi-dwarf pyramidal form with bright yellow new growth, darkening to light green by fall; best with regular light pruning. Color is brightest in full sun, but an eastern or northern exposure is best in hot-summer valleys. Several other golden-foliaged forms are available, all very similar. To 8 ft. × 5 ft. (2.4 m × 1.5 m).

'Pendula' (weeping hemlock). Vigorous prostrate form ideal for training over large rock, wall, or slope. Stake leader to desired height; branches may trail 10 ft. (3 m) or more. Takes pruning well.

TSUGA (HEMLOCK)

Origin: North America, Japan, eastern Asia

Hardiness zones: 4 to 9

Size: Varies

Exposure: Cool sun to partial shade

Soil preference: Average to moderate fertility; moist but not soggy; acidic to neutral

Water needs: Moderate

Maintenance needs: Moderate

Subregions best suited: Puget Sound, Pacific Coast, Georgia Basin/Puget Trough

Subregions not suited: None

Possible problems: Hemlock woolly adelgid, balsam woolly adelgid

Beautiful, graceful conifers preferring cool conditions, high humidity, and moist soil. Very fine-textured, short-needled foliage with silvery undersides; tiny brown cones are also decorative. Sprouts from old wood, making good hedging subject. Hemlocks grow well in partial shade; afternoon shade is recommended in hot-summer valleys.

Tsuga heterophylla

Tsuga heterophylla (western hemlock). Native to the Pacific Northwest. Species is a large timber tree, easily recognizable from a distance by its drooping "flop-top." Shallow-rooted and prone to blowdown in strong winds, but makes a beautiful, shade-tolerant hedge. Slow growing but worth the wait. Less subject to aphids than *T. canadensis*, but still needs regular checking.

Tsuga mertensiana (mountain hemlock). Native to high elevations in the Pacific Northwest. Species is a tall, narrowly conical tree; very beautiful foliage is blue-gray, soft to touch, slightly drooping at tips.

    'Elizabeth'. Chance seedling found on Mount Rainier in the late 1940s. Good in average garden conditions; takes more sun and drier soil than species. Very slow growing; eventually to 12 ft. × 6 ft. (3.6 m × 1.8 m).

CHAPTER 7

Shrubs

Mixed shrubs in July, authors' garden. Left to right: *Philadelphus* ×*virginalis* (white), *Spiraea japonica* 'Goldflame' (center foreground), *Lonicera nitida* 'Baggesen's Gold', *Erica carnea* 'Vivellii' (right foreground)

The Pacific Northwest is truly an Eden for shrubs, most of which prefer a slightly acidic soil, fairly high rainfall, and a moderate climate without extremes of temperature. Broadleaved evergreen shrubs in particular—especially those notorious for their exacting needs for moderately to strongly acidic soil, mild winters, relatively cool summers, and high humidity as well as high rainfall—find an ideal home here. It's no accident that "difficult" shrubs such as rhododendrons and azaleas, heaths and heathers, camellias, pieris, enkianthus, hebes, daphnes, and skimmias thrive in our climate with little or no attention.

However, our imperfect climate also accommodates heat-lovers such as photinia and firethorn (*Pyracantha*), sun-lovers such as rosemary and lavender, and very drought-tolerant, even water-shy shrubs such as California lilac (*Ceanothus*) and purple-leaved smoke tree (*Cotinus coggygria*). The only shrubs that don't grow well in our climate are those native to harsh continental climates with cold dry winters, such as Russian olive (*Elaeagnus angustifolia*).

Keeping this chapter to a manageable size meant leaving out a great many other shrubs that thrive beautifully here. We

153

would have loved to have included more shrubs that excel in windy coastal conditions, such as *Escallonia* and hardy fuchsia; more thoroughly drought-tolerant shrubs that accommodate our wet winters, such as beautybush (*Kolkwitzia amabilis*); more Pacific Northwest natives and their derivatives, such as snowberry (*Symphoricarpos albus* var. *laevigatus*); more deliciously fragrant shrubs such as *Daphne odora* and Korean spice viburnum (*Viburnum carlesii*); and more ever-reliable old favorites such as flowering quince (*Chaenomeles*), forsythia, kerria, and weigela.

Suffice it to say that shrubs, more than any other plant form, are the defining feature of most Pacific Northwest gardens. No rigid stylistic rules guide our choices; we simply plant what we like, and what likes our local conditions. The shrubs that grace our gardens—shrubs that flower in every month of the year, in every color, in every size from ground-hugging miniatures to the size of small trees—are both old and new, evergreen and deciduous, hardy and near-tender, attention-grabbing and quietly elegant. These are just a few of the most essential.

CALLICARPA BODINIERI VAR. GIRALDII 'PROFUSION' (PROFUSION BEAUTYBERRY)

Origin: China

Hardiness zones: 6 to 9

Size: 6 ft. × 5 ft. (1.8 m × 1.5 m)

Season of interest: September to December

Exposure: Sun to partial shade

Soil preference: Moisture-retentive but well drained; slightly acidic

Water needs: Drought tolerant when established

Maintenance needs: Low

Subregions best suited: All

Possible problems: None serious

Deciduous. A must-have in the Pacific Northwest for its clusters of tiny, truly profuse fall fruits of luminous violet. An arresting sight when the leaves drop in October, these are exactly the right color at exactly the right time to perfectly complement

Callicarpa bodinieri var. *giraldii* 'Profusion'

our subtle fall colors of yellow, orange, tan, dark red, and deep maroon, all set against a backdrop of shades of green.

The fruits alone would make it well worth growing (*Callicarpa* literally means "beautyberry"), but everything else about this shrub is also well suited to our growing conditions. It likes cool climates with not-too-severe winters, but needs dry, reasonably warm summers to fruit well. Established plants tolerate our normal summer droughts with no problem, but do not object to our heaviest winter deluges as long as drainage is reasonable. It's not fussy about soil type, but is happiest in slightly to moderately acidic conditions.

It's also a nice size, growing quickly but never outgrowing its space. No regular maintenance is needed, but vigorous new growth can be encouraged by removing the oldest stems every few years in early spring. No insects or diseases bother it. Its only fault, if it can be called such, is its habit of leafing out very late; the not-terribly-interesting winter silhouette persists until May. However, with so much else happening in early spring, this is hardly noticeable, and small spring bulbs such as crocus, squill, and erythroniums help make up the difference.

Although fall is the peak season of interest, Profusion beautyberry also bears attractive clusters of tiny violet-pink flowers in July, and September foliage colors of pastel pink, yellow, and purple are beautiful in their own right. The flower and foliage colors of heaths, heathers, and daboecias blend beautifully with those of beautyberry in all seasons, making them natural companions.

Fruits remain attractive until they finally shrivel in January. Small birds such as chickadees and juncos may sample them, creating an entertaining show themselves, but plants are never completely stripped; fruits are still in beautiful condition against the pristine background of an early snowfall.

CAMELLIA

Origin: Southern China, southeastern Asia, Japan, Korea, Taiwan

Hardiness zones: Varies

Size: Varies

Blooming season: February to late May; *Camellia sasanqua* November to February

Exposure: Sun to partial shade; protected from wind, intense sun, and sudden frosts

Soil preference: High in organic matter; moderately acidic; moisture-retentive but well drained

Water needs: Moderately drought tolerant when established, but best with regular water

Maintenance needs: Low

Subregions best suited: All

Possible problems: Bud drop, chlorosis, petal blight, root weevils

Evergreen. With the possible exception of water lilies, no flowers are more exquisitely formed than camellias. This alone would make them worth growing, but considering that the Pacific Northwest is one of only three climates in North America where camellias can be grown successfully (the others being the southeastern American states and non-desert parts of California), it would almost be a crime not to grow them here.

Most of us lump camellias with rhododendrons and consider them rather delicate, but we're mistaken on both counts. Although camellias are not as cold-hardy as most rhododendrons, they're less fussy about acidic soil. They also take considerably more sun and heat—often more than they're given in our cool, sun-challenged climate.

It helps to think of their close relative, *Camellia sinensis*, whose leaves provide the beverage we know as tea. All camellias are native to tropical or near-tropical latitudes, but the tropical climate and bright light is moderated by their habitats on the sides of high mountains, under the shade of tall trees. In the moist but well-drained acidic soils of these sheltered sites, protected from wind and extremes of temperature, camellias enjoy moderately high light levels, warm but not hot temperatures, a cool root run, and high humidity year-round. To grow camellias to perfection, these conditions need to be duplicated as closely as possible.

In the Pacific Northwest, year-round humidity comes gratis, although some summer misting is appreciated in the Rogue subregion. Cool root runs are provided by mulch; high organic content keeps soils acidic. In the Pacific Coast and Puget Sound subregions, full sun is best; in our hotter valleys, midday shade, intermittent shade, or a northern exposure open to the sky is advisable. Camellias will not bloom well in cool, dark, dry shade such as found under tall conifers.

Contrary to intuition, a western exposure (given the summer shade of a deciduous tree in our hotter valleys) is preferable to an eastern exposure. Because camellias bloom so early, their flowers are often frosted at night, which in itself does no harm. However, early morning sun on iced petals browns their edges, spoiling their looks. Camellias should always be sited where direct sun cannot reach them until late morning at the earliest.

Good flowering is dependent on protection from excessive winter wetness, extreme summer dryness, very high heat, sudden changes in temperature, and hot or cold drying winds, all of which can cause excessive bud drop. (A small amount of bud drop is normal on all camellias.) Cultivars with light-colored or variegated flowers are especially dependent on consistent growing conditions. Camellias will also flower poorly, if at all, if planted too deeply. Like rhododendrons, they should be planted with the top of the fibrous root ball even with the soil surface, then covered with a layer of loose, organic mulch.

Unlike rhododendrons, camellias need some calcium as well as magnesium (they're more acid-tolerant than lime-hating) and will tolerate any soil on the acid side of neutral (pH 7.0). In our climate, yellowing camellia leaves don't necessarily indicate chlorosis; more likely causes are soil dryness in summer, excessive soil wetness in winter, or normal aging of the oldest leaves. Camellias are not heavy feeders; more have been killed by over-fertilizing than by lack of nutrients. Modest feedings of compost will usually provide all the food they need.

CAMELLIA FLOWER SIZES AND BLOOMING TIMES

Small: 2.5–3 in. (6–7.5 cm) in diameter

Medium: 3–4 in. (7.5–10 cm)

Large: 4–5 in. (10–13 cm)

Very large: Over 5 in. (13 cm)

Early: Early to late March

Midseason: Late March to late April

Late: Late April or later

(*Camellia sasanqua* and its relatives bloom from late fall through late winter.)

Petal blight is the only serious disease in our climate. This fungus affects only the flowers; plants remain healthy. Brown petal edges may be mistaken for frost damage, but if browning runs into the centers of flowers and turns grayish, petal blight is to blame. Since the fungal spores are airborne, prevention is all but futile. Diligent and prompt removal of all infected flowers, including fallen petals, is the only effective control.

No regular pruning is required, but camellias do accept pruning exceptionally well and can be trained into espaliers, standards, or even hedges. They also make excellent container subjects. Since they sprout from old wood, aged or neglected specimens can be rejuvenated by heavy pruning immediately after flowering. Established camellias should also be pruned fairly severely when being transplanted (even large specimens can be moved successfully in early fall) to compensate for inevitable root loss.

Camellia flowers are classified by shape, theoretically being either single, semi-double, anemone form, peony form, rose form, or formal double. In reality, all but single and formal double shapes can look confusingly similar, especially since the same cultivar or even the same plant can produce two or three different flower forms and even different colors (sports). Flower color can also vary slightly from plant to plant or season to season. Except for exhibition purposes, none of this matters; whatever their shape, size, or color, all camellias are beautiful.

All the possible variations add up to thousands of cultivar names, many of which are synonyms. New camellias are constantly coming on the market, but recommendations need careful scrutiny: many cultivars are developed specifically for the summer-humid southeastern states or for nearly frost-free California. By all means try some new camellias, but don't neglect older cultivars. The following selections are all proven performers in the Pacific Northwest.

Camellia japonica 'Carter's Sunburst'. Flower of *C. j.* 'Bob Hope' is just visible at upper left.

Camellia japonica 'Kumasaka'

Camellia japonica. Native to Japan, China, Korea, and Taiwan. Usually a fairly slow growing, medium-sized shrub to 6–8 ft. × 4–6 ft. (1.8–2.4 m × 1.2–1.8 m), but old, well-maintained specimens can easily top 15 ft. × 12 ft. (4.5 m × 3.6 m). Often rated as cold-hardy only to Zone 8, but established plants have no problem handling Zone 7 winters as long as low temperatures don't come on suddenly. Established camellias even survive our Big Freezes, although they may lose their leaves; however, winter mulch is always recommended.

'Bob Hope'. Large, very dark red semi-double flowers; compact, slow growing habit. Very glossy foliage. Midseason to late.

'Carter's Sunburst'. Large semi-double, peony form, or formal double flowers of pale pink striped deep pink; compact habit. Early to late.

'Coquettii' (syn. 'Glen 40'). Medium-sized formal double flowers of deep red; much used for bouquets and boutonnieres. Classic compact French cultivar is cold-hardy and reliable; good in containers. Midseason to late.

'Debutante'. Medium-sized peony form flowers of clear light pink; popular and reliable for over 100 years. Vigorous upright habit. Early to midseason.

'Elegans' (syn. 'Chandleri Elegans'). Large to very large anemone form flowers of rose-pink with white-marbled central petaloids (modified stamens resembling small petals). Vigorous, upright, spreading plant is a true classic; also available are 'Elegans Champagne' (white wavy petals with frilled edges), 'Elegans Splendour' (soft pink with white serrated petals), and 'Elegans Supreme' (rose-pink with serrated petals). All bloom early to midseason.

'Guilio Nuccio'. Large to very large semi-double flowers of deep coral-pink; inner petals stand upright, giving flowers a distinctive look. Vigorous upright plant with slightly drooping branches. Midseason.

'Kumasaka'. Medium-sized rose form or peony form flowers of deep rose-pink; very heavy flower production on vigorous compact plant. Hardy to Zone 6; takes morning sun with little or no damage. Midseason to late.

'Shiragiku'. Often sold as 'Shiragiku Purity' or 'Purity'. Medium-sized rose form to formal double flowers of pure white,

often showing a few golden stamens. Vigorous upright habit; late blooming time means flowers escape worst of unsettled spring weather.

'Tom Knudsen'. Hybrid of *Camellia japonica* and *C. reticulata*, a very large-flowered but slightly tender Chinese species. Medium to large rose form or peony form flowers of deep red with darker veins; vigorous but compact growth habit. Mulch for winter in colder subregions. Early to midseason.

Camellia sasanqua. Native to Japan. Small spreading plants with slender, somewhat lax branches that lend themselves well to espaliering and take pruning exceptionally well. Attractive, glossy evergreen leaves are smaller and narrower than those of *C. japonica*. Much valued for their fragrant flowers that bloom over a long period from late fall through winter.

Plants themselves are hardy to Zone 7, but bloom well only after a hot, sunny summer and a warm fall; best suited to Willamette, Rogue, and Cascade Slopes/Outflow Valleys subregions. Elsewhere, sasanquas need to be positioned against a warm sunny wall in summer or grown in containers (all make excellent container subjects) that can be exposed to summer heat but brought into a sheltered site for winter. In all areas, blooming plants need protection from wind and heavy rains as well as flower-spoiling frosts. Containerized plants can be sheltered in an unheated porch or garage during very inclement weather.

Cultivars of *Camellia hiemalis* and *C.* ×*vernalis* (hybrids between *C. sasanqua* and *C. japonica*) are usually classed with

Camellia 'Tom Knudsen'

Camellia × *vernalis* 'Yuletide'. Photo by Judy Newton

Camellia × *williamsii* 'Donation'

sasanquas (and often sold as such) because of their similar growth habit and blooming season.

'Bonanza' (*Camellia hiemalis*). Large semi-double or peony form flowers of deep red; long blooming season. Upright, spreading habit.

'Fukuzutsumi' (syn. 'Apple Blossom'). Large single to semi-double white flowers flushed rose-pink; spreading habit.

'Jean May'. Large double flowers of shell-pink; foliage is particularly glossy. Bushy habit.

'Showa-no-sakae' (*Camellia hiemalis*). Small to medium-sized semi-double or rose form flowers of soft pink. Small, fast growing plant with willowy branches; good espalier.

'Yuletide' (*Camellia* × *vernalis*). Small single flowers of orange-red with showy golden stamens; classic winter bloomer. Slow, compact pyramidal habit.

Camellia × *williamsii*. Hybrids of various *C. japonica* cultivars with *C. saluenensis*, a hardy, free-flowering Chinese species. Hybrid vigor, superior cold hardiness, extended blooming season, and abundance of graceful, slightly more relaxed flowers make these camellias must-haves in the Pacific Northwest. Growth is similar to *C. japonica*, with slightly more open habit and more pendulous branches. All are fully hardy in Zone 7.

Many of the most beautiful *Camellia* × *williamsii* hybrids were bred in New Zealand by Les Jury; of the following selections, all but 'Donation' are Jury hybrids.

'Anticipation'. Large peony form flowers of deep rose-pink with great petal substance; narrowly upright habit. Midseason.

'Daintiness'. Large semi-double flowers of clear salmon-pink; vigorous, slightly open rounded habit. Midseason.

'Debbie'. Large peony form flowers of bright deep pink; compact pyramidal habit. Very adaptable; buds well and flowers prolifically no matter what our spring weather. *Camellia japonica* parent was 'Debutante'. Midseason.

'Donation'. One of the first *Camellia* × *williamsii* hybrids (bred in England in 1941) and still considered by many to be the finest camellia bred in the 20th century. Large semi-double flowers of orchid-pink bloom in unbelievable profusion over an extended period. Compact vigorous habit; an outstanding plant. Midseason.

'Elsie Jury'. Large peony form flowers of pure medium pink. Neat small plant with slightly open habit is good in containers. Midseason to late.

'Jury's Yellow'. Medium-sized anemone form flowers with wavy-edged ivory petals surrounding primrose-yellow petaloids. Compact upright habit; best in site sheltered from wind, hot sun, and severe winter cold. Early to late.

Related species
Stewartia pseudocamellia (Japanese stewartia), a small deciduous tree with beautiful camellia-like single white flowers in August, is a close relative of camellias and enjoys the same conditions, although performance is more dependent on sufficient soil moisture in summer. Hardy in zones 7 to 9, it's attractive in all seasons, with fresh green leaves in spring, good fall foliage of bronze/burgundy/orange, and a pleasing winter silhouette.

Corylus avellana 'Contorta' in February

Hamamelis ×intermedia 'Arnold Promise' in early March

CORYLUS AVELLANA 'CONTORTA' (CONTORTED FILBERT)

Origin: Spontaneous mutation of *Corylus avellana* native to Europe, western Asia, and North Africa; found in English hedgerow about 1863

Hardiness zones: 5 to 9

Size: To 10 ft. × 12 ft. (3 m × 3.6 m) or more

Season of interest: Winter, early spring

Exposure: Full sun to light shade

Soil preference: Moderately rich; moisture-retentive but well drained

Water needs: Drought tolerant when established

Maintenance needs: Low

Subregions best suited: All

Possible problems: None serious

Deciduous. This distinctive shrub has no faults except its own popularity; it's considered a cliché by some. However, its perfect health, very low maintenance, and incomparable winter interest of bare branches and catkins are all undeniable.

All parts of the shrub—short trunk, branches, twigs, leaves—are contorted except for its long, beautiful greenish yellow catkins in February and March. (In our garden, contorted twigs are greatly favored by ravens for Velcro-like nesting material.) Congenitally weak roots mean it's almost always grafted; any non-contorted shoots growing from the rootstock should be removed promptly.

Although very slow growing, it definitely reaches small tree size eventually; a very common mistake is leaving it too little room. The crown can be raised as it matures by removing lowest limbs to reveal the strong, gnarled, satin-sheened trunk.

Winter-blooming heaths make superb companions, especially when catkins are out. (Make sure the heaths won't eventually be shaded.) Plant where both can be enjoyed from windows most often looked out of in winter. Underplanting with snowdrops, snow crocus, or hellebores adds even more winter interest. From late spring through fall, the shrub blends into the background as a large, pleasant green mound.

HAMAMELIS (WITCH HAZEL)

Origin: Eastern Asia, eastern North America

Hardiness zones: 5 to 9

Size: 8 ft. × 12 ft. (2.4 m × 3.6 m) or more

Season of interest: Winter (flowers); fall (foliage)

Exposure: Full sun to partial shade

Soil preference: Moderately rich, moderately acidic; moisture-retentive but well drained

Water needs: Drought tolerant when established

Maintenance needs: Low

Subregions best suited: All

Possible problems: None serious

Deciduous. Not related to hazels or filberts, although large, handsome rounded leaves look similar; closer kin to *Corylopsis, Parrotia, Liquidambar, Fothergilla,* and other choice ornamentals and a must-have in Pacific Northwest gardens.

Regardless of weather or temperature, many-petalled spidery flowers cover bare branches in midwinter and bloom for six to eight weeks. Fall foliage is gloriously colored; in most cases, the exact hue echoes the flower color.

Long, very slender branches on short trunks ("witch" may derive from "switch") grow in an attractive vase shape, spreading very wide in maturity. Reserve plenty of room for a witch hazel; slow-to-establish plants resent being moved, and pruning spoils their graceful silhouette.

Witch hazels are almost always grafted (even species); seeds take two years to break dormancy, and cuttings, for reasons unknown, seldom survive their first winter. Any suckers should be removed as soon as noticed.

Contrary to the rule of thumb that smaller plants are easier to establish, witch hazels should be large at time of purchase—preferably 3–4 ft. (0.9–1.2 m) tall with roots balled and burlapped for early spring planting—but in nothing smaller than a five-gallon container. Smaller plants need dedicated care; even then, they may not establish well. Size makes them expensive but worth it: the reward is decades of stellar performance.

Hamamelis ×*intermedia* 'Jelena' in late December

Hamamelis ×*intermedia* 'Diane' in October

Hamamelis mollis in October

Summer watering is crucial until plants are established (a minimum of three years, often longer) with care taken that the actual clay root ball, not just soil surrounding it, is adequately moistened. Once finally established, witch hazels tolerate our normal summer drought and heavy winter rains with equal aplomb. No pruning is necessary; wayward branches can be trained to better placement or removed at the trunk when young.

Hamamelis ×*intermedia*. Hybrids of *H. mollis* and *H. japonica*, a large, variable spreading shrub with twisted flower petals and richly colored fall foliage.

'Arnold Promise'. Freely borne flowers of bright primrose-yellow, February and March; fall color is blend of apricot, orange, and yellow. More compact and upright than most.

'Diane'. Fragrant, deep red flowers in February and March; color shows best against light background. Fall color is bright red and orange.

'Feuerzauber' (Fire Charm, Magic Fire). Orange-red flowers in January and February. Fall foliage is flaming red; considered the best red-leaved cultivar.

'Jelena' (syn. 'Copper Beauty'). Yellow flowers with dark red bases appear orange; bloom late December to mid-February. Fall foliage is beautiful orange with yellow and red highlights.

'Pallida'. Seedling of *Hamamelis mollis*; considered a hybrid. Large, abundant flowers of sulfur-yellow are strongly but sweetly scented; bloom late December to mid-February. Fall foliage is yellow.

'Westerstede'. Canary-yellow flowers in February and March; fall foliage is deep golden yellow.

Hamamelis mollis (Chinese witch hazel). Native to China. Popular for more than a century and still considered the best witch hazel by many. Deep yellow-gold flowers with red bases bloom January to March with subtle, sweet scent; fall foliage is the clearest, purest yellow imaginable.

Related species

Distylium racemosum (evergreen witch hazel) is closely related to *Hamamelis* and thrives in the same conditions. Native to Japan, Korea, and China; similar in size and shape to *Hamamelis* but with smaller, shiny, leathery evergreen leaves. Clusters of small petal-less flowers with conspicuous red stamens bloom in March and April. Small tree in wild; in gardens, slow growth to 6 ft. × 8 ft. (1.8 m × 2.4 m). Zones 6 to 9.

HEATHS AND HEATHERS:
ERICA, *CALLUNA*, AND *DABOECIA*

Origin: Northern and western Europe, British Isles, northern Africa, Asia Minor

Hardiness zones: Varies

Size: Varies; most low and mounding

Blooming season: Varies

Exposure: Cool sun

Soil preference: Well drained, acidic, moisture-retentive; low to average fertility

Water needs: Moderate to high in youth, drought tolerant when established

Maintenance needs: Low

Subregions best suited: Puget Sound, Pacific Coast, Georgia Basin/Puget Trough

Subregions not suited: None

Possible problems: None serious

Evergreen. Heaths (*Erica*), heathers (*Calluna vulgaris*), and daboecias (*Daboecia cantabrica*) are so well suited to Pacific Northwest conditions that it's something of a mystery why they're not grown much more widely here, especially since this is the best climate in all of North America for them. Their incomparable ability to provide ever-changing year-round color, especially in our long, wet, dismally gray winters, would make them well worth growing even if they were difficult and finicky, which they definitely are not.

It's no wonder the words "heath," "heather," and "heathen" are so similar. (In German, they're even closer; "heathland" is *die Heide*, "heathens" *der Heide*.) Like the unenlightened, self-reliant heathens of yore who chose to dwell far outside the city walls and shunned the comforts of civilization, these true dwarf shrubs disdain horticultural coddling and thrive on exposure to the natural elements. In true testimony to their heritage, most well-known cultivars and even hybrids of these highly variable plants are natural wildlings, chance seedlings, or sports. (This is changing; recent breeding efforts, notably by Kurt Kramer in Germany, have resulted in some outstanding new introductions, especially in winter-blooming heaths.)

All heaths and heathers are ideally suited to maritime-influenced climates with mild, wet winters and relatively cool summers. Their only absolute needs are full sun (light shade where summers are hotter) and acidic, very well-drained soil that's not too dry and not too rich. Since they grow naturally on bleak, desolate, windswept moors and exposed mountainsides, they can take just about anything else nature can dish out.

Our own heaths and heathers have survived Big Freezes, summer temperatures of 95°F (35°C), snow loads exceeding 3 ft. (0.9 m), hurricane-force winds, a drought that lasted from March to October (they did get some supplemental water then), and a deluge of 48 in. (1200 mm) of rain in less than four months. They also tolerate salt spray, making them excellent seaside plants,

and are reputed to regenerate quickly following forest fires. These plants do not need pampering.

What they do need, and what is likely to do them in if not supplied, is regular watering while becoming established. Their very fine roots eventually develop into massive systems that enable most species to survive our normal summer drought with ease, but the small roots of very young plants dry out quickly. Unfortunately, heaths and heathers show no warning signs of water stress; by the time a young plant looks wilted, it's already dead. Close attention to soil moisture is essential for the first and second summers (even the third), especially with summer-blooming species.

Established plants of most species are reliably drought tolerant in cool-summer gardens, but a couple of deep soakings are necessary in extended summer droughts and in our hot-summer river valleys, where an eastern or northern exposure open to the sky is advisable.

Copious amounts of peat moss or well-rotted sawdust mixed into the soil before planting will help retain summer moisture without compromising winter drainage, which is also essential. (No heaths, heathers, or daboecias tolerate wet feet.) Fertilizer should be avoided, but a few feedings of half-strength liquid fish fertilizer helps get young plants off to a good start.

Mulch is a huge help in keeping roots cool, conserving soil moisture, and keeping weeds down until plants fill in. (Be sure to consider the recommended spacing for each species; due to their large but fragile root systems, transplanting is traumatic if not fatal.) Mulch also encourages rooting of the lowest stems, making specimens more vigorous and drought tolerant. These rooted stems are also a convenient source of new plants.

All heaths and heathers, including daboecias, need regular shearing after flowering to keep them compact and free-flowering. (In the wild, browsing deer or sheep do the job.) Exact needs vary by species; for timing and severity of these bowl haircuts, see the descriptions that follow.

Perhaps the best feature of heaths and heathers is their ability to combine so beautifully and seamlessly with each other, making a never-ending tapestry of subtly blended flower and foliage color that changes month by month. Massing them is much more effective than dotting them here and there; single plants always look lonely and a bit forlorn. For greatest impact, use relaxed drifts of three to five plants of a long-blooming cultivar accented by single cultivars that bloom at different times. No real mistakes are possible—the term "heather tones" doesn't exist for nothing—but some of the brighter winter foliage colors can require careful placement.

Massed heaths and heathers also combine beautifully with other species needing cool, sunny conditions and acidic, not-too-fertile soil, such as conifers, hebes, ornamental grasses, and deciduous azaleas. Spring bulbs, especially daffodils, also make good companions.

Sizes given for all heaths, heathers, and daboecias are approximate after being established for three years. All will spread in time, some considerably; the spacing recommended takes this into account.

Winter-blooming heaths with Scottish heathers in late February. *Erica ×darleyensis* 'Silberschmelze' (white, center left and center right), *Calluna vulgaris* 'Beoley Gold' (golden foliage, left foreground and center), *Erica carnea* 'Myretoun Ruby' (deep pink, right foreground)

Calluna vulgaris 'Mair's Variety'

HEATHS AND HEATHERS FOR YEAR-ROUND BLOOM

	Jan–Apr	May	June	Jul–Sep	Oct	Nov	Dec
Calluna vulgaris	*			X	X	X	*
Daboecia cantabrica			X	X	X		
D. c. subsp. scotica		X	X	X	X		
Erica carnea	X					X	X
E. ciliaris				X	X		
E. cinerea			X	X	X	X	
E. ×darleyensis	X	X				X	X
E. ×stuartii		X	X	X			
E. tetralix			X	X	X	X	
E. vagans				X	X	X	
E. ×watsonii			X	X	X	X	
E. ×williamsii			X	X	X	X	

* colorful winter foliage or new tips

Most drought tolerant: *Calluna vulgaris, Erica ×darleyensis, E. vagans*

Most shade tolerant: *Daboecia cantabrica, Erica carnea, E. ciliaris, E. vagans*

Most tolerant of non-acidic soil: *Erica carnea, E. ×darleyensis, E. vagans, E. ×williamsii*

Longest-blooming: *Daboecia cantabrica, Erica cinerea, E. ×darleyensis, E. vagans, E. ×watsonii*

Calluna vulgaris (Scottish heather). Native to British Isles, northern and western Europe, northern Africa, and western Asia. All true heathers (as opposed to heaths) belong to this one species, but over 600 cultivars have been named, encompassing an amazing range of both flower and foliage colors. True heathers can always be distinguished from heaths (*Erica*) by their scaly, overlapping leaves resembling cedar foliage; leaves of *Erica* species stand straight out from stems like fir needles.

Peak flowering season is August and September, but some bloom as early as July and a few late bloomers are still in flower in November. As with most heaths, the majority of well-known heather cultivars are findlings, sports, or chance seedlings; white heathers and those with double flowers are considered lucky. However, much new breeding work is being done; bud bloomers, for instance, are cultivars with flowers that never fully open. Marketed as Painted Heathers, these flowers take much longer to wither and so provide color for an exceptionally long time, even into December.

No *Calluna* cultivars bloom in winter, spring, or early summer. However, some have colored foliage of yellow, gold, silver, chartreuse, or orange that is very attractive all year round, especially in combination with other heathers and heaths. In winter, many of these colored-foliage types take on deeper hues of old gold, orange-red, bright red, brick-red, or mahogany, with full sun and colder temperatures intensifying the colors. Other heather cultivars have brightly colored new tips in late winter and early spring that are as showy as flowers.

Except for dwarfs such as 'J. H. Hamilton', 'Mousehole', and 'Soay', which lack an extensive root system, Scottish heathers are highly drought tolerant once established. However, in the kind of extended drought that kills even established native plants, one or two deep soakings in summer are greatly appreciated. Shade is not well tolerated; poor drainage is almost always fatal. Dwarf, silver-foliaged, and double-flowered cultivars are especially sensitive to wet feet.

Scottish heathers must be sheared back every year without fail. Without shearing, new blooms begin only where last year's flowers left off, making plants open, lanky, and less and less inclined to flower; with annual shearing, plants become larger, bushier, and more floriferous. Remove the faded flower spikes at or even slightly below their bases. Just be sure not to cut into leafless wood, since bare stems will not resprout.

Since heathers bloom well into fall, shearing can be delayed until late March or early April, just before new growth begins.

Calluna vulgaris 'Elsie Purnell'

Calluna vulgaris 'Silver Queen'

(The dried flowers add their own pleasant notes of tan and brown to the winter garden.) However, cultivars grown mainly for their brightly colored new tips should be sheared as soon as their flowers fade in fall so that no new tips are sacrificed by spring pruning.

Of the many hundreds of heather cultivars, these are some of the best performers in the Pacific Northwest, categorized by their most striking features. Most cultivars should be spaced at 30–36 in. (75–90 cm); vigorous or spreading forms at 36–42 in. (90–105 cm). Zones 5 to 9.

Free-flowering, single

'Allegro'. Ruby-red flowers bloom July to October; vigorous mounding foliage is dark green. 20 in. × 24 in. (50 cm × 60 cm).

'Corbett's Red'. Crimson flowers on long spikes, August to October; compact dark green foliage. Good performer in the Pacific Northwest; a British Columbia introduction. 10 in. × 16 in. (25 cm × 40 cm).

'Dark Beauty'. Profuse semi-double flowers of cherry-pink darkening to deep ruby-red, August to October; compact dark green foliage. 10 in. × 18 in. (25 cm × 45 cm).

'Fritz Kircher'. Bud bloomer with long spikes of purplish pink buds, lighter at bases, August to December; compact green foliage. 12 in. × 18 in. (30 cm × 45 cm).

'Mair's Variety'. A classic; still considered the best vigorous single white heather. Pure white flower spikes on tall, dense mounds of dark green foliage, August and September. Good

cut flower. 18 in. × 20 in. (45 cm × 50 cm). Giving similar color effect is 'Melanie', a white-flowered bud bloomer.

Double flowers

'Annemarie'. Rose-pink flowers on tall mounds of dark green foliage, late August to October. Excellent cut flower. 20 in. × 24 in. (50 cm × 60 cm).

'County Wicklow'. Beautiful flowers of soft shell-pink on compact green foliage from August to October. Deservedly popular since discovered in Ireland in the 1920s. 10 in. × 18 in. (25 cm × 45 cm).

'Elsie Purnell'. Long spikes of silvery lavender flowers August to October; vigorous, spreading mounds of gray-green foliage. 16 in. × 30 in. (40 cm × 75 cm).

'Kinlochruel'. Abundant spikes of white flowers on compact, rounded mounds of green foliage, August to October. Sport of 'County Wicklow'; considered the best double-flowered white heather. 10 in. × 16 in. (25 cm × 40 cm).

'Peter Sparkes'. Very long flower spikes of silvery rose-pink on spreading mounds of dark green foliage, August to October; excellent for cutting. 12 in. × 24 in. (30 cm × 60 cm).

Foliage color, summer

'Beoley Gold'. Excellent yellow-gold foliage keeps its bright color all winter; small white flowers in August and September. 16 in. × 20 in. (40 cm × 50 cm).

'Kerstin'. Gray-green foliage with a distinct lilac cast deepens in color in winter; new growth is tipped cream and pink. Mauve flowers in August and September. 12 in. × 18 in. (30 cm × 45 cm).

'Lime Glade'. Lime-green summer foliage is creamy chartreuse in spring; protect from hot or intense sun. Sparse white flowers in September and October. 12 in. × 18 in. (30 cm × 45 cm).

'Silver Knight'. Vigorous, upright silver-gray foliage covered with lavender flowers from July to September; one of few excellent foliage heathers also having abundant and attractive flowers. Foliage takes on purple tints in winter. 20 in. × 24 in. (50 cm × 60 cm).

'Silver Queen'. Soft, spreading silvery foliage and lavender-pink flowers in August and September make a beautiful combination. Handle carefully when pruning; stems can be brittle. 12 in. × 20 in. (30 cm × 50 cm).

Foliage color, winter

'Boskoop'. Summer foliage of deep gold turns bright orange in winter, deepens to brick-red in cold spells. Sparse lavender flowers in late summer. 12 in. × 20 in. (30 cm × 50 cm).

'Copper Glow'. Yellow-green summer foliage turns bright bronze to deep copper in winter; new growth is tipped bright coppery pink. Vigorous grower; mauve flowers in late summer. 18 in. × 24 in. (45 cm × 60 cm).

'Firefly'. Yellow-orange summer foliage turns salmon-orange in winter, intensifying to bright red in cold spells; one of the best winter reds. Deep mauve flowers in late summer. 18 in. × 24 in. (45 cm × 60 cm).

'Red Carpet'. Golden summer foliage turns an intense orange-red to dark brick-red in winter. Low, spreading habit; mauve flowers in late summer. 8 in. × 18 in. (20 cm × 45 cm).

'Winter Chocolate'. Yellow-gold summer foliage turns bronze in cool weather; deep chocolate-brown in cold weather. New tips are salmon-pink. Lavender flowers in late summer. 18 in. × 24 in. (45 cm × 60 cm).

Colorful new tips

'Easter-bonfire'. Very bright spring tips of creamy white and red on dark green foliage give three-toned effect until summer. Light purple flowers in August and September. 16 in. × 20 in. (40 cm × 50 cm).

'Hillbrook Sparkler'. Multi-colored spring tips of cream, pink, orange, red, and copper look like fireworks on dark green foliage. Mauve flowers from August to October. 18 in. × 24 in. (45 cm × 60 cm).

'Spring Cream'. Bright cream tips on very dense green foliage look like thousands of tiny lights in early spring. White flowers from August to November; foliage tips darken to yellow in fall and winter. 14 in. × 18 in. (35 cm × 45 cm).

'Spring Torch'. Prolific spring tips of yellow, pink, and dark red look like sparks from a bonfire on dark green foliage. Mauve flowers from August to October. 20 in. × 24 in. (50 cm × 60 cm).

Daboecia cantabrica (St. Dabeoc's heath, Irish bell heather). Native to northern Spain, western France, and northwestern Ireland. Large, attractive bell-shaped flowers look like heather flowers on steroids. Small triangular leaves are glossy dark green on top; whitish underneath. Blooms non-stop from late spring until mid-fall, but is less drought tolerant and slightly more tender than other heaths and heathers. Best with regular watering; in hot-summer valleys, light shade is advisable.

Shear hard annually in late winter as soon as danger of hard frost is past; these vigorous growers can get away from you. Some stem growth can be removed, even into bare wood, as long as at least half the stems retain some leaves. Except for compact cultivars, which can be spaced closer, space at 36 in. (90 cm). Average height is 16–18 in. (40–45 cm). Hardy in Zones 7 to 9.

Daboecia cantabrica subsp. *scotica* 'William Buchanan'

'Alba'. Very large bells of pure white on light green foliage; vigorous.

'Arielle'. Large flowers of bright glowing magenta; compact dark green foliage.

'Cinderella'. Semi-dwarf with white bells tinged pink at bases; compact dark green foliage. 12 in. × 18 in. (30 cm × 45 cm).

'Hookstone Purple'. Large, clear lilac-purple bells on very dark green foliage.

'Praegerae'. Cherry-pink bells on vigorous mid-green foliage.

subsp. *scotica*. Usually listed as a hybrid, *Daboecia ×scotica*. Shorter, more compact, and even longer flowering than the species, blooming from May to at least October. Space at 24–30 in. (60–75 cm); dwarf forms closer. Zones 7 to 9. 'Seattle Purple', a dwarf selection of this subspecies with pretty lilac bells on dark green spreading foliage, was raised from seed at the Rhododendron Species Foundation and Botanical Garden near Seattle; it grows to 8 in. × 18 in. (20 cm × 45 cm). Another selection, 'William Buchanan', offers profuse bells of bright crimson-purple on dark green foliage and grows to 16 in. × 20 in. (40 cm × 50 cm).

Erica (heath). Although often called heathers in the general sense of belonging to the heather family (Ericaceae), this genus differs from true heathers in several important ways. Unlike heathers, which belong to a single genus (*Calluna vulgaris*), there are nearly 800 *Erica* species, most of which are frost-tender natives of South Africa. Of the dozen or so hardy species native to Europe, some bloom from late spring to late summer, some from midsummer to fall, and (most importantly to gardeners, especially in our mild but gray winters), some from late fall right through midwinter and into early spring. Flowers of the different species vary by shape, configuration, and color range. We have profiled only a few of the most outstanding cultivars of the most important *Erica* species; even more choices are available through specialty growers.

Winter-blooming heaths in March. *Erica carnea* 'Springwood White' (center front), *E.* ×*darleyensis* 'Mary Helen', right foreground

Erica carnea. Native to European Alps and Carpathian Mountains. Peak blooming season is January to March, but some cultivars begin blooming in December or even November, while others are still in bloom in April. Most of the brightest winter-blooming cultivars are found in this hardiest and most adaptable species. Good drainage is a must, but anything from acidic to neutral soil will do. Light shade is also acceptable and is highly recommended where summers are hot, since this mountain-dwelling species needs cool conditions. Suffers in prolonged heat or drought; good mulching and a few deep soakings in summer are advisable, especially in hot-summer valleys.

Habit is low-growing and spreading, making good groundcover. Space at 30–36 in. (75–90 cm) for good root development and reasonably fast fill-in; vigorous cultivars can be spaced at 36–42 in. (90–105 cm). Shear lightly in early spring every two to three years to keep plants compact and bushy. To keep them from becoming bald at centers, lift the branchlets near the crown and cut them back more severely, but not into bare stems. Zones 4 to 9.

'Adrienne Duncan'. Bright reddish purple flowers from January to April; dark green foliage turns bronze-green in cold weather. Even more vigorous and longer flowering than the older, very popular 'Vivellii', which it closely resembles. 6 in. × 18 in. (15 cm × 45 cm).

'Golden Starlet'. White flowers from December to March; golden summer foliage turns lime-green in winter, making excellent contrast with darker foliage. Compact grower. 6 in. × 16 in. (15 cm × 40 cm).

'Myretoun Ruby'. Deep ruby-magenta flowers completely obscure the vigorous dark green foliage from January to April. Its hybrid progeny 'Winterfreude' (Winter Joy) and the cultivar 'Challenger' are both very similar. All 6 in. × 18 in. (15 cm × 45 cm).

'Pink Spangles'. Profuse bicolored flowers of shell-pink and white bloom from January to April; deepen to rose-pink. Vigorous, time-tested, and dependable. 6 in. × 18 in. (15 cm × 45 cm).

'Rosalie'. Large flowers of bright pink on compact, upturned bronze-green foliage, January to April. Hybrid involving 'Myretoun Ruby'. 6 in. × 16 in. (15 cm × 40 cm).

'Springwood White'. Outstanding classic with pure white flowers on bright green, non-bronzing foliage from December to April. Vigorous creeping or trailing habit with upturned branchlets, 4 in. × 20 in. (10 cm × 50 cm). Its more compact, larger-flowered hybrids 'Ice Princess', 'Isabell', and 'Schneekuppe' (Snow Crest) are now considered even better, but the longer-blooming, far-wandering 'Springwood White' will always be welcome in gardens.

'Wintersonne' (Winter Sun). Bright magenta flowers from February to April; compact bronze-green foliage turns mahogany-red in cold weather. 6 in. × 16 in. (15 cm × 40 cm).

Erica ciliaris (Dorset heath). Native to coast of western Europe. Relatively large bell-shaped flowers bloom from July to

Erica ×darleyensis 'Arthur Johnson' (center) in April

Top to bottom: *Erica ×darleyensis* 'Silberschmelze', *E. ×darleyensis* 'Furzey', *Abies balsamea* 'Nana'

October at the tips of stems; leaves are gray-green. Less cold-hardy than most heaths and heathers, but tolerates fairly dry soils and light shade. To keep compact, prune hard (not into bare wood) in early spring. Height 12 in. (30 cm); space at 24 in. (60 cm). Zones 7 to 9.

'Corfe Castle'. Large flowers of unusual salmon-pink; compact green foliage turns bronze in winter.

'Mrs. C. H. Gill'. Long flower spikes of deep crimson on dark green foliage; showy.

'Stoborough'. Large white flowers on bright green foliage; vigorous and very long blooming.

Erica cinerea (bell heather). Native to northern and western Europe. Small but prolific bell-shaped flowers bloom over a very long season beginning in June; wide range of flower colors. Habit is mounding and spreading, making good groundcover. Needs full sun, acidic soil, and excellent drainage; in the wild, grows on seaside cliffs, mountain slopes, and moist but very well-drained moorland.

Good drought tolerance when established, but protect from drying winds; don't ever let young plants dry out. Prune as for *Calluna vulgaris*, removing entire flower spikes in early spring. Space vigorous cultivars at 30–36 in. (75–90 cm); smaller ones at 24–30 in. (60–75 cm). Zones 7 to 9.

'C. D. Eason'. Magenta-pink flowers on dark green foliage are a standout in early summer; bloom from June to September. 10 in. × 24 in. (25 cm × 60 cm).

'Eden Valley'. White flowers with lavender-pink tips give cool, pastel effect from June to October. Spreading habit. 8 in. × 24 in. (20 cm × 60 cm).

'Lime Soda'. Profuse lavender flowers from June to October on vigorous lime-green foliage. Great color combination. 12 in. × 24 in. (30 cm × 60 cm).

'P. S. Patrick'. True purple flowers on compact dark green foliage, June to September; unusual deep color is nice contrast with other summer bloomers. 8 in. × 18 in. (20 cm × 45 cm).

'Pink Ice'. Masses of large, light rose-pink flowers from July to November on low-growing, spreading foliage of dark green. 6 in. × 18 in. (15 cm × 45 cm).

Erica ×darleyensis. Hybrid of *E. carnea* and *E. erigena*, a very tall but slightly tender winter-blooming species native to northern Spain and Ireland. Invaluable winter-blooming species; taller, wider, longer blooming, and more tolerant of summer heat than *E. carnea*, although not quite as cold-hardy. Established plants are reliably drought tolerant even in our extended summer droughts but look better with at least one soaking in very dry summers. Dense vigorous growth effectively smothers weeds.

Many cultivars open a few blooms in November and are still going strong in April or even May; peak blooming season is February to April. Besides brightening gardens with broad swaths of very early color, their late winter/early spring blooms are one of very few sources of sustenance for early-emerging bees. All cultivars have a spreading habit and show hybrid vigor.

Erica vagans 'Mrs. D. F. Maxwell', right foreground. Top to bottom at left: *Calluna vulgaris* 'Peter Sparkes', *E. v.* 'Saint Keverne', *E.* ×*williamsii* 'P. D. Williams'

Spacing of 48 in. (120 cm) is not too much, since sizes given are for just-established plants; some of our older specimens are over 7 ft. (2.1 m) wide.

Shear as soon as possible after flowers fade to avoid accidentally cutting off the attractive tips of the fast-emerging new growth (or even worse, next winter's flower buds); very late bloomers may have to be pruned while still in flower. Less vigorous cultivars can get by with a light trim or even skip a year, but vigorous cultivars need vigorous annual haircuts. Zones 5 to 9.

'Arthur Johnson'. Very tall, vigorous, and late blooming; long spikes of lilac-pink flowers from January to May on boulder-sized mounds of mid-green foliage. Outstanding. 24 in. × 30 in. (60 cm × 75 cm).

'Furzey'. Deep rosy purple flowers on bronze-green foliage that deepens to almost black-green in cold weather; January to May. Excellent. 16 in. × 24 in. (40 cm × 60 cm). 'W. G. Pine', similar but lower growing, flowers even more prolifically.

'Ghost Hills'. Pink flowers in long spikes on vigorous, wide-spreading mounds of light green foliage, November to May. 12 in. × 30 in. (30 cm × 75 cm).

'Kramer's Rote' (Kramer's Red). Bright magenta flowers on vigorous mounds of bronze-green foliage, January to April; very attractive and reliable. 14 in. × 24 in. (35 cm × 60 cm).

'Mary Helen'. Deep pink flowers on compact foliage of deep gold that darkens to bronze-gold in cold weather. Unusual and very attractive color combination; blooms February to April. 10 in. × 18 in. (25 cm × 45 cm).

'Silberschmelze' (Molten Silver). Profuse, lightly fragrant flowers of silvery white with brown anthers on very vigorous mounds of dark green foliage. Flowers may begin opening in October; many are still fresh in May. An outstanding cultivar. 'White Perfection', its more compact sport, is also excellent. 16 in. × 30 in. (40 cm × 75 cm).

'Spring Surprise'. Dark rose flowers on upright bushy mound of dark green foliage, March to May. Very free-flowering tetraploid. 18 in. × 24 in. (45 cm × 60 cm).

Erica ×*stuartii*. Natural hybrid of *E. tetralix* and *E. mackayana*, a moisture-loving species native to northern Spain and western Ireland. Large flowers held in terminal clusters bloom over a very long season; tips of new growth show bright colors for many weeks in late winter and early spring. Needs moist, acidic soil in sun or light shade; space at 24–30 in. (60–75 cm). To avoid having to cut off bright new tips in early spring, trim flowers after they fade in fall. Give more severe haircuts every few years to keep plants tidy. Zones 6 to 9.

'Irish Lemon'. Bright lemon-yellow new tips on mid-green foliage are a show in themselves, persisting even after flowering begins. Mauve flowers bloom from May to September. 10 in. × 24 in. (25 cm × 60 cm).

'Irish Orange'. New orange tips on compact, dark green foliage are brighter than but not as long-lasting as those of 'Irish Lemon'. Lilac-pink flowers bloom from June to September. 10 in. × 18 in. (25 cm × 45 cm).

Erica ×*watsonii* 'Dawn' with *Campanula cochlearifolia*

Erica tetralix (cross-leaved heath). Native to northwestern Europe and British Isles. Flowers held in dense terminal clusters bloom reliably from midsummer well into fall; tiny gray-green leaves arranged in whorls of four form an X in cross section. Prefers moist, acidic soil (it grows in boggy areas in the wild), but tolerates drier conditions in cool-summer gardens. Habit is mounding, spreading, and usually compact; space at 18–24 in. (45–60 cm) except for vigorous cultivars, which can be spaced at 24–30 in. (60–75 cm). Prune hard in early spring, but not into bare wood. Zones 6 to 9.

'Alba Mollis'. Pure white flowers from June to October on compact gray-green foliage with silvery tips. 8 in. × 12 in. (20 cm × 50 cm).

'Con Underwood'. Large flowers of an unusual brick-red shade bloom from July well into November on vigorous gray-green hummocks. 10 in. × 20 in. (25 cm × 50 cm).

'Pink Star'. Lilac-pink flowers from July to October are held at almost right angles to the stems, making star-like patterns. Low, spreading gray-green foliage. 8 in. × 18 in. (20 cm × 45 cm).

Erica vagans (Cornish heath). Native to northern Spain, western France, and the tip of southwest England. A superb summer-blooming species with tiny flowers held in dense cone-shaped spikes; these bloom from base upward over a very long period and remain attractive even when faded. Dome-shaped mounds of dark bluish green foliage are very dense and handsome even when out of flower. Tolerates light shade and non-acidic soil; reliably drought tolerant when established.

To leave plenty of room for mature mounds, space at 30–36 in. (75–90 cm). Leave flowers on plants over winter for their beauty; shear hard in early spring to keep domes compact. Zones 5 to 9.

'Lyonesse'. Dainty white flowers on bright green, non-bronzing foliage, July to October. 12 in. × 24 in. (30 cm × 60 cm).

'Mrs. D. F. Maxwell'. Deep cherry-red flowers smother vigorous domes of very dark green foliage, July to October. Faded early flowers contrast nicely with very late flowers; attractive in all seasons. Outstanding cultivar; reputed to be the most popular worldwide of all heaths and heathers. 16 in. × 24 in. (40 cm × 60 cm).

'Saint Keverne'. Deep pink flowers on dark green foliage bloom from July to November. 12 in. × 24 in. (30 cm × 60 cm).

Erica ×*watsonii*. Natural hybrid of *E. ciliaris* and *E. tetralix*, showing variable characteristics of both. Sterile flowers in terminal clusters bloom over a very long season; plants are hardy, vigorous, adaptable, and have colorful new tips. Drought tolerant when established, but keep new plants well watered. Space at 24–36 in. (60–90 cm) depending on vigor. As with *E.* ×*stuartii*, trim off flowers in fall to avoid cutting off early new growth in spring; give a more severe haircut every few years. Zones 5 to 9.

'Dawn'. Deep pink bell-shaped flowers bloom June to November on spreading, downy gray-green foliage. New growth is tipped red in late winter, becoming yellow in early spring. Very reliable. 10 in. × 20 in. (25 cm × 50 cm).

Erica ×*williamsii*. Natural hybrid of *E. tetralix* and *E. vagans*, resembling a shorter version of *E. vagans* with lighter green foliage. Sterile flowers bloom over a long season; new growth is tipped yellow. Best in light shade. Space at 24–30 in. (60–75 cm); shear lightly in early spring. Zones 5 to 9.

'P. D. Williams'. Dainty pink flowers on light green foliage from July to November. 10 in. × 20 in. (25 cm × 50 cm).

HEBE

Origin: New Zealand; a few species in Australia and southern South America

Hardiness zones: Varies

Size: Varies

Blooming season: Late spring to late summer

Exposure: Cool sun to light shade

Soil preference: Well drained, average fertility (not too rich); preferably light-textured

Water needs: Drought tolerant when established

Maintenance needs: Low

Subregions best suited: Pacific Coast, Puget Sound, Georgia Basin/Puget Trough, Olympic Rain Shadow

Subregions not suited: None

Possible problems: Lack of winter hardiness

Evergreen. In all of North America, only the Pacific Northwest has a climate mild enough in winter and cool enough in summer to grow hebes successfully. This alone would be reason enough to grow them, but their versatility and variability—not to mention their unusual attractiveness—make them must-haves.

Sizes range from rock garden miniatures to broad, head-high specimens; habits range from prostrate groundcovers to dwarf globes to upright columns. Flower spikes of white, purple, blue, or pink vary greatly in size and effect. Most remarkable is the diversity of their foliage, consisting of stalkless leaves that sit right on the curiously flexible, almost rubbery branches. Leaves may be tiny and round, angular and pointed, long and thin, or

Hebe 'Emerald Gem', right; *H. odora* 'New Zealand Gold', left

Hebe cupressoides

shaped like those of a jade plant (with a look almost as succulent); the foliage of the so-called whipcord hebes could easily be mistaken for that of a conifer.

Leaves are often arranged in four geometrically precise columns on the stems, forming an X in cross section. The color may be green or glaucous, golden-tipped or red-edged, silver-blue, purplish, variegated, or olive-copper. All make excellent low hedges and are especially nice mixed in with heaths and heathers, having just enough difference of flower type and foliage texture to keep things interesting.

All hebes are superb seaside plants, taking salt spray and any amount of wind in stride. They're also reputed to tolerate industrial pollution, making them good city plants. Remarkably, they're thoroughly drought tolerant in our normal summer droughts and in fact do not like regular summer water. In an extended drought they do appreciate a drink or two, but not in the heat of the day, since warm wet soil may lead to root rot. Snow is no problem; although the limber stems get flattened, they pop right back up, and any broken stems are soon replaced.

Hebes need little or no regular pruning, but a light haircut after flowering keeps them compact and bushy. Overgrown, leggy, or winter-damaged plants can be pruned hard in early spring. They'll respond with vigorous growth (they're named for Hebe, the Roman goddess of youth) and will bloom as usual in summer.

Although they have long been grown in the British Isles, hebes are just beginning to become well known here, mainly because they have been considered borderline hardy at best. Most references lump all 100 or so *Hebe* species into Zone 8, but in real life there are considerable differences. Some species and hybrids are hardy only to Zone 9, making them too tender for most parts of the Pacific Northwest, but established specimens of others have survived Big Freezes.

There is some truth to the rule of thumb that the smaller the leaf, the hardier the hebe; the small-leaved alpine species come from the mountains of New Zealand's South Island. Whipcord species are also reliably hardy in our climate, but even some of the showier large-leaved hybrids are proving hardier than once thought. Oregon State University is evaluating the hardiness of many species and hybrids at its North Willamette Research and Extension Center in Aurora, Oregon (near Portland), so the guesswork in choosing cultivars suitable for our gardens will eventually be eliminated.

In the meantime, it's well worth experimenting. Plant hebes in spring only (not fall) so their roots can get established before winter, and protect new plants in their first winter by mulching around their bases with loosely piled conifer branchlets. In a sudden cold snap, some of these can be pulled over the tops as well, but don't forget to remove them once the weather warms again.

A protected microclimate near a heated building is good winter insurance for those rated less hardy; in our hottest river valleys, all hebes should be planted where they get afternoon shade in summer. Cuttings taken in midsummer root very easily and can serve as extra insurance against winter losses. Container growing is another option for tender species (they make excellent container subjects), but be sure to protect the pots from direct sun to avoid heating the roots.

Hardiness of the following taxa is based on personal experience and reports of other gardeners' experiences in the Pacific Northwest.

Hebe ochracea in May

Hebe 'Patty's Purple'

Hebe albicans. Dense rounded dwarf with small glaucous leaves and short but dense spikes of white flowers in midsummer. 2 ft. (0.6 m) high and wide; Zone 7.

Hebe 'Autumn Glory'. Broad, leathery spoon-shaped leaves of dark green shaded purple; red-edged when young. Short plump spikes of deep violet flowers from late August to October. 3 ft. (0.9 m) high and wide; Zone 8.

Hebe 'Blue Gem' (syn. *H. ×franciscana* 'Blue Gem'). Compact dome of rounded, glossy light green leaves; showy flower spikes of bright violet-blue in midsummer. Good in dry conditions and takes salt spray, but needs winter protection when young. 4 ft. (1.2 m) in height and width; Zone 7b when established.

Hebe cupressoides. Bright, slightly glaucous green whipcord foliage could easily be mistaken for a cypress or upright juniper—except for tiny pale violet flowers on mature specimens in midsummer. Upright growth to 6 ft. × 4 ft. (1.8 m × 1.2 m). Zone 7, possibly hardier; established plants have survived Big Freezes.

   'Boughton Dome'. Compact dwarf to 2 ft. (0.6 m) in both dimensions; good in rock gardens. Seldom flowers.

Hebe 'Emerald Gem' (syns. 'Emerald Green', 'Green Globe', 'McKean', 'Milmont Emerald', *H. mackenii, H. mckeanii*). This densely foliaged dwarf with tiny glossy green leaves on upright stems is probably a natural hybrid; hebes interbreed freely. Tiny white flowers are seldom produced but are not missed; this is a terrific foliage plant suitable for rock gardens. 12 in. × 18 in. (30 cm × 45 cm); Zone 7.

Hebe 'Marjorie'. Relatively large rounded green leaves on bushy, spreading mounds; short flower spikes of light blue, fading white, bloom from July to September. 3 ft. × 4 ft. (0.9 m × 1.2 m); Zone 7. One of the hardiest larger-leaved hebes. *Hebe* 'Margret' is similar but lower growing, with brighter blue flowers.

Hebe 'Midsummer Beauty'. Long narrow green leaves, reddish on undersides when young; long, slender, very showy flower spikes of pinkish lavender bloom sporadically all summer and into fall. One of the hardiest large-flowered hebes, but a winter-protected site is advisable. 4 ft. × 5 ft. (1.2 m × 1.5 m); Zone 8.

Hebe ochracea. Ochre-green whipcord foliage brings to mind some prehistoric, rather sparse fern. Often confused with and sometimes sold as *H. armstrongii*, a very similar whipcord hebe with yellowish green to olive-green foliage. Both bear very short spikes of tiny white starry flowers that cover the foliage. Most books say this happens in July and August, but either the books or the plants are wrong: every specimen of *H. ochracea* (including 'James Stirling') and *H. armstrongii* we have ever grown or seen blooms in May and June. Rounded growth to 4 ft. × 5 ft. (1.2 m × 1.5 m). Zone 7 or better; established plants have survived Big Freezes.

   'James Stirling'. Compact, flat-topped growth to 2 ft. × 4 ft. (0.6 m × 1.2 m).

Hebe odora (syn. *H. buxifolia*; boxleaf hebe). Neat rounded domes of small, light green box-like leaves stacked up in perfect geometric columns on stems. Short spikes of white flowers in midsummer have slight but pleasant scent. Very tolerant of heat and cold; takes dry conditions well. Variable in size, but usually about 3 ft. (0.9 m) high and wide. Zone 7, possibly hardier.

Hebe pinguifolia 'Pagei'

Hebe 'Youngii'

'New Zealand Gold'. Yellow stems and larger, sharply pointed leaves tipped gold; geometric arrangement of leaves is even more prominent. Tiny white flowers in midsummer, but shy to flower at all in cool summers. 3 ft. × 4 ft. (0.9 m × 1.2 m); Zone 7b.

Hebe 'Patty's Purple'. Compact rounded plant with small, neat, dark green leaves and showy spikes of lavender and white flowers in midsummer. A hybrid involving *H. odora*, but definitely lacking that parent's cold tolerance; a winter-protected site is mandatory for this very appealing plant. 3 ft. (0.9 m) high and wide; Zone 8b at best.

Hebe 'Pewter Dome'. Lower growing than one of its parents, *H. albicans*, with gray-green foliage. 18 in. × 24 in. (45 cm × 60 cm); Zone 7.

Hebe pimeleoides 'Quicksilver'. Low-growing spreading shrub with tiny silvery blue leaves on purple-black stems; leaves show thin red edging, especially in colder weather. Small but profuse short flower spikes of pale violet bloom June to August. 18 in. × 24 in. (45 cm × 60 cm); Zone 7b.

Hebe pinguifolia 'Pagei'. Low-growing but very wide-spreading mounds of tiny glaucous-green leaves that are completely covered with short white flower spikes in May. Hardy and reliable; attractive all year. 1 ft. × 5–6 ft. (0.3 m × 1.5–1.8 m); Zone 7.

Hebe 'Red Edge'. A hybrid involving *H. albicans* and similar to that species, but with leaves outlined with a thin red edge especially prominent in winter; pink-tinged winter tips are as showy as flowers. Actual flowers (in midsummer) are lilac. Zone 7.

Hebe 'Silver Queen' (syn. *H.* ×*franciscana* 'Variegata'). Often sold as *H.* 'Variegata'. Dense mounds of fairly large, fleshy green leaves edged creamy white. Rarely flowers; foliage is the main attraction. Needs a sheltered site protected from both summer heat and winter cold. 3 ft. (0.9 m) high and wide; Zone 8.

Hebe 'Youngii' (syn. 'Carl Teschner'). Low-growing spreading plants with small dark green leaves and short but profuse spikes of blue-violet flowers in June and July. Very free-flowering; excellent small-scale groundcover in a site protected from cold winter winds and late frosts. 12 in. × 18 in. (30 cm × 45 cm); Zone 7b.

HYDRANGEA

Origin: Eastern Asia, the Himalaya, North America

Hardiness zones: Varies

Size: Varies

Blooming season: July to September

Exposure: Partial shade to full sun

Soil preference: Rich, moisture-retentive; slightly to strongly acidic

Water needs: Moderate

Maintenance needs: Low

Subregions best suited: All

Possible problems: None serious

Deciduous. These popular easy-care shrubs are seen all over the Pacific Northwest, most often in the mophead form of *Hydrangea macrophylla*. Hydrangeas are at their near-perfect best in the moist, cool-summer Pacific Coast and Puget Sound subregions, but grow well even in hot-summer valleys when planted in humus-rich soil in partial shade, mulched well, and watered as needed.

As well as blooming all summer (showy colored "petals" are actually the sepals of sterile flowers), hydrangeas have the added attraction of changing color as summer shifts into fall. Light blue fades to green; deep blue to wine red; light pink to reddish purple, deep pink to deep purple; white to pink.

In addition, on *Hydrangea macrophylla*, *H. aspera*, and *H. serrata*, flower color can be changed from pink to blue, or vice versa. Strongly acidic soils allow these species to take up aluminum from the soil, making the flowers blue; soils with higher pH block the uptake of aluminum, so on very slightly acidic soils, flowers are pink.

To turn blue flowers pink, add dolomite lime to the soil to raise the pH to about 6.0–6.2. (Higher levels may cause iron-deficiency chlorosis.) High phosphorus levels also lead to pink flowers, which is why heavily fertilized "blue" hydrangeas in nurseries are often pink.

To turn pink flowers blue or make blue ones even bluer, add aluminum sulfate in the amount recommended on the package. Soils high in organic matter also tend to turn flowers blue, so good helpings of compost are in order for blue shades.

Given all these options, do we Pacific Northwesterners ever love to fool around with our hydrangea colors. Everything from startling near-turquoise to deep red can be seen, along with every conceivable shade (and a few inconceivable ones) in between. Plant developers seem focused on flowers that remain pink, while gardeners seem to prefer blue (or perhaps just have highly acidic soil), so the most amazing violets, deep purples, and even navy blues are also common.

Any soil amendments must be added well before blooming time, preferably the season before bloom, but small amounts added monthly starting in April should give good results. If the soil is not at least somewhat conducive to the color desired, it's best to grow the specimen in a container, where soil adjustments are much easier to control. Keep in mind that color intensity will not change; light pink, for instance, can change to light mauve or light blue, but not deep blue. White flowers of any species cannot be changed to pink or blue by any soil amendments, although most naturally fade to pink.

Not all *Hydrangea* species are ideally suited to all Pacific Northwest subregions. White-flowered *H. quercifolia* (oakleaf hydrangea), prized mainly for the red fall color of its oak-shaped leaves, is native to Georgia and Florida and needs a long, consistently hot summer with plenty of moisture to bloom best. The white, globular flowerheads of *H. arborescens* (native to the Appalachian Mountains) are spectacular but are so enormous that they tend to flop to the ground in cool rainy weather or even with heavy dew. However, both these species are successfully grown in our warmer subregions.

All *Hydrangea* species need little maintenance beyond mulching, occasional feedings of compost, and the removal of faded flowerheads and any winter-killed stem tips before spring. Mature specimens of *H. aspera*, *H. macrophylla*, and *H. serrata*

can be rejuvenated by pruning oldest stems to the ground in March; *H. arborescens* and *H. paniculata* cultivars can be pruned to any height in early spring to control size. For a discussion of *H. anomala* subsp. *petiolaris* (climbing hydrangea), see Chapter 11, "Vines and Groundcovers."

Hydrangea aspera. Native to the Himalaya. Noted for its long, dark green, velvety-textured leaves; large, domed lacecap flowerheads have an almost fuzzy texture. Needs a sheltered, lightly shaded site protected from strong winds that can tatter leaves and late frosts that can nip flowers. Stunning in the right setting, but must have room; this large plant cannot be pruned without sacrificing most of either this year's or next year's flowers. 7 ft. (2.1 m) high and wide; Zones 7 to 9.

Villosa Group. One of the best forms; deep blue fertile flowers surrounded by large sterile flowers of light mauve bloom in August and September. Needs consistently moist soil.

Hydrangea macrophylla (mophead hydrangea, lacecap hydrangea). Native to maritime habitats in Japan. Reliable, adaptable, and easy to grow; tolerates wind and salt spray and is an excellent seaside plant. Mophead flowers are very large and globular; lacecap flowers flatter and very wide. Both are blue on strongly acidic soils and pink on slightly acidic soils.

Hydrangea macrophylla 'Nikko Blue'

Hydrangea macrophylla 'Glowing Embers'

Flowers grow only on new wood produced from buds that form on old wood in late summer (not on new wood that grows from the ground), so any regular pruning more severe than deadheading will sacrifice some of next summer's flowers. Late frosts may also nip buds in some years, but even if all buds are winter-killed, new growth from the ground will bloom the following year. Newer cultivars such as Endless Summer bloom even on new wood from the ground, so are better choices where late frosts are common.

Mophead types

Although often listed as full-shade plants, mophead hydrangeas do not bloom well in the cool, dark full shade of the Pacific Northwest. An eastern or northern exposure open to the sky is usually ideal; they can take full sun in coastal areas. Afternoon shade is advisable in hot-summer valleys. Adaptable to any soil except very dry or very lean, but best in rich soil with regular water. Average size 5 ft. × 6 ft. (1.5 m × 1.8 m), spreading wider with age. Zones 6 to 9.

'Alpenglühen' (Alpenglow). Reliably deep pink to rosy red even on slightly acidic soil; vigorous growth. Leaves have a thin red edge.

'Ayesha'. Large, domed, slightly fragrant flowerheads consisting of small, waxy, pale pink to pale mauve flowers resemble lilacs; foliage is glossy.

'Bailmer' (Endless Summer). Small globular flowerheads on compact plants are pastel to medium pink or blue, depending on soil. Blooms on new wood anywhere on the plant; good choice where late frosts may kill old-wood buds.

'Blauer Zwerg' (Blue Dwarf). Newer introduction with deep blue flowers on compact plants to 3–4 ft. (0.9–1.2 m). Best on strongly acidic soil for good blue color.

'Glowing Embers'. Very large (8 in., 20 cm) flowerheads on compact plants are deep rosy red, fading to a rich wine-purple. One of the reddest cultivars; even foliage has reddish tints. Often confused with Alpenglow, but red color is deeper and brighter.

'Masja'. Small, tough, adaptable plant to 3 ft. (0.9 m). Rich deep pink to wine-purple flowerheads, depending on soil.

'Merritt's Supreme'. Compact plant with large flowerheads easily changed from rosy pink to mid-blue. Blue color is best in light shade.

'Nikko Blue'. Best on strongly acidic soils for good blue color; cool sun or very light shade recommended. Reliable and popular, but may be slow to establish.

'Pia' (syns. 'Piamina', 'Pink Elf', 'Winning Edge'). Dwarf form to 2 ft. (60 cm). Small round flowerheads of deep pink to mauve, depending on soil. Good in containers.

Lacecap types

Despite their larger plant size, lacecaps have a more delicate look than mopheads; they tolerate slightly drier conditions but need more shade. Blooming is not as profuse, but flowerheads may be 8–10 in. (20–30 cm) in diameter. Like mopheads, their color can change according to soil pH. To 7 ft. (2.1 m) high and wide, or more; Zones 6 to 9.

'Mariesii Grandiflora' (syn. 'White Wave'). Flowerheads emerge white; small fertile flowers fade to pink or blue, depending on soil, but large sterile flowers always fade to pink.

'Mariesii Perfecta' (syn. 'Blue Wave'). Best in partial shade on strongly acidic soil for rich, true blue flowers; outstanding in right setting. Huge plant to 7 ft. × 10 ft. (2.1 m × 3 m) or more.

Hydrangea paniculata (tree hydrangea). Native to Japan, China, and Taiwan. Tall, upright shrub can be trained as a small single-trunked tree. Very large, cone-shaped, fragrant flower panicles need shelter from strong winds and heavy rains. Best in full sun; any soil except very dry or very lean. Blooms late July to September; at its peak in August. 7 ft. (2.1 m) high and wide, or more; Zones 3 to 8.

'Grandiflora' (PeeGee hydrangea—P.G. for *paniculata* 'Grandiflora'). Enormous cones of sterile white flowers can reach 18 in. × 12 in. (45 cm × 30 cm); remain showy for many weeks as they slowly fade to deep pink.

'Kyushu'. Elegant compact plant with slender white flower cones; attractive dark green foliage is glossy.

'Limelight'. Flowers open bright lime-green, fade to creamy white, then pink. Compact plant.

'Tardiva'. Similar in looks to 'Unique', but blooms August to October, extending the season.

'Unique'. Similar to 'Grandiflora' but on smaller scale; compact but vigorous mix of sterile and fertile flowers gives a more delicate look.

Hydrangea macrophylla 'Pia'

Hydrangea macrophylla 'Mariesii Perfecta'

Hydrangea paniculata 'Grandiflora'

DRYING HYDRANGEAS

Mopheads dry best, but lacecaps are also worth trying. The trick is not to cut them in full bloom (they'll just rot), but to wait until the flowerheads are beginning to fade and feel slightly papery. Late August is usually about right. Cut the heads with 12–18 in. (30–45 cm) of stem on a sunny day after all dew has evaporated. Remove the leaves and place stems in a vase, with or without a small amount of water, in a well-ventilated place out of direct sun. Do not add any more water once it is all absorbed.

Flowerheads are completely dry when they become stiff and individual sepals have a slightly leathery feel, which takes a week or two. Although their colors will continue to fade slowly, dried hydrangeas remain attractive for many months.

Hydrangea 'Preziosa'. Hybrid of *H. macrophylla* and *H. serrata*. Small mophead flowers open pale green, change to creamy white, then pink, finally fade to rosy red regardless of soil type.

Hydrangea serrata. Native to Japan and Korea. Similar to *H. macrophylla*, with both mophead and lacecap types represented, but plant is smaller and needs more consistently moist soil. Best in partial shade; good choice for smaller gardens. 4 ft. (1.2 m) high and wide; Zones 6 to 9.

'Beni-gaku'. Lacecap type. Sterile flowers are white, fading to pink, then reddish; fertile flowers are dark purple fading to light blue.

'Bluebird'. Outstanding small lacecap with flowerheads of pale blue to reddish purple; best on strongly acidic soils.

LAVANDULA (LAVENDER)

Origin: Mediterranean region, western Asia, northern Africa

Hardiness zones: Varies

Size: Varies

Blooming season: May to August

Exposure: Cool sun

Soil preference: Average fertility; very well drained; slightly acidic to slightly alkaline

Water needs: Drought tolerant when established

Maintenance needs: Low

Subregions best suited: All; ideal in Olympic Rain Shadow

Possible problems: None serious

Evergreen. Universally popular for its incomparable fragrance, lavender has a 2000-year-plus history of cosmetic, herbal, and even culinary use, but its popularity as a garden plant has never been far behind. Although usually thought of, used, and sold as perennials, lavenders are true dwarf shrubs renowned for their versatility in perennial beds, as edging along paths (where their fragrant gray-green foliage can be brushed against frequently), and as low hedges. Their spiky wands of bluish, pinkish, or purple flowers add welcome cool notes to summer gardens—if they haven't already been picked for cut flowers, crafts, sachets, or potpourri.

All lavenders are perfectly at home in the Pacific Northwest. Being native to seaside areas of the Mediterranean, they're happiest in coastal climates where summers are dry and sunny but fairly cool; despite their natural drought tolerance, they dislike both hot-dry and hot-humid climates. Near-perfect conditions are found in the Olympic Rain Shadow subregion: lavender growing is now a major part of the economy of Sequim, Washington, which hosts a three-day Lavender Festival every summer; open-house weekends are held at lavender-growing farms near Victoria, B.C.

Lavender is a superb seaside plant, tolerating frequent fog and high humidity as long as temperatures remain cool. Being well adapted to a wet-winter Mediterranean climate, it accepts our prolonged rainy season graciously as long as drainage is excellent. Full sun is a must except in our hottest, driest river valleys, where light shade or an eastern or northern exposure is appreciated. A deep soaking just before or during bloom is also appreciated if conditions are abnormally hot or dry.

Other than a yearly shearing after their flowers fade (assuming they have not already been harvested), lavenders require no maintenance. No insects or diseases bother them; as true shrubs, they never need lifting or dividing. Average, well-drained garden soil suits them just fine; they accept poor soil but will not grow as large. Rich soil and high-nitrogen fertilizer should be avoided, since they make plants floppy and reduce the concentration of aromatic oils. Strongly acidic soils should ideally be amended with a sprinkling of dolomite lime every couple of years, but even this is negotiable. In fact, once established in a congenial site, lavender seems to thrive best on benign neglect.

Lavandula angustifolia 'Munstead'

Lavandula angustifolia 'Jean Davis'

When we moved to our present garden, we brought many plants from our previous garden with us, including a forlorn English lavender whose survival seemed doubtful. Not quite having the heart to compost it, we planted it outside our deer fence (lavender is one of very few plants that are truly deer-proof) in full sun in rather poor but well-drained soil.

That was 23 years ago. It has not been watered, fertilized, or limed since, and the only care it gets is a haircut once a year. It thinks it's in heaven. Lavender has a reputation for being short-lived, but this plant just gets bigger and blooms more prolifically every year.

Lavandula angustifolia (English lavender). Native to the Mediterranean region; long cultivated in England. Sweetest-scented of all lavenders and the best choice for cool-summer subregions. The species itself grows to 3–4 ft. (0.9–1.2 m) in height and width and tends to be rangy; its more compact cultivars are much better known. The two most popular, 'Hidcote' and 'Munstead', are both seed-grown strains and can vary slightly in size, habit, and flower color—a point to keep in mind when massing or planting as a hedge. Most cultivars bloom in June and July. Zones 7 to 9.

'Hidcote'. Medium-purple flowers on short mounds of greenish gray foliage bloom over a long season. Prefers cool summers that are not too dry. 12–24 in. × 18–24 in. (30–60 cm × 45–60 cm).

'Hidcote Pink' (syn. 'Rosea'). Pastel pink flowers on compact plants. Easiest of the pink lavenders to grow, but dislikes heat. Same size as 'Hidcote'.

'Jean Davis'. Pale pink flowers with mild fragrance; reputed to be best-tasting form for culinary use. Sets seed, but does not come true; for pink flowers, plants must be propagated by cuttings. Upright habit, 12–18 in. (30–45 cm) in both dimensions.

'Munstead'. Most widely grown cultivar. Bright lavender-blue flowers bloom early in season on dense, compact mounds of foliage. Most heat-tolerant of *Lavandula angustifolia* cultivars. 18–24 in. × 24–30 in. (45–60 cm × 60–75 cm).

'Twickel Purple'. Deep purple flowers held in fan-like sprays on tall stems; felt-textured foliage is silvery green. Blooms July and August. 24–36 in. (60–90 cm) high and wide.

Lavandula dentata (French lavender). Native to southern and eastern Spain. Small shrub with silvery felt-textured foliage; each leaf is serrated with squared notches at the tip. Short, dense spikes of powdery lavender-blue flowers with tufted petals at their tips bloom from May to August. Hardy to Zone 7, but needs warm summers to bloom well. Dislikes winter wetness; may need to be grown in a container so it can be moved out of heavy winter rain. 24–30 in. × 30–36 in. (60–75 cm × 75–90 cm).

Lavandula ×*ginginsii* 'Goodwin Creek Grey'. Usually sold as *L. dentata* 'Goodwin Creek Grey'. Same size, needs, and hardiness as *L. dentata*. Silvery felt-like foliage topped by violet-purple flowers in midsummer; both flowers and foliage have strong spicy fragrance.

Lavandula ×*intermedia* (lavandin). Hybrids of *L. angustifolia* and *L. latifolia* (spike lavender), another Mediterranean native with longer, broader leaves and a more branching habit. Larger, free-flowering plants are more tolerant of heat and drought than *L. angustifolia*; fragrance is stronger but not as sweet. Bloom period is later, in July and August. Good all-around performance

Lavandula stoechas

Lonicera nitida 'Baggesen's Gold'

for landscaping, low hedges, crafts, drying, and oil production. Most cultivars are sterile and must be propagated by cuttings. 3–4 ft. (0.9–1.2 m) high and wide. Zones 6 to 9.

Dutch Group (Dutch lavender). Despite its name, considered the "true" English lavender; formerly considered a species (*Lavandula vera*). Late-blooming blue-purple flowers and relatively broad grayish green leaves; plants are tall and robust. Considered the best variety for herbal use. 3–4 ft. (0.9–1.2 m) high and wide.

'Fred Boutin'. Large, long-stemmed, light purple flowers with excellent fragrance; felty silver-green foliage. Good cut flower.

'Grosso'. Highly valued for strongly scented oil production; used in cosmetics industry. Popular for making lavender wands, as buds remain on stems when dried.

'Provence'. Long slender stalks with light purple flowers. Valued for sachets, potpourri, and other crafts where buds must be separated from stems.

Lavandula stoechas (Spanish lavender). Native to the Mediterranean region. Distinctive dark purple flowers shaped like miniature pineapples are topped by two large petals of bright purplish pink. Narrow leaves are dark green with a grayish cast; habit is more lax and spreading than other lavenders. Strong camphor fragrance. Excellent for landscape use; blooms prolifically from May to July with sporadic blooms continuing until October. 18–24 in. × 30–36 in. (45–60 cm × 75–90 cm). Zones 7 to 9.

'Anouk'. Newer cultivar with greater cold hardiness (Zone 5) and more upright, compact habit. Early blooming.

'Otto Quast'. Strong-growing selection with large flowers and a very long blooming period.

LONICERA NITIDA 'BAGGESEN'S GOLD' (BAGGESEN'S GOLD BOX HONEYSUCKLE)

Origin: Sport of species native to China

Hardiness zones: 7 to 9

Size: 3 ft. (0.9 m) high and wide

Season of interest: Year-round

Exposure: Cool sun to light shade

Soil preference: Fertile; moisture-retentive but well drained

Water needs: Low

Maintenance needs: Low to moderate

Subregions best suited: All

Possible problems: None serious

Evergreen. This unassuming small shrub is a real sweetheart, welcome to add its bright but unobtrusive color and intricate texture to virtually any landscaping situation except hot, dry sun. New growth is an especially attractive buttery yellow; unlike many golden-foliaged shrubs, it remains true deep yellow in winter. It's particularly effective with heaths and heathers, dwarf conifers, and hebes; it can also be used as a low hedge.

Its stiff stems covered with very small shiny leaves (*nitida* means "shining") grow at seemingly random rates, giving the shrub a slightly tousled, pleasingly informal outline. Although it does need yearly pruning to keep long shoots from getting out of hand, its upkeep is nowhere near that of the plain green species, which grows so rampantly it needs pruning two or three times yearly. Shearing does it no harm—it will stubbornly revert to its normal irregular outline—but a lighter touch is more in keeping with its relaxed character.

Its one fault is that like the species, its lowest branches tend to root where they touch ground, sending up very vigorous suckers that can spoil its shape. It's a good idea to check around the base for suckers during its annual haircut; these can be pulled up and cut off or transplanted elsewhere.

Cool sun brings out the brightest foliage color, but leaves will burn in intense or very hot sun. Established plants are reasonably drought tolerant in cool conditions, but cannot take extended drought or drought combined with high heat. It handles our wet winters with ease (anything short of waterlogged soil) and is an excellent choice for coastal areas, since it takes wind and even salt spray in stride.

MAHONIA

Origin: Western North America, eastern Asia, the Himalaya

Hardiness zones: Varies

Size: Varies

Blooming season: Early winter to spring

Exposure: Partial shade to cool sun

Soil preference: Moderately fertile, moisture-retentive but well drained; preferably acidic

Water needs: Drought tolerant when established

Maintenance needs: Low

Subregions best suited: All

Possible problems: None serious

Evergreen. Every Pacific Northwest garden should feature at least one species of mahonia, native or non-native. Best in cool-summer, mild-winter climates, these beautiful foliage plants need ample moisture while in bloom in winter and spring; they also tolerate our normal summer droughts with ease. Their fragrant yellow flowers are especially welcome in our gray winters and early springs, and their showy, non-toxic, blue-black fruits attract birds in early summer. Fruits of the native species are not only edible but make delicious jelly.

In many cases, mahonia's glossy, spiny, leathery dark green foliage takes on shades of red, yellow, orange, brown, purple, and/or near-black for winter, making these low-maintenance plants truly four-season shrubs. Garden uses range from awe-inspiring specimens to accents to informal hedges to lightly shaded woodland companions to native/wildlife gardens to groundcover.

Members of the barberry family, mahonias share a number of features with heavenly bamboo (*Nandina domestica*), another member of the same family. The inner wood and roots of both are a startlingly bright golden yellow and are still used as a source of natural yellow dye. Both have an upright, somewhat top-heavy growth habit consisting of many slender canes; both need no regular pruning but are more vigor-

Mahonia aquifolium

Mahonia japonica Bealei Group

Mahonia japonica 'Hivernant'

ous and compact when the oldest, leggiest canes are removed every few years.

Any overly long stems on both can also be cut back to just above a node at whatever height desired in early spring; bushy new growth will sprout from that point. Both can have stems broken by heavy, wet snow, but damaged or overgrown specimens can be rejuvenated by pruning to within 6–8 in. (15–20 cm) of the ground in early spring. Both are pest-free and impervious to disease; both are highly deer-resistant; both tolerate dry shade.

Unlike heavenly bamboo, which likes heat, mahonias prefer cool conditions. Plants are most compact and flower most prolifically in cool sun, but light shade is recommended in hot-summer valleys. A site protected from strong winter winds (especially cold ones) is appreciated by all species and is mandatory for the more tender Asian species. Trunks on young plants of Asian species are very tender and vulnerable to cold; wrapping them at ground level for the first two winters will allow them to get established and start developing their characteristically thick, beautifully furrowed protective bark. Eventually, these trunks can become the size of small trees.

Mahonia aquifolium (Oregon grape). Native to the Pacific Northwest; state flower of Oregon. Grows everywhere from sandy beaches in full sun to deep woods on the Cascade slopes, which speaks volumes about its toughness and adaptability. Perfectly adapted to our peculiar climate, it has survived many thousands of our dry summers and the same number of our winter monsoons. Good drainage, though, is a necessity; Oregon grape will not tolerate saturated soil.

Although it can be scraggly in the wild, garden performance in well-drained soil in cool sun or light shade is top-notch. Shiny dark green holly-like foliage is highlighted with bright red and purple accents in winter; new growth is bright coppery pink. Dense clusters of fragrant yellow flowers burst into bloom in late February or early March, long before most shrubs even think about blooming. These are followed in midsummer by showy, edible blue-black berries that make great jelly—if the birds don't get them first.

Plants sucker slowly, gradually making a sizeable clump; genetic variation means a few plants sucker rapidly, but unwanted suckers are easily removed. No regular pruning is necessary, but an occasional trim and removal of oldest stems keeps plants compact and bushy. 5–6 ft. × 3-4 ft. (1.5–1.8 m × 0.9–1.2 m); Zones 5 to 9.

'Apollo'. Suckering dwarf with deep golden yellow flowers; height 24–30 in. (60–75 cm).

'Atropurpurea'. Winter foliage of rich reddish purple.

'Compactum'. Semi-dwarf form to 4 ft. × 3 ft. (1.2 m × 0.9 m).

'Orange Flame'. Low-growing; new growth is bronzy orange. Height 24–36 in. (60–90 cm).

Mahonia × media 'Winter Sun'

Mahonia × media 'Winter Sun', new growth

Mahonia japonica. Native to Japan and China. Long leaves densely set with paired spiny leaflets; fragrant flowers are held in long, lax clusters. Blooms February to April; best in lightly shaded site sheltered from strong winds. 6–8 ft. (1.8–2.4 m) high and wide; Zones 7 to 9.

Bealei Group. Wide leaflets almost overlap; foliage is tinted yellow to light orange in winter and spring, sometimes with touches of red. Flower clusters are shorter and more upright than species; purple-blue fruits are large and decorative. Vigorous.

'Hivernant' (Winter Resident). Winter foliage of bright yellow, orange, green, and red persists through spring; growth habit is dense and rounded. Flowers are rather sparse, but robins relish the large berries that follow and will spend hours stealing them one by one. We're always amused, in our Canadian garden, to watch these American robins stealing berries from the Japanese mahonia with the French name.

Mahonia lomariifolia. Native to the Himalaya. Large, rather gaunt upright shrub with very long leaves (to 24 in., 60 cm) composed of 15 to 23 pairs of narrow, spined, shiny dark green leaflets. Very fragrant lemon-yellow flowers held in long, lax clusters bloom in early to midwinter. Needs a cool, lightly shaded site protected from hot sun in summer and cold winds in winter. 6–10 ft. × 3–4 ft. (1.8–3 m × 0.9–1.2 m); Zones 8 to 9.

Mahonia ×*media.* Hybrids of *M. japonica* and *M. lomariifolia.* These magnificent focal-point large shrubs have the hardiness and dense habit of the former; the long leaves and winter-blooming habit of the latter. All need light shade, protection from both hot and cold winds, and lots of space. All can be pruned in early spring to control size. Blooms in late fall/early winter; Zones 7 to 9.

'Arthur Menzies'. Compact upright habit; flowers are golden yellow. A chance natural hybrid selected in 1964 at Seattle's Washington Park Arboretum from a batch of seedlings of *M. lomariifolia* sent from Strybing Arboretum in San Francisco; named for its assistant director, in whose garden the seed originated. 6–8 ft. × 4–5 ft. (1.8–2.4 m × 1.2–1.5 m).

Mahonia nervosa in August

'Charity'. Enormous, breathtaking shrub with soft yellow flowers held in lax clusters; can reach tree-like proportions. Best in sheltered site. 10–15 ft. (3–4.5 m) high and wide.

'Lionel Fortescue'. Similar in size to 'Charity' but with frost-resistant flowers of bright yellow held in upright clusters. May bloom as early as November.

'Winter Sun'. Relatively compact plant with dense foliage and bright yellow flowers in long clusters; blooms mid-December. New growth is shrimp-pink to orange. To 10 ft. (3 m) in height and width.

Mahonia nervosa (Cascade Oregon grape). Native to the Pacific Northwest; familiar colonizer of forest floor from British Columbia to northern California. Also known as low Oregon grape and longleaf mahonia; its notched (rather than spined) leaves can reach 18 in. (45 cm). Long, very lax clusters of yellow flowers in mid-spring are followed by large, decorative, edible blue-black berries; winter foliage takes on shades of red, yellow, orange, purple, and brown.

Spreads widely by underground stems but is not invasive. Good under large native trees such as Pacific dogwood, in shady borders, or as groundcover in woodland or native garden. Best in cool, loose, humusy acidic soil in light shade, where it is very drought tolerant; grows more compactly in cool sun, taking on reddish tints, but may then need summer watering.

NANDINA DOMESTICA (HEAVENLY BAMBOO)

Origin: China, Japan, India

Hardiness zones: 7 to 9

Size: Varies

Season of interest: Summer through winter

Exposure: Full sun to partial shade

Soil preference: Average fertility; moisture-retentive but well drained

Water needs: Drought tolerant when established

Maintenance needs: Low

Subregions best suited: All

Possible problems: None serious

Evergreen. Not a bamboo at all, but a member of the barberry family; slender, graceful leaflets on thrice-compound leaves resemble bamboo foliage. Leaves that grow from nodes on tall, slim stalks are reddish purple when young; mature to shiny deep green; turn shades of red, purple, pink, and orange in fall and winter, especially in sun. Panicles of small white flowers in July are followed by bright red persistent berries. Better crops are borne if two or more plants are present.

Heavenly bamboo is not fussy about soil texture or exposure (leading to overuse in commercial plantings), but likes heat better than cold. Strong winds can tatter leaves; somewhat brittle stalks may be broken by snow but regrow quickly when cut back. Leaves may drop in very cold winters, but not until March—and by then, bronzy pink new growth is appearing.

Nandina domestica

Winter flower buds of *Pieris* 'Brouwer's Beauty'

PIERIS (LILY-OF-THE-VALLEY SHRUB)

Origin: Japan, China, Taiwan, the Himalaya, eastern North America

Hardiness zones: 6 to 9

Size: 4–6 ft. (1.2–1.8 m) high and wide

Blooming season: Early March to May

Exposure: Partial shade to cool sun

Soil preference: Cool, rich, moisture-retentive but well drained; acidic

Water needs: Moderately drought tolerant when established

Maintenance needs: Low

Subregions best suited: All

Possible problems: None serious

Clumps spread slowly from bright yellow creeping rhizomes but are never invasive; in our climate plants do not self-seed. Any leggy, top-heavy stalks are easily rejuvenated by cutting them almost to the ground or just above a node in early spring. Vary height of cuts for balanced, full-foliaged look.

The species itself is an excellent upright specimen or mixed shrub companion, making good seasonal contrast with rhododendrons and azaleas. Can reach 8 ft. (2.4 m).

'Fire Power'. Dwarf form with relatively large leaflets; yellow-green in summer, reddish orange in winter. Good in containers. Height 24 in. (60 cm).

'Gulf Stream'. Compact growth with blue-green summer foliage; best sited in sun to bring out excellent fall/winter color. Seldom flowers. Height 3–4 ft. (0.9–1.2 m).

'Harbor Dwarf'. Dense, twiggy stalks and small leaves give fine texture. Winter color orange-red. Spreads moderately from creeping rhizomes; good groundcover. Height 24 in. (60 cm).

'Moon Bay'. Semi-dwarf form with dense, compact growth; leaves are lime-green in summer, bright red in winter. Height 30 in. (75 cm).

'Moyer's Red'. New leaves purple-red, fall color brilliant scarlet. Best in sun. Height 7 ft. (2.1 m).

Evergreen. If ever there was a perfect four-season shrub, pieris is it. All winter, prominent flower buds on densely foliaged, compact evergreen plants are almost as showy as flowers. In very early March (sometimes even earlier), these open to profuse clusters of small, lightly fragrant, bell-shaped flowers resembling those of heathers. (Both are members of the family Ericaceae.) By May, while many flowers are still in full bloom, colorful new growth makes a show-stopping appearance.

New growth continues changing color until early summer, when the attractive leaves settle back into shades of green. The bead-like seedpods of spent flowers are also attractive in summer (some people mistake them for flower buds) and do not necessarily need deadheading, although some gardeners prefer to do so. By fall, these will have dropped off by themselves, and next year's flower buds will have replaced them for visual interest.

Pierises are as perfectly adapted to the Pacific Northwest climate as are rhododendrons, flourishing in the same cool conditions. If anything, pierises need a bit more fertile soil, a bit more wind protection, and a bit more protection from hot sun, although full sun is fine in coastal areas. On the plus side, they are more reliably drought tolerant when established in a congenial site.

As with rhododendrons, pierises are theoretically subject to chlorosis, root rot, and root weevils, but in reality they are con-

Pieris japonica 'Dorothy Wyckoff'

Pieris 'Forest Flame'

Pieris japonica 'Valley Rose'

siderably less vulnerable to all three. Pruning is not required, although plants can be lightly trimmed after flowering; the naturally compact forms of most cultivars remain attractive for the life of the plants.

If anything, these adaptable and very low-maintenance shrubs are a victim of their own success, often being planted in less-than-ideal or even abusive situations (hot sun, deep shade, dry or alkaline soil) where their looks and performance are compromised. However, this is not the fault of the plants. When properly sited, fed, and watered as necessary during dry spells, few shrubs give so much and ask for so little in return.

Pieris 'Bert Chandler'. Australian introduction grown for its foliage, which is bright salmon-pink when new, changing to creamy yellow, then white, then green; winter foliage is pale green to creamy yellow. Sparse white flowers are a bonus. Best in partial shade.

Pieris 'Brouwer's Beauty'. Deep red buds open to abundant creamy white flowers held almost horizontally on brownish red stalks; foliage is light green.

Pieris 'Forest Flame'. Vigorous and very popular hybrid between *P. formosa*, a tall but slightly tender Himalayan species with bright red new foliage, and *P. japonica*, a smaller, hardier, free-flowering Japanese species. 'Forest Flame' inherited the best of

both parents: profuse, showy white flowers on a compact and hardy plant, and bright red new foliage that turns pink, then white, then green.

Pieris japonica. Compact glossy foliage with colorful new leaves of bronzy pink to red; bright winter buds open to waxy, slightly fragrant flowers of white, pink, or red. Parent of many excellent hybrids.

'Cavatine'. Dwarf form growing to only 3–4 ft. (0.9–1.2 m); suitable for large containers. Clusters of large creamy white flowers almost completely obscure the dark green glossy foliage; new growth is coppery bronze.

'Dorothy Wyckoff'. Deep red buds open to flowers of pale pink to white; new growth turns from red to green. Compact habit and refined, elegant appearance.

'Flamingo'. Free-flowering clusters of bright pink flowers are very showy, perhaps a bit too flouncy. (They've been compared to Shirley Temple's curls.) Cheerful and bright in the right setting.

'Valley Fire'. New growth is brilliant red, fading directly to green; short flower clusters are white. Very disease-resistant; an improvement over the similar *Pieris japonica* 'Mountain Fire' (see photo on page 47), which is more susceptible to root rot. Upright growth to 6–7 ft. (1.8–2.1 m). The "valley" of this and the following two cultivars is the Willamette Valley, where

RHODOSPEAK

blotch. Large, conspicuous area of different color on upper petal

deadhead. To break off faded trusses to prevent seed set and rangy growth

elepidote. Leaves without minute scales; broadly used to mean large-leaved "typical" evergreen rhododendrons

flare. Different color on upper petal

hose-in-hose. Semi-double flowers appearing to consist of one flower inside another

indumentum. Dense felt-like covering of very short hairs, usually on underside of leaves

lepidote. Leaves with minute scales; broadly used to mean small-leaved or dwarf evergreen rhododendrons

section. Secondary divisions of the genus *Rhododendron* based on common characteristics

subgenus. One of the main divisions of the genus *Rhododendron*; includes *Pentanthera* (deciduous azaleas) and *Tsutsusi* (evergreen azaleas)

truss. Cluster of individual flowers; may be two to 20 or more

RHODODENDRON PLANT SIZES AND BLOOMING TIMES

Tall: 6 ft. (1.8 m) or more in ten years

Medium tall: 5 ft. (1.5 m) in ten years

Medium: 4 ft. (1.2 m) in ten years

Low: 3 ft. (0.9 m) in ten years

Semi-dwarf: 24–36 in. (60–90 cm) in ten years

Dwarf: 12–24 in. (30–60 cm) in ten years

All rhododendrons will grow somewhat taller and considerably wider in maturity.

Very early: January to mid-March

Early: Mid-March to mid-April

Early midseason: Mid-April to late April

Midseason: Late April to mid-May

Late midseason: Mid-May to late May

Late: Late May to mid-June

Very late: Mid-June or later

---

all three were developed at Oregon State University by Robert Tichner.

'Valley Rose'. Deep pink buds open to two-toned flowers that are pink at bases and white at tips, giving an overall effect of pastel pink. Free-flowering; plant habit is rounded and compact.

'Valley Valentine'. Deep red buds open to small but profuse flowers of dark red that fade to reddish pink with white bases; new foliage is bronze-copper. Highly disease-resistant and easy to grow.

'Variegata'. Compact, refined foliage plant considered by some to be the best variegated foliage plant of all. Dense grayish green leaves are edged white; new growth is pinkish bronze. Pure white flowers make it especially attractive in spring. Better form and more vigorous constitution than *Pieris* 'Flaming Silver', a variegated form with bright red new growth.

'White Cascade'. Profuse, early-blooming white flowers in large clusters are frost-resistant; new foliage is coppery bronze.

RHODODENDRON

Origin: Asia, Europe, North America; usually from mountainous areas

Hardiness zones: Varies

Size: Varies

Blooming season: Varies; main season March to May

Exposure: Partial shade to cool sun

Soil preference: Cool and loose, well drained, high in organic matter; acidic

Water needs: Low to moderate; many are drought tolerant when established

Maintenance needs: Low to moderate

Subregions best suited: All

Possible problems: Chlorosis, mildew, root rot, root weevils

Evergreen, semi-evergreen, or deciduous. If one plant genus defined Pacific Northwest gardens, it would be *Rhododendron*— a genus that now includes not just the typical large-leaved evergreen rhododendrons and the smaller-leaved dwarf forms, but azaleas, both deciduous and evergreen (formerly *Azalea japonica* hybrids). Although there is no longer any such botanical name as *Azalea*, the common name is still very much in use for practical reasons. Since it is so much more widely understood than *Rhododendron* subgenus *Pentanthera* (deciduous azaleas) and *Rhododendron* subgenus *Tsutsusi* (evergreen, or Japanese, azaleas), we have described these plants under their more familiar names.

Whatever they're called, all these fantastic spring-blooming shrubs (a few bloom in late winter or early summer) are ideally suited to Pacific Northwest conditions. All grow best in high-rainfall climates without extremes of temperature; all need cool, acidic soil; all prefer a consistently moist but cool atmosphere; all dislike hot or intense sun.

BY THE NUMBERS: RATING RHODODENDRONS

5 definitely superior (not given lightly)

4 very good

3 good

2 adequate

1 lacking in some way

In the descriptions that follow, the first number refers to the flower, the second to the foliage, the third to overall form and performance. Bear in mind that ratings are essentially personal opinions and somewhat subject to current fashion, so there is no such thing as objective ratings—or even consistent ones. (Where our sources differ, we have averaged them.) If you really like a certain rhododendron and it performs well in your own garden, it's a "5" no matter what its official ratings. However, as collective opinions, higher ratings are valuable predictors of long-term satisfaction with a plant.

Rhododendron augustinii subsp. *augustinii*

Rhododendrons grow so well here with or without care that it's the rare front yard that doesn't sport at least one. Gardener involvement can range from those who plunk in a "pink rhodie" from a big-box store to fanatics (the term "rhodoholic" is well understood) who carefully nurture hundreds of rare and unusual forms and speak knowingly of subgenera, sections, subsections, lepidotes, elepidotes, indumentum, and other strange things.

With so many forms from which to choose, at least one form of rhododendron is ideally suited to each of our subregions. Very large-leaved evergreen rhododendrons, which have the highest need for a cool, moist atmosphere and protection from hot sun, grow to perfection in the Puget Sound subregion. Tender species from the Himalaya thrive in the Pacific Coast and (with adequate water) Olympic Rain Shadow subregions. Deciduous azaleas, which have high tolerance of drought, cold, and sun, are right at home in the Rogue and Cascade Slopes/Outflow Valleys subregions. Evergreen azaleas, which are the most tolerant of heat and sun but are not always very cold-hardy, thrive in the warm-summer, mild-winter Willamette subregion. And small-leaved or dwarf evergreen rhododendrons, which tend to be the most widely adaptable of all, are perfectly happy in all subregions in any conditions except very hot and/or dry.

Of course, all forms can be grown in all subregions when given appropriate siting. A good rule of thumb for evergreen types is the larger the leaf and/or the plant, the more shade needed; the smaller the leaf and/or the plant, the more sun-tolerant. In cool, misty coastal areas, all rhododendrons can take full sun; in hot-summer valleys, open shade (such as a northern exposure) or light shade is best for almost all.

In our climate, rhododendrons will not flower well in deep shade. An ideal situation is one in which plants are protected from direct sun between 11:00 a.m. and 3:00 p.m. (just as people should be), but can receive plenty of cooler morning and late afternoon light. Coolness, not darkness, is the goal.

All forms need plenty of air in the soil to allow their dense fibrous roots to breath as well as to provide good drainage for our heavy winter rains. (Standing water can be fatal.) Working bark mulch or coarse peat moss into the soil helps provide these air spaces and also helps retain needed moisture in summer. Although no rhododendrons can take extended drought in hot conditions, many of the larger types (and some dwarfs) easily tolerate our normal summer droughts in cool conditions, which can often be provided by light or afternoon shade. Evergreen rhododendrons—large-leaved ones in particular—enjoy a light misting in early morning or evening during dry weather.

Rhododendrons should always be planted shallowly, with the top surface of their fibrous roots just even with or slightly above the surrounding soil, then mulched. Other than appropriate siting, mulch is the best thing gardeners can do for their rhododendrons, and Douglas fir bark is ideal. Bark mulch keeps the soil acidic, helps cool the roots, allows them to breath, and provides just enough nourishment (all rhododendrons are light feeders) as it slowly breaks down. Don't overdo it; 2–3 in. (5–7.5 cm) is enough, although it should be topped up as necessary.

Rhododendron bureavii

Rhododendron degronianum subsp. *yakushimanum*

Other than root weevils and root rot, rhododendrons have no truly serious problems in our climate. They are, however, subject to a host of minor or cosmetic conditions, most of them due to environmental stresses (see Chapter 14). For more information on specific problems, or simply to find out more about these endlessly fascinating plants, consider joining the local chapter of the American Rhododendron Society, which includes members worldwide.

Species rhododendrons range in size from tiny ground-hugging dwarfs to tree-sized giants and represent every conceivable flower color, shape, and size. Even more importantly for year-round gardens, they encompass an astounding range of foliage shapes, sizes, colors (especially of new growth), and textures; some foliage is even aromatic. Species rhododendrons may be evergreen or deciduous, with or without indumentum, densely or sparsely foliaged, easy or difficult to grow, tender or iron-clad hardy, but are always and endlessly fascinating.

The flower trusses of most species are generally not as large, formal, or showy as those of the large-leaved midseason hybrids, but their more relaxed natural look is part of their charm: since they're not subject to fads or passing styles, their appeal is genuine and eternal. (Not to mention they come true from seed.) A visit to the Rhododendron Species Foundation and Botanical Garden in Federal Way, Washington, in April or May is an experience not soon forgotten. (For a virtual experience, go to www.rsf.citymax.com and click on Rhododendron Photos.) Warning: collecting species rhododendrons is definitely habit-forming; enthusiasts who get hooked on species are hooked for life.

With well over 800 species from which to choose, it is very difficult to limit our descriptions. However, these few selections are all proven performers in Pacific Northwest gardens and are most likely to be available locally. Unless indicated otherwise, all are native to western China and/or the eastern Himalaya, where climatic conditions closely approximate our own.

Rhododendron augustinii subsp. *augustinii*. Tall, early midseason to midseason, 4/3/4, Zone 6b. Small bell-shaped flowers range from deep violet-blue to pale blue to electric-blue to white. Still the bluest of blues, although exact shade may change on same plant in different years. Lepidote; short pointed leaves on upright plants. Several named forms are available; parent of many fine hybrids. Excellent in cool sun to partial shade.

Rhododendron barbatum. Medium, very early to early, 4–5/3/3, Zone 7b. Nicely shaped flowers of true bright red in rounded trusses bloom in February or early March. Elepidote; very long dark green leaves hang downward. Easy to grow in woodland conditions.

Rhododendron bureavii. Medium, midseason, 3/5/3, Zone 6a. Dark green foliage covered with thick ivory-white indumentum that changes to cinnamon-brown; one of the finest foliage species. Elepidote. Flowers are white flushed pink with red spotting. Needs cool site, protection from hot sun, and excellent drainage.

Rhododendron calostrotum subsp. *keleticum* (syn. *R. keleticum*). Dwarf, midseason, 4/4/4, Zone 7a. Lepidote; tiny oval aromatic leaves cover low creeping mounds. Small flowers of deep purplish red open flat. Great in rock gardens, as small-scale groundcover, or for bonsai; best in cool sun.
    Radicans Group (syn. *Rhododendron radicans*). Completely prostrate form with tiny glossy green leaves and purple flowers. Lowest-growing plant in the genus.

New foliage of *Rhododendron degronianum* subsp. *yakushimanum*

Rhododendron fortunei subsp. *discolor*

Rhododendron campanulatum subsp. *aeruginosum*. Dwarf, early midseason, 3/5/4, Zone 6b. Short rounded leaves are metallic bluish green on top with rusty brown indumentum below. Elepidote; foliage and compact mounding habit make it a winner even without the relatively large bell-shaped flowers of pink or white.

Rhododendron campylogynum. Dwarf, midseason, 4/4/3, Zone 6b. Lepidote; small, smooth, shiny dark green leaves grow densely on low mounds. Small trumpet-shaped flowers are widely flared at the rim; rounded petals give rim a scalloped appearance. Slightly nodding flowers are held on upright stems may be reddish, pink, pinkish purple, salmon-pink, deep purple, or creamy white. Several forms available, all very appealing.

Rhododendron davidsonianum. Tall, early midseason, 4/3/3, Zone 7a. Fragrant funnel-shaped flowers of pale pink to purplish pink, sometimes spotted red. Lepidote; short, shiny lance-shaped leaves on upright plants.

'Ruth Lyons'. Deep rose flowers with gold and magenta spotting; very floriferous.

Rhododendron degronianum subsp. *yakushimanum* (syn. *R. yakushimanum*). Dwarf to semi-dwarf, early midseason to midseason, 5/5/4, Zone 5b. Native to Japan. Although the American Rhododendron Society now considers the "yaks" a subspecies of *R. degronianum*, the switch is not universal; many plants will be labelled *R. yakushimanum* for a long time to come.

Whatever it's called, this species from tiny, mountainous Yaku Island (Yakushima or Yaku Jima) at the southern tip of Japan is an exceptional plant in all ways: beautiful, hardy, adaptable, and perfectly suited to Pacific Northwest conditions. Pink buds open to well-formed pale pink flowers that fade white; trusses are neither too stiff nor too lax. Elepidote. Long narrow leaves on dense mounding plants have beautiful woolly brown indumentum; new growth is so completely covered with fine white hairs it appears silvery blue. Cool sun to light shade suits it best.

Parent of innumerable hybrids, many of which are rated 4/4/4. Besides those described elsewhere in this entry, a few of them include 'Bob Bovee' (yellow with red and green spotting),

'Caroline Allbrook' (clear rosy violet), 'Dopey' (bright glossy red), 'Fred Peste' (red with deeper red spotting), 'Grumpy' (yellow tinged pink), 'Ken Janeck' (a superb seedling selected in the Seattle area; considered a hybrid), 'Noble Mountain' (purplish pink with red spotting), and 'Schneekrone' (Snow Crown; white flushed pink).

'Koichiro Wada'. Selected form with rosy buds opening pink, fading white. Rated a rarely achieved 5/5/5.

Rhododendron fortunei subsp. *discolor*. Tall, late midseason to late, 4/4/4–5, Zone 6a. Native to central and eastern China. Large pale pink to white bell-shaped flowers are slightly fragrant. Elepidote; leaves are large and very handsome. Vigorous plant tolerates both heat and cold and is easy to grow; can become small tree. The type, *R. fortunei* subsp. *fortunei*, is very similar but flowers in midseason.

Rhododendron impeditum. Dwarf, early midseason, 4/4/4, Zone 5b. Lepidote; densely twiggy mounds are covered with very tiny, narrow, grayish green aromatic leaves. Small flat-faced flowers are pinkish purple to violet. Very hardy, healthy, sun-tolerant, and widely adaptable; popular choice for rock gardens. A must-have.

Rhododendron keiskei. Dwarf to semi-dwarf, early midseason, 4/4/4, Zone 6b. Native to southern Japan, including Yakushima. Small funnel-shaped flowers of pale to lemon-yellow are very prolific. Lepidote; narrow pointed leaves on compact mounds are bronzed when young. Easy to grow but needs excellent drainage.

'Yaku Fairy'. Clone of *Rhododendron keiskei* var. *ozawae*. Clear yellow flowers on dense, completely prostrate plant; new growth is copper-red.

Rhododendron lutescens. Tall, early to early midseason, 4/3/4, Zone 7b. Small, widely funnel-shaped flowers of pale to primrose-yellow, spotted green. Lepidote; new leaves are deep red. Upright willowy habit; floriferous and easy.

Rhododendron macabeanum. Tall, early to early midseason, 4/5/3, Zone 8a. Native to northern India. Truly a tree rhodo-

Rhododendron impeditum

Rhododendron 'Maureen'

Rhododendron 'Anna Rose Whitney'

Rhododendron 'Mrs. Furnivall'

dendron; in ideal conditions it can reach 40 ft. (12 m). Elepidote; enormous leaves can reach 12–18 in. (30–45 cm) and have woolly-white indumentum on undersides. Huge lemon-yellow flowers blotched purple at bases are also impressive. Easy to grow, but needs mild winters and summer watering. Best in light shade protected from strong winds.

Rhododendron macrophyllum. Medium tall, midseason to late midseason, 3/3/3, Zone 7a. Native to the Pacific Northwest;

state flower of Washington. Bell-shaped flowers of pale to deep pink; occasionally white or magenta. Elepidote. Long smooth leaves on vigorous plants; mature specimens can become small trees. Tolerates heat, drought, sun, shade, winter wet (with good drainage), and salt spray; perfectly adapted to our wet-winter, dry-summer climate. Excellent in informal gardens or light woodland.

Rhododendron 'Scintillation'

Rhododendron 'Taurus'

Rhododendron 'Elizabeth'

Rhododendron 'Dora Amateis'

Rhododendron oreotrephes. Tall, early midseason, 3/4/4, Zone 7a. Prolific bell-shaped flowers of pale pink to pinkish lavender, sometimes lightly spotted. Lepidote; short, slightly rounded leaves are grayish to bluish green. Upright but compact habit; easy to grow. (See photo on page 50.)

Rhododendron pemakoense. Dwarf, very early to early, 4/4/4, Zone 7a. Profuse, relatively large funnel-shaped flowers of pink to pinkish purple on compact creeping plants. Lepidote; small oblong leaves are glossy green. Easy to grow in sun or light shade; parent of many fine hybrids.

Rhododendron pseudochrysanthum. Medium, early midseason, 3/5/4, Zone 6a. Native to Taiwan. Small bell-shaped flowers are pink to blush-pink with red flecks. Elepidote; small rounded leaves are lightly covered with silvery white indumentum. Slow grower in sun or light shade, making compact mounds.

Rhododendron williamsianum. Dwarf to semi-dwarf, early midseason, 3/4/4, Zone 6b. Nodding, rather sparse pink flowers shaped like wide bells on compact spreading plants. Elepidote. Distinctive compact leaves are nearly round; new growth is bright coppery bronze. Species itself is seldom grown; parent of many excellent hybrids that retain its outstanding foliage. A few well-known and highly rated examples include 'Bow Bells' (deep pink), Cowslip Group (creamy yellow), 'Gartendirektor Glocker' (pink with deeper pink edging), 'Gartendirektor Rieger' (cream with red spotting), 'Jock' (deep rose), 'Kimberly' (pastel pink, slightly fragrant), 'Maureen' (orchid-pink), Moonstone Group (pale yellow), 'Sea-Tac' (bright red), and Temple Belle Group (soft pink). All are excellent in Pacific Northwest gardens.

Large-leaved hybrids

With over 1000 cultivars on the market at any given time and outstanding new introductions added yearly, large-leaved hybrid rhododendrons (mainly elepidotes) offer gardeners virtually unlimited choice. In time, some of the older cultivars do fall off the back of the wagon, but a surprising number remain popular after a century or more despite what could be considered faults by more recent standards. For instance, 'Sappho' (a tall white cultivar with a striking deep purple blotch on each flower) has a strong inclination to become leggy and has a non-starter rating of 4/1/2; however, it's still in demand after almost 150 years for its health, vigor, and ability to provide decades of reliable bloom. Just place it in the background to hide its bare legs and less-than-perfect foliage.

Choosing cultivars is very much a matter of personal taste, but it's always advisable to be guided by local sources, such as an independent nursery or the nearest chapter of the American Rhododendron Society, rather than by a continent-wide guidebook or catalog. Cultivars that thrive on the East Coast do not necessarily do well in our cooler summers (although some do); conversely, cultivars termed "difficult" in such sources are often the very ones that thrive best in Pacific Northwest conditions.

The large-leaved selections described here, presented alphabetically first by flower color group (pink, red, and so forth) and then by season (very early or late bloomers), are all well-tested successes in our climate; their names appear consistently on the "proven performers" lists of every Pacific Northwest (including Canadian) chapter of the American Rhododendron Society.

Pink. This largest color group contains every shade from the palest blush-pink to deep rose-pink. Most are best in cool sun but are very adaptable, vigorous, and trouble-free, accepting everything but blazing hot sun or very dry conditions.

'Anna Rose Whitney'. Tall, late midseason, 4/3/5, Zone 6b. Large, unspotted flowers of deep rose; large leaves are densely set. Vigorous and sun-tolerant.

'Bruce Brechtbill'. A sport of the yellow-flowering 'Unique'; same outstanding foliage and plant form, but flowers are pastel pink.

'Cilipinense'. Medium, early, 4/3/4, Zone 7a. Delicate flowers of apple-blossom pink with deeper pink accents; smallish leaves are deep forest-green. Easy to grow in woodland conditions, but early flowers need protection from late frosts.

'Fantastica'. Low, late midseason, 4/4/4, Zone 6b. Rose-pink flowers fading to white in centers with light green spotting; long narrow leaves have woolly reddish brown indumentum. Hybrid involving *Rhododendron degronianum* subsp. *yakushimanum*.

'Janet Blair'. Tall, late midseason, 4/3/4, Zone 5b. Distinctively frilled light pink flowers with light green flare; vigorous and very adaptable.

'Lem's Monarch' (syn. 'Pink Walloper'). Tall, midseason, 4/4/4, Zone 6b. Magnificent sturdy specimen plant with huge, perfectly formed trusses; pale pink flowers blend to white centers. Very large leaves are deep green.

'Mrs. Furnivall'. Also spelled Mrs. Furnival. Medium, early midseason, 5/4/3, Zone 5b. Classic well-formed rosy pink flowers with reddish flare. Compact plant is very well mannered but can be slow to establish.

'Point Defiance'. Tall, midseason, 5/4/4, Zone 6b. Absolutely gigantic trusses of pastel pink flowers with deep rose edges blending to white centers; sometimes classed as white. Named in honor of the rhododendron garden of Point Defiance Park, Tacoma, Washington.

'Scintillation'. Medium tall, midseason, 4/4/5, Zone 5b. Pastel pink flowers with light orange-brown flare bloom profusely; shiny dark green foliage on compact upright plants. Very adaptable and reliable; good mixer.

'Teddy Bear'. Low, early midseason, 4/5/4, Zone 6a. Light pink flowers in delicate trusses on compact mounding plants; dense, shiny dark green leaves have reddish indumentum. Hybrid involving *Rhododendron degronianum* subsp. *yakushimanum*.

Red. Red-flowered hybrids grow vigorously but need cool conditions and protection from hot or intense sun. Most also appreciate a site not too exposed in winter, such as the edge of woodland.

'Elizabeth'. Low, early midseason, 3/4/4, Zone 7a. Unmistakable plant with wide-spreading habit and very narrow fir-green leaves; excellent for landscaping. Lax trusses of relatively large trumpet-shaped flowers of clear red; often reblooms in September. The sport 'Elizabeth Red Foliage' has reddish new growth.

'Etta Burrows'. Tall, early, 4/4/4, Zone 7b. Very deep red flowers in well-shaped trusses; handsome fir-green foliage. Sturdy and dependable.

'Halfdan Lem'. Medium tall, midseason, 5/4/4, Zone 6b. Huge trusses of cherry-red flowers on strong sturdy plants with dark green foliage; good specimen.

'Taurus'. Tall, early midseason, 5/4/4, Zone 6b. Red winter buds open to bright flowers of deep red; deep green leaves are pointed at tips. Strong stems on vigorous plant; excellent performance in Pacific Northwest conditions.

'The Honourable Jean Marie de Montague'. Medium tall, midseason, 4/4/4, Zone 6b. Classic red usually sold as 'Jean Marie de Montague'; widely known among enthusiasts simply as Jean Marie. True red flowers, thick heavy foliage, good form, and all-around dependable performance; tolerates full sun better than most reds.

Rhododendron 'Snow Lady'

Rhododendron 'Crest'

Rhododendron 'Hotei'

Rhododendron 'Purple Lace'

White. Although they appear delicate and fragile, most white-flowered hybrids are vigorous, very healthy, and very adaptable. Whites are often passed over in favor of the more spectacularly colored hybrids but always add light, grace, and classic beauty to gardens.

'Dora Amateis'. Low, early midseason, 4/4/4, Zone 5b. Wide-spreading plants well clothed with dense, deep green foliage are covered head to toe with small, lightly fragrant, slightly nodding white flowers in early spring. Grows to perfection in cool sun; essential landscaping plant perfect for low borders or massing.

'Loderi King George'. Tall, midseason, 4/3/4, Zone 7a. Pink buds open to large white flowers that are noticeably fragrant, as are all the Loderi Series; very long narrow leaves have burgundy stems. Needs protection from hot sun and wind along with plenty of space; can become a small tree.

'Loder's White'. Tall, midseason, 5/3/3, Zone 7a. Large white flowers with frilly pink edges and yellow throats held in tall trusses; handsome foliage. Good background plant; glowing white flowers will shine through.

'Sir Charles Lemon'. Medium tall, early midseason, 4/5/3, Zone 7b. White flowers with sparse red spotting are produced only on mature plants, but foliage is a knockout year-round. New leaves are almost white as they unfold; mature leaves have bright cinnamon-colored indumentum. Can become a small tree. Best in light shade; needs protection from hot sun.

'Snow Lady'. Semi-dwarf, early, 4/4/4, Zone 7a. Graceful, slightly fragrant flowers of pure white with black-tipped stamens bloom in early March; need protection from late frosts. Beautiful foliage is softly fuzzy and irresistible. Best in partial shade; tolerates deep shade. Lepidote.

Yellow. As a group, yellow hybrids tend to be the most dependent on good growing conditions to look and perform best. Cool woodland conditions and excellent drainage are almost always mandatory, but given these conditions, they make outstanding specimens. A winter-sheltered site is usually appreciated.

'Crest'. Tall, midseason, 4–5/3/3, Zone 6b. Large, well-shaped flowers are clear sunny yellow. Still the finest tall yellow hybrid, but best as background plant or in informal woodland setting; large plants can become open-limbed. Can be shy to flower when young; flowers heavily in maturity.

'Hotei'. Low, midseason, 5/4/3, Zone 7b. Canary-yellow flowers in relaxed trusses on spreading, compact plants. Needs a cool, well-drained site in partial shade. Parent of many choice hybrids.

'Odee Wright'. Medium, midseason, 5/4/4, Zone 6b. Large, profuse flowers of clear yellow with faint red spotting; thick-textured green leaves on compact, slightly spreading plants.

'Paprika Spiced'. Low, early midseason, 5/3/3, Zone 7b. Light yellow flowers heavily speckled red; handsome foliage on broad spreading plant.

Rhododendron 'Canadian Sunset'

Rhododendron PJM Group

'Top Banana'. Low, early midseason, 5/4/4, Zone 7b. Hybrid involving 'Hotei', with similar flowers but more upright in habit; blooms more consistently at an earlier age.

'Unique'. Medium, early midseason, 3/4–5/4, Zone 6b. Compact dome-shaped plants are clothed with dense rounded foliage all the way to the ground. Pink buds open to creamy yellow flowers that fade to pale cream; on mature plants flowers completely obscure foliage. Healthy, reliable classic; best in light or filtered shade.

Blue/purple. Large-leaved blue or purple hybrids love sun and are usually heat-tolerant, but also thrive in light shade. They tend to bloom late in the season (as opposed to the small-leaved blue/purple lepidotes, which tend to bloom very early) and are one of the best choices for exposed sites. They also tend to be remarkably drought tolerant when established. Excellent drainage is a must; most are sensitive to root rot. Watch for root weevils, which seem to prefer blue/purple shades to all others.

'Blue Boy'. Medium tall, late midseason, 4/3/4, Zone 6a. Violet-purple flowers with wavy edges and very dark purple blotch bloom heavily on upright plant with long narrow leaves.

'Blue Peter'. Medium tall, midseason to late midseason, 4/2/3, Zone 6a. Lavender-blue flowers with frilled edges and dark purple blotch are among the bluest of large-leaved hybrids, most of which are violet-purple at best. Vigorous, cold-hardy, sun- and heat-tolerant, drought tolerant when established. Consistent good performance in Pacific Northwest gardens proves the fallibility of ratings.

'Purple Lace'. Medium tall, late midseason, 4/4/4, Zone 6b. Dark reddish violet flowers with very frilly edges have white-tipped stamens that contrast nicely; well-shaped plant has glossy deep green foliage.

'Purple Splendour'. Medium tall, late midseason, 4/3/3, Zone 6b. Deep purple flowers with very dark blotch; still the truest and darkest purple. Good-looking foliage on upright, well-mannered plant, but roots are slightly weak; protect plant from strong winds. Best in sun; good drainage is imperative. (Note: 'Purple Splendor', the evergreen azalea, is spelled differently.)

Orange and orange/yellow/peach blends. Truly orange hybrids are tricky to grow, needing moist but very well-drained soil and a warm (not hot) site protected from intense sun; most

are also on the tender side. Many gardeners (and breeders) are attracted to the orange shades precisely because they are challenging, but gardeners simply wanting a good bright orange are advised to look among deciduous azaleas, where excellent choices abound. However, many of the orange/yellow/peach evergreen hybrids give excellent performance in Pacific Northwest gardens.

'Canadian Sunset'. Low, late midseason, 4/5/4, Zone 6b. Red buds open to pink flowers with salmon undertone, fading to creamy yellow at centers. Compact habit and excellent indumentum; *Rhododendron degronianum* subsp. *yakushimanum* was a parent.

Fabia Group. Low, late midseason, 3/3/4, Zone 7b. Lax trusses of trumpet-shaped flowers in varying shades of orange and peach. 'Fabia Tangerine', a selected clone with lighter orange flowers with pink rims, performs more reliably in Pacific Northwest conditions.

'Lem's Cameo'. Medium tall, midseason, 5/4/4, Zone 7a. Huge flowers of creamy apricot and pink, fading to white in centers. New growth is coppery bronze; mature leaves shiny deep green.

'Nancy Evans'. Low, midseason, 4/4/4–5, Zone 7b. Hybrid of 'Hotei' and 'Lem's Cameo'. Orange-red buds open to frilly, funnel-shaped, hose-in-hose flowers of butterscotch-yellow with orange edges, blending to light yellow centers. New growth is bronze; mature leaves shiny green. Excellent performance in Pacific Northwest conditions.

'Percy Wiseman'. Low, midseason, 4/4/4, Zone 6a. Flowers are a subtle blend of soft apricot and pastel yellow, fading to white with yellow centers. Excellent foliage and compact habit; hybrid of *Rhododendron degronianum* subsp. *yakushimanum* and 'Fabia Tangerine'.

Very early bloomers. Few large-leaved hybrid rhododendrons that bloom before mid-March can compete with later-blooming hybrids for outstanding looks, but their super-early blooms that bring the promise of spring are perhaps even more appreciated. Although they're hardy, most need some shelter to protect their flowers from our heavier late-winter rains and winds.

Rhododendron 'Gomer Waterer'

Rhododendron 'Cream Crest'

'Bric-à-brac'. Semi-dwarf, 3/3/3, Zone 7b. Pink buds open to white flowers, usually in February; rounded leaves are bronze-green. Lepidote. Best in light shade.

'Christmas Cheer'. Medium, 3/4/4, Zone 6a. Bright pink buds open to pale pink flowers; exact shade can change from year to year. Very reliable old standby; late February/early March bloom is a sure sign of spring's approach. (Name refers to practice of forcing budded branches for Christmas decorations.) Good in cool sun; quite drought tolerant.

'Gable's Pioneer'. Tall, 4/3/4, Zone 5b. Usually sold as 'Pioneer'. Bright flowers of rosy mauve-pink bloom all along stems in February or even January in very mild winters. Tolerates sun, heat, cold; foliage is semi-deciduous. 'Pioneer Silvery Pink', which blooms slightly later, is pastel pink and has red fall foliage. Lepidote.

'Olive'. Medium, 3/3/3, Zone 5b. Small but abundant orchid-pink flowers on vigorous upright plants. One of the first to bloom every year, usually in February. Lepidote.

PJM Group. Medium, 4/4/4, Zone 4b. Bright lavender pink flowers bloom in early March against small rounded leaves that still retain their winter color of dark maroon. Foliage slowly turns green for summer. A very easy, adaptable, and reliable must-have; takes sun (best for foliage color), cold, heat, partial shade, exposure. Lepidote.

Late bloomers. Late May can be a real letdown as the great and varied show of rhododendron trusses begins to wind down for the year, so hybrids and species that bloom in late May/early June or even later are greatly appreciated. They not only help prolong the show, but help ease us into the reality of summer's warmer, drier, sunnier conditions. Not surprisingly, many late bloomers are heat-tolerant, but most need some protection from direct afternoon sun, which is at its highest intensity of the year. Light shade will prolong their flowering.

Aladdin Group. Tall, 4/4/4, Zone 7a. Large, fragrant, deep pink trumpet-shaped flowers with a hint of peach bloom on upright plant in late June/early July; leaves are large and narrow. Deadhead to prevent legginess.

'Anah Kruschke'. Tall, 4/3/5, Zone 5b. Bright reddish purple flowers are attractive, but outstanding feature is its immense mounding domes of variably shaped leaves that clothe branches to the ground. Mature specimens can easily exceed 12 ft. (3.6 m) in diameter. Best in sun; tolerates heat, cold, and drought.

'Goldsworth Orange'. Medium tall, 4/4/3, Zone 6b. Widely flared trumpet-shaped flowers of salmon-orange held in loose trusses; dark green leaves have red stems. Heat- and cold-tolerant.

'Gomer Waterer'. Tall, 4/4/4, Zone 5b. Lavender-pink buds open pearly white with yellow-brown flare; stubby, leathery, variably sized dark green leaves have slight downward curve. Very reliable and sun-tolerant; an old favorite.

'Mrs. T. H. Lowinsky'. Medium tall, 4/3/4, Zone 5b. Often sold as 'Mrs. Tom Lowinsky' or 'Mrs. Tom H. Lowinsky'. Lavender buds open to white flowers with large conspicuous blotch of deep orange; very showy. Vigorous.

'Polar Bear'. Tall, 4/3/4, Zone 6b. Large, very fragrant white flowers with green centers are among the latest (July) to bloom. Leaves are large and growth vigorous; can become a small tree. Unlike most late bloomers, it's best in woodland conditions.

Small-leaved hybrids

Although they appear dainty and even fragile, small-leaved hybrid rhododendrons (mainly lepidotes) as a group are more sun-tolerant than their large-leaved relatives and are also more tolerant of windy or exposed sites. Most are thoroughly cold-hardy in our climate and surprisingly drought tolerant when established, although their smaller root systems cannot cope with extended summer drought. Since they need no deadheading or special coddling, they make excellent subjects for landscaping, rock gardens, and containers. All the selections given here are proven performers in Pacific Northwest gardens.

'Blaney's Blue'. Medium, early midseason, 5/4/4, Zone 6b. Silver-dollar-sized open flowers of light violet-blue bloom prolifically on vigorous plants; foliage is bronzed in winter. Bred for and extensively tested in Pacific Northwest conditions; excellent. Hybrid of 'Blue Diamond' and a *Rhododendron augustinii* clone.

'Blue Diamond'. Semi-dwarf, early midseason, 4/4/4, Zone 6b. Densely branched upright stems are covered their entire length with small blue flowers; popular for borders and landscaping.

Rhododendron 'Ginny Gee'

Rhododendron 'Ramapo'

'Bob's Blue'. Semi-dwarf, midseason, 4/4/4, Zone 7a. Small flowers of electric blue on compact mounds; foliage turns maroon in winter. Free-flowering and easy to grow.

'Carmen'. Dwarf, early midseason, 4/5/4, Zone 6b. Dense spreading mats of small, rounded, bright green leathery leaves; small bell-shaped flowers of dark red have waxy texture. Elepidote.

'Cream Crest'. Semi-dwarf, early midseason, 3/4/4, Zone 7a. Dense twiggy mounds of small leaves smothered with tiny flowers of creamy yellow. Vigorous and totally reliable; highly tolerant of sun and drought.

'Curlew'. Dwarf, early midseason, 5/4/4, Zone 6b. Relatively large flowers of light lemon-yellow on dense mounds of dark green leaves. Needs good drainage.

'Egret'. Dwarf, early to early midseason, 4/4/4, Zone 6b. Nodding funnel-shaped flowers of creamy white on compact mounds; small shiny green leaves. Protect flowers from late frosts.

'Ginny Gee'. Dwarf, early midseason, 5/5/4, Zone 6b. Incredibly profuse thumbnail-sized flowers of pale pink dappled white; habit is ground-hugging and spreading. Newer introductions of similar habit include 'Patty Bee' (pastel yellow, slightly larger flowers), 'Ernie Dee' (pinkish lavender), 'June Bee' (creamy white), 'Too Bee' (bell-shaped pink flowers with red spotting), and 'Wee Bee' (red/pink blend). All perform beautifully in Pacific Northwest gardens.

'Ramapo'. Semi-dwarf, early midseason, 3/4/4, Zone 4a. Outstanding landscape plant with a constitution of iron. Small pinkish violet flowers contrast nicely with glaucous aromatic foliage; new leaves are light bluish green. Tolerates sun, shade, heat, cold, and drought.

'Shamrock'. Dwarf, early, 4/4/4, Zone 6b. Tiny but prolific yellowish green flowers bloom just in time for St. Patrick's day on spreading prostrate plants.

'Vibrant Violet'. Semi-dwarf, early midseason, 4/4/4, Zone 7a. Very bright, truly vibrant violet flowers; small dark green leaves are pointed at tips. Hybrid of *Rhododendron impeditum* and an *R. augustinii* clone.

Azaleodendrons

Hybrids between azaleas (deciduous or evergreen) and evergreen rhododendrons, these compact, very floriferous plants blend the characteristics of both. Most azaleodendrons are semi-deciduous.

'Glory of Littleworth'. Medium tall, midseason, 5/3/3. Relatively large, slightly fragrant creamy white flowers with large blotch of bright orange. Attractive foliage is bluish gray.

'Hardijzer Beauty'. Low, early midseason, 4/4/4, Zone 6b. Small but exquisitely formed flowers of clear bright pink bloom freely all along stems; small green leaves on upright plants remain evergreen. Vigorous and sun-tolerant.

'Ria Hardijzer'. Low, early midseason, 4/4/4, Zone 6b. Very similar to 'Hardijzer Beauty' but with deeper pink flowers; leaf stems are red.

Deciduous azaleas

Besides shedding their foliage for winter, deciduous azaleas differ from evergreen rhododendrons in several ways important mainly to botanists. For gardeners, the main differences are greater tolerance of sun, heat, drought, and cold (Zone 5, some hardier); most cultivars are derived from species native to Europe or North America and are adapted to more continental climates. In most parts of the Pacific Northwest, they're best sited in full but cool sun, although light shade will prolong their blooms. Afternoon shade is advisable in hot-summer valleys.

The color range is also different, being strongly skewed to the yellow-orange-pink range (along with white) and totally lacking in true blue. Individual flowers are somewhat smaller but much more profuse, completely covering the branches before the leaves appear.

Size, leaf form, and blooming times are also much more consistent. In our climate, almost all deciduous azaleas bloom in May (a few start in late April) and grow to 4–5 ft. (1.2–1.5 m) in both height and width in ten years. However, as with evergreen rhododendrons, they can get considerably taller and wider after several decades. Colorful fall foliage is a valuable bonus; many deciduous azaleas have excellent fall colors of yellow, orange, red, or burgundy.

Rhododendron 'Hardijzer Beauty'

Rhododendron 'Irene Koster'

Rhododendron luteum

Rhododendron 'Gibraltar'

Although slightly less vulnerable to root rot and root weevils, deciduous azaleas are much more subject to powdery mildew, especially in late summer if the soil is dry. This is seldom serious, since the leaves will soon drop anyway, but it does spoil the fall foliage. Good air circulation and moisture-retaining mulch are the best preventatives.

At one time, deciduous azaleas were always classified by hybrid groups (Exbury, Ghent, Knapp Hill, Mollis, Occiden-

tale), and many older cultivars are still identified as such. However, since all the hybrid groups share some of the same species ancestors, and newer hybrids are of increasingly complex parentage, the differences between them are less and less relevant. Scores of good hybrids are available; unlike evergreen rhododendrons, they are not individually rated.

Deciduous azalea species are seldom grown; the three noted here are popular and garden-worthy exceptions.

Rhododendron 'Louise Gable'

Rhododendron 'Girard's Rose'

Rhododendron 'White Lights'

Rhododendron luteum (syn. *Azalea pontica*). Native to Europe and the Caucasus. Small funnel-shaped flowers of deep yellow are powerfully fragrant and sticky to the touch; flowers open just before leaves. Easy to grow and very adaptable.

Rhododendron occidentale (western azalea). Native to the Pacific Northwest. Dark pink buds open to fragrant flowers of pale pink with yellow-orange blotch; glossy green foliage turns yellow or red in fall. Can grow very large, over 8 ft. (2.4 m) tall and wide, in time. Beautiful enough in itself, this species was the main one used in the development of the very beautiful and fragrant Occidentale hybrids. Several selected forms are available.

Rhododendron schlippenbachii (royal azalea). Native to northeastern Asia and Manchuria. Open-faced flowers of pastel to blush-pink have very delicate appearance; beautiful soft green leaves appear shortly after buds open. Foliage turns red, orange, and/or yellow in fall. Compact plant with pleasing natural form; needs lightly shaded woodland conditions and protection from late frosts.

The hybrid deciduous azaleas next described are time-tested winners that perform consistently well in Pacific Northwest conditions.

'Cannon's Double'. Creamy white flowers with apricot-pink tinge are double-layered rather than many-petalled; new growth is bronze. Vigorous and easy to grow.

'Gibraltar'. Flowers are bright vermilion-orange with ruffled edges; very floriferous. Habit is compact but vigorous; excellent and reliable performance in the Pacific Northwest.

'Homebush'. Small semi-double flowers of rose-pink held in distinctive, perfectly round trusses with stamens protruding; popular.

'Irene Koster'. Large, very fragrant pastel pink/peach flowers with yellow flare; best in cool sun to partial shade. Hybrid involving our native *Rhododendron occidentale*.

'Klondyke'. Orange-yellow buds open to flowers of bright deep gold with bronze tints; new growth is bronze.

'Oxydol'. Large flowers of pure white with faint greenish yellow spotting; new growth is bronze. Free-flowering, best in partial shade to extend blooming time.

'Strawberry Ice'. Frilly flowers of pink shading to pale apricot with yellow flare; flowers are held in large rhododendron-like trusses.

DEADHEADING AND PRUNING RHODODENDRONS AND AZALEAS

Rhododendrons and azaleas do not require regular pruning, but when it becomes necessary to increase bushiness, repair damage, or to reduce a plant's size, the ideal time to prune is immediately after bloom.

Where to cut and how much to prune depends on plant type. Some large-leaved evergreen rhododendrons will resprout even if they're cut to within a few inches of the ground; others won't resprout at all from old wood, even when dormant buds are visible. Since many hybrids have complex ancestry, it's best to err on the side of caution and prune only to a healthy side branch or to just above a whorl of leaves. The plant will bloom more sparsely the spring following drastic pruning, but will then resume its normal flowering habit.

The best way to prevent large-leaved evergreen rhododendrons from getting lanky in the first place is to deadhead them every year as soon as the flowers fade. This takes time and patience (and gets your fingers very, very sticky), but will result in more blooms on a more compact plant next year. Keep in mind that some cultivars are naturally leggy, especially as they mature—but this gives a good excuse for planting lower-growing cultivars in front of them. Very mature, out-of-reach tall specimens are best left to their own devices; attempts at deadheading can cause too much accidental breakage.

To deadhead faded flowers, grasp the base of the truss and give it a sharp bend. It should snap off cleanly above the new growth buds located just below it. If the truss bends but doesn't break, wait a few days before trying again; rubbery trusses make it too easy to accidentally snap off the new growth buds as well. Wearing disposable gloves solves the sticky-finger problem, but if gloves are uncomfortable, rubbing a dab of butter (not margarine) into your hands will remove the stickiness.

Evergreen azaleas and small-leaved evergreen rhododendrons do not need deadheading. It's also not essential for deciduous azaleas, but it doesn't hurt, either; deadheading prevents seed formation, which can sap a plant's energies, and seedpods on some deciduous azaleas can be an eyesore.

Young deciduous azaleas send up long, bare branches that make them look awkward and leggy. In time, plants will bush out by themselves, but for a more nicely shaped plant sooner, just cut the branches to whatever height you want, whether or not leaves are present at that point. Unlike evergreen rhododendrons, deciduous azaleas quickly sprout dozens of brand new leaves from these bare branches, thanks to latent leaf buds that lie hidden under the bark.

Mature deciduous azaleas can be kept vigorous by pruning out a few of the oldest branches every few years, thus encouraging new stems. Overgrown or neglected deciduous azaleas can be rejuvenated by hard pruning as soon as the flowers fade, leaving 6–8 in. (15–20 cm) on each stem.

Evergreen azaleas are easiest of all to prune. When the flowers have faded, simply give the plant a bowl haircut. New growth will begin almost immediately, so the closer the haircut, the bushier next year's plant will be. As with deciduous azaleas, there's no worry about cutting into any long, bare branches; these too will soon sprout dense, leafy new stems—all of which will bear flowers next spring—from latent buds hidden inside the branches.

Mature evergreen azaleas do not object to a light trim every year right after flowering, but this is not absolutely necessary; most specimens look just fine with little or no pruning. However, even mature specimens can always be made more compact and floriferous by shearing them back.

'White Lights'. Pink buds open to fragrant blush-pink flowers with yellow stripe, fading pure white; very floriferous. Part of the Northern Lights Series of fragrant, ultra cold-hardy (Zone 3 or colder) deciduous azaleas developed at the University of Minnesota.

In marked contrast to most plants developed for extreme cold hardiness, all Northern Lights azaleas do very well in our climate. Their compact growth habit is well suited to smaller gardens, and their sterile flowers mean no deadheading is needed. Other cultivars include 'Golden Lights' (deep yellow, mildew-resistant), 'Lemon Lights' (light yellow, reblooms in fall), 'Mandarin Lights' (red-orange, ruffled), 'Orchid Lights' (soft pinkish violet, very compact), 'Rosy Lights' (deep pink), and 'Western Lights' (clear pink).

Evergreen azaleas
These dwarf shrubs with very dense, twiggy foliage and small but very profuse flowers differ markedly from both deciduous azaleas and evergreen rhododendrons. Native only to eastern and southeastern Asia, evergreen azaleas are much more tolerant of sun and heat, but are less tolerant of drought and especially of cold. Few are hardier than Zone 6b, and many hybrid groups are semi-tender.

"Evergreen" is something of a misnomer, since two types of leaves are produced every year. Both are small, rounded, and not as thick or leathery as those of evergreen rhododendrons. Leaves that appear in spring are dropped in fall, while the smaller, darker green summer leaves remain on the plants over winter before dropping in spring. Young plants and those in very cold gardens tend to be semi-deciduous, but mature plants are covered with dense, shiny, attractive foliage year-round.

Nothing can match evergreen azaleas for sheer masses of bright color in the pink-red-purple range (plus white). Ideal for landscaping, massing, borders, and containers, these wide-spreading, trouble-free dwarf shrubs are completely smothered with flowers in late April and May. Most do not exceed

Rhododendron 'Amoenum'

Rhododendron 'Hino-crimson'

3–4 ft. (0.9–1.2 m) in height even after decades of growth, but can easily spread twice as wide. All can be kept dense and compact indefinitely by shearing back as soon as flowers fade (see sidebar).

Other than needing more winter protection than most other rhododendrons, evergreen azaleas are remarkably healthy and pest-free. Azalea leaf gall, a fungus, can occasionally cause leaf tips to swell into horrible-looking white tumor-like growths, but these are quite harmless. Just cut them off and spray with sulfur to prevent its spread; providing good air circulation is the best preventative.

There are several major groups of evergreen azaleas, some of them tender (florist's azaleas, for example) and some not well suited to our climate. Like camellias, certain evergreen azaleas thrive in the warmer late spring conditions of the East Coast and/or California, but the same selections do not always do well here—and vice versa. All those described here are proven performers in Pacific Northwest conditions.

Gable hybrids. Developed from Kurume hybrids. Flowers and habit are slightly larger than Kurumes; many forms have double flowers. Height 2–4 ft. (0.6–1.2 m); Zone 6b. Some of the best include 'Caroline Gable' (bright rose-pink, hose-in-hose, reddish winter foliage), 'Louise Gable' (salmon-pink, semi-double), 'Purple Splendor' (violet-purple, hose-in-hose), 'Rosebud' (shell-pink, double; buds look like perfect miniature rosebuds), and 'Stewartstonian' (deep orange-red; reddish winter foliage).

Girard hybrids. Developed from Gable hybrids, with greater cold hardiness in mind. Single flowers are fairly large; leaves of compact bushy plants turn reddish in winter. Many cultivars. Height 2–3 ft. (0.6–0.9 m); Zone 5b. Popular choices include 'Girard's Fuchsia', 'Girard's Hot Shot' (deep orange-red), and 'Girard's Rose'.

Glenn Dale hybrids. Larger plants, larger leaves, and larger flowers; over 400 varieties have been named. Habit may be low and spreading or upright. Height 3–5 ft. (0.9–1.5 m); Zone 7a. Popular choices include 'Buccaneer' (orange-red; vigorous upright habit, best in light shade), 'Everest' (white with chartreuse blotch, low-growing), 'Gaiety' (large rose-pink flowers with violet flare; spreading habit), and 'Helen Close' (large, pure white flowers with faint greenish spotting, dense habit).

Kurume hybrids. Derived from *Rhododendron kiusianum* var. *kiusianum* (syn. *R. obtusum* f. *japonicum*; Kurume azalea). Very popular; one of the best-suited groups for the Pacific Northwest. The flowers of the Kurume azalea are tinier and even brighter than those of the Kyushu azalea; may be pink, bright purple, salmon-red, or white. The neon-bright reddish purple *R*. 'Amoenum' (syn. *R. obtusum* f. *amoenum*) is typical of the species. Dense, almost congested growth is completely covered with small but very profuse flowers; habit is very low and spreading. Height 18–30 in. (45–75 cm); Zone 7a. Perennially popular choices include 'Hershey's Red' (bright red, double), 'Hino-crimson' (tiny single crimson-red flowers and very small leaves; much prized), 'Hinode-giri' (bright rose-red; red winter foliage), 'Kirin' (pinkish hose-in-hose flowers, very early bloom; often sold as 'Coral Bells'), and 'Mother's Day' (semi-double flowers of rose-red).

Kyushu azalea (*Rhododendron kiusianum*). Native to the island of Kyushu, Japan. An outstanding densely branched dwarf shrub with rounded leaves and spreading habit; profuse small flowers may be pink, red, or purple. Several selections are available. Height 24 in. (60 cm); Zone 6a.

Other groups, such as the late-blooming, semi-hardy Satsuki hybrids, do well in local microclimates; local nurseries and garden clubs are the best place to seek advice.

RIBES SANGUINEUM (FLOWERING CURRANT)

Origin: Pacific Northwest

Hardiness zones: 5 to 9

Size: 6–8 ft. × 4–6 ft. (1.8–2.4 m × 1.2–1.8 m)

Blooming season: March to May

Exposure: Light shade to cool sun; protected from hot or intense sun

Soil preference: Heavy, moderately acidic; moisture-retentive but well drained

Water needs: Moderately drought tolerant when established

Maintenance needs: Low

Subregions best suited: All

Possible problems: Leaf spotting

Ribes sanguineum

Deciduous. Of all the plants native to the Pacific Northwest, flowering currant has enjoyed the widest popularity for the longest time. First described (to Europeans) in 1793 by Archibald Menzies, surgeon-naturalist on Captain George Vancouver's ship, it was introduced to British horticulture by plant explorer David Douglas in 1826 and has been popular on that side of the Atlantic ever since.

Ironically, one of the main attractions of this remarkable shrub is entirely missing in Europe. Its flowers of bright pink to red attract hummingbirds like a magnet, but hummingbirds are endemic to the New World and are not found in Europe.

In the Pacific Northwest, flowering currant is a crucial source of nectar for hummingbirds returning from their wintering grounds in Mexico. The timing of their return is in fact linked to the first blooming of this shrub, which is early March in our warmest southern coastal regions and progressively later northward and inland. In our own garden, the first flowers almost always open on 1 April—and on the same day, we invariably see our first hummingbird. From then until the flowers fade in late May, these feisty little bundles of energy are never far from the plants from dawn until dusk.

Flowering currant is nearly as attractive to gardeners, especially since its graceful drooping clusters of bright pink flowers with white or pinkish petaloids (modified stamens resembling small petals) and white stamens start blooming before the leaves open. Flower color varies in the wild from light to dark pink, but plants with larger white petaloids or even all-white flowers are occasionally found. At least two dozen cultivars are available in England and Europe, but 'King Edward VII', a dark red, is the only English cultivar widely available here.

Being fairly compact and upright in form, flowering currant is a natural for informal hedges; it needs no regular pruning, although it responds well to shaping right after the flowers fade. Good winter drainage is essential, but soil should not be too light-textured; if it is, plants will suffer in summer drought, especially if spring has been dry. However, keeping the soil moist through June will see them through normal dry summers. Flowering is most prolific with at least some direct but cool sun; an eastern exposure is ideal.

As beautiful as it is, flowering currant is best sited in a not-too-prominent spot. The soft maple-shaped leaves are handsome enough, but prone to fungal leaf-spotting by midsummer. Although relatively harmless, the spotting is unsightly; in severe cases resulting from an overly wet spring, plants can be defoliated by August. If appearance is a concern, the fungus can be halted with a copper spray, but plants will bounce back next spring even if defoliated.

Small blue-black berries with a glaucous bloom appear in late summer and add a certain charm. If left on the ground where they fall, many will sprout and provide a source of new plants. Although their color makes them appear somewhat toxic, don't worry if your kid eats one, or even a handful; although mealy and insipid, they're perfectly edible.

'King Edward VII'. The cultivar most likely to be found in the general nursery trade. Slightly smaller than the species, with large drooping flower clusters of deep crimson.

'Ubric' (White Icicle). Clusters of large white flowers, fading pink. Not as attractive to hummingbirds (although they do visit), but an outstanding sight in full bloom. Introduced in the 1980s by the Plant Introduction Scheme of the Botanical Garden of the University of British Columbia (PISBG).

Sarcococca confusa

SARCOCOCCA (SWEET BOX)

Origin: China, the Himalaya

Hardiness zones: 6 to 9

Size: Varies

Blooming season: January to March

Exposure: Partial shade

Soil preference: Humus-rich; moisture-retentive but well drained; slightly acidic to slightly alkaline

Water needs: Drought tolerant when established

Maintenance needs: Low

Subregions best suited: All

Possible problems: None serious

Evergreen. These small shrubs are handsome enough for year-round general landscaping purposes, but if truth be known, they're quite unremarkable except for their unique flowers. These are small, white, and visually insignificant, being half hidden behind the dense foliage, but their fragrance—a powerful but deliciously subtle perfume noticeable from many feet away—makes them must-haves in Pacific Northwest gardens.

That these shrubs perfume the air for several months starting in January (sometimes even December) makes them even more valuable in our dull, gray winters—the scent is like walking into a florist shop. The ideal site for this plant is near an entryway or frequently used path, where passersby can get maximum enjoyment of the winter perfume, but any semi-shaded site protected from wind and late frosts is good. Fragrance is most pronounced on still, relatively warm afternoons.

Plants are quite slow growing at first and may be difficult to establish, especially if they have been tissue-cultured, but will eventually spread enthusiastically and may even become gangly. Keep shrubs full and compact by cutting stems back by one-third their length in April, after flowers have faded. A sprinkling of dolomite lime in October every two or three years will give them ideal conditions; an organic mulch or annual layer of leaf litter is their only other request.

Sarcococca confusa. Shiny, wavy-edged, leathery dark green leaves somewhat resemble skimmia. Profuse flowers; small berries that follow are red at first but soon turn shiny black. Densely foliaged clumps spread very slowly, eventually becoming broader than tall. 4 ft. × 5 ft. (1.2 m × 1.5 m).

Sarcococca hookeriana. Erect, suckering shrub with pointed leaves and black fruits. Species itself is rarely grown; varieties are popular.

var. *digyna.* Spreads very quickly by suckers; may become untidy in habit. Slightly hardier than the species, with narrower leaves. Flowers are pink-tinged, fruits are black. 4 ft. × 6 ft. (1.2 m × 1.8 m).

var. *humilis.* Dwarf, densely foliaged suckering shrub spreads quickly to make a patch; good medium-scale groundcover in shade. Narrow, shiny leaves are deep green; fruits are glossy blue-black. Height 12–18 in. (30–45 cm); can spread to 3–4 ft. (0.9–1.2 m).

Sarcococca ruscifolia. Broad, thick, glossy dark green leaves. Flowers are almost hidden behind foliage; fruits are dark red. Best known by its Chinese variety.

var. *chinensis.* More vigorous than species, with narrower leaves; very similar in size and appearance to *Sarcococca confusa* except that fruits are dark red, habit is more upright. May begin blooming as early as December. 4 ft. (1.2 m) high and wide.

SPIRAEA (SPIREA)

Origin: China, Japan, the Himalaya, western North America

Hardiness zones: Most 4 to 9

Size: Varies

Blooming season: Early spring through summer

Exposure: Full sun to light shade

Soil preference: Heavy; moisture-retentive but well drained

Water needs: Most species drought tolerant when established

Maintenance needs: Low

Subregions best suited: All

Possible problems: Slightly susceptible to verticillium wilt

Deciduous. Although spireas grow well just about everywhere, they're a must-have in the Pacific Northwest. These members of the rose family love our heavy soil, perform beautifully in full sun to light shade, and need very little maintenance.

Never the stars of the show, these hardworking, underappreciated shrubs nevertheless provide four-season interest with their colorful new growth, masses of spring or summer flowers, beautiful fall foliage that often persists into winter, and attractive winter stems and dried seedheads.

There's always a place for one more spirea; at last count we have over 40 in our modest-sized garden. Whether strategically placed as accents, combined with early-blooming bulbs and perennials, massed under high-branching trees, associated with other shrubs, or used as informal flowering hedges (a role at

Spiraea douglasii

Spiraea japonica var. *albiflora*

Spiraea 'Arguta'

Spiraea japonica 'Anthony Waterer'

Spiraea japonica 'Goldflame'

which all excel), spireas are trouble-free, long-lived, and always attractive.

As with all shrubs, most need periodic rejuvenation. The taller fountain-shaped species and cultivars (*Spiraea* 'Arguta', *S. nipponica* 'Snowmound', *S. prunifolia* 'Plena', *S. thunbergii*, *S.* ×*vanhouttei*) need only the removal of a few of the oldest stems every few years as soon as flowers fade. Our native

hardhack, which blooms on new wood, can be renewed by hard pruning (nearly to the ground) in early spring. *Spiraea japonica* cultivars also blooms on new wood; overgrown shrubs are easily rejuvenated by cutting all stems to about 4 in. (10 cm) in early spring when all danger of hard frost is past and new shoots are expanding. New growth will be very vigorous, but flowering will be slightly delayed that year. Alternatively,

Spiraea japonica 'Little Princess'

Spiraea japonica 'Walbuma' (Magic Carpet)

Spiraea nipponica 'Snowmound'

S. japonica cultivars can be trimmed yearly in fall or early spring as needed.

Spiraea 'Arguta' (syn. *S.* ×*arguta*). Hybrid of two species native to China. One of at least three spireas called bridal wreath. (The other two are *S. prunifolia* 'Plena' and *S.* ×*vanhouttei*.) Tiny but very prolific flowers of dazzling pure white cover slender cascading stems in April and May. Slender apple-green leaves appear soon after flowers, giving a fresh, delicate look; attractive fall foliage is soft yellow/peach/orange. Graceful winter stems are attractive bronze-purple. Needs excellent drainage; moderately drought tolerant, but needs summer watering in prolonged droughts. 5–6 ft. (1.5–1.8 m) high and wide; Zones 4 to 9.

Spiraea douglasii (hardhack). Native to the Pacific Northwest. Tall, moisture-loving, rampantly suckering shrub topped with pink flower plumes in June and July; flower color and shape make it clear why astilbe is sometimes called false spirea. Narrow leaves are dark green on top, felty-gray on bottom. Needs heavy acidic soil, plentiful water, and lots of space; best suited to wild/native gardens or natural bogs in sun or light shade. Height 6–8 ft. (1.8–2.4 m); Zones 5 to 9.

var. *menziesii*. Smaller version of species with purplish pink flowers in July and August; tolerates drier sites but still needs summer watering. Height 4–6 ft. (1.2–1.8 m).

Spiraea japonica (Japanese spirea, dwarf spirea). Native to China; long cultivated in Japan. Small rounded shrub with profuse flat-topped flowerheads from late spring through summer. New foliage of hybrids is often brightly colored; attractive fall foliage often persists well into winter. Best in full sun (light shade in hot-summer valleys). Drought tolerant when established; tolerates wind and dry soil but flowers bloom longer with adequate soil moisture. 3 ft. × 3–4 ft. (0.9 m × 0.9–1.2 m); spreading wider in maturity. Zones 4 to 9.

var. *albiflora* (syn. 'Shirobana'). Unique compact shrub bears both pink and white flowerheads on same plant from July to frost; new shoots of red or green correspond to flower color. Two-toned effect continues through winter, with pink flowers producing black seedheads; white ones green. Nice fall foliage of dark red, purple, yellow, and green.

'Anthony Waterer'. Deep rose-red flowerheads in great profusion bloom June to frost, and rusty brown seedheads remain attractive all winter. New shoots are deep red; mature leaves dark reddish green with a few creamy white leaves variegated bright pink. (These will not grow from cuttings: lacking chlorophyll, they cannot produce their own food.) Fall foliage is deep maroon and purple; habit is dense and spreading.

'Froebelii'. Very similar to 'Anthony Waterer' but more upright in habit.

'Goldflame'. Dark red buds open to new leaves of impossibly bright orange, fading to deep gold with rusty red tips. Rosy pink flowerheads in early June do not make the most attractive combination, but are fortunately short-lived. Long-lasting fall foliage is a beautiful mixture of yellow, orange, red, green, and rusty brown. Best in cool sun or very light shade. Largely replaced by the smaller, more tasteful 'Walbuma' (Magic Carpet), but many gardeners (including ourselves) will always have a soft spot for the over-the-top exuberance of 'Goldflame'.

'Lisp' (Golden Princess). Similar to 'Little Princess' but smaller and slower growing; rarely needs renewal pruning. Small flowerheads of rosy pink look good with tiny golden leaves; attractive fall foliage is red/orange/brown. 2–3 ft. (0.6–0.9 m) high and wide.

'Little Princess'. Dense, twiggy stems covered with tiny light green leaves; small, dense, short-lived flowerheads of silvery pink bloom late May/June. Showy fall foliage of yellow, orange, red, and green lasts until early December; black seedheads remain attractive all winter, making a stark contrast in snow. Low-growing shrub is little in height only: unpruned plants can spread to 6–8 ft. (1.8–2.4 m). Excellent for massing, taller groundcover in full sun, or (with hard pruning every four to five years) low hedges or borders. 2–3 ft. × 4–6 ft. (0.6–0.9 m × 1.2–1.8 m).

'Walbuma' (Magic Carpet). Newer dwarf cultivar with soft yellow foliage that takes full sun without burning; small clusters of rosy pink flowers in late May/June are a bonus. New growth is bronze-orange, not as bright as 'Goldflame'; fall foliage is gold/orange/bronze. Well mannered (needs little or no pruning) and very popular, especially in commercial plantings. 18 in. × 24–30 in. (45 cm × 60–75 cm).

Spiraea nipponica 'Snowmound' (syn. *S. nipponica* var. *tosaensis* 'Snowmound'). Native to Japan. Versatile and well-mannered upright shrub; slender arching branches are covered with tiny white flowers in late May and June. Flowers are held on short stems on upper sides of branches, almost completely obscuring small, rounded leaves of bluish green. Dense habit and low maintenance make it a good privacy screen even in winter; black winter stems and seedheads add touch of elegance. Best in sun. 5–6 ft. (1.5–1.8 m) high and wide; Zones 4 to 9.

Spiraea prunifolia 'Plena'. Native to China. Tiny, fully double stemless flowers of pure white sit right on branches in April and May, looking like miniature roses or wedding decorations. Also called shoe-button spirea. Rounded dark green leaves turn bright orange-red in fall. 5–6 ft. (1.5–1.8 m) high and wide; Zones 5 to 9.

Spiraea thunbergii (garland spirea). Native to China; introduced from Japan. Very dainty arching shrub blooms in March and April with tiny white single flowers all along wiry stems. Small narrow leaves are light green; long-lasting fall foliage is bright yellow/orange/bronze. Best in sun. 5 ft. (1.5 m) in both dimensions; Zones 4 to 9.

'Fujino Pink'. Red buds open to white flowers tinged pink, giving effect of soft pink.

'Ogon' (Gold). New foliage is butter-yellow, fading to bright green.

Spiraea ×vanhouttei. Older hybrid still valued for tall, gracefully arching form, rounded blue-green leaves, and small white flowers borne in dense rosettes in late May and June. Easy and adaptable; good mixer. 6 ft. (1.8 m) high and wide; Zones 4 to 9.

CHAPTER 8

Roses

Roses in June, authors' garden. Left to right: Alba Meidiland, Bonica, Roseraie de l'Haÿ (background), *Rosa glauca*

The Pacific Northwest is an ideal home for roses. As everybody knows, roses love sunshine, which many places have in abundance in summer. But they also like their sunshine not too hot or intense, and even slightly on the cool side—a much harder-to-meet condition easily supplied by our unique climate. In addition, our mineral-rich river valley soils and abundant rainfall go a long way toward satisfying their notoriously hearty appetites for both food and water. (Summer irrigation is of course required in most locations.)

Add our mild winter climate, meaning virtually no winter-kill or necessary exclusion of less hardy types, and we truly have a paradise for roses. Portland isn't known as The City of Roses for nothing, and every other major city—and not a few smaller ones—also has its own thriving Rose Society.

This doesn't mean there are no problems in paradise; as usual, our beloved Eden is far from perfect. Our cold, wet springs are ideal incubators of black spot, and the dry soils, cooler temperatures, and moist atmosphere of our late summers are made to order for powdery mildew. Rust, aphids, and all the other well-known pests of roses are also always lurking in the background. To top things off, roses are one of the favorite browse foods of deer.

There are a few other rose-growing problems unique to the Pacific Northwest. Roses bred primarily for extreme cold-hardiness, such as the Brownell Series (also known as sub-zero roses) or the Manitoba-bred Parkland Series, are usually not good choices because of their susceptibility to black spot in our milder but wetter climate. Cold-hardy roses may also break dormancy too early, fooled by those mild spells in February, and get their new growth killed by later frosts. The Explorer Series of cold-hardy roses is an exception; these roses do very well here.

Yellow roses, most of which are derived from species requiring sandier soils and/or hotter summers than we can supply, tend to be poor performers here. (Fortunately, there are some notable exceptions.) White or very pale roses grow well, but most are prone to developing ugly pink splotches if the weather remains cool and rainy through June, as it often does.

Very large and/or very double flowers tend to be major disappointments here. Large flowers get bent almost to the ground in rain or heavy dew, and wet weather means roses with over 40–45 petals (some have 80 or more) may open poorly or not at all. When this happens, flowers look more like disgusting wads of wet, discarded tissue than like roses.

On the plus side, many other factors more than compensate for these drawbacks. More and more roses have been bred for good to excellent disease resistance as well as great beauty. Success with any rose with flowers up to 4 in. (10 cm) in diameter is almost guaranteed in our climate, and many outstanding roses have petal counts between five and 40. Most fully double roses actually have only 25 to 35 petals, even though it looks like much more.

Even better, rose roots absolutely love our heavy, slightly acidic soils. (Lime should be added to strongly acidic soils.) In our area, *Rosa rubiginosa* (syn. *R. eglanteria*; sweetbriar rose) has naturalized; we've dug out roots extending over 6 ft. (1.8 m) wide and 4 ft. (1.2 m) deep. This typical extensive rooting not only means great vigor, but in most cases means established roses will easily survive summer-long drought. However, "survive" and "flourish" are quite different things, and all roses will grow better and have much better repeat bloom when given a good deep soaking every two weeks in summer (more often in hot weather). To avoid disease, always water at ground level, never overhead.

Specific details about planting, feeding, watering, and maintaining roses are available in any good book on the subject. Suffice it to say proper planting is crucial to the establishment of a new rose; no pains should be spared in preparing a good home for one. The needs for deadheading, treating/preventing disease, and coping with insect pests are also not to be taken lightly, and this brings up two distinct trends in rose-growing in the Pacific Northwest.

The first is a move away from growing roses for cutting or exhibition (mainly hybrid teas) and enjoying them instead *in situ* on low-maintenance shrub or landscape roses. These are not a specific type of rose, but any of a wide variety in which growth is dense, shrubby, attractive, and covered all summer with small to medium-sized flowers that don't require deadheading. In short, landscape roses are shrubs—as versatile and beautiful as any other sun-loving shrubs—with roses for flowers. Not coincidentally, landscape roses are also much more vigorous, disease-resistant, and drought tolerant than rose-garden-type roses—factors that figure strongly in the busy but casual, outdoor-oriented, environmentally conscious lifestyles of Pacific Northwesterners.

The other trend is toward roses grown on their own roots rather than as grafts. Own-root roses grow more slowly at first, but the advantages are many: much longer life (up to 100 years versus ten years or less for grafted roses), no chance of viruses being passed on from contaminated rootstock, no unwanted suckers to contend with, more and firmer rooting against winter wind-rock, and excellent chances of regrowth should some accident befall the top growth.

Not all roses succeed on their own roots, so there is still a definite place for grafted roses. However, more and more shrub roses, old garden roses, and vigorous climbers and ramblers are being offered on their own roots by popular demand.

There are thousands of named roses, each with its own merits, and it would be impossible to list all or even most that do well in the Pacific Northwest. The few examples that follow each type description are—besides being personal favorites—only a taste of the many great choices available.

Winners of AARS awards (All-America Rose Selections) are not automatically superior to other choices, but an AARS award does mean the rose is a strong grower and prolific bloomer as well as being disease-resistant and adaptable to a wide range of conditions. It may also possess a unique color, fragrance, form, or growing habit.

Most older roses have only one name, such as 'Golden Showers', but increasingly, the names of hybrid roses are trademarked (Heritage, Sun Sprinkles, Olympiad), with another code-like name ('Ausblush', 'Jachal', 'Macauk') being botanically correct. Rather than listing the correct but confusing names, we have followed the common practice of listing all roses by their selling names only, whether registered or trademarked, but without the single quotation marks that are rightfully reserved only for registered names.

Hybrid teas

Aristocrats of the rose world, these classic "long-stemmed roses" are characterized by large, high-centered, fully double flowers, each held on a single stem. Requiring considerably more maintenance than other roses, these are also less disease-resistant and less cold-hardy (winter mulch is recommended even in our mild climate), so they're best grown in dedicated beds where their flowers can be cosseted and groomed for cutting and exhibition purposes. Still, a well-grown hybrid tea rose is a sight to behold, and many hybrid teas, including the few samples that follow, perform very well indeed in the Pacific Northwest.

Dainty Bess. 1925. Medium-sized single flowers (most unusual for a hybrid tea) with equally unusual wine-red stamens; compact, sturdy plant is outstanding in full bloom. Light fragrance.

Elina (syn. Peaudouce). 1985. Primrose-yellow buds open to very large, well-formed flowers of rich ivory-white that hold up to rain and cool temperatures without becoming mottled pink.

Iceberg (floribunda)

Fragrant Cloud (hybrid tea)

Sunsprite (floribunda)

Vigorous, free-flowering, and highly disease-resistant. Light fragrance.

Fragrant Cloud. 1963. Large geranium-red flowers hold their unusual color best in cooler weather. Slightly subject to black spot, but worth growing for the intensity of its fragrance. Considered by many to be the most fragrant of all hybrid teas.

Just Joey. 1972. Wavy-edged petals on informal but beautifully formed double flowers of pale peach/orange/yellow make this vigorous rose irresistible even if disease resistance is not perfect. Holds up well to rain. Strong spicy-fruity fragrance.

Olympiad. 1982. Large, classically formed, beautifully textured flowers of bright, clear red bloom in repeated flushes all summer. Excellent, long-lasting cut flower; very good disease resistance—a real plus in a large red hybrid tea. Alas, no fragrance.

Floribundas

Shorter, bushier, and more shrub-like than hybrid teas, floribundas are well named: abundant medium-sized flowers, held in clusters, cover the plants. Quick succession of flushes means virtually continuous bloom all season. Lower maintenance and wide color range make them suitable for massing, borders, low hedges, general landscaping, and even containers. Some popular choices follow.

Angel Face. 1968. Unusual color—an indescribable silvery pinkish lavender—and exquisite, porcelain-like form of newly opened flowers keep this one perennially popular despite slight susceptibility to black spot. Strong lemony fragrance. AARS winner 1969. The fragrant, similarly colored Blueberry Hill (1997) is more disease-resistant, but its flowers are not quite as beautifully formed.

Hot Cocoa. 2002. Newer introduction with unusual color as well as great promise for disease resistance. Large, fully double flowers of smoky, orange-tinged chocolate-red are especially dark in cooler weather. Strong old-rose fragrance. AARS winner 2003.

Iceberg. 1958. A classic in the rose world; deservedly popular. Cool, rainy weather does cause pink spotting of the pure white flowers, but free-flowering habit and reliability make it well worth growing. Vigorous and disease-resistant; moderate sweet fragrance. Climbing Iceberg, a much taller sport, has similar qualities.

Nicole. 1985. Pure white petals strongly edged in bright pink. Vigorous, very strong-growing plant is highly rated in the Pacific Northwest even though it's slightly susceptible to black spot. Slight spicy fragrance.

Sexy Rexy. 1984. Despite too-cute name, a very dependable performer in our climate. Pink flowers look like slightly ruffled formal double camellias; neat, compact plant is always in bloom

Queen Elizabeth (grandiflora)

American Pillar (rambler)

Dortmund (climber)

and looks good no matter what the weather. Highly disease-resistant. Moderate spicy-sweet fragrance.

Sunsprite (syn. Friesia). 1977. One of the best yellow floribundas ever, and arguably the best-performing pure yellow rose for the Pacific Northwest. Loosely double flowers are clear sunshine-yellow; compact plant is vigorous and disease-resistant. Strong sweet fragrance.

Grandifloras

Combining the attributes of hybrid teas and floribundas, these strong, tall-growing roses bear medium-sized to large flowers with the form and substance of hybrid tea roses, but with the multi-stemmed, continuous blooming habit of floribundas. Some good picks:

Gold Medal. 1982. Red-tipped buds open to high-centered flowers of deep yellow edged in old gold to pink. Good cut flower. Vigorous plant with good disease resistance; good performer in our climate. Light fruity-spicy fragrance.

Queen Elizabeth. 1954. Properly named 'The Queen Elizabeth'. Truly a sovereign among roses, this statuesque plant—to 7 ft. (2.1 m) or more—still commands respect. Large flowers of unfading clear pink are reliable in any weather. Highly resistant to disease, insects, and neglect, but performs even better with care. Light fragrance. AARS winner 1955.

Tournament of Roses. 1988. Medium-sized coral-pink flowers with classically beautiful form; blooms continuously throughout the season on compact, highly disease-resistant plant. Light spicy fragrance. AARS winner 1989.

Climbers and ramblers

Roses do not actually climb, but those with long, pliable canes can be tied to a vertical trellis or pillar, trained along the top of a fence, or allowed to scramble up into a tree for support. Roses classified as climbers are usually 8–15 ft. (2.4–4.5 m) in length, may have relatively large flowers, and are almost always repeat blooming. In addition to varieties designated as climbers, any tall rose with flexible canes can be trained against a trellis or wall.

Ramblers have especially long, thin, flexible canes—up to 20 ft. (6 m) or more—that bear masses of small to medium-sized flowers; romantic looks keep them sentimental favorites in spite of being highly subject to mildew. Ramblers bloom only on canes that grew the previous season or earlier, and are usually not repeat blooming.

In comparison to hybrid teas and floribundas, most of which are here today and gone tomorrow, climbers and ramblers have remarkable staying power. Most are noticeably long in the tooth and some are downright ancient, but in this category a winner remains a winner. Those well suited for the Pacific Northwest include the following.

Albéric Barbier. 1900. Rambler, 15–20 ft. (4.5–6 m), non-repeat blooming. Medium-small double flowers of creamy yellow cover the vigorous plant; foliage is dense and nearly evergreen. Tolerates shade and poor soil, but needs good air circulation to avoid mildew. Moderate sweet fragrance.

Altissimo. 1966. Climber, 10–14 ft. (3–4.2 m), repeat blooming. Large single flowers of shiny Chinese-lacquer-red with prominent yellow stamens. Hard to place, but a real knockout in the right location. Very light fragrance.

American Pillar. 1902. Rambler, 15–20 ft. (4.5–6 m), non-repeat blooming. Small to medium-sized single, wavy-edged flowers of bright pink with prominent white eye, held in clusters. Long-lasting flowers followed by red hips; vigorous plant takes shade, drought, and total neglect, but watch for mildew. Slight fragrance.

Dortmund. 1955. Climber, 8–10 ft. (2.4–3 m), repeat blooming. Large red flowers with small white eye are single, but wide, wavy-edged petals make them appear semi-double. Foliage is thick, disease-resistant, and very glossy, almost like holly. Deadheading prolongs blooming season; if not deadheaded, sets attractive orange hips. Very light fragrance.

Dublin Bay. 1975. Climber, 8–10 ft. (2.4–3 m), repeat blooming. Medium-sized, weatherproof double flowers of rich, deep red. Blooms prolifically all season; highly disease-resistant. Moderate fragrance.

Golden Showers. 1956. Climber, 10–12 ft. (3–3.6 m), repeat blooming. Medium-sized, loosely double flowers of cheerful light yellow fade to creamy white, bloom over long season. Perfect in informal country settings; healthy, adaptable, shade tolerant, and unfailingly reliable. Moderate sweet fragrance. AARS winner 1957.

Handel. 1965. Climber, 12–15 ft. (3.6–4.5 m), repeat blooming. Medium-sized, semi-double flowers of creamy pink with deep pink edges hold up well to rain; good performance in cooler weather. Strong grower, but slightly subject to black spot. Slight fragrance.

New Dawn. 1930. Climber, 15–20 ft. (4.5–6 m), repeat blooming. Often but mistakenly considered a rambler for its size and for its profusion of medium-small, semi-double flowers of blush-pink. Climber-type flowering habit, near-continuous bloom, and good disease resistance keep it extremely popular. Tolerates light shade and some neglect, but looks better with care. Moderate sweet fragrance.

Royal Sunset. 1960. Climber, 8–15 ft. (2.4–4.5 m), repeat blooming. Large flowers of apricot-orange are shaped like hybrid tea roses; very disease-resistant. Highly rated in the Pacific Northwest. Strong fruity fragrance.

Old garden roses

Roses have been grown with a passion since antiquity, and attempts at perfecting them through hybridization have been continuous for at least five centuries. The dividing line between "old" and "modern" roses is drawn at 1867, the year the first hybrid tea rose was introduced. Hybrid groups existing prior to this time include, in roughly chronological order, Gallicas, Damasks, Centifolia or "cabbage" roses, moss roses, Albas, China roses, tea roses (not to be confused with hybrid teas), Portland roses, Noisettes, Bourbons, and Hybrid Perpetuals.

Many named roses belonging to these groups are still in cultivation—a fact that speaks volumes about them—and many

New Dawn (climber)

Madame Alfred Carrière (OGR, Noisette)

rose fanciers swear by their special qualities of long life, strong fragrance, full flowers, and tolerance of shade and other less-than-ideal growing conditions. These qualities are very real, but old garden roses (OGRs) also have a limited color range, tend to grow too large for today's gardens, and are almost all non-repeat blooming. Some are cold-tender even in our mild climate, and in our moist atmosphere many are prone to black spot.

Long life is a definite asset, but this can be attributed mainly to being grown on their own roots. Given the hardiness, adaptability, relatively compact size, strong fragrance, and high disease resistance of modern shrub roses—especially when grown on their own roots, as more and more of them are—there is little reason for the average gardener to choose an "old" hybrid over a modern one.

However, the charm and romance of old garden roses (not to mention their fragrance) are powerful draws, and few collectors or serious aficionados can resist indulging in at least a few of these legendary plants. Larger garden centers usually carry a limited selection of old garden roses; Königin von Dänemark or Queen of Denmark (Alba, medium pink), Madame Alfred Carrière (Noisette, pale pink climber), Madame Hardy (Damask, white with small green center), Madame Isaac Pereire (Bourbon, deep pink), and Zéphirine Drouhin (Bourbon, pink, thornless; can be used as climber) are often available. Much wider choices are available through specialty nurseries.

Shrub roses

Originally, this category consisted of species roses, various "old" non-climbing roses, and modern shrubby types such as rugosas and polyanthas. However, the introduction of a wide variety of free-flowering, low-maintenance, disease-resistant shrubby hybrids has led to several new subcategories of shrub roses. These include David Austin (or "English") roses, modern rugosa hybrids, the super-cold-hardy Explorer Series, and an ever-increasing number of groundcover types. Each of these subcategories is described separately elsewhere, but there are still some outstanding, must-have shrub and species roses that defy classification. Among them are these:

Alba Meidiland. 1987. Very vigorous, dense, spreading form to 4 ft. × 7 ft. (1.2 m × 2.1 m). Completely covered with very small but fully double white flowers (fading to buff-pink) all season long. Tolerates poor soil and neglect; highly disease-resistant. No fragrance.

Ballerina. 1937. Small, cup-shaped single flowers of pale pink with dark pink edges are held in prolific, hydrangea-like clusters; deadheading is advised to prolong blooming season. Grows to 4 ft. (1.2 m) in height and width; stems are nearly thornless. Tolerates poor soil and part shade; disease-resistant. Sweet fragrance.

Bonica. 1982. Medium-small, perfectly formed double flowers of medium pink with hint of fruit-punch pink in cen-

Alba Meidiland (shrub)

Bonica (shrub)

Carefree Delight (shrub)

Rosa glauca

ters bloom from June to November. Prolific, showy hips of burnt-brick orange persist all winter, along with an occasional flower bud. Compact growth to 5 ft. × 4 ft. (1.5 m × 1.2 m), tolerates poor soil and part shade. Good but not perfect disease resistance. A favorite in spite of having no fragrance. AARS winner 1987.

Carefree Delight. 1994. Abundant clusters of tiny, pointed, orange-pink buds open to small, cup-shaped, slightly ruffled single flowers of peachy pink with white centers. Prolific bloom over long season; leaves are small, shiny, and very disease-resistant. Very low maintenance; dense growth to 3 ft. × 5 ft. (0.9 m × 1.5 m). AARS winner 1996.

Rosa gallica 'Versicolor'. Prior to 1310. Technically an old garden rose but often listed as a shrub rose; widely known as Rosa Mundi. Profuse, medium-sized semi-double flowers are striped rose-red and white (may revert to plain rose-red); no repeat bloom. A sport of *R. gallica* var. *officinalis*, the "Apothecary's rose." Small suckering shrub to 4 ft. (1.2 m) high and wide; tough and adaptable; healthy foliage is gray-green. Moderate fragrance.

Rosa glauca. The outstanding feature of this species is its foliage—smoky blue-purple on top, purplish red underneath. Arching purple canes are nearly thornless when young;

dense, upright shrub to 6 ft. × 5 ft. (1.8 m × 1.5 m) is totally impervious to disease. (At least all five of our specimens are.) Small single flowers of bright pink with white eye in spring. No repeat bloom, but flowers are followed by prolific clusters of small attractive hips that go through several color changes (green, brown, light red) before settling on cranberry-red. Light fragrance.

Knock Out. 1999. Small single or semi-double flowers of light red are held in clusters; good repeat bloom. Compact shrub, to 3 ft. (0.9 m) high and wide, is proving to be highly disease-resistant, drought tolerant, and a reliable performer. Light fragrance. AARS winner 2000. Double Knock Out (2004) is a slightly larger plant with smaller but fully double red flowers.

The Fairy. 1932. Small but extremely prolific clusters of light pink flowers begin blooming in July and continue nonstop into November. This adaptable, no-maintenance, easy-to-grow spreading shrub to 3 ft. × 6 ft. (0.9 m × 1.8 m) is often just touched by black spot, but never seriously. Slight fragrance. Always listed under T, for "The."

David Austin (English) roses

Bred in England, these modern shrub roses combine the strong fragrance and full, often "quartered" look of old roses

Evelyn (David Austin)

Golden Celebration (David Austin)

with the greater disease resistance, repeat blooming habit, and more compact size of modern hybrids. These roses are particularly well suited to Pacific Northwest temperatures (protect for winter in Cascade Slopes/Outflow Valleys subregion). However, our stronger rains can spoil the most super-double flowers—some have over 100 petals—and bend the canes of the tallest varieties almost to the ground when in flower. Disease resistance is generally good, but mild black spot can be bothersome. Some good choices for our climate, all wonderfully fragrant, follow.

Belle Story. 1984. Delicate pink, semi-double flowers are freely produced; strong growth to 5 ft. (1.5 m) high and wide; healthy foliage.

Evelyn. 1991. Profuse, saucer-shaped double flowers of a beautiful apricot-pink blend; delicious fragrance is used in perfumes made by the British firm Crabtree and Evelyn. Bushy foliage on small, vigorous shrub to 4 ft. × 3 ft. (1.2 m × 0.9 m).

Fair Bianca. 1982. Profuse, saucer-shaped double flowers of pure white; disease-resistant foliage, 3 ft. × 2 ft. (0.9 m × 0.6 m).

Golden Celebration. 1992. Similar in color and parentage to Graham Thomas, but growth is much more compact at only 4 ft. (1.2 m) in height and width. Good performer in our climate.

Graham Thomas. 1983. Deep golden yellow double flowers bloom well in cooler weather. Tall shrub to 7 ft. × 5 ft. (2.1 m × 1.5 m); best trained as small climber to keep flowers from bending to ground under weight of rain or heavy dew.

Heritage. 1984. Soft blush-pink double flowers with excellent rebloom. Good performance in cooler temperatures; takes part shade. Strong, nearly thornless shrub reaches 5 ft. × 4 ft. (1.5 m × 1.2 m). Old-rose/lemony fragrance.

Rugosa hybrids

Dense, bushy, low-maintenance hybrids of *Rosa rugosa* are one of the best choices for Pacific Northwest gardens, especially near the coast. As well as being highly resistant to disease and insects, these iron-clad shrubs tolerate wind, salt spray, sandy soil, heat, cold, and our normal summer drought. Their leathery, attractively wrinkled (rugose) foliage is very sensitive to chemicals and should never be sprayed—but given their robust constitutions, there's no need to. Some excellent choices follow.

Blanche Double de Coubert. 1892. A true classic. Medium-large, semi-double white blooms are free-flowering, but dead-heading is advised to prolong season. Dense, dark green foliage is highly disease-resistant. Shrub reaches 5 ft. (1.5 m) in height and width; tolerates light shade. Strong rich fragrance.

Fru Dagmar Hastrup. 1914. Large single flowers of light pink are followed by enormous bright red hips; flowers and hips appear together all summer. Suckering, disease-resistant shrub reaches 4 ft. × 5 ft. (1.2 m × 1.5 m); foliage turns rich gold in fall. Moderate spicy fragrance.

Hansa. 1905. Medium-sized, loosely double flowers of reddish purple are followed by large orange-red hips. Nearly indestructible shrub reaches 6 ft. (1.8 m) in both dimensions; tolerates just about everything except alkaline soil. Extremely strong, rich fragrance.

Roseraie de l'Haÿ. 1901. Medium-sized double flowers of deep rose-red bloom over a very long season; sets few hips. Majestic, dense, drought-tolerant growth to 7 ft. (2.1 m) high and wide; foliage turns gold with red highlights in fall. Excellent disease resistance. Very strong, rich fragrance.

Explorer roses

Although most roses specifically bred for cold hardiness do not perform well in the moist atmosphere and mild climate of the Pacific Northwest, those of the Canadian-bred Explorer Series are exceptions due to the strong rugosa strain in the ancestry of most. Three in particular stand out, not the least for their excellent disease resistance.

Henry Hudson. 1976. Medium-sized semi-double white flowers bloom repeatedly and reliably if deadheaded regularly. Low, spreading, suckering shrub to 2 ft. × 4 ft. (0.6 m × 1.2 m). Strong spicy fragrance.

Jens Munk. 1974. Large semi-double flowers of medium pink have good repeat bloom. Extremely tough, vigorous shrub reaching 6 ft. × 4 ft. (1.8 m × 1.2 m) is drought tolerant; said to be more deer-resistant than most roses. Strong spicy fragrance.

John Davis. 1986. Medium-sized semi-double flowers of clear pink are gracefully formed and profuse; very vigorous shrub reaching 8 ft. × 6 ft. (2.4 m × 1.8 m) is often trained as a climber. Strong spicy fragrance.

Miniature roses

Miniature only in the relative size of their beautifully formed, usually double flowers, these floriferous roses can grow knee-high and spread as wide as a floribunda. Although perfectly cold-hardy (more so than most hybrid teas) and surprisingly vigorous, they need close attention for summer watering (their smaller root systems just cannot tolerate drought), and their disease resistance is usually not as good as that of normal-sized roses. However, their size is perfect for containers, small spaces, and balcony gardens, where they can be monitored daily and admired at close range. Most are fully double; some have hybrid-tea form.

A truly amazing range of choices—old moss roses, fragrant roses, even a few climbers and groundcovers—is available, and collecting them can be addictive. A few proven performers in our climate are Gourmet Popcorn (single white with yellow stamens, upright and vigorous; sometimes classed as a shrub rose), Jean Kenneally (pale ivory with apricot centers, beautifully formed), Jeanne Lajoie (pink climber, lightly fragrant), Rainbow's End (showy red-yellow blend), Starina (orange-red and very reliable; a classic), Sun Sprinkles (clear deep yellow, very fragrant; AARS winner 2001), and Sweet Chariot (lavender, very double and very fragrant).

Groundcover roses

Although any low-growing or lax-stemmed rose can theoretically be grown as groundcover, the realities of weeding, deadheading, and pruning severely limited their use as such—until recently. New long-blooming, low-maintenance hybrids are now available in a good assortment of colors and sizes for mass planting on banks, along sidewalks, in parking strips, or as low borders. Far from being novelties, these tough but beautiful newcomers are here to stay.

All are characterized by smaller but continuously blooming flowers that completely cover the plant and need no deadheading. Other attributes are bushy spreading growth that effectively smothers weeds, high disease tolerance, and good tolerance of heat, cold, and neglect. Most importantly, all are grown on their own roots, meaning they'll have long life; all canes being true to type, their growth is dense and naturally spreading.

Flower Carpet Series. Overly aggressive marketing can get nauseating, but plants do have many good points: very long bloom season, an abundance of flowers (2000 to 4000 are claimed for a mature plant), and good—not perfect—disease resistance. Low, compact growth averaging 3 ft. × 4 ft. (0.9 m × 1.2 m). Varieties include Appleblossom, Coral, Pink, Red Velvet, Sunshine, and White. Slight fragrance.

Pavement Series. Developed in Germany specifically for landscape use. Rugosa parentage makes them tolerant of heat, cold, drought, wind, and salt from winter roads as well as highly resistant to disease. Medium-sized semi-double flowers bloom all summer and are followed by attractive hips; low, spreading, suckering shrubs average 3 ft. × 4 ft. (0.9 m × 1.2 m). Excellent for groundcover, massing, or as low hedges along sidewalks (pavements) or paths. Varieties include Dwarf (rosy purple), Foxy (dark pink), Pierette (large, double, deep pink), Pink (salmon-pink), Purple, Scarlet, and Snow. Very strong fragrance.

Sunblaze Series. Derived from miniature roses, these sport small but fully double, brightly colored flowers that cover plants all season. Very low, spreading shrubs averaging 12 in. × 18 in. (30 cm × 45 cm) have good disease resistance but need regular watering. Varieties include Cherry, Golden, Lavender, Mandarin, Orange, Red, and Sweet (clear pink). Slight fragrance.

Pruning roses

Because the canes of all types of roses become exhausted after several years, the production of vigorous new canes needs to be encouraged through regular pruning. How much wood should be removed, how often, and when varies according to the type of rose, but the goal is always the same: to keep the plant vigorous, healthy, and productive. Always wear gloves when pruning or handling roses—thorns that penetrate deeply can cause wicked infections.

The perfect time to prune most roses is in very late winter just as new leaf buds start swelling, but before full leaves actually emerge. In the Pacific Northwest this is usually early to

Blanche Double de Coubert (rugosa)

Roseraie de l'Haÿ (rugosa)

Jens Munk (Explorer)

Fru Dagmar Hastrup (rugosa)

Flower Carpet Pink (groundcover)

mid-March, but timing may vary slightly, depending on location and weather. The exceptions are non-repeat-blooming ramblers, old garden roses, and species roses. Unlike most modern roses, these produce their new wood after flowering, so removal of exhausted wood and any other extensive pruning is best done in summer as soon as flowers fade. Dead, damaged, or diseased wood should of course be removed as soon as noticed.

After basic pruning, you should be left with a well-shaped plant bearing only healthy, vigorous, true-to-type canes; the only thing left to do is prune for height, which varies by type (see sidebars).

Propagating roses

In the Pacific Northwest climate, most roses are easy to propagate from cuttings taken in mid-September. The main advantage of this method, other than its utter simplicity, is that the resulting roses will be on their own roots regardless of whether the parent plant is own-root or grafted.

The disadvantages are that cuttings take two full years to reach the size of plants sold in nurseries, and that some roses are not suitable for this method, either because their propagation is protected by patent (which should be respected), or because their natural root systems are very weak. Hybrid teas—particularly yellow-flowered ones—make doubtful candidates, as do some large-flowered climbers. However, this leaves most floribundas, ramblers, vigorous climbers, groundcover roses, and virtually all shrub and species roses with which to experiment.

1. Fill as many pots as you'll need with coarse, free-draining potting mix or sharp black builders' sand (never beach sand); water well. A pot 6 in. (15 cm) in diameter holds three to five cuttings nicely, but allow some extras; success rate is 75 to 80 percent.

2. Choose healthy, vigorous stems of this year's growth. Test for ripeness by snapping off a thorn—it should break cleanly from the stem. Take 10 in. (25 cm) cuttings from where stems are about as thick as a pencil, not from the thinner growth right at the tips. Make bottom cuts just below a leaf, using a straight cut; use slanting cuts on top ends to make it impossible to mistake which end goes up. If planting will be delayed by more than a few minutes, pop cuttings into a zippered plastic bag to keep from drying out. Keep bag out of direct sunlight.

3. Remove all leaves and large thorns from lower half of each cutting, leaving four leaves on top half (trim if necessary). Insert cuttings into potting medium up to their lowest leaves. Firm in, water well, then firm again to eliminate air pockets.

BASIC PRUNING

Groundcover roses
When growth becomes overly woody and flowering diminishes, simply cut whole planting down to about one-third its normal height in March.

Climbing roses and repeat-blooming ramblers
For first two or three years, limit pruning to removal of dead, damaged, or diseased wood. In subsequent years, cut back lateral branches (the flower-bearing wood arising from the long, horizontally trained canes) to two or three growth buds. Trim back canes as necessary for size or shape. As oldest canes become unproductive, remove them completely by cutting to within 4–6 in. (10–15 cm) of the ground.

All other established roses
Begin by removing all dead, damaged, or diseased wood. Next, remove the most exhausted canes; these are identifiable by their larger diameters, pale/dull color of gray or brown, weaker growth buds, and dead tips. Their bark may also be starting to crack. Then remove any weak, spindly canes—those skinnier than a pencil—since these will never become productive. Finally, cut back to a side branch or remove completely any canes rubbing against each other, crossing over the center of the rose, or growing in an awkward direction. Be sure at least three canes remain on the plant. On grafted roses, remove any suckers (canes arising from below the graft) by pulling sharply downward. This pulling removes suckers completely; cutting them would leave growth points that result in even more suckers.

PRUNING FOR HEIGHT

Shrub roses, rugosas, Explorers, and repeat-blooming old garden roses
No pruning required for first two or three years; after that, start removing exhausted wood. Longer canes may be shortened by up to one-quarter of their height every few years to encourage larger flowers that bloom lower on the canes.

Floribundas and most grandifloras
Cut back annually, shortening by no more than one-quarter of their height. Do not remove any healthy, vigorous, well-placed canes; the goal here is more flowers, not super-large ones.

David Austins and very vigorous grandifloras
Cut back annually, shortening by one-third to one-half their height. Lower pruning results in larger flowers; higher pruning in a greater number of them.

Hybrid teas
Thin canes annually to three to five of the strongest, then reduce their height by one-half. At one time, it was standard practice to prune hybrid teas very hard every year—to as low as 4 in. (10 cm) from the ground—but this is no longer recommended except when planting a new hybrid tea rose in early spring. Prune established hybrid teas no closer than 12 in. (30 cm) from the ground.

Standard or "tree" roses
Prune in March according to their type (floribunda, species, or other). Any especially tall or top-heavy roses, especially if recently planted, can be cut back by about one-third in fall to help prevent wind-rock (loosening of roots in winter by partially blowing over). Normal spring pruning still applies.

4. Set pots in a lightly shaded place and keep well watered through fall. Do not cover, but protect pots from freezing in winter by packing bark mulch or fir boughs around them. Check periodically for dryness, especially in late winter.

5. In March, when tiny new leaves have emerged, gently tip pots on their sides and tease out cuttings with their fragile new roots. Plant in individual pots at least 6 in. (15 cm) in diameter filled with good-quality potting soil. Water well.

6. Place pots in a sunny spot and keep well watered over summer, feeding dilute liquid fish fertilizer every two weeks.

7. Plant out in late September or early October when the weather has cooled but the ground is still warm.

CHAPTER 9

Perennials and Ferns

Perennials in early June, authors' garden. Center: foliage of *Romneya coulteri* 'White Cloud'. Background, left to right: bearded iris, *Asphodeline lutea*, Bowles' Mauve wallflower. Foreground, left to right: lavender, *Thymus serpyllum* 'Pink Chintz', *Hypericum olympicum* f. *uniflorum* (yellow), *Euphorbia polychroma*, daylily.

To paraphrase Abraham Lincoln, you can grow some perennials everywhere in the Pacific Northwest, and you can grow every perennial somewhere in the Pacific Northwest, but you cannot grow every perennial everywhere in the Pacific Northwest. Our subregions are just too different from each other in summer, which is of course when most perennials bloom. (For more information on which do well where, see chapters 2 and 4.)

Popular perennials that grow well throughout our region are astilbes, daylilies, hostas, iris, peonies, rudbeckias, and many others, but since these also grow well just about everywhere, we

have restricted our descriptions to a very few must-haves that are particularly at home in our unique climate. Those that made the list are long-lived, trouble-free, and as maintenance-free as perennials can be. More importantly, since the great majority of these do not need regular lifting or dividing, they can be used as permanent elements of the garden.

Many, many excellent books on perennials thoroughly cover the basics of planting, deadheading, lifting and dividing, watering, and pest control; most also provide extensive lists of best choices for sun, shade, dry sites, moist soil, and so on.

MORE PERENNIALS

For general information on a wide range of perennials, visit the Web site of Heritage Perennials at http://www.perennials.com/. Although not every plant listed is suitable for our climate, the information usually indicates which ones are; Valleybrook Gardens, one of Heritage Perennials' two extensive growing areas, is located in Abbotsford, B.C. The site also contains many useful Pacific Northwest gardening links.

For information on public and private Pacific Northwest perennial gardens, educational organizations, and special-interest plant societies, visit the Web site of the non-profit Northwest Perennial Alliance at http://www.northwestperennialalliance.org/.

Aubrieta 'Red Carpet'

However, the source of the information may make some translation necessary. Perennials rated highly drought tolerant in eastern North America, where it rains in summer, may not be at all drought tolerant here; those that are highly drought tolerant in California may drown in our wet winters. Most perennials needing a warm wall in England are fine in the open here; many of those needing cool shade in the rest of the North America need only light shade or even partial sun in our climate.

In general, good winter drainage is important for all perennials, but especially those with fleshy roots and/or open crowns, such as baby's breath, Oriental poppies, hardy gloxinia (*Incarvillea delavayi*), or red hot poker (*Kniphofia*). Periodic liming is also usually necessary, since most perennials prefer a fairly high pH. But with these two guidelines and the characteristics of your own subregion in mind, the sky's the limit: most perennial species and cultivars grow as fast and as easily as weeds in our climate.

ROCK GARDEN PERENNIALS

Rock garden or alpine perennials are a special case. Neither term is quite accurate; neither rocks nor scree (gritty soil composed of fine bits of rock) are required to grow most "rock garden" species, and not all "alpines" are native to mountaintop habitats. What most people (including ourselves) actually mean by either term is any very low-growing (under 12 in., 30 cm) tufted or spreading perennial that flowers profusely with tiny but colorful flowers, usually in spring or early summer.

True alpines come by their appealing habit honestly, since they're exposed to constant harsh winds that limit their stature. Since they also have a very short growing season to contend with, most do not rely on setting seed to perpetuate themselves, but spread horizontally by rhizomes or rooting stems. Most flower in early to mid-spring, taking advantage of the abundant moisture of snowmelt before summer's drought arrives. (There are no water tables on mountaintops.)

Since most are fully exposed in their native habitats, true alpine plants need full sun—but since they grow at such high

Lithodora diffusa 'Grace Ward'

altitudes, they like cool sun; most need protection from hot sun. In addition, since mountaintops lack a thick buffering layer of soil to hold summer heat in, they need cool summer nights and a cool root run.

If all this sounds familiar, it should: although alpine-growing conditions are hard to replicate in most climates, they're a near-perfect match for the peculiar climate of the Pacific Northwest. The only thing that needs careful watching is drainage: most true alpines need very well-drained soil, especially in winter. Some, but by no means all, prefer alkaline conditions (it depends on which mountains they're from), but lime is easily supplied.

Other so-called rock garden perennials are native to wind-swept seashores or to harsh Arctic conditions that similarly limit their stature; still others are simply low-growing compact plants. But whether true alpines or not, these dainty and very attractive perennials can be as rare and difficult or as easy and commonplace as a gardener chooses. Alpine/rock garden societies are very popular in our region; rock garden plants are available at every nursery.

These are just a few of the easiest and most popular perennials suitable for rock gardens. Unless stated otherwise, all are evergreen, very low-growing, hardy to at least Zone 5, and need cool sun and excellent drainage. Rock walls are a natural for providing cool root runs, but mulch or gravel also work well. For more choices, see the perennials marked (R) in the "In Fresh Bloom" lists for March, April, May, and June in Part 2.

Other compact, low-growing plants such as dwarf conifers, small bulbs, and hebes and other dwarf shrubs also make good rock garden subjects. Slowly creeping groundcovers can also be included, but watch out for beautiful aggressive spreaders—including some "alpines" such as snow-in-summer (*Cerastium tomentosum*)—that can overwhelm slower-growing plants.

Arabis (wall cress). Billowing mounds of small mustard-like flowers of white or lilac-pink bloom from April to June. Prefers a high pH. Clip back hard after flowering to keep plants compact.

Armeria (thrift). Tiny globular flowers of bright pink or white held above grassy tufts of foliage bloom non-stop from April through summer if kept deadheaded. Self-seeds moderately. Drought tolerant when established; excellent seaside and edging plant.

Aubrieta (rock cress). Spreading carpets of tiny deep purple, mauve, violet, or purplish red flowers from late March through June are most spectacular when spilling over a low wall. Very easy in our climate; a must-have. Thrives with or without attention such as a light trim after flowering; survives summer drought by going dormant in hot weather. Seed-grown strains vary in color; for best satisfaction, buy small plants in bloom.

Dianthus (pinks). Many species are suitable for rock gardens; some are true alpines. Main blooming time is May and June; some bloom longer. Pinks are happiest with some lime in the soil but are not fussy.

Gentiana (gentian). Species vary considerably: alkaline to acidic soil; easy to difficult culture; blooming time spring, summer, or fall. All have deep true-blue trumpet flowers; summer-blooming *G. septemfida* (everyman's gentian) is one of the easiest.

Helianthemum (sun rose). Low spreading mounds of small narrow leaves, often grayish green; relatively large potentilla-like

Saxifraga ×arendsii, pink form

flowers in the yellow/pink/orange/red range cover plants from May to September. Drought tolerant when established.

Lithodora diffusa 'Grace Ward'. Small, very bright flowers of rich deep blue cover the prostrate foliage from late April to July. Needs acidic soil and excellent winter drainage; tolerates light shade. Best with some summer water; plants blacken in drought (or with severe cold) but recover quickly. Spreads vigorously enough to be groundcover, but color can be overwhelming on a large scale.

Saxifraga ×arendsii (mossy saxifrage). Small rounded hummocks of bright green foliage are covered by perky cup-shaped flowers of pink, white, or red from late March to June. Needs a cool site in partial shade; not drought tolerant. One of the first perennials to welcome spring every year.

BORDER PERENNIALS

BERGENIA

Origin: Siberia, the Himalaya

Hardiness zones: 3 to 9

Size: Foliage 10–14 in. (25–35 cm), flowers 12–20 in. (30–50 cm)

Blooming season: February to May

Exposure: Any

Soil preference: Any, as long as well drained

Water needs: Drought tolerant when established

Maintenance needs: Low

Subregions best suited: All

Possible problems: None serious

Bergenia cordifolia with *Arabis procurrens* 'Variegata' in March

Evergreen. In our climate, this nearly indestructible Victorian favorite (then called saxifrage) takes heavy or light soil, acidic or alkaline conditions, full sun or full shade, moist or dry atmosphere—anything but wet soil—but is best in partial shade in cool, moisture-retentive soil of reasonable fertility. Perfect for borders, massed in dry shade under deciduous trees, or as a small-scale groundcover. Its large, rounded leaves add structural texture while beautifully complementing all other plant forms; for whatever reason, no weeds grow among them. Root weevils are fond of leaf edges but do no discernible harm other than cosmetic notching.

Attractive green foliage shows some bright red leaves in fall; winter color is deep red to maroon. Long-stalked flower clusters bring welcome brightness in late winter/early spring. Some magenta shades can border on garish for the first few days, but soon mellow; returning hummingbirds love them in any color.

Slowly creeping fleshy rhizomes at soil surface should not be covered with soil or mulch. Seldom if ever needs dividing, but clumps that have outgrown their space can be reduced in girth by pulling up outermost rhizomes in early fall. This maneuver can double as propagation, since rhizomes with shoelace-like black roots reestablish easily.

Bergenia 'Abendglut' (Evening Glow). Reddish purple leaves lie almost flat; flowers and stalks are beet-red. Blooms March and April. Height 10 in. (25 cm).

Bergenia 'Baby Doll'. Compact (not dwarf) foliage; baby-pink flowers bloom freely March to May. Height 10 in. (25 cm).

Bergenia 'Bressingham Ruby'. Leaves turn deep wine-red in winter, almost glowing when backlit by afternoon sun. Flowers dark red, March to May. Height 14 in. (35 cm).

Bergenia cordifolia (heartleaf bergenia). Native to Siberia. Robust, somewhat heart-shaped leaves turn maroon in winter. Flowers and stalks are both deep magenta-pink; blooms from March to May. Very reliable. Height 14 in. (35 cm).

Bergenia crassifolia foliage in September

'Purpurea'. Strong-growing cultivar; flowers are more purple-pink than species.

Bergenia crassifolia (winter-blooming bergenia). Native to eastern Siberia. Despite its name, more refined than *B. cordifolia*. Spoon-shaped leaves lie almost flat and remain mostly green in

Bergenia 'Silberlicht'

winter. Needs a sheltered site; very early-blooming light pink flowers are often caught by late frosts. Blooms February to April. Height 12 in. (30 cm).

Bergenia 'Silberlicht' (Silver Light). White flowers with a hint of pink bloom very freely March to May. Height 14 in. (35 cm).

Bergenia stracheyi. Native to the Himalaya. Smaller and less robust than other species, but parent of many excellent hybrids. Small pink to white flowers bloom March and April. Height 10 in. (25 cm).

CAMPANULA (BELLFLOWER)

Origin: Europe, Balkans, Turkey, Asia, Japan, southeastern Siberia

Hardiness zones: Varies

Size: Varies

Blooming season: June to September

Exposure: Cool sun to partial shade

Soil preference: Well drained, light, moist; slightly acidic to slightly alkaline

Water needs: Moderately drought tolerant when established

Maintenance needs: Low to moderate

Subregions best suited: All

Possible problems: Slugs and snails. Most species have a spreading habit; a few can be invasive

Herbaceous; some species semi-evergreen in mild winters. At first glance, plants that prefer light alkaline soil that's moist in summer may seem a questionable fit for the Pacific Northwest, but campanulas thrive here. It's true that a few obscure species are finicky enough to challenge connoisseurs, but for the most part, these are among the easiest and most dependable perennials of all. Widely tolerant of growing conditions, most of the 300 or so species of *Campanula* accept just about anything except poorly drained or strongly acidic soil, intense sun, or very high heat. (Zones 8 and 9 are included here in the context of the Pacific Northwest only.)

Since many are native to mountainous areas with sunny summers but cool nights, campanulas actually seem to consider the Pacific Northwest a perfect home regardless of our not-so-perfect soil conditions for them. In fact, these shortcomings work in our favor: since many campanulas have a tendency to spread to the point of invasiveness on light, moist, alkaline soils, our heavy, summer-dry, acidic soils constrain them just enough to keep them vigorous without any danger of them running amok.

In the wild, campanulas grow in stiff competition with other plant species, which accounts for their sometimes overenthusiastic vigor, but this also explains their companionability. They seem to prefer the company of other plants and are remarkably easygoing, neither intimidating not being intimidated by their neighbors regardless of species. (All the same, keep very small, delicate plants out of the way of the most vigorous spreaders.)

They're also great mixers in the visual sense, knitting together disparate garden elements with their cool, calming shades of blue that go with everything and are never (well, hardly ever) overwhelming in themselves. Campanulas are also incredibly versatile, ranging from back-of-the-border stalwarts to carefree edging to exquisite cut flowers to go-anywhere clumps of color to groundcover and underplanting for shrubs.

Good drainage is their only absolute requirement. Heavy winter rains are well tolerated as long as water doesn't remain standing on their roots, but they can be quite sensitive to soggy soil when new growth is resuming in spring. Potted plants may have to be moved under an overhang in early spring to keep

Campanula lactiflora

Campanula medium

from drowning. Slugs and snails can also wreak havoc on newly emerging foliage.

Campanulas tolerate our normal summer drought very well indeed, especially in partial shade (recommended in our hottest river valleys), but most look better and bloom longer with a modest amount of summer water. Regular liming is also beneficial, but many species, especially the more vigorous ones, are quite content on all but the most strongly acidic soils.

A few widely recommended species are not well suited to Pacific Northwest conditions. *Campanula punctata* has large, beautiful, rosy pink tubular flowers, but tends to die out on heavy soils; *C. latifolia* (not to be confused with *C. lactiflora*) has an atypically short flowering season and a coarse growth habit. As well, both these border types have definite invasive tendencies, and neither tolerates drought. *Campanula rotundifolia* (bluebells of Scotland), an alpine type, is appealing in the first flush of bloom but tends to get weedy-looking very quickly. This spreading species is best relegated to wild gardens or meadows, where it can be quite charming.

Campanula rapunculoides (rover bellflower) is another story. Although sometimes recommended for wild gardens, this border type is a pernicious, hard-to-eradicate invader that rightfully deserves to be called "the bell from hell." Undeniably attractive and somewhat resembling peach-leaved bellflower with its blue,

slightly drooping bells on tall stems, it self-seeds like crazy while also spreading rapidly by deep underground rhizomes. Unlike other campanulas, this one overwhelms and even kills other plants, including grass. Don't plant it. (And never be tempted to dig up any pretty "wild" campanula.)

Border campanulas
Campanula carpatica (Carpathian bellflower). Native to the Carpathian Mountains. Low-growing, spreading mounds of heart-shaped notched leaves covered with relatively large, cup-shaped blue flowers from June to September. Truly a rock garden plant (it loves growing among rocks), but also suitable for perennial beds, fronts of borders, and as edging. Best known by its cultivars, all of which are lower growing and more compact than the species. All self-seed moderately but not invasively; most come true from seed. Long-lived and very reliable. Zones 3 to 9.

'Blue Clips' (correctly, 'Blaue Clips'). Large flowers of China blue; neat, compact habit to 6 in. × 10 in. (15 cm × 25 cm).

'Blue Moonlight'. Pale sky-blue flowers, very dense foliage. 4 in. × 8 in. (10 cm × 20 cm).

'Chewton Joy'. Dusky blue flowers fading to pale blue centers; later blooming than most. 8 in. × 12 in. (20 cm × 30 cm).

Campanula cochlearifolia

Campanula ×haylodgensis 'Plena'

'White Clips' (correctly, 'Weisse Clips'). Similar to 'Blue Clips' but with taller, looser habit and large white flowers. 10 in. × 12 in. (25 cm × 30 cm).

Campanula lactiflora (milky bellflower). Native to the Caucasus. Very tall, strong stems with large nettle-like notched leaves are topped with starry funnel-shaped flowers of milky blue from June to September. One plant makes a feature. Can self-seed prolifically on bare soil, but seedlings are easy to pull. (Mulch helps.) If cut back in July when first blooms start to fade, plants will rebloom. Cut stems to ground in late fall.

Needs partial shade and cool, moisture-retentive soil; accepts dry shade but performs better with a bit of summer water. Deep roots compete well with tree roots, even cedars, and tall stems don't need staking as long as they're sheltered from strong winds. Even strong-colored cultivars tend to revert back to skimmed-milk blue, very pale pink, or off-white—sometimes on the same plant—but these muted colors are strangely attractive. 5 ft. × 2 ft. (1.5 m × 0.6 m); Zones 4 to 9.

'Loddon Anna'. Flesh-pink flowers; does not self-seed. Good cut flower.

'Pouffe'. Dwarf form to 16 in. × 12 in. (40 cm × 30 cm); lavender-blue flowers.

'Prichard's Variety'. Dark violet-blue bell-shaped flowers on compact plants to 36 in. × 24 in. (90 cm × 60 cm).

'Superba'. Even larger than species, with large, starry flowers of soft lavender-blue.

'White Pouffe'. White-flowered sport of 'Pouffe'.

Campanula medium (Canterbury bells). Native to mountains of southern Europe. Sturdy biennials with very large, rounded bell-shaped flowers. These cottage-garden plants, which have been cultivated throughout Europe since the Middle Ages, are still popular for massing, summer color, and as cut flowers. Many named strains in blue, pink, white, dark rose, deep purple, and lilac; all are free-flowering and bloom for many weeks in June and July if kept deadheaded. Since it does not self-seed reliably, seeds should be sown every spring for bloom the following summer. Best in sun; needs regular watering for good flower production. 24–36 in. × 12 in. (60–90 cm × 30 cm); Zones 2 to 9.

Two double forms are popular, especially with kids. In the hose-in-hose form, the calyx (the protective outer part of a flower bud) becomes a second bell surrounding the bell; in the other, *Campanula medium* var. *calycanthema*, the broad, flattened calyx provides the "saucer" for the old-fashioned favorite known as cup-and-saucer flower.

Campanula persicifolia (peach-leaved bellflower). Native to Europe, northern Africa, across Asia to Siberia. Classy, refined good looks and well-behaved habit make this a garden classic. Slightly nodding, graceful bell-shaped flowers of violet-blue bloom profusely on tall stems in June and July; if cut back, will repeat until September. Long, narrow leaves droop slightly, resembling peach leaves.

Takes poor soil and holds up well to rain and wind, but best with discreet support to keep weight of blooms from bending stems. Good cut flower. Adaptable and easy to grow, but best when divided frequently; place where digging will not be a problem. Self-sows very modestly and is never invasive. 36 in. × 24 in. (90 cm × 60 cm); Zones 3 to 9.

var. *alba*. Large flowers of pure white; scarce seedlings tend to revert to blue.

'Chettle Charm'. White flowers edged in pale blue; outstanding. Propagate by division.

'Telham Beauty'. Flowers larger than species; vigorous clumps to 4 ft. × 2 ft. (1.2 m × 0.6 m).

Campanula takesimana (Korean bellflower). Native to Korea. Quite different from most campanulas; tall stalks covered with large, lush, heart-shaped notched leaves bear large, pale lilac-pink tubular flowers with rosy spots on their insides. Unusual but attractive dangling flowers bloom from June to August.

Best performance in partial shade. Creeping roots eventually make a large patch and can border on invasiveness in moist soil, but are more constrained in dry shade, which they tolerate well. Competes well with tree roots; good woodlander that thrives on slightly acidic soils. 30 in. × 18 in. (75 cm × 45 cm); Zones 5 to 9.

'Alba'. Similar to species but with white flowers spotted maroon on insides.

Campanula poscharskyana

Campanula portenschlagiana

'Elizabeth'. Large flowers of satiny rose-pink with darker spotting; blooms June and July.

Alpine campanulas

Although all low-growing campanulas are genuine alpines, not all are suitable for rock gardens. Some choice, hard-to-find collector's species have to be coaxed into growing, but the most popular and readily available types grow almost too easily. However, none are truly invasive in our climate and soils, and any too-ambitious growth is easily pulled.

These campanulas all have small rounded or heart-shaped leaves with notched edges; all are covered in summer with profuse, usually blue flowers that completely obscure the foliage and never need deadheading. Unlike border types, alpine types rarely set seed, but spread—often vigorously—just beneath the soil surface. Where winters are very mild, many remain almost evergreen.

Although very sun-tolerant, alpine campanulas also tolerate dry shade, making them excellent choices for underplanting shrubs and as small-scale groundcover under deciduous trees. They survive even extended summer drought with no ill effects, but flowering will stop in early August if no water is forthcoming.

Campanula 'Birch Hybrid'. Hybrid names are not supposed to include the word "hybrid," but avoiding the common practice of combining the names of the two parent species is a no-brainer in this case: it's a cross of *C. portenschlagiana* and *C. pos-*

charskyana. This small but vigorous plant, smothered with small bell-shaped flowers of mauve-blue from June to September, is deservedly popular. Compact growth to 6 in. × 12 in. (15 cm × 30 cm); Zones 4 to 9.

Campanula cochlearifolia (syn. *C. pusilla*; fairy thimbles). Also spelled *cochleariifolia*. Native to European Alps. Ground-hugging spreading mats of tufted foliage are covered from June to August with thimble-shaped flowers of bright sky-blue. Each flower is just the right size and shape to barely accommodate one small bee; at any given time in early summer, dozens of flowers are so occupied.

This species runs everywhere, poking into every available nook and cranny like an inquisitive puppy, but it's impossible not to like it. The bright color can be a bit much in large patches (which it's perfectly capable of covering), but it's a real plus when scrambling around the edges of staid conifers, silver-foliaged plants, or among plants with white or yellow flowers. Shallow-rooted, it dislikes long dry spells and high temperatures but will take full sun in cool-summer subregions. Height 4 in. (10 cm), spread indefinite. Zones 2 to 9.

'Alba'. Dainty, pure white flowers would be welcome even in large patches, but plants are not very vigorous and tend to revert to blue.

'Elizabeth Oliver'. Double flowers; spreads less aggressively than species.

Campanula garganica (Adriatic bellflower). Native to Greece, Italy, and the former Yugoslavia. Compact mounds of nearly evergreen foliage; long, lax stems bear profuse star-shaped mauve flowers, rather like a smaller version of Serbian bellflower. Good in rock gardens; tolerates poor soil and considerable drought even in full sun. 6 in. × 16 in. (15 cm × 40 cm); Zones 4 to 9.

'Dickson's Gold'. Sport with greenish golden foliage. Fewer flowers than species, but they contrast beautifully with foliage. Compact habit; excellent in rock gardens. Protect from intense sun. 6 in. × 12 in. (15 cm × 30 cm); Zones 5 to 9.

Campanula ×*haylodgensis* 'Plena'. Selection of a cross of *C. carpatica* and *C. cochlearifolia* made at Hay Lodge, Scotland, in 1885. Small ruffled flowers of powder blue are exquisite. Spreads extremely slowly; choice rock garden plant. Needs excellent drainage. 4 in. × 8 in. (10 cm × 20 cm); Zones 4 to 9.

Campanula portenschlagiana (syn. *C. muralis*; Dalmatian bell-flower). Native to the former Yugoslavia. Low-growing rosettes of rounded, heart-shaped notched leaves; flowers are small, funnel-shaped bells of satiny violet-purple that bloom prolifically in June and July, more sporadically until late September or even later. Although it has a reputation as a rampant spreader, it is well-behaved on heavier soils, creeping slowly but not invasively. (Keep it out of the rock garden, though.) Long-lived and reliable. Great for underplanting shrubs, mixing with other vigorous perennials, and as cover for snowdrops and other very early bulbs. 6 in. × 16 in. (15 cm × 40 cm); Zones 4 to 9.

Campanula poscharskyana (Serbian bellflower, trailing bell-flower). Native to the former Yugoslavia. Rampant, spreading growth can be invasive on lighter soils, but makes excellent filler/mixer/groundcover in dry shade on heavier soils. Dense mounds of heart-shaped notched leaves, larger than most alpine types, bear long, lax stems that clamber over everything in their path but do not take root (it spreads underground). Each stem is covered from June through August by small, profuse star-shaped flowers of a beautiful shade of mauve-blue.

Keep it away from weak or delicate plants, but let it run wherever it wants among vigorous perennials, shrubs, and grasses. It looks terrific scrambling through the large, dark green leaves of hellebores or reclining against the sides of *Spiraea japonica* var. *albiflora*, whose pink and white flowers bloom at the same time. Very drought tolerant, but blooms longer with a couple of good soakings in summer. 10 in. × 36 in. (15 cm × 90 cm); Zones 3 to 9.

'Blue Waterfall'. Outstanding newer selection with sturdy stems and long blooming period.

'E. H. Frost'. Large milky-white flowers with pale mauve centers; larger leaves than species. Not quite as rampant.

GERANIUM (CRANESBILL, HARDY GERANIUM)

Origin: Europe, western Asia, the Himalaya

Hardiness zones: Most 4 to 9

Size: Varies

Blooming season: May to frost

Exposure: Cool sun to woodland shade; light shade usually ideal

Soil preference: Well drained, especially in winter; fertile, moisture-retentive

Water needs: Low to moderate; some species drought tolerant when established

Maintenance needs: Low

Subregions best suited: All

Possible problems: None serious

Mainly herbaceous; some semi-evergreen. Every Pacific Northwest garden needs at least a few hardy geraniums. (The name cranesbill, describing the odd shape of their seedpods, has never quite stuck in the Pacific Northwest.) Not to be confused with the tender bedding plants called geraniums, which belong to the genus *Pelargonium*, these true hardy perennials are not only versatile and trouble-free, but thrive best in temperate climates with cool summers and, especially, cool summer nights.

Their flowers, while not spectacular individually, are produced so prolifically and over such a long season that their use in general landscaping (as opposed to being strictly relegated to flower beds) is almost unlimited. Although large clumps may eventually need their girth reduced, hardy geraniums never actually require lifting or dividing, so can become—and should become—permanent elements of ornamental gardens.

Like campanulas, geraniums excel at knitting together disparate parts of the garden; somehow, even though many have very bright flowers, they're never in-your-face obtrusive. Depending on habit, they may be used for borders, edging, underplanting shrubs, in rock gardens, or simply scrambling under, on, or through other perennials and shrubs. *Geranium macrorrhizum* (bigroot geranium), a valuable groundcover, is described in Chapter 11.

With very few exceptions (such as the gorgeous but finicky purple-foliaged *Geranium pratense* Midnight Reiter strain and the barely less finicky *G. p.* Victor Reiter Junior strain), all are ridiculously easy to grow. All they need is reasonably fertile soil, an appropriate site, and a modest amount of summer watering. A few species are reliably drought tolerant in our normal summer conditions, but most look best and bloom longest in soil that is not too dry. Root weevils may nibble on the roots or leaves, but are rarely a serious problem; diseases are virtually unknown.

In most cases, flowering can be extended well into fall by cutting back hard after the first flush of blooms starts to fade in early summer. There's no need to be delicate here; hardy geraniums are tough plants and will bounce back almost immediately with fresh foliage and blooms after the most severe haircut. (Some gardeners have been known to use a lawn mower on more vigorous species such as *Geranium ×oxonianum*.) Following the second flush of bloom, many have attractive red fall foliage that further extends their seasonal display. The spent stems and leaves of herbaceous types can be tidied up by cutting back in late fall or early spring, but no great harm is done if they're not.

The over 1000 hardy geranium cultivars known to horticulture can be divided (as they are here) into categories based on their best use, but these are by no means rigid. As long as its cultural needs are met, any cultivar can be used wherever it seems most fitting. These are only a few of the best.

Border geraniums

Geranium 'Ann Folkard'. Large flowers of bright magenta-pink with striking black centers bloom June to September; new foliage is bright chartreuse in spring, darkening slightly in summer. Flowers resemble those of Armenian cranesbill (*G. psilostemon*),

Geranium 'Johnson's Blue'

Geranium ×*oxonianum* 'Wargrave Pink'

Geranium ×*magnificum*

Geranium ×*cantabrigiense* 'Cambridge'

which is one of its parents, but habit and vigor are better. Not for the faint of heart, this plant has a magnificently bold visual presence and an equally bold habit of spreading and scrambling over other plants. Surprisingly, its colors combine beautifully with many different hues. Best in a cool site in moist, fertile soil—in large gardens. 2 ft. × 6 ft. (0.6 m × 1.8 m).

Geranium 'Gerwat' (Rozanne). Very large, bright purple-violet flowers on compact mounds of foliage bloom June to October; being sterile, there is no risk of self-sown seedlings running amok. An outstanding newer cultivar. Best in cool sun; light shade in hot-summer valleys. 15 in. × 18 in. (38 cm × 45 cm).

Geranium himalayense (syn. *G. grandiflorum*). Native to the Himalaya. Very large, deep violet-blue flowers with red veining bloom in June and July on vigorous mounding clumps; deeply cut leaves turn red in fall. Spreads slowly but not invasively by creeping rhizomes. Quite drought tolerant, especially in light shade. 18 in. × 24 in. (45 cm × 60 cm).

  'Plenum' (syn. 'Birch Double'). Fully double purple-blue flowers are sterile and bloom longer than species, but are not as large or effective.

Geranium 'Johnson's Blue'. Hybrid of *G. himalayense* and *G. pratense*, a European species. Very popular classic; large, saucer-shaped lavender-blue flowers appear true blue in evening

light. Blooms June to October if cut back after first flush. Deeply cut mounding leaves turn red and gold in fall. Although its flowers are unbeatable, 'Johnson's Blue' foliage does tend to flop open by midsummer; the newer cultivar 'Brookside', which has somewhat similar lavender-blue flowers with white eyes, has a sturdier, more upright habit.

Geranium ×*magnificum*. Hybrid of two species native to Asia Minor. Large flowers of rich violet-blue bloom all too briefly, but are truly a magnificent sight when they completely cover the vigorous mounds in June and early July. Deeply cut foliage with velvety texture turns red in fall. Best in cool sun; light shade in hot-summer valleys. 24 in. × 30 in. (60 cm × 75 cm).

Geranium ×*oxonianum*. Hybrid of *G. endressii* and *G. versicolor*, both native to the Mediterranean; hybrids often listed under *G. endressii*. Tough, vigorous, drought-tolerant spreading plant makes an excellent medium-scale groundcover in cool sun or light shade. Small but prolific pink flowers bloom profusely June and July; if cut back hard and watered well, plants quickly regrow and rebloom until October. Good weed suppressor except for vetch, which disguises itself as geranium stems. Evergreen in mild-winter subregions. Self-seeds moderately; not for small spaces. 24 in. × 36 in. (60 cm × 90 cm).

  'A. T. Johnson'. Silvery pink flowers, lower growing than species.

'Claridge Druce'. Clear rose-pink flowers with darker veining; foliage is slightly glaucous. Very vigorous; give it lots of room.

'Phoebe Noble'. Prolific hot pink flowers; slightly shorter and more wide-spreading than species. Named for a retired professor of mathematics at the University of Victoria who made hardy geraniums a consuming hobby.

'Wargrave Pink'. Open-faced small flowers are often described as salmon pink, but color is closer to clear silvery pink with only a faint peach undertone. Vigorous.

Geranium 'Patricia'. Clear magenta-pink flowers with black centers similar to those of 'Ann Folkard' but considerably more subdued in tone; blooms May to August. Habit is also more subdued, although it will scramble; foliage has nice fall color. Best in moist soil in cool sun. 18 in. × 30 in. (45 cm × 75 cm).

Creeping/groundcover geraniums

Geranium ×*cantabrigiense*. Hybrid of *G. dalmaticum* and *G. macrorrhizum*. Ground-hugging, spreading plants quickly knit together to make a semi-evergreen groundcover. Best in light shade; dislikes heat and intense sun, but needs good light to flower well. Excellent for underplanting shrub roses. Fragrant foliage takes on red tints in fall and remains attractive all winter.

'Biokovo'. Relatively large flowers of very pale pink with deeper pink centers bloom in May and June; best in cool light shade. Takes occasional foot traffic when not in flower. Height 8 in. (20 cm).

'Cambridge'. Magenta-pink flowers bloom May to August; more vigorous and sun-tolerant than 'Biokovo', but doesn't take foot traffic. Height 10 in. (25 cm).

Geranium 'Mavis Simpson' (syn. *G.* ×*riversleaianum* 'Mavis Simpson'). Hybrid of *G. endressii* and a New Zealand species. Silvery pink flowers that bloom May to September resemble those of *G. endressii* but are larger and more rounded; slightly glaucous foliage has a velvety texture. Habit is low, spreading, and vigorous. 16 in. × 48 in. (40 cm × 120 cm).

Geranium sanguineum (bloody cranesbill). Native to Europe and Asia Minor; common name comes from dark red sap seen when roots are cut. This vigorous, self-reliant, adaptable spreading plant is reliably drought tolerant in our normal summers and thrives in any non-extreme garden situation. Small but bright magenta flowers bloom June to August on lax stems that make low mounds or scramble through nearby shrubs; excellent companion for golden or chartreuse foliage. Small, deeply lobed dark green leaves have good fall color. 12 in. × 36 in. (30 cm × 90 cm).

'Album'. Milk-white flowers on tall stems. Best combined with other plants it can lean on or scramble through; isolated upright stems look a bit odd but strangely appealing by themselves. 24 in. × 30 in. (60 cm × 75 cm).

'Max Frei'. Abundant flowers of deep magenta; compact habit. Good small-scale groundcover. 8 in. × 24 in. (20 cm × 60 cm).

Geranium sanguineum var. *striatum*

var. *striatum* (syn. var. *lancastriense* 'Splendens'). Abundant flowers of beautiful soft pink with darker pink veining; low spreading mounds of finely cut dark green foliage. Best in partial shade; excellent for underplanting shrubs. 12 in. × 30 in. (30 cm × 75 cm).

Woodland geraniums

Geranium clarkei. Native to Kashmir. Low mounds of deeply cut foliage topped with large cup-shaped purplish pink flowers with prominent veining. Blooms June to August; best in a moist, cool site in partial shade. 12 in. × 24 in. (30 cm × 60 cm).

'Kashmir White'. A classic; pure white flowers with lilac veining are almost luminescent in shade.

Geranium phaeum (mourning widow). Native to Europe and the Balkans. Odd but curiously attractive small nodding flowers of dark maroon held on tall upright stems; each large green leaf is marked with a small black blotch. Blooms May to August if cut back after first flush. Tolerates deep shade well, but best in moist shade; although it will live in dry shade, powdery mildew can be a problem. Self-seeds prolifically; best in woodland gardens where it can spread to its heart's content. 36 in. × 24 in. (90 cm × 60 cm).

'Lily Lovell'. Large deep purple flowers with white eyes; showy.

'Samobor'. Deep maroon flowers with small white eyes; foliage is very boldly marked black.

Geranium sylvaticum. Native to Europe. Violet-pink flowers bloom in May and June on long stems held high above bold, handsome leaves. Best in moist soil in woodland shade. 36 in. × 24 in. (90 cm × 60 cm).

'Album'. More compact than species with large, pure white flowers and attractive light green leaves. Many gardeners consider it the best white-flowered geranium.

Alpine geraniums

Geranium Cinereum Group (syn. *G. cinereum*). Native to the Pyrenees. Beautiful and choice alpine with gray-green velvety foliage; pink or purplish flowers with prominent dark veining bloom in June and July. Likes cool sun and is quite drought tolerant, but needs near-perfect drainage in winter; best planted on a slope or in very light-textured soil. 6 in. × 12 in. (15 cm × 30 cm).

'Ballerina'. Relatively large flowers of lilac-pink with deep red veining; silvery green foliage.

'Laurence Flatman'. Deep pink flowers with dark red veining on longer stems; foliage is green.

Geranium dalmaticum. Native to the former Yugoslavia. Shell-pink flowers bloom May to July on compact mounds of glossy green foliage. Best in cool sun. Needs good winter drainage, but is more adaptable and reliable in our wet winters than most alpine geraniums. 6 in. × 18 in. (15 cm × 45 cm).

HELLEBORUS × HYBRIDUS (LENTEN ROSE)

Origin: Hybrid of species from Europe and Asia Minor

Hardiness zones: 4 to 9

Size: 16–24 in. × 24–36 in. (40–60 cm × 60–90 cm)

Blooming season: February to April

Exposure: Partial shade

Soil preference: Rich, heavy, well drained; neutral to slightly acidic

Water needs: Drought tolerant when established

Maintenance needs: Low

Subregions best suited: All

Possible problems: None serious

Evergreen. More permanent than stinking hellebore (*Helleborus foetidus*), more versatile than Corsican hellebore (*H. argutifolius*), more reliable and much better suited to our wet winters than Christmas rose (*H. niger*), hybrid hellebores (formerly classed as hybrids of Lenten rose, *H. orientalis*) are absolutely essential in Pacific Northwest gardens. Subtle color blends, exotic speckling, and intricate veining make the long-lasting nodding flowers mesmerizing in themselves, but other assets include late winter bloom time, dark green leathery foliage, and the ability to thrive in dry shade. Selected as Perennial Plant of the Year for 2005 by the Perennial Plant Association.

Needs ample water in winter and spring (provided gratis), but easily tolerates our summer drought, especially under deciduous trees where their early-blooming flowers also receive the light they need. With dolomite lime added every few years to neutralize acidity, hellebores thrive in our heavy soils. Handsome clumps are long-lived, free of insects and diseases (root weevils may sample leaf edges), and practically indestructible in our climate.

Flowers of original Lenten rose, *Helleborus orientalis*, are often somber-hued, but hybridization now gives the choice of pink, plum-purple, dark red, slate-blue, creamy white, yellow, green, near black, pure white, and picoteed forms (petals edged in a different color), all with or without spotting. Double-flowered forms are also available but are usually not as effective as singles. Propagation by division is very slow, so most plants are

Helleborus ×hybridus

Helleborus ×hybridus 'White Lady'

sold as seedling strains of a particular color or pattern, such as the Lady Series (available in blue, pink, red, white, and yellow). For top satisfaction, buy in bloom—but don't neglect unnamed seedlings. This is one plant that could be improved to death by breeding out the very somberness and mystery that made it so fascinating in the first place.

New plants take a year or so to settle in and resent being moved, so choose planting site carefully. Hybrid hellebores seldom if ever require division; some of our own clumps are 4 ft.

Helleborus ×*hybridus* seedlings

(1.2 m) across and bear over 350 flowers (we stopped counting) with no indication of slowing down after 15 years. However, young clumps can be lifted and divided right after flowering if the exact clone is wanted elsewhere.

Handsome, lustrous, deeply divided foliage can look ratty by winter's end; old leaves can be removed as soon as flowers start to open. Flowers are attractive even when faded but are best removed before the four swollen seedpods burst open; self-sown seedlings can be prolific. Seedlings take a year to germinate and three years or more to flower, but "potluck" colors can be very rewarding. If they're wanted, seedlings can be left in place, transplanted immediately to better sites, or potted up until they reach flowering size before planting out.

HEUCHERA AND ×HEUCHERELLA

Origin: Eastern North America; mountains of western North America

Hardiness zones: Most 4 to 9

Size: Varies

Blooming season: April to September

Exposure: Partial shade to cool sun; protection from hot or intense sun

Soil preference: Moisture-retentive but well drained, moderately fertile, slightly acidic

Water needs: Drought tolerant when established

Maintenance needs: Low

Subregions best suited: All

Possible problems: Root weevils, sunburn

Evergreen. Heucheras and the closely related heucherellas (an intergeneric cross between *Heuchera* and *Tiarella* or foam-flower) are extremely well suited to Pacific Northwest conditions. These versatile, low-maintenance plants, which cannot abide the combination of high temperatures and high humidity, are sometimes considered rather difficult in other climates, but our dry, relatively cool summers and especially our cool summer nights are made to order for them. In fact, *H. glabra* and *H. micrantha* (an important parent of many garden hybrids) are native to the Pacific Northwest.

Our mild winters aren't strictly necessary, since most are quite cold-hardy, but they do give us ample opportunity to enjoy beautiful evergreen foliage of unmatched color range. The tiny flowers that bloom on tall, delicate stalks in late spring and summer are by no means insignificant, especially with *Heuchera sanguinea* cultivars and most heucherellas, but with most heuchera cultivars, foliage is the outstanding feature. Ruffled varieties are especially beautiful in winter when frost outlines their edges. Smaller-growing cultivars are suitable for rock gardens in cool sun.

Being either crevice dwellers on steep cliffs or woodland plants preferring dry shade, all heucheras are naturally very drought tolerant; in our climate, heucherellas are only slightly less drought tolerant. As long as the soil is well drained, neither objects to our wet winters. Both dislike hot or intense sun; morning sun/afternoon shade is a good formula for most and is the best preventative for sunburn. Plants should not be overwatered, but leaves may show edge burning if soil is allowed to become bone dry. A slightly acidic soil suits them best.

Heuchera

Until the 1980s, *Heuchera sanguinea* (coral bells) and its cultivars were the only heucheras familiar to most gardeners, and these were known for their small but bright coral-red flowers. Then came *H. micrantha* var. *diversifolia* 'Palace Purple' (syn. *H. villosa* 'Palace Purple'), an unusual foliage plant with new leaves of deep purple, fading in summer to bronze-brown with burgundy undersides. As worthy as this cultivar is, and despite being named Perennial Plant of the Year for 1991, newer cultivars with even more spectacular foliage have pretty well left 'Palace Purple' in their dust.

Heuchera micrantha 'Ruffles', a chance seedling, offered beautifully ruffled leaves. Then came 'Eco-magnififolia', a selection of *H. americana* (a species found in the southern Appalachian Mountains), which introduced foliage marked with metallic silver and dark veining. More recently, genetic mutations have yielded foliage colors of chartreuse, peach/orange, and rose-red.

Not surprisingly, possible combinations among these features have generated an explosion of new hybrids. Terra Nova Nurseries of Canby, Oregon, has alone introduced more than 80 heuchera and heucherella cultivars since 1992. Some of these will undoubtedly fall by the wayside, but others are already clas-

Heuchera Crème Brûlée

Heuchera 'Pewter Veil'

Heuchera 'Plum Pudding'

sics. (A word of caution in an otherwise rosy picture: some gardeners may notice a lack of vigor in the newest cultivars; this is not necessarily inherent in the cultivar but is more likely due to its being propagated by tissue culture.)

Heucheras make wonderful subjects for general landscaping, mixed perennial beds, and edging for paths, and are invaluable in the dry shade of trees and shrubs, especially on their eastern edges. They also make excellent container subjects; the smaller cultivars can even be used in hanging baskets.

Plants spread slowly, soon becoming wider than tall, but seldom if ever need dividing. Clumps do have a tendency to push themselves out of the soil, so should be lifted and resettled every few years. Alternatively, more mulch can be added, but eventually resettling will be needed. Make sure the crown is not buried; it should be just flush with the soil surface.

Unless noted otherwise, the following selections bloom in June and July. Heights given are for foliage only; flower stalks are generally twice the height of the foliage.

Heuchera 'Chocolate Ruffles'. Huge, very ruffled leaves, chocolate brown on top and burgundy on reverse, can reach 8 in. (20 cm) in diameter. Plentiful flowers of burgundy/purple bloom from June to September. Robust grower; best in good light but surprisingly shade tolerant. Height 14 in. (35 cm).

Heuchera Crème Brûlée. Registered as 'Tnheu041' (Dolce Series), but don't ask for it by this name at your local nursery. Large leaves are a warm blend of copper, orange, amber, and bronze, fading lighter by summer; flowers are not showy. Height 12 in. (30 cm).

Heuchera 'Green Spice' (syn. 'Eco-Improved'). Improved version of *H. americana* 'Eco-magnififolia' with brighter green and silver markings that hold up longer in summer. Excellent fall color with reddish tints and red veining; good in shade. Height 16 in. (40 cm).

Heuchera 'Lime Rickey' (Rainbow Series). Ruffled foliage is bright chartreuse in spring, darkening to lime green in summer; pure white flowers are a bonus. Needs good light for best color, but protect from hot sun. Slow growing. Height 8 in. (20 cm).

Heuchera 'Marmalade'. Large leaves with slightly wavy edges range from orange to butterscotch-yellow to copper with rosy overtones. All colors become paler by summer; although very scorch-resistant, best in light shade in hot-summer valleys. Abundant yellow-green flowers; vigorous wide-spreading habit. Height 10 in. (25 cm).

Heuchera 'Obsidian'. Shiny, smooth leaves of darkest burgundy appear near black when new; pale greenish white flowers are a nice contrast. Height 10 in. (25 cm).

Heuchera 'Pewter Veil'. One of the first "veiled" or silver-overlaid hybrids and still one of the best. Large metallic silver leaves with dark veining and edges are tinged pink in spring; numerous flowers on tall stalks are green and purple. Good in shade, where it is striking. Vigorous. Height 14 in. (35 cm).

Heuchera 'Plum Pudding'. Beautifully textured, lustrous foliage is a pleasing blend of burgundy, purple, and chocolate brown; flowers are white. Robust grower that maintains its good looks year-round; one of the best dark-foliaged hybrids. Height 12 in. (30 cm).

Heuchera sanguinea (coral bells). Native to high mountains of the southwestern United States and Mexico. Nearly indestructible cottage perennial with dense, rounded green foliage and small, coral-red flowers shaped like tiny bells on tall, graceful stalks. Extremely drought tolerant once established; in the Pacific Northwest, adaptable to any well-drained soil in sun or part shade. Excellent for attracting hummingbirds. Blooms May to August if deadheaded; benefits from division every two to three years. Long-lasting cut flower. Height 10 in. (25 cm); flower stalks to 24 in. (60 cm).

'Alba'. Smaller and daintier than the species, these white coral bells bloom just as the old campfire song says, upon slender stalks. Height 8 in. (20 cm).

Firefly. Registered as 'Leuchtkäfer'. Seed-grown hybrid strain with fragrant dark red flowers on sturdy stalks. Height 12 in. (30 cm).

'Snow Storm'. Small white leaves edged and spattered with dark green; flowers and stalks are bright cherry red. Give it good drainage and good light, but protect from hot or intense sun. Slower growing than most heucheras. Height 8 in. (20 cm).

'Splendens'. One-hundred-year-old seed strain still performing beautifully. Tight clumps of green foliage; clear red flowers bloom over a long season. Height 10 in. (25 cm).

'Splish Splash'. Foliage is irregularly splashed green and white, tinged pink with prominent red veining in colder weather. Flowers are pink. Needs good drainage. Height 10 in. (25 cm).

Heuchera 'Stormy Seas'. Showy leaves with ruffled edges are a blend of purple, silver, and charcoal gray; flowers are creamy white. Vigorous and reliable. Height 16 in. (40 cm).

×*Heucherella*

Heucherellas are the result of an intergeneric cross of *Heuchera* and *Tiarella* (foamflower), a woodland groundcover native to eastern North America. Generally smaller than heucheras, they have taller and more numerous flower stalks with slightly larger, showier flowers. Foliage is more deeply divided—in some cases almost like oak leaves or needlepoint ivy—and may have darker markings in centers; flowers bloom earlier than heucheras, starting in April and continuing through early summer. Unlike their

×*Heucherella alba* 'Bridget Bloom'

tiarella parent, heucherellas are clump-forming, not stoloniferous, but do spread slowly to make a small patch.

With a few exceptions (×*Heucherella alba* 'Bridget Bloom' is one), heucherellas need slightly more shade and moisture than heucheras (although they should not be overwatered) and are happiest in woodland settings with good drainage. They appreciate our dry, moderately cool summers and cool summer nights even more than heucheras do; as with heucheras, recent breeding programs have resulted in many new cultivars of this once-obscure species.

×*Heucherella alba* 'Bridget Bloom'. One of the first crosses, developed by Alan Bloom in 1955 and named for his daughter. Vigorous and long-lived, with a constitution of cast iron; takes sun, shade, and any soil (as long as well drained) and requires no regular maintenance, although plants do look better when deadheaded. Unbelievably drought tolerant when established. Compact green foliage with rounded lobes spreads slowly; profuse tall stalks to 18 in. (45 cm) bear numerous small, round, pinkish white flowers from April to June. Nearly sterile, as are all heucherellas, but seedlings are not unknown—we have found several. Height 8 in. (20 cm).

×*Heucherella* 'Chocolate Lace'. Reddish brown leaves are deeply divided, with scalloped edges; flowers are pale pink. Needs good light. Height 10 in. (25 cm).

×*Heucherella* 'Kimono'. Narrow, deeply divided leaves with notched edges are a brocade-like blend of green and metallic silver with purple markings and dark purple veining. Summer foliage is larger and more rounded; leaves take on rose-red tints in winter. Yellow-brown flowers are not showy. Height 8 in. (20 cm).

×*Heucherella* 'Quicksilver'. Compact bronze foliage with silver overlay and dark veining; contrasting pink-tinged white flowers on dark stems bloom May to July. Height 8 in. (20 cm).

Romneya coulteri 'White Cloud'

ROMNEYA COULTERI (MATILIJA POPPY, CALIFORNIA TREE POPPY)

Origin: Southern coastal California, Baja California

Hardiness zones: 7 to 9; established clumps probably hardier

Size: 7 ft. × 6 ft. (2.1 m × 1.8 m), spreading habit

Blooming season: Late June to October

Exposure: Full sun

Soil preference: Lean to average fertility; excellent drainage

Water needs: Very drought tolerant when established

Maintenance needs: Low

Subregions best suited: Rogue, Willamette, Olympic Rain Shadow

Subregions not suited: None

Possible problems: Spreads by underground runners; very difficult to propagate

Herbaceous. This spectacular shrub-like perennial blooms all summer with huge but fragile-appearing poppy-like flowers measuring 8 in. (20 cm) or more across. The wide, pure white petals surrounding large central domes of yellow stamens are so wonderfully crinkled and airy they seem to be made of delicate crepe paper, yet they hold up to the strongest, hottest sun. Flowers have a subtle but pleasant fragrance. Deeply divided gray-green foliage on strong, sturdy stalks is a perfect foil.

Coming from a Mediterranean climate (albeit one much warmer than ours), romneyas are right at home with our wet winters and dry summers. Because their rhizomes grow at a very deep level, established clumps are reliably hardy everywhere in the Pacific Northwest. They don't seem to mind our heavier, colder, more prolonged winter rains at all as long as drainage is somewhere between excellent and perfect. (Planting on a slope is recommended.)

Spring rains while they're growing are beneficial, but once they start blooming, established clumps are die-hard drought tolerant even in our extended summer droughts. They don't object to a few summer showers, but should be planted where they will not be watered regularly. Heat is not a requirement—they're perfectly happy in cool-summer conditions—but full sun is a must. No pests or diseases seem to bother them.

In spite of growing like weeds once they're established, romneyas are devilishly hard to propagate by any method, making potted plants extremely scarce (most nurseries that do carry them have waiting lists) and outlandishly expensive when they are available. Even then, success is not guaranteed.

Because their propagation is so iffy, potted plants tend to be weakly rooted. Best chance for survival is to plant in September, using generous amounts of bone meal, and mulch for winter. (Mulch only in this first year; do not cover crown.) Monitor carefully over the growing season; water at first signs of stress but do not overwater. Be prepared to shelter new plants from intense sun and/or drying winds if necessary. Once plants make it through their first year, they're on their own.

Ironically, these hard-to-propagate plants soon develop vigorous, deep-growing rhizomes and increase with abandon, quickly making large clumps and sending up errant shoots as far as 20 ft. (6 m) away. This habit, plus their size and dislike of regular summer watering, makes romneyas unsuitable for mixed perennial beds, but nobody who has one seems to mind. Let it dominate a bed of its own, keeping it company with other drought-tolerant Mediterranean plants such as lavenders, creeping thymes, alliums, and Bowles' Mauve wallflower, perhaps with a backdrop of ceanothus or columnar yews. Unwanted shoots are easily pulled, but wear gloves—stems have small but prickly spines. Cut old stalks to the ground in late fall or very early spring.

Best chance for small-scale propagation is to dig up a shoot and section of rhizome in September (hopefully with some feeder roots attached) and replant immediately. Rhizomes may be as deep as 18 in. (45 cm) underground, so dig deeply—and cross your fingers.

'White Cloud' (syn. *Romneya* ×*hybrida*). Floriferous cultivar, possibly a subspecies or a natural hybrid with the very similar *R. trichocalyx*. More multi-branched than species; best choice for garden settings.

FERNS

Ferns are a must-have in all Pacific Northwest gardens. Living as we do in one of the world's best fern-growing climates, we're sometimes inclined to take these remarkable plants for granted, but they have many more horticultural possibilities than they're given credit for.

Far from being the plant of last resort for a what-else-can-you-do-with-it damp, shady corner, ferns—both native and introduced—also excel in lightly shaded perennial beds, as foundation plantings for eastern and northern exposures, as groundcover under deciduous trees, as companions for shade-tolerant shrubs and grasses, and in containers. Ferns are also excellent for controlling erosion on shady slopes; native ferns in particular make an ideal bridge between cultivated gardens and nature's own landscaping.

Contrary to popular belief, ferns do best in light to medium shade, not dense shade; in our climate, many types are sun-tolerant. They don't necessarily need constantly moist soil, but do need cool roots, protection from wind and hot sun, and an open-textured, usually acidic soil. Damp woodland is ideal, but shelter from wind is as important as shade; coolness as important as light level; air spaces in the soil as important as water. Very few ferns actually like boggy conditions; most will not survive poorly drained soil.

Leaf litter (not to mention old decomposed fronds) makes ideal loose, cool mulch, but bark mulch is also good. Even stone mulch works surprisingly well, since many ferns grow naturally among root-sheltering rocks. Light, sandy soils should be heavily amended with bulk organic materials before planting ferns, but heavier, well-drained soils need only a loose-textured mulch. Shelter from wind is crucial: wind lowers humidity, desiccates fronds and soil, and can break stems of some species.

Beyond appropriate choice of species and careful siting, no plants are easier to grow. Ferns pre-date humans by a good 350 million years, give or take a few hundred thousand, and can get along quite nicely with no help from us at all. (Most cultivars are not deliberate crosses, but natural mutations.) Established ferns prefer to be left alone and are best not disturbed except for minor tidying up of old fronds in early spring.

However, not all fern species—including many recommended as "easy to grow" or "widely adaptable" in British or North American gardening books—are well suited to Pacific Northwest growing conditions. Spleenworts (*Asplenium*) need well-drained neutral to alkaline soil; ostrich fern (*Matteuccia struthiopteris*) and most soft shield ferns (*Polystichum setiferum*) need constant moisture and prefer neutral to alkaline soil. Christmas fern (*P. acrostichoides*) sounds well suited to our conditions but is one of those plants native to eastern North America that for whatever reason just does not translate well into our corner of the continent. Royal fern (*Osmunda regalis*) is best in

Native western sword ferns as informal groundcover

Western maidenhair fern (*Adiantum aleuticum*)

swampy conditions but also prefers hot summers—conditions often hard to combine in the Pacific Northwest.

This still leaves hundreds of beautiful ferns with which to indulge ourselves. The ones included here are among the easiest to grow and most widely available; many more can be found through specialty nurseries.

ADIANTUM ALEUTICUM (SYN. *A. PEDATUM*; WESTERN MAIDENHAIR FERN)

Origin: Western North America

Hardiness zones: 2 to 9

Size: 12–24 in. (30–60 cm) in height, spreading wider

Exposure: Medium to light shade in cool conditions

Soil preference: Average to rich heavy loam, moist; acidic

Water needs: High

Maintenance needs: Low

Subregions best suited: All

Possible problems: None serious

Herbaceous. Formerly thought to be a western variation of *Adiantum pedatum* (northern maidenhair fern), found throughout eastern and northern North America; now considered a separate species but often still sold as *A. pedatum*. Dainty and delicate in appearance, with airy leaflets arranged in unmistakable finger-like pattern on wiry black stems, but tough as nails in the right conditions. Needs summer water. Easily naturalized on stream banks or other moisture-retentive soils, forming dense colonies.

'Imbricatum'. Smaller than species, with overlapping leaflets.

'Subpumilum' (dwarf maidenhair fern). Miniature version only 3–4 in. (7.5–10 cm) tall. Occurs naturally but rarely in Washington and on Vancouver Island; nursery-raised specimens are popular.

Japanese painted fern (*Athyrium niponicum* var. *pictum*)

ATHYRIUM

Origin: Europe, northern Africa, North America, South America, Asia

Hardiness zones: Most 4 to 9

Size: Most 12–24 in. (30–60 cm) in height, spreading wider

Exposure: Partial shade

Soil preference: Humus-rich, moderately acidic

Water needs: Moderate

Maintenance needs: None

Subregions best suited: All

Possible problems: None serious

Herbaceous. Adaptable, dependable growers; genus includes over 180 species and hundreds of cultivars. Most have very finely divided fronds, giving a graceful, lacy look. Best in moist, humus-rich soil in partial shade, but most adapt well to ordinary garden conditions. Stems are brittle and easily broken; provide shelter from wind, pets, and boisterous children.

Athyrium filix-femina (lady fern). Native to Europe and Asia. Natural tendency to mutate has given hundred of lacy, frilled, or filigreed forms. Horticultural divisions include Cristatum Group (crested or forked at frond tips); Cruciatum Group (leaflets arranged in crossed pattern); Plumosum Group (feathery, much-divided fronds); and many dwarf, congested forms so finely divided that some resemble parsley. Despite their fragility of appearance, all are surprisingly reliable when given adequate shelter.

Athyrium 'Ghost'. Hybrid of *A. filix-femina* and *A. niponicum* var. *pictum*. New growth of upright, arching fronds is silvery white, turning pale greenish white with maroon midribs. Needs bright light (will go mint-green in shade), but will burn in hot sun; an eastern or northern exposure is best. Best in moist soil, but quite drought tolerant in cool conditions. Height 24–36 in. (60–90 cm).

Athyrium niponicum var. *pictum* (Japanese painted fern). Native to Japan. Metallic silver fronds with green, red, and blue shadings and dark red to burgundy stems. Sends up new fronds all summer. Several cultivars are available; all are easy to grow in a cool, lightly shaded site in moist but well-drained acidic soil. Selected as Perennial Plant of the Year for 2004 by the Perennial Plant Association. Height 10–18 in. (25–45 cm).

Athyrium otophorum. Native to Japan. Related to *A. niponicum* var. *pictum* and needing similar growing conditions; several hybrids exist. Similar in size and looks except fronds are light silvery green, stems and fiddleheads (unfurled fronds) dark maroon.

Deer fern (*Blechnum spicant*)

Fragile fern (*Cystopteris fragilis*)

BLECHNUM SPICANT (DEER FERN)

Origin: Pacific Northwest, northeastern Asia, Europe

Hardiness zones: 5 to 9

Size: To 36 in. × 16 in. (90 cm × 40 cm)

Exposure: Medium shade to cool sun

Soil preference: Average to rich, acidic; moisture-retentive but well drained

Water needs: Moderate

Maintenance needs: None

Subregions best suited: All

Possible problems: None serious

Evergreen. This elegant, graceful fern retains a flattened cluster of short, leathery, sterile fronds all year round. In spring and summer, tall, upright, very slender fertile fronds appear in the center; these turn black when the spores mature. A natural for Pacific Northwest gardens. Several fancy forms exist, but none can top the species itself for informal yet elegant looks.

CYSTOPTERIS FRAGILIS (FRAGILE FERN)

Origin: Temperate regions of northern hemisphere, including the Pacific Northwest

Hardiness zones: 6 to 9

Size: 12–18 in. × 10–15 in. (30–45 cm × 25–38 cm)

Exposure: Cool sun to partial shade, sheltered from wind

Soil preference: Loose, moisture-retentive but well drained; moderately to slightly acidic

Water needs: Drought tolerant when established

Maintenance needs: None

Subregions best suited: All

Possible problems: None serious

Herbaceous; semi-evergreen in mild winters. The only thing fragile about this native fern is its stems, which are easily broken by rough handling. Everything else about it, despite its lacy, delicate looks, is indestructible. It may have to be sought in specialty or native plant nurseries, but is well worth the hunt.

We first noticed it growing on the side of a rocky, west-facing beachside bluff, bearing the full brunt of afternoon sun. When the bluff was partially cleared, we rescued half a dozen small plants and transplanted them in our garden.

Since then, they have multiplied steadily, and 15 large clumps now thrive in three different difficult but well-drained sites, including one in afternoon sun. Beyond watering them for the first summer, they have lived—and lived well—on natural rainfall only, even through the unnaturally dry summers of recent years. They've also grown half again as tall as they do in the wild.

Some greenery remains in mild winters, darkening to a very deep olive-green that is especially attractive when the lacy fronds are outlined with frost. Small clumps sometimes disappear over winter, seemingly for good, but most reappear from the underground rhizomes after an absence of one or even two years.

DRYOPTERIS (WOOD FERN)

Origin: Temperate regions worldwide

Hardiness zones: Most 4 to 9

Size: Varies

Exposure: Partial shade to cool sun

Soil preference: Humus-rich, moderately acidic; cool, well drained

Water needs: Low to moderate

Maintenance needs: None

Subregions best suited: All

Possible problems: None serious

Herbaceous, semi-evergreen, or evergreen, depending on species. Although native to moist woodlands and even swamps, the "dry" in *Dryopteris* is quite accurate in regard to some of the most garden-worthy species of this huge genus. In our climate, some species are thoroughly drought tolerant in shade on heavier soils, even in our rainless summers. Among the sturdiest of ferns, *Dryopteris* species are robust, adaptable to most ordinary garden conditions, and very reliable.

Dryopteris affinis (golden-scaled male fern). Semi-evergreen. Erect fronds; many crested forms with frond tips displaying multiple little finger-like growths. Height 24–48 in. (60–120 cm).

Polydactyla Group (many-fingered male fern). One of the best forms; takes drought in part shade, tolerates sun if soil is moist.

Dryopteris dilatata (broad wood fern, broad buckler fern). Deciduous. Broadly triangular bluish green fronds with divided leaflets give richly textured look. Best in humus-rich woodland soil, but very adaptable. Several fancy forms are available. Height 24–36 in. (60–90 cm).

Dryopteris erythrosora (autumn fern). Evergreen. New spring growth (but not fall color) is rich autumnal coppery orange; clumps become full and lush in time. Needs good drainage.

Many-fingered male fern (*Dryopteris affinis* Polydactyla Group)

Autumn fern (*Dryopteris erythrosora*) in spring

Tolerates drought in partial shade; we have some thriving autumn ferns in the shade of a large witch hazel that have not been watered in 20 years—and that includes several extended-drought summers. Height 18–24 in. (45–60 cm).

Dryopteris filix-mas (male fern). Very similar to *D. affinis*, with tall, erect fronds. Good-looking but tough, tolerating sun (in moist soil), rocks, and considerable drought. Likes cool conditions. Many crested and linear-leaved forms are available. Height 24–48 in. (60–120 cm).

    'Barnesii'. Attractive, upright form with very narrow fronds.

    'Undulata Robusta'. Vigorous form with broad, wavy fronds.

POLYSTICHUM (SHIELD FERN)

Origin: North America, Europe, eastern Asia

Hardiness zones: Most 5 to 9

Size: Varies

Exposure: Partial shade to cool sun

Soil preference: Cool, moderately acidic; moisture-retentive but well drained

Water needs: Low to moderate

Maintenance needs: None

Subregions best suited: All

Possible problems: None serious

Evergreen or semi-evergreen, depending on species. Dense, handsome clumps of arching, leathery, lustrous fronds. Robust, reliable growers; excellent garden subjects. Need rich soil with good drainage, especially around crowns in winter; perform well in everything from moist shade to open, rocky sites in cool sun.

Polystichum braunii (Braun's holly fern). Evergreen. Native but uncommon in the Pacific Northwest. Thick, shiny fronds in dense clumps; stems and fiddleheads are covered with attractive silvery scales that turn golden brown. Very hardy, but new growth may need protection from late spring frosts. Height 12–24 in. (30–60 cm).

Polystichum munitum (western sword fern). Evergreen. Pacific Northwest native; deserves a place of honor in all gardens. Perfectly suited to our soils, climate, rainfall, and light levels; performs beautifully in medium shade to cool sun. Excellent on shady slopes. Survives almost anywhere, but most outstanding in good, well-drained garden soil with shelter from wind and strong sun. Tidy up as needed in early spring. Can reach 5 ft. (1.5 m) in shade; more compact in sun.

    var. *imbricans*. Dwarf form sometimes available in nurseries.

Western sword fern (*Polystichum munitum*) unfurling

Polystichum polyblepharum (Japanese tassel fern). Evergreen. Very handsome, oval-shaped dark green fronds with shiny surfaces. Stems and leaflets heavily scaled; name means "many eyelashes." Needs moist site in partial shade. Height 12–24 in. (30–60 cm).

Polystichum tsussimense (Korean rock fern). Semi-evergreen. Glossy, pointed fronds have showy black veins. Needs good drainage; good in lightly shaded rock gardens. Drought tolerant on heavier soils when established. Height 8–12 in. (20–30 cm).

CHAPTER 10

Bulbs and Bulb-like Plants

Bulbs and mixed perennials in late May, authors' garden. Background, center right: *Iris* 'Pink Horizon'. Center, left to right: *Erysimum* 'Bowles' Mauve' (with faded foliage of *Narcissus* 'Actaea' below), *I.* 'Gold Galore', *Allium hollandicum* 'Purple Sensation', *I.* 'Caliente', *Asphodeline lutea* (yellow). Foreground, left to right: *Allium karataviense*, *I.* 'Dusky Challenger' (in bud), *A. cristophii* (just opening), foliage of *Salvia ×superba*, foliage of *Romneya coulteri* 'White Cloud'.

Many climates around the world have at least one harsh element—severe winter cold, searing summer heat, prolonged drought—that limits the growth of indigenous plants. But nature abhors a vacuum, and these very climates are the ones richest in bulbs and bulb-like plants (those growing from corms, tubers, tuberous roots, or rhizomes).

In an ingenious solution to dealing with conditions that would kill them if they grew above ground all year, these unique plants grow, bloom, and set seed when conditions are optimal—often only a very short period in spring—then literally go underground to wait out the siege of unfavorable conditions, with up to ten months of life-sustaining food stored in their fleshy tissues.

Climatic conditions in the mild Pacific Northwest may appear to differ drastically from the harsh native habitats of most bulbs, and in fact they do. But it is the combined climatic quirks of our imperfect Eden that allow us to grow bulbs from virtually every other part of the world.

235

Our winters are cold enough for long enough to give hardy spring bulbs such as crocuses and tulips the required winter chill they need to keep them going perennially—yet they're mild enough and short enough to grow not-so-hardy bulbs from the southern hemisphere, such as alstroemerias and calla lilies.

Our summers are dry enough to keep Mediterranean bulbs such as *Narcissus bulbocodium* from rotting, and just hot enough to give Middle Eastern bulbs such as hyacinths the summer-dormant baking they need, yet we can easily supply summer water and/or cool conditions to keep bulbs such as crocosmias and Oriental lilies happy. Our soils are moist enough and cool enough in early spring to grow erythroniums, trilliums, and English bluebells, but warm enough and dry enough in late summer to grow colchicums, saffron crocus, and belladonna lilies (*Amaryllis belladonna*).

Our bulb blooming season begins in January with snowdrops, spring snowflakes, winter aconite, and *Cyclamen coum*; it continues uninterrupted through November with ivy-leaved cyclamen. In between come an incredible assortment of hardy bulbs (for blooming times, see Part 2, the gardening calendar), along with summer-blooming tender bulbs that can be lifted and stored for winter.

The only hardy bulbs likely to disappoint in our climate are foxtail lilies (*Eremurus*) and crown imperials (*Fritillaria imperialis*), both of which are prone to rotting in winter. For the most part, we also have a less-than-perfect climate for tulips, which object to our prolonged moist springs by developing fungal leaf spots that weaken the bulbs. Nonetheless, tulips are planted by the millions every year and are among our most popular bulbs. Although fancy types such as parrot and fringed tulips are unlikely to give a good show beyond the first year, others have remarkable staying power. Best bets in most areas are the botanical species, Darwins, and single late tulips.

With the exception of meadow-dwellers such as camas (*Camassia*) and snake's head fritillary (*Fritillaria meleagris*), all hardy bulbs need good drainage. They also need abundant moisture from the time their roots start into regrowth—usually with the first fall rains—until their blooms fade, followed by drier conditions as they go dormant.

Most importantly, bulbs need to keep their foliage until it withers away naturally. The leaves are needed to convert sunlight into stored food that keeps bulbs alive while dormant; pulling, cutting, or tying up bulb foliage for the sake of neatness deprives them of stored energy and seriously affects their vigor. Withering bulb foliage is definitely unsightly, but it can be conveniently camouflaged with perennials that leaf out just as bulb leaves start to yellow. Which ones work best depends on the blooming time of the bulbs as well as on personal preference; a little experimenting is usually necessary. Just don't use water-dependent summer perennials to cover bulbs that require summer dryness.

With the exception of crocosmias and calla lilies, which should be planted in spring, hardy bulbs should be planted in fall. As a rule of thumb, the depth to the bottom of the hole should be two to three times the length of the bulb from tip to base (the lighter the soil, the deeper the planting). However,

Dahlia hybrids in July

even small bulbs should be covered with a good 2 in. (5 cm) of soil. A generous pinch of bone meal beneath each bulb helps roots get off to a good start; all should be watered in well to settle the soil around them.

A layer of organic mulch or leaf litter helps provide ideal conditions for most bulbs by keeping their roots cool and evenly moist. Alternatively, hardy bulbs can be planted in non-mowed grassy areas that imitate the natural habitat of many species. The earliest-blooming spring bulbs are very short, with later spring bulbs somewhat taller and summer-blooming bulbs tallest of all, so flowers will peek over the top of the grass at all stages of its growth. One mowing in August (if the grass has not yet died down naturally) then gives short fall-blooming bulbs such as colchicums their place in the sun.

Another whole world of bulbs exists in the semi-hardy and tender species, most of which are native to the southern hemisphere. Bulbs that keep our summer gardens and containers ablaze with color include agapanthus (lily of the Nile), caladiums, canna lilies, dahlias, freesias, gladioli—including the tall, fragrant, fall-blooming *Gladiolus murielae* (syns. *G. callianthus*, *Acidanthera bicolor*)—ixias, pineapple lily, sparaxis, tuberous begonias, zephyr lilies (*Zephyranthes*), and many others, including a host of lesser-known species from South Africa. It is beyond the scope of this book to describe any of these in detail,

Tuberous begonias in hanging basket

but two deserve special note for their prominence in the Pacific Northwest.

Dahlias as we know them are all hybrids, but are derived from species native to mountainous areas of Mexico and Guatemala, where summer days are sunny but only moderately warm, while nights are noticeably cool. Since our own unique summer conditions closely echo this combination, dahlias thrive here better than anywhere else outside their native habitats. Dahlias are found in almost every summer garden in the Pacific Northwest; dahlia societies abound throughout our region.

No other flower is so varied in height—from ground-hugging dwarfs to monsters reaching 6 ft. (1.8 m) or more—or in flower size, color, or shape. Sizes range from golfball-sized miniature ball form to so-called dinner-plate dahlias (decorative forms). Colors include every shade of red and yellow, white, cream, orange, pink, purple, maroon, and an astounding range of bicolors. Standard forms include anemone-flowered, ball, cactus (straight and incurved), collarette, formal decorative, informal decorative, laciniated, miniature ball, mignon single, orchid-flowering, pompon, peony-flowering, single, semi-cactus, stellar, and water lily, as well as several novelty classes. All make wonderful cut flowers.

The tuberous roots can be planted outside as soon as danger of hard frost is past (they can take a light frost) and the soil no longer feels cold. Dig a hole 12 in. (30 cm) deep and drive a sturdy stake for varieties that will grow taller than about 3 ft. (0.9 m). Place the tuber close to the stake with the eye facing it, since this is where the stem will grow, and cover with about 3 in. (7.5 cm) of soil. As the shoots grow, gradually fill in the hole and tie up the stems as necessary. Regular watering is needed all summer, but if planted in reasonably rich soil, no extra fertilizer is necessary; nitrogen in particular will make stems floppy. Watch for earwigs, especially when plants are young.

Dahlias are hardy enough to overwinter in Zones 8 and 9, but since they come from a dry-winter climate, the tubers are inclined to rot. Even in light, well-drained soils the clumps will likely have to be divided before next summer, so in the long run the best strategy is to lift them in fall and store them over winter (see sidebar).

Tuberous begonias are truly tender, being hybrids of species native to the shady understories of tropical jungles in South America and southern Africa. However, their bright jewel-like colors of pink, red, yellow, white, orange, salmon, or picoteed color combinations never seem gaudy or out of place in our more subdued light and cooler temperatures; the pendulous types in particular are indispensable for our legendary hanging baskets. Connoisseur choices include saucer-sized flowers on upright plants, ruffled petals, unusual colors or forms, and even scented flowers.

All forms of *Begonia* ×*tuberhybrida* excel in the Pacific Northwest, but here they need treatment that is slightly different from what is generally recommended. Although considered shade plants, the shade in their close-to-the-equator native habitats is warm and quite bright. Full shade anywhere in the Pacific Northwest is simply too dark and too cool to keep these tropical beauties happy; in our more sun-challenged subregions, even all-day light shade can be too much. In general, tuberous begonias are at their best here with four hours of morning sun. In the Pacific Coast and Puget Sound subregions, this can be increased to six hours or even full sun as long as the site is protected from intense sun, high heat, and wind.

The relatively high humidity needed by these jungle-shade dwellers can usually be taken for granted here, but protection from drying winds (which can also snap the thick but brittle flowering stems) is important in all subregions. However, the common recommendation to spray or mist the foliage frequently is an open invitation to powdery mildew and/or botrytis blight in our climate. Just give tuberous begonias a warm but not hot site, good air circulation, bright but cool light, and keep the soil (but not the leaves) evenly moist but not wet, and they'll grow to perfection.

Shop for fancy begonias starting in early February, choosing large, plump tubers with small pink eyes (growing points). If none are visible, place tubers in a warm, dark place until they appear. Then fill a shallow tray or a few pots with loose-textured potting soil and plant the tubers, concave side up, so their tops are barely covered. Thoroughly moisten the soil, taking care not to create puddles in the concave tops, and place the trays or pots in a cool area (60–70°F, 15–20°C) with good light. Unless soil shrinks from the sides of the containers, do not water again until green shoots appear; then water just enough to keep the soil barely but evenly moist.

When the sprouts have two leaves, transplant the tubers into individual pots, covering them with 1–2 in. (2.5–5 cm) of potting soil. For large upright varieties, one tuber per 6–8 in. (15–20 cm) container is sufficient; for pendulous types, use three large or four to five smaller tubers per large basket. Plant with leaf tips pointing outward, since the flowers always face the leaf tips.

Move the containers into a bright, well-ventilated area where the temperature will not fall below 60°F (15°C) and water them only when the soil surface feels dry. When shoots reach

LIFTING AND STORING TENDER BULBS

Cut all stems to within 2–4 in. (5–10 cm) of the soil in mid-October or right after the first frost has blackened the leaves, whichever comes first. Lift clumps and carefully shake excess dirt from bulbs, but do not wash. Let dry in a covered, well-ventilated area until the remaining stems detach naturally; any excess dirt should then be dry enough to brush off with your fingers.

With corms, separate new corms and tiny cormels and discard the old shriveled corm; sort by size, dust with sulfur, and store by hanging in mesh bags or old nylons. True bulbs, tubers, tuberous roots, and rhizomes can be divided now, although spring division is preferable; undivided bulbs are less prone to shriveling over winter. In either case, sort by size, dust with sulfur, and insert, not touching, in well-labeled shallow trays or open boxes filled with dry peat moss, vermiculite, sawdust, or shavings.

Store all bulbs in a dry, well-ventilated area that remains very cool (45–50°F, 7–10°C) but does not freeze. If mice can possibly enter the storage area, cover boxes or trays with wire mesh before storing. Check periodically over winter, and discard any bulbs that have started to rot. If bulbs start to shrivel, sprinkle with a few drops of water and move to a cooler area.

In spring, divide bulbs, tuberous roots, and rhizomes as necessary, making sure each section contains at least one eye or new growing point. True tubers such as tuberous begonias are best left whole; they can be propagated by stem cuttings of the new shoots. Let cuts heal over by drying in an open area for several days before planting.

the length of a finger, start feeding every two weeks with half-strength liquid fish fertilizer. When flowers appear, switch to a balanced organic liquid fertilizer.

Plants can be set out (after hardening off) as soon as nighttime temperatures are consistently above 15°F (60°C), but be prepared to cover them or move them back in if the weather suddenly reverts to March-like conditions.

As flowers appear, watch for and pinch off the smaller, single female flowers. Their removal not only prevents seed set that could slow or stop flower production, but ensures that all blooms will be the larger, fully double, much showier male flowers. (This said, there are a few very showy varieties with all-single flowers.) With a bit of practice, female flowers can be spotted even before they open by looking for the tiny but distinctive three-winged seedpods visible just behind the buds.

Since some fancy begonia tubers can cost an arm and a leg, be sure to lift them in fall for winter storage. Withholding water for a week or so before lifting helps nudge the tubers into dormancy.

ALLIUM (FLOWERING ONION, FLOWERING GARLIC)

Origin: Europe to Asia; North America

Hardiness zones: Most 4 to 9

Size: Varies

Blooming season: May to July

Exposure: Full sun

Soil preference: Average to rich, well drained; slightly acidic to slightly alkaline

Water needs: Moist in spring, dry in summer

Maintenance needs: Low

Subregions best suited: All

Possible problems: None serious

True bulb; dormant late summer through winter. Close relatives of culinary onions, garlic, chives, and leeks, these eye-catching flowering bulbs grow on light, gravelly soils in their native habitats, but adapt well to our heavier soils as long as winter drainage is good. Our ample spring rains provide the moisture they need while growing; our late spring/early summer weather prolongs their blooms; our dry summers are ideal as they enter their long period of dormancy. Most are lime-tolerant but do not object to moderately acidic soils. Strongly acidic soils, though, need periodic liming.

Alliums are free of pests and diseases and are not eaten by deer, mice, rabbits, moles, or birds. It's true their leaves and stems give off an onion-y odor, but only when crushed; the flowers of several species actually have a very agreeable sweet fragrance. All attract bees and butterflies.

Alliums do have one major drawback: their foliage. Although the narrow strap-shaped leaves are actually very handsome in themselves, they start fading at the tips just as the flowers open. At peak bloom, the foliage looks the pits, being partially or fully withered. This is not attributable to late frosts, untimely drought, lack of micronutrients, or any other adverse growing condition: it's simply how alliums grow. The very few species that do retain their foliage are exceptions.

The solution is simple: plant alliums among leafy summer perennials whose emerging foliage will deftly hide the withering allium leaves. This happy association works both ways; alliums provide a much-appreciated bridge between spring bloomers, most of which have finished flowering, and summer bloomers, most of which have not yet started. Alliums also happen to look great with bearded iris, whose blooming season and cultural needs are very similar.

For gardening purposes, alliums can be divided into two overlapping groups roughly corresponding to their height. Because their habits and needs differ, we are listing the few examples of each group separately.

Lower-growing alliums

These look and behave more like herbaceous perennials, spreading slowly by underground stolons. (Some also spread quickly by seed.) Because of their creeping habit, they never need lifting or dividing and can be left indefinitely where they look best:

wandering among, around, and through herbaceous perennials. Very adaptable, these creepers grow happily in damp or dry soils; many tolerate light shade. Flowers are smaller and more relaxed in form than taller types, but bloom longer. Most make good cut flowers; all are long-lived and very easy to grow.

Allium cernuum (nodding onion). Native to North America, including the Pacific Northwest. Small bell-shaped flowers of pink, purple, or white in nodding clusters bloom July and August; good for naturalizing among grasses and wildflowers. Needs excellent drainage. Height 12–18 in. (30–45 cm).

Allium flavum. Native to the Mediterranean region. Dozens of tiny yellow florets held in loose globes look like holiday sparklers; bloom July and August. Easy and reliable; retains its foliage all summer, making it suitable for front-of-border use. Height 12–18 in. (30–45 cm).

Allium moly (golden garlic). Native to the western Mediterranean. Small, shiny, star-shaped flowers of bright yellow held in loose umbels bloom June and July; thrives in warm shade as well as in sun. Height 10–16 in. (25–40 cm).

Allium neapolitanum (Naples garlic). Native to the Mediterranean region. Small, glistening white cup-shaped flowers in loose umbels bloom in May with a sweet freesia-like scent. Excellent cut flower (grown commercially) and container plant. Height 12–18 in. (30–45 cm); Zones 6 to 9.

Cowanni Group. Superior selection with slightly larger flowers.

Allium oreophilum (syn. *A. ostrowskianum*; pink lily leek). Native to the Caucasus and Central Asia. Bright rose-pink flowers in large, loose clusters bloom in July; narrow gray-green leaves remain attractive all summer. Good cut flower and excellent rock garden subject; very long-lived. Height 6–10 in. (15–25 cm).

'Zwanenburg'. Selection with deeper rose-red flowers.

Allium schoenoprasum (chives). Native to Europe. Familiar culinary plant; grass-like, nearly perennial leaves have a mild onion flavor. Small, rosy purple flower globes are pretty but can self-

seed like crazy. To prolong fresh foliage for culinary use, cut clumps to ground when flowers appear; new leaves will soon grow. Height 12–18 in. (30–45 cm).

'Forescate' (giant chives). Free-flowering ornamental form is sterile (no self-seeding); large reddish purple flowers bloom May to July. Foliage can be used like chives.

Allium tuberosum (garlic chives, Chinese chives). Native to eastern Asia. Small, pretty, violet-scented globes of white flowers bloom in June and July. Narrow, flattened gray-green leaves with very mild garlic flavor can be eaten like chives. Likes moist soil. Self-seeds as enthusiastically as regular chives. Height 12–18 in. (30–45 cm).

Allium unifolium. Native to coastal mountains of Oregon and California. Beautiful lavender-pink flowers with satiny sheen bloom in large, loose globes in May and June. Sun or part shade; needs excellent drainage. Height 18–24 in. (45–60 cm).

Taller-growing alliums

Flowerheads of these spectacular alliums resemble fireworks in arrested motion, with star-shaped florets on radiating stems forming perfect spheres. In the wild, these function like tumbleweeds after seeds ripen, breaking from the stems and rolling over stony landscapes to spread seed far and wide. In garden settings, seedheads are more likely to be picked for dried arrangements or left to add interest to summer gardens. No garden species are truly invasive, but those that self-seed freely are best deadheaded after flowering.

All need full sun and very good drainage, especially in winter. Best in warm sites (all are very heat-tolerant); they prefer soil on the dry side but do not object to occasional summer watering even when dormant. Plant among vigorous, leafy summer perennials that will hide their withering foliage and fill the gaps left when the alliums go dormant in mid- to late summer.

Lift and divide clumps in fall when they become crowded and flowering diminishes, usually after five or six years. Since the bulbs will be completely dormant then, be sure to mark the site before the clumps disappear from view.

Allium caeruleum (syn. *A. azureum*; blue globe onion). Native to Central Asia. Densely packed globes the size of golfballs are deep cornflower-blue; bloom June and July. Self-seeds, but seedlings are attractive scattered throughout perennial beds. Good cut flower. Height 12–18 in. (30–45 cm).

Allium cristophii (star of Persia). Native to northern Iran and Central Asia. Enormous, rather sparse starry globes of metallic lavender flowers can reach the size of soccer balls; bloom June and July. Long-lasting dried seedheads are if anything even more striking as conversation pieces. Height 18 in. (45 cm).

Allium 'Gladiator'. Large, dense, grapefruit-sized globes of rosy lilac bloom in June and July on very tall stems. Effect is something like chive flowers on an enormous, Alice-in-Wonderland scale. Similar to but larger and more vigorous than the older

Allium moly

A. 'Lucy Ball' (often sold as *A. giganteum* 'Lucy Ball'). Height 48 in. (120 cm).

Allium 'Globemaster'. Huge melon-sized balls of violet-purple bloom from late May to August, longer than any other globe allium. Attractive dried seedheads stay attached to strong, robust stems until September, prolonging summer interest. Height 42–48 in. (105–120 cm).

Allium hollandicum 'Purple Sensation'. Species (syn. *A. aflatunense*) native to Central Asia. Slightly dome-shaped flowerheads of deep reddish purple bloom in May and June. Sweetly scented flowers attract butterflies like a magnet, especially elegant swallowtails. Height 24–36 in. (60–90 cm).

Allium karataviense (Turkestan allium). Native to Central Asia. Pale silvery mauve flowerheads the size of tennis balls appear to sit on a nest of broad, showy blue-green leaves with thin red edges. Leaf tips may fade early, but foliage remains attractive until flowers start to fade. Can self-seed prolifically; deadheading is advisable. Height 12 in. (30 cm).

'Ivory Queen'. Ivory-white flowers and green foliage; nice in combination with species.

Allium schubertii. Native to Asia Minor and Israel. Stems of individual violet-purple florets vary in length, making a large (10 in., 25 cm in diameter), bizarre flowerhead that looks like something from outer space. Needs excellent drainage. Height 18 in. (45 cm).

Allium sphaerocephalon (drumstick allium). Native from Europe to the Caucasus; northern Africa to Israel. Egg-sized, pointed flowerheads of bright, deep rosy purple resemble giant clover flowers. Good cut flower; excellent for dried arrangements since it keeps its attractive color when dried. Self-seeds with abandon; plant with caution in perennial bed or confine it to a cut-flower bed. Height 24–36 in. (60–75 cm).

ANEMONE (WINDFLOWER)

Origin: Europe to Central Asia

Hardiness zones: Varies

Size: Varies

Blooming season: February to May

Exposure: Partial shade; some species take sun

Soil preference: Humus-rich; well drained, slightly acidic

Water needs: Moist in winter and spring, dry in summer

Maintenance needs: None

Subregions best suited: All

Possible problems: None serious

Tubers or rhizomes; dormant summer through winter. Since *Anemone* comes from the Greek *anemos*, meaning "wind," the term "windflower" applies to all members of this genus,

including the magnificent fall-blooming, moisture-loving Japanese anemones, *A.* ×*hybrida*. But it's the spring-blooming species—tuberous or rhizomatous, low-growing, large-flowered, fine-foliaged, and inclined to wander—that truly deserve the name.

Springing up suddenly in late winter to early spring, almost as if the passing wind drew life from the bare ground, these bloom with abandon for several weeks. Then, just as suddenly, they're gone. Some disappear completely; others leave behind (for a while) attractive fern-like foliage or fluffy seedheads resembling those of clematis, which belong to the same buttercup family (Ranunculaceae).

Being related to buttercups, it's not surprising that all windflowers are spreaders, whether by seed, underground rhizomes, or both. But none are invasive and none are remotely weedy; in fact, most gardeners can't get enough of them.

The Pacific Northwest is a natural home for these early-blooming beauties, which prefer their springs cool and moist and their summers relatively dry. Most prefer heavy soils, although good drainage is a must. A site under deciduous trees, where they just happen to look most perfect, also gives these plants made-to-order growing conditions of cool sun in late winter, followed by increasing shade as temperatures rise in spring. Annual leaf litter also provides the loose mulch and humusy conditions needed to grow them to natural perfection; no maintenance is needed.

Anemone blanda (Grecian windflower). Native to Greece and Asia Minor. Relatively large daisy-like flowers of blue, pink, or white with white eyes and yellow centers appear on very short stems as early as February. Blooms may last until early May, closing at night and on cloudy days; finely dissected foliage remains an attractive groundcover right up until dying down in June. Best in large drifts, which expand naturally through self-seeding. A few bird-sown seedlings may pop up far afield, but most remain close to the main patch. (Just the same, keep it away from rock gardens.)

Plant the small, lumpy, very hard black tubers in fall; in our sodden climate, pre-soaking is not necessary. If the tiny growing tips indicating tops of the tubers are hard to discern, plant them on their sides; flowers will find their way to the surface. Several cultivars are available, but the majority of seedlings will be the beautiful soft mauve-blue of the species. Some seedlings have unique and unexpected colors, but all blend together beautifully. Height 4–6 in. (10–15 cm); Zones 6 to 9.

'Blue Star'. Large flowers of mauve-blue with white eye; late February through early April. Vigorous.

'Radar'. Purple-red flowers with white eye, March and April.

var. *rosea*. Usually sold as 'Rosea'. Bright rose-pink flowers with white eye, late February through early April; foliage is darker green.

'White Splendour'. Very large flowers of pure white flushed pink on backs of petals, February and March.

Anemone coronaria (poppy-flowered anemone). Native to eastern Mediterranean. Naturally short-lived and not reliably hardy

Seedheads of *Allium cristophii*

Allium hollandicum 'Purple Sensation'

Allium 'Globemaster'

Allium karataviense

Anemone blanda

Anemone nemorosa 'Vestal'

sets them off to perfection. Best in heavy, slightly acidic soil with plenty of leaf litter. Perfect in deciduous woodland with other early spring bloomers, but also takes full sun in moisture-retentive soil. Good in rock gardens. The roots of this very long-lived plant creep very slowly to form a spreading carpet with no maintenance necessary. Plants can be increased by divisions taken as soon as the blooms fade. Height 4 in. (10 cm); Zones 5 to 9.

'Allenii'. Large silvery lavender flowers on vigorous plants; taller than species at 6–10 in. (15–25 cm).

'Robinsoniana'. Violet-blue flowers; spreads very slowly.

'Rosea'. Pink-tinged buds open to white flowers, fade to violet-rose.

'Vestal'. Exquisite flowers of pure white are double in center, surrounded by ring of tiny single petals. Growth is dense and healthy, but increase is very slow; suitable for rock gardens. Often confused with 'Flore Pleno', a very similar cultivar.

CAMASSIA (CAMAS, QUAMASH)

Origin: North America, especially Northwest

Hardiness zones: 4 to 9

Size: 24–48 in. (60–120 cm) in height

Blooming season: April to June

Exposure: Full sun to light shade

Soil preference: Heavy, rich, moderately acidic

Water needs: Moist to wet in winter and early spring, dry in summer

Maintenance needs: Low to none

Subregions best suited: All

Possible problems: None serious

True bulb; dormant summer through winter. No Pacific Northwest garden should be without at least one species of these native bulbs, if only because they revel in heavy soil in our wet winters, even taking waterlogged soil in winter and early spring. They also like heavy soil in our dry summers (of course they're highly drought tolerant); in fact, they actually need both plant-unfriendly conditions. They also happen to be beautiful. Several new cultivars have been developed in Europe, where they're considered exotic and chic and are very popular.

All three northwestern native species bear spikes of star-like flowers held high above the narrow, strap-like foliage; flowers open from the base upward over a period of several weeks in spring. Withering spikes can be removed if their looks detract; if left to self-seed, plants will bloom from seed in three to five years and take care of themselves indefinitely.

Common camas, *Camassia quamash*, was once an important food for both Plains and Coast Indian tribes, who tended large beds of them and cooked and dried them in great quantities. Bulbs were harvested before blooms completely withered in order to distinguish them from the similar-looking but toxic bulbs of a white-flowered species with the grimly accurate name death camas (*Zigadenus*). Home tasting is definitely not recommended; even edible camas bulbs have mild toxins

in all parts of the Pacific Northwest, but worth growing as an annual for large (up to 3 in., 7.5 cm), bright, beautifully formed flowers in a wide range of colors, all with attractive dark centers. Prefers full sun and light-textured soil. Excellent cut flowers; successive sowings in early spring provide fresh blooms from May to July. Tubers can also be planted in fall in subregions with very mild winters.

If planting in spring, soak tiny claw-shaped tubers before planting claw side down; keep soil moist until growth appears. Flowers bloom about three months from planting; will bloom with minimal water as long as moisture was plentiful while growing. Plants go dormant in midsummer. Height 12 in. (35 cm); Zones 8 and 9.

Saint Bridgid Group has double flowers in many colors; flowers of De Caen Group are single but larger and showier. Many of these are named; the vibrant dark blue 'Mister Fokker' (often sold as Blue Poppy) and the pure white 'Die Braut' (usually sold as The Bride) are especially popular and make a terrific combination.

Anemone nemorosa (wood anemone). Native to eastern Europe and Asia Minor. Technically a rhizomatous-rooted perennial, but resembles bulb-type windflowers in blooming (far too briefly) in late March and April, then going dormant in June. Small, starry, usually single flowers with a satiny sheen are white to palest lavender to violet-blue; finely dissected foliage

Camassia cusickii

(only partially removed by cooking) that can cause gastrointestinal distress.

Plant bulbs when soil has started to cool in October, covering with 3–4 in. (7.5–10 cm) of soil. Wet soil in winter and early spring is perfect, but these are not bog plants; soil should dry out naturally in late spring and summer and stay dried out. In the wild, camas beds are found in winter-wet swales and depressions, but only in areas where summers are dry.

Camassia cusickii (Cusick's camas). Native to Oregon and northern California. Dense clusters of large, starry, pale blue flowers on tall spikes in May and June; one spike may bear over 100 flowers. Fist-sized bulbs, much larger than other camas bulbs, multiply freely to make huge clusters. New clumps can be started by stealing bulbs from top of cluster without having to lift clump. Height 30–36 in. (75–90 cm).

'Zwanenburg'. Large flowers of deep blue; leaves are slightly wavy.

Camassia leichtlinii (great camas). Native to the Pacific Northwest; especially plentiful in Oregon's Umpqua Valley. Robust plants with tall spikes, each bearing 20 to 40 flowers in May and June; excellent cut flower. Best in full sun. Height 3–4 ft. (0.9–1.2 m).

subsp. *leichtlinii*. Creamy white flowers open from yellow buds. 'Alba' has the whitest flowers of any camas; 'Plena' has double flowers of creamy yellow.

subsp. *suksdorfii*. Flower color ranges from mid-blue to purple-blue. Cultivars include 'Blauwe Donau' (sold as Blue Danube, dark blue), Caerulea Group (variable deep blue), 'Electra' (rich bright blue), and 'Lady Eve Price' (lavender-blue).

Camassia quamash (common camas, quamash). Native to northwestern North America; large patches were once very abundant. As noted by Meriwether Lewis of the Lewis and Clark Expedition in 1806 (in his own unique spelling), "The quawmash is now in blume and from the colour of its bloom at a short distance it resembles lakes of fine clear water, so complete is this deseption that on first sight I could have sworn it was water."

Flower color varies but is most commonly deep purple-blue; sturdy spikes hold ten to 40 flowers near their tops in April and May. Foliage is often slightly glaucous. Multiplies freely by bulb offsets and seed; excellent for naturalizing. Height 24–30 in. (60–75 cm).

'Blue Melody'. Foliage edged in creamy white contrasts beautifully with dark blue flowers.

CROCOSMIA

Origin: Mountains of southern and eastern Africa

Hardiness zones: Most 6 to 9

Size: Varies

Blooming season: June to October

Exposure: Full sun to light shade

Soil preference: Rich, moisture-retentive but well drained

Water needs: Low

Maintenance needs: Low

Subregions best suited: All

Possible problems: Can spread quickly

Corm; dormant in winter. Once a mainstay of Victorian gardens, these hardy relatives of gladioli and freesias nearly disappeared from cultivation in World War II, but never quite vanished from gardening consciousness. Nearly everyone who sees the bright yet delicate late-summer flowers recollects seeing them somewhere, but their name—any name—escapes most memories.

This is hardly surprising, since the plants have been bounced in and out of the genera *Antholyza, Curtonus, Montbretia,* and *Tritonia* as well as *Crocosmia*; species names are even more hopelessly tangled. Oddly enough, they've never had a universally accepted common name, at least in English; only montbretia has stuck for long, and even this is now deemed incorrect. (All montbretias are crocosmias, but not all crocosmias are montbretias.) Most of the modern introductions responsible for the strong comeback of these timelessly appealing plants are complex hybrids, potentially muddying the waters even more, but common sense has finally prevailed: crocosmia is now the accepted common name as well as the genus name.

Despite their bright, bold colors, the slender sprays of crocosmia flowers are held with such delicacy on slender,

Crocosmia 'Blacro' (Jenny Bloom)

Crocosmia ×crocosmiiflora

arching stems that even bright reds, flaming oranges, and brilliant yellows appear almost fragile. But there is nothing fragile about these plants, which look and behave more like hardy perennials. In fact, they're ridiculously easy to grow—so easy that *Crocosmia ×crocosmiiflora* tends to escape cultivation in mild, moist climates and become naturalized. (So far, it's not considered invasive.)

No pests or diseases bother them; even deer don't eat them. All they ask is a place in the sun (light shade in hot-summer valleys) in reasonably fertile, moisture-retentive soil that's given a couple of good soakings in dry weather. Clumps will survive and bloom without summer water if well mulched, but suffer visibly in prolonged drought.

All bloom for six to eight weeks, combining beautifully with both hot and cool colors, and make excellent cut flowers that last up to two weeks. The narrow, sword-shaped foliage is also very attractive; in some cases lengthwise veins are folded into shallow pleats. Leaves can be almost as kinetic as ornamental grasses, with sometimes a single leaf vibrating, sometimes the whole plant swaying with the breeze.

Plant the marble-sized corms in early spring, spacing 4–6 in. (10–15 cm) apart and covering with 2–4 in. (5–10 cm) of soil; deeper planting helps keep taller varieties windfirm. Keep soil

moist until growth appears, then water only in dry periods. Crocosmias bloom best when slightly crowded, but eventually, new corms that grow on underground rhizomes create overcrowded conditions. When annual flowering declines after four or five years, lift and divide clumps just as new growth resumes in early spring. Replant vigorous sections from edges and discard older, exhausted sections.

Crocosmia 'Blacro' (Jenny Bloom). Prolific small flowers of bright deep gold bloom from July to September on vigorous plants; leaves are long and slender. Height 30 in. (75 cm).

Crocosmia ×crocosmiiflora (common crocosmia, montbretia). Hybrid vigor is still very apparent in this cross of *C. aurea* and *C. pottsii*, initially made in 1879. Dainty flowers variably shaded scarlet/orange/yellow bloom in profusion from late July to October; vigorous foliage is narrow and sword-like. Multiplies quickly and can make large patches in a short time; has naturalized in coastal southern Oregon and northern California. Can be kept in check by removing excess corms every few years in early spring. Species is striking in large borders and excellent for naturalizing, but too rampant for smaller gardens; its cultivars multiply more sedately and are an excellent choice in gardens of any size. Height 30 in. (75 cm).

Crocosmia 'Lucifer'

Crocosmia ×*crocosmiiflora* 'Solfatare'

'Emberglow'. Very large flowers of burnt orange with red overtones from July to September; narrow reed-like foliage. Height 24 in. (60 cm).

'Emily McKenzie'. Huge (to 4 in., 10 cm), gladiolus-like outfacing flowers of golden orange with mahogany-red throats in August and September; leaves are broad and slightly pleated. Height 24 in. (60 cm).

'George Davison'. Bright yellow-orange buds open to small, clear yellow flowers from July to September; leaves are medium narrow. Height 30 in. (75 cm).

'Solfatare'. Also spelled Solfaterre. Soft apricot-yellow flowers and bronze-green foliage make a very attractive combination; popular for over 100 years. Slow growing; best in a bright but sheltered site protected from late frosts and hot or intense sun. Height 24 in. (60 cm); Zones 7 to 9.

Crocosmia 'Lucifer'. Probably the most popular cultivar of all. This cross, made by British plantsman Alan Bloom circa 1966, was the spark that led to the renaissance of hardy crocosmia hybrids. Large flowers of brilliant fire-engine red bloom early, June to August; large, broad leaves are strongly pleated. Indispensable for summer borders, but protect from wind that can

flatten the top-heavy stems. Plant corms deeply to increase windfirmness. Height 4–5 ft. (1.2–1.5 m).

Crocosmia masoniorum (giant montbretia). Relatively large, wide-petalled, upfacing flowers of deep orange bloom July to September; flower sprays are held almost horizontally at tips of arching stems. Leaves are broad and strongly pleated. Height 30 in. (75 cm).

'Firebird'. Selected form with very large flowers of flaming orange-red with bright yellow throats.

'Rowallane Yellow'. Long, upfacing sprays of deep yellow flowers on dark stems. Takes partial shade.

Crocosmia 'Severn Sunrise'. Bright salmon-orange flowers with yellow throats fade to pink; bloom from July to September on vigorous plants. Height 30 in. (75 cm).

CYCLAMEN HEDERIFOLIUM (SYN. *C. NEAPOLITANUM*; IVY-LEAVED CYCLAMEN)

Origin: Mediterranean region

Hardiness zones: 5 to 9

Size: 4–6 in. × 6–8 in. (10–15 cm × 15–20 cm)

Blooming season: Late August to November

Exposure: Partial shade

Soil preference: Well drained, high humus content; moderately acidic to neutral

Water needs: Moist in winter, dry in summer

Maintenance needs: None

Subregions best suited: All

Possible problems: Root weevils, slugs and snails

Tuber; dormant in summer. Of all the different species of hardy cyclamen that bloom at different times of the year, ivy-leaved cyclamen is the most vigorous and most perfectly adapted to our dry summers, long falls, and wet winters.

Dainty, delicate-looking flowers resembling florist's cyclamen (*Cyclamen persicum*) on a miniature scale appear suddenly,

Cyclamen hederifolium in early September

Cyclamen hederifolium foliage in April underneath blooming *Viburnum carlesii*

without leaves, at the height of summer's heat and drought. A few weeks later, handsome ivy-shaped leaves—beautifully marbled silver and green on top; maroon on the undersides—start to emerge, soon making a dense, low carpet of foliage that remains fresh all winter. In late spring the foliage begins to die down; by summer, the tubers are completely dormant. Here they stay, safely tucked away from drought and heat, until the reemergence of the naked flowers in late summer brings the welcome promise of soon-to-come cooler temperatures and much-needed moisture.

No maintenance is needed; the tubers never need lifting or dividing. Shaped somewhat like begonia tubers, with smooth, rounded bottoms (roots grow from the sides) and slightly concave tops, these tubers simply grow larger every year, eventually reaching the diameter of dinner plates and producing hundreds of flowers apiece every year. Several named strains are available (at a premium), but potluck seedlings are just as unusual and beautiful in both leaf and flower. Mid-pink is the usual flower color, but pale pink, dark pink, and white seedlings are also common.

Instead of making offsets, these plants self-seed freely (perhaps a little too freely) in a method noteworthy in itself. Seed capsules that begin to form after the flowers fade are encircled by the flower stems, which twist and spiral around them and eventually corkscrew them down to the ground. Capsules soon grow to the size and shape of large marbles; the several dozen sticky seeds inside them are quickly dispersed by birds and insects, which are attracted to the sweet coating. Germination rate is high.

Seeds sown nearby quickly fill in any bare spots; plants somehow sort out their own spacing without ever becoming overcrowded. Seeds sown elsewhere in the garden may or may not be wanted; if not, the tiny tubers are easily dislodged. They can even be transplanted elsewhere, producing their first blooms in two more years.

Store-bought tubers should be planted as soon as they become available in early fall, since they have already broken dormancy. Cover with about 1 in. (2.5 cm) of soil; water regularly until fall rains begin. If the soil is strongly acidic, a sprinkling of dolomite lime will also be appreciated. Don't plan on mixing *Cyclamen hederifolium* with winter-blooming *C. coum* or other hardy cyclamens for multi-season bloom; the much more vigorous *C. hederifolium* will soon crowd out all other species. These can, of course, be planted in other parts of the garden for year-round interest.

Few serious pests bother these tubers, although root weevils may nibble their roots and slugs may nibble their leaves. The ideal planting site (where they just happen to look their best) is beneath vigorous drought-tolerant shrubs and trees, which are essential for several reasons. They provide shelter not just from hot sun in August and September, which can burn the delicate flowers, but from wind and excess rain in winter, which can rot the tubers. (Tubers also dislike constantly moist soil during their dormant period; summer sprinkling should definitely be avoided.)

The yearly leaf litter of the shrubs or trees provides needed humus; their roots help draw excess moisture from the soil in winter, keeping the tubers from rotting. Although these Mediterranean natives are adapted to dry-summer, wet-winter climates, the wetness they get in Pacific Northwest winters is more than they want—or need. Tubers sited in the open are apt to drown, especially in heavier soil. However, chance seedlings located closer to sheltering shrubs or trees will survive and start making new colonies—proving once again that the most reliable source of information about any plant's likes and dislikes is the plant itself.

ERYTHRONIUM (FAWN LILY, TROUT LILY)

Origin: Pacific Northwest, eastern North America, Europe to Asia

Hardiness zones: 3 to 9

Size: 8–12 in. (20–30 cm) in height; spreading habit

Blooming season: March to June

Exposure: Partial shade

Soil preference: Leafy, loose, humus-rich; moisture-retentive but well drained

Water needs: Moist in winter and early spring, dry in summer

Maintenance needs: None

Subregions best suited: All

Possible problems: Slugs and snails

Erythronium californicum 'White Beauty'

Bulb; dormant summer through winter. Erythroniums are quite literally a natural for the Pacific Northwest; of the two dozen or so species known worldwide, most are native here. All are perfectly suited to our cool, wet springs and dry summers. The western natives in particular have been thriving in these very conditions for hundreds of thousands of years, if not longer, with no artificial assistance.

The common names fawn lily (for the two large, broad basal leaves shaped like the ears of a deer), trout lily (for the brown-purple mottling on the leaves of some species), glacier lily, avalanche lily, and dog's-tooth violet (for the shape of the long, slightly pointed bulbs) are widely but inconsistently used, often meaning completely different species and in some cases meaning the whole genus.

Whatever they're called, it would be hard to imagine anything more graceful or delicate-looking than their nodding, gently reflexed flowers that are held on slender stems just high enough above the basal leaves to set them off to perfection. Superb for naturalizing, they're perfectly sited in the shade of deciduous trees. Here, their early blooms are exposed to cool sun, yet the dry-shade conditions of summer give the summer-dormant bulbs exactly the cool, dry conditions they need. Natural leaf litter that accumulates over them provides ideal and ample humus.

Plant bulbs as soon as possible in early fall, pointed end up, with at least 4–5 in. (10–13 cm) of soil covering them; water them in well. After that, erythroniums should not be disturbed at all. The bulbs will continue to pull themselves down to a depth of 12 in. (30 cm) or more, making digging for them a futile and probably destructive exercise. Division is never necessary; these plants sort out any problems of congestion all by themselves.

Once established, erythroniums self-seed freely, but they can be helped along (or introduced into other areas) by collecting and sowing the abundant seeds produced in upright, papery capsules soon after the flowers fade. Most books recommend sowing fresh seed, but for western natives, more seed will survive if saved and sown in late September, just before fall rains begin. Collect the upright capsules when they turn brown and are just beginning to open; store in well-labeled paper (not plastic) bags until early fall. Scatter seed on humus-rich soil in partial shade; do not cover.

Erythronium revolutum. Photo by Judy Newton

The only sign of life the following spring will be short, very slender, grass-like single leaves, so make sure they're not pulled as weeds. In the spring following, growth will be slightly more recognizable, but plants will not reach flowering size for another two to three years. Cultivars will not come true from seed, but if more than one species is planted, some interesting hybrids may arise.

Small amounts of seed can be collected from the wild as long as it does not threaten the plants' natural increase. Needless to say, wild plants should never be dug up unless to rescue them from a site slated for destruction.

Erythronium californicum (fawn lily). Native to coastal ranges of northern California. Creamy white flowers with darker yellow centers bloom March and April; leaves are strongly mottled brown. Needs a cool site in partial to full shade.

'White Beauty'. Much confusion exists over the classification of this beautiful and popular plant, which has also been considered a vigorous form of the very similar *Erythronium oregonum*, or of *E. revolutum*, or a natural hybrid. Large white flowers are very similar to *E. oregonum* but have a distinct dotted band of maroon near centers; leaves are moderately mottled brown. Excellent, vigorous garden cultivar; easy to naturalize in partial shade. Blooms April and May.

Erythronium 'Pagoda'. Photo by Judy Newton

Erythronium dens-canis (dog's-tooth violet). Native to Europe and Asia. Purplish pink, rose, or white flowers on short stems; leaves are variably spotted maroon-brown. Best in cool sun to very light shade; blooms April to June. Several cultivars are available.

Erythronium grandiflorum (glacier lily). Native to higher elevations from southern British Columbia to northern California; eastward to Rocky Mountains. Large flowers of creamy to deep yellow, sometimes with red or purple anthers; non-mottled green leaves. Needs cool conditions; may be shy to flower until established. To 24 in. (60 cm) tall; blooms March to May.

Erythronium montanum (avalanche lily). Native to high elevations of Vancouver Island Ranges, Olympic Mountains, and northern Cascades, where it blankets alpine meadows as snow melts in spring. Not the easiest to grow, needing cool, moist, well-drained soil and very cool sun, but a choice alpine in the right situation. Delicate white to cream flowers; light green leaves are non-mottled. Blooms May and June.

Erythronium oregonum (white fawn lily). Native to lower elevations from Vancouver Island to northern California. Pristine white to cream flowers with yellow anthers; leaves are strongly mottled brown. One of the easiest and most adaptable erythroniums in garden conditions; increases readily in partial shade. Blooms April and May.

Erythronium revolutum (pink fawn lily, western trout lily). Native to lower elevations from Vancouver Island to northern California. Beautiful pale pink flowers mature to darker pink with pale centers; deep green leaves are mottled mahogany-brown and lighter green. Needs abundant moisture in early spring; best in cool woodland conditions. Blooms March to June. Several selections are available.

Erythronium tuolumnense. Native to lower elevations of Sierra Nevada of California. Vigorous species bearing bright yellow, slightly fragrant flowers with brown band near centers; leaves are non-mottled. Best known by 'Kondo' and 'Pagoda', vigorous hybrids with another (unknown) western species. Blooms March to May.

'Kondo'. Lemon-yellow scented flowers; otherwise similar to 'Pagoda'.

'Pagoda'. Large, deep yellow flowers on tall stems; leaves are very lightly mottled. Very adaptable to garden conditions; naturalizes easily in partial shade.

LILIUM (LILY)

Origin: Asia, North America, Europe

Hardiness zones: Most 4 to 9

Size: Varies

Blooming season: June to September

Exposure: Cool sun to light shade, protected from strong wind

Soil preference: Rich, well drained, high in humus (sandy loam ideal); slightly acidic

Water needs: Moderate to high while growing and blooming; drier period after blooming

Maintenance needs: Low to moderate

Subregions best suited: All

Possible problems: Botrytis blight

True bulb; dormant in winter. To live in the Pacific Northwest and not grow lilies would be a crime: not only do we have a world-class climate for growing these incomparable bulbs, but the entire history of today's healthy, adaptable, long-lived hybrid lilies is solidly rooted in the Pacific Northwest.

Not so long ago, the only lilies available anywhere were botanical species, most of which are quite narrowly adapted and deserving of their reputation for being finicky, short-lived, and/or sickeningly prone to disease when grown outside their native habitats. That all changed in the 1950s when Jan de Graaf, a Dutch immigrant operating Oregon Bulb Farms near Portland, succeeded in raising the first truly adaptable, vigorous, healthy hybrids on a commercial scale. Appropriately called Mid-century hybrids, these were the forerunners of today's extremely popular Asiatic hybrids.

Mid-century and other hybrid groups of the same era have since been eclipsed by newer hybrids, but many of their names—Bellingham hybrids (now Bellingham Group), San Juan hybrids, Olympic hybrids—bear witness to their origins. The Netherlands, New Zealand, and to some extent Canada and Japan are also important lily-breeding centers today, but the Pacific Northwest connection is as strong as ever.

In Washington, Port Townsend is home to B&D Lilies, a major grower and distributor; in Vancouver, Judith Freeman, an internationally recognized pioneer in breeding interdivisional lilies, owns and operates The Lily Garden, where she and her daughter continue their hybridization program (Columbia-Platte Lilies) and grow and sell garden lilies worldwide.

Aurora, Oregon, near Portland, is where Cebeco Lilies USA, a Dutch-owned company, specializes in developing and selling lilies worldwide, especially for the cut flower trade. And a narrow strip of coastline on the Oregon–California border has grown virtually all the Easter lilies (*Lilium longiflorum*) sold in North America since World War II. With recent changes in demographics, markets, and lilies themselves, this area now grows many Oriental hybrids and interdivisional hybrids as well.

Most lilies, like clematis, prefer cool conditions with their heads in sun and their feet in shade. Root shade can be provided by low-growing shrubs, perennials, annuals, clumping-type ornamental grasses (many lilies are native to grassy meadows), or non-competitive groundcovers. Do not plant near cedars or maples, which have greedy surface roots. A 2–3 in. (5–8 cm) layer of organic mulch helps keep bulbs cool and moist; mulching with aged compost or well-rotted manure keeps them well fed.

Keep the soil consistently moist but never soggy from the time bulbs are planted until three to four weeks after blooming, then withhold water so bulbs can go into their necessary resting period. (Except for late-blooming varieties, our climate provides these very condition naturally.) But since lily bulbs are never completely dormant, never allow soil to become bone dry.

After flowers fade, cut them off to direct the plants' energies back into the bulbs instead of into seed-making, but leave the leafy stems until they wither naturally in fall. When fully shriveled, tug gently to remove; cut if necessary.

Bulbs may be planted in fall (recommended for better first-year performance) or spring. Plant as soon as purchased; the bulbs are never truly dormant. If delay is unavoidable, open the plastic wrapping slightly to prevent excess condensation and store, plastic and all, in the crisper drawer of a refrigerator.

Plant lily bulbs deep, covering with a layer of soil three times the measurement of the bulb from tip to base. Err on the shallow side in heavy soils; bulbs will pull themselves down if necessary. However, if drainage is at all doubtful, plant on a slope or in raised beds. If planting in containers, place bulbs near the bottom to encourage stem rooting.

Lilies need dividing when yearly flower production starts to decline; this is best done in fall when withered stems flag the location of the bulbs. Lift the whole clump, separate bulbs, and replant the largest, spacing them 6–12 in. (15–30 cm) apart. Smaller bulbs can be grown on or replanted elsewhere. Lilies can also be propagated from individual bulb scales or stem bulbils, but these will take several years to reach blooming size.

Modern hybrids are highly disease-resistant, but in continuously warm, humid conditions such as a rainy June, botrytis blight may cause leaf spotting or even dieback. Good air circulation, adequate spacing, and minimal shade are effective preventions. Some straight species from which these hybrids derive

Lilium henryi

can be grown here; the following are those *Lilium* species that are best suited to Pacific Northwest conditions.

Lilium columbianum (Columbia tiger lily). Native throughout our region. Small orange "tiger lilies" with red spots bloom in July; best in woodland conditions or damp meadows. Height 24 in. (60 cm).

Lilium henryi. Native to China. Small, strongly reflexed flowers of light orange bloom in August on towering stems. Lime-tolerant, but accepts mildly acidic conditions; best in light shade. Highly disease-resistant; parent of many important hybrids. Height 8 ft. (2.4 m) or more.

Lilium lancifolium (tiger lily). Native to Japan, Korea, and China. Easygoing, very adaptable old favorite blooms in August, eventually making huge clumps of black-spotted orange flowers. *Lilium lancifolium* var. *splendens* is especially vigorous; hybrids also come in white, yellow, pink, and red. Height 3 ft. (0.9 m).

Lilium regale. Native to China. Parent of many if not most trumpet hybrids. Very fragrant July-blooming flowers with

Lilium regale

Lilium 'Connecticut King'

Lilium speciosum var. *rubrum*

Lilium 'Côte d'Azur'

petals white on inside, rosy purple on reverse; *L. r.* 'Album' is pure white. Both are adaptable and long-lived. Height 4–6 ft. (1.2–1.8 m).

Lilium speciosum (Japanese showy lily). Large white flowers with red spotting; parent of many Oriental hybrids. Blooms August or later. Best in moist soil in partial shade. Vigorous and healthy; thrives in our climate. Pure white *L. s.* var. *album* is less robust than species; *L. s.* var. *roseum* has pink centers and red spotting;

L. s. var. *rubrum* has deep pinkish red petals and deep red spotting. Height 3–4 ft. (0.9–1.2 m).

Asiatic hybrids

Sturdy, healthy, and very adaptable. Open, mainly upfacing medium-sized flowers bloom in sun or light shade in June and July. High bud count, ease of growing, and almost unlimited color range make up for lack of fragrance; their necessary drying-off period coincides perfectly with our normal summer drought. Lift and divide when yearly flower production diminishes, usually every three to four years. Cultivars listed are just a few proven performers among scores available. Height 3–4 ft. (0.9–1.2 m).

'Aphrodite'. Double flowers (no stamens, no pollen) of blush-pink.

'Centrefold'. Bright white with maroon brushstrokes and spotting.

'Connecticut King'. Profuse outfacing flowers of glowing yellow. One of the original Mid-century hybrids and still going strong; superbly healthy. Multiplies quickly.

'Côte d'Azur'. Wide petals of deep clear pink; high bud count and strong, short stems. Good in containers.

'Grand Cru'. Also spelled Gran Cru. Cheery yellow with dark red mark at base of each petal.

'Landini'. Very dark burgundy; buds and flowers appear black. Vigorous grower; best in full sun.

'Lollypop'. White flowers with hot-pink tips on each petal. Very bright eye-catcher; popular. Early bloomer.

'Menton'. Wide, rounded petals of creamy light orange with great substance; vigorous. Late bloomer.

'Montreux'. Late-blooming, freely produced flowers of medium pink with light spotting.

Other lilies considered Asiatic hybrids due to their parentage include the dwarf Pixie Series, ideally suited to container culture; some outfacing reflexed cultivars; and some pendent reflexed cultivars, such as the popular Tiger Babies Group (pastel peach "tiger lilies") and 'Tinkerbell' (dainty lavender-pink).

Trumpet hybrids

Powerfully fragrant, outfacing trumpet-shaped flowers bloom in July on tall, strong stems. Best in full sun; stems will lean toward the light they crave. Need ample water before and during bloom, followed by drier conditions. Height 5–8 ft. (1.5–2.4 m).

Classic color strains include African Queen Group (variable deep orange-gold), 'Anaconda' (coppery orange), 'Black Dragon' (petals white on inside, deep maroon on reverse), 'Golden Splendor' (petals clear yellow on inside, pinkish purple on reverse), and Pink Perfection Group (variable purplish pink). Newer forms involving complex crosses are still evolving; these are some of the most promising.

Hood Canal Series. Newer introductions named for geographic features near Hood Canal in the Olympic Peninsula. Wide range of colors; flowers are mostly upfacing. Height 4–6 ft. (1.2–1.8 m).

Sinfonia strain. Huge ivory-white petals with deep pink on reverse and rosy pink edging; tetraploid vigor and substance. Height 3–4 ft. (0.9–1.2 m).

Temple Series. Very large trumpets; popular members include 'Amethyst Temple' (deep violet-pink), 'Golden Temple' (deep yellow), 'Marble Temple' (white), and 'Moon Temple' (clear lemon yellow). Height 4–6 ft. (1.2–1.8 m).

Oriental hybrids

Very large, slightly reflexed flowers with strong coloring, prominent raised spotting, and intense, exotic perfume. Main

Lilium Tiger Babies Group

Lilium Pink Perfection Group

blooming time is August, but many hybrids bloom slightly earlier; a few slightly later. Best in moist soil in light or afternoon shade; protect from intense sun and drying winds. Because Oriental hybrids need watering while they're growing and blooming, keep them separate from Asiatic hybrids, which need to start drying out at the same time. Height 2–4 ft. (0.6–1.2 m).

'Acapulco'. Outfacing flowers of deep pink with magenta-pink ribs; tall stems. Late blooming.

Lilium 'Casa Blanca'

'Arena'. White with narrow pink and yellow ribbing and red spotting. Early blooming.

'Casa Blanca'. Worldwide classic with enormous, pure white outfacing flowers. Height 4–5 ft. (1.2–1.5 m).

'Dizzy'. White with pinwheel-like red ribbing and dark red spotting.

'Joy' (syn. 'Le Rêve'). Outfacing flowers of soft clear pink. Early blooming.

'Star Gazer'. Famous upfacing flowers of deep pinkish red with white edging; short stems. 'Starfighter' is similar but with wider edging, larger flowers, shorter stems.

'Tom Pouce'. Soft pink with yellow ribbing and yellow spotting; short stems. Early blooming.

Interdivisional hybrids

Until fairly recently, crosses between the eight different divisions of lily hybrids (a ninth includes all species) were considered biologically impossible, since fertilized seed invariably failed to develop normally. But in the 1970s, a technique called embryo rescue, which involves removing the just-fertilized seeds and growing them in a sterilized medium, opened a new door. Not all crosses are compatible—nature still decides this—but these "test-tube babies" display forms, shapes, colors, and combined characteristics never before seen in lilies.

Naturally, the Pacific Northwest is again at the cutting edge of breeding these new lilies, which if anything are even healthier and more vigorous than earlier hybrids. Besides the types listed here, there are now also Oriental-Asiatic crosses, Trumpet-Longiflorum crosses, Longiflorum-Oriental crosses, and others.

Asiapets. Sturdy, vigorous, sun-loving crosses of Asiatic and trumpet hybrids bloom in late June. Large, wide-petaled, fragrant flowers may be gently reflexed and pendent, as in 'China Express' (peach with orange-gold centers) or the self-descriptive 'Peach Butterflies'; or more bell-shaped and outfacing, as in the Canadian Belles Series ('Blushing Belles', 'Creamy Belles', 'Fiery Belles', 'Silky Belles', and others). Height 3–4 ft. (0.9–1.2 m).

LA hybrids. Developed for the cut flower trade, these crosses of the traditional Easter lily (*Lilium longiflorum*) and Asiatic hybrids bloom in July. Large flowers may be outfacing or upfacing; fragrance is sweet but light. Superb, long-lasting cut flowers; pastel colors hold best in part shade. Clumps need frequent division for continued garden presence, but bulbs multiply easily and quickly. Height 3–4 ft. (0.9–1.2 m).

Orienpets or OTs. Ultra-vigorous, ultra-adaptable crosses of Oriental and trumpet hybrids bloom in July in full sun to light shade. Most are powerfully fragrant and reasonably drought tolerant in our climate. New cultivars are being developed constantly. A few classics include 'Catherine the Great' (large, silky yellow flowers; deepest color in cool weather), 'Scheherazade' (long-blooming, deep red reflexed flowers edged in gold), and 'Silk Road' (enormous, long-blooming white flowers with wide, deep pink centers and intense perfume). Height 3–6 ft. (0.9–1.8 m); some established cultivars even taller.

NARCISSUS (DAFFODIL)

Origin: Mountainous regions of western Mediterranean; central Europe, Balkans

Hardiness zones: Most 3 to 9

Size: Varies

Blooming season: February to May

Exposure: Full sun to dappled shade

Soil preference: Heavy but well drained; slightly acidic

Water needs: Moist in winter and spring, dry in summer

Maintenance needs: Low to moderate

Subregions best suited: All

Possible problems: Narcissus bulb fly

True bulb; dormant summer through winter. Whether any or all are called by their Latin name, narcissus, or by their English name, daffodil, all species and cultivars of this indispensable genus have one thing in common: near-perfect adaptation to the climate of the Pacific Northwest. Our winter and summer temperatures, soils, and rainfall pattern are so like their native habitats that these spring bulbs don't seem to realize they're not native here as well.

Even hybrids naturalize readily, popping up in all sorts of places on their own, and most also interbreed freely. (Our own garden contains several beautiful hybrids that were definitely not planted.) They're also deer-proof—bulbs are toxic if eaten, and deer are not stupid—making them highly desirable for that reason alone.

It's no wonder over 1000 acres (405 ha) of daffodils are grown commercially here, mainly in the Olympic Rain Shadow and Georgia Basin/Puget Trough subregions. Our mild winters are nevertheless cold enough to give them proper winter chill; our wet season comes just when they need ample water for good root growth, flowering, and foliage. Our dry summers are timed just right for their necessary dry resting period; our summer temperatures also suit them, since they require dryness without high heat while dormant.

Although we take them for granted, daffodils are considered difficult to grow in wet-summer parts of the world. A few showers or occasional sprinklings while dormant do them no harm, since light summer showers do occur in their native habitats, but they should not be planted in areas slated for constant irrigation. (Daffodils in planters or flower beds should be lifted before adding summer annuals.) In the Pacific Coast subregion, where early summer showers are frequent, they're best planted under deciduous trees or shrubs, where leafy canopies and moisture-sucking roots keep them sufficiently dry.

Planting under deciduous trees or shrubs also gives daffodils adequate sunlight while blooming (not to mention a perfect visual setting) without having to leave an open space in the garden all summer. When choosing which side of a tree (or a path) to plant them on, consider the prevailing light: although flowers do not turn constantly to follow the sun, they will all face the brighter side. Planting in lawns also requires some forethought.

Although they look terrific there in full bloom, the grass should not be cut until the daffodil foliage dies down—in late May at the earliest—by which time the lawn may well be knee-high.

Daffodils are gregarious flowers and always look best in groups, with clumps or drifts of the same cultivar being more effective and more natural-looking than a mixture of varying heights, colors, and blooming times. Novelty daffodils (double flowers, split coronas, unusual colors or shapes) are always intriguing, but can be disappointing or look out of place in informal garden settings; some are so novel they don't look like daffodils—or any other work of nature—at all.

Catalog photographs can be misleading. "Pink" daffodils are at best peach, apricot, or salmon pink, and then only on first opening. The tiny, fully double 'Rip Van Winkle' that looks so irresistible in photographs looks distressingly like a dandelion in real life. Very large double flowers can soak up rain and flop over, but smaller doubles such as 'Cheerfulness' hold up very well and even naturalize.

Daffodils of all types should be planted as soon as they become available in late August or early September so their roots can become established before the soil cools. Water well after planting. Little yearly maintenance is needed; after flowers fade, snap them off to prevent seed set (unless wanted for naturalizing), but do not remove foliage until it withers. Clumps need lifting and dividing when yearly flowering diminishes and foliage becomes crowded; this is best done before withered foliage disappears completely and location becomes uncertain.

The larvae of the narcissus bulb fly can tunnel into bulbs, eating the hearts out and/or inviting fungi that cause rot. If bulbs do not bloom and foliage is spindly, dig up bulbs after the foliage dies down and destroy any soft, rotten, or damaged bulbs. Planting in rough grass is said to help by confusing the bumble-bee-like adult fly, which lays its eggs at the base of decaying foliage in May. Scuffling the dirt at the base of the foliage also helps discourage this pest.

The genus *Narcissus* is split into 12 divisions based on flower shape, size, and parentage. Dozens of choices are available in most divisions, with new introductions every year; these are just a few proven favorites.

Division 1 (trumpet daffodils). Large flowers, one per stem, midseason bloom. Trumpet length equal to or greater than petal length. Height 16–20 in. (40–50 cm).

'Dutch Master'. Now the standard for large yellow daffodils; superior performance and greater vigor has replaced (not always with customer knowledge) the older 'King Alfred', which has far greater name recognition. Light fragrance.

'Mount Hood'. Very large, slightly fragrant flowers open creamy white with light yellow trumpets; these quickly fade to a beautiful pale cream and mature as white as the snow on their namesake. Very long blooming time.

Division 2 (large-cupped daffodils). Large flowers, one per stem, midseason to late bloom. Cup (reduced trumpet) length more than one-third of but less than equal to petal length. Reliably perennial; good for naturalizing. Height 14–18 in. (35–45 cm).

Narcissus 'Carlton'

Narcissus bulbocodium

Narcissus 'Thalia'

Narcissus 'Actaea'

'Carlton'. Yellow with frilled cup. Very reliable; naturalizes into large drifts. Strong vanilla scent.

'Flower Record'. White petals; small yellow cup rimmed in red. Popular for forcing as well as in gardens.

'Ice Follies'. Light lemon-yellow; wide, frilled cup matures to pale cream.

'Mon Cherie'. White petals; large frilled cup of peach-pink.

Division 3 (small-cupped daffodils). Medium-sized flowers, one per stem, later blooming. Cup length no more than one-third of petal length. Height 14–16 in. (35–40 cm).

'Barrett Browning'. White petals; wide, showy orange-red cup. Midseason bloom.

'Mint Julep'. Greenish yellow petals; small yellow cup with green eye.

Division 4 (double-flowered daffodils). May be any size, height, color, or blooming time; doubling may include both petals and cup, or cup alone.

'Cheerfulness'. Medium-small, fully double flowers, six or more per stem; creamy white with some yellow in center. Very fragrant. 'Yellow Cheerfulness' is identical except for all-yellow color. Both 16 in. (40 cm); reliably perennial.

'Flower Drift'. Medium-large, fully double flowers, one per stem; white with orange-red in center. Naturalizes well. Spicy fragrance. Height 12–16 in. (30–40 cm).

'Tahiti'. Large, fully double flowers of butter-yellow with orange-red in center. Strong stems hold up to rain; reliably perennial. Height 14–16 in. (35–40 cm).

Division 5 (*Narcissus triandrus* hybrids). Small to medium-sized slightly pendent flowers, two to three per stem, late midseason bloom. Strong sweet fragrance. Height 6–14 in. (15–35 cm). Species is sometimes called Angel's Tears, commemorating the frustration and fatigue of a very young guide named Angelo on an arduous 19th-century bulb-gathering expedition in the mountains of Spain.

'Hawera'. Cross of *Narcissus triandrus* and *N. jonquilla*. Small, gracefully pendent yellow flowers; height 6–8 in. (15–20 cm). Very popular and reliable.

'Thalia'. Large, gently nodding, very fragrant flowers of pure white; a classic since 1916. Multiplies quickly, tolerates drier soils. Height 14 in. (35 cm).

Division 6 (*Narcissus cyclamineus* hybrids). Small flowers, one per stem, with slightly to strongly reflexed petals and straight-sided trumpets; early blooming. Shade tolerant and easy to naturalize; also excellent for rock gardens, containers, and forcing.

'February Gold'. Always the first to bloom, but may be later than February, depending on weather. Fragrant, gently nodding flowers have bright yellow petals and slightly deeper yellow trumpets. Height 12 in. (30 cm).

'Jack Snipe'. Sturdy and reliable; relatively large early-blooming flowers have white petals and frilled yellow trumpets. Blooms for a good six weeks. Height 10 in. (25 cm).

'Jetfire'. Small flowers have deep yellow petals and long, tubular orange trumpets; very early bloom. Height 12 in. (30 cm).

'Tête-à-tête'. Gently nodding miniature flowers with light yellow petals and brighter yellow trumpets are perfectly formed. Very early bloom; good for naturalizing and very popular for forcing. One to three flowers per stem; sometimes placed in Division 12. Height 6–8 in. (15–20 cm).

Division 7 (*Narcissus jonquilla* hybrids). Small flowers, three or more per stem, with short, wide petals held at right angles to cups. Strongly fragrant. Latest to bloom, usually in May. Narrow, rush-like foliage; excellent for naturalizing but prefers warm soils and humid conditions. Heat-tolerant if not too dry.

'Baby Moon'. Miniature flowers of soft yellow; prolific bloom. Height 8–10 in. (20–30 cm).

'Bell Song'. Ivory-white petals and apricot-pink cups; very free-flowering. Tolerates sun and heat without fading. Height 12–14 in. (30–40 cm).

'Quail'. Deep gold flowers with rounded, overlapping petals and sweet fragrance. Height 14 in. (40 cm).

Division 8 (*Narcissus tazetta* hybrids). An anomaly among *Narcissus* species, being native or naturalized from central Europe to Asia, China, and Japan (perhaps due to ancient trade routes) and being less cold-hardy (Zone 5 at best). Bunch-flowering, with 6–8 small early-blooming flowers per stem; powerfully fragrant. Excellent for forcing (this division includes the well-known but tender paperwhites), but also naturalizes readily in wet-winter, dry-summer climates.

'Geranium'. Creamy white petals and orange-red cups; strong grower. Height 16 in. (45 cm).

'Minnow'. Miniature flowers with light yellow petals and deeper yellow cups; tolerates part shade. Height 6–10 in. (15–25 cm).

Division 9 (*Narcissus poeticus* hybrids). Large, powerfully fragrant, late-blooming flowers with pure white petals, very small red-rimmed yellow cups, and green eyes. Good in damp soil; virtually always in growth either above or below ground. Species is known as poet's daffodil. The variety *N. poeticus* var. *recurvus*, with narrower, slightly recurved petals, is known as pheasant's eye daffodil. Hybrids, all very similar, have broad, overlapping white petals. Most popular is 'Actaea', a vigorous grower that multiplies quickly. Height 16 in. (40 cm).

Division 10 (species). Includes all true species regardless of size, shape, or blooming time. Ideally suited to the Pacific Northwest but considered tricky almost everywhere else is *Narcissus bulbocodium* (hoop petticoat daffodil). Small, bright yellow flowers, three to five per tiny bulb, have short, very narrow petals and huge, flaring, funnel-shaped cups. Prolific bloom over long season; excellent for naturalizing as it multiplies quickly and self-seeds as well. Needs dry summers. Attractive dark green foliage resembling clumps of chives is nearly evergreen; new growth emerges with fall rains and lasts all winter and spring. Height 6–10 in. (15–25 cm). The selection 'Golden Bells' bears up to 15 flowers per bulb.

Division 11 (split corona or butterfly daffodils). Trumpets or cups (technically called coronas) are split and lie nearly flat, giving semi-double effect very unlike all other daffodils. Flowers are mainly upfacing. Many new introductions; average height 14–16 in. (35–40 cm).

'Cassata'. Creamy white petals; broad, ruffled lemon-yellow cup matures white.

'Orangery'. Large white petals; broad, flat orange cup.

Division 12 (all other daffodils). A provision for future developments.

OXALIS ADENOPHYLLA (CHILEAN WOOD SORREL)

Origin: Mountains of southern Chile and Argentina

Hardiness zones: 4 to 9

Size: 4 in. × 8–10 in. (10 cm × 20–25 cm)

Blooming season: May to July

Exposure: Cool sun to partial shade

Soil preference: Rich; moisture-retentive but well drained, especially in winter

Water needs: Moderately drought tolerant

Maintenance needs: Low

Subregions best suited: All

Possible problems: None serious

Bulb-like rhizome; herbaceous. *Oxalis* is not a term dear to the hearts of most Pacific Northwesterners, who associate it with ho-hum clover-like perennials or groundcovers—or worse, with the tiny yellow-flowered pernicious lawn weed. But *O. adenophylla*, a true alpine, is a gem of a plant with impeccable manners as well as nearly year-round beauty.

The pink-edged flowers with white throats, dark red eyes, and dark but faint veining are a treat in themselves in late spring and early summer, especially because the wide-petalled, relatively large blooms (1 in., 2.5 cm) are so unexpected on such short plants. These open from violet-pink upright buds that are furled like tiny closed umbrellas; opened flowers also furl at night and on cloudy days. Individual flowers bloom for only a few days, but the abundance of buds makes a good show over many weeks.

The foliage, which sets off the flowers in perfect nosegays, is if anything even more attractive; the deeply divided, scalloped leaflets of silvery gray-green are folded into dainty pleats. Foliage goes briefly dormant in midwinter; it may also go briefly dormant in dry summers but will reappear (along with a flower or two) in September.

Plant the shaggy brown bulbs in fall (they're sometimes sold under the misleading and irritating name "pink buttercups") with the stringy, hairy roots pointing downward. Finding an ideal site—the best compromise between adequate sunlight and adequately cool/moist soil—can be something of an experiment. Dappled shade under a lightly branched tree or shrub is usually ideal, but flowers will not open fully (if at all) in too much shade. In the sun-challenged Pacific Coast and Puget Sound subregions, full sun is recommended; in the hotter, sunnier Rogue and Willamette subregions, partial shade is preferable.

If the site turns out to be less than perfect, Chilean wood sorrel can be relocated in fall with no harm done. Although perfectly happy in our prevailing heavy-textured, acidic soils, it's not terribly particular and will adapt to almost any site as long as winter drainage is excellent. Saturated soil in winter is the only condition likely to do in this trouble-free plant. Plants accept summer watering well, keeping their foliage, but summer drought is also well tolerated; plants simply go dormant.

Good looks and good behavior make this an excellent edging plant, small-scale groundcover, rock garden subject, container subject, or even houseplant. When annual flowering starts to diminish, lift plants in fall, separate the shaggy bulbs, and replant every one of them—it's impossible to have too many.

Oxalis adenophylla

CHAPTER 11

Vines and Groundcovers

Vines and groundcovers share some similar traits, such as the need for cool root runs. Most groundcovers evolved in the shade of larger plants, while vines grew to depend on trees and shrubs to shade their roots while their long stems clambered through them to enable their flowers to reach the sun. Not surprisingly, both tend to be drought tolerant, since the canopies of larger plants act as umbrellas and limit the amount of rain reaching the soil beneath them.

By necessity, both vines and groundcovers tend to be very vigorous, due to their long history of coping with dense root competition and the less-than-ideal growing conditions of dry shade. All are very self-reliant; many are fully capable of growing to indefinite size with no help whatsoever. (Gardeners, however, prefer to set firm limits on their potential size and spread.)

Even their categorization is not mutually exclusive. Many vines can be used as groundcover (some more successfully than others), and most groundcovers will climb or scramble over rocks, small plants, or any other obstacles in their way, including tree trunks. However, the main reason for their close association in gardening terms is their unique usefulness. Vines allow us to garden on vertical surfaces, adding height without width; groundcovers allow us to garden on horizontal surfaces, filling in and defining broad spaces without adding height.

Both are indispensable in adding color, texture, and fullness to gardens without competing for space with plants that are bulkier in all three dimensions. In fact, both vines and groundcovers seem to enjoy the company of other plants, thriving best and looking best when combined with a variety of other plant forms. Fortunately, Pacific Northwest gardeners have no shortage of either from which to choose.

VINES

All hardy vines grow very well in our climate—if anything, a little too well, as if they realize there is no threat of freezing back in our mild, wet winters. All too often, romantic visions of flower-covered walls, fences, or rooftops end up as nightmares of tangled growth that threaten to engulf everything in their paths.

The main trick with vines is to fit their mature size and weight (which they're bound to reach eventually) to the space and support available. Self-clinging Boston ivy (*Parthenocissus tricuspidata*) can easily cover the sides of three-story buildings; looser-growing Virginia creeper (*P. quinquefolia*) can cover large cottages or sheds—and then some. However, the much smaller, slower-growing silvervein creeper (*P. henryana*) is suitable for normal-sized walls or fences, where it can show off its beautiful white-veined green leaves in summer as well as its blazing red color in fall.

Clematis 'Jackmanii' and *Hypericum calycinum* in July, authors' garden

Wisterias and grapevines can also get enormous, which may or may not be the intended goal. Both can be kept to a reasonable size, but only through regular hard pruning. Silver lace vine (*Fallopia baldschuanica*, syn. *Polygonum aubertii*) also needs plenty of space despite its delicate-looking flowery tendrils; one of its other names is mile-a-minute vine.

Other vines to approach with caution are trumpet vine (*Campsis*), which can sucker a bit too enthusiastically, and most Japanese honeysuckles (*Lonicera japonica*), which tend to have a rampant and even invasive growth habit. Hall's honeysuckle (*L. j.* 'Halliana') should definitely be avoided, but the purple-leaved *L. j.* var. *repens* (usually sold as *L. j.* 'Purpurea') is well behaved, and the beautiful golden reticulated honeysuckle (*L. j.* 'Aureoreticulata') can be safely grown in the smallest gardens.

Other well-behaved honeysuckles include the very fragrant Early Dutch (*Lonicera periclymenum* 'Belgica') and Late Dutch (*L. p.* 'Serotina') honeysuckles as well as the scentless but visually arresting orange-flowered *L.* 'Mandarin', an introduction of the Plant Introduction Scheme of the Botanical Garden of the University of British Columbia (PISBG). Both ornamental and edible kiwi vines grow well in our climate; the pink, white, and green variegation of *Actinidia kolomikta* is particularly showy, but even the large leaves and fuzzy red stems of edible kiwis (*A. deliciosa*) are highly ornamental.

Although they're not technically vines, climbing roses are also extremely popular in the Pacific Northwest. Star jasmine (*Trachelospermum jasminoides*) is another great favorite, although it is not always reliably hardy in our colder-winter subregions. However, the most popular and best-suited vines of all for the Pacific Northwest are clematis, described in detail in the first entry.

All hardy vines get off to a better start in our climate when planted in early fall rather than spring. In September's warm soil, the massive root systems necessary to support all that incredible top growth can begin to get established long before they're called on to feed stems, leaves, and flowers, and the soon-to-come fall rains will keep them well watered. Spring planting is also acceptable, but vines will not grow as fast as fall-planted specimens and will need considerably more water and fertilizer the first summer. Generous amounts of bone meal at planting time, whether in fall or spring, will help get roots off to a good start and encourage good flowering as well.

CLEMATIS

Origin: Europe, Asia, North America, New Zealand

Hardiness zones: Varies

Size: Varies

Blooming season: Varies

Exposure: Cool sun to light shade; protected from hot or intense sun

Soil preference: Rich, deep, cool; moisture-retentive but well drained; slightly acidic to neutral

Water needs: Moderate when young; most are moderately drought tolerant when established

Maintenance needs: Low to moderate

Subregions best suited: All

Possible problems: Clematis wilt, powdery mildew, earwigs

Mainly deciduous; a few species semi-evergreen or evergreen. Like roses, clematis are beautifully suited to Pacific Northwest conditions. They grow most vigorously in moist climates without extremes of temperature, and bloom best in sunny but relatively cool summers. They also love our heavy, moisture-retentive but well-drained loamy soils.

With flower sizes ranging from tiny to immense, vine sizes from 6 ft. (1.8 m) to 30 ft. (10 m), blooming times from late winter to fall, and an incredible choice of flower color and form, the choices are almost unlimited—and most of us take advantage of as many as we can. Fortunately, most clematis are small vines, so it's possible to plant a dozen or more even in the smallest garden without being the least bit overwhelmed by jungle-like growth. Some Pacific Northwest gardeners grow 100 or more on city-sized lots.

More importantly, clematis have impeccable manners, which among vines is truly an amazing asset. Since they support themselves very delicately by twisting their leaf stems around slender supports, clematis vines will not tear apart house siding, lift roof shingles, strangle trees, break trellises with their weight, smother nearby plants, or invade neighbors' gardens—with one exception. *Clematis vitalba*, a European species known as traveler's joy or old man's beard, is so vigorous, drought tolerant, and invasive (it spreads both by rooting stems and seed) that it has been declared noxious in Oregon and Washington.

However, the rest of the dozen or so popular species and the many hundreds of complex hybrids are ideally suited to garden conditions. Depending on size, they can be grown on trellises, along fences, around posts (with netting for support), on freestanding obelisks or teepees, in containers, or as groundcover. They can also be allowed to scramble through roses, shrubs, or other vines, or trained up into trees, in whose canopies they flower with abandon. Several popular species (*Clematis* ×*durandii*, *C. heracleifolia*, *C. integrifolia*) do not climb but are treated as herbaceous or semi-woody perennials.

"Heads in the sun and feet in the shade" is a well-known and useful guideline for siting; all clematis flower best in at least morning sun, but they also need a cool root run. This can be supplied by a good layer of mulch, flat stones laid over the root area, or small shrubs planted on their sunny side. A clematis intended for growing into a tree should be planted on the drip line (not near the trunk) on the shady side of the tree; it will work its way to the sunny side to expose its flowers.

Many clematis formerly considered cultivars of a particular species are now classified as hybrids; for example, *Clematis alpina* 'Willy' is now *C.* 'Willy'. However, since almost all Group A hybrids and many Group C hybrids retain strong characteristics of a certain parent species (and are usually sold as such),

PLANTING A CLEMATIS

Great care is required in planting a clematis, both in preparation of the hole and in handling the new vine. Even for small nursery plants, dig a round hole at least 18 in. (45 cm) wide and deep, which is much bigger than it sounds—use a measuring tape to check. Strongly acidic soil should be amended with dolomite lime, but unless the soil is very infertile, no other amendments are needed. (Their need for alkaline soil is greatly exaggerated; although clematis are very tolerant of alkaline conditions, they do not require them and are perfectly happy in slightly acidic soil.) Compost or manure is best added on top of the soil, where there is no danger of burning tender roots.

The reason for deep planting is partly to keep the roots cool, but mainly as insurance against clematis wilt. This fungal disease, which causes leaves and stems to suddenly wilt and die, has no cure, but its spread can be halted by cutting the affected stems well below the lowest wilted leaves and destroying them. (Disinfect pruners after each cut.) Even if all stems are affected, as long as the vine is planted deeply, new stems should eventually arise from dormant buds well below ground.

The fungus that causes clematis wilt can enter the vine through any break or wound in the all-too-fragile stems, so it's a good idea to plant clematis well away from high-traffic paths, children's play areas, and the favorite haunts of pets. Plants must also be handled very carefully when pruning, training, and especially when planting. A common cause of damage to young plants while planting is failing to notice that the small sticks on which they're trained are securely stapled to the nursery pots. The long staples must be removed before attempting to dislodge the plant. It's far safer to sacrifice a 15-cent pot by cutting it off the plant than to try to shake the plant out of the pot, which is certain to break some stems and perhaps sacrifice a 15-dollar plant to clematis wilt.

Sprinkle a handful of bone meal in the bottom of the hole, then add some of the soil removed from the hole so that the crown of the vine will be 6–8 in. (15–20 cm) below the level of the top of the hole. Carefully set the new plant in the center of the soil, disturbing the roots as little as possible. Any curled-up roots on the bottom should be gently loosened, but don't dig into the main root ball. While you can still see where the roots are, position a slender bamboo cane for the vine to cling to, then backfill with the rest of the soil and water in well. However, if the clematis stem is unripe (greenish in color), leave a small space around it until it ripens (turns brownish) before covering it with soil.

Clematis armandii in June. New shoot at right (bronze foliage) bears a very late small flower.

we have described these newly reclassified hybrids under the appropriate species. Any straight selections of the species are so noted.

Early-blooming species and their cultivars (Pruning Group A)

These earliest-blooming clematis need no regular pruning, but any dead or weak stems should be removed as soon as flowering is finished. They can also be lightly trimmed for shape then, but since they bloom only on old wood (stems that grew last year or earlier), drastic pruning merely reduces the number of flowers possible. However, the more rampant species often need periodic reduction of their size.

Clematis alpina. Native to northern Europe, mountains of central Europe, and northern Asia. Small, very cold-hardy vines bear small, nodding, bell-shaped single flowers consisting of four broad tepals (petals and/or sepals) that partially reveal creamy white stamens. Blooms April and May; large fluffy seedheads that follow are very attractive. Likes cool conditions; needs northern exposure or light shade in hot-summer valleys. Good on low fences, growing through small shrubs, covering stumps, on small trellises or posts, and in containers. Height 6–10 ft. (1.8–3 m); Zones 3 to 9.

'Constance'. Relatively large, deep pink semi-double flowers. Vigorous and free-flowering; a seedling of the smaller-flowered purplish pink *C.* 'Ruby'.

'Frances Rivis'. Long, broad, slightly twisted tepals of pale blue; free-flowering.

'Pamela Jackman'. A selection of the species. Bell-shaped flowers of deep rich purple-blue.

'Willy'. Pale mauve-pink flowers, darker at bases. Vigorous.

Clematis armandii. Native to China. Although several not-so-hardy *Clematis* species are evergreen, this is the one known throughout the Pacific Northwest simply as "evergreen clematis." Although perfectly hardy in our climate, *C. armandii* needs a sheltered site; late frosts can nip the early flowers, and sudden cold spells or dry winter winds can cause dieback. However, its long, narrow, leathery leaves and sweetly scented small white flowers in March and April make it very popular.

Growth is rampant, needing sturdy support and regular thinning to remove buildup of dead stems. Good privacy screen. Best in cool conditions or afternoon shade; leaf tips can burn in strong sun. Height 15–20 ft. (7.5–6 m); Zones 7 to 9.

'Apple Blossom'. White flowers blushed pink.

'Snowdrift'. Large, pure white flowers.

Clematis cirrhosa. Native to the Mediterranean. Interesting rather than beautiful; very small greenish yellow bell-shaped flowers with purplish markings bloom in late winter. Attractive, deeply divided foliage remains evergreen in mild winters, turning bronze in colder weather. Needs a winter-sheltered site. Takes full sun in summer and is very drought tolerant, but may go briefly dormant in late summer. Height 10–15 ft. (3–4.5 m); Zones 8b to 9.

Clematis montana var. *rubens* 'Pink Perfection'

var. *balearica* (fern-leaved clematis). Very finely divided foliage bronzed in winter; yellowish flowers are speckled reddish brown.

var. *purpurascens* 'Freckles'. Larger greenish yellow flowers are heavily spotted red. First flush of flowers appears in late fall, escaping worst frosts; blooms sporadically over winter.

Clematis macropetala (downy clematis). Native to Mongolia and northern China. Very similar in looks and uses to *C. alpina*, to which it is closely related, but flowers are slightly larger and semi-double, with a ruffled appearance. Takes cold, exposed sites, but the fluffy flowers that bloom in April and May are best when protected from heavy spring rain. Height 8–12 ft. (2.4–3.6 m); Zones 3 to 9.

'Blue Bird'. Mauve-blue flowers; very vigorous and free-flowering.

'Lagoon' (correctly, 'Lagoon Jackman 1959'). Larger flowers of very deep blue; slightly later blooming time.

'Markham's Pink'. Fully double flowers of deep pink set off by light green foliage. Vigorous.

'Rosy O'Grady'. Larger flowers of mauve-pink are darker on outsides, lighter on insides.

'White Wings'. Free-flowering Swedish hybrid with larger, fully double flowers of creamy white.

Clematis montana (Himalayan clematis). Native to the Himalaya. Beautiful but rampant vine completely smothered in May and June with thousands of small, slightly fragrant four-petalled flowers of pink or white. Not for small spaces, but a magnificent sight scrambling through a large tree or covering a sturdy fence, large arbor, chimney, or porch. Likes cool conditions. Best in cool sun but very adaptable; tolerates shade (at the expense of full blooming) and moderately acidic soil.

Needs a site sheltered from late frosts, which can kill flower buds; since it blooms only on old wood, loss of buds means no flowers that year. Pruning is not necessary, but may be desirable immediately after blooming to control size. Height 25–30 ft. (7.5–10 m); Zones 6 to 9.

var. *alba* (syn. 'Alba'). White flowers; now considered synonymous with species.

'Elizabeth'. Light pink flowers with pleasant vanilla fragrance; new growth is bronze but matures green.

'Freda'. Deep rose-pink flowers and deeply bronzed foliage.

var. *grandiflora*. Large flowers of pure white.

'Marjorie'. Semi-double flowers of creamy pink; best in cool sun.

var. *rubens* 'Pink Perfection'. Large flowers of soft pink; bronzed foliage.

var. *rubens* 'Tetrarose'. Large flowers of deep mauve-pink with heavy substance; bronze new foliage matures bronze-purple.

Early-blooming large-flowered hybrids (Pruning Group B)

The largest, showiest flowers are combined with compact vines in this group, making them ideal for smaller trellises, covering posts, displaying on freestanding obelisks or teepees, or growing in containers. Smaller-flowered hybrids can be combined with roses or grown through small shrubs, but the very largest flowers are best displayed (flaunted?) on their own. Most tolerate light shade well; pastel shades in particular hold their color better with at least afternoon shade. On the down side, this is the group most susceptible to clematis wilt, so very careful handling is mandatory.

Flowers of Group B hybrids bloom mainly on old wood in May and June, with a second flush of slightly smaller flowers blooming on the current season's growth in September. Double-flowered varieties are double only on old wood, that is, in spring; September flowers that bloom on new wood are single.

To prune Group B hybrids, remove dead and weak stems in early spring, just as the leaf buds begin to swell, and give the whole vine a light pruning for shape. Cut each stem separately, varying the lengths for a more natural look.

Some Group B clematis bloom on both old and new wood, with at least a few flowers appearing continuously all summer. For pruning purposes, these May-to-September bloomers can be treated as either Group B or Group C.

Unless stated otherwise, the following selections—a few from among hundreds—bloom in May, June, and September on vines 6–9 ft. (1.8–2.7 m) in length and are hardy in Zones 4 to 9. "Large" flowers are 6–8 in. (15–20 cm) in diameter; "very large" flowers reach 7–9 in. (18–23 cm). All are smaller in September.

Clematis 'Lasurstern'

'Alice Fisk'. Very large full-petalled flowers of light purplish blue on compact vine.

'Asao'. Large flowers of deep rosy pink with showy yellow stamens; compact vine.

'Blue Ravine'. Immense flowers with blue-mauve pointed tepals can reach 10 in. (25 cm) in diameter. Free-flowering and vigorous; best in sun. Introduced through the Plant Introduction Scheme of the Botanical Garden of the University of British Columbia (PISBG).

'Daniel Deronda'. Very large flowers of deep purple-blue with a few white edges are semi-double in May and June, single in September. Showy seedheads have unusual form.

'Doctor Ruppel'. Large flowers of rosy red with deeper red bar; vigorous and showy.

'General Sikorski'. Enormous mauve flowers with showy white stamens can reach 8–10 in. (20–25 cm) in June; flowering continues until September but size diminishes. Vigorous vine can be pruned as Group B or Group C.

'Haku-okan'. Also written 'Haku Ookan'; Japanese name means "white royal crown." Large flowers of rich, deep violet-purple with prominent pure white stamens are double in May and June, single in September.

'Lasurstern' (Azure Star). Very large mauve-blue flowers have wide, overlapping tepals with wavy edges; showy stamens are creamy white. Vigorous and free-flowering; seedheads are large and attractive.

'Marie Boisselot'. Large open-faced flowers have wide, rounded, pure white tepals and white stamens. Flowers are held almost horizontally; best sited at or below eye level. Blooms June to September, sometimes as late as November. Can be pruned as Group C.

'Nelly Moser'. Introduced in France in 1897 and still the most popular Group B clematis; very reliable and adaptable. Very large flowers of pale pink with deeper pink bars are free-flowering; seedheads are large and attractive. Best in light shade or northern exposure; color fades quickly in full sun. Excellent performer in our climate.

'Snow Queen'. New Zealand introduction. Large rounded tepals are white with a hint of light blue; showy stamens are tipped dark red.

'Vyvyan Pennell'. Large, fully double, very frilly flowers of rosy purple-mauve in May and June; one flower floating in a bowl is a sight to behold. Single flowers in September are light violet. Best in cool sun. Young plants are prone to clematis wilt; handle very carefully when planting.

Late-blooming large-flowered hybrids
(Pruning Group C)

These large, vigorous vines bloom continuously and heavily from June to September or later, bearing profuse flowers that

Clematis 'Nelly Moser'

average 4–6 in. (10–15 cm) in diameter. Because of their vigor and flowering habit, members of this group are ideal for covering walls, rambling over fences or large arbors, scrambling through roses or large shrubs, or growing into trees.

Hybrids in this group are highly resistant to clematis wilt, but some have a slight susceptibility to powdery mildew, especially if the soil is dry in late summer. Most are best in sun and are quite heat-tolerant as long as they have a cool root run; they're also moderately drought tolerant when established. However, a couple of good soakings will keep them blooming longer.

Flowers of Group C hybrids are borne only on new wood (stems of the current season), so the vines need to be pruned hard every year in late winter to stimulate strong new growth. This is best done just as the new buds begin to swell, not while they're completely dormant. Midwinter pruning won't necessarily harm the plant, but it's very hard to tell whether or not a dormant stem will bear buds—or even if it's alive. (Nothing looks deader than a deciduous clematis vine in winter. Many a perfectly healthy specimen has been summarily dispatched, usually by a well-meaning but non-gardening spouse.)

On new plants, cut each stem back to two strong sets of leaf buds—one to grow and the other for insurance. Prune established vines to within 24 in. (60 cm) or so of the ground, but not into bare wood; leave at least two sets of leaf buds on each stem. Hard pruning every year guarantees flowers over the entire length of the new stems, some of which can reach 10–15 ft. (3–4.5 m) in a single season.

Left unpruned, Group C hybrids will still bloom, but only on new wood, which will begin growing where last year's growth ended, leaving long stretches of flowerless stems. This is not always a negative; shorter, spring-blooming Group A clematis (which can also be left unpruned) can be planted in front to hide the flowerless stems of the taller vine and extend the blooming season. Unpruned Group C hybrids are also excellent for covering sheds or large fences and for growing through tall trees, where they will send their flowers higher every year.

Unless stated otherwise, the following cultivars grow 8–12 ft. (2.4–3.6 m) annually and are hardy in Zones 3 to 9.

'Allanah'. New Zealand introduction with deep violet-red rounded tepals and showy white stamens with dark tips. Vigorous but compact vine is suitable for containers.

'Comtesse du Bouchard'. Popular classic with satiny rose-pink tepals and yellow stamens. Blooms June to August; excellent for combining with roses.

'Gipsy Queen'. Large velvety flowers of rich violet-purple with small white stamens; vigorous and free-flowering. Similar to 'Jackmanii Superba' and sometimes sold as such.

'Hagley Hybrid'. Nicely formed flowers of mauve-pink to shell pink with red-tipped stamens; pink color is purest in light shade. Free-flowering; compact vine is suitable for containers.

'Huldine'. Smallish but very abundant flowers are pearly white on insides and striped pale reddish purple on outsides. Blooms July to October; can grow to 20 ft. (6 m). Best in sun.

'Jackmanii'. The most popular clematis of all time; over 150 years old and still an excellent performer. Deep velvety-purple flowers bloom profusely and reliably on strong-growing, disease-resistant vines. Very adaptable, vigorous, and versatile. Blooms best in sun, especially in cool-summer areas. Height 12–20 ft. (3.6–6 m).

'Jan Pawel II'. Usually sold as 'John Paul II'. Creamy white flowers have rounded, overlapping tepals with faint pink bars. Blooms June to August.

'Kardynal Wyszynski'. Usually sold as 'Cardinal Wyszynski'. Deep carmine-red flowers with rounded tepals and carmine stamens. Color, vigor, growth habit, and disease resistance make it the best red-flowered clematis yet.

Late-blooming species and their cultivars
(Pruning Group C or A)

For pruning purposes, the mainly large and vigorous late-blooming species are included in Group C. However, many are most spectacular when left unpruned and allowed to scramble through trees, along fences, over arbors or sheds, or even used as groundcover. In this case, they can be classed with Group A, pruning only for repair and size control in early spring. Again, the cultivars listed are hybrids involving the species, unless otherwise noted.

Clematis orientalis (orange peel clematis). Native from Asia Minor to western China. Small, nodding, lantern-shaped yellow flowers have four leathery tepals that curl back on themselves, revealing reddish purple stamens. Blooms July to September;

attractive foliage is grayish green. Very drought tolerant. Blooms best in warm summers; may need the help of a southern exposure or warm wall in cool-summer subregions. Height 10–20 ft. (3–6 m); Zones 5 to 9.

Clematis tangutica (golden clematis). Native to northeastern Asia and Mongolia. Small, nodding, lantern-shaped yellow flowers are similar to (and often confused with) those of *C. orientalis*, but tepals do not curl back so strongly and foliage is bright green. Blooms late June to September. Very large, silky seedheads appear at same time as later flowers, making an attractive combination, and remain fluffy and showy far into winter. Very drought tolerant. Vigorous but not rampant; best left unpruned to grow into trees or cover large supports. Makes an excellent, weed-free, mounding groundcover; just cut back to a radius of about 4 ft. (1.2 m) in early spring. Height 15–20 ft. (4.5–6 m); Zones 3 to 9.

'Bill MacKenzie'. Hybrid with *Clematis orientalis*; often sold as a cultivar of one or the other. Large, bright yellow lantern-shaped flowers with thick tepals and purple stamens; foliage is bright green. Very free-flowering.

Clematis terniflora (syn. *C. maximowicziana*; sweet autumn clematis). Native to Japan. Tiny white hawthorn-scented flowers bloom in great abundance from late August to October, especially after a warm summer. Foliage is semi-evergreen. Vigorous

Clematis 'Jackmanii'

Clematis 'Kardynal Wyszynski' on weeping silver pear (*Pyrus salicifolia* 'Pendula')

Seedheads of *Clematis tangutica* in November

Clematis terniflora in October

WHICH PRUNING GROUP?

With many hundreds of different cultivars of complex parentage available, it's impossible to remember which pruning group each one belongs to. Most nursery-grown clematis come with a tag identifying them as belonging to Group A, B, or C—but what if the tag is missing, or you forget what it said, or you're not sure of the identity of a mature clematis? Not to worry. As Yogi Berra once said, you can observe a lot just by watching—in this case, watching it grow through an entire season. It won't do any clematis a bit of harm to go completely unpruned for a year.

If it blooms only between late March and June, it belongs to Group A (no pruning necessary except for repair and to control size). If it blooms in May and June and again in September, it belongs to Group B (moderate pruning and shaping in early spring). If it blooms continuously from June or July until early fall, it belongs to Group C (hard pruning in late winter). Alternatively, vigorous cultivars that bloom continuously all summer can be treated as Group A and left unpruned to cover large areas or grow into trees.

If planting two or more clematis together, make sure they belong to the same pruning group or at least have compatible pruning needs; sorting out which thoroughly tangled stems belong to which plant is impossible.

Overgrown or neglected clematis of any type can be invigorated by pruning hard (to about 24 in., 60 cm, but not into bare wood) in early spring. New growth will appear very quickly thanks to the vine's large, established root system; however, flowers may not appear until next season if it's a type that blooms on old wood only.

but nonrampant growth is very attractive when left unpruned to cover a long sunny fence or large arbor. Species has naturalized in eastern North America but does not self-seed in our climate. Height 20–25 ft. (6–7.5 m); Zones 5 to 9.

Clematis texensis. Native to Texas. Very atypical climbing species, being fully or partially herbaceous. Very small, nodding, pitcher-shaped flowers of bright red are showy against the glaucous foliage; distinctive leaves are shallowly lobed or rounded. Subject to powdery mildew, especially in late summer; must have sun and excellent air circulation in our climate. Needs neutral to slightly alkaline soil. Hybrids are easier to grow and more vigorous than the species. Height 8–12 ft. (2.4–3.6 m); Zones 5 to 9.

'Duchess of Albany'. Upright flowers of bright pink with darker pink bars are slightly larger than those of the species, resembling miniature tulips. Good container subject or cut flower.

'Pagoda'. Medium-sized nodding flowers of creamy mauve-pink with darker mauve-pink bars; flowers open slightly at tips, revealing greenish anthers. Vigorous; easiest of the texensis hybrids to grow.

Clematis viticella. Native to Italy and Turkey. Parent of many if not most late-blooming large-flowered hybrids. Species itself blooms June to September, bearing small, nodding mauve to purple flowers on vigorous stems, and is highly resistant to clematis wilt. Good drought tolerance, but subject to powdery mildew in our climate. Needs include a warm (not blazing hot) sunny site, good air circulation, and slightly acidic to slightly alkaline soil. Best known by its numerous outstanding selections and hybrids. Height 10–15 ft. (3–4.5 m); Zones 3 to 9.

'Abundance'. Small flowers of bright mauve-red are truly abundant, completely covering vines.

'Étoile Violette'. Very free-flowering and vigorous, with small, rounded, slightly nodding flowers of reddish purple with creamy stamens. A classic; good performer in our climate.

'Madame Julia Correvon'. Small but very showy flowers have four slightly twisted tepals of bright wine-red. Compact growth to 10 ft. (3 m).

'Minuet'. Tiny but abundant white flowers have broad reddish purple margins and veining; very showy.

'Polish Spirit'. Medium-sized flowers have six tepals of intense deep purple-blue with dark stamens. Usually classed with Group C hybrids, but *Clematis viticella* influence is strong.

HUMULUS LUPULUS (HOP)

Origin: Southern Europe to western Asia

Hardiness zones: 4 to 9

Size: To 15–25 ft. (4.5–7.5 m) annually

Blooming season: August and September

Exposure: Full sun to light shade

Soil preference: Rich, heavy, moisture-retentive but well drained

Water needs: Moderate

Maintenance needs: Moderate

Subregions best suited: All; ideal in Willamette

Possible problems: Spider mites, powdery mildew

Herbaceous. Hop vines have a natural affinity for the Pacific Northwest. A few generations ago, hops were a major agricultural crop in the Willamette Valley and required a great numbers of pickers, many of whom were women. Although not nearly as labor-intensive today, hops—the papery, feather-light fruits of the hop vine used to flavor beer—are still very important commercially. Between Washington (by far the largest hop producer in the United States, although the main growing area is in the Yakima Valley east of the Cascades) and Oregon, over 75 million pounds (34 million kilograms) of hops are produced annually.

It's no wonder this European native does so well here. It likes rich, heavy soil and excels in temperate climates where spring is abundantly moist but September is warm and dry for harvesting. In these conditions, a hop vine can easily grow 25–30 ft. (7.5–9 m) in one season. (The *lupulus* part of its name refers to its wolf-like rapacity.) Understandably, new plants need lots of water in their first year of growth, but in our cooler subregions at least, established plants can rely on abundant spring rainfall to carry them through summer. In our warmer, drier subregions, some summer water is advisable; plants will survive but leaf edges may burn, spoiling their looks. Adequate water also lessens the likelihood of spider mite damage and powdery mildew in late summer.

Although the vine is totally herbaceous, leaving not even a bare framework in winter, hop vines are a handsome and easy solution for adding summer privacy or summer screening of large ugly objects such as sheds or stumps. We also have the option of growing the vine on a fence, large trellis, or rustic teepee, where its handsome lobed leaves and attractive late-summer hops can be admired at close range.

Old vines should be cut to the ground when they start withering in fall, but this is just for cleanup and to make sure next year's new shoots do not get hopelessly tangled in the remains of last year's stems. There is no danger of invasiveness; although new shoots appear every spring, neither they nor the roots creep or travel underground. There is also no danger of self-sown seedlings, since both male and female vines are required for seeds; only female vines bear hops and only female vines are sold as ornamentals.

Humulus lupulus

Hop vines sold in nurseries in early spring appear to be the ultimate hoax: no growth at all is visible in the labelled pots. However, they do contain a vertical section of root, planted thick end up. Shoots will not appear until late April or May, but will then grow with unbelievable speed. New shoots need just a bit of training to fill out a space well; most want to grow straight up

'Aureus' (golden hop). Very decorative leaves and hops are a soft golden color. Not as rampant as species; needs good light but protection from hot sun.

HYDRANGEA ANOMALA SUBSP. *PETIOLARIS* (CLIMBING HYDRANGEA)

Origin: Japan, Korea

Hardiness zones: 4 to 9

Size: To 65 ft. (20 m)

Blooming period: late June, July

Exposure: Shade to cool sun

Soil preference: Lean, cool; moisture-retentive but well drained

Water needs: Moderately drought tolerant when established

Maintenance needs: Low

Subregions best suited: All

Possible problems: None serious

Deciduous. This trouble-free, adaptable vine is excellent for climbing large, rough-barked trees, training on a fence or pillar, or covering large north- or east-facing walls—as long as they will never need painting. Aerial rootlets are self-clinging, like ivy, making unpainted masonry walls the best surface. Without a support to climb on, it makes an attractive spreading mound.

Slow to establish (vine may need training until aerial roots are fully developed), but a truly impressive sight when mature. Leaves are small, deep green, and somewhat heart-shaped; the loosely formed white lacecap flowers are 6–10 in. (15–30 cm) in diameter. Little care is needed; once established it will even tolerate poor, dry soil. No pruning is necessary other than to control size.

Related species
Schizophragma hydrangeoides (Japanese climbing hydrangea) looks very similar but has coarsely toothed leaves and slightly smaller flowerheads. The petals of 'Roseum' are tinged pink.

A similar vine of note is *Schizophragma integrifolium*. Hardy in Zones 7 to 9, this smooth-leaved native of China has the same self-clinging habit as *Hydrangea anomala* subsp. *petiolaris* but is much less vigorous, reaching only 20 ft. (6 m). It needs moist, humus-rich soil in sun or shade and is more tolerant of heat. Lacecap flowers are fewer but larger; the very showy, teardrop-shaped white sterile flowers surrounding the small fertile flowers can reach 3.5 in. (9 cm) in length.

PASSIFLORA CAERULEA (BLUE PASSION FLOWER)

Origin: Southern Brazil, Argentina

Hardiness zones: 7b to 9

Size: To 10 ft. (3 m) high and wide annually; more in warm-summer areas

Blooming season: July to hard frost

Exposure: Full sun

Soil preference: Well drained; reasonably fertile but not too rich

Water needs: Moderate

Maintenance needs: Low to moderate

Subregions best suited: All, but needs winter protection in colder areas

Possible problems: None serious

Evergreen or semi-evergreen; deciduous in colder winters. No one can call blue passion flower beautiful—its flowers look uncomfortably like plastic dollar-store decorations—but the sheer improbability of this 100 percent natural, non-hybrid species makes it fascinating. Almost as remarkable is the fact that this subtropical native is quite at home in the Pacific Northwest.

Hydrangea anomala subsp. *petiolaris*

Passiflora caerulea. Photo by Judy Newton

Even if cold winters cut down its normally evergreen top growth, established plants send out vigorous new flowering shoots from the roots the following spring.

In fact, regular hard pruning in early spring is a good idea even if the stems do not die back over winter. In hot-summer, mild-winter climates, this vine's vigorous habit is rampant to the point of invasiveness. However, in our relatively cool summers, established plants grow just fast enough in one season to fill a trellis, decorate a porch column, or even be grown in a large tub that can be moved to a sheltered site in winter if necessary. Wherever it's planted, some kind of support is needed for the wispy tendrils to cling to.

The sunniest site possible is advisable in our coolest-summer subregions; although high heat is not necessary, bright light is. Good drainage is (as usual) essential, especially in winter, but the soil should be kept evenly moist—not soggy—through the growing season. Slightly acidic soil suits it well, although it is not fussy. In normally fertile garden soil it needs no additional fertilizing; in containers, excess nitrogen should be avoided to prevent rampant growth at the expense of flowers.

The large lobed leaves and delicate tendrils of blue passion flower are attractive in themselves, but of course it is the large, slightly fragrant flowers that make it popular. These consist of ten ivory-white tepals (five petals and five sepals) topped by a ring-shaped corona of showy filaments—startling blue at the tips, white in the middle, and purple at the base—crowned by five stamens and an ovary bearing three conspicuous stigmas. The flowers were given their name by devout Spanish priests in colonial South America, who saw in them symbols of the passion or crucifixion of Christ: three nails, five wounds, a crown of thorns, ten faithful apostles (minus Judas and Simon Peter), and so on.

Individual flowers, which are attractive to butterflies and bees, live for only a couple of days. However, fat balloon-like buds, decorative in themselves, open almost daily from mid-summer through September or even October to give a continuous show. In warm summers, decorative yellow-orange fruits the size and shape of small eggs follow. These are edible but bland; true passion fruit belongs to the tender species *Passiflora edulis*.

GROUNDCOVERS

Strictly speaking, a groundcover can be any low-growing, reasonably dense plant that covers the ground, whether it's a perennial, ornamental grass, spreading shrub, rose, vine, or conifer—or even a bulb, such as *Cyclamen hederifolium*. However, what gardeners usually mean by groundcover is a low-growing, preferably evergreen perennial that spreads and knits together by itself, forming a maintenance-free, drought-tolerant, weed-smothering carpet that can fend for itself beneath taller plants while providing its own color, texture, and beauty.

As with vines, this is where it can get hard to draw the line between vigorous growth, aggressively spreading habit, and invasiveness. For very small shaded areas, best bets for our climate are low-growing perennials with definite (or at least stated)

CAUTION: PLANTS SPREADING

Tough situations call for tough plants, and sometimes one of the more aggressive groundcovers is just the thing for a very difficult site where nothing else will grow, such as very poor, dry soil in the shade of a surface-rooting tree, at the base of an established cedar hedge, or on large slopes. However, extreme caution is advised in their use.

Confine securely on all sides

Aegopodium podagraria 'Variegatum' (variegated goutweed)

Convallaria majalis (lily-of-the-valley). Useful in large woodland settings.

Houttuynia cordata (chameleon plant)

Hypericum calycinum (St. John's wort)

Vinca minor (periwinkle). 'Argenteovariegata' is not as aggressive; neither is *V. major*.

Do not plant (highly invasive)

Aegopodium podagraria (green-leaved goutweed)

Hedera helix (English ivy). Species is noxious in Oregon and Washington; check cultivar names locally.

Lamium galeobdolon (yellow archangel). 'Hermann's Pride', a non-invasive cultivar, is acceptable.

Sasa veitchii (Veitch's bamboo)

limits to their width, such as *Bergenia*, *Epimedium*, or *Primula*. Alpines such as *Aubrieta* or *Lithodora* make excellent small-scale groundcover in sunny sites, since they have a naturally spreading habit. For a few more useful and well-behaved options, see Chapter 9's listings of alpine campanulas and creeping/groundcover geraniums.

For larger spaces, plants classed as groundcover are more useful, since they have the necessary vigor and creeping habit to fill in quickly. Well-mannered choices for partial shade include carpet bugle (*Ajuga reptans*), Japanese spurge (*Pachysandra terminalis*), or wintergreen (*Gaultheria procumbens*); good choices for sunnier areas are bearberry or kinnikinnick, sedums, or thymes.

The few groundcovers we have profiled here are all vigorous but definitely non-invasive; all perform beautifully in our climate. Many others just don't know where to stop and can become real nuisances (see sidebar).

Geranium macrorrhizum

GERANIUM MACRORRHIZUM (BIGROOT GERANIUM)

Origin: Balkan region and southeastern Alps

Hardiness zones: 3 to 9

Size: 15 in. × 30 in. (38 cm × 75 cm); creeping habit

Blooming season: May

Exposure: Cool sun to full shade; partial shade ideal

Soil preference: Any, as long as well drained

Water needs: Drought tolerant when established

Maintenance needs: Low

Subregions best suited: All

Possible problems: None serious

Semi-evergreen. This amazingly tough, spreading, but non-invasive plant grows so densely and vigorously that weeds don't stand a chance against it. This alone would make it valuable groundcover, but it also thrives in dry shade, competes successfully with tree roots (even cedars), and never needs lifting or dividing. Its aromatic foliage has a subtle but arresting citrus/pine/mint fragrance, making it an excellent choice along semi-shady paths, where its distinctive fresh scent can be released by brushing against it frequently.

It's also beautiful in four seasons. In spring and summer, the slightly fuzzy, deeply divided seven-lobed leaves create an intricately textured pattern that invites a closer look. In fall, the leaves take on red, orange, and yellow highlights. In winter, frost outlines the smaller leaves that remain on the plants, defiant of any and all weather conditions, until spring. Small magenta-pink flowers in May are a bonus; although pretty enough, this is a foliage plant, and an outstanding one.

Although happiest in partial shade, bigroot geranium will take cool sun if conditions aren't too dry. It will also accept deep shade, but growth will be slightly looser. The only conditions it can't abide are intense or hot sun and humid heat. It may even sulk for a few days in May's usual sudden combination of high temperatures, strong sun, and high humidity, but it soon recovers.

Best in medium-scale settings, bigroot geranium is most effective where it can be seen (and smelled) up close, but it's a little too vigorous for edging. It excels in the shade of deciduous trees but should be kept away from small, delicate plants in the same area. Left alone, it will creep slowly to make a large patch, but any unwanted growth is easily pulled from the outer edges. These sections (or occasional self-seeded small plants) can be transplanted to other garden areas in fall or early spring.

'Album'. Near-white flowers with coral-pink centers; light green leaves.

'Czakor'. Large, very bright magenta-pink flowers; an improvement over the older 'Bevan's Variety'.

'Ingwersen's Variety'. Large flowers of clear bright pink.

LUZULA SYLVATICA (GREATER WOOD RUSH)

Origin: Europe

Hardiness zones: 4 to 9

Size: Foliage 12 in. (30 cm) in height, spreading wider

Blooming season: April to June

Exposure: Partial to medium shade

Soil preference: Heavy, rich; acidic

Water needs: Drought tolerant when established in shade; also thrives in damp soil

Maintenance needs: Low

Subregions best suited: All

Possible problems: None serious

Evergreen. Usually listed with grasses, but best use is as beautifully weed-proof groundcover, even in hard-to-garden-in areas of dry shade. Not as popular as the smaller related *Luzula nivea* (snowy wood rush), which has more esthetic appeal in nursery containers with its white flowers (good for cutting) and thread-like white hairs on leaf edges. But there is more than one reason *L. sylvatica* is called greater wood rush: although single specimens are not particularly impressive, their combined effect when massed as groundcover is extremely attractive.

Grass-like in appearance (wood rushes are related to both true rushes and true grasses), their ribbon-like, satiny foliage is loosely piled into pleasingly tousled tussocks. Plants set 12–16 in. (30–40 cm) apart in spring or fall will soon fill in, making a dense and totally weed-proof mat, but expanding clumps are never invasive; any not wanted are very easily pulled.

Clusters of tiny brown flowers held on slender, arching stems in spring are not showy individually, but add just-right complementary airiness and delicacy to broad ribbons of massed foliage. Self-seeds moderately. Seeds can be collected when ripe in late July and broadcast into other areas in September; if no seeding is wanted, flowers can be trimmed off before July.

Takes moist to damp sites, but is also perfectly drought tolerant in moisture-retentive soil in shade or cool morning sun. If old foliage looks tatty by late winter, cut it back before new

Luzula sylvatica with frost in December

Mahonia repens

Luzula sylvatica in April

growth begins. Best as small- to medium-scale groundcover; particularly effective under deciduous trees or large shrubs.

'Aurea'. Foliage yellow-green; best color in light shade or cool sun with adequate moisture. Zones 6 to 9.

'Marginata'. Leaves thinly edged with creamy white; elegant and refined. Grows and spreads more slowly; good mixer in woodland garden. Zones 6 to 9.

MAHONIA REPENS (CREEPING MAHONIA)

Origin: Northwestern North America

Hardiness zones: 3 to 9

Size: Variable; average 12–18 in. × 24 in. (30–45 cm × 60 cm), creeping wider

Blooming season: March and April

Exposure: Full sun to full shade

Soil preference: Any, as long as well drained

Water needs: Very drought tolerant when established

Maintenance needs: Low

Subregions best suited: All

Possible problems: None serious

Evergreen. Resembles Oregon grape (*Mahonia aquifolium*) with cheerful yellow flowers in March, edible blue berries in summer, and lustrous compound leaves with holly-like spines, but growth is much lower and habit much more strongly creeping. New growth is copper-colored; a few leaves turn bright red in fall, especially in full sun.

Seedlings are extremely variable. Some have rounded, barely notched leaves while others are narrow and spiny; some have many small leaves while others have fewer but larger ones; some are shaped like a miniature shrub while others are ground-hugging spreaders. None are invasive. All are very adaptable, but growth is more compact and flowers and berries more prolific in at least partial sun.

Being native to the eastern side of the Cascades, creeping mahonia will take any amount of drought once established. Iron-clad constitution enables it to survive almost any conditions, including total neglect, but performance is even better with reasonable care. If growth becomes rangy, shear back to desired height right after blooming.

Although not overly dense, weed suppression is excellent, perhaps due to the secretion of some substance that inhibits weed growth. Best as medium- to large-scale groundcover; excellent for stabilizing banks in sun or shade.

Easily propagated by fresh-sown seed, although only about half the seeds planted will sprout. However, since seedlings are so variable, cuttings are preferable for massed plantings. Rooted sections from the outside edges of plants can also be separated and replanted in fall.

'Rotundifolia'. Selected tall form with nearly round leaves; very few spines.

RUBUS ROLFEI (SYNS. R. CALYCINOIDES, R. PENTALOBUS; TAIWAN CREEPER)

Origin: Taiwan

Hardiness zones: 7 to 9

Size: 6–12 in. (15–30 cm) in height; spread indefinite

Blooming season: June

Exposure: Full shade to cool sun

Soil preference: Average fertility, heavy, moderately acidic; well drained

Water needs: Very drought tolerant when established

Maintenance needs: Low

Subregions best suited: All

Possible problems: None serious

Evergreen or semi-evergreen. Low-growing creeping stems bear five-lobed, leathery dark green leaves (whitish on undersides) with unusual but attractive rough texture. This easy-care plant adapts to Pacific Northwest gardens as effortlessly as do other, more familiar *Rubus* species such as raspberry, blackberry, salmonberry, and thimbleberry. Stems and leaves have small rough hairs characteristic of the genus but are not prickly. Pretty white flowers in June are partially hidden by foliage; these are followed by edible, bright orange berries resembling small blackberries. Flavor is pleasant and sweet, but birds usually get to them first.

Best in partial to full shade; tolerates full sun in moisture-retentive soil but does not like high heat. Plants are hardy but can be defoliated in exposed areas by late or prolonged frosts, so shelter of overhanging branches of trees or shrubs in winter is advisable. Invaluable in the dry shade under trees; once established, never needs watering.

Stems creep slowly, rooting as they go, but cannot be considered invasive, since any overly ambitious stems are easily cut back before they take root. Growth is sparse for the first few years but eventually becomes dense, effectively smothering all but the most persistent perennial weeds. Established plantings can be kept compact by cutting back hard every two or three years in early spring.

Rubus rolfei

Best as medium- to large-scale groundcover; good for controlling erosion on banks. Doesn't mind occasional foot traffic but cannot take being walked on regularly.

'Emerald Carpet'. Vigorous selection with larger leaves and faster growth, introduced through the Plant Introduction Scheme of the Botanical Garden of the University of British Columbia (PISBG).

VERONICA UMBROSA 'GEORGIA BLUE'

Origin: Caucasus

Hardiness zones: 6 to 9

Size: 8–10 in. × 12–16 in. (20–25 cm × 30–40 cm), spreading wider

Blooming season: March to late May; September

Exposure: Partial shade to cool sun

Soil preference: Moisture-retentive but well drained; not too rich

Water needs: Moderate

Maintenance needs: Low

Subregions best suited: Pacific Coast, Puget Sound, Georgia Basin/Puget Trough

Subregions not suited: None

Possible problems: None serious

Semi-evergreen. Earlier misidentified as a selection of *Veronica peduncularis* and often sold as such. Name refers not to the southern American state, but to the other Georgia, in the western Caucasus, where it was found by British plantsman Roy Lancaster in 1979. This absolute gem of a plant is perfectly at home in our mild, moist climate.

Small (0.5 in., 12 mm) flowers of true blue are not a surprise, since this is a veronica, but there the similarity ends. Unlike most of its relatives, 'Georgia Blue' is not the least bit invasive (lax stems do eventually root, but are easily controlled if desired). It does not self-seed, never needs deadheading, is impervious to mildew, and blooms so prolifically that the small, narrow, bronze-tinted leaves can hardly be seen.

Veronica umbrosa 'Georgia Blue'

Waldsteinia ternata

Flower shape and color are also unique. The rounded, four-petalled flowers with white eyes start out cornflower-blue and fade not to purple, as do most "blue" flowers, but to a pale bluish gray that remains attractive until the flowers drop off, which they do cleanly.

As with dandelions, flowering is triggered by cool but not cold daytime temperatures (50–60°F, 10–15°C) at any time of year, so a few flowers may bloom in mild spells even in January or February. Where daytime temperatures remain in this range most of the year, 'Georgia Blue' will flower continuously except in midwinter and midsummer. Flowering is best in full sun, but since it dislikes heat, partial shade is usually preferable, especially in hot-summer valleys. It will even flower (although more sparsely) in full shade, where it is reasonably drought tolerant on heavier soils.

Plants in full sun need summer watering, or they will show their discomfort by shriveling and turning brown or black. However, they recover amazingly quickly when adequate water is restored. They also dislike very cold temperatures and cold winter winds, but are hardy everywhere in the Pacific Northwest.

Because of its bright color, 'Georgia Blue' is best suited for small-scale groundcover or underplanting trees and shrubs. It also makes an excellent bulb companion, rose companion (especially white, pink, or yellow roses), or even rock garden plant. To propagate, transplant small sections from outside edges of plants directly into place in fall (preferably) or early spring.

WALDSTEINIA TERNATA (BARREN STRAWBERRY)

Origin: Northeastern Asia and Japan; central Europe

Hardiness zones: 4 to 9

Size: 4 in. (10 cm) in height; spread indefinite

Blooming season: April and May

Exposure: Partial shade to cool sun

Soil preference: Any, as long as well drained; sandy loam ideal

Water needs: Drought tolerant when established

Maintenance needs: Low

Subregions best suited: All

Possible problems: None serious

Evergreen. Dense, good-looking, weed-smothering, reliable, trouble-free, and far underused. Abundant potentilla-like flowers of bright yellow in early spring are attractive, but real value is in the strawberry-like foliage. Just on the olive side of green, it complements all other foliage colors while remaining handsome but unobtrusive year-round. Take occasional foot traffic.

Creeping but non-invasive stems never stray far, keeping foliage wonderfully dense, and grow quickly enough to fill in fairly large areas. Any unwanted growth is easily pulled or clipped back. Prefers cool conditions; best in partial shade, where it is reliably drought tolerant, but also performs well in cool sun if not too dry.

Since it does not set fruit or seed, and creeping stems do not root immediately, this plant is difficult to propagate for the container trade and is not always easy to find. However, small unrooted sections of stem planted in place in fall or early spring will usually take root if kept well watered, so a few small plants can eventually go a long way.

Excellent small- to medium-scale groundcover, especially in the dry shade under trees and shrubs. Mixes well with small spring bulbs and is especially companionable with *Anemone blanda*, since their blooming times and heights are similar.

Ornamental grasses in July, authors' garden. Clockwise from top right: *Miscanthus sinensis* 'Gracillimus', *M. s.* 'Morning Light', *Deschampsia cespitosa* 'Bronzeschleier' (with *Carex albula* in front), *Pennisetum alopecuroides* 'Hameln', *Calamagrostis* ×*acutiflora* 'Karl Foerster'.

ORNAMENTAL GRASSES

That our climate is ideal for growing grasses is obvious to anyone who has ever seen a Pacific Northwest lawn grow in April, or looked at a hayfield in June. Ornamental grasses are relative latecomers to the gardening scene here, as they are everywhere, but we have lost no time in embracing them enthusiastically for their unique contributions of texture, habit, flower type, fall and winter interest, and above all, movement. No plants are more kinetic than grasses as they respond to every nuance of wind, temperature, and humidity through the changing seasons.

Grasses are different from all other plants in other ways as well. In the first place, they're all invasive in their native habitats, either through prolific self-seeding or aggressively running roots—or both. By design, grasses are meant to colonize huge areas and create their own monocultures.

And it's a good thing they do, or we would have no wheat, rice, oats, rye, barley, corn, or other grains for our daily bread; and cattle, dairy cows, horses, sheep, migrating waterfowl, and many other animals would have precious little to eat. There would of course be no lawns, no meadows, no grasslands, no savannahs, no prairies, and no steppes.

272

TOO MUCH OF A GOOD THING

Prolific self-seeders (use at own risk)

Briza media (quaking grass)

Chasmanthium latifolium (northern sea oats)

Eragrostis species (love grass)

Festuca amethystina (big blue fescue)

Milium effusum (wood millet)

Pennisetum alopecuroides 'Moudry'

Pennisetum alopecuroides 'National Arboretum'

Aggressively running ornamental grasses (containerize or confine securely)

Bromus inermis 'Skinner's Gold'

Elymus species (wild rye)

Eriophorum species (cotton grass)

Imperata cylindrica. The popular red-bladed Japanese blood grass, *I. c.* 'Rubra', can spread freely in moist soil; reversion to the invasive green form may be possible.

Leymus species (blue lyme grass)

Miscanthus sacchariflorus (Amur silver grass)

Phalaris arundinacea var. *picta* (ribbon grass, gardener's garters). Green/white/pink variegated form 'Feesey' is much less aggressive but is still a spreader, especially in moist soil.

Spartina pectinata 'Aureomarginata' (variegated prairie cord grass)

Do not plant

Arundo donax (giant reed). Potentially noxious.

Cortaderia jubata (Jubata grass). Potentially noxious.

Hordeum jubatum (foxtail barley). Often used in dried arrangements; can self-seed and become a nuisance weed in grazing pastures.

Spartina species (cord grass). Invasive in wetlands; some species (but not *S. pectinata*) are noxious in Oregon and Washington.

This is one place where it pays—with appropriate precautions—to plant exotic species rather than naturally invasive native ones. For instance, pampas grass self-seeds rampantly in its native Argentina, and can self-seed to the nuisance stage in similar hot, dry climates such as southern California, but seeds don't have a chance to mature here in our shorter, much cooler summers—and if they did, they wouldn't survive our wet winters. Similarly, *Miscanthus sinensis* (Japanese silver grass) covers whole hillsides in Japan, where summers are hot and humid (both conditions are necessary for successful seed germination), but since our summers are dry as well as much cooler,

miscanthus cultivars—even early-flowering varieties—rarely if ever self-seed here.

Some grasses, such as *Deschampsia* or hair grass, do self-seed modestly on moist soil in our climate, but these are easily kept under control simply by not watering them in summer. (Alternatively, self-seeding may be a desirable trait for a difficult site such as a large bank.) Grasses with a moderately spreading or running habit can also be somewhat restrained by withholding summer water, since rhizomes spread most freely in moist soil. However, prolific self-seeders should be approached with extreme caution, and aggressively running grasses should always be held in maximum security, either by containerizing (well rings make terrific bold planters) or planting in between inescapable barriers such as sidewalks, pavement, and buildings.

Ornamental grasses are divided into two distinct groups: cool-season and warm-season. Cool-season types grow very rapidly in spring, flower in late spring or early summer, then more or less stop growing, even though most continue to look good. (A few go dormant in hot weather.) Warm-season types start slowly in spring, grow rapidly in hot weather (over 80°F, 27°C), and flower in late summer or early fall. Deciduous warm-season grasses often have attractive fall foliage.

In general, cool-season grasses are better suited to Pacific Northwest conditions, but two of our most spectacular successes, pampas grass and miscanthus, are warm-season types. Most warm-season grasses native to continental-climate prairies, though, are either unsuitable or underwhelming in the Pacific Northwest, except perhaps in well-watered sites in the Rogue or Willamette subregions.

All ornamental grasses are best planted or divided in early spring to early summer, just as they resume growth. This is an iron-clad rule for warm-season grasses, but cool-season evergreen grasses (including the grass-like carexes) can also be successfully planted or divided in September.

The selections that follow are among those most perfectly suited to Pacific Northwest conditions, with the fewest known problems and the lowest need for maintenance.

ARRHENATHERUM ELATIUS VAR. *BULBOSUM* 'VARIEGATUM' (VARIEGATED BULBOUS OAT GRASS)

Origin: Europe

Hardiness zones: 4 to 9

Size: Foliage to 12 in. (30 cm), flowers to 24 in. (60 cm)

Season of interest: Late winter to early summer; fall

Exposure: Cool sun to full shade

Soil preference: Average fertility; moisture-retentive but well drained

Water needs: Drought tolerant when established

Maintenance needs: Low to moderate

Subregions best suited: All

Possible problems: Rust

Arrhenatherum elatius var. *bulbosum* 'Variegatum' in June

Calamagrostis ×*acutiflora* 'Karl Foerster' in June

Cool-season; evergreen or semi-evergreen. This neat, white-variegated, shade-tolerant grass is perfect for Pacific Northwest conditions: it blooms only in cool temperatures, prefers dry summers with cool nights, and remains evergreen in mild winters. Near-white appearance is bright enough to light up shady corners but subtle enough to blend beautifully with perennials, shrubs, and spring-blooming bulbs. It also makes an outstanding low border.

Its one drawback is that it tends to "brown out" with rust by July, especially in full sun; clumps can look so wretched, the only recourse is to cut them back hard. Clumps in shade are less affected but can still look bedraggled by midsummer.

Fortunately, cut-back clumps with their swollen, bulb-like stems are attractive enough (or at least interesting) in themselves and will make up for temporary lack of foliage by putting on fresh new growth in September. New growth remains attractive through fall and winter and is most appreciated in late winter. Vigorous new growth begins as early as February, just in time to be a perfect foil for purple-flowered crocus.

Clumps are fast growing but not invasive. Divide every three or four years by pulling up or rubbing off surplus swollen stems in February or September.

CALAMAGROSTIS (REED GRASS)

Origin: Northern temperate regions

Hardiness zones: 4 to 9

Size: Varies

Season of interest: Spring to winter

Exposure: Full sun to light shade

Soil preference: Average to rich; moisture-retentive but well drained

Water needs: Drought tolerant when established

Maintenance needs: Low

Subregions best suited: All

Possible problems: Some species can be invasive

Cool-season; herbaceous. Most reed grasses (including Pacific Northwest natives) prefer moist to wet soil and tend to spread fairly aggressively; some species also self-seed a little too freely. Fortunately, forms most often cultivated are well behaved; the genus includes some of the most outstanding ornamental grasses ever developed.

Calamagrostis ×acutiflora 'Karl Foerster' in September

Calamagrostis ×acutiflora (feather reed grass). Hybrid of two Eurasian species, *C. epigejos* and *C. arundinacea*, which sometimes cross in the wild. Both parents have strongly running habits and can self-seed prolifically, but hybrid form does not run and very rarely sets viable seed. Like both parents, hybrid is tall, upright, clump-forming grower and tolerates heat well, even though technically a cool-season species.

'Karl Foerster'. Truly an all-season ornamental grass; named Perennial Plant of the Year for 2001 by the Perennial Plant Association and deservedly popular worldwide. Slowly expanding clumps are long-lived, seldom needing dividing, and are adaptable to all reasonable garden situations, including heavy clay. Needs little or no maintenance beyond cutting back old stalks in late winter. New growth is mounding, followed in June by tall flower stalks topped with large, feathery, pink-tinged flower plumes. Plumes turn golden tan by August and are held close to stems in upright, stiffly vertical bundles. Stems gradually fade to buff but remain upright and attractive through fall and winter, providing both visual and kinetic interest. (In our wilder windstorms, they do double duty as weathervanes and wind-speed indicators.) Foliage to 36 in. (90 cm), flowers to 6 ft. (1.8 m).

'Overdam'. Similar to 'Karl Foerster' but slightly smaller, with white-variegated foliage and more relaxed habit. Likes summers with low humidity and cool nights. Foliage to 30 in. (75 cm), flowers to 5 ft. (1.5 m).

Calamagrostis brachytricha (Korean feather grass). Clumping foliage is unremarkable, but large, feathery, rosy purple flower plumes are very showy. In use, more like a warm-season grass; flowers bloom in late summer. Needs a sunny spot in moisture-retentive soil but will accept partial shade in hot-summer valleys. Flowers fade to silvery white but remain open and feathery; attractive through winter. May self-seed on moist soil, but not aggressively. Foliage to 30 in. (75 cm), flowers to 4 ft. (1.2 m).

CAREX (SEDGE)

Origin: New Zealand, Japan, Europe, Asia, North America

Hardiness zones: Varies

Size: Varies

Season of interest: Spring to winter

Exposure: Cool sun to light shade

Soil preference: Average to rich, moderately acidic; moisture-retentive

Water needs: Varies

Maintenance needs: Low

Subregions best suited: All

Possible problems: None serious

Cool-season; evergreen, semi-evergreen, or herbaceous, depending on species. Grass-like plants (sedges are not true grasses, but related to them) grown for variously colored, variously textured, attractively mounding foliage rather than for flowers, which are inconspicuous. Most are native to moist to wet habitats and make good waterside subjects; many are also amazingly drought tolerant in our cool-summer conditions. Sedges are hardy, durable, adaptable, and absurdly easy to grow. Optional maintenance consists of cutting back old foliage of broader-leaved types in early spring; fine-textured "hair" sedges can be combed out with fingers in spring, but benefit from a hard clipping-back every five years or so.

Carex albula (frosty curls sedge). Evergreen. Native to New Zealand. Often sold as a cultivar or as *C. comans* 'Frosty Curls', but actually a true species, as occasional self-sown seedlings attest. Very long, finely textured, light silvery green foliage resembling blonde hair is stunning beside water (especially when draped over a bank), in raised containers, or just spilling languidly over the ground. Drought tolerant and adaptable, but best in light shade. 12 in. × 24 in. (30 cm × 60 cm). Zones 7 to 9.

Carex buchananii (leatherleaf sedge). Evergreen. Native to New Zealand. Fine coppery red foliage blending to reddish tan grows in upright, slightly vase-shaped habit. Tips of foliage

Carex albula

Carex buchananii

are attractively curled, especially in drier weather. Unusual but quite vibrant color (no more "dead" looking than the bark of healthy shrubs) is excellent for combining with winter-flowering heaths, accenting brightly colored summer perennials, mixing with other grasses, and in mixed planters. Drought tolerant. 30 in. × 24 in. (75 cm × 60 cm). Zones 6 to 9.

Carex comans (bronze hair sedge). Evergreen. Native to New Zealand. Hair-like texture and mounding form are very similar to *C. albula*, which looks great with it. Bronze-brown foliage is darker and less red than that of *C. buchananii*, but the two species are easily confused when young. Self-seeds moderately, but seedlings are easy to pull or scratch out. Very drought tolerant; sun or partial shade. 12 in. × 24 in. (30 cm × 60 cm). Zones 6 to 9.

Carex elata 'Aurea' (Bowles' golden sedge). Semi-evergreen. Native to moist sites in northern and eastern Europe. Narrow flattened leaves are truly golden in spring and early summer, with a few faint green variegations, but become yellow-green by late summer. Graceful fountain-shaped form is best in a very moist site, even in shallow water. Light shade protects foliage from burning, but leaves turn lime green in too much shade. Excellent on stream banks or beside pond in light shade, especially when foliage is fresh. 30 in. × 24 in. (75 cm × 60 cm). Zones 5 to 9.

Carex flagellifera (orange hair sedge). Evergreen. Native to New Zealand. Another bronze-colored sedge, distinguished by slightly wider, flattened leaf blades and larger, more vigorous mounding form. This bronze foliage has a definite orange tinge, especially in full sun. Easy and adaptable; drought tolerant. May self-seed a bit too enthusiastically on moist soil. 24 in. × 30 in. (60 cm × 75 cm). Zones 7 to 9.

Carex morrowii 'Ice Dance'. Evergreen. Native to Japan. Broad, flattened, leathery green leaves narrowly outlined in white grow in graceful, spreading clumps. Roots creep slowly, eventually making a patch, but are not invasive. Excellent small-scale groundcover in light shade, which it prefers. Drought tolerant

in heavy soil; very long-lived. 18 in. × 24 in. (45 cm × 60 cm). Zones 5 to 9.

Carex oshimensis 'Evergold'. Evergreen. Native to Japan. Narrow, flattened, leathery green leaves have broad yellow stripe in center; yellow becomes creamy white in cool shade, bright gold in sun. Prefers cool temperatures; foliage may burn in hot sun if soil is too dry. Highly ornamental and very popular for reliable year-round color that blends well with everything. Best in light shade; drought tolerant in heavy soil. Slow to establish, but very long-lived. 16 in. × 24 in. (40 cm × 60 cm). Zones 6 to 9.

Carex siderosticha 'Variegata'. Herbaceous. Native to Japan, Korea, and China. White-edged green leaves are unusually broad for a sedge, almost like a narrow-leaved hosta. Very attractive foliage is heavily tinged pink in spring and in cooler weather. Excellent non-invasive woodland groundcover; slowly creeping roots make dense mats. Needs moist, fertile, acidic soil in partial shade. Height 8 in. (20 cm); Zones 6 to 9.

Carex tenuiculmis 'Cappuccino'. Native to New Zealand. Graceful weeping form; narrow arching leaves of light brown with green and cinnamon tints hold color well in sun or shade. Drought tolerant. 12–16 in. × 24 in. (30–40 cm × 60 cm); Zones 7 to 9.

Carex morrowii 'Ice Dance'

Cortaderia selloana in September

Carex oshimensis 'Evergold'

CORTADERIA SELLOANA (PAMPAS GRASS)

Origin: Argentina, Chile, southern Brazil

Hardiness zones: 8 to 9; hardier when established

Size: To 10 ft. (3 m) high and wide, or more

Season of interest: Late summer to winter

Exposure: Full sun

Soil preference: Average to rich; well drained

Water needs: Very drought tolerant when established

Maintenance needs: Moderate

Subregions best suited: All

Possible problems: None serious

Warm-season; evergreen. Among the most familiar and best loved of all ornamental grasses. Pampas grass revels in our wet-winter, dry-summer climate; although it blooms best in warm to hot summers, it will grow just about anywhere in the Pacific Northwest except in shade or poorly drained soil. Plants are not terribly cold-hardy, but established clumps survive Big Freezes; winter losses are more often due to drowning than freezing. Planting in spring or early summer—not fall—gives its roots a chance to get established before winter.

Clumps are very long-lived (well over 50 years) and never need dividing—they just get bigger and bigger, bearing even more of their magnificent white plumes. (Plumes of most cultivars described as "pink" are disappointingly dull-colored and anemic.) Clumps do look better when cut back occasionally in early spring, although yearly pruning is not necessary.

Never burn clumps to renew them: it may start an out-of-control grass fire, and even if everything goes right, it leaves an unnecessarily ugly mess. Powered hedge trimmers or even hand-held loppers work just fine, but be sure to wear eye protection, long sleeves, and heavy leather gloves. Leaf edges are very sharp (*cortaderia* derives from the Spanish for "to cut") and can easily slice through skin.

'Monvin' (Sun Stripe). Bright yellow leaves with lime-green margins make a stunning all-year focal point. Needs a warm site, adequate soil moisture, and shelter from hot sun. Good in very large containers. To 7 ft. (2.1 m). Zones 8 to 9.

'Pumila' (dwarf pampas grass). Compact but very floriferous; mature plants can bear over 100 large, fluffy plumes. More cold-hardy than species. Height 4–6 ft. (1.2–1.8 m). Zones 6 to 9.

'Silver Comet'. White-variegated foliage is very attractive year-round; modest white flower plumes are a bonus. Best in warm site sheltered from cold winter winds. To 8 ft. (2.4 m). Zones 8 to 9; established clumps may be hardier.

DESCHAMPSIA CESPITOSA (TUFTED HAIR GRASS)

Origin: Temperate regions worldwide, including the Pacific Northwest

Hardiness zones: 4 to 9

Size: Foliage 12–24 in. (30–60 cm), flowers to 48 in. (120 cm)

Season of interest: Late spring to winter

Exposure: Cool sun to medium shade

Soil preference: Average to rich, heavy; moderately acidic

Water needs: Drought tolerant when established on heavy soil

Maintenance needs: Low

Subregions best suited: All

Possible problems: May self-seed in moist soil

Cool-season; evergreen. Epithet is sometimes spelled *caespitosa*. The rather coarse foliage of this clumping grass is nothing to write home about, but the incredibly delicate, shimmery, long-lasting flowers are outstanding. Silky, almost shiny flower stems practically obscure foliage in late spring, with unbelievable numbers of minuscule flowers opening in June. Flowers remain attractive well into winter, when frost or heavy dew outlines their delicacy.

Withholding summer water once plants are established keeps self-seeding to a minimum without compromising flower production. Clumps are long-lived and seldom need dividing; optional maintenance consists of cutting off any remaining old flower stems in early spring.

'Bronzeschleier' (Bronze Veil). Popular form with bronze-green flowers; one of the best performers in Pacific Northwest.

'Fairy's Joke'. Novelty form bearing live plantlets instead of seeds at tips of stems. Sometimes sold as *Deschampsia cespitosa* var. *vivipara*.

'Goldtau' (Gold Dew). Similar to 'Bronzeschleier' except that flowers open lemon yellow, fade to green. 'Goldgehänge' (Golden Pendant), 'Goldschleier' (Gold Veil), and 'Goldstaub' (Gold Dust) are similar.

'Northern Lights'. White-variegated foliage, strongly tinged pink in cooler conditions; bronze flowers on upright stems. Best in partial shade. Foliage to 10 in. (25 cm), flowers to 36 in. (90 cm).

HAKONECHLOA MACRA (HAKONE GRASS)

Origin: Japan

Hardiness zones: 5 to 9

Size: 16–30 in. (40–75 cm) in height; spreading wider

Season of interest: Spring to fall

Exposure: Cool sun to partial shade

Soil preference: Rich, moist but well drained; acidic

Water needs: Moderate to high

Maintenance needs: Low

Subregions best suited: Puget Sound, Pacific Coast, Georgia Basin/Puget Trough

Subregions not suited: None

Possible problems: None serious

Warm-season; herbaceous. One of the most beautiful of all grasses grown for foliage (flowers are insignificant); resembles a small, very graceful bamboo. Slow growing, arching, one-sided form is especially attractive near water; makes excellent container subject in a wooden half-barrel. Needs cool, moist conditions. Green-leaved species itself is robust and adaptable, with beautiful orange-copper fall foliage, but variegated forms are much more widely cultivated.

Plant in spring or early summer only (not in fall, when plants are approaching dormancy). Slow to establish but long-lived; seldom if ever needs division. Trim back any remaining old foliage just as new growth resumes in early spring.

'Albovariegata'. Vigorous white-variegated form to 36 in. (90 cm) in height, spreading wider. More sun-tolerant than 'Aureola'.

Deschampsia cespitosa 'Bronzeschleier' in May

Hakonechloa macra 'Aureola'

'All Gold'. Foliage bright, clear yellow without green variegation. Needs shelter from strong sun.

'Aureola'. Most popular and arguably the most beautiful form, with golden leaves variegated with thin green stripes. Yellow color is paler in cooler climates or partial shade, stronger in warmer conditions or cool sun. New growth and fall color is strongly tinged pink; fall color is especially beautiful as it slowly fades to buff.

HELICTOTRICHON SEMPERVIRENS (BLUE OAT GRASS)

Origin: Western Mediterranean

Hardiness zones: 4 to 9

Size: Foliage 24–30 in. (60–75 cm), flowers to 48 in. (120 cm)

Season of interest: Spring to winter

Exposure: Full sun

Soil preference: Well drained, especially in winter; average fertility

Water needs: Drought tolerant when established

Maintenance needs: Low

Subregions best suited: All

Possible problems: None serious

Cool-season; evergreen. Stiff, spiky-looking but not prickly blue foliage makes a stunning, geometrically perfect dome. Tan flowers in June, held on slender stems well above foliage, exactly echo its domed shape. A near-perfect fit for the Pacific Northwest, it grows best in climates with cool, moist springs and moderate but dry summers. Good winter drainage is essential.

Self-seeds modestly on moist soil, but seedlings are usually welcome as additional garden subjects. Flowerheads become very sticky soon after blooming and are best removed in midsummer. Divide every four or five years; rejuvenate in late winter by combing out old, tan leaves with fingers, as if grooming an Old English sheepdog whose coat is shedding.

Helictotrichon sempervirens in June

MISCANTHUS SINENSIS (JAPANESE SILVER GRASS)

Origin: Japan, Korea, China

Hardiness zones: 5–6 to 9

Size: Varies

Season of interest: Summer to winter

Exposure: Full sun to light shade

Soil preference: Average fertility; moisture-retentive

Water needs: Moderate

Maintenance needs: Moderate

Subregions best suited: Willamette, Rogue, Georgia Basin/ Puget Trough, Cascade Slopes/Outflow Valleys

Subregions not suited: None

Possible problems: Miscanthus mealybug

Warm-season; herbaceous. Among the most popular and showiest of all ornamental grasses, especially from late summer through late fall. Although a warm-season species that loves both heat and moisture, *Miscanthus sinensis* performs beautifully in our relatively cool but dry summers. In fact, our climate is ideal for enjoying its spectacular visual benefits without the

Miscanthus sinensis 'Adagio' in September

Miscanthus sinensis 'Hinjo' in July

Miscanthus sinensis 'Rotsilber' in August

attendant danger of self-seeding, as can happen in hotter, wetter summers than ours. On the down side, some late-blooming cultivars may bloom poorly (if at all) in cooler subregions. However, others bloom as early as July and can be enjoyed anywhere in the Pacific Northwest.

Established clumps on heavy, moisture-retentive soil can take our normal summer drought in stride, especially if there has been lots of rain between April and June, but no miscanthus will grow well on a dry, gravelly slope. Fertility is a different question: gravelly soil would probably be acceptable if it could be kept moist all summer. Miscanthus is not a heavy feeder; excess nitrogen should be avoided as it makes plants lax and floppy.

Although winter interest is considerable, most clumps start breaking up and scattering long leaves far and wide from December onward, necessitating garden-wide pick-up chores. Whether to leave plumes as long as possible or cut them early is a personal choice, but all stems should be cut to within 6 in. (15 cm) of the ground well before growth resumes in early spring. Loppers or powered hedge trimmers work well for this job.

Eventually, clumps die out in center and need dividing in late winter or early spring. This can involve major excavation for older, larger specimens, but the reward is at least a decade of renewed vigor and better flower production. Use a large serrated

knife or saw to divide clump into sections; discard the worn-out center and replant a vigorous outer section.

A great many miscanthus cultivars are available—probably too many, since so many closely resemble each other—but the best ones have a way of sorting themselves out over time. These are a few of them.

'Adagio'. Narrow foliage with silvery sheen and good yellow-tan fall color; white flower plumes open pinkish in August and are held well above foliage. Graceful, refined choice, especially in smaller gardens. Foliage to 4 ft. (1.2 m), flowers to 5 ft. (1.5 m).

'Blütenwunder' (Flower Wonder). Very showy, silvery pink flower plumes in late summer are held at varying heights—some very high—above medium-textured foliage; flowers fade to almond. Foliage to 4 ft. (1.2 m), flowers to 7 ft. (2.1 m).

var. *condensatus*. Native to coastal Japan and at higher elevations. Taller and more robust than species, with much broader leaves.

var. *condensatus* 'Cabaret'. White-variegated form with very broad white central stripe outlined with narrow green edges; any all-green stems should be removed. Foliage is tinted pink in cooler weather. Strong upright growth makes a knockout specimen in right location, but don't try to blend this one into the background. Sun or partial shade; needs a long, hot summer to

Miscanthus sinensis 'Rotsilber' in December

Miscanthus sinensis 'Silberfeder' in August

produce bronzy flowers by October. Foliage to 7 ft. (2.1 m), flowers to 8 ft. (2.4 m).

var. *condensatus* 'Cosmopolitan'. Similar to 'Cabaret' except variegation is the more familiar pattern of green leaves edged in white. White midrib typically found on miscanthus leaves helps create a markedly striped effect; some leaves have a series of narrow white variegations. Similar in effect and use to 'Variegatus', but leaves are twice as wide; plant is much larger. Foliage to 8 ft. (2.4 m), late-blooming bronzy flowers to 9 ft. (2.7 m).

'Gracillimus' (maiden grass). One of the oldest cultivars, still valued for its fine-textured foliage and upright, gently rounded form. Slender reddish flowers do not bloom until late September or October. May not bloom at all in cooler summers, but architectural form and good reddish fall color make it worth growing anyway. Foliage to 5 ft. (1.5 m), flowers to 6 ft. (1.8 m).

'Graziella'. Fine-textured, upright foliage turns bright copper-orange in fall. Silvery plumes in late August are held high above foliage, become white and very fluffy as they age. Foliage to 5 ft. (1.5 m), flowers to 7 ft. (2.1 m).

'Hinjo' (syn. 'Little Nicky'). Compact form of zebra grass, a form of miscanthus characterized by horizontal yellow banding on each leaf blade. More prominent banding, smaller size, and stronger, non-flopping upright habit are improvements over the original zebra grass, 'Zebrinus', and even over its more upright form 'Strictus' (porcupine grass). Copper-colored flowers in September are a bonus; zebra grasses are never floriferous. Foliage to 5 ft. (1.5 m), flowers to 6 ft. (1.8 m).

'Morning Light'. Variegated form of 'Gracillimus'; even more graceful and elegant. Bronze-red flower plumes appear very late in season; fall foliage is attractive blend of pink, green, white, purple, and tan. Foliage to 4 ft. (1.2 m), flowers to 5 ft. (1.5 m).

'Rotsilber' (Red Silver). Flower plumes open shiny candy-apple red in early August; slowly fade to pinkish silver, then fluffy white. Medium-textured, strong-growing foliage turns orange-red in fall. Foliage to 4 ft. (1.2 m), flowers to 5 ft. (1.5 m).

'Silberfeder' (Silver Feather). Robust, strong-growing form with broad, arching foliage; makes wide mound spreading to 8 ft. (2.4 m) or more. Shiny silver flower plumes open with slightest touch of pink in August; turn pure white and arch gracefully high above foliage. Foliage to 5 ft. (1.5 m), flowers to 7 ft. (2.1 m).

'Variegatus'. Older cultivar still proving its worth with strongly white-variegated, medium-textured foliage that turns pleasantly pink and orange in fall. Late-blooming coppery red flowers are nice contrast. Good in partial shade, although flowering will be diminished. Foliage to 5 ft. (1.5 m), flowers to 6 ft. (1.8 m).

Miscanthus sinensis 'Variegatus' in July

A PEST TO WATCH FOR

Although serious pests (or even trivial pests) of grasses are rare in the Pacific Northwest, it's probably only a matter of time before the miscanthus mealybug, *Miscanthiococcus miscanthi*, makes its appearance here. Native to Asia, this tiny (3/16 in., 5 mm) miscanthus-specific insect was found in the eastern United States in the 1980s and has since made its way to California via infested nursery stock.

Because they live under the lower leaf sheaths, miscanthus mealybugs go unnoticed until their numbers build up and damage is severe. Infested plants are not killed outright but are stunted and misshapen, with twisted flower plumes that open—if they open at all—within the foliage rather than above it. Lower stems may have a white powdery coating and/or may turn dark red where insects are feeding, especially by fall. At this point, pulling a lower leaf sheath away from the stem will reveal a telltale white, waxy substance.

Unfortunately, vigilant checking of new miscanthus plants by wholesalers, retailers, and home gardeners alike is the only way to prevent the spread of this destructive insect. No completely effective natural, chemical, or mechanical controls have yet been found, so infested plants must be dug up and discarded, preferably by burning. Because some insects may remain in the soil, do not plant another miscanthus in its place. (Other grasses should be safe.)

'Yaku-jima'. Catch-all name for all dwarf forms similar to those found on Japanese island of Yaku Jima, or Yakushima. Typical forms are 3–5 ft. (0.9–1.5 m) in height, including flowers, and have a fountain-like habit. Flower plumes are narrow and dainty; pleasingly prolific but not as showy as larger forms. Good dark red fall color; plants remain attractive well into winter.

MOLINIA CAERULEA (PURPLE MOOR GRASS)

Origin: Northern Europe to the Caucasus and Siberia

Hardiness zones: 4 to 9

Size: Varies

Season of interest: Spring to fall

Exposure: Cool sun to partial shade

Soil preference: Lean to average, acidic; moisture-retentive

Water needs: Moderate

Maintenance needs: Low

Subregions best suited: Puget Sound, Pacific Coast, Georgia Basin/Puget Trough

Subregions not suited: None

Possible problems: None serious

Cool-season; herbaceous. Mounding, clump-forming foliage is topped in summer by tan flowerheads on tall, slender stems that sway in every breeze, arch fountain-like in wet weather, and stand upright in dry weather. In fall, most forms turn golden yellow; upright stems create pillars of brightness. Stems break off naturally over winter, meaning little or no maintenance. Likes cool, moist summers but tolerates heat if soil is sufficiently moist. In hot-summer valleys, needs protection from afternoon sun. Established clumps are reasonably drought tolerant on heavy soil in partial shade. Selections of the type (subsp. *caerulea*) are best choice for most gardens, being compact, well-behaved plants.

subsp. *arundinacea*. Similar to subsp. *caerulea* but on much larger scale: foliage can reach 3 ft. (0.9 m); flowers 7 ft. (2.1 m) or more. Needs lots of room, but provides unmatched kinetic display as flower stems arch outward, then upward, then bend with the wind. Fall color is bright yellow with stems held in vertical bundle. Best in cool summers, but surprisingly adaptable, even tolerating alkaline soil. Self-seeding may be a problem on moist soil. Most popular form is 'Skyracer', with flowers exceptionally tall, to 8 ft. (2.4 m) or more; 'Transparent' and 'Windspiel' (Wind-play) are very similar, slightly smaller selections.

Molinia caerulea subsp. *caerulea* 'Variegata'

Pennisetum alopecuroides 'Hameln' in November

Pennisetum orientale in July

'Heidebraut' (Heath Bride). Graceful straw-blond flowering stems are held well above the foliage; fall color is pure gold. Foliage to 18 in. (45 cm), flowers to 36 in. (90 cm).

'Moorhexe' (Moor Witch). Deep, almost olive-green foliage in compact clumps; very dark flowers held on stiffly vertical stems. Fall color is brilliant yellow. Very adaptable, tolerating quite dry soil. Foliage to 18 in. (45 cm), flowers to 36 in. (90 cm).

'Variegata'. Older cultivar, but still one of the best yellow-variegated grasses. Foliage brightens up shady spots; purplish flowers on graceful stems move in the slightest breeze. Foliage to 18 in. (45 cm), flowers to 24 in. (60 cm).

PENNISETUM (FOUNTAIN GRASS)

Origin: Warm temperate regions and tropics worldwide

Hardiness zones: Varies

Size: Varies

Season of interest: Summer to winter

Exposure: Full sun to light shade

Soil preference: Average fertility; moisture-retentive but well drained

Water needs: Low to moderate

Maintenance needs: Low

Subregions best suited: All

Possible problems: Some cultivars self-seed prolifically

Warm-season; herbaceous. Aptly named, fountain grasses are characterized by arching foliage topped with long bottlebrush-like flowerheads on graceful arching stems. Flowers appear in midsummer and remain attractive through winter, especially when dew or frost sparkles on them. Fast growing clumps need dividing every three to five years; annual maintenance consists of cutting back old foliage in early spring. Loves sun, warm temperatures, and ample moisture, but most species are reasonably drought tolerant when established on heavy soils.

Pennisetum alopecuroides. Native to Japan and eastern Asia.

'Caudatum'. Near-white flowers are pleasing addition in perennial beds and borders and among mixed grasses. Self-seeds moderately. Foliage to 3 ft. (0.9 m), flowers to 4 ft. (1.2 m).

'Hameln'. Compact, reliable form popular for its sterile (no self-seeding) creamy white flowers, which bloom from July onward. Whole plant turns almond-tan by late fall; holds up well until late winter. Foliage to 18 in. (45 cm), flowers to 24 in. (60 cm). Zones 5 to 9.

Pennisetum setaceum 'Rubrum' in late September

Stipa tenuissima in September

STIPA TENUISSIMA (SYN. *NASSELLA TENUISSIMA*; MEXICAN FEATHER GRASS)

Origin: Mexico, New Mexico, Texas

Hardiness zones: 6 to 9

Size: To 24 in. (60 cm) tall; becoming pendulous

Season of interest: Spring to winter

Exposure: Full sun

Soil preference: Lean to average; well drained

Water needs: Very drought tolerant when established

Maintenance needs: Low

Subregions best suited: Olympic Rain Shadow, Cascade Slopes/ Outflow Valleys, Georgia Basin/Puget Trough

Subregions not suited: None

Possible problems: May self-seed in moist soil

Cool-season; evergreen. Very graceful, silky, fine-textured grass; especially beautiful when massed, with long, hair-like foliage billowing like waves. Foliage is light green in spring, turns the color of ripe wheat by midsummer, and remains attractive through winter. Long, slim, silvery flowerheads appear in June, becoming indistinguishable from foliage.

Can be invasive in hot, dry climates, but few seeds survive our wet winters. Best in sunny, dry, but cool summers; will go summer-dormant in high heat. Light shade is advisable in hot-summer valleys. Good on slopes, among rocks, on low walls, in containers. Seldom needs dividing. Trim back old foliage just before new growth resumes in early spring.

BAMBOOS

Although bamboos are also grasses (and very ornamental ones at that), there are major differences between them and all other ornamental grasses, especially in the cool-temperate Pacific Northwest climate.

Since bamboos are native mainly to subtropical and tropical regions in Japan, Korea, and China, they prefer warmer temperatures than ours in both summer and winter. Our relatively cool summers prevent them from growing as tall or as fast as they

'Little Bunny'. Dwarf seedling of 'Hameln' with cute little tufts of flowers; big hit with children. Foliage to 12 in. (30 cm), flowers to 16 in. (40 cm). 'Little Honey' is an even smaller variegated seedling of 'Little Bunny'; flowers barely reach 12 in. (30 cm). Both are slow growing; need good, moisture-retentive soil in full sun.

Pennisetum orientale. Native to Central Asia and northern India. Large, showy, pearly white flowerheads are pink-tinged in cooler weather; bloom from June to October. Although hardy to Zone 6, it requires full sun, a long hot summer, and moist soil with excellent winter drainage to be reliably perennial. Good choice in hot-summer valleys; worth growing as an annual elsewhere. Foliage to 12 in. (30 cm), flowers to 18 in. (45 cm). Zones 6 to 9.

Pennisetum setaceum 'Rubrum' (purple fountain grass). Native to tropical Africa and southwestern Asia; widely grown as a sun-loving annual. Relatively broad, burgundy-red foliage; graceful, arching, smoky pinkish purple flowerheads can be over 12 in. (30 cm) long. Blooms July to hard frost, with flowers gradually fading to tan. Well worth overwintering or replacing every year. Foliage to 4 ft. (1.2 m), flowers to 5 ft. (1.5 m). Zone 9.

Bambusa multiplex 'Golden Goddess'

Fargesia nitida

normally would, and our winters are at the low end of the scale of their cold-hardiness.

To look their best, bamboos need fertile, preferably acidic soil that's consistently moist but well drained (they will not grow in wet or boggy soil), along with consistently high humidity. Fertile, acidic soil is not in short supply here; we can also supply consistently moist soil and high humidity in spades for eight to ten months of the year. However, our dry summers create a serious water deficit for these very popular plants. Some species are moderately drought tolerant when well established, but most non-watered bamboos are visibly stressed by summer drought, with leaf edges curling downward and culms (the botanical term for all grass stems, including bamboo "canes") drooping sadly.

With adequate summer water, though, well-chosen bamboos can and do thrive in the Pacific Northwest. They even look very much at home here, probably because so many of our other well-suited garden plants are their natural compatriots, being native to Japan or China. Bamboos are especially comfortable in the year-round high humidity, very mild winters, and reasonably warm summers of the Puget Sound subregion.

All bamboos spread via underground rhizomes, but are divided into two groups according to how fast and how far they spread. Clumping types expand by slowly creeping rhizomes, with new shoots emerging very close to the clump; running types spread rapidly and in some cases very invasively by strong-running rhizomes, with new shoots emerging as much as several feet away.

In some ways, our less-than-ideal climate for bamboos works in our favor, as these heat- and moisture-lovers grow and spread more slowly in our cooler, drier summers. But this is false security. All bamboos take several years to become well established here, and it's easy to be lulled into thinking running types will pose no problem—until it's too late. Once established, running bamboos will do exactly what they're designed to do: run rampant.

Since eradicating unwanted bamboo shoots is never an easy task, all running-type bamboos should be securely confined right from the start, either by immovable boundaries, solid in-ground containers such as concrete well rings at least 24 in. (60 cm) in depth, or in equally secure above-ground containers. These need not be overly large; bamboos actually do best when slightly rootbound.

A few very attractive bamboos are so invasive they should not be planted at all. These included *Sasa palmata*, a semi-dwarf species with unusually long, broad, finger-like leaves, and the similar but even lower-growing *S. veitchii*, whose leaf margins turn light tan to white in fall, giving a very attractive variegated effect. *Sasaella ramosa* (syn. *Arundinaria vagans*) is another very low-growing, very attractively yellow-variegated species sometimes recommended as a groundcover. Don't be tempted. All three have extremely aggressive running habits and are dubious choices even for containers, since they outgrow them so quickly.

The bamboos listed here are a few of those best suited to our climate and most likely to be available. The heights given are not their maximums but indicate the most likely size to be achieved in Pacific Northwest conditions.

Many bamboos have been botanically reclassified in recent years—often several times over, and sometimes back again—so genus and species names can be misleading. To be very sure the plant you buy is the one you actually want, check with the grower or a reliable reference book.

Bambusa multiplex. Clumping habit. Moderate height and dense, leafy growth; good choice for privacy screening. Protect from cold winter winds. Zones 8 to 9.

'Alphonso-Karrii'. Usually sold as 'Alphonse Karr'. Medium-thick yellow culms variegated with thin, bright green stripes; new culms tinted pink. Needs full sun and good drainage. Height 8–10 ft. (2.4–3 m).

'Golden Goddess'. Slender, densely foliaged yellow-green culms arch gracefully; especially nice in containers. Height 6–8 ft. (1.8–2.4 m).

Fargesia (Chinese mountain bamboo). Clumping habit. Slender, arching culms in dense clumps; does not run, but wide-arching habit takes considerable space. Culms that grow in late summer remain leafless through winter, giving a semi-deciduous look, but become densely foliaged with slender new leaves in spring. One of the hardiest bamboos; can be completely flattened by wet snow but will spring back up again when snow melts. Prefers cool sun or light shade; evenly moist soil. Protect from hot sun and high winds. Zones 6 to 9.

Phyllostachys aurea in summer

Phyllostachys aurea in winter

Fargesia murielae (syns. *Arundinaria murielae*, *Sinarundinaria murielae*; umbrella bamboo). Slender yellow-green culms are very lax; mature, wide-arching clumps can exceed 12 ft. (3.6 m) in diameter. Introduced in 1913 by Ernest "Chinese" Wilson and named for his daughter Muriel. Height 6–8 ft. (1.8–2.4 m).

Fargesia nitida (syns. *Arundinaria nitida*, *Sinarundinaria nitida*; fountain bamboo). Similar to *F. murielae* but more upright in habit, arching at top like a sheaf of wheat; mature culms are dark purple to near black. Best in partial shade. For the record, this is the staple food of the now-rare giant panda in China. Several selections are available, all similar. Height 6–8 ft. (1.8–2.4 m).

Fargesia robusta 'Green Screen'. Newer, fast growing selection with deep green leaves; mature culms retain yellow sheaths. Clumping form, but leave lots of room: culms can arch to 12 ft. (4.2 m) in width. Good privacy screen. Height 15–18 ft. (4.6–5.5 m).

Phyllostachys. Running habit. Tall, graceful, easy-to-grow bamboos give classic Oriental feeling, but running habit must be strictly controlled. Zones 7 to 9.

Phyllostachys aurea (golden bamboo). Adaptability, robust health, and considerable drought tolerance make this the most widely planted bamboo in the Pacific Northwest. Yellow-tan culms are brightest in spring. Beautiful choice when controlled, but can become a nightmare (especially between neighbors) when uncontrolled. Height 8–10 ft. (2.4–3 m).

Phyllostachys nigra (black bamboo). Similar to *P. aurea* but slightly slower growing and slower to spread. Green culms turn black when mature; popular for Oriental-themed gardens. Shade tolerant. Height 8–10 ft. (2.4–3 m).

Pleioblastus variegatus (syn. *Arundinaria fortunei* 'Variegata'; dwarf whitestripe bamboo). Running habit. Low-growing, very slender green culms with green-and-white striped leaves look delicate and innocuous, but can quickly become invasive if allowed out of captivity. Very attractive in tubs or confined areas, but don't let it loose. Height 3 ft. (1 m). Zones 6 to 9.

Phyllostachys nigra

PART FOUR

COMMON PROBLEMS AND THEIR SOLUTIONS

Approximately two-thirds of all plant problems presented to nursery staff, master gardeners, and government services are caused not by diseases or insects, but by environmental factors or inappropriate cultural conditions. In addition, many cases of actual insect damage or disease are attributable to choosing plants unsuited to our climate, siting them inappropriately, and/or feeding or watering them inappropriately.

One of the main reasons for writing this book was to raise awareness of the unique gardening conditions created by the Pacific Northwest climate in general and by conditions in the different subregions in particular. Healthy plants are seldom seriously bothered by diseases or insects, and choosing plants suitable for a specific site is by far the most effective way to reduce or eliminate the use of pesticides, even organic ones.

Although most organic pesticides are much less harmful to humans, animals, and the environment than are chemical fungicides, insecticides, and herbicides, no substance meant to kill living things of any kind can be considered completely harmless or without unintended consequences. Just because a substance is natural does not mean it's safe to use; rotenone, for instance, is highly toxic to fish and hogs as well as to non-target insects and is no longer approved for use on certified organic crops. Prevention, good cultural practices, tolerance of minor or cosmetic damage, and mechanical controls such as physical barriers or hand-picking pests should always be the main priorities; pesticides of any kind should be used only as a last resort.

It is not our intention to describe every problem and situation that can possibly affect plants in the Pacific Northwest; these are just the most common and/or most potentially serious. Much more specific information can be found through gardening clubs, master gardener programs, County Extension Services (in British Columbia, the Ministry of Agriculture and Lands), and in books.

MORE SOLUTIONS FOR MORE PROBLEMS

The following Web sites provide a wealth of information on plant problems, including (but not limited to) cultural and non-toxic methods of pest prevention and control. In addition, the 526-page handbook *Sustainable Gardening: The Oregon-Washington Master Gardener Handbook* is available for sale through Oregon State University and Washington State University county extension offices.

An Online Guide to Plant Disease Control, Oregon State University Extension

http://plant-disease.ippc.orst.edu/

This site also has links to online versions of the current (yearly) *Pacific Northwest Insect Management Handbook* and the *Pacific Northwest Weed Management Handbook*.

Integrated Pest Management Manual for Home and Garden Pests in BC, Environmental Protection Division, Ministry of Environment, Government of British Columbia

http://www.env.gov.bc.ca/epd/ipm/docs/envirowe/default.htm

Washington State Pest Management Resource Service, Washington State Tri-Cities

http://wsprs.wsu.edu/

CHAPTER 13

General Problems

A doe and her fawn find a perennial border very tastefully designed

DEER

Nothing brings out stronger feelings—or more mixed ones—in the hearts of Pacific Northwesterners than deer. It's impossible not to appreciate the gentle beauty of these creatures of nature, which after all were here first. But it's also hard not to become apoplectic when they devour our carefully nurtured garden plants.

The only sure way to protect plants is with a continuous fence deer can't jump over, crawl under (their preferred method), or squeeze through. However, dealing with gates is awkward for people and vehicles, and fences of the necessary minimum height (7 ft., 2.1 m) may not be allowed locally. One compromise is to fence the backyard only, using the house as part of the barrier. Another is to purposely set aside a portion of your own property as a wildlife corridor, preferably as a joint project with neighbors.

Most oddball scent repellents claimed to be foolproof—bags of human hair, cakes of Irish Spring soap, lion manure from animal preserves—have limited success. One homemade repellent that is effective is a spray of one beaten egg in one gallon (four liters) of water, but this scent also tends to repel people. The spray also has to be reapplied after every rain, as do most commercial repellents.

The best option short of a continuous fence is to choose plants deer are less likely to relish. Many lists of supposedly deer-proof plants exist, but there's a catch: deer don't read them. So much depends on so many variables—the time of year, the availability of food and water elsewhere, the size and age of the plant, and even the experience and taste preferences of individual deer—that no plant can be declared totally and absolutely deer-proof. A plant that's bitten off and spit out is still destroyed. But it is possible to figure out what might make a plant unpalatable to most deer.

These intelligent animals instinctively avoid plants that are actually poisonous to them, such as daffodils, foxgloves (source of the drug digitalis), hellebores, daphnes, monkshood (*Aconitum*), and autumn crocus (*Colchicum autumnale*). But since most of these are also poisonous to humans—particularly small, curious ones—they can't be recommended for gardens where young children might play.

Native plants, contrary to popular belief, are not automatically deer-proof. (What have deer lived on since time immemorial?) Tender new growth of virtually all native species, including Pacific madrone (*Arbutus menziesii*) and western red cedar (*Thuja plicata*), is fair game. This makes cedar hedging a special problem, since deer absolutely love the two most popular non-native alternatives, Emerald and pyramidal cedars (*T. occidentalis* 'Smaragd' and *T. o.* 'Pyramidalis'). However, native hemlock is usually left alone, as is Leyland cypress (×*Cupressocyparis leylandii*), a cross between our native yellow cedar and a true cypress. Yews are unpredictable; they can be shunned in one area and stripped in another.

Once they're a certain size, spruce, pine, fir, and oak trees (both native and non-native) are usually ignored, but native and non-native maples, alders, crabapples, poplars, and willows are devoured at any age. Fortunately, all large shrubs and trees—even fruit trees—tend to become less palatable to deer as they mature. (The plants, not the deer.)

Although new plants in unfenced gardens need the protection of wire cages for several years, mature plants are able to survive deer even if regularly sampled. However, there is still the hazard of bucks rubbing the velvet off their horns on mature trees and shrubs, which can be nearly as damaging as browsing.

Thorns are no deterrent to browsing deer—roses are an all-time favorite—but leaf texture does play a role. Plants with tough, leathery leaves such as rhododendrons (but not deciduous azaleas), camellias, skimmia, holly, mahonia, boxwood, pieris, bearded iris, and yucca are not very appealing to deer.

Neither are plants with fuzzy-textured leaves, such as lamb's ears (*Stachys byzantina*), dusty miller, mullein, silver sage (*Salvia argentea*), rose campion (*Lychnis coronaria*), or leatherleaf viburnum (*Viburnum rhytidophyllum*). Nor are plants whose leaves contain very little water, such as junipers, butterfly bush (*Buddleja*), chrysanthemums, Shasta daisies, marguerites, yarrow (*Achillea*), smoke tree (*Cotinus*), heaths and heathers, and most ornamental grasses, including pampas grass. Deer also avoid plants with strongly scented foliage, such as lavenders, artemisias, alliums, and virtually all herbs. Any foliage that smells strongly of mint or lemon is usually shunned as well.

Emerald cedars (*Thuja occidentalis* 'Smaragd') killed by drought

Plants deer tend to leave alone for reasons best known to themselves include rock cress (*Arabis*), leopard's bane (*Doronicum*), euphorbias (the sap is an irritant, if not an outright poison), crocosmias, poppies, black-eyed Susans (*Rudbeckia*), dahlias, most ferns, and the annuals ageratum, cosmos, nicotiana, and zinnia.

DROUGHT

Drought is not always a complete negative. On the principle of what doesn't kill you makes you stronger, occasional drought can improve plant performance by forcing roots to delve deeper into the subsoil to find moisture. The result is a larger and stronger root system capable of supporting more top growth and enduring more drought next year. But it's up to the gardener to make sure prolonged drought (or drought combined with unusually high heat) does not indeed kill instead of strengthen, because even the survival of so-called drought-tolerant plants is not a given: drought tolerance must be grown.

There is no way around having to water new plantings regularly for the first full year; new root systems are just not capable of searching for water at the same time they're getting established. Regular, slightly less frequent but deeper soakings for the following two summers are also very important, especially for trees and shrubs. As with humans, the first three years of a plant's life have enormous effect on its future growth, stamina, and health. Given a good beginning (adequate fertilizer as well as adequate water), plants are much more likely to withstand normal summer drought later in life.

Even drought-tolerant plants that dislike summer watering, such as ceanothus or our native Pacific dogwood, need some summer water while getting established. In these cases, fewer but deeper soakings should be given starting the first summer; an organic mulch helps even out moisture between soakings. Water very early in the morning, or better yet in the evening, to keep the soil cool while wet; the risk of root rot is greatest in warm, wet soil. For water-shy species, allow the soil to dry out slightly between soakings, but not to the point where leaves droop. In the second summer, one or two soakings should see the plant through the season; in the third summer, water only if the plant shows signs of stress.

For all established plants, effective drought remedies are adding water, conserving existing moisture, or both. Adding water seems the best option at first glance, but due to sprinkling restrictions, limited well-water supply, poor water quality (high chlorine content, high alkalinity, salt water intrusion in deep wells), or simply the growing awareness of a global scarcity of water, this option is not always feasible.

Conserving moisture

Well-chosen, well-mulched established plants on organically amended soils should easily withstand normal summer drought in the Pacific Northwest. Well-chosen plants include those originating in places with low summer rainfall (especially important in the Rogue and Olympic Rain Shadow subregions), such as artemisias, candytuft, or lavender; those with naturally deep or extensive root systems, such as hollies, yews, or rugosa roses; and/or those requiring less-than-average moisture when they're appropriately sited, such as epimediums and carpet bugle (*Ajuga reptans*), which are drought tolerant in shade but not in full sun. Of course, this being the Pacific Northwest, plants must be chosen for their ability to withstand winter wetness as well—plants from truly arid regions are likely to drown in the first fall rainstorm.

Organically amended soils are those into which large quantities of bulk organic materials such as compost, fish compost (a commercial blend of composted bark and fish by-products), aged manure, peat moss, well-rotted sawdust (not fresh), shredded leaves, or other shredded plant materials have been well mixed. If using sawdust, Douglas fir or hemlock is best; avoid using red cedar or yellow cedar sawdust, which contain natural preservatives. Pine and alder sawdust use up considerable nitrogen as they break down and can end up robbing the soil of more benefits than they add.

These bulk amendments improve the moisture-holding capacity of both sandy and clay soils. Paradoxically, they also improve drainage by binding soil into a crumb-like texture containing many tiny air pockets. Don't skimp on bulk soil amendments—spread a layer 4–6 in. (10–15 cm) thick before tilling or spading in thoroughly.

Finally, "well-mulched" means a material—preferably organic—spread over the soil in such a way that it completely covers the roots of all plants in the area. (A small space is left around plant trunks to avoid causing bark decay.) More and deeper is not necessarily better; a depth of 2–3 in. (5–7.5 cm) is usually ideal. The very best mulch is a plant's own naturally shed leaves or needles, but since it may be 20 years or more before the yearly amount is adequate, introduced mulches are usually necessary. Bark mulch is the most popular and readily available, but make sure the bark is either Douglas fir or hemlock. As with sawdust, most other kinds have more drawbacks than benefits.

Other excellent organic mulching materials include homemade compost, fish compost, well-rotted manure, dry leaves, grass clippings (as long as they haven't been treated with weedkillers), and well-chipped branches of trees and shrubs. Do not use walnut or cedar branches; both contain natural growth inhibitors. Peat moss and sawdust, although good soil amendments, do not make good mulches. Both become impervious to water once they dry out, so any rain or irrigation water simply flows off their thatch-like surfaces instead of soaking in.

Non-organic mulches include stones, decorative chipped rock, and gravel. These can be attractive, but do not add food to the soil as they break down. It's also very hard to pull weeds in them without drawing soil to the surface.

As counterintuitive as it seems, non-invasive groundcovers and other low-growing plants are excellent living mulches. Far from robbing larger plants of soil moisture, they actually help conserve it. Their leaves shade the soil and keep roots cool, slowing the evaporation of moisture from the soil and reducing the plant's need for transpiration.

Extreme drought

The bad news is that all these moisture-conserving measures are effective only in our normal summer drought period—July and August—or, in a pinch, our extended-normal summer droughts, say from mid-June to late September. When summer drought follows a dry spring, no amount of water conservation is adequate: you can't conserve what isn't there. If dry summers follow dry springs year after year, as they have throughout the Pacific Northwest in recent years, even well-established native trees, 20 to 30 years old or more, can succumb to drought. Large, dead, native trees of many species are increasingly visible throughout the Pacific Northwest.

What this means for gardeners is that it's even more important to irrigate in April and May, if normal spring rains don't materialize, than it is to irrigate in summer. With adequate moisture in spring, while they're actively growing, most established plants are well able to handle drought in summer. (Adequate water in June also greatly improves the performance of summer bloomers such as hydrangeas, even if they get no extra water in July and August.) But if they're already stressed by the time summer arrives, no amount of catch-up watering can make up for their earlier deprivation. To sum up: in a dry spring, add water. Lots of it.

All of us have been conditioned to spare the hose until late June or July, so it takes some conscious effort to monitor the amount of actual rainfall (not just overcast or drizzly days) in spring. Use of a rain gauge is highly recommended. Normal rainfall for April in most parts of the Pacific Northwest is 0.75–1 in. (19–25 mm) per week; in May, 0.5–0.75 in. (12–19 mm) per week. Amounts are higher in the Pacific Coast subregion; in the Rogue and Olympic Rain Shadow subregions, where they're considerably less, watering of non-established plants is usually mandatory starting in April.

Late summer has also become problematic. It used to be a good idea to stop watering woody plants at the beginning of September to allow them to harden off their new growth before winter. But that was when at least some rain could be expected by late September or early October. Now, there's no telling when—or if—genuine fall rains will arrive. (In our area, one year in the early 1990s, it was December.) Late summer watering is now a judgment call. But if plant leaves are dull and drooping, or if the soil feels dry to the depth of your second finger joint, go ahead and water. In these conditions, no new growth is likely to be made anyway. When the soil is this dry, irrigation efforts are more of an ambulance service, simply keeping plants on life support until real rain arrives.

FROST POCKETS

Cold air behaves exactly like water. Being heavier than warm air, it sinks, always seeking the lowest level. It also flows downhill, fills up depressions, dams up behind barriers, and runs out drains. Frost pockets are literally pools of cold air that remain trapped in low-lying areas, much as rainwater remains trapped in puddles. The Puget Sound subregion, especially around Olympia, abounds in these frost-collecting shallow depressions.

To visualize frost pockets, imagine standing at the highest point of your property pouring out great quantities of thick, slow-moving syrup from a giant bucket. Where does the imaginary syrup flow, and how fast? This is the existing air drainage.

If the property is sloped, air drainage is good—provided there are no obstacles in the way. Buildings, solid fences, hedges, and large evergreen shrubs all obstruct the flow of cold air, forcing it to slow down as it seeks another route around the obstacle. The longer cold air lingers, the more damage it can cause, especially in spring when late frosts may damage emerging buds. Good air drainage is especially important for early-blooming fruit trees, which is why orchards are usually planted on slopes.

If neighboring properties (including those across the street) are higher, cold air will flow downhill from them—right into your garden. Streets, roads, and driveways are also excellent river-like conduits for cold air that can either flood a property with cold air or help drain it, depending on their orientation.

Solid fences or evergreen hedges at the lowest part of a garden cause cold air to pool up just like water behind a dam. However, this cold air can be drained through any openings allowing it to flow out, such as a driveway, wire gate, or series of smaller, spaced openings in the fence or hedge. Use imagination to "see" whether puddles of cold air remain trapped in corners.

A solid barrier such as an evergreen hedge planted on the high side of the property can sometimes prevent cold air from entering the garden, or at least help deflect the flow. Strategically placed outbuildings, fences, and evergreen shrubs can also help direct air flow toward natural drains; plants that require extra winter protection can be sited in the lee of these barriers. Deciduous trees and shrubs do not greatly affect air flow, so may be safely used wherever an evergreen plant might cause problems.

Very small natural depressions—cold air "puddles"—can be filled in to grade level, but larger ones can seldom be completely drained. Options for large depressions include planting only hardier, later-blooming plants; limiting the area to annuals and later-blooming perennials; or reserving that space for a lawn, gazebo, or other non-plant use.

LACK OF VIGOR AND GENERAL DECLINE

Poor siting

Inappropriate siting—planting water-lovers in dry soil, sun-lovers in shade, lime-lovers in acidic soil, or vice versa—is the most common cause of failure to thrive and general decline. Trees and shrubs planted close to busy roads can also go into

Spiraea japonica 'Little Princess' with heavy frost

Lack of vigor in a young *Chamaecyparis pisifera* 'Filifera'. Probable causes include too much shade, poor or compacted soil, and slight chlorosis from being planted next to a concrete sidewalk.

decline from continual exposure to road salt and/or motor vehicle exhaust fumes.

Lack of vigor in specimen trees and shrubs can often be attributed to planting them in lawns with grass up to their trunks. Grass outcompetes the specimen's roots for water and nutrients, and undetected damage from string trimmers (not to mention the use of chemical weedkillers on the lawn) can stunt or even kill trees or shrubs. Landscape specimens are healthiest, and best displayed, in large beds filled in with small shrubs, perennials, bulbs, and/or non-aggressive groundcovers.

Planting near a black walnut tree can also cause poor growth and decline, since the roots of these trees secrete juglone, a substance that inhibits the growth of many other plants. Birch, cotoneaster, crabapple, hydrangea, lilac, true lilies, mountain laurel, peony, pine, potentilla, privet, and yew are among the most susceptible; rhododendrons and azaleas are most sensitive of all and should not be planted within 50 ft. (15 m) of a black walnut.

Root girdling

Another cause of inexplicable decline in woody plants is root girdling, either from a misplaced small root that crosses a larger one or from roots that were forced to wrap around each other in their nursery containers. As these roots grow, they gradually strangle other roots (or even the trunk) and cut off the flow of water and nutrients. If such strangling roots are visible, they should be cut; roots should always be gently unwound and untangled before planting. Norway maples are especially subject to root girdling.

When buying a "multi-trunked" tree or shrub, be sure the trunks are indeed growing from the same rootstock and not from two or three plants jammed together. We once had to remove a large *Viburnum* ×*burkwoodii* because of continual unexplained dieback; when we dug it up we discovered three separate plants all strangling each other. The trunk of one, which was the thickness of a broom handle above ground, had been squeezed just below the soil to a mere fraction of an inch.

Winter-kill

Sudden death of plants in early spring may be due to winter-kill, which is not usually suspected if the plant flowers as usual and then collapses. However, early spring flowering is the result of stored energy and can happen even though the plant is in fact dead. (Think what happens when you turn off the faucet to a hose: water continues to come out for some time.) Since most winter losses in the Pacific Northwest are due to overly wet soil, not overly cold temperatures, winter-kill is also seldom suspected in the spring deaths of conifers and broadleaved evergreens, which do not wilt or turn brown until temperatures rise in April.

Propagation methods and longevity

As a rule, the faster and more productive the method of propagation, the less vigorous and shorter lived (in relation to its expected life span) the resulting plant is likely to be. The most popular cultivars, both recent and classic, are disproportionately affected by this problem, which has no easy answers. No single method of propagation—seed, division, cuttings, grafting, or tissue culturing—is best; all have merits and drawbacks.

Seed. Plants grown from seed have the longest possible natural life spans and are least likely to be affected by slowly declining vigor. Seed-grown annuals, of course, live for only one growing season, but seed-grown trees such as oaks and Japanese flowering cherries can live in good health for hundreds of years, and some seed-grown conifers such as redwoods and bristlecone pines can live for thousands of years.

However, seeds of woody ornamentals may be very slow to sprout, and flowering and fruiting are similarly delayed. Most seedling fruit trees will not bear for at least ten years; seedlings of *Wisteria sinensis* and many *Magnolia* species may not flower for 15 years or more. Choice is also limited: hybrids—by far the majority of garden plants—do not come true from seed, and seedlings of species can vary considerably in flower color, shape, and even size.

Division. Plants propagated by division, including named hybrids, can be expected to have the same vigor and life span of the original plant, since they are literally part of it: all divisions are clones (genetically identical to the parent plant) with exactly the same characteristics as the parent plant.

The main drawback of plant division is that this method is limited to perennials, groundcovers, bulbs, and other non-woody plants; those with a single stem cannot be divided. There is also a limit to how many divisions can be taken from a single plant, which can be a major problem for growers—especially when stock is limited, as it is with new introductions.

Cuttings. Most hybrid plants are propagated by cuttings (stem, leaf, or root) that naturally grow their own root systems, resulting in new plants that, like divisions, are clones of the parent plant. Cutting-grown plants flower much earlier than seedlings; wisterias and magnolias, for instance, may bloom at three years. However, life spans will not be as long as those of seedlings of the species. Like Dolly the sheep, the cloned plants are the same physical age as the parent plant, even though the parent has existed for a longer time.

The main drawback of cuttings is that in time (cuttings of cuttings of cuttings) the vigor, health, and other attributes that made the original hybrid worth cloning always tend to decline; they never improve. The more popular the cultivar, the more rapidly this happens. The Peace rose, the most popular rose of all time, has lost much of its vigor, most of its scent, and virtually all its disease resistance since its introduction in 1946. Italian prune plums are another victim of their own popularity; these once-vigorous and healthy trees are now very susceptible to black knot, a fungal disease. Cuttings can also pass on undetected viruses, which can cause unexplained plant decline and eventual death.

Grafts. Grafting of trees, shrubs, and roses greatly increases the availability of new hybrids, since it produces a saleable plant at least a year sooner than waiting for a cutting to grow its own roots. It also greatly speeds maturity: grafted fruit trees start bearing as early as their second year. Many hardwood trees and some conifers (notably spruces, firs, and pines) do not propagate

Rhododendrons (*Rhododendron* 'Kimbeth' is shown here) need acidic soil (low pH)

Mock orange (*Philadelphus*) prefers neutral or slightly alkaline soil (high pH)

well from cuttings, so their cultivars are almost always grafted. Plants such as hybrid witch hazels and some hybrid roses have naturally weak root systems of their own and perform much better when grafted onto more vigorous stock.

Unfortunately, grafting shortens plant life spans considerably. Although it initially speeds maturity, the graft itself tends to grow into a callous-like knot that affects the flow of water and nutrients to the top growth. Most grafted trees start to show signs of decline after about 30 years, as opposed to seedlings living in good health for hundreds of years. Grafted roses start to decline at about ten years, as opposed to thriving for possibly 100 years on their own roots.

Tissue culture. Propagation by tissue culture (also called micropropagation) can cause the most immediate and obvious problems with vigor and longevity. In this method, which has become widespread in the last couple of decades and is certain to become more so, plants can be reproduced from very small sections of plant tissue—sometimes only a few cells—grown in a test tube containing sterile nutrients and plant hormones. One advantage of this method is the ability to regenerate stock that has become infected with a virus; another is to make rare or hard-to-propagate plants such as orchids available to gardeners at reasonable prices.

Its main advantages, however, are incredible speed and volume. With this method, millions of clones of a single plant such as a brand-new hybrid can be grown in one year, as opposed to perhaps a score from cuttings or a mere handful from division. Virtually all "instant hit" new cultivars of daylilies, heucheras, hostas, pulmonarias, and other perennials—especially those showing rare or unusual features—are now propagated by tissue culture to meet the huge demand they generate.

Part of this demand is undoubtedly created by market-savvy plant promoters, but a very large part comes from gardeners' insatiable appetite for the new, the novel, and the trendy, which keeps plant breeders busy trying to gratify us. (This demand has already opened the door to never-before-seen genetically engineered ornamental plants such as blue carnations. Although tissue culturing involves propagation only and does not alter the genetic structure of the plant being propagated, the technologies of genetic engineering and tissue culturing are linked, and

the temptation for plant breeders to embrace genetic engineering is great.)

The downside of tissue-cultured plants is that they are often noticeably lacking in vigor when grown in garden conditions in the natural world, as opposed to the highly artificial environments in which they began their existence. When planted in real soil, some specimens—it's impossible to predict which ones—begin a relentless downward decline from the moment they're set into the earth. Others, apparently healthy, may die a sudden and premature death. Mountain laurels (*Kalmia latifolia*), which are almost always propagated by tissue culture because more conventional methods are not very successful, are notorious for sudden collapse, as are some tissue-cultured rhododendrons.

If tissue-cultured plants can be babied and coddled through their initial shock of adjustment to the natural world, something like normal vigor can eventually be restored. However, many gardeners who have had one bad experience with a tissue-cultured plant are unwilling to risk another, especially if the plant in question was highly desired and priced at a premium. For peace of mind in such cases, find out by what method a plant has been propagated before buying it.

pH NEEDS AND ADJUSTMENTS

Technically an indicator of hydrogen ion concentration, the abbreviation pH is commonly used by gardeners for convenience in expressing soil acidity or alkalinity. On the pH scale of 0 to 14, a value of 7.0 is neutral; lower values are increasingly

pH PREFERENCES

The examples given here are meant as a rough guide only. Most plants have a wide range of pH tolerance—which, considering the tenfold difference between whole-number pH values, is quite phenomenal. As long as plants with strong preferences for acidic or alkaline soils are accommodated (and obviously not planted too close together), there is no need to obsess about precise numbers.

Very strongly acidic (pH 4.0–4.5)

Blueberries and other *Vaccinium* species; cranberries

Strongly acidic (pH 4.5–5.5)

Azaleas (deciduous and evergreen), most native ferns, heaths and heathers, rhododendrons, potatoes, strawberries

Moderately acidic (pH 5.5–6.0)

Trees: Douglas fir, true firs, larch, pine, most spruces, most other conifers; flowering dogwood, holly, Japanese maple, magnolia, oak, stewartia, styrax, willow

Shrubs: Camellia, enkianthus, fothergilla, pernettya, pieris, witch hazel

Bulbs: Camas

Grasses: *Carex, Deschampsia, Molinia*

Small fruits and vegetables: Blackberry, raspberry, rhubarb

Slightly acidic (pH 6.0–6.5)

Trees: Birch, flowering cherry, flowering crabapple, most maples, mountain ash

Shrubs and vines: Roses; barberry, flowering currant, forsythia, spirea, most other shrubs; honeysuckle, hops, most other vines

Perennials and bulbs: Aubrieta, hardy geraniums, heuchera, most primulas, most other perennials; grape hyacinth, narcissus, and most other spring bulbs except tulips; most true lilies

Grasses: Most ornamental grasses and bamboos

Fruits, nuts, and vegetables: Apple, cherry, pear, peach, plum; corn, lettuce, peas, peppers, tomatoes, most other vegetables except those of the cabbage family

Slightly acidic to slightly alkaline (pH 6.5–7.2)

Trees: Ash, beech, blue spruce, hawthorn

Shrubs and vines: Boxwood, buddleja, deutzia, lavender, lilac, mock orange, rock rose, rosemary, weigela, juniper, yew; clematis, wisteria

Perennials and bulbs: Arabis, artemisia, aster, baby's breath (*Gypsophila* literally means "lime-loving"), campanula, catmint, delphinium, dianthus, gas plant (*Dictamnus albus*), hellebore, peony, pulsatilla, thrift, wallflower, many alpine plants; allium, bearded iris, tulip

Grasses: Lawns (any pH between 6.0 and 7.5 is acceptable)

Fruits and vegetables: Currant, gooseberry; asparagus, beet, Swiss chard, leek; all members of the cabbage family, including broccoli, Brussels sprouts, cabbage, cauliflower, collards, kale, kohlrabi, and most Chinese vegetables

---

acidic and higher values increasingly alkaline. Soils capable of supporting plant life seldom test below pH 4.0 or above pH 8.5, since at both these extremes essential nutrients in the soil are locked up and unavailable to plants.

The preferences of almost all plants can be accommodated between about pH 5.0 and pH 7.0. With the notable exception of acid-lovers such as rhododendrons, the vast majority of ornamental plants are happiest in slightly acidic soil measuring between about 6.0 and 6.5 on the pH scale. This may seem a very narrow range, but since this scale is logarithmic, like the Richter scale for earthquakes, pH 4.0 is ten times more acidic (or less alkaline) than pH 5.0, one hundred times more acidic than pH 6.0, and a mind-boggling one thousand times more acidic than pH 7.0.

In most parts of the Pacific Northwest, as in other climates with high rainfall, unamended soils are strongly acidic, about pH 4.5 to 5.5. This is partly because rain itself is slightly acidic, and partly because high rainfall leaches lime (various forms of calcium, an element that neutralizes acidity) from the soil. Where rainfall is lower, as in the Rogue and Olympic Rain Shadow subregions, the pH of raw land is slightly higher; in the very rainy Pacific Coast subregion, soils are even more strongly acidic.

However, soils containing the calcium-rich remains of clam or oyster shells, as in parts of the Puget Sound subregion and some waterfront properties on eastern Vancouver Island, can be near-neutral or even alkaline. Soils underlain by limestone, as on parts of northern Vancouver Island or on Texada Island in the Strait of Georgia (where limestone is quarried) can also be neutral or slightly alkaline. Deep drilled wells usually produce alkaline water, especially if drilled in shale; irrigating with such water also raises soil pH.

Liming

For those of us with strongly to moderately acidic soil, adding lime is a simple and effective way to raise the pH to the point preferred by most plants. (Since it is constantly being leached away, lime must be reapplied regularly in high rainfall areas.) Neutralizing acidic soil increases its fertility by making essential nutrients available to plants. It also improves soil texture and workability, encourages earthworms with their nutrient-rich castings and soil-aerating activity, and even discourages slugs. Nitrogen-fixing bacteria require the presence of lime, as do other beneficial soil microorganisms.

Calcium itself is an essential plant nutrient (calcium, magnesium, and sulfur are secondary only to the "big three" nutrients, nitrogen, phosphorus, and potassium). However, some plants such as vacciniums are actively averse to its presence and will develop chlorosis if exposed to calcium even in minute amounts. Such plants are known as calcifuge or lime-hating. Other plants such as rhododendrons are more accurately termed acid-loving, that is, preferring strongly acidic conditions but tolerating pH levels up to about 6.0 before developing chlorosis.

Balancing pH, calcium, soil fertility, and acid-loving plants can be tricky business, but in general, new gardens in high-rainfall areas benefit greatly by broadcasting lime over the entire area and digging or tilling it in before planting, even when planting acid-lovers. Once planted, though, acid-lovers should never be limed; an initial application to boost earthworm and beneficial bacteria activity is sufficient. Fortunately, acid-lovers are not heavy feeders (acidic soils tend to be infertile), so merely incorporating lots of organic material into the planting site and giving them an occasional light helping of compost will keep them happy.

For the rest of the garden, including vegetable gardens and lawns, periodic liming is a fact of life in the Pacific Northwest. Ordinary garden lime or ground limestone (calcium carbonate) gives quick results but must be reapplied more often, so this form is best confined to lawns and vegetable gardens (for more information on liming lawns and vegetable gardens, see Chapter 3). Slower-acting dolomite lime (calcium magnesium carbonate) is preferable for ornamental plantings because results last longer and because it contains magnesium, another essential plant element. Do not use slaked or hydrated lime (calcium hydroxide), which is very caustic and will burn plants.

How much lime is necessary and how often it should be reapplied depends on many factors: the original pH, the target pH, local rainfall, and the type of soil. (Clay soil needs about half again the amount of lime to raise the pH to a given target level.) Test the soil before liming, using an inexpensive kit available at garden centers; if the pH needs to be raised drastically, don't even think about doing it all at once. Apply at the rate recommended on the bag, realizing it may take several years to reach the target. Fall is the ideal time for applying lime, since the coming rains will carry it down to the root zone of plants, but early spring is also good. If applying fertilizer, do not lime at the same time, since their reaction can diminish the effects of both; separate their applications by about two weeks.

Garden results are always more satisfying (and look much more natural) when playing the hand that's dealt—concentrating on acid-lovers if the natural soil is strongly acidic and on lime-lovers if it's neutral or slightly alkaline. But, being human, we always want what we don't have, so there will always be pH exceptions in every garden. Just remember to group these together so their special needs can be met. To increase the acidity of soils with a high pH, add garden sulfur or aluminum sulfate at the rate recommended on the package; to help maintain acidity, keep the organic content of the soil high.

POOR DRAINAGE

The heavy soil so common in the Pacific Northwest is a blessing in summer for its ability to hold water and release it slowly, but in our wet winters these blessings become liabilities. Walking or even stepping on saturated soil compacts it into an impervious water-holding layer, so garden beds should not be entered at all in the rainy season. If such entry is necessary, for instance for removing a broken tree limb, lay a wide board or piece of plywood on the ground to distribute your weight.

If not compacted by foot traffic, winter drainage in cultivated loam soils (a mixture of clay, silt, and sand) is usually adequate. However, unamended soils with high clay content swell when wet, effectively plugging any air spaces through which water could drain. The same soils shrink in summer, causing wide and deep cracks.

The solution to both problems is the same: work in copious amounts of bulk organic materials such as peat moss, well-rotted coarse sawdust (Douglas fir or hemlock only), compost, well-rotted manure, or leaf mold. Aim for adding a layer one-quarter to one-half the depth of the unamended soil and till in thoroughly.

Addition of this humus stimulates activity by worms and beneficial microorganisms, which in turn binds soil into coarse crumbs. Numerous small air spaces are created between the crumbs, allowing excess water to drain in winter but still allowing moisture to be retained and released slowly in summer. The addition of dolomite lime also aids in the formation of a desirable crumbly texture.

Sand can also be added, but sand particles alone merely become individually encased in clay, creating a texture like concrete. Sand used in combination with bulk organic materials should be coarse builders' sand only, never beach sand.

New house construction often creates hardpan (an impervious, water-holding layer of hard-packed heavy soil), the result of subsoil being dumped on topsoil and driven over by heavy machinery. Hardpan is often disguised with a thin layer of beautiful-looking imported topsoil, so deep tilling of all soil surrounding a new house is highly recommended. Till as deeply as possible first, add amendments, then till again.

Even well-drained loam soils can have difficulty handling our non-stop rains in November and December, so ditching may also be necessary. Ditches may be open or closed (drain pipe laid at the bottom and covered with drain rock or crushed gravel), but should be slightly deeper than the subsoil. The ditch should extend all across the highest side of property and drain into an approved municipal or highway department ditch. (Check local bylaws to see if a permit is necessary.) Driveways, sidewalks, and garden paths can create mini-dams and may need additional covered drains to allow water to flow around or underneath them.

Draining roof gutters into holes filled with rock, as is often recommended in drier climates, is not a good idea in the Pacific Northwest. Gardeners in the Rogue and Olympic Rain Shadow subregions may get away with it due to their lower rainfall, but elsewhere, such holes are likely to become permanently filled

Rain-saturated soil in January

sunken bathtubs in winter. Instead, gutters should be drained into underground pipes that terminate on the surface of the soil or into an existing ditch. Only a slight slope of about 1 in. in 10 ft. (2.5 cm in 3 m) is needed.

On dead-level land, the only solutions for poor drainage (beyond adding humus) may be choosing plants with known tolerance of winter wetness and/or planting in raised beds. Any slight slope should be exploited, and any low spots filled with soil of the same texture. Ideally, this would be done before planting, so the new soil can be mixed with the existing soil.

Very heavy winter rains inevitably leave puddles even in well-drained heavy soil. These are not too worrisome as long as they drain completely within three to four hours of the rain stopping. However, areas that consistently remain under water for longer than four hours require improvement by one means or another.

CHAPTER 14

Physiological and Environmental Problems

CHLOROSIS

Although it sounds like a disease, chlorosis is a physiological condition indicating poor production of chlorophyll, the green coloring matter of plants essential to the vital process of photosynthesis. Chlorotic leaves (those lacking sufficient chlorophyll) turn yellow, with veins remaining green in mild cases.

The most common cause, especially with acid-loving plants such as rhododendrons, is a lack of an essential element—usually iron, but sometimes magnesium—due not to a deficiency in the soil itself, but to an excess of calcium in the soil. The calcium binds up these essential elements, making them unavailable to the plant. Common causes of chlorosis in acid-loving plants include liming the soil around them, using non-acidic fertilizers, and planting them close to concrete sidewalks or foundations, which slowly but continually leach lime into the soil.

Iron-deficiency chlorosis, which almost always shows up as yellow or pale leaves with prominent green veins, is easily treated with chelated iron, either applied to the soil or sprayed directly on the plants. Magnesium-deficiency chlorosis, characterized by yellowing leaves with edges and midveins remaining green, is similarly treated with magnesium sulfate, commonly known as Epsom salts. Since veins also remain green in the initial stages of iron-deficiency chlorosis, it's sometimes hard to tell the difference between the two. However, iron deficiency affects younger leaves first; magnesium deficiency affects older leaves first.

Before jumping to the conclusion that chlorosis is due to the presence of lime, other causes of chlorotic leaves must be ruled out. Camellias, for instance, need some calcium as well as magnesium, so a light application of dolomite lime (calcium magnesium carbonate) to aid their uptake of soil nutrients may be exactly what their yellowing leaves need.

If yellow leaves occur only on the oldest foliage, the cause may be normal aging (see "Flagging and Senescence," later in this chapter). If they occur only on the side of the plant most exposed to the sun, the cause may be sudden exposure to strong sunlight—sunburn in summer, sunscald in winter. If leaves are

Magnesium-deficiency chlorosis on rhododendron, aggravated by sunburn

uniformly yellow all over, the cause may be a simple lack of fertilizer, especially nitrogen. A sudden shock to the root system, whether due to accidental damage, transplanting, or attack by root weevils, can also cause chlorotic leaves.

If all acid-loving plants in a particular area have yellowish leaves, the cause is probably environmental—most likely an extended dry period in summer or a prolonged wet period causing waterlogged soil in winter. In addition, our long, gray, sun-

Fasciated stem on squash plant

Cedar flagging on *Thuja occidentalis* 'Pyramidalis'

Senescent leaves on rhododendron in late August

starved winters cause the leaves of many acid-loving broadleaved evergreen shrubs and even the needles of some conifers to look a little wan by winter's end—not quite yellowish, but not quite true green, either. In all these cases, the problem will correct itself when conditions return to normal. However, if chlorotic leaves are netted or mottled with green, the problem may be a virus, which is probably incurable and may spread to other plants.

Obviously, a bit of sleuthing to determine the most likely cause of chlorosis is necessary before settling on a treatment and the prevention of future occurrences. If in doubt, take a sample of leaves (securely enclosed in a zippered plastic bag in case of disease) to a garden center for a second opinion.

FASCIATION

Flattened, apparently fused stems of herbaceous perennials, annuals, and bulbs are commonly seen, especially in lilies, Shasta daisies, delphiniums, gaillardias, lupines, and even squash and cucumber vines. Multiple small flowers may appear on the grotesquely flattened stems, and/or the terminal growth may consist of multiple fused flowers.

Fasciation, as this condition is known, is not very well understood, but is an entirely natural "mistake" that was well documented long before air pollution, environmental toxins, or radioactive fallout were common concerns. It is thought that the growing tip of the plant somehow becomes confused, perhaps by weather conditions at some critical point in spring. Other abnormal growth patterns include leaves growing out of flower petals and needles growing out of conifer cones.

No control is necessary for fasciation; it is not "catching" and does no harm to the plant, although its looks and production are compromised for that season. On perennial plants, growth should be perfectly normal next spring.

Fasciation has always been very common in ferns and cacti, and fasciated or crested (cristated) forms are highly prized. These can be perpetuated through division or cuttings, or through grafts on cacti. Sometimes crested forms can even be perpetuated in seed-grown strains, such as in cockscomb celosia, a popular bedding plant.

FLAGGING AND SENESCENCE

Although the leaves of some broadleaved plants and the needles of most conifers are evergreen, they are not immortal. Some live for two years, others for three or more, but eventually they turn yellow, then reddish brown, then shrivel and fall off.

Sunburn on rhododendron

Most of the time this normal leaf shedding isn't even noticed, partly because the shedding leaves are hidden behind two or three years' growth and partly because it takes place gradually, usually in late summer and fall. Sometimes, though, the process is condensed and becomes very noticeable.

On conifers, this is called flagging. Cedars (*Thuja* species, that is, not *Cedrus*) are particularly prone to this condition—it's sometimes called cedar flagging—but it also shows up often on pines, false cypresses (*Chamaecyparis*), and sequoias. The condition is most noticeable when a dry summer follows an exceptionally wet spring.

The condition is perfectly normal, but always be suspicious of sudden yellowing and dropping of inner needles on spruces, since this could indicate spider mites. To speed the demise of unsightly yellow needles on cedar hedges and dwarf conifers, rub the foliage lightly between your hands.

Senescence, which is really just a ten-dollar word for aging, applies to the same process on broadleaved evergreen leaves, especially those of rhododendrons. In most cases this process happens quite discreetly, but weather conditions in some years make it show up like a sore thumb. Some *Rhododendron* species and hybrids have a yearly tendency for their oldest leaves to turn yellow all at once. There is no point in doing anything about it,

since the leaves will fall soon anyway. However, if in doubt that senescence is the cause, take a few leaves to a local nursery or garden center for analysis.

LEAF ABNORMALITIES

Blotches
Yellow or tan blotches on thick-leaved species such as hellebores or rhododendrons may be due to sudden exposure to intense sunlight in summer (sunburn); in winter, it may be due to sudden bright or intensified sunlight reflected off snow or a nearby picture window (sunscald).

Crisp or dry brown blotches, especially on variegated foliage or thin-leaved species, are usually due to sunburn or windburn. Soft, rubbery blotches of light brown are most likely due to salt injury, which could be from salt spray near the ocean, salt water intrusion into deep wells used for irrigation, or salt applied to nearby roads in winter. Puffy tan blotches on lilac, though, are almost certainly caused by lilac leafminers. Pick these off and destroy them as soon as the first small tunnels are noticed.

Black blotches indicate tissue death from any cause. Parts of aucuba leaves, for instance, can be killed in early spring by late frosts, especially if exposed to direct morning sun, and new magnolia leaves often develop small squarish blotches of dead tissue in changeable spring weather. Unless black blotches appear everywhere, indicating widespread tissue death, there is no reason for concern.

There is a very slight possibility that brown or black leaf blotches, especially on camellias, pieris, rhododendrons, or viburnums could be due to ramorum blight and tip dieback.

Cold-weather colors
The foliage of many conifers, especially *Thuja*, turns color in winter in response to cold. Green foliage turns purplish or brownish; golden foliage turns deep gold to orange. Many broadleaved evergreens with variegated foliage respond to cold weather by taking on pink tints; green-leaved boxwoods often turn orange; and some very small-leaved evergreen groundcovers turn purple-brown. Some vegetables, notably tomatoes and broccoli, turn purple soon after planting in our cold springs due to a temporary inability to take up phosphorus from the soil. In all these cases, colors will right themselves when the weather warms up.

Distortion and puckering
New leaves of deciduous species can be severely distorted by aphids; snowball bush (*Viburnum opulus* 'Roseum') and most honeysuckles are notoriously prone to such distortion. Damage can be controlled by controlling aphids.

New broadleaved evergreen leaves can be distorted by spring weather that fluctuates rapidly between cold and hot. Conflicting messages of "stop" and "grow" result in shortened, puckered leaves, as if someone held onto the leaf while pulling on the midrib. The distortion causes no harm but can be unsightly.

Cold-weather color on dwarf boxwood (*Buxus sempervirens* 'Suffruticosa')

Leaf puckering on *Viburnum opulus* 'Roseum' due to aphids. Photo by Whitney Cranshaw

On peaches or any of their relatives (nectarine, almond, apricot, flowering peach, flowering nectarine, flowering almond, flowering apricot, *Prunus mume*), distorted, puffy, reddish leaves are undoubtedly caused by peach leaf curl.

Twisted, grossly misshapen leaves are likely due to herbicide damage, especially lawn weedkillers containing 2,4,D. Damage can result from aerial drift from neighboring properties or from using a sprayer that formerly held weedkiller.

Drooping

The most obvious cause of drooping leaves is soil dryness, but even plants in moist soil will droop in high or unaccustomed heat, especially if humidity is high. In this case, which is very common in May, leaves revive in evening or when the weather cools. However, if only one plant or only the plants in a certain area consistently wilt during the day and revive in the evening, suspect verticillium wilt.

The leaves of some broadleaved evergreens with large leaves, such as *Viburnum rhytidophyllum* and larger-leaved rhododendrons, will droop markedly in response to low temperatures in winter but will resume their normal position when milder weather resumes.

Drooping leaves, especially on rhododendrons, could also indicate root rot. Since this can look very much like the effects of severe drought, soil moisture should always be checked before soaking with water.

Leaf scorch

Reddish or brown crispy edges in late summer are almost always due to soil dryness, especially on thin-leaved species such as maples. In early spring, brown edges on new leaves are probably due to frost damage or windburn. Reddish brown edges on roses could be due to a deficiency of potassium, especially in sandy soils.

The sudden appearance of crisp brown leaf edges on any plant could be due to fertilizer burn, the result of overfertilizing or of applying fertilizer to a plant with dry roots. Always water first before fertilizing; if burning is evident, flood with water to prevent further damage.

Irregular dark brown or grayish edges on rhododendrons and other broadleaved evergreens are usually due to frost damage and/or windburn over the winter. This dead tissue often falls off in spring; the remaining parts of the leaves can give the impression of having been chewed by giant caterpillars.

Rolled edges

In root rot and physiological response to cold, leaf edges are almost always rolled downward along the midribs. Leaves rolled upward along the midribs usually indicates soil dryness, but this is not infallible: tomato leaves roll upward in wet soil, and filbert (hazelnut) leaves roll downward in dry soil.

Rolled leaves in late spring are likely caused by leafrollers, small caterpillars that pupate inside them. Check by unrolling a leaf; control by hand-picking or spraying with BTK (*Bacillus thuringiensis* var. *kurstaki*). This is a caterpillar-specific stomach poison, so spray the leaves they're eating, not the caterpillars themselves.

Spotting

For unknown reasons, some species and cultivars are prone to purplish leaf spotting in late summer; spireas, hydrangeas, and the hybrid rhododendrons 'Blue Ensign' and 'Mrs. G. W. Leak' are noted for this. Photinias and other broadleaved evergreens are often spotted by late winter. Although unsightly, such spots are harmless.

Fertilizers, chemical sprays, and the drift of dormant winter sprays onto non-target species can also cause leaf spotting. Overhead watering in midday can also cause spotting (the sun's rays are magnified in each droplet).

Very small purplish leaf spots, especially on roses, are often simply a consequence of poor growing conditions and/or lack of nutrients. Orange or yellowish powdery spots on the undersides of leaves indicate rust. Most other leaf spotting is likely due to fungal disease such as anthracnose, black spot, or scab.

Leaf droop on rhododendron due to low temperature

Leaf scorch on *Viburnum davidii* caused by frost and windburn in winter

Leaf spotting on *Photinia* × *fraseri* in late winter

LIVERWORTS

Liverworts—primitive, spore-producing, low-growing plants related to true mosses—are commonly found on moist, acidic, humus-rich soils throughout the Pacific Northwest and are part of the natural ecology of our region. However, they are not welcome on the moist, acidic, humus-rich, peat-based potting soil of nursery containers and decorative planters. These flattened, spongy, greenish growths with the consistency of raw liver soon spread to cover the soil surface and can choke out small plants and even seedling trees.

Any moss-like growth on the soil surface of containerized plants should be removed by hand as soon as noticed. A narrow flat tool such as the handle of a spoon is helpful in removing extensive growths. This procedure usually removes some of the potting soil as well, so most containers will need topping up. If the problem is extensive, liverworts can be killed off by spraying with a mixture of one part white vinegar to two parts water—but take great care not to spray the plants as well, since vinegar is a natural herbicide and can kill leaves and tender new growth.

Liverwort on soil surface of containerized plant. Photo by Judy Newton

Mosses, lichens, and algae on trunk of filbert

Liverworts can be discouraged by adding a shallow layer of coarse sand or fine gravel to the soil surface. In very rainy weather—the kind liverworts love—smaller pots are best moved under a roof to keep their soil from being constantly soggy.

MOSSES, LICHENS, AND ALGAE

True mosses, lichens, and algae all thrive in the humid atmosphere of the Pacific Northwest and are very common on the trunks and limbs of native trees (particularly bigleaf maples) as well as on fallen logs, rocks, the forest floor, and any other stationary objects within reach of their reproductive spores. These green, gray, or whitish growths, which come in an astounding and often beautiful array of shapes and textures, also make themselves at home on many garden plants. They seem especially fond of deciduous azaleas, filberts (hazelnuts), hollies, maples, fruiting and ornamental plums, viburnums, and witch hazels.

Although heavy or extensive growths can make it look as though branches are being strangled by them, these plants are not parasitic and do no direct harm. In fact, their almost inevitable appearance on the trunks of older trees adds an attraction of its own, along with the assurance of good air quality. (Mosses, lichens, and algae do not fare well in polluted atmospheres.) However, the tight, heavily textured growths hold water against the branches, which adds considerable weight to them and can contribute to breakage during windstorms, wet snows, or freezing weather.

These growths can be removed by rubbing with bare hands or a soft nylon-bristled scrub brush, taking care not to injure tender bark. Annual dormant sprays of lime sulfur will discourage their growth on deciduous trees and can also be used half-strength on hollies if applied before March. Read the label for accurate concentrations, timing, and a list of species that may be harmed by lime sulfur.

Do not use proprietary moss killer sprays on plants, since these are meant only for fences, sidewalks, roofs, siding, and other non-living surfaces. Although most of these preparations are environmentally safe, they contain ingredients that could harm plants.

CHAPTER 15

Diseases

Due to our high rainfall and mild climate, fungal plant diseases in particular are very common and easily spread in the Pacific Northwest. The same conditions are also conducive to the spread of bacterial diseases, although their spread is more localized. Viral diseases, which are relatively uncommon, are not dealt with here; other than controlling aphids, which can spread viruses, there are no effective measures to prevent them and no cures except the removal of infected plants.

Many fungal and bacterial diseases can be prevented by following good cultural practices and practicing good sanitation. Whenever possible, choose species and cultivars known to be highly disease-resistant, plant them in sites appropriate to their needs, and keep them appropriately fed and watered—including not feeding or watering, if that's what they need. Healthy, thriving plants are much less likely to be infected by disease than are plants under stress.

Since fungal and bacterial diseases are most easily spread in wet weather at temperatures of 60°F (15°C) or above, never prune or deadhead plants in these conditions, and avoid handling or even brushing against wet foliage. Do not compost or bury diseased plant parts, but dispose of them promptly in household garbage (preferably in tightly sealed bags) or by burning. Clean up all fallen diseased leaves as soon as possible and dispose of them.

In addition to good cultural practices, three disease-preventing organic sprays are very helpful in Pacific Northwest weather conditions. Lime sulfur is mainly used as a dormant spray to prevent anthracnose and scab on deciduous trees, while wettable sulfur is useful year-round in preventing an assortment of fungal diseases. Fixed copper is an effective bactericide as well as a fungicide, but should be used sparingly since it is toxic to earthworms and can build up in the soil. Always read the labels of these sprays thoroughly before using, taking note of appropriate concentration, timing, temperature, and species that might be sensitive to the substance.

If a plant shows repeated susceptibility to disease despite good cultural practices, preventative measures, and appropriate controls, it should be "shovel-pruned" (dug up and disposed of) and a plant of a different species tried in its place.

DISINFECTING PRUNING TOOLS

To avoid inadvertently spreading disease when pruning out infected plant parts, every pruning tool used—hand pruner, knife, loppers, pole pruner, or saw—must be disinfected after each cut it makes. Dip tools or wipe blades in either 70 percent denatured alcohol (isopropyl rubbing alcohol) used full strength, or in a solution of one part household bleach to nine parts water. Make sure all cutting surfaces are thoroughly covered. If using bleach, wash and dry steel blades when finished to avoid corrosion.

AIRBORNE FUNGAL DISEASES

Anthracnose
This catch-all category of leaf, shoot, and twig blights is caused by a number of different fungi that target trees and shrubs in early spring, notably fruiting apple, fruiting pear, ash, dogwood, maple, and sycamore (*Platanus*) trees, and privet hedges. All the fungi require the presence of abundant moisture, especially in spring; anthracnose cannot be spread in dry conditions. Since Pacific Northwest springs are virtually guaranteed to be wet, except possibly in the Rogue subregion, anthracnose is a common hazard.

Fortunately, with the exception of dogwood anthracnose (described under *Cornus*, in Chapter 5), this disease is generally less serious among ornamental plants than are other fungal diseases such as scab. It can, however, be a real problem in fruiting apple trees, where repeated infections can lead to cankers (sunken areas of dead tissue on limbs) and dieback of whole branches.

The first sign of infection is brown or purplish spots on new leaves. Spotting may progress to blotches of dead tissue; in severe cases, mature leaves may also become infected and drop off. Leaves are usually replaced by new growth, and with any luck these will escape infection as the weather dries out. In most cases, the disease is easily controlled by removing and destroying

Sycamore anthracnose on London plane (*Platanus ×hispanica*). Photo by Heide Hermary

European canker on apple tree. Photo by Heide Hermary

Black spot on rose

infected leaves and twigs. A dormant spray of lime sulfur the following winter helps prevent future infection next spring.

Some apple varieties, however, are sensitive to lime sulfur and even wettable sulfur, so this is not always an option for them. (Pear trees may be safely sprayed.) On apple trees, remove all infected leaves and twigs promptly and prune out any cankers at least 6 in. (15 cm) below the lowest visible sign of infection. Monitor trees throughout the growing season, and remove any cankers as soon as noticed.

A copper spray following apple harvest but before fall rains begin helps prevent future infections of anthracnose as well as infections of European canker, a similar fungus affecting apple trees in wet-spring climates. However, copper is toxic to earthworms and, with repeated use, can build up in the soil, so this should not be relied on. Where wet springs are a fact of life, avoid susceptible varieties such as Gala, McIntosh, and Yellow Transparent. Apple varieties showing some resistance to anthracnose include Golden Delicious, Gravenstein, Jonagold, Liberty, and Northern Spy.

Black spot
Exposure to this most common disease of roses cannot be avoided in the Pacific Northwest. The fungus responsible for the small, circular, unmistakable black spots on rose foliage—especially new leaves—not only overwinters very comfortably in our mild climate, but can infect wet foliage in as little as nine hours in temperatures between 50°F and 80°F (10–27°C).

Since these temperatures dominate our climate, black spot can be spread in winter, spring, summer (by overhead watering), or fall, but infection is most prevalent in spring. The fungus lives on both living and dead plant tissue, and spores are easily splashed onto healthy foliage in wet weather. Once contracted, the cycle continues virtually uninterrupted, with as few as ten to 18 days between new infections. In severe cases, leaves turn yellow and drop off. Repeated infections can seriously weaken plants, cause dieback, and even kill them.

Planting roses in full sun with plenty of space around them for good air circulation is a good start for preventing black spot; watering at ground level (not overhead) also helps avoid the disease by keeping foliage dry. However, the most effective defense is to choose black-spot resistant varieties, of which there are many. Bear in mind that the fungus is variable, and a rose that is highly resistant in one area may not be resistant in another. (For the record, two roses on which we have never found a single black spot are *Rosa glauca* and Roseraie de l'Haÿ, a rugosa hybrid.)

Botrytis blight (gray mold) on zucchini. Photo by Linda Gilkeson

Late blight on tomato. Photo by Linda Gilkeson

There's no need to panic at the first sign of black spot; the rose may be perfectly fine next year under different weather conditions, or it may need to be moved to a sunnier spot. However, any rose showing strong or repeated susceptibility to black spot is best uprooted and replaced: no matter what its reputation, the only performance that counts is the one in your own garden.

Pick off any leaves showing signs of black spot to prevent the fungus from spreading. If mild, wet weather is likely to continue, consider spraying weekly with wettable garden sulfur, which will prevent further infections but will not eradicate established ones. (Keep picking and destroying diseased leaves.) Spray to the point of runoff, including the undersides of the leaves, and alternate occasionally with copper so the fungus does not develop resistance. A truly all-organic preventative spray that has proven quite effective is plain milk—skim, two percent, whole, or powdered—diluted in nine parts water.

Since spores can be splashed onto healthy leaves by rain falling onto infected leaves on the ground, pick up as many fallen leaves as possible. Mulch, low-growing companion plants, or non-aggressive groundcovers help prevent spores from being splashed back, so don't tear them up looking for diseased rose leaves; black spot is rose-specific and will not infect other plants.

At season's end, gather up as much fallen litter as possible and dispose of it in household garbage or by burning (never by composting). Prune off any dead or diseased cane tips and dispose of them as well. Some gardeners strip and dispose of any leaves remaining on the canes before fall rains arrive to help deprive the fungus of a place to overwinter.

Botrytis blight

Often simply called gray mold, this fungal disease appears most commonly on perennials, bulbs, greenhouse plants, small fruits (strawberries are very prone), vegetables, and some shrubs. The first signs are water-soaked areas on leaves, stems, and spent flowers; these quickly turn into a disgusting growth of gray fuzz that looks like something left too long in the refrigerator. Plant tissue seemingly dissolves into this gray mold as the plant dies back or collapses.

Infection is most likely to occur in warm, humid conditions with poor air circulation, such as is often found in greenhouses, but in warm, wet springs many herbaceous plants—particularly peonies, tuberous begonias, and strawberries—are also vulnerable in outdoor conditions. Botrytis on lilies is different in that the disease spreads most rapidly in cool but wet conditions. Fortunately, although lily top growth may be ruined in severe cases, the bulbs themselves are seldom affected.

Prevention of botrytis blight consists mainly of providing good air circulation. Plant on a slight slope if possible, avoid the creation of "dead air zones" by objects or plants that obstruct natural air flow, and do not crowd plants, especially in humid conditions. In greenhouses, increasing ventilation and lowering the temperature slightly goes a long way toward prevention. Other preventative measures include making sure plants are not shaded more than necessary, watering at soil level to avoid wetting foliage, and allowing the soil to dry out slightly between waterings.

Since the fungus enters plant tissue mainly through wounds and spent flowers, good sanitation is also very important, especially for vulnerable species. Avoid touching or handling foliage when wet or damp, and avoid damaging fragile stems by rough handling. Prune any broken stems cleanly and keep plants dead-headed, especially during windless, humid conditions such as fog. In fall, rake up and destroy all plant debris on the ground to prevent the fungus from overwintering.

Remove and destroy any infected plant parts promptly to avoid spreading infection to healthy tissue or to nearby plants, and wash your hands thoroughly with hot water and soap before handling other plants.

Late blight

This fungus appears literally overnight in the form of greenish brown leathery lesions on ripe and nearly ripe tomatoes, rendering them inedible. Smaller green tomatoes are affected as well; even if they're picked immediately for indoor ripening, the blight shows up as soon as they turn color.

Until fairly recently, late blight fungal spores were not able to overwinter in Pacific Northwest gardens, but new strains that emerged in the 1990s are much more virulent. Since both tomatoes and potatoes can now be infected from soilborne spores, crops should be rotated so neither is planted in the same soil for at least three consecutive years.

Late blight tends to come and go in cycles but is always worse in cool, wet summers. Once plants are infected, the blight cannot be halted, so prevention—keeping the foliage as dry as possible—is the only cure. Water at ground level, avoiding splashback, and do not handle foliage that is wet with rain, dew, or fog. Always water tomatoes early in the day (never in late afternoon or evening) to allow any dampened foliage to dry quickly. High nitrogen, which encourages lush, moisture-holding foliage, should be avoided.

Choosing early-maturing tomato varieties can sometimes beat the late-summer onset of late blight, and some varieties such as Early Cascade, Oregon Spring, and Sweet Cluster are more blight-resistant than others. However, no variety is completely immune.

Spraying weekly with fixed copper is an effective control, but this amount of copper is unacceptable for both human consumption and the soil. The only sure prevention is to grow tomatoes under cover: a greenhouse is foolproof, but plastic tents will do as long as they protect foliage from all sides.

Late blight is much less frequent but just as devastating on potatoes. (It was responsible for the terrible Potato Famine in Ireland in the mid 19th century.) If foliage starts to turn black and die down prematurely, cut off the blackened foliage immediately, disinfecting pruning tools after each cut. Do not harvest potatoes for at least two weeks, and then only if the weather is dry. Unless infection is very severe, potatoes are still edible, although they may have to be peeled thickly.

Do not compost any foliage, fruit, or tubers even suspected of having late blight, but dispose of in household garbage or by burning.

Peach leaf curl

This fungal disease is endemic in the Pacific Northwest and is virtually guaranteed to affect peaches, nectarines, and their flowering counterparts. The disease also affects the related apricots, flowering apricots, almonds, and flowering almonds, although not as seriously. However, these last four are so prone to other

Peach leaf curl. Photo by Linda Gilkeson

fungal and bacterial diseases, along with assorted environmental stresses, that none are recommended in our climate.

Determined gardeners can and do succeed in growing peaches and nectarines, especially in the Rogue and Olympic Rain Shadow subregions. But most of us are better advised to grow some other fruit that actually likes our climate—raspberries, strawberries, blueberries, even kiwis—and buy our peaches from sources on the eastern side of the mountains.

The fungus that causes peach leaf curl requires surface moisture and is most active at temperatures around 65–70°F (18–21°C). Since these temperatures occur just as new peach leaves emerge and are accompanied by frequent showers, infection is swift and unmistakable: swollen, puckered, wart-like areas on twisted and distorted leaves that often turn red.

No fungicides of any kind are effective at this point, so the only remedy is to pick off all infected leaves. New ones will replace them, and by that time rains have usually eased and temperatures have risen slightly. However, if mild, wet weather continues, the second set of leaves will also be infected, leading to stunted growth, twig dieback, blossom and fruit drop, and a greater likelihood of winter injury. Repeated infections cause gradual deterioration of the tree and may even kill it.

The peach varieties Renton, Pacific Gold, and Frost are resistant to peach leaf curl but not immune. One effective preventative measure is to espalier peaches or nectarines against a wall where they can be sheltered from spring rains by a wide roof overhang. As long as the leaves stay dry, they remain healthy. However, any foliage that extends beyond the overhang will be infected, and wind-driven rain or protracted fog can spoil the whole scheme.

All fallen leaves should be raked up and destroyed to prevent the fungus from overwintering. A dormant spray of lime sulfur just before bud break helps prevent the disease, but don't spray trees growing against a house wall—lime sulfur stains. A copper spray in late September is extra insurance against peach leaf curl; copper can also be used as a dormant spray and is most effective just before bud break

Powdery mildew

Powdery mildew is the common cold of the plant world, and in September the entire Pacific Northwest sneezes. This is

Powdery mildew on bigleaf maple in September

Rust on St. John's wort (*Hypericum calycinum*)

when the combination of dry soil, warm days, cool nights, and increasingly high humidity—which happens to be the perfect recipe for powdery mildew—is most widespread.

Some plants, notably asters, delphiniums, lupines, monarda, *Phlox paniculata*, scabiosa, tuberous begonias, *Viburnum tinus*, zinnias, and most rambler roses are well known for their susceptibility to powdery mildew and may exhibit telltale grayish white withering leaves any time these conditions prevail, even in spring. But in late summer and fall, the leaves of deciduous azaleas, cucumber and bean vines, spent perennials, zucchini and squash leaves, and many other plants—even native bigleaf maples—are very commonly affected.

However, like the common cold, which is almost impossible to avoid when conditions are highly favorable for it, powdery mildew is rarely a serious concern for home gardeners. Unlike downy mildew, a more serious fungus that starts deep within leaves and kills tissues, powdery mildew affects only the surfaces of mature leaves, and usually deciduous ones at that. Vegetables are perfectly edible, perennial plants are not permanently affected, and the soil not at all. But, just as repeated heavy colds can weaken a person's immune system, repeated heavy infestations of powdery mildew can weaken a plant and leave it vulnerable to other diseases and/or insect attack.

The first line of defense, as with all fungal diseases, is to allow plenty of space between plants so air can circulate freely. (Mature gardens may need periodic plant thinning or pruning of overhanging branches.) Susceptible species should be planted in as much sun as possible, since shade also contributes to powdery mildew and other fungal diseases. However, if a particular plant is severely affected year after year, it's best to give up on it and replace it with a species better suited to the conditions of that site.

As counterintuitive as it seems, keeping plants well watered helps prevent the disease; powdery mildew is actually much less of a problem where summer rain is frequent than in our dry-summer subregions. Be sure to water early in the day so foliage can dry quickly. With susceptible species, always water at ground level, especially in late summer.

Spraying healthy foliage with wettable sulfur will prevent powder mildew spores from germinating there. So will a solution of one tablespoon (45 ml) baking soda to one gallon

(4 liters) of water, with a dash of dishsoap added as a sticker-spreader. (Don't mix these two preventatives; they'll cancel each other out.) To minimize sources of infection, keep up with regular deadheading of annuals and perennials and remove and destroy garden debris such as withered foliage.

Rust

Many different rust-producing fungi target their own specific plants, but all have similar causes, symptoms, and methods of prevention. In the Pacific Northwest, the major victims by far are hawthorns, St. John's worts (*Hypericum*), and hollyhocks; other susceptible plants include carnations, mountain ash, roses, snapdragons, and willows. Even rhododendrons and lawn grass can be infected.

The distinctive yellow or orange spots that indicate rust appear first on the undersides of leaves and are only later seen on the tops. Rust is most likely to occur in spring and late summer, when days are mild and nights are cool and damp; infections seldom occur in midsummer. This is because infection spreads very rapidly on wet foliage in mild weather—in as little as two hours at temperatures in the high 60s F (18–21°C)—but is halted if temperatures remain above the high 80s F (29–32°C) for two days or more. (In case of infection, hope for a heat wave.) Dry weather also halts the spread of rust, as long as nights aren't too cool, but disfigured leaves remain until leaf fall, which in severe cases may be almost immediately.

To help prevent rust, avoid overhead watering and provide good air circulation to speed drying of foliage. Since rust fungi overwinter on fallen leaves, rake and destroy them in early fall to break the cycle of infection. Following these precautions and planting rust-resistant varieties of roses, perennials, and annuals is usually sufficient to keep the disease at bay on these plants; if only a few rusted leaves appear, they can simply be picked off and destroyed. (Rust on lawns, although fairly common, is rarely serious enough to treat.) If rust-inducing weather continues, spraying vulnerable plants with wettable sulfur at weekly intervals will prevent more fungal spores from germinating. Be sure to spray undersides of leaves thoroughly.

Some plants, though, are so notoriously prone to rust in our climate that they're best avoided completely, at least in areas where mild temperatures and damp conditions go hand in hand most of the growing season. Hawthorns, for instance, are vulnerable to at least nine different kinds of rust-causing fungi; the red, double-flowered 'Paul's Scarlet' (*Crataegus laevigata* 'Paul's Scarlet') is extremely susceptible.

Most shrubby St. John's worts are very vulnerable to rust, although the superb *Hypericum* 'Hidcote' and the alpine *H. olympicum* f. *uniflorum* (syn. *H. o.* 'Grandiflorum') are two notable and garden-worthy exceptions. The widely planted groundcover *H. calycinum* is intermediate in susceptibility, being infected only when rust-inducing conditions are prolonged.

Hollyhocks, even rust-resistant varieties, are a write-off in all but the warmest and driest parts of the Pacific Northwest. (The dwarf French hollyhock *Malva sylvestris* 'Zebrina' is very healthy and very pretty, but since it's not of the genus *Alcea*, it isn't really a hollyhock.) Even with weekly sprayings of sulfur, new rust infections appear quickly and plants tend to defoliate. Growing hollyhocks under an overhang to keep the foliage dry helps somewhat, but even this measure can be defeated by high humidity.

Scab

This fungal disease, which looks as ugly as it sounds, is a very common problem in flowering crabapples and fruiting apples in the Pacific Northwest. Scab also affects fruiting pear trees, but apple scab cannot cause pear scab and pear scab cannot cause apple scab. Two other different but related fungi cause scab in firethorns (*Pyracantha*) and willows, but infections are not as widespread or severe and can usually be controlled by picking off diseased leaves.

Flowering crabapples, apples, and pears are most likely to be infected just before bloom, especially if the weather is wet, as it usually is then. The warmer the temperature at this time, the more likely scab will develop. At 50°F (10°C), infection can begin if foliage stays wet for 12 hours; at 70°F (20°C), it takes only six hours.

The first sign of infection is olive-green leaf spots that soon run together in brown or black blotches; badly infected leaves turn yellow, shrivel, and fall off. Severe scab can cause defoliation, which greatly weakens the tree even though new leaves are produced. In mild cases, fruit is somewhat stunted and shows hard, corky brown lesions ("scabs"), but is still edible. With moderate infection, fruit develops numerous lesions and may be cracked; in severe cases fruit is grossly distorted, shrunken, and covered with deep cracks and lesions, making it totally worthless.

Fortunately, scab infections become more difficult to produce as spring approaches summer, partly because our weather tends to dry out as it warms up. Even if rain continues, though, infections require longer and longer periods of foliage wetness as the season progresses.

The best defense against scab is choosing resistant varieties. Scab-resistant flowering crabapples are described under *Malus* in Chapter 5, along with cultivars to avoid. In pears, scab-resistant varieties include Bartlett, Bosc, Comice, and Olympic; Seckel is prone to scab and should be avoided.

Scab on flowering crabapple

In fruiting apples, Chehalis, Freedom, Enterprise, Goldrush, Liberty, Prima, and Redfree are highly scab resistant (Enterprise is reputedly immune); Jonafree and MacFree are also scab-resistant but of poor eating quality. King, Tydeman's Red, and Yellow Transparent are somewhat resistant; Spartan gets mixed reviews, being resistant in some areas and slightly susceptible in others. In wet-spring areas, moderately or very susceptible varieties such as Gala, Empire, Golden Delicious, Fuji, McIntosh, Mutsu, Red Delicious, and Rome Beauty are simply not worth growing. New scab-resistant apples are being developed all the time, so there is plenty of choice.

Rake and destroy leaves in fall to help prevent the fungus from overwintering and lime the soil as necessary to keep pH at ideal levels. Planting fruit trees on a slope to increase air circulation helps foliage dry quickly after spring rains; keeping trees well pruned also helps air circulation.

If infection is severe, pear trees should be sprayed with lime sulfur when dormant to help prevent infection the following spring. Some apple varieties such as Red Delicious can be harmed by lime sulfur or sulfur sprays, so copper is a better alternative if infection has been particularly bad.

SOIL- AND WATERBORNE FUNGAL DISEASES

Ramorum blight and tip dieback (sudden oak death)

Phytophthora ramorum, a potentially devastating fungus-like pathogen primarily spread in soil and water, was first detected in 1995 in the San Francisco Bay area, where it was killing tanoak trees (*Lithocarpus densiflorus*). Because this particular pathogen can also be spread by airborne spores, it quickly spread throughout northern California and into southern coastal Oregon (a few isolated sites near Brookings), infecting hundreds of tanoaks, coast live oaks (*Quercus agrifolia*), southern red oaks (*Q. falcata*), holly oaks (*Q. ilex*), black oaks (*Q. kelloggii*), and other related oaks, killing many of them. (Garry oak, *Q. garryana*, is more distantly related and so far does not appear to be highly susceptible.) The fungus also killed many Pacific rhododendrons (*Rhododendron macrophyllum*) and evergreen huckleberries (*Vaccinium ovatum*).

At approximately the same time, a slightly different form of the same disease was detected in Europe on nursery-grown rho-

KEEP INFORMED

For continually updated information on ramorum blight and tip dieback, including the latest lists of susceptible species and photographs of species-specific symptoms, visit the Web site of the California Oak Mortality Task Force (an international umbrella group) at http://www.suddenoakdeath.org. If there is reason to suspect ramorum blight and tip dieback in any native or cultivated plant after checking species-specific symptoms, contact the nearest office of your County Extension Service (in B.C., the Ministry of Forests and Range).

dodendrons and viburnums. On these plants, the fungus caused leaf blotches and tip dieback, but did not necessarily kill the host plant. At this time there is no way to prevent or cure either form of the disease.

In 2003 ramorum blight and tip dieback was found on nursery-grown camellias, pieris, rhododendrons, and viburnums in California, Oregon, Washington, and British Columbia. (An international shipment was the suspected source.) These infected plants were quickly destroyed, but in a nightmarish scenario, the number of native and cultivated species susceptible to the fungus began to escalate. Oregon myrtle/California bay laurel (*Umbellularia californica*) was identified as a very significant host for the disease, and many of our most widespread native plants—Pacific madrone, bigleaf maple, cascara, coast redwood, Douglas fir, kinnikinnick, salmonberry, even poison oak—were also found to be hosts. So too were an ever-increasing number of cultivated garden plants, including many of those most widely grown in the Pacific Northwest.

In 2004, ramorum blight and tip dieback was found in several large West Coast ornamental nurseries. The plants were destroyed and the nurseries quarantined, but some 2.3 million potentially infected plants had already been shipped to retail nurseries throughout the United States and Canada. A massive emergency program then ensued, involving tracking the shipments and holding them until they could be inspected, issuing educational warnings, implementing strict export controls, and establishing mandatory inspection of nurseries. Master gardeners were recruited to help identify the disease on any plants already purchased.

With the amount of governmental regulatory control that now exists for the disease, plus mandatory compliance of nurseries with these regulations and thorough inspection of plants, it is highly unlikely that any plant purchased from any nursery is infected with *Phytophthora ramorum*. However, ideal conditions for infection—mild temperatures, wet soil, wet foliage, and high humidity—are very frequent throughout the Pacific Northwest, especially in spring. Given the enormous range of hosts now found capable of spreading the disease, and the potentially devastating effects of its spread, it behooves all gardeners in the Pacific Northwest, especially those in the Rogue and southern

Pacific Coast subregions where soils are warmer in spring, to learn to identify the symptoms. These vary considerably by species, but can be divided into two types.

Bark cankers, found on susceptible oak species, are characterized by bleeding cankers on the trunk that can girdle the tree, causing death within months. The open cankers also invite insects and other diseases, which may kill the tree more slowly over a matter of years.

Host plants generally show only leaf spotting and/or blotching, usually at the tips or along the midribs where rain and irrigation water tend to pool before drying. Blights on new shoots and twigs can also occur, causing tip dieback. The disease is not usually fatal on host plants.

Root rot (phytophthora diseases)

The main hazard to plant roots in Pacific Northwest winters is not freezing, but rotting. When prolonged heavy rains combine with heavy soils and a high water table, there is no way for excess water to drain away. The soil becomes saturated, with water filling all available air spaces.

If water remains standing on plants roots for more than a few hours at most, any species is at risk. However, some plants are especially sensitive to wet soil and can succumb to root rot even when the soil is not actually flooded. If soil is moist enough to squeeze water out of a fistful of it, whatever the time of year, rhododendrons (especially purple-flowered cultivars), true firs (*Abies*), daphnes, junipers, lilacs, and yews are in grave danger of succumbing to root rot. Boxwoods, camellias, dogwoods, hemlocks, pieris, pines, blueberries, raspberries, and strawberries are also very sensitive to wet soil.

Root rot in these and other species is not actually due to drowning, but to infection by fungus-like soilborne water molds of the genus *Phytophthora*, which gradually kill roots and leave them to decay. There are no preventatives or cures for these water molds, of which there are several species; by the time symptoms are obvious, infection is usually fatal.

Port Orford cedar/Lawson cypress (*Chamaecyparis lawsoniana*) is so prone to root rot caused by *Phytophthora lateralis* that it is not recommended in the Pacific Northwest, even though it is native to the southern Oregon coast. Lilacs also have their own species-specific phytophthora, *P. syringae*; rhododendrons and most of the other plants just mentioned succumb to *P. cinnamomii*.

Although most root-kill happens in late winter or early spring, damage may not be apparent until temperatures rise in early summer and the plant can no longer draw sufficient water through its roots. The plant then wilts. Because it looks as if it is not getting enough water—which it isn't, because most of its roots are dead—many people mistakenly give the plant a lot more water, which speeds the infection and spreads it. If a wilted plant doesn't perk up almost immediately after being watered, suspect root rot.

In rhododendrons, dull, off-color leaves that wilt slowly but feel stiff almost certainly indicate root rot. A related phytophthora, *Phytophthora cactorum*, usually causes dieback on only one branch, in which case the plant may be saved by cut-

Dieback on rhododendron due to *Phytophthora cactorum*

ting that branch out and replanting in a site with better drainage. But by the time most cases of *P. cinnamomii* root rot become obvious, rhododendrons usually cannot be saved and should be removed and destroyed. In both instances, root rot will continue to be a problem as long as drainage remains poor. Because phytophthora molds live in the soil, any plant that has succumbed to root rot should not be replaced with the same species or with any other species sensitive to wet soil.

The best way to avoid root rot is to improve soil drainage long before planting (see "Poor Drainage" in Chapter 13). Rhododendrons, camellias, pieris, and other plants needing moist soil should have plenty of coarse organic bulk material worked into the soil to provide the essential air spaces through which water can pass freely. Mulch also helps; infections are most likely in warm, wet soil, so if roots can be kept cool, the growth of phytophthora fungi is further discouraged.

Sensitive plants in containers are especially vulnerable to root rot because most pots (especially black or dark green plastic) tend to absorb heat and most potting mixes are formulated with peat moss to help retain water. If sensitive plants must be kept in containers over summer, repot them into breathable fiber containers or sink them into a deep layer of mulch. To

make sure drainage is adequate, add coarser materials such as bark to the potting mix.

Automatic sprinklers that turn on for set times regardless of weather conditions can also cause root rot in sensitive species. There is no one-size-fits-all watering schedule; plants with low water requirements and those sensitive to root rot should be grouped separately from those with high water requirements and preferably watered by hand.

Verticillium wilt

The fungus *Verticillium dahliae*, commonly found in many of our soils, is particularly worrisome to Pacific Northwest gardeners because it affects woody ornamentals, especially maple trees. (A similar soilborne fungus, *V. albo-atrum*, affects tomatoes, potatoes, peppers, eggplants, and many other herbaceous plants.) Japanese barberry (*Berberis thunbergii*), lilac, redbud (*Cercis*), smoke tree (*Cotinus coggygria*), spirea, and weigela are somewhat susceptible to verticillium wilt, but maples are most widely and seriously affected. Japanese maples are particularly vulnerable.

Unlike damage from airborne fungi, verticillium wilt is hard to recognize. The fungus invades plants through their roots, then moves upward through the plant's vascular system and produces toxins. In an attempt to seal off the toxin, the plant itself produces gums that slowly clog its water-conducting tissues at the point of infection. Due to lack of water, leaves beyond this point become stunted, curled up, brown-edged, and/or yellowish. Leaves may also wilt, especially during the heat of the day, but revive somewhat in the evening. In mild cases, the plant may succeed in containing the infection and show normal growth the following spring. In other cases, the disease progresses slowly, sometimes over several years, and eventually becomes fatal.

There is no practical way of eradicating the fungus from the soil, where it can live indefinitely, but healthy, vigorously growing plants are rarely affected. However, very young plants, unthrifty plants, those in decline, and those under stress, especially from summer drought, are at risk. Damage, which shows up in midsummer, is more widespread following cool, wet weather in late spring; in prolonged wet springs, even healthy, established maples may be affected.

Because initial symptoms on established plants are often very mild, and because progress of the disease is often very slow, symptoms are often mistaken for sunburn, windburn, lack of water or fertilizer, general lack of vigor, or mechanical injury. However, verticillium wilt is unique in usually affecting only one side or section of a plant. On maples, and especially on Japanese maples, verticillium wilt should always be suspected when only one branch looks peaked or stunted. The appearance of olive-green streaks and/or a long, slightly sunken canker on that branch is almost certain confirmation of the disease.

No fungicides are effective against verticillium wilt, so small, weak, or badly infected plants usually need to be removed and burned to avoid spreading the fungus to healthy plants. However, established maples can often be saved by removing the affected limb before leaf fall. Olive-green streaks indicating infection may be found just beneath the bark; be sure to cut well below such marks. Disinfect pruning tools after each cut, and clean your shoes before walking into other areas of the garden.

Because the fungus does not necessarily cross over from last season's wood into new wood, maples can often be restored to health by making sure new growth is vigorous. Keep the tree well watered the following summer, and give it a small amount of compost (or seaweed, if available) if the soil is not very fertile. Avoid high nitrogen, which can make the problem worse. Moderate applications of potassium-containing fertilizer such as kelp meal or greensand can be beneficial, and a foliar spray of seaweed "tea" or liquid seaweed extract acts as a general tonic.

For shrubs, prompt removal of the affected branches is often sufficient to halt the disease. Maintaining plant vigor with adequate water and fertilizer (avoiding high nitrogen) is the best insurance against recurrence.

If a shrub must be removed, do not replace it with the same species, or with any other susceptible species. If a maple must be removed, do not replace it with a maple of any kind. Alternative trees resistant to verticillium wilt include flowering crabapple, flowering dogwood, hawthorn, mountain ash (*Sorbus*), and sweetgum (*Liquidambar styraciflua*).

BACTERIAL DISEASES

Bacterial blight

A number of ornamental plants are subject to bacterial infections, especially during mild, rainy spring weather when new leaves are just emerging. Infection on perennials and annuals, particularly carnation, cosmos, delphinium, nasturtium, primula, and verbena, usually shows up as extensive dark leaf spotting and blotching; on bulbs such as dahlias, freesias, and gladioli, symptoms are usually a sudden drooping and wilting.

These symptoms can easily be mistaken for fungal disease or even mechanical damage such as broken stems, but bacterial disease usually progress so quickly that small plants are beyond salvaging before an accurate diagnosis can be made. The best remedy then is to remove and dispose of all parts of the infected plants as quickly as possible. Be sure to disinfect any tools used, including trowels or shovels, and wash your hands with hot water and soap before handling other plants. Good sanitation, including planting replacements in fresh soil in a different spot in the garden, usually prevents recurrence.

In woody plants, bacterial infections usually show up as blackened and wilting leaves, flowers, and shoots, which may be followed by twig and branch dieback. Barberries, flowering cherries, fruiting cherries, maples, poplars, and walnuts are slightly susceptible to bacterial blights, but in Pacific Northwest conditions, lilacs are the most notoriously susceptible, especially in very wet springs. White-flowered cultivars and very young specimens seem to be affected most often, but all species and cultivars are vulnerable.

The first response to bacterial blight in any woody species is to remove all infected shoots well below the diseased portion. Disinfect pruning tools after each cut and dispose of all diseased plant parts promptly by burning or wrapping securely and placing in household garbage. To prevent further infections, apply a copper spray two or three times at intervals of ten to 14 days, spraying only when conditions are such that foliage can dry quickly.

Bacteria can overwinter on infected trees and shrubs, causing sunken cankers and subsequent dieback on limbs. To prevent recurrence of infection the following spring, spray vulnerable plants with copper as soon as leaves fall.

Fireblight

Although fireblight is seen much less often in the Pacific Northwest than on the eastern sides of the mountains, it is ruthlessly destructive when it does occur. The main victims are members of the family Rosaceae, especially apple, pear, fruiting quince (but not flowering quince), flowering crabapple, hawthorn, mountain ash, and serviceberry. Cotoneaster and firethorn can also be affected.

Fireblight appears very suddenly (one bacterium can theoretically multiply to 17 million in 24 hours under ideal conditions), leaving telltale evidence of twigs or even whole branches with dead, hanging, reddish leaves that look as if they have been scorched by fire.

If left on the plant, dead leaves remain all winter, allowing bacteria to overwinter on twigs and branches in sunken cankers. Bacteria oozing from these cankers are then spread by splashing rain in spring. The disease can also be spread by contaminated pruning tools and by insects, including foraging bees.

Fireblight is best prevented by avoiding high-nitrogen fertilizers, which cause the succulent growth most susceptible to the disease. If it does occur, infected twigs and branches should be removed and burned immediately. Make pruning cuts at least 12 in. (30 cm) below the affected foliage and disinfect pruning tools after each cut.

Plants can be given added protection by spraying with fixed copper at blossom time, following recommendations on the label. However, unless a specimen has special value, seriously affected plants are best removed and burned to prevent spreading the disease to healthy plants.

CHAPTER 16

Insects

Of the over 750,000 species of insects so far known to exist in the world, only a few dozen cause serious ecological or economic harm, and only a handful are likely to cause problems for gardeners. In the Pacific Northwest, as elsewhere, we are just beginning to appreciate how much we don't know about the roles of the vast majority of insects that share our complex planet. Broad-spectrum insecticides that kill all insects they contact—even supposedly "safe" organic ones such as pyrethrum—cause more problems than they solve, since they kill off neutral, harmless, and beneficial insects as well. Some of these are important pollinators, some perform the vital function of breaking down organic material into soil, and others prey on or parasitize the very insects most likely to cause damage to crops, forests, or garden plants.

Although most of us have been conditioned to a mentality of there's-a-bug-squish-it, a garden totally free of insects—or even just of the ones we consider pests—is neither possible nor desirable. Beneficial and predator insects have to have something to eat, and left to their own devices, they do an excellent job of keeping problem insects under control. Insect-eating birds, bats, spiders, frogs, and garter snakes also help keep the balance of nature truly in balance.

Even low-toxicity insecticidal sprays are rarely necessary in a well-tended mixed garden and should be used only as a last resort. For instance, expected outbreaks of known nuisance pests on fruit trees and vegetables can often be controlled by physical means. Dormant oil sprays smother overwintering insect eggs; floating row covers prevent flying insects from laying their eggs on target crops; bands of sticky paste prevent flightless insects from reaching their intended goals. If sprays must be used, read the label carefully to make sure the product is the right one for the right pest at the right time, and heed all warnings. Spray only on a windless, overcast day, and be especially leery of spraying when fruit trees are in bloom, since pollinating insects can be affected.

Again, choosing plants well suited to the peculiar climate of the Pacific Northwest goes a long way toward preventing insect damage. Like jackals, insects tend to target the most vulnerable

ALL-PURPOSE ORGANIC FERTILIZER BLEND

4 parts seed meal (e.g., canola or cottonseed meal)

1 part dolomite lime

1 part bone meal

1 part greensand (optional)

½ part kelp meal

All measurements are by volume.

prey available—the very young, the very old, the weak, and the stressed—but healthy, vigorously growing plants are seldom bothered by insects and can easily withstand minor or cosmetic damage. Adequate water and fertilizer are of course important in keeping plants vigorous, but too much nitrogen causes succulent, over-forced growth that practically begs insects to come take a bite. Unlike annuals and vegetables, most ornamental plants have a fairly slow but steady rate of natural growth, and occasional modest feedings of compost, seaweed, aged steer or horse manure, fish fertilizer, or all-purpose organic fertilizer blend are more than adequate.

It would clearly be impossible to identify each and every one of the thousands of insects likely to be encountered in the Pacific Northwest and determine the purpose of each; it makes much more sense to learn to recognize the very few likely to cause harm. All others should be presumed innocent until proven guilty. Chances are overwhelming that any very unusual-looking insect is harmless or even somewhat beneficial. Actually, some of our most highly beneficial insects can look quite ferocious on first sight, so it's important to be able to identify these as well.

BENEFICIAL INSECTS

Beetles and centipedes

Lady beetles are universally recognized as "good" insects for their renowned appetite for aphids, but far fewer gardeners recognize their larvae, which are equally beneficial. These soft-bodied, wingless, orange-and-black larvae look like tiny alligators and can be found near any aphid-prone plant in June. Other beneficial beetles include several flightless ground beetles—all of them large, black, and robust-looking—that eat slug and snail eggs, leatherjacket larvae, cutworms, and other soil-dwelling grubs.

Rove beetles are slender, shiny black, fast-moving insects that look like oversized earwigs without the pincers; they live in compost piles and cultivated soil, where they eat insect eggs and prey on root maggots and other grubs. Centipedes, which are shaped like flat worms with many legs, are also fast-moving residents of compost piles. These are strictly insect-hunters and -eaters and do no harm whatsoever to plants.

Flying insects

Lacewings are small flying insects with large, transparent oval wings that seem too large for their bodies; both adults and larvae feed on aphids, mealybugs, spider mites, thrips, and other nuisance insects. Hover flies, so named for their habit of hovering like hummingbirds over flowers, look like small, black-and-yellow or black-and-white bees; their larvae devour great quantities of aphids. Tachinid flies, which are large and gray and look more like flies, parasitize western tent caterpillars and other insect larvae.

Ichneumonid wasps look terribly menacing with their long, slender bodies ending in very long "stingers," but these appendages are actually ovipositors used to lay parasitizing eggs in the bodies of western tent caterpillars, spruce budworms, and other harmful larvae. They do not sting. Several other stingless wasps also parasitize more harmful insects; even yellowjackets, which do sting, prey on large quantities of flies, caterpillars, and other insect larvae to feed their young.

Leafcutter bees, which are native to western North America, look like small honeybees. Although seldom seen in action, their presence is unmistakable from their habit of cutting large, smooth-edged, perfectly rounded semi-circles from the leaves

Leaves of *Epimedium grandiflorum* cut by leafcutter bees

Lady beetle, adult. Photo by Ken Gray

Lady beetle, larva. Photo by Ken Gray

Ground beetle. Photo by Ken Gray

Centipede. Photo by Ken Gray

Rove beetle. Photo by Ken Gray

Green lacewing. Photo by Ken Gray

Hover fly. Photo by Ken Gray

Tachinid fly. Photo by Ken Gray

Ichneumonid wasp. Photo by Whitney Cranshaw

Yellowjacket wasp. Photo by Ken Gray

of roses, lilacs, clematis, Virginia creeper, and various perennials with leaves of a certain thickness and texture. They do not eat these leaves, but use them to make amazingly well-constructed liners for the nests for their young, which are often located underground.

Although damage can be unsightly, it is never serious and never reason to harm these small bees, which are very important pollinators. Like our native blue mason bees, to which they're closely related, leafcutter bees are actually more efficient pollinators than honeybees; their presence should if anything be encouraged.

Spiders

Spiders are not insects (insects have six legs, spiders have eight), but as beneficial predators, they're hard to beat. In its lifetime, each one will catch and eat many hundreds of potentially harmful insects while doing absolutely no harm to plants. (Spiders are strictly meat-eaters; they never even nibble on green things.)

Most spiders—even large, scary-looking ones—are shy, completely harmless creatures that shrink from human contact, but some species can and will bite if suddenly disturbed. Since all spider bites are painful, and some (such as that of the brown recluse) can be dangerous, always wear gloves when working around dense grass or low-growing perennial foliage. If gloves are temporarily removed and laid on the ground, shake them out well before putting them back on.

NEUTRAL INSECTS

Sowbugs and pillbugs (or wood lice) are both ubiquitous in moist Pacific Northwest gardens, especially where organic content is high. Gray or black in color, these many-legged small creatures that look like miniature Volkswagens are actually not insects at all, but land-based crustaceans related to crabs, lobsters, crayfish, and shrimp. When disturbed, pillbugs (but not sowbugs) roll themselves into perfect flattened balls that look like shiny ornamental black buttons.

Since their main function is to break down organic matter into soil, sowbugs and pillbugs are often found in or near compost piles. However, they're also commonly found in vegetable gardens, on wet or rotting wood, in coarse potting mixes, in leaf litter, and just about anywhere else where moist conditions exist in, on, or above the ground. (We have found them motoring around atop the chimney of our two-story house.) Although they do nibble on plant roots, vegetable skins, and occasionally on stems, their presence near a newly dead plant rarely means they killed it. More than likely they're just Johnny-on-the-spot, doing their essential job of turning waste matter into soil.

Like the shrimp to which they're related, sowbugs occupy a low rung on the food chain and are an important food source for many birds, especially in winter. Robins, towhees, and wrens seem particularly fond of them.

Most true bugs such as green or brown shield-shaped stink bugs do little or no harm to plants, although they're often found on them. Some are important insect predators whose good points far outweigh whatever minor damage they may cause.

Garden spider. Photo by Ken Gray

Sowbug. Photo by Whitney Cranshaw

MORE GOOD BUGS

For more information on identifying and attracting beneficial insects in the Pacific Northwest, visit

http://www.govlink.org/hazwaste/house/yard/problems/goodbugs.cfm.

This guide was written by Annette Frahm, Brendan Jordan, and Andrea Imler and produced by the Local Hazardous Waste Management Program in King County, Washington.

Pillbugs. Photo by Whitney Cranshaw

Spittlebugs, tiny green sucking insects hidden inside small bits of wet froth, do very little harm, although the globs of "spit" commonly seen on plants in early summer are unsightly. If they're too much of an eyesore, they can be hosed off with a strong stream of water.

Earwigs, night-feeding scavengers that eat aphids and other soft-bodied insects, are basically harmless. (The pincers don't pinch but are used for grabbing ants.) Unfortunately, they also eat the soft parts of plants, such as leaves and petals, and are particularly fond of dahlias. However, damage is usually minor and confined to cosmetic concerns, such as holes in leaves or missing petals. If damage goes beyond tolerable levels, earwigs can be controlled by placing rolled-up newspapers near infested plants at night; earwigs will crawl into them to hide and can be disposed of in the morning. Diatomaceous earth sprinkled on the ground also helps control them. As a last resort, plants can be sprayed with a pyrethrin-based spray, which has some short-term residual effect and so does not have to contact the elusive insects directly.

NUISANCE INSECT PESTS

Aphids
Aphids are never a direct lethal threat to plants, although they can spread viruses. But they're the number one nuisance pest on almost everybody's list for their ability to distort and pucker new leaves (snowball bush is a favorite target) and to produce sticky honeydew (especially on birches), which drips onto cars and patio furniture and encourages the growth of sooty mold. They also have the annoying ability to appear almost instantly on fast growing, succulent new growth on almost any species. The growing tips of honeysuckle vines and the tips of vigorous new rose canes are almost sure to attract aphids, and anything grown in a greenhouse—especially green peppers—is vulnerable.

Their sheer numbers can seem daunting, but fortunately, just about every other insect out there either eats or parasitizes aphids. If nature does not take care of the problem, aphids can easily be dispatched by gently squeezing the affected stem tips or leaves. They can also be hosed off with plain water; once knocked off the plant, they cannot climb back up. As a last resort, affected plant parts can be sprayed with insecticidal soap. Anything more powerful is unnecessary and should be avoided, since it is likely to kill off aphid predators as well.

Ants actually farm aphids for their sweet honeydew, so controlling ants also controls aphids. Both can be kept off the leaves of filberts (a favorite) and fruit trees by banding their trunks with tape or foam and applying sticky paste such as Tanglefoot to the band.

Caterpillars
Aside from western tent caterpillars and the larvae of winter moths, most caterpillars can be classed as nuisance pests. Although they do chew large, ragged holes in leaves, damage

Green stink bug. Photo by Frank Peairs

Spittlebug froth. Photo by Whitney Cranshaw

Earwigs. Photo by Whitney Cranshaw

Caterpillar (green fruitworm). Photo by Whitney Cranshaw

is usually localized and within tolerable limits; hand-picking is sufficient control. Fluttery white butterflies hovering near any member of the cabbage family (including flowering cabbage and kale) are notice of impending cabbage worms; if hand-picking can't keep up, try dusting plants with flour, or spray with BTK (*Bacillus thuringiensis* var. *kurstaki*, a caterpillar-specific stomach poison).

Not all caterpillars need control. Butterfly larvae, for instance, are also caterpillars; although fewer in number and less voracious than most, they also chew holes in leaves and are also affected by BTK. Caterpillars such as the familiar, fuzzy, black-and-orange woollybear that are seen mainly in early fall do very little harm; the leaves they have just finished chewing will soon fall off anyway.

Leafrollers
Leafrollers, very small caterpillars commonly found on deciduous ornamental trees and fruit trees in early spring, roll themselves up with sticky webbing inside leaves during the day and emerge at night to feed. Eventually they pupate inside the rolled-up leaves, emerging as small brown moths that lay eggs on the tree bark and branches and start a whole new cycle next year. Damage is seldom serious and can usually be managed by pinching any rolled-up leaves, or by picking them and dropping them into a bucket of soapy water. If infestation is heavy, a dormant oil spray just before the leaves open next spring will kill most overwintering eggs.

Pear slugs
Pear slugs (or rose slugs) are not true slugs, but very small, slimy, green or black legless caterpillars that look like miniature tadpoles. These nuisances eat the surface layers of leaves of pear, apple, and quince trees as well as roses, leaving them skeletonized and withered. Damage is unsightly but rarely serious except on very young trees, which may be nearly defoliated. Since pear slugs are most active in late summer, badly affected leaves (especially those with pear slugs still on them) can simply be picked off and destroyed. If there are too many to pick, insecticidal soap gives effective control.

Scale
Scale insects can be hard to recognize, since these plant-sucking insects spend most of their lives as immovable, barnacle-like small bumps on twigs and small branches. Damage is usually minor, but plant vigor can be reduced and small twigs may be killed. Sprays are ineffective once scale insects are glued down and protected by their hard shell-like coverings, but they can be removed by scraping gently with a fingernail or stiff brush. Daubing them with rubbing alcohol helps loosen their hold.

If infestation is heavy, the cycle can be broken by spraying deciduous plants with dormant oil just before buds open. Broadleaved evergreens such as hollies can be sprayed with insecticidal soap in early summer to kill scale insects while still in their vulnerable crawler stage.

Spider mites

Spider mites, having eight legs, are not true insects; although related to spiders, which are beneficial, spider mites do cause damage to plants by sucking their juices. Because they're so small—almost too small to be seen with the naked eye—their telltale damage is the only sign of their presence. Deciduous leaves take on a dry yellowish or bronze color with characteristic stippling or mottling. To control, pick off the worst-affected leaves and spray plant with insecticidal soap three times at weekly intervals. A dormant spray will help reduce infestations the following year.

For identification and control of spider mite damage on conifers, see under *Picea* in Chapter 6. Spider mite damage on both deciduous and coniferous plants can be greatly discouraged by misting plants or giving them occasional overhead sprinklings, especially during hot, dry weather. Do any such sprinkling early in the morning or in the evening, not in full sun.

SERIOUS INSECT PESTS

Because gardens are not monocultures and have healthy populations of beneficial insects, birds, and other insect predators, they are unlikely to experience devastating insect attacks of any kind. However, since the following all-too-common pests can inflict serious or even fatal damage on young, very old, weak, or stressed plants, it pays to keep a vigilant eye out for them at all times. Whenever possible, steps should be taken to prevent damage before it can occur.

Insects capable of causing serious damage to a particular genus only are described under that genus in Part 3; for instance, the cherry bark tortrix is described under *Prunus* (Japanese flowering cherries) in Chapter 5.

Borers

These caterpillar-like larvae of certain beetles live inside trees, doing their damage just under the bark, rather than chewing them from the outside. They gain their entry via eggs laid on tree trunks or branches by adult borers (beetles); when the eggs hatch, the tiny larvae bore their way inside the wood and feed on the cambium layer, growing bigger all the time. If the cambium layer is completely girdled, water and nutrients cannot pass through and all plant tissue beyond that point will die.

Hardwood trees are most likely to be attacked by borers, although similar insects do attack softwood forest trees. Favorite targets include fruit and nut trees (especially chestnuts, for unknown reasons), ash, birch, horse chestnut, maple, poplar, and willow. Unfortunately, once borers gain entry, they're so well protected behind the bark that no physical barriers or sprays are effective against them, and hand-picking is impossible. In fact, there is no sign of their presence except for very small holes (about the diameter of the point of a pen) in the bark.

If borer holes are found on an upper branch, the safest course is to remove the branch and burn it before the insects

Leafroller larva. Photo by Whitney Cranshaw

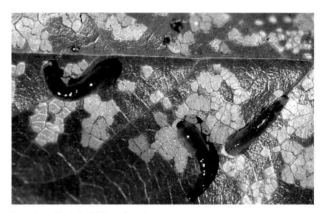
Pear slugs. Photo by Whitney Cranshaw

Brown scale, parasitized. Photo by Linda Gilkeson

Spider mite damage on leaf. Photo by Linda Gilkeson

have a chance to spread further. Little can be done to eradicate borers in the main trunk, although they can sometimes be killed by poking a wire through the holes, especially if fresh sawdust is seen directly underneath them.

The only real cure is prevention, and it works. Trees stressed by drought, injury, lack of fertilizer, or poor growing conditions are most at risk, as are newly planted young trees, but healthy mature trees are seldom if ever attacked. Keeping trees well watered and in good growing condition is excellent insurance, especially when planting a new specimen of a susceptible species.

Root weevils

Although the black vine weevil is the species responsible for most damage in the Pacific Northwest, several other species of root weevils are very similar and cause similar damage. Adult root weevils—small, dark, somewhat beetle-shaped insects with distinctive long "snouts"—are bad enough, disfiguring rhododendron leaves in particular by chewing their signature squared-off notches in leaf edges. They occasionally try other large and/or leathery leaves such as bergenias, camellias, hellebores, photinias, or viburnums, but rhododendron leaves are by far their favorite.

Root weevil larvae are even worse. These small, fat, legless white grubs chew off the bark and cambium layer on the trunks of rhododendrons (including azaleas), yews, and hemlocks just below the soil surface. Young plants are particularly vulnerable, but even large plants can be killed if the cambium layer is completely girdled. Root weevil larvae of several different species also attack the roots of strawberries, raspberries (adults also chew unopened buds), blueberries, cranberries, grapes, heucheras, hardy cyclamen, hardy gloxinias, and primroses. All species can be distinguished from other soil grubs by their dark heads, accordion-pleated bodies, small size (about the length of a thumbnail), and their habit of curling up in the shape of the letter C.

Because adult root weevils feed only at night, they're almost impossible to catch in the act for hand-picking or spraying with contact insecticides, and of course the larvae are virtually invisible underground. To make matters worse, root weevils multiply rapidly and can overwinter, so that adults, eggs, and larvae can all be present at the same time and wreak havoc from late spring until fall. May is the peak season of activity; this is when overwintered adults resume feeding, overwintered larvae start eating roots and the underground parts of stems, and eggs from overwintered adults start hatching into new larvae. It's also only a short time until adults start laying new eggs to start a whole new cycle.

To top off this already nightmarish scenario, all adults are female, each capable of laying hundreds of eggs without male assistance. A single egg can start a whole new infestation.

The unwelcome reality is that it's impossible to eradicate root weevils completely, even with the most heavy-duty synthetic pesticides. Chemical baits only partially control adults, and there are no chemicals at all—at least none available to home gardeners—that control root weevil larvae. (Chemicals formerly applied to the soil are no longer allowed because of their persistence in the environment.)

FRIEND OR FOE?

For positive identification of many insects commonly seen in the Pacific Northwest, good close-up photographs can be found through the Pacific Northwest Nursery IPM page of the Oregon State University Horticulture Department Web site at http://oregonstate.edu/Dept/nurspest/Insects.htm.

Our only option—fortunately, a successful one—is to work with nature to keep populations and damage to tolerable levels. Our normal dry weather in July and August helps kill off many newly hatched larvae, so keeping summer irrigation to a minimum on well-mulched established plants helps reduce their number. (Even rhododendrons can easily handle normal summer drought when they're mature, especially if they're mulched.) Avoid planting rhododendrons and azaleas underneath large Douglas firs; weevil activity seems more concentrated there, perhaps because the protected site and abundant needle litter make it easier to overwinter.

Sometimes one plant can protect another. In our own garden, for instance, every one of the many bergenias planted beneath a large rhododendron is well-notched, but so far—touch wood—not a single rhododendron leaf has been chewed. Meanwhile, the bergenias are holding their own, so everybody's happy.

One ace in gardeners' hands is that adult weevils cannot fly. This makes it possible to trap them on rhododendrons and other woody ornamentals by banding their trunks with nontoxic sticky paste such as Tanglefoot. Don't apply the paste directly to the bark; wrap trunks with waterproof paper, foam, or surveyor's tape first, then apply the paste to that.

Diatomaceous earth, a non-toxic insecticide harmless to people, pets, birds, wildlife, and plants, gives reasonable control of adults when applied to the soil around small plants such as strawberries or perennials. However, the fine powder must be reapplied after every rain to remain powdery and effective. (Wear a face mask whenever applying any fine dust.)

Another promising solution is biological control of larvae with microscopic nematodes. These tiny creatures sold in packaged form (BioSafe is one brand) do a credible job, but control is effective only if they're applied to very warm, moist, loose soil in late summer.

The best and most effective root weevil control is eternal vigilance. Although both adults and larvae undoubtedly have some place in the scheme of things, it's OK to do search-and-destroy missions on them at any time. (Don't worry, there'll be plenty left.) Make it a habit to thoroughly inspect the soil of all new plants before popping them into your garden. (We once found several dozen root weevil larvae in the soil of a one-gallon potted yew, which still looked fine even it was actually dead from girdling.) Learn to recognize the first signs of weevil damage, which include drooping, off-color, or dull-surfaced plants as well as newly notched leaves.

Such signs are a signal to gently brush the soil away from the main stem, right down to the roots, and check for signs of chewing. Any larvae found should be squished on the spot or dropped into a bucket of soapy water. To control any adults in the area, apply diatomaceous earth and/or band the trunks with Tanglefoot. Be especially vigilant with young plants, since they're most susceptible to damage.

Slugs and snails

Slugs are the bane of all Pacific Northwest gardeners, but especially those who garden in moist, shady conditions. These slimy, soft-bodied non-insects—they're actually mollusks, like clams and oysters—are such a constant fact of life that they're even featured in community celebrations (largest slug contests, slug costumes, slug races). They could almost be considered regional mascots if they didn't do so much damage so consistently.

At least a dozen different species of slugs inhabit our region, including the black, orange-rimmed native species and the huge, dark-spotted, greenish brown banana slug. Up to two dozen species inhabit very moist areas such as parts of the Olympic Peninsula. All, along with the less prevalent snails (essentially slugs with shells), are most commonly found in damp, cool, shady conditions and do the same ragged-hole damage. Large, lush, succulent foliage such as hosta leaves are favorite targets; small transplants may be devoured or felled like timber by having their stems eaten through. Slugs do their dirty work mainly at night, but are also active in the daytime in damp, cloudy weather.

Elimination is impossible, as well as undesirable (like it or not, slugs are part of our ecosystem), so keeping damage to an acceptable minimum is the only realistic goal. The number one priority is to search for and destroy their eggs to keep them from multiplying. These clusters of small translucent "pearls" are most likely to be found under boards, rocks, or pots set directly on the ground, but are also laid on the undersides of low-lying foliage. Gardeners get a lot of help in this task from other insects and especially from garter snakes, but it also helps to clean up garden debris and thin out overhanging branches to allow more sunlight to penetrate. In cool, shady gardens, the use of straw or hay as mulch should be avoided; slugs multiply exponentially in it.

Physical barriers are effective in keeping slugs away from prized plants or small areas. Being soft-bodied, both slugs and snails are reluctant to cross rough surfaces such as sharp gravel or crushed eggshells. Copper tape (sold commercially) is an excellent barrier; it causes a mild electric shock when damp slug or snail bodies touch it. Applied to the tops of boards surrounding raised beds, it will keep slugs from entering from the outside, but they can still come up from the bottom inside the beds.

Traps are the next line of defense, with the simple, time-honored method of a cottage cheese container filled with stale beer being most popular and effective. The beer-filled tub (a solution of sugar and yeast in water also works) is set into the ground almost up to its rim, with several dime-sized holes cut into the part above ground and the lid in place. Slugs are attracted to the yeasty smell, crawl through the holes, cannot escape, and drown. Then it's simply a matter of disposing of dead slugs in the morn-

Rhododendron leaves notched by root weevils

Black vine weevil, adult. Photo by John Capinera

Borer trails under tree bark. Photo by David Leatherman

Black slug, red form. Photo by Whitney Cranshaw

Western tent caterpillar web on native black cottonwood (*Populus trichocarpa*)

ing (or when the container is full), refilling the container with stale beer, and repeating until no more slugs appear.

Another effective trap is a wide board or piece of plywood held just off the ground by two sticks. Slugs and snails crawl underneath to hide in its damp shade during the day and can easily be hand-picked into a bucket of soapy water. Hand-picking after dark is also very productive on warm, moist nights in spring or early fall. Wear gloves whenever handling slugs, since they may harbor parasites.

Many commercial slug baits are available, but most contain metaldehyde, which also attracts and can be fatal to dogs, other pets, and wildlife, especially in the form that looks like kibble. Since it is not even very effective (it deteriorates quickly in the moist conditions slugs like most) and also kills earthworms and slug predators, metaldehyde cannot be recommended, even when placed inside traps.

Newer slug baits based on iron phosphate appear to be only mildly toxic to non-target species and are quite effective, since they will hold up for about two weeks in wet conditions. Iron phosphate is a naturally occurring substance found in soil, but all-natural does not automatically mean all-safe; arsenic, mercury, and derris (the source of rotenone) are natural substances, too. Although it looks promising, the jury is still out on the long-term effects of concentrations of iron phosphate in the environment.

Gardeners in rural areas might consider keeping ducks, which are super-efficient slug hunters. Garter snakes relish both slugs and slug eggs and do an excellent job keeping their populations to a minimum. A few rock walls strategically placed where the sun can warm them provide excellent habitat for garter snakes and ensure long-lasting, efficient, and safe slug control.

Western tent caterpillars and fall webworms

Unlike most insects that camouflage themselves to avoid detection, western tent caterpillars and fall webworms are impossible not to notice once their webbed "tents" reach a certain size. Those of western tent caterpillars (or simply tent caterpillars, as they're commonly known), which start becoming noticeable in early May, can reach mammoth proportions by summer, sometimes enclosing whole branches. Fall webworm tents, found in August and September, are smaller and wispier, but serve the same purpose: caterpillars shelter inside them at night and move

out during the day to devour nearby leaves and begin enclosing them in their webs. As the caterpillars grow through voracious feeding, so does the tent.

Fruit trees (especially apples) are a favorite target of both pests, but tent caterpillars are also commonly found on flowering cherry, flowering plum, alder (a favorite), ash, birch, cottonwood, and willow. When their cyclical populations reach peak levels, they can be found on virtually any plant with green leaves, including shrubs and roses. Fall webworms target roses and wisteria as well as fruit and nut trees; apples and walnuts are most commonly affected.

Of the two, tent caterpillars—yellowish brown with a line of blue dots, hairy, wriggly, and reaching 2 in. (5 cm) in length—are more likely to cause serious damage, partly because of their greater size and numbers, and partly because they attack leaves just as they start to unfold in spring. Unlike fall webworms, which skeletonize leaves, tent caterpillars eat every leaf right down to nothing before moving further down the branch. Young trees and whole branches on larger trees may be completely defoliated.

Even defoliation is unlikely to be fatal, because trees usually push out new leaves after the caterpillars stop feeding in late June and drop to the ground to pupate. However, repeated or severe defoliation can seriously weaken trees and leave them vulnerable to winter damage as well as to attack by disease and/or other insects.

Fortunately, tent caterpillar populations are strongly cyclical, so that a widespread or serious infestation every dozen years or so is sure to "crash" within a year or two and give trees a chance to recover. However, populations then begin rebuilding. Although they are parasitized by some other insects, few predators actually eat tent caterpillars (even birds seem to shun them), so it's up to gardeners to deal with them.

If possible, tents should be cut out as soon as they're noticed and the whole thing dropped into a bucket of soapy water or placed in a securely fastened plastic bag for garbage disposal. On very young trees with no branches to spare, tents can be pulled by hand, taking care not to spill any caterpillars. Since caterpillars are away from the tent during the day, do this very early in the morning or just before dark.

On large, mature trees, tents may be beyond the reach of even a pole pruner. Adult moths prefer to lay their eggs on twigs about the diameter of a pencil, and of course these are at the outer tips of branches. A few small out-of-reach tents do no serious harm on a large tree, but if a large, fast growing tent can't be physically removed, spray the leaves just behind the tent with BTK. Once they ingest leaves covered with this caterpillar-specific stomach poison, tent caterpillars will stop feeding, although it may take several days before they're killed.

Although eggs are laid in midsummer, they do not hatch until the following spring, so a dormant oil spray can be effective in smothering them. On branches within reach, winter is a good time to look for the grayish bands of tiny eggs on pencil-sized twigs and scrape them off.

Fall webworms, which are yellowish or green and about 1 in. (2.5 cm) long, are less of a concern since the leaves they eat would have fallen off soon anyway. However, they tend to pick the same trees and the same sites as tent caterpillars and can add considerably to the stress of infested trees. They're also best controlled by pruning out tents, or, if they can't be reached, spraying with BTK.

Winter moths

If the leaves of maples, oaks, or flowering cherry trees are full of gaping holes as soon as they unfold in spring, suspect the larvae of the winter moth—little green caterpillars about 1 in. (2.5 cm) long. These voracious feeders hatch out inside leaf or flower clusters in early spring and begin feeding immediately. When finally satiated in June, they lower themselves to the ground on fine threads (easy targets for squishing) and pupate in the soil.

On very young trees, caterpillars can be hand-picked, or leaves can be sprayed with BTK as soon as damage is visible. Keep in mind that BTK is deadly to all caterpillars, including butterfly larvae. Read instructions on the label carefully and remember to spray the leaves, not the caterpillars.

Between November and January, especially following a hard frost, the cycle begins again as adult moths emerge from the soil and begin mating. Only the male winter moth has wings; these gray-brown insects, about 1 in. (2.5 cm) long and triangular in outline, are often attracted to lighted window panes after dark. The wingless females are brownish humps barely more than 0.25 in. (6 mm) long.

Since the flightless females must climb the trunks of trees in order to lay their eggs on upper branches, banding the trunks with sticky paste such as Tanglefoot will literally stop the winter moth in its tracks. (Don't apply sticky paste directly to tree bark, but to strips of foam, waterproof paper, or surveyor's tape wrapped securely around the trunk. Make sure the band is placed high enough that pets and small children will not get tangled up in it.) Any gaps between wrapping material and bark should be stuffed with cotton batting or similar material.

Winter moth infestations tend to be heavy one year and lighter the next, but are always worse following a wet summer and mild fall. If infestation has been heavy, an egg-smothering spray of dormant oil in late winter is good insurance against a repeat performance the following year.

Egg mass of western tent caterpillar. Photo by Whitney Cranshaw

Fall webworms on crabapple. Photo by Whitney Cranshaw

Leaves of Japanese flowering cherry damaged by winter moth larvae

CHAPTER 17

Weeds

A useful definition of "weed" is "a plant growing where it is not welcome." Lawn grass is a weed when it comes up in a bed of hardy geraniums; various small creeping geraniums are weeds when they come up in lawns. "Weed" also applies to plants that outcompete most plants around them by growing faster, spreading more aggressively, and/or self-seeding prolifically. Many weeds, such as Himalayan jewelweed or policeman's helmet (*Impatiens glandulifera*), get their start as deliberately planted ornamentals because of their attractiveness and ease of growing. However, when they start taking over, they become nuisances at best and in some cases are declared noxious. (*Impatiens glandulifera* is noxious in Washington and Oregon.)

Although "noxious" seems a fitting description of any hard-to-control invasive plant, this is actually a legal term with much more than collective opinion backing it up. Applied only to introduced weeds known to cause extensive ecological or economic damage, it means the sale, transport, or distribution of that plant in any form, including seed, is prohibited by law. It also obligates landowners, including governments, to control or eradicate the weed on their property.

However, not all invasive weeds can or should be designated noxious. Some, such as field horsetails and trailing blackberry, are native plants; troublesome as they are, no one has the right to legislate them out of existence. Others, such as Himalayan blackberry and Scotch broom, are so widespread that control (let alone enforcement of control) is impossible. Legal designation as noxious varies with local jurisdictions: a given plant may be a severe problem in one area, a minor nuisance in another.

With its year-round growing climate, the Pacific Northwest has more than its share of weeds, and chemical herbicides can be tempting. However, such herbicides can damage non-target plants, harm the environment (especially if they get into streams), poison pets and wildlife, and endanger the long-term health of human beings, especially children. Weeds invariably end up growing back anyway, since their seeds can remain viable in the soil for decades. The safest and most permanent way of dealing with weeds in gardens remains the ten-finger method: hand-pulling.

A great deal of unnecessary weeding can be avoided by making sure garden soil is covered at all times with dense but non-invasive groundcover, natural leaf litter, or mulch. Nature abhors a vacuum, and weeds invariably win the race to cover bare soil. Mulch also goes a very long way toward suppressing weeds, especially annual weeds, and makes persistent perennial weeds much easier to pull. Most perennial weeds will eventually succumb if totally deprived of light for a full growing season, but there are exceptions to this rule (see "Horsetails," later in this chapter). Landscape cloth laid on the ground beneath the mulch can help suppress many persistent weeds, but stout, aggressive species such as thistles and tansies will poke through anyway.

If there are no ornamental plants in an area badly infested with aggressive weeds, they can be cut to the ground, then covered with a layer of heavy cardboard weighted down with stones or boards. New shoots will start coming up thick and fast around the edges and between overlapping layers of cardboard, and these must be kept pulled regularly to deprive the roots of energy. If this process is started in very early spring and new shoots are kept pulled until late fall, even very deep-rooted weeds will become exhausted and the plants will be killed.

No garden will ever be completely weed-free, but hand-pulling is actually an excellent opportunity to get on really intimate terms with a garden. Besides being a chance to check closely on the health and vigor of individual plants, crawling around on hands and knees gives entirely new and enlightening perspectives of the garden. It's also an opportunity to find new seedlings of desirable plants to pot up or transplant, and to closely observe birds, bees, butterflies, snakes, frogs, spiders, insects, and other co-inhabitants of our gardens.

Best of all, it's an entirely justifiable time out from other concerns—time to literally stop and smell the flowers. (And the foliage, too.) Setting a time limit or a physical goal such as "one bucketful" or "just to the end of the hedge" keeps weeding from becoming too much of a good thing all at once. The weeds will still be there tomorrow. But if they're starting to go to seed, they should at least be deadheaded immediately: the saying "one year's seeding is seven years weeding" is all too true.

Taprooted weeds such as dandelions and dock can be removed with various ingenious tools designed for that purpose. (Diggit is an excellent gardener-designed tool made in the

Seattle area; for more information, visit http://diggitinc.com.) Weeds in rock walls or between paving stones can be scraped out with various knife-like tools. (Again, the Diggit Duck is excellent.) Weeds in non-garden areas such as driveways or tiled patios can be killed by spraying them on a hot, sunny day with a non-toxic (to people, pets, wildlife, and the environment) solution of one part white vinegar to one part water. Most weeds will eventually grow back, but not for a long time.

Since most weeds prefer full sun and lean soil, they become less and less of a problem as the garden matures and fills in, especially when natural leaf litter is added to the equation. However, eternal vigilance is always required to prevent new or persistent weeds from gaining a toehold, and in the Pacific Northwest, this really does mean eternal. Chickweed matures in cool weather and can start seeding as early as March. So can pepperweed (hairy bittercress), that infuriating small plant with a flat rosette of tiny green leaves and even tinier white flowers that's often found in nursery containers. Grassy weeds of all kinds burst into explosive growth in April. Dandelions appear in mild spells any time from midwinter on and abound from March to June. Hawkweed, a smaller dandelion look-alike, grows, blooms, and goes to seed from midsummer to frost even in the worst droughts.

Since all these weeds and dozens of others can be well controlled by mulching, preventing seed set, and hand-pulling, we have profiled only the most troublesome and most invasive weeds commonly found throughout the Pacific Northwest. For lawn weeds and methods of controlling them, see Chapter 3.

Canada thistle

Cirsium arvense (Canada thistle) has the dubious distinction of being designated noxious throughout Oregon, Washington, and British Columbia. Although not native to Canada (it hitchhiked from Europe in colonial times), this well-known, prickly, deciduous weed does grow best where winters are cool to cold, making it most invasive in North America between the latitude of San Francisco and the Arctic Circle. It also likes moderate to high rainfall and is especially prolific on heavy soils with good drainage. It loves the Pacific Northwest.

Although plants are unisexual (either male or female), they have no problem getting together to produce thousands of fertile seeds, each of which has a 95 percent chance of successful germination. Each new plant then sends out very deep vertical roots that can penetrate 20 ft. (6 m) or more. Each also starts spreading by horizontal rhizomes located at least 24–30 in. (60–75 cm) below the soil surface. New shoots start popping up from these interconnected rhizomes in late winter and quickly cover a large patch of ground surrounding the original plant. Such a patch can be likened to an underground tree with its trunk and branches hidden far below the soil surface and only its upper "leaves" showing above ground.

"Pruning" the tree by pulling shoots seems almost futile, since they can be spaced less than 4 in. (10 cm) apart and replaced in as little as five days. But pulling them is essential, especially from July to September, when seedheads are form-

ing. New spring shoots take several months to form flowers, but summer shoots form them almost immediately, even on very short stems. Once the flowers start showing their characteristic purple color, seeds will continue to ripen even if the flowers are cut off. Under no circumstances should deadheaded thistle flowers be added to the compost pile or allowed to remain on the ground; always pick them up and put them in the garbage.

Unfortunately, pulling shoots is the only way to eradicate an established patch of Canada thistle, and it takes many, many pulling sessions over the growing season. In fact, it can take five to seven years before a badly infested part of the garden is completely thistle-free, but it will then remain that way.

On the plus side, the job gets easier as the thistles get weaker and desirable garden plants begin to shade them out. It helps to remember that Canada thistle is actually a soil builder, bringing up minerals from deep in the subsoil, and can actually increase garden fertility. For this reason, as long as the flower buds have not started to swell or show color, thistles are a welcome addition to the compost pile, where they also make an excellent accelerator.

Being a soil builder, Canada thistle is most likely to appear on recently disturbed soil, especially if it's on the lean side or is mixed with subsoil. To minimize new seeding (and subsequent years of hand-weeding), avoid cultivating or exposing bare soil between July and September, when seeds of Canada thistle and other species are floating through the air on their white, airy thistledown. Whenever possible, pick up or catch these seed-containing balls of fluff and destroy them to prevent them from germinating anywhere.

For established patches of Canada thistle, a thorough pulling session in mid-October is important because it helps deprive the soon-to-be-dormant roots of sustenance over the winter. For the same reason, another session in early spring as soon as the shoots are big enough to grasp will also do much to weaken the rhizomes. Allowing shoots to grow large at any time strengthens the rhizomes, so keeping at them while they're small will shorten the total time necessary to get rid of them.

Thistles in fields, meadows, or rough grass can easily be controlled by mowing once a year, but timing is critical. Mid- to late July, just before the flowers start showing color, is perfect. Mowing any sooner just stimulates new growth, and mowing any later risks the formation of viable seeds.

Field bindweed

With its mind-boggling capacity for self-reproduction, it's a wonder field bindweed doesn't cover even more of the Pacific Northwest than it already does. No one can be unfamiliar with the white funnel-shaped flowers, long heart-shaped leaves, and twining stems of *Convolvulus arvensis*. Although everyone here calls it morning glory, this plant is not even in the same genus as true morning glories (*Ipomoea*), which are not invasive; to be fair (and to make true morning glories less of a hard sell), we really should make an effort to call it bindweed.

Field bindweed appears everywhere, from vacant lots to cultivated fields to neglected gardens (and even well-tended ones) to commercial landscaping. It even comes up through cracks in

Canada thistle (*Cirsium arvense*) in early summer

Field bindweed (*Convolvulus arvensis*)

sidewalks. The less common hedge bindweed (*Calystegia sepium*) is virtually identical except for having larger flowers and leaves; it has the same habit of sprawling and climbing over everything, including fences.

Field bindweed absolutely loves heavy clay soil, sending its roots as deep as 20 ft. (6 m) into the subsoil to make itself totally drought-tolerant. Its seeds, which are scattered far and wide by birds, can remain viable for 60 years. It also spreads underground by lateral roots or rhizomes located 12–24 in. (30–60 cm) below the soil surface; these grow as thick as a rope and send up new shoots every few inches. Every new shoot quickly becomes a new plant; if pulled, it stimulates the rhizome to send up another in its place. As little as 2 in. (5 cm) of a vertical shoot left in the ground can regrow into a new plant. In short, field bindweed is a nightmare. In Oregon and Washington, it's noxious.

But there is hope. The rhizomes can eventually be starved out by completely depriving them of sunlight. First, all above-ground parts of the plant must be pulled or cut to the ground. Covering the soil with landscape cloth is of some help, since field bindweed stems are fairly soft and will not penetrate it. (Invest in good quality; it will last much longer. Do not use plastic sheeting, which causes more problems than it solves.) Then cover the landscape cloth with mulch to block out all light.

Shoots will try their best to find their way through any holes, including those deliberately made for planting desirable species, so these must be watched for and pulled immediately. It may take as long as three years, but as long as light-tightness is maintained and all shoots are pulled, the weed will eventually die out.

Then it's just a matter of preventing new infestations. Since prevention is much easier than cure, keeping a sharp eye out for seedlings is essential throughout the growing season. Any new seedling with two true leaves shaped like arrowheads should be pulled first and questioned later. Even if it turns out to be an epimedium or some other garden plant, it's better to be safe than sorry.

In Oregon and Washington, owners of neighboring lands infested with field bindweed are obligated to control it, but, bureaucracy being what it is, it's good idea to keep an eye on any bindweeds on nearby empty lots or roadsides and pick and destroy the flowers before they go to seed.

Himalayan blackberry

We Pacific Northwesterners are ambivalent about Himalayan blackberry (*Rubus discolor*). Its dense but open growth provides protective cover for birds and small animals, and its large, tasty, prolific berries are relished by birds, bears, and ourselves. Picking blackberries along country roadsides for fresh eating, pies, desserts, jams, jellies, and wines is an integral part of late-summer life for most of us. But Himalayan blackberry is also very thorny, notoriously invasive, and devilishly hard to eliminate.

Being a member of the rose family, it grows extremely well—and extremely fast—in our heavy soils and is perfectly suited to our climate. Although it grows absolutely everywhere in the Pacific Northwest, it is noxious only in Oregon, where it is a threat to berry-growing agricultural regions and physically lim-

Himalayan blackberry (*Rubus discolor*) in June

its access to recreational lands. Elsewhere, designating it noxious is considered unenforceable and therefore futile.

Regardless of spring weather, there will always be good fruit set, since blackberry flowers pollinate themselves without the assistance of bees. With dozens of seeds per berry, thousands of berries per mature clump, and wide dispersal via many species of far-flying birds, virtually no garden can escape the introduction of seedlings.

Unless pulled while very young—preferably at the two-leaf stage—blackberries soon develop large, tough, deep-growing crowns that send out new canes almost as fast as they can be pulled. Even when very small, canes tend to break off at ground level, leaving the crown intact and ready to throw out a replacement. Each semi-evergreen cane quickly grows as long as 10 ft. (3 m) in a single season, complete with vicious curved thorns, and each will readily take root when its arching tip touches the soil. One plant soon becomes a huge, impenetrable mass.

The only solution to unwanted blackberries (many people want them, but only on someone else's property) is complete removal of the crown. This is a job requiring leather gloves, long sleeves, long-handled loppers, a shovel, and in many cases a pickaxe, since the crown can be over 12 in. (30 cm) deep and almost as wide. Late fall, when rains have softened the ground, is the best time for this, but any time between October and March is fine.

Any part of the crown left in the soil will eventually send out new shoots again, although it may take a while, so all "cleared" sites must be closely monitored for at least two years. Any new canes should be promptly pulled to further weaken the crown; if possible, excavation is even better.

Digging out the crown is also the only way to eradicate other invasive blackberries. Evergreen blackberry (*Rubus laciniatus*), an introduced species similar in size and habit to Himalayan blackberry, is the one with deeply divided evergreen leaves. The low-growing, much smaller semi-evergreen plant with the slender, lax, prickly stems that spread quickly at ground level is our native trailing blackberry or dewberry (*R. ursinus*).

Horsetails

Common or field horsetails (*Equisetum arvense*) are those primitive-looking green or brownish stems, usually about 12–18 in.

Foliage of evergreen blackberry (*Rubus laciniatus*)

Trailing blackberry or dewberry in fall (*Rubus ursinus*)

(30–45 cm) tall, with tufts of thin, wiry green leaves arranged in whorls at each stem joint. Because they're perennial, fast growing, and spread quickly via underground runners, two or three harmless-looking horsetails (also called mare's tails and a good many other names that aren't printable) can quickly overwhelm a large planted area. This is one invasive weed that can't be blamed on an alien introduction: the ancient, prehistoric plants are native here, as they are over most of the temperate world.

Once established, a patch of horsetails seems destined to remain forever, because these plants are virtually indestructible. To add insult to injury, every seemingly sensible method of trying to eradicate them ends up backfiring. Here's what does *not* work:

➤ Pulling stems. A new plant will reappear at each newly created scar on the underground runner.

➤ Digging out roots. Besides the futility of excavating the entire garden, any tiny piece of root left will resprout. In fact, digging seems to invigorate them.

➤ Covering with black plastic. No matter how long it's left on, a forest of tangled roots will form underneath it, just waiting to regrow. Horsetails thrive in warm, dank, oxygen-starved conditions.

➤ Covering with landscape cloth. They'll poke right through—immediately in the cheaper kind, not long afterward in even the toughest, most expensive kind.

➤ Covering with bark mulch. While it appears to work temporarily, the horsetails will soon reappear stronger than ever. A deep covering of bark mulch aggravates the problem (and may help create it in the first place) by providing a moist, airless, acidic "wet blanket" with no nutrient value.

➤ Spraying with weedkillers. Horsetails are impervious to all but the most toxic chemicals, and even these kill only the top growth, which will eventually regrow.

The only sure way to rid a garden of horsetails takes time and effort, but it works: improve the drainage, raise the pH, and increase the fertility of the soil.

As living fossils, virtually unchanged for millions of years, horsetails thrive in conditions mimicking those that existed millions of years ago—soil that's acidic (low pH), low in oxygen (lacking minute air pockets), and very low in nutrients. Moist or boggy soil provides all three conditions, but in many cases dry soil is also acidic, compacted, and lean. Changing these conditions seems to give horsetails an evolutionary signal that their reign is over, and it's time for other kinds of plants to take their place.

Improving poor drainage (see Chapter 13) is the first step. Next, remove any mulch and/or plastic from the soil—there's no need to dig up existing plants—and apply dolomite lime at the rate recommended on the package. Wait at least two weeks before adding any fertilizer, since lime and fertilizer tend to cancel each other out if applied together. Meanwhile, water the lime in.

Common or field horsetails (*Equisetum arvense*)

Scotch broom (*Cytisus scoparius*) showing variability of flower color

For large areas, spread fish compost, home-grown compost, or aged cow or horse manure in a layer at least 2 in. (5 cm) deep. For smaller areas, a balanced blend of organic meals (see the first sidebar in Chapter 16, "All-purpose Organic Fertilizer Blend") will also do the trick. Both the fertilizer and the lime will encourage earthworm activity, which will start aerating the soil. If weeds other than horsetails are a concern, consider a non-acidic mulch such as stones or gravel, but do not use bark mulch at this time. The best weed suppressor of all is a living one, so this is an excellent time to get some good groundcovers established.

Considerable improvement should be apparent in one year, but it may be as long as five years before all horsetails are gone. In severe cases, liming and fertilizing may have to be repeated, but once all three steps have been followed, horsetails will gradually start disappearing all by themselves. Sound far-fetched, but it works. Bark mulch can even be reintroduced as long as the area is limed beforehand and the mulch is not over 2–3 in. (5–7.5 cm) thick.

To avoid introducing horsetails into the garden accidentally, keep an eye out for the shorter, leafless stems of fertile horsetail plants in April—a good month before the yearly reappearance of the much more noticeable, rampantly spreading infertile forms—and avoid walking through patches of them. The small, pinkish yellow pointed domes atop these fertile stems contain zillions of extremely small spores, and given the right conditions, each could become a new plant. Domes that have not yet opened can be carefully pinched off, securely contained in a zippered plastic bag, and disposed of in household garbage.

Scotch broom

As everybody in the Pacific Northwest knows all too well, Scotch broom (*Cytisus scoparius*) spreads prolifically by seed. (Yes, it could be called Scots or Scottish broom, but with all due respect to people of Scots heritage, the common name is as firmly entrenched as the plant itself.) That popping sound heard in open areas on hot summer days is seedpods splitting open with a bang to fling their seeds—up to 18,000 per plant—far and wide. Each pod contains a dozen or so seeds, and each mature plant bears hundreds of seedpods. Seeds that don't sprout right away remain viable for up to 30 years.

Originally native to the Mediterranean region but now covering all of Europe and many other parts of the world, Scotch broom is very drought tolerant and is extremely well adapted to climates with mild wet winters and dry sunny summers that are not terribly hot. Because it grows quickly, adapts to many different sites, and is not eaten by any animals (it's mildly toxic), it soon takes over pastures, ranchland, Christmas tree farms, recently reforested sites, grasslands, and any other open sunny sites. Because of its impact on forest regeneration, it's noxious in Washington and Oregon.

The good news is that Scotch broom is not a threat to gardens, lawns, vegetable plots, or any other well-tended, continuously cultivated areas. This opportunistic colonizer takes hold mainly on land that has been massively disturbed by logging, clearing, forest fire, bulldozing for subdivisions, road cuts for highways (until recently, some forms were deliberately planted as bank stabilizers), or on formerly cultivated land that has been let go. Unfortunately, from nature's point of view, cleared lands such as pastures and ranchland are also artificially "disturbed," since they prevent natural succession.

It's almost possible to feel sorry for Scotch broom. Being a nitrogen-fixing legume, it could be considered one of nature's remedies for healing what it considers scarred landscapes and starting over—a kind of temporary band-aid. In most such sites in the Pacific Northwest, nature's plan after a few years would be a second succession of fast growing native deciduous trees such as red alder, which would begin to shade and crowd out the broom. A third succession of conifers such as native Douglas firs would give year-round shade, and the Scotch broom—a short-lived species that must have considerable sunlight to survive—would die off. In 20 years, we have personally seen acres of Scotch broom in our neighborhood (including our own very overgrown lot, which we hand-cleared) slowly but surely disappear as this natural succession has taken place.

However, given the legitimate demands of our own species for new housing, roads, logging, ranchland, pastures, open recreational areas, and the like, *Cytisus scoparius* is far too much of a threat to ignore and let nature take its course. Even cultivated forms of the species, which are very beautiful and supposedly set very little or no seed, should be avoided; by law in Oregon and Washington, they must be. As with cultivated forms of purple loosestrife (*Lythrum salicaria*), even claims of complete sterility are likely to prove mistaken. Property owners are well advised—and in Washington and Oregon, legally obligated—to control wild broom, especially near open land. Fortunately, this can be done quite easily.

➤ Cut mature plants just as they begin to flower—when their bright blooms make them hard to miss, but before they can form seedpods. Cutting them at this time is most likely to weaken or kill them; cutting at other times merely rejuvenates them. Many will resprout, so several years of monitoring and cutting will be necessary.

➤ Pull seedlings and younger plants, which will come out by their single taproots much more easily if the soil is moist. For more pulling power, wrap the top growth around the handle of a shovel and use it as a lever. (The Weed Wrench is a great tool made in the Pacific Northwest specifically for pulling broom and other unwanted woody plants; for more information, visit http://www.weedwrench.com.) Make sure pulling does not expose bare soil, creating ideal places for dormant broom seed or other noxious species to sprout.

➤ Keep cultivated land cultivated: weed regularly and dig over empty beds.

➤ Use a heavy-duty string trimmer, scythe, or brush cutter to mow fields, meadows, or grassy areas yearly just as the flowers begin to bloom. Scotch broom takes two to three years to reach blooming size, so seedlings are easily controlled with regular annual mowing. However, if mowing is stopped, new seedlings will soon take over.

PLANT HARDINESS ZONES

Zone	Average Minimum Winter Temperature	
	Fahrenheit	Celsius
1	-50° and below	-46° and below
2	-50° to -40°	-46° to -40°
3	-40° to -30°	-40° to -34°
4	-30° to -20°	-34° to -29°
5	-20° to -10°	-29° to -23°
6	-10° to 0°	-23° to -18°
7	0° to 10°	-18° to -12°
8	10° to 20°	-12° to -7°
9	20° to 30°	-7° to -1°
10	30° to 40°	-1° to 4°
11	over 40°	over 4°

Each of Zones 2 through 10 can be further divided into two sections, "a" and "b," with "a" being the colder half and "b" the milder half. For instance, Zone 8a would be 10° to 15°F (-12° to -9°C) and Zone 8b would be 15° to 20°F (-9° to -7°C). However, since many factors other than cold affect the winter survival of plants, these zones should be considered a rough guide only.

Wind, humidity, aspect (northern or southern exposure, for example), soil texture, overhead protection, and the presence or absence of mulch all play a role. In the Pacific Northwest, winter drainage is at least as important a factor in winter survival as low temperatures. Improving drainage tends to increase cold hardiness, while wet winter soil decreases it. Timing is also important: a cold snap in November or late February does considerably more harm than if the same low temperature occurs in January, when most plants are fully dormant.

Established plants are much more likely to survive cold at the limit of their range than are very young specimens or those newly planted. Plants that are borderline hardy in a particular zone, those that bloom in late summer or fall, and very small specimens are best planted in spring only (not fall) so they can get established before winter.

Protected sites such as those close to a heated building or in the lee of large evergreens can create plant-favorable microclimates at least half a zone higher than the prevailing hardiness zone. However, such protection cannot be relied on if minimum temperatures plunge well below the norm (Big Freezes), as they do every 15 to 20 years in the Pacific Northwest.

MAJOR BOTANICAL GARDENS OF THE PACIFIC NORTHWEST

British Columbia

GLENDALE GARDENS AND WOODLAND
505 Quayle Road
Victoria, BC V9E 2J7
phone: (250) 479-6162
fax: (250) 479-6047
e-mail: info@hcp.bc.ca
Web site: http://www.hcp.bc.ca/

Five acres of intensively cultivated gardens managed by the non-profit Horticulture Centre of the Pacific, which also operates Pacific Horticultural College, offers a community education program, and manages the natural and restored greenspace of the 103-acre site where all are located. Demonstration gardens include heather, herb, lily, dahlia, native, rhododendron/hosta, Mediterranean, and a drought-tolerant garden. Of special note are the Takata Japanese garden and the Doris Page Winter Garden, the latter dedicated to the hundreds of plants with winter interest in the Pacific Northwest.

UNIVERSITY OF BRITISH COLUMBIA BOTANICAL
   GARDEN AND CENTRE FOR PLANT RESEARCH
6804 SW Marine Drive
Vancouver, BC V6T 1Z4
phone: (604) 822-9666
fax: (604) 822-2016
e-mail: botg@interchange.ubc.ca
Web site: http://www.ubcbotanicalgarden.org/

Combined teaching, research, display, plant development, and public interest/education facility dedicated to collecting, documenting, displaying, studying, conserving, and developing plants. Major collections include maple, clematis, dogwood, hebe, magnolia, rhododendron, and alpines; major gardens include the David C. Lam Asian Garden, E. H. Lohbrunner

Alpine Garden, Food Garden, Native Garden, Nitobe Memorial Garden (Japanese; considered one of the top five in North America), and Winter Garden. Widely planted cultivars introduced or recommended by the Plant Introduction Scheme of the Botanical Garden (PISBG) include *Arctostaphylos uva-ursi* 'Vancouver Jade', *Lonicera* 'Mandarin', *Veronica umbrosa* 'Georgia Blue' (as *V. peduncularis* 'Georgia Blue'), and several others.

VAN DUSEN BOTANICAL GARDEN
5251 Oak Street
Vancouver, BC V6M 4H1
phone: (604) 878-9274
Web site: http://www.vandusengarden.org

Fifty-five acres containing over 255,000 plants from around the world. Specialty gardens include a Children's Garden, Rose Garden, Mediterranean Garden, Sino-Himalayan Garden, Heather Garden, Stone Garden, Herb Garden, Rock Garden, Rhododendron Walk, Southern Hemisphere Flora, Western North America Flora, and many others. Host for the Master Gardeners of British Columbia program; offers courses for adults, children and families, and schools.

Oregon

HOYT ARBORETUM
400 SW Fairview Boulevard
Portland, OR 97221
phone: (503) 865-8733
e-mail: info@hoytarboretum.org
Web site: http://www.hoytarboretum.org/

A living museum of over 1000 species of trees grown from seeds collected around the world, the Arboretum is jointly managed by Portland Parks and Recreation and the Hoyt Arboretum Friends. About half of the 185-acre site is devoted to conifers, making it one of the largest collections of conifers (over 240 species) in North America; other major collections are magnolias and maples. Total number of trees and other plants is over 8000. A library of over 500 horticultural books and other publications is available at the Visitor Center, and several programs are available for children. Volunteers at the Center answer questions and help interpret the Arboretum; self-guided tour brochures are also available.

THE BERRY BOTANIC GARDEN

11505 SW Summerville Avenue
Portland, OR 97219
phone: (503) 636-4112
fax: (503) 636-7496
e-mail: register@berrybot.org
Web site: http://www.berrybot.org/

Formerly the estate of Rae Selling Berry; now a non-profit botanic garden of growing regional importance. Garden began as collections of Asian plants—many grown from seed obtained from famous British plant explorers such as Frank Kingdon-Ward—combined with collections of Pacific Northwest native plants, particularly lilies and alpines. Major collections include primulas, rhododendrons, alpines (the largest public rock garden on the West Coast), and species lilies native to the West Coast. Educational program includes classes and workshops in Pacific Northwest gardening with a strong emphasis on conservation of native species; the garden maintains the Seed Bank for Rare and Endangered Plants of the Pacific Northwest.

THE OREGON GARDEN

879 W. Main Street
Silverton, OR 97381
phone: (503) 874-8100
toll-free: (877) 674-2733
e-mail: info@oregongarden.org
Web site: http://www.oregongarden.org/

Display and botanical garden established by the Oregon Association of Nurserymen in the mid-1990s with a strong emphasis on ecologically appropriate gardening. The 80-acre site utilizes treated wastewater from the city of Silverton, and its wetlands provide a natural filtration system. (One goal of the garden is to foster research and development of plants to solve environmental challenges.) More than 20 specialty gardens include a Native Garden and the Lewis and Clark Garden, featuring Pacific Northwest native plants; a Conifer Garden, featuring dwarf and miniature conifers; a Sensory Garden, featuring fragrance and texture; a Dinosaur Garden, featuring living fossils such as cycads, ginkgos, and magnolias; and a 400-year-old

Garry oak (*Quercus garryana*). The garden also sponsors environmental and forestry educational programs for schools and youth groups.

Washington

BELLEVUE BOTANICAL GARDEN

12001 Main Street
Bellevue, WA 98005
phone: (425) 452-2750
Web site: http://www.bellevuebotanical.org/

Display gardens, woodlands, meadows, and wetlands covering 53 acres. Major gardens include Alpine Rock Garden, Waterwise Garden, Perennial Border, Shorts Ground Cover Garden, Native Discovery Garden, and Yao Japanese Garden; in summer, lavish displays of fuchsias and dahlias are featured. A Living Lab program provides popular botany-related educational activities for local elementary schools. Docent-led tours are offered on weekends. In late November and December, the garden is lit each evening with half a million colored lights shaped as three-dimensional plants.

ELISABETH CAREY MILLER BOTANICAL GARDEN

P.O. Box 77377
Seattle, WA 98177
phone: (206) 352-8612
fax: (206) 362-4136
Web site: http://www.millergarden.org/

Private estate garden (tours available); over 4000 different kinds of well-chosen plants are displayed on three acres. Parent organization of several extraordinary outreach programs promoting greater gardening success in the Pacific Northwest. The Elisabeth C. Miller Library at the Center for Urban Horticulture, University of Washington Botanic Gardens, is the largest horticultural library in the Pacific Northwest, containing over 15,000 volumes; it also hosts a Plant Answer Line by e-mail, hortlib@u.washington.edu, or phone, (206) 897-5268. The library has its own Web site: http://depts.washington.edu/hortlib/index.shtml. The Gardening Answers Knowledgebase link under Resources answers hundreds of regionally common gardening questions.

Great Plant Picks, an educational awards program of the Elisabeth Carey Miller Botanical Garden, provides a forum for horticulturists from Washington, Oregon, and British Columbia to share the results of recent growing trials and other cultural information with the gardening public. Great Plant Picks can be reached at the mailing address and phone number above; its Web site is http://www.greatplantpicks.org/.

RHODODENDRON SPECIES FOUNDATION AND
    BOTANICAL GARDEN

2525 South 336th Street

P.O. Box 3798

Federal Way, WA 98003

phone (Seattle): (253) 838-4646

phone (Tacoma): (253) 927-6960

fax: (253) 838-4686

e-mail: rsf@rhodygarden.org

Web site: http://www.rhodygarden.org/

One of the largest collections of species rhododendrons in the world, with over 10,000 rhododendrons (including azaleas) displayed on a 22-acre woodland site located between Seattle and Tacoma. Peak blooming season is March through May, but at least some species are in bloom between January and late July. Conifers, Japanese maples, alpines, perennials, and water plants are also included in the display for year-round interest. Seeds, pollen, and plants are available for sale to the public to help support the non-profit organization. Mail order plants and seeds are available through a link on the Web site; the Rhododendron Photos link shows scores of species.

WASHINGTON PARK ARBORETUM

2300 Arboretum Drive East

University of Washington

Box 358010

Seattle, WA 98195-8010

phone: (206) 543-8800

Web site: http://depts.washington.edu/wpa/

Huge, overwhelming living museum of woody plants on 230 acres just east of downtown Seattle; plant collections and green space are jointly supported by the University of Washington, the City of Seattle, and the Arboretum Foundation. Internationally recognized collections of trees and other woody plants; major collections include maple, camellia, holly, mountain ash, oak, and conifers. Offers free guided tours, plant stewardship/conservation programs, and a wide variety of educational programs to the gardening public as well as to professionals. The associated Center for Urban Horticulture also offers a wide variety of educational services, including the Master Gardener Foundation of King County.

BIBLIOGRAPHY

Bloom, Adrian. 2002. *Gardening with Conifers*. Buffalo, N.Y.: Firefly Books.

Bloom, Alan, and Adrian Bloom. 1992. *Blooms of Bressingham Garden Plants: Choosing the Best Hardy Plants for Your Garden*. London: HarperCollins Publishers.

Church, Glyn. 2001. *Hydrangeas*. Buffalo, N.Y.: Firefly Books.

Coats, Alice M. 1969. *The Quest for Plants: A History of the Horticultural Explorers*. London: Studio Vista.

Darke, Rick. 1999. *The Color Encyclopedia of Ornamental Grasses, Sedges, Rushes, Restios, Cat-tails, and Selected Bamboos*. Portland, Ore.: Timber Press.

Editors of Sunset Books and Sunset Magazine. 1994. *Sunset Western Garden Book*. Menlo Park, California: Sunset Publishing Corporation.

Erickson, Jon. 1992. *Plate Tectonics: Unraveling the Mysteries of the Earth*. The Changing Earth Series. New York: Facts on File.

Evison, Raymond J. 1998. *The Gardener's Guide to Growing Clematis*. Portland, Ore.: Timber Press.

Fisher, John. 1982. *The Origins of Garden Plants*. London: Constable and Company.

Gardiner, Jim. 2000. *Magnolias: A Gardener's Guide*. Portland, Ore.: Timber Press.

Gildemeister, Heidi. 2004. *Gardening the Mediterranean Way*. New York: Harry N. Abrams, Inc.

Glattstein, Judy. 2005. *Bulbs for Garden Habitats*. Portland, Ore.: Timber Press.

Grant, John A., and Carol L. Grant. 1990. *Trees and Shrubs for Coastal British Columbia Gardens*. 2nd ed, revised by Marvin E. Black, Brian O. Mulligan, Joseph A. Witt, and Jean G. Witt. Portland, Ore.: Timber Press.

Greer, Harold E. 1996. *Greer's Guide to Available Rhododendrons*. 3rd ed. Eugene, Ore.: Offshoot Publications.

Heims, Dan, and Grahame Ware. 2005. *Heucheras and Heucherellas*. Portland, Ore.: Timber Press.

Hillier Nurseries Ltd. 1993. *The Hillier Manual of Trees and Shrubs*. 6th ed. Melksham, Wiltshire, U.K: Redwood Press.

Jermyn, Jim. 2001. *The Himalayan Garden*. Portland, Ore.: Timber Press.

Kruckeberg, Arthur R. 1996. *Gardening with Native Plants of the Pacific Northwest*. 2nd ed. Seattle: University of Washington Press.

Kuitert, Wybe, with Arie Peters. 1999. *Japanese Flowering Cherries*. Portland, Ore.: Timber Press.

McRae, Edward Austin. 1998. *Lilies: A Guide for Growers and Collectors*. Portland, Ore.: Timber Press.

Mickel, John T. 2003. *Ferns for American Gardens*. Portland, Ore.: Timber Press.

Phillips, Roger, and Martyn Rix. 1989. *The Random House Book of Bulbs*. New York: Random House.

———. 2002. *Perennials*. Buffalo, N.Y.: Firefly Books.

Pirone, Pascal P. 1978. *Diseases and Pests of Ornamental Plants*. 5th ed. The New York Botanical Garden. New York: John Wiley and Sons.

Pojar, Jim, and Andy MacKinnon, eds. 1994. *Plants of Coastal British Columbia Including Washington, Oregon and Alaska*. Rev. ed. Vancouver: Lone Pine Publishing. Published simultaneously as *Plants of the Pacific Northwest Coast, Washington, Oregon, British Columbia, and Alaska*. Rev. ed. Richmond, Wash.: Lone Pine Publishing.

Valder, Peter. 1999. *The Garden Plants of China*. Portland, Ore.: Timber Press.

Vertrees, J. D. 2001. *Japanese Maples*. 3rd ed, rev. and expanded by Peter Gregory. Portland, Ore.: Timber Press.

Wright, Michael. 1984. *The Complete Handbook of Garden Plants*. London: The Rainbird Publishing Group.

Zhao, Ji, ed., with Zheng Guangmei, Wang Huadong, and Xu Jialin. 1990. *The Natural History of China*. New York: McGraw-Hill.

Booklets and bulletins

Antonelli, A. L., et al. 1984. *How to Identify Rhododendron and Azalea Problems*. Pullman: Washington State University Cooperative Extension, Bulletin 1229.

Clearview Horticultural Products Inc. 1996. *The Concise Guide to Clematis in North America*. Aldergrove, B.C.: Clearview Horticultural Products Inc.

Gilkeson, Linda. 1994. *Safe and Sensible Pest Control* (Brochure Series). Victoria, B.C.: Pesticide Management Branch, Ministry of Environment, Lands and Parks, Government of British Columbia.

Ministry of Agriculture, Fisheries, and Food, Province of British Columbia. 1995. *A Gardener's Guide to Pest Prevention and Control in the Home Garden*. Victoria, B.C.: Crown Publications.

Valleau, John M. 1995. *Perennial Gardening Guide*. 2nd ed., ed. by John D. Schroeder. Abbotsford, B.C.: Valleybrook Gardens.

Web sites

An Online Guide to Plant Disease Control. Oregon State University Extension. http://plant-disease.ippc.orst.edu/.

California Oak Mortality Task Force. http://www.suddenoakdeath.org.

Canadian Climate Normals or Averages 1971–2000. Environment Canada Weather Office. http://climate.weatheroffice.ec.gc.ca/climate_normals/index_e.html.

Great Plant Picks. An educational awards program of the Elisabeth Carey Miller Botanical Garden. http://www.greatplantpicks.org/.

Integrated Pest Management Manual for Home and Garden Pests in BC. Environmental Protection Division, Ministry of Environment, and Government of British Columbia. http://www.env.gov.bc.ca/epd/ipm/docs/envirowe/default.htm.

Invasive and Noxious Weeds. Natural Resources Conservation Service, United States Department of Agriculture. http://plants.usda.gov/java/noxiousDriver.

Invasive Plant Lists. Canadian Botanical Conservation Network. http://www.rbg.ca/cbcn/en/projects/invasives/i_list.html.

Plants of Southern Africa. http://www.plantzafrica.com/.

Rhododendron Database Search. American Rhododendron Society. http://www.rhododendron.org/search_intro.htm.

Rose Name Search. Help Me Find. http://www.helpmefind.com/rose/roses.php.

The Heather Society's Handy Guide to Heathers. 3rd ed. http://www.heathersociety.org.uk/handy_guide.html.

The Royal Horticultural Society Horticultural Database. http://www.rhs.org.uk/databases/summary.asp.

Washington State Pest Management Resource Service. Washington State Tri-Cities. http://wsprs.wsu.edu/.

Western Regional Climate Center. National Climatic Data Center. http://www.wrcc.dri.edu/.